# EMPIRES AND
# BARBARIANS

*Also by Peter Heather*

# THE FALL OF THE
# ROMAN EMPIRE

PETER HEATHER

# EMPIRES AND BARBARIANS

MACMILLAN

First published 2009 by Macmillan
an imprint of Pan Macmillan Ltd
Pan Macmillan, 20 New Wharf Road, London N1 9RR
Basingstoke and Oxford
Associated companies throughout the world
www.panmacmillan.com

ISBN 978-0-333-98975-3

Map artwork by ML Design
Typeset by SetSystems Ltd, Saffron Walden, Essex
Printed in the UK by CPI Mackays, Chatham ME5 8TD

To my Father and Father-in-Law

ALLAN FREDERICK HEATHER
28.2.1923–14.1.2008

RICHARD MILES SAWYER
30.7.1917–3.9.2007

## PICTURE ACKNOWLEDGEMENTS

AKG Images: 4, 6, 10, 11, 12, 17, 18, 26

Bodleian Library: 14

Bridgeman Art Library: 5, 7, 8, 16, 22, 25

British Museum: 13

British Museum Press: 19, 20
(from *The Early Slavs* by P. M . Barford, 2001, pp. 333, 335.
After V. D. Baran and O. M. Prikhodniuk.)

Corbis: 15

Getty: 1, 2, 3, 21, 23, 24, 28, 29

Mary Evans Picture Library: 9

Oxford University Press: 27
(from *The Oxford Illustrated History of the Vikings*, ed. P. Sawyer, 1997, p. 154)

Every effort has been made to contact copyright holders of photographs
reproduced in this book. If any have been inadvertently overlooked,
the publishers will be pleased to make restitution
at the earliest opportunity.

# CONTENTS

# PREFACE

This book has taken me an extremely long time to write. I signed the original contract when my son William was in the womb. He will be taking GCSEs when the book is finally published (for those of you not familiar with the British education system, this means he's sixteen . . .). In part, it has taken so long because I have being doing other things as well in the meantime, but this project has of and in itself consumed four separate periods of academic leave, which is more time than I have ever spent on anything else, and this does reflect the real difficulties of the task as it evolved. To start with, it covers a huge range in time and space, and consequently a number of entirely separate specialist literatures. There are several of these which I make absolutely no claim to have mastered in full, not least Slavic history and archaeology, where I am exceedingly grateful for the long-standing habit of its major scholars to publish versions of their key arguments in Western European languages. Here, and in many other intellectual contexts in what follows, I am often rushing in where no self-respecting angel would be seen dead. This, of course, is a second reason why the project has taken so long.

But treating so many different contexts in such a thoroughly comparative fashion is central to the design of the project. My original design involved writing about the transformation of barbarian Europe in the first millennium from two separate perspectives. First, it seemed to me that similar patterns of development could be observed in Germanic societies around the fringes of the Roman Empire in the first half of the millennium, and in Slavic societies around the fringes of the Frankish and Byzantine Empires in the second. This could surely not be accidental. Second, I felt that some modern approaches to the phenomenon of barbarian migration in the same period had reacted too strongly to a previous overemphasis on its importance, and were now taking an overly reductive line. To help myself think again about first-millennium migration, it then seemed a good idea to read about its more modern and better-documented counterparts, and from that reading the outline of the book as it now stands eventually took shape. What gradually dawned on me from my reading in the comparative literature on migration is that, first, its patterns and forms are usually intimately linked to prevailing patterns of social and economic development, and, second, that they are also often decisively shaped by the political context(s) in which they are operating. In other words, although it took me a long time to realize it, the two separate strands of my original approach to barbarian Europe in the first millennium were not separate strands at all, but mutually dependent aspects of one broader process of transformation. The patterns of barbarian migration in the first millennium were bound to be dictated by the broader socioeconomic and political transformations of barbarian society in the same period, and shaped, too, by the ways in which those societies were interacting with the imperial powers of their day. This is the central argument of the book, and it could only emerge from the very broadly comparative approach that the project has eventually taken. It is of course for the reader to judge whether the overall gains from adopting such a strategy compensate for the deficiencies in detail that have undoubtedly been generated in its wake.

Otherwise, I would like here only to acknowledge with great pleasure and gratitude all the help that I've had with this project over the many years I've been pursuing it. There are some straightforwardly institutional debts. The Classics and History departments of Yale University provided me with a year-long refuge in 1999–2000, during which I acquired much of my understanding, such as it is, of patterns of modern migration. The AHRC awarded me an extra term's study leave for autumn 2004, giving me some eight months off in total, during which time I was able to draft most of the later chapters of the book. Part of this time was also spent in the extremely pleasant surroundings of Dumbarton Oaks in Washington DC, where it is so wonderfully easy to work surrounded by so many books and such stimulating company. It gives me great pleasure to thank the Director and Trustees for the award of a fellowship for the Fall Term of 2004. A small grant under the AHRC's Migrations and Diasporas project also allowed me to run a series of seminar sessions on Migration and the First Millennium in spring and summer 2005, which proved extremely fruitful for myself, and, I hope, for the other participants as well.

The more particular academic debts I have built up over the past sixteen years are enormous, and I can't thank everyone individually. In my initial years of thinking about the topic, I was lucky enough to be invited to participate in one of the sub-groups of the Transformation of the Roman World project, funded by the European Science Foundation. It remains a formative intellectual experience for me, and I cannot even begin to lay out how much I owe to the many exchanges of ideas and information that both occurred at the time and have flowed from it subsequently. I am particularly grateful, however, to Przemysław Urbanczyk who subsequently invited me to Poland and allowed me to take my understanding of the early medieval Slavs beyond the highly superficial level at which it then stood. Otherwise, I would also like to thank everyone who made the AHRC-funded Migration seminars such a stimulating and enjoyable experience. And among the many scholars who have helped me more particularly along the way with gifts of their thoughts and publications, I would like to thank especially Paul Barford, Andrzej Buko, James Campbell, David Dumville, Guy Halsall, Wolfgang Haubrichs, Lotte Hedeager, Agnar Helgason, Christian Lübke, Walter Pohl, Mark Shchukin, Mark Thomas, Bryan Ward Perkins, Mike Whitby, Mark Whittow, Chris Wickham, Ian Wood, and Alex Woolf. This is a far from exhaustive list, but these names can at least stand as a symbol of the intellectual debt to others that I know to be enormous.

At a still more immediate level, I would like to thank my editor Georgina Morley, my copy-editors Sue Philpott and Nick de Somogyi, together with my editorial manager Tania Adams. I know I've not made life easy for them, but they have all contributed hugely to the project, and I am immensely grateful for every incoherence, error, and infelicity identified and corrected. Those that remain, of course, are certainly my own responsibility. Thank you too to Neil McLynn and other particular friends and colleagues who have read so much of what follows for me in various drafts. I am deeply grateful for their patience, encouragement and correction. I also owe everyone at home, as usual, a huge debt of gratitude for putting up with me during these last few months. Bongo and Tookey have endured the lack of exercise with patience, and William and Nathaniel have generously forgiven my distraction and bad temper. Above all, though, I want to thank Gail, who, alongside an enormous amount of logistic and emotional support, has also laboured long and hard on the final stages of this book's production. If my debts here are too great to measure, then so, at least, is my love and gratitude in return.

# PROLOGUE

IN THE SUMMER OF AD 882, close to the Hungarian Plain where the River Danube flows between the Alps and the Carpathians, Zwentibald, Duke of the Moravians, and his men captured Werinhar, 'the middle of the three sons of Engelschalk, and their relative Count Wezzilo, and cut off their right hands, their tongues, and – horrible to relate – their genitals, so that not a trace of [the genitals] could be seen'. Two aspects of this incident stand out against the broader backdrop of European history in the first millennium AD.

First, the Moravians were Slavic-speakers. Moravia lay north of the Danube largely in the territory of what is now Slovakia, and from a modern perspective it seems unremarkable to find Slavic-speakers dominating this part of central Europe. They still do. But at the start of the first millennium and for all of the next five hundred years, Slovakia, and much else around it, was controlled by Germanic-speakers. Where had the Slavic-speaking Moravians come from?

Second, the incident itself. Despite the fact that we hear about it only from a non-Moravian, Frankish commentator, and despite the appalling mutilations, our source is not unsympathetic to the Slavs. The Moravians took such drastic action, we are told, out of a mixture of pre-emptive strike and revenge. Revenge because of the way in which Werinhar's father Engelschalk and his uncle William had treated them when the two had earlier been in joint charge of the Frankish side of the same frontier. But pre-emption too, because they were trying to prevent Engelschalk's sons from seizing their father's old job from a new appointee. If certainly ferocious, the Moravians were not motiveless barbarians, therefore, and even a Frankish commentator could recognize a defined and coherent agenda behind the brutality. They wanted their part of the frontier to be run in a way acceptable to them. Archaeological evidence helps put this demand in perspective. Moravia was the first Slavic state of any size and cohesion to appear in the late first millennium, and its physical remains are impressive. At

Mikulčiče, its capital, excavators uncovered a series of massive stone-built enclosures and the remains of a fabulous cathedral covering an area of 400 square metres: as big as anything being constructed anywhere else, even in areas of Europe supposedly more advanced at this date.[1] Again, all this is hugely arresting when set against a bigger first-millennium picture. Not only was Moravia run by Germanic-speakers at the birth of Christ, but these populations customarily organized themselves only in small chiefdoms, and never built anything more substantial than slightly larger – as opposed to slightly smaller – wooden huts.

A frontier incident of the late ninth century thus beautifully captures the problem that lies at the heart of this book: the fundamental transformation of barbarian Europe in the first millennium AD. 'Barbarian' is being used here and throughout this book in a very specific sense, one which incorporates only part of the meaning of the original Greek *barbaros*. For Greeks first and then imperial Romans, 'barbarian' carried huge connotations of inferiority, in everything from morals to table manners. It meant the opposite, the 'other', the mirror image of the civilized imperial Mediterranean which the Roman Empire united. It is in a limited sense, denuded of its moral connotations, that I am using the word. Barbarian Europe for this study is the non-Roman, non-imperial world of the east and north. For all the Mediterranean's astonishing sophistication in everything from philosophy to engineering, it was also a world happy to feed people to wild animals in the name of entertainment, so I would anyway have no idea of how even to begin comparing imperial with non-imperial Europe in moral terms.

When this story opens at the birth of Christ, the European landscape was marked by extraordinary contrasts. The circle of the Mediterranean, newly united under Roman imperial domination, hosted a politically sophisticated, economically advanced and culturally developed civilization. This world had philosophy, banking, professional armies, literature, stunning architecture and rubbish collection. Otherwise, apart from some bits west of the Rhine and south of the Danube which were already beginning to march to the tune of a more Mediterranean beat, the rest of Europe was home to subsistence-level farmers, organized in small-scale political units. Much of it was dominated by Germanic-speakers, who had some iron tools and weapons, but who worked generally in wood, had little literacy and never built in stone. The further east you went, the simpler it all became: fewer iron tools, less productive agricultures and a lower population density. This was, in fact, the ancient world order in western Eurasia: a dominant Mediterranean circle lording it over an undeveloped northern hinterland.

Move forward a thousand years, and the world had turned. Not only had Slavic-speakers replaced Germanic-speakers as the dominant force over much of barbarian Europe, and some Germanic-speakers replaced Romans and Celts in some of the rest, but, even more fundamentally, Mediterranean dominance had been broken. Politically, this was caused by the emergence of larger and more solid state formations in the old northern hinterland, as exemplified by the Moravians, but the pattern was not limited to politics. By the year 1000, many of the Mediterranean's cultural patterns – not least Christianity, literacy and building in stone – were also spreading north and east. Essentially, patterns of human organization were moving towards much greater homogeneity right across the European landmass. It was these new state and cultural structures that broke for ever the ancient world order of Mediterranean domination. Barbarian Europe was barbarian no longer. The ancient world order had given way to cultural and political patterns that were more directly ancestral to those of modern Europe.

The overall significance of this massive shift of power shows up in just how many of the histories of modern European countries trace themselves back, if at a pinch, to a new political community which came into existence at some point in the mid- and later first millennium. Sometimes the pinch is pretty severe, but it would be absolutely impossible for most of Europe's nations to think of stretching their sagas back further, to the birth of Christ and beyond. In a very profound sense, the political and cultural transformations of the first millennium really did witness the birth pains of modern Europe. For Europe is fundamentally not so much a geographic as a cultural, economic and political phenomenon. In geographical terms, it is just the western portion of the great Eurasian landmass. What gives Europe its real historical identity is the generation of societies that were all interacting with one another in political, economic and cultural terms on a large enough scale to have certain significant similarities in common, and the first emergence of real similarity was one direct consequence of the transformation of barbarian Europe in the first millennium.

For the very reason that it marks such a crucial point of both national and regional emergence, this period has long attracted the attention both of academics and of the general public. Versions of the narrative sweeps in which the ancestral national communities were thought to have emerged have generally been taught at school, and since the institution of general public education there can be few modern Europeans who have not some familiarity with at least the outlines of their own national sagas. It is precisely at this point, however, that the plot starts to thicken.

Until very recently, both scholarly and popular understandings of the period tended to feature a starring role in the story for immigrants of various kinds who cropped up in different places at different stages of the millennium. In its middle years, Germanic-speaking immigrants destroyed the Roman Empire and, in the process, generated one set of ancestral states. They were succeeded by more Germans and, above all, Slavs, whose activities put many more pieces of the European national jigsaw in place. Still more immigrants from Scandinavia and the steppe, towards the end of the period, completed the puzzle. Quarrels over details were fierce, but no one had any doubt that the mass migration of men and women, old and young, had played a critical role in the unfolding saga of Europe's creation.

In the last generation or so, scholarly consensus around these big ideas has broken down because they have been shown to have been far too simple. No new overview has emerged, but the overall effect of a wide variety of work has been massively to downgrade the role of migration in the emergence of at least some of those distant first-millennium ancestors of the modern nations of Europe. It is now often argued, for instance, that only a few people, if any, moved in the course of what used to be understood as mass migrations. Whereas whole large social groups used to be thought of as having regularly shifted around the map of first-millennium Europe, a picture has been painted more recently of few people actually moving, and many gathering behind the cultural banners of those who did move, thus acquiring a new group identity in the process. Much more important than any migration to the reordering of barbarian Europe in the thousand years after the birth of Christ, this work implies, were its internal economic, social and political transformations.

The fundamental aim of *Emperors and Barbarians* is to provide that missing overview of European emergence: one which takes full account of all the positive aspects of the revisionist thinking, while avoiding its traps. As the Moravian anecdote forcibly reminds us, state formation in previously undeveloped, barbarian Europe – the growth of larger and more coherent political entities – is at least as big a part of the first-millennium story as migration, if not bigger. It was the appearance, by its conclusion, of entities like Moravia right across the north European political landscape that made it no longer possible for a Mediterranean-based state to exercise supraregional hegemony, as the Roman Empire had done a thousand years before. Nonetheless, it is important not to jump too quickly into a world view of ever-changing identities and few migrants. The way forward, this study will argue, is not to reject migration, sometimes even of quite large groups of people, but to analyse its varying patterns in the context of all the transformations then unfolding in barbarian Europe.

Overall, this book has still wider ambitions than trying to put certain large-scale migrations back on the menu of important first-millennium phenomena, setting them passively alongside the other transformations. It will argue instead that it is possible to identify a kind of unified field theory behind the broader transformation of barbarian Europe. Looked at closely, the processes bound up both in state formation and in the precise migratory forms operating in the first millennium are best understood not as two different types of transformation, but as alternative responses to the same set of stimuli. Both must be understood as responses to the massive inequalities between more and less developed parts of Europe with which the millennium began. And both, in my view, were instrumental in undermining those inequalities. Migration and state formation are closely related phenomena, which between them destroyed the ancient world order of Mediterranean domination and set in place the building blocks of modern Europe.

# 1

# MIGRANTS AND BARBARIANS

IN APRIL 1994, ABOUT two hundred and fifty thousand people fled from Rwanda in East-Central Africa into neighbouring Tanzania. The following July a staggering one million people followed them into Zaire. They were all running away from a wave of horrific killing which had been set off by probably the most unpleasantly successful assassination of modern times. On 6 April that year, Presidents Juvénal Habyarimana of Rwanda and Cyprien Ntaryamira of Burundi were killed when their plane crashed as it attempted to land at Rwanda's capital, silencing the two leading moderate voices of the region at one stroke. Other moderate voices in the government, bureaucracy and judiciary of Rwanda were silenced with equal dispatch, and the killing began, not only in the towns but in the countryside as well. The UN estimates that one hundred thousand people were massacred in the month of April alone, and probably about a million altogether. The only escape lay in flight, and in both April and July, men, women and children fled for their lives. Most of the refugees' possessions were left behind, and with them secure access to good-quality food and water. The results were predictable. Within the first month of the July flight to Zaire 50,000 of the refugees had died, and altogether some-where close to 100,000 – one tenth – would succumb to cholera and dysentery.

Rwanda is only the most dramatic of many recent examples of migration as a response to political crisis. Only slightly later, 750,000 Kosovan Albanians fled to neighbouring countries in a similar response to escalating violence. But large-scale flight from danger is only one cause of migration. More numerous are all the people who use movement to a 'richer' country as a strategy for improving the quality of their lives. This phenomenon is found right around the globe. Two hundred thousand people out of a total of three and a half million left the Irish Republic in the 1980s, largely for destinations in economically more dynamic areas of Europe, though many of them have since returned as the Irish economy has boomed, with Ireland itself becoming a major destination for migrant labour. And economic migration is even more prevalent where living standards are poorer. Of different sub-Saharan populations, fifteen million are currently to be found in the Middle East, fifteen million in South and South-East Asia, another fifteen million in North America and thirteen million in Western Europe. The causes of this staggering phenomenon – the numbers are so large as to be virtually unimaginable – lie in massive inequalities of wealth. The average income in Bangladesh, for instance, is one-hundredth of that prevailing in Japan. This means that a Bangladeshi who can get work in Japan at only half the average Japanese wage will earn in only two weeks the equivalent of two years' income in Bangladesh. Political violence and economic inequality combine to make migration – in its many forms – one of the big stories of the modern world.

Nor was it so different in the past. 'The history of mankind is the history of migration.'[1] This is a truism, but, as with most truisms, one that is in a broad sense correct. It is a basic implication of the currently available evidence for human evolution that, having evolved in one favourable context on the continent of Africa, different hominid species then used the adaptive skills provided by their extra brain power to colonize most land environments on the planet. The whole world, in essence, is peopled by the offspring of immigrants and asylum seekers.

The recorded history of the last millennium, too, throws up many examples of migration, some of them – especially those originating from within Europe – remarkably well documented. The modern USA, of course, is a phenomenon created by immigrants. Up to sixty million Europeans migrated overseas between 1820 and 1940 to destinations worldwide, thirty-eight million of them to North America. Continuing waves of especially Hispanic-speaking immigration mean that the US story has not yet reached any kind of conclusion. Likewise, a quarter of a million people emigrated from Spain to the New World in the sixteenth century, another two hundred thousand in the first half of the seventeenth. In the same centuries, respectively, eighty thousand and half a million British braved the North Atlantic. Moving still further back in time, the documentation becomes scrappy, but migration was certainly a significant phenomenon. In the high medieval period, perhaps two hundred thousand Germanic-speaking peasants

moved east of the Elbe during the twelfth century alone to take lands
in Holstein, west Brandenburg and the Saxon marches.²


# THE PEOPLING OF EUROPE


This book is concerned with a still more distant past: Europe in the
first millennium AD. It is a world that hovers between history and pre-
history. Some parts of it are studied primarily through written historical
sources, others through the material remains that are the preserve of
archaeologists. This range of evidence and its combinations pose
particular challenges, but there is no doubt that migrants of all kinds
were busy within the frontiers of Europe in the thousand years after
the birth of Christ. Given the overall part that migration has played in
human history, it would be bizarre if they had not been. The first two
centuries AD saw Romans move outwards from Italy to bring the joys
of town life and central heating to large parts of western Europe. But
it is the migration of so-called barbarians from beyond the borders of
imperial Europe that has long been seen as fundamentally characteristic
of the first millennium.

    Who were these barbarians, and where and how were they living
at around the time that Christ was born in Bethlehem?


## Barbarian Europe

At the start of the first millennium, imperial Europe, defined by the
reach of Rome's legions, stretched out from the Mediterranean basin
as far north – broadly speaking – as the River Danube and as far east
as the Rhine. Beyond these lines lay Europe's barbarians, who occupied
some of the central European uplands and most of the Great European
Plain, the largest of Europe's four main geographical regions (Map 1).
The unity of this vast area, however, lies in geological structure, not
human geography. While heavy clay soils are characteristic throughout
its wide expanses, distinct variations in climate and hence vegetation
generate marked differences in its farming potential, both because of

the growing seasons and the basic fertility of the soil. Western parts, particularly southern Britain, northern France and the Low Countries, are governed by Atlantic weather systems, bringing mild, damp winters and cooler summers with, again, plenty of rain. Why it was the British who invented cricket, the only game that cannot be played in the rain, remains one of history's great mysteries. Central and eastern reaches of the plain enjoy a more continental climate, with colder winters and hotter, drier summers. Average winter temperatures fall as you move further east, and summer rainfall declines in a south-easterly direction. Historically, this has had huge effects on farming, particularly in pre-modern eras employing only limited agricultural technologies. In the south-east, even in the famously fertile black-soil region of Ukraine, productivity was limited by low summer rainfall, with settlements clinging to the river valleys. North and east, winter cold imposed serious limitations. Because of the cold, the characteristic deciduous and mixed deciduous/coniferous forests which comprise the natural vegetation of most areas of the plain eventually give way, first to purely coniferous taiga forest and then to arctic tundra. Broadly speaking, the northern boundary of the mixed woodland zone marks the edge of that part of the European landscape where enough humus built up in the soil in the dim and distant past to make normal farming, or an adapted version of it, possible.

At the start of the first millennium AD, much of this plain was still heavily wooded, and northern Europe was a long way from developing its full agricultural potential. This was not just because of the trees, but also because of the soil. Potentially highly productive, the thick clay soils of the North European Plain required heavy ploughs to maintain their fertility: ploughs capable not just of cutting furrows but of turning the soil over, so that the nutrients in weeds and crop residues could rot into the soil and be reclaimed for the next growing season. In the mid- and high Middle Ages, this problem was solved by the *carruca*, the four-wheeled iron-shod plough drawn by up to eight oxen, but at the start of the millennium most of Europe's barbarians were doing little more – literally – than scratching the surface. So the inhabitants of the European plain were farming at very little, if anything, above subsistence level, and the population was distributed between isolated, cultivated islands amidst a sea of green.

Mediterranean commentators were always much more interested in themselves than in the barbarian 'other' across the frontier, but even they could see that there were more of these islands of cultivation, and hence a denser overall population, the further west you went. More specifically, they divided the barbarian occupants of the Great European Plain into Germani and Scythians. There had previously been Celts – Keltoi – too, but most of previously Celtic western- and central-southern Europe had been swallowed up by the advance of Roman might. And already at the start of the millennium, these areas were set on a non-barbarian trajectory towards Latin, towns and rubbish collection. The archaeological evidence suggests that the placing of the new boundary of imperial Europe wasn't just an accident. Pre-Roman Celtic material culture is famous for a distinctive art style, expressed particularly in beautifully crafted metalwork. Celtic settlements of the period also shared a general sophistication in other aspects of material culture: amongst other things, technologically advanced wheel-turned pottery, substantial and often walled settlements (so-called *oppida*), and the considerable use of iron tools to generate a comparatively productive agriculture.[3]

The material remains thrown up by Germanic-speakers in the same period, by contrast, were generally of a much less rich and developed kind. Typical finds from Germanic Europe consist of cremation burials in urns with few or no gravegoods, only hand-worked rather than wheel-made pottery, no developed metalwork style and no *oppida*. The general level of agricultural productivity in Germanic-dominated areas was also much less intense. It was precisely because the economy of Germanic Europe produced less of an agricultural surplus than neighbouring Celtic regions, of course, that there was smaller scope for the employment of the specialist smiths and artists required to produce sophisticated metalwork. And while the Romans never took a broad strategic decision to absorb just Celtic Europe, the narratives of attempted conquest indicate that Roman commanders on the ground eventually came to appreciate that the less developed economy of Germanic Europe just wasn't worth the effort of conquest. Traditional accounts of Rome's failure to conquer the Germani, as these Germanic-speakers are now often called, emphasize the latter's destruction of Varus' three legions at the battle of the Teutoburger Wald in 7 AD. Reality was more prosaic. The defeat was heavily avenged by the Romans in the years that followed, but this couldn't hide the fact that potential taxes from a conquered Germanic Europe would pay neither for the costs of conquest nor for its subsequent garrisoning.

As a result, shortly after the birth of Christ, different Germanic-speaking groups were left in control of a vast tract of Europe between the Rivers Rhine and Vistula (Map 1). The primary social and political units of these Germani were characteristically small. Tacitus in the first century and Ptolemy in the second provide an almost bewildering list of group names, which you can only approximately plot on a map. The key point emerges nonetheless with total clarity. There were so many of these political units ('tribes' if you like, but that word carries a lot of potentially inappropriate baggage) that, individually, they must have been extremely small-scale.

Not all of this area had always, or perhaps even for long, been the preserve of Germani. Graeco-Roman sources document that Germanic Europe had grown in size periodically, even if they provide almost no circumstantial detail about the processes involved. The Germanic-speaking Bastarnae moved south-east of the Carpathians at the end of the third century BC, for instance, to become the dominant force north-west of the Black Sea. Around the turn of the millennium, the Germanic-speaking Marcomanni evicted the Celtic Boii from the upland basin of Bohemia. When we talk of Germanic Europe, therefore, we are really talking about Germanic-*dominated* Europe, and there is no reason to suppose that the entire population of this truly vast area – some of it militarily subdued in the fairly recent past – was culturally homogeneous in terms of belief systems or social practice, or even that it necessarily spoke the same language.[4]

'Scythia' was a catch-all term among Graeco-Roman geographers for inhabitants of eastern parts of the North European Plain, stretching from the River Vistula and the fringes of the Carpathian Mountains to the Volga and the Caucasus (Map 1). In Greek geographical and ethnographic tradition, it was often portrayed as a chill wilderness, the archetypal 'other', the mirror image of Greek civilization. And to the inhabitants of this world, every imaginable type of uncivilized behaviour was ascribed: blinding, scalping, flaying, tattooing, even drinking wine unmixed with water. In reality, the territory designated by this term encompassed a wide variety of habitats. In the valleys of the great rivers flowing gently south out of the eastern reaches of the Great European Plain good farming country could be found, within, at least, the temperate zones marked by the extent of the forested steppe. To the south lay the much drier landscape of the steppe proper, whose expansive grasslands provided a natural home for the herds of the nomad. Further north and east, less intensive farming regimes gradually faded out, leaving the landscape for the hunter-gatherers of the Arctic Circle.[5]

Of these different population groups, nomads will play a major role in our story of the transformation of barbarian Europe in the first millennium, but only an indirect one, so there is no need to explore their world in detail. Suffice it to say that by the start of this period nomad populations had long tended to roam the lands south-east of the Carpathians and north of the Black Sea. Geologically, this landscape is again part of the European plain, but a general lack of summer rainfall makes farming precarious or impossible. East of the River Don, there isn't enough rain to make farming viable without irrigation, a technology which singularly failed to penetrate these lands in antiquity, and the land retained its natural vegetation: steppe grassland. West of the Don, enough water for farming is to hand in some of the river valleys, but these valleys sit in close proximity to a large swathe of territory, just inland from the Black Sea coast, which is again natural steppe country. Perhaps not surprisingly, therefore, political domination of this landscape in antiquity tended to switch backwards and forwards between nomad and more settled agricultural groups. At the birth of Christ, the Germanic-speaking Bastarnae and Peucini who had moved into the region in the third century BC still retained their domination, but it was about to be overturned by nomadic Sarmatians, who swept through the area in the first century AD.[6]

North of the forested steppe, the eastern reaches of the North European Plain are swathed in vast stretches of increasingly coniferous forest. Here, as average winter temperatures fall lower and there is less humus in the soil, conditions become much tougher for farming. It was a world little known to the Mediterranean at the start of the first millennium. In his *Germania*, Tacitus places the hunter-gatherer Fenni (Finns) in the far north, and another group, the Veneti (or Venethi), between them and the Germanic Peucini on the fringes of the Carpathians:

> The Veneti have taken a great many customs from the Sarmatians, for in plundering forays they roam through all the forests and hills that rise between the Peucini and Fenni. Still, they are more properly classed as Germani, because they have fixed homes and bear shields and take pleasure in moving fast by foot.

Pliny, a little earlier, had likewise heard of the Venedae, as he names them, but reports no detailed information, and even the second-century geographer Ptolemy knew little more about them than a few of their group names. The area was a touch less mysterious than what lay beyond, where people had 'human faces and features, but the bodies and limbs of beasts', but only just.

Archaeologically, the picture of the inhabitants of these wooded and forested zones of eastern Europe around the birth of Christ is reasonably straightforward. As Tacitus' comment about permanent settlements implies, it was a world of farmers, but farmers with an extremely simple material culture, less developed even than that prevailing further west in Germanic Europe. The remains of its pottery, tools and settlement are so simple, in fact, that they frustrate any attempt at stylistic or even chronological categorization, being extremely slow to change before the second half of the first millennium AD. This archaeological evidence suggests that it was a world of small, isolated farming settlements, operating at a lower subsistence level than the Germani, with little sign of any surplus, and none of trade links with the richer world of the Mediterranean to the south. The ethnic and linguistic identity of these forest-dwelling Veneti has generated much discussion, in particular regarding their relationship, if any, with the Slavic-speakers who become so prominent in European history after about 500 AD. We will return to this discussion in Chapter 8, but it would appear that the likeliest place to find Slavs – or their most direct ancestors – at the birth of Christ was somewhere among these simple farming populations of the easternmost stretches of the Great European Plain.[7]

With only a little simplification, therefore, barbarian Europe at the start of our period can be divided into three main zones. Furthest west and closest to the Mediterranean was the most developed, with the highest levels of agricultural productivity and a material culture that in its pottery and metalwork was already rich and sophisticated. This had long been controlled largely by Celtic-speakers, and much of it had just been brought under Roman rule. Further east lay Germanic-dominated Europe, where agriculture was less intensive, and which consequently lacked the same richness of material culture. Even Germanic Europe practised a relatively intensive agriculture, however, compared with the inhabitants of the woods and forests of eastern Europe, whose material culture has left correspondingly minimal remains. Nothing in this brief survey is really controversial, except, perhaps, where Slavs might be found. What has become highly disputable, however, is the role played by migration in the astounding transformation of barbarian Europe which unfolded over the next thousand years.

## Barbarian Migration and the First Millennium

That some migration occurred within and out of barbarian Europe in the first millennium would be accepted by everyone. The big picture, however, is now very polemical. Before the Second World War, migration was seen as a phenomenon of overwhelming importance in the transformation of barbarian Europe: a spinal column giving the millennium its distinctive shape. Large-scale Germanic migration in the fourth and fifth centuries brought down the western Roman Empire, and established new linguistic and cultural patterns in the north. This was the era when Goths from the northern Black Sea littoral moved over two thousand kilometres to south-western France in three discrete leaps over a thirty-five-year period (c.376–411 AD). Vandals from central Europe went nearly twice that distance and crossed the Mediterranean to end up, again after three discrete moves, in the central provinces of Roman North Africa. This took thirty-three years (c.406–39), including a lengthy sojourn in Spain (411–c.430). It was in these centuries, too, that the history of the British Isles took a decisive turn with the arrival of Anglo-Saxon immigrants from Denmark and northern Germany.

Of greater importance still, arguably, was Slavic migration. Slavic origins were always hotly debated, but, wherever they came from, there was no doubting the fact that from relative obscurity in the sixth century Slavic-speakers spread across vast tracts of central and eastern Europe over the next two hundred years. Substantial parts of this landscape had previously been dominated by Germanic-speakers, so the rise of the Slavs represented a huge cultural and political shift. It created the third major linguistic zone of modern Europe alongside the Romance and Germanic tongues, and the boundaries between the three have remained little altered since they were first created. Scandinavian migration in the ninth and tenth centuries then completed a millennium of mass migration. In the Atlantic, entirely new landscapes were colonized for the first time in Iceland and the Faroes, while Viking migrants in western Europe established Danelaw in England and the Duchy of Normandy on the continent. Further east, other Scandinavian settlers played a key role in creating the first, Kievan, Russian state, whose limits established and delineated the boundaries of Europe down to the modern era.[8]

No single view of any of these migrations and their significance ever won universal acceptance. Many of the details, as we shall see in the chapters that follow, have always been and will remain highly controversial. But the conviction that barbarian migration played a hugely formative role in the history of Europe in the first millennium was a distinctive feature of all European scholarly traditions up to 1945. It was true of history on the very grandest scale. Here first-millennium migrants were seen as establishing the main linguistic divides of modern Europe: between its Romance-, Germanic-, and Slavic-speaking populations. But migration was given a critical role at more intimate levels too. Particular sets of migrants were considered to have laid the foundations of such long-lived and geographically widespread political entities as England, France, Poland and Russia, not to mention all the Slavic states who clawed their way to independence from Europe's multinational empires in the nineteenth and twentieth centuries. In the interwar era, the proportion of modern European nation states who traced the origins of their distinctiveness back to first-millennium migrants was staggering. This shared vision of the past is what more recent scholarship has come to call a Grand Narrative. Argument never ceased over the details, but that didn't really matter. The important point was that so many of the population groupings of modern Europe considered the roots of their own distinctiveness to lie in a continuous history stretching back to a migratory moment some-where in that specific thousand years.[9]

An integral part of this narrative was a particular vision of the nature of the population units doing the migrating. Many of these moves were not well documented in the historical sources, some not at all. But what historical information there was did sometimes talk of large, compact groups of men, women and children moving together in highly deliberate fashion from one habitat to the next. This information struck a chord. Since the migrant groups were seen as the start of something big – entities with a long future of continuous distinctiveness ahead of them leading inexorably to the nations of modern Europe – it was natural to apply this vision to them all. Thus all the migrant groups of the first millennium – documented or not – came to be viewed as large, culturally distinctive and biologically self-reproducing population groupings which moved, happily unaffected by the migratory process, from point A to point B on the map. These distant ancestors had to be numerous and distinctive enough to explain the existence of their many and now politically self-assertive descendants in the modern era. A good analogy for the migration process envisaged might be billiard balls rolling around the green baize table. Something might make the balls roll from one part of the table to another – overpopulation at the point of departure was the usual suspect – but any one ball was straightforwardly the same ball in a different place when the movement had finished. This view was applied particularly to Germanic groups involved in the action of the fourth to sixth centuries, but also to a considerable extent to Slavs and Scandinavians as well. Modern Slavic groupings such as Serbs, Croats and Slovenes, for instance, all traced their history back to coherent migratory populations of the first millennium.[10]

This first-millennium narrative was itself part of a still grander narrative accounting for the whole peopling of Europe in prehistoric times. The birth of Christ marked the moment when written historical information started to become more or less available for large parts of Europe north of the Alps. Reconstructing the more distant past relied entirely upon archaeological evidence and tended to be written up – before 1945 – in terms of a sequence of 'more advanced' population groups succeeding one another as the dominant force in the European landscape. The first farmers of the late Stone Age arrived from the east to displace the hunter-gatherers, the copper users did the same for the stone users, the bronzesmiths for the copper users, until eventually we reached the Iron Age and the first millennium AD. The details of this bigger picture do not concern us, but to understand what follows it is necessary to realize that a migration model taken from some first-millennium texts – one where coherent groups of men, women and children moved intentionally to take over landscapes – was imported back into the deeper past, wholesale, to explain the developing patterns of archaeological remains from prehistoric Europe. It was because of what people thought they knew about first-millennium migration that the first farmers, then subsequently those who worked copper, bronze and iron, were all viewed – successively – as outside population groups moving in to take over the European landscape.[11] Within this grandest of all grand narratives about the peopling of Europe, our period represented an end and a beginning. It saw the last in the sequence of major migrations by which the whole history of the continent had been shaped since the last Ice Age, and marked the start of a Europe peopled by entities with a continuous history – that's to say, groupings largely untouched by further migration – down to the present. It also provided the migration model by which all of this European history was ordered. Its sheer prevalence is the key to understanding the virulence of subsequent intellectual response.

## THE GREAT MIGRATION DEBATE

Since 1945, so many key elements of this migration-driven narrative of the European past have been challenged that the old certainties have been eroded. In some parts of Europe, the narrative continues broadly to hold sway, but particularly in English-speaking academic circles, migration has been relegated to a walk-on part in a historical drama that is now largely about internally driven transformation. This intellectual revolution has been so dramatic, and its effects on more recent accounts of first-millennium migration so profound, that none of what follows will make sense without some understanding of its major outlines. A key starting point is the completely new understanding, which emerged in the postwar era, of how human beings come together to form larger social units.

### Identity Crisis

It may seem strange that the first port of call in thinking about migration should be group identity, but the old grand narrative of European history has ensured that migration and identity are inextricably linked, at least when it comes to the first millennium AD. This is for two basic reasons. First, the billiard ball model of migration that powered this narrative assumed that human beings always came in compact groupings of men, women and children who were essentially closed to outsiders and reproduced themselves by endogamy (marrying someone who was already a member of the group). Second, in what is essentially the same view of group identity played out over the long term, it was presumed that there was a direct and tangible continuity between immigrant groups of the first millennium and similarly named nations of modern Europe. Thus the Poles were the direct descendants of the Slavic Polani, the English of Anglo-Saxons, and so forth. National identities were ancient, unchanging 'facts', and their antiquity gave them a legitimacy which overrode the claims of any other form of political organization. Where they did not prevail as the prime mode of political organization, then some other power structure (such as the old multinational empires of central and eastern Europe) had in the meantime erected itself by the illegitimate use of force, and needed to be overturned. Both assumptions have been shown to be flawed.

Nazi atrocities played a key role in stimulating historians to think again about the presumption – generated at the height of European nationalism in the late nineteenth and early twentieth centuries – that nations had always existed, and were the fundamentally correct way to organize larger human communities. In Nazi hands, these ideas led straight to claims for *Lebensraum*, based on how much of Europe the ancient Germani had once controlled, and, with the added dimension of claimed German racial superiority, to the horror of the death camps. Historians would probably have got there anyway at some point, but the excesses of runaway nationalism provided a powerful stimulus to corrective reflection. On closer examination, the assumption that ancient and modern speakers of related languages somehow share a common and continuous political identity has proved unsustainable. The kinds of national identities that came to the fore in nineteenth-century Europe were created in historical time, and did not represent the re-emergence of something fundamental but long submerged. Without the kind of mass communications that became available in the eighteenth and nineteenth centuries, it would have been totally impossible to bind together numerically huge and geographically dispersed populations into national communities. Group identity simply did not function in the same way in earlier eras without canals, railways and newspapers, a world where 'country' meant 'county', for instance, for the vast majority of the British population. The creation of modern nationalism also required the conscious input of intellectuals, who created national dictionaries, identified national costumes, and collected the dances and folktales which were then used to 'measure' ethnicity (I've always thought of these men as looking a bit like Professor Calculus out of *Tintin*). These same individuals then also generated the educational programmes that solidified the elements of national culture that they had identified into a self-reproducing cultural complex which could be taught at school, and by that means reach a still larger body of humanity in an era when mass primary education was rapidly becoming – for the first time – a European norm. The emergence of nationalism is a great story in itself, and has rightly attracted a lot of attention in the last generation or so of scholarship. The point for us, though, is straightforward. Europe has not been peopled since the first millennium by large blocks of population conscious of distinct nationalist affiliations which fundamentally shaped their lives and activities. Nineteenth- and early twentieth-century affiliations cannot be imposed on the deeper past.[12]

Feeding into this reconsideration of the nationalist phenomenon was an equally revolutionary set of conclusions emerging from the work of social scientists studying exactly how, and how strongly, individual human beings are ever attached to any kind of group identity. In this field, the world was turned upside down in the 1950s by an anthropologist called Edmund Leach, who investigated how identity worked in the hills of northern Burma. Leach was able to show that an individual's group identity does not necessarily vary with measurable cultural traits, whether material (types of houses or pottery, for example) or non-material (shared social values, belief systems and so on). People sharing the same set of measurable cultural traits (including language: the great symbol of group identity in the nationalist era) can think of themselves as belonging to different social groups, and people with different cultures can think of themselves as belonging to the same ones. Fundamentally, therefore, identity is about perception, not a check-list of measurable items: the perception of identity the individual has inside his or her head, and the way that individual is perceived by others. Cultural items may express an identity, but they do not define it. A Scotsman may wear a kilt, but he remains a Scotsman even if he doesn't.

As a great deal of further work has confirmed, this suggests an entirely different view of the bonds that create human group identities from that which prevailed before the Second World War. Up to 1945, identity was viewed as an unchanging given, a defining aspect of any individual's life. But studies inspired by Leach's work have shown both that an individual's group identity can and does change, and that a particular individual can have more than one group identity, sometimes even choosing between them according to immediate advantage. In our post-nationalist world, this seems less surprising than it might have done sixty years ago. My sons will have both American and British passports, where before 1991 they would have had to opt for one or the other at eighteen (at that point you could be a joint American citizen only with Israel and Ireland – an interesting combination); EC citizens have both their home-national and a European identity. And instead of being seen, as used to be the case, as an overriding determinant of life choices, group identity is now sometimes relegated to a much more minor role. Particularly influential in first-millennium studies, for instance, has been a set of essays published by the Norwegian anthropologist Fredrick Barth in 1969. The collective view emerging from these papers portrays identity as no more than a strategy for personal advancement. As circumstances change, making first one group identity then another more advantageous, the individual will vary his or her allegiance. As Barth famously characterized it in the introduction to these essays, group identity must be understood as an 'evanescent situational construct, not a solid enduring fact'.[13]

This work transports us a million miles from the expectation that individuals will have one fundamental identity that defines them for life, a notion that not only seemed unchallengeable in the era of nationalism, but was also the basic assumption behind the migration model that drove the Grand Narrative of European development in the first millennium (and, indeed, the deeper past as well). The billiard-ball view of migration absolutely assumed that migrants moved in complete social groups that were closed to outsiders, that replicated themselves by endogamy and that possessed their own culture, which was identifiably different from that of any other group they might encounter on their travels. This vision rested in part, as we've seen, on some historical texts, but mostly on prevailing assumptions about how human groupings were organized, since the historical texts were actually few and far between. Once nationalist assumptions about group identity had been undermined, it was open season on the old Grand Narrative that had rested so firmly upon them.

## The New Millennium?

The lead in thinking again about the deep European past from a post-nationalist perspective has been taken by archaeologists. Traditional approaches to European archaeology worked by mapping patterns of similarity and difference in archaeological finds of broadly the same date across a given landscape, so that defined sub-areas – called 'cultures' – came to be marked out. Originally such definitions tended to be based almost exclusively on pottery types, since pottery fragments are both indestructible in themselves and relatively easy to find, but any kind of similarity, whether in burial customs, house types, metalwork or whatever, might have been used in principle, and has been since. The empirical fact that boundaries can sometimes be drawn between areas of archaeological similarity and difference emerged quickly in the nineteenth century with the rise of archaeology as a scientific discipline. In that intellectual and political context – again we're talking the height of European nationalism – it proved irresistible to equate the cultures depicted on the maps with ancient 'peoples', who were, after all, each presumed to have had their own material (and non-material) cultures. If you were very lucky, and were working on a late enough period, you might even be able to name the bearers of the culture you had found in the ground on the basis of information from a historical text such as Tacitus' *Germania*.

Now often called 'culture history', the development of this approach is particularly associated with the German scholar Gustav Kossinna, who was active from the late nineteenth into the early twentieth century. His approach was a touch more sophisticated than is sometimes appreciated. He did not say that all areas of archaeological similarity should be equated with independent ancient peoples. This was only true, he argued, in cases where sharp boundaries could be drawn between different archaeological areas, and where the similarities within the bounded area were marked and distinct. But terms such as 'sharp', 'marked' and 'distinct' were always made to be argued over, and the fundamental assumption of archaeological investigation in this era was that you would normally find your remains neatly packaged in distinct 'cultures', and that these cultures were the remains of 'peoples'.

The key point for us is that Kossinna's culture history underpinned much of the Grand Narrative. Thinking of archaeological cultures as 'peoples' carried within it a powerful tendency to explain major archaeological change in terms of migration. Where particular and distinct assemblages of material remains – archaeological 'cultures' – were each equated with ancient 'peoples', who were also viewed as the basic unit of human social organization, it was only natural to think any change to an existing pattern of remains represented the impact of a new 'people'. Given that each people had its own 'culture', when you suddenly found a new 'culture' on top of another, you then might well think that one 'people' must have replaced another. Migration, particularly in the form of the mass replacement of one population group by another, thus became the characteristic means by which observable changes to archaeological remains were explained. In modern parlance, although the term had not yet been coined, the peopling of Europe was envisaged as being driven forward by one massive episode of ethnic cleansing after another, in what has been evocatively dubbed the 'invasion hypothesis' view of the past.[14]

The impact of new understandings of group identity on this old intellectual structure has been profound. Once the assumption was removed that the material remains of the past would present themselves in neatly packaged 'cultures' left by ancient 'peoples', it became much less clear that they did. As more material has come to light and existing finds have been subjected to closer scrutiny, many of the boundaries between supposedly distinct cultures have started to blur, while the identification of important local variants has often undermined the homogeneity of supposed cultures from within. Equally, and perhaps even more important, while patterns of similarity do nonetheless sometimes exist, and, where they do, usually mean something important, it has also become clear that no simple rule (such as 'cultures' = 'people') can be applied universally. The precise significance of any particular pattern of similarity and difference will depend in fact on exactly what is similar and different about it. An observable archaeological 'culture' might represent the physical remains of anything from an area of general social or economic interaction, to an area of shared religious belief (where, for instance, funerary rites are similar), or even, in some cases, an area of political association (as Kossinna essentially supposed). A good way to summarize the difference in approach, it seems to me, is that Kossinna thought of archaeological cultures as the remains of entities – 'peoples' – but modern archaeologists regard them as the remains of systems of interaction, and the nature of that interaction does not have to be the same in every case.[15]

Rethinking the nature of cultures in this way has allowed archaeologists to demonstrate that even major material cultural changes can have causes other than outside invasion. Since patterns of observable archaeological similarity can be generated for a variety of reasons – trade, social interaction, shared religious belief or anything else you can think of – then changes in one or more of any number of these areas might be responsible for an observable change. Changes do not have to reflect the arrival of a new social group but might be caused by any substantial alteration in the system that originally created it. Indeed, it was deep dissatisfaction with the intellectual limits of the invasion hypothesis, overemployed as a monolithic model of change, as much as the impact of the new understandings of group identity, that drove a whole generation of archaeologists in the English-speaking world to reject its tenets in the 1960s, and in many other parts since.

For very good reasons, therefore, archaeologists have increasingly looked beyond the invasion hypothesis to other types of explanation altogether, since the 1960s. These new approaches have been highly fruitful, and in the process undercut much of the broader sweep of the old Grand Narrative. Up to about 1960, European prehistory was envisaged as one population group after another using their new skills – in farming technology or metallurgy – to establish dominance over the landmass and expel their predecessors. Nowadays, much of the evolution of central-western European society between the Bronze Age and the Roman Iron Age (roughly the last two millennia BC) can be convincingly explained without recourse to mass migration and ethnic cleansing. Instead of one set of invaders after another overthrowing each other, the European past is now peopled with human beings who could learn new skills and, over time, develop new economic, social and political structures.[16]

There is one further element to this intellectual revolution that has had a huge impact on more recent approaches to the story being explored in this book. In the process of freeing themselves from the undoubted tyranny of culture history and the invasion hypothesis, certain (particularly British and North American) elements of the archaeological profession have come to dismiss migration almost entirely as an agent of significant change. Such has been their collective sigh of relief at escaping from Kossinna's conceptual straitjacket that some have resolved never to have anything to do with migration again. For these archaeologists, migration is associated with a previous, less advanced era in the intellectual development of their discipline, when in their view archaeology was subordinated to history. The billiard-ball migration model found some of its justification in historical sources, as we have seen, and when cultures were thought of as 'peoples' it was possible to write about prehistoric archaeological transformation as a quasi-historical narrative, with people X succeeding people Y, and so forth.

As a result, a basic equation has grown up in the minds of some archaeologists between any model of the past involving population movement, and simple-mindedness. As a recent introduction to early medieval cemeteries put it, avoiding migration in explanations of archaeological change 'is simply to dispose of an always simplistic and usually groundless supposition in order to enable its replacement with a more subtle interpretation of the period'. Note the language, particularly the contrast between 'simplistic' and 'groundless' (the world dominated by migration) with 'more subtle' (any other kind of explanation). The message here is loud and clear. Anyone dealing with the geographical displacement of archaeologically observable artefact types or habits, who wants to produce an account of the past that is at all 'subtle' or 'complex', should avoid migration at all costs. The tables have turned. From a position of overwhelming dominance before the 1960s, migration has become the great Satan of archaeological explanation.[17]

Such a major intellectual U-turn was bound to have a profound impact on the way historians approached the first millennium, where archaeological evidence was always of vital importance, and, of course, historians had in the meantime been thinking about the significance of the great identity debate for themselves. The consequential landmark of change in historical thinking, the starting point for all subsequent approaches to identity and hence first-millennium migration, was a book published in 1961 by the German scholar Reinhard Wenskus. Entitled *Stammesbildung und Verfassung* (*The Generation and Bonding of Tribes*), it showed that you don't have to read far even in the pages of the first-century Roman historian Tacitus to find some Germanic groups being totally exterminated, and other entirely new ones being created. And when you get to the great migrations of the fourth to the sixth centuries, the evidence for discontinuity only multiplies. As we will explore in more detail later, all the Germanic groups at the heart of the successor states to the Roman Empire in this era – Goths, Franks, Vandals and so on – can be shown to be new political units, created on the march, many of them recruiting from a wide range of manpower sources, some of which were not even Germanic-speaking. The political units formed by the Germani in the first millennium were thus not closed groups with continuous histories, but entities that could be created and destroyed, and which, in between, increased and decreased in size according to historical circumstance. There has been much discussion since of the details of how group identity might have worked among first-millennium Germani, and on its likely strength, and we will need to return to these arguments in due course. But all subsequent discussion has accepted and started from Wenskus's basic observations.[18]

These observations have had a profound knock-on effect upon understandings of Germanic migration. Under the old view of unchanging closed group identities, if group X was suddenly encountered in place B rather than in place A, it was only natural to conclude that the whole group had moved. Once it is accepted that group identities can be malleable, then in principle only a few – maybe even a very few – of group X need have moved to provide a core around whom a population from disparate sources then gathered. The billiard-ball view has thus come to be replaced by the snowball. Instead of large, compact groups of men, women and children moving with determination across the landscape, many now think in terms of demographic snowballs: originally small groupings, probably composed largely of warriors, who, because of their success, attract large numbers of recruits as they travelled.

Such post-nationalist readings of the historical evidence for barbarian Europe in the first millennium had similar but independent roots to the new dawn that was sweeping simultaneously through archaeology. But the vehemence of the archaeologists' new mindset has added further momentum to the evident potential for rewriting the story of barbarian migration from historical sources. So convinced now are some historians that large, mixed migration units could never have been a feature of the past that they have started to argue that the handful of historical sources that apparently report the opposite – the source of the invasion-hypothesis model of migration – must be mistaken. Graeco-Roman sources, it has been suggested, are infected with a migration topos, a cultural reflex that made Mediterranean authors describe any barbarians on the move as a 'people', whatever the real nature of the group. A European history composed of long-distance, large-scale population moves is being replaced by a history of small-scale mobile groupings, gathering in followers as they went. Migration – though the word is now scarcely used – remains part of this story, obviously, but with the scaling-down of the numbers of people envisaged as participating in those journeys, the key historical process is no longer the movement itself but the gathering-in of new recruits afterwards.[19]

There is a beautiful symmetry here. The old Grand Narrative subdued archaeology to the demands of history, with archaeological cultures that were understood as 'peoples' and a migration model derived from first-millennium historical sources which ordered the progression of these cultures into a historical narrative punctuated by episodes of large-scale migration and mass ethnic cleansing. Now, the credibility of these same historical sources has been undermined by a reaction against migration which started with the archaeologists' ferocious rejection of culture history and the invasion hypothesis that was its natural corollary. History used to lead archaeology; now archaeology is leading history. In the process, a vision of early European history driven by outside emigration has given way to another characterized by few immigrants but by many people adapting to whatever stimuli were provided by the few who did move: a story largely of internal development. This is in its own right a beautiful pattern. We have now reached a point that is the mirror image of where we were fifty years ago. But while this is satisfyingly symmetrical as an intellectual progression, is it convincing history? Should migration be relegated to such a minor, walk-on part in the history of barbarian Europe in the first millennium AD?

# MIGRATION AND INVASION

The invasion hypothesis is dead and buried. No longer would we even want to litter prehistoric and first-millennium Europe with a succession of ancient 'peoples' carving out their chosen niches via a lethal cocktail of large-scale movement and ethnic cleansing. Arguably, such a cocktail should never have existed. At least the ethnic-cleansing element of the old Grand Narrative finds little support that I know of in the sources. The demise of the invasion hypothesis does not mean, however, that migration has entirely disappeared from the story. Nor could it. Even if you accept that a migration topos operated among Mediterranean authors, their cultural fantasies would still have had to be underpinned by population movements of some kind, and some of the archaeological evidence is likewise suggestive of humanity somehow on the move. Two alternatives to the invasion-hypothesis model of mass migration have consequently come into use.

The first is the 'wave of advance' model. Applicable to small migration units, it provides an alternative view of how a group of outsiders might take over a landscape. It has been applied in particular to the spread across Europe of its first proper farmers in the Neolithic period, and shows how, even with individually undirected moves, farming populations might nonetheless have come to dominate all suitable points in that landscape. According to this model, Neolithic farmers did not arrive en masse and oust the hunter-gatherers in an invasion. Rather, the farmers' capacity to produce food in much greater quantities meant that their population numbers grew so much more quickly that, over time, they simply swamped the hunter-gatherers, filling up the landscape from the points nearest the first farming sites, as individual farmers grew to maturity and sought their own lands. It is a model for small-scale, family- or extended-family-sized moves and unintentional takeover, which, by virtue of these qualities, also allows for the possibility that some of the indigenous hunter-gatherers might have learned farming skills for themselves as the process slowly unfolded. What could be more attractive for scholars trying to free themselves from a world of mass moves and conquest?[20]

Even more popular among archaeologists, because of its greater range of potential applications, is the 'elite transfer' model. Here, the intrusive population is not very large, but does aggressively take over a territory by conquest. It then ousts the sitting elite of the target society and takes over its positions of dominance, while most of the underlying social and economic structures which created the old, now expelled or demoted, elite are left intact. The classic example of this phenomenon in medieval history is the Norman Conquest of England, where, because of the astonishing wealth of information surviving in *Doomsday Book*, we know that a few thousand Norman landholding families replaced their slightly more numerous Anglo-Saxon predecessors at the top of the eleventh-century English heap. Again the vision of migration suggested by this model is much less dramatic than that envisaged under the invasion hypothesis. It retains the latter's intentionality, and some violence, but because we're talking only of one elite replacing another, with broader social structures left untouched, this is a much less nasty process than the ethnic cleansing that was central to the old model. And because it is merely a question of swapping a few elites around, the outcome is likewise much less dramatic and in one sense less important, since all the main existing social and economic structures are left in place, as they were in England by the Norman Conquest.[21]

The intellectual response to the oversimplicity of the invasion hypothesis has thus taken the form of developing two models which in different ways minimize the importance of migration, whether by cutting back on the likely numbers involved, the degree of violence, the significance of its effects or, in one of the two, the extent to which there was any real intent to migrate-cum-invade at all. These models are obviously much more compatible than the invasion hypothesis with those visions of group identity that deny that large, compact groups of humanity could ever intentionally move as a cohesive block from one locality to another. But while these models are certainly more sophisticated, and are to that extent a step in the right direction, they do not yet, even in combination, add up to a satisfactory overall approach to migration in first-millennium Europe. Confining discussion to a framework supplied by just these two models involves three specific problems, and one much more general one.

## Mistaken Identity?

The first problem stems from the fact that in their excitement that human beings do not always organize themselves in self-reproducing, closed population groups (and, I think too, in their determination to banish for ever the abominations of the Nazi era), historians and archaeologists of the first millennium have tended to concentrate on only one half of contemporary discussions of identity in the social-scientific literature. At the same time as Leach, Barth and others were focusing on group behaviour and observing individuals swapping allegiance according to immediate benefit, a second group of scholars turned their attentions to the close observation of individual human behaviour. These have sometimes been called 'primordialists', because they argue that group affiliations have always been a fundamental part of human behaviour. Some of these studies seemed to come up with different conclusions from those generated by Leach and Barth in that they showed that, in some cases, inherited senses of group identity apparently cannot be manipulated at will, but constrain individuals into patterns of behaviour that go against their immediate interests. Differences in appearance, speech (whether language or dialect), social practice, moral values and understandings of the past can – once they have come into existence – act as formidable barriers to individuals who might wish, for personal advantage, to attach themselves to a different group.[22]

The two lines of research have sometimes been held to contradict each other, but in my view they do not. They actually define the opposite ends of a spectrum of possibility. Depending upon particular circumstances, not least past history, inherited group identities can exercise a more or less powerful constraint upon the individual, and provide a greater or lesser rallying cry to action. Again, this is firmly in line with observable reality. In terms of larger group identities now, the rhetoric of Britishness strikes a much stronger chord in the United Kingdom in contemporary debates about the EU, for instance, than does, say, Luxembourgeoisness in its home corner of Europe, neatly located between Germany, France and Belgium. And so too at the level of the individual: individual members of any larger group show marked differences in their levels of loyalty to it. Accepting the fact that group identity is sometimes a stronger and sometimes a weaker force in people's lives does not, I would stress, really contradict what Barth had to say (even though *he* might think it did). His famous aphorism is that identity must be understood as a 'situational construct'. Fair enough, but a crucial point is that all situations are not the same. Influenced in part by the old Marxist dogma that any identity that is not class-based (as group identities will not be, unless every member has the same status) must be 'false consciousness', and partly by the fact that he was primarily reacting against a world dominated by nationalist ideologies, Barth stressed, and was most interested in, the kinds of situations that produced weak group affiliations. But even the logic of his own phrasing implicitly allows that there might be other situations that produced stronger types of group affiliation, and the so-called primordialist research has explored some of them.

Two entirely different types of constraint can act as barriers. On the one hand, there are the informal constraints of the 'normal', whether we're talking food, clothing, or even moral values. Research has suggested that the individual picks up many of these group-defining characteristics in the earliest years of life, which helps explain, of course, why they might sometimes have a profound effect, making individuals feel so uncomfortable outside the norms of their own society that they cannot happily live anywhere else. On the other hand, and sometimes operating alongside such senses of discomfort, there can also be much more formal barriers to changing identities. As an individual, you can in theory claim any identity you want to, but that doesn't mean it will be recognized. In the modern world, group membership usually means having the appropriate passport, and hence the ability to satisfy the criteria for obtaining it in the first place. In the past, of course, passports didn't exist, but some ancient societies monitored membership carefully. Rights to Roman citizenship were jealously guarded, for instance, and a whole bureaucratic apparatus was set up to monitor individual claims. Greek city states had earlier followed similar strategies. Such bureaucratic methods relied on literacy, but there is no reason why non-literate ancient societies might not also have controlled membership closely in certain conditions. There can also be degrees of group membership. America and Germany, in the modern world, have more and less officially accepted large groups of foreign workers without necessarily giving them full citizenship rights, and herein lies the key, in my view, to a total understanding of the identity question. When full group membership brings some kind of legal or material advantage – a set of valuable rights, in other words – we should expect it to be closely controlled.[23]

The underlying conclusions to emerge from the identity debate are more complex, therefore, than has sometimes been realized. For individuals born into all but the simplest of contexts, group identity comes in layers. Immediate family, wider kin, town, county, country, and these days international affiliations (such as citizenship of the EU), together with their own life choices – the desire, for instance, to live somewhere else entirely – all provide the individual with possible claims to membership of a larger group. But any claim he or she makes does have to be recognized, and, according to context, these possible affiliations might exercise a more or less powerful hold upon them. Essentially, Barth's famous aphorism sets up a false contrast. All group identities are 'situational constructs' – they are created, they change, they can cease to exist entirely – but some are more 'evanescent' than others.

From this follows a first potential problem in current approaches to migration in the first millennium. They are predicated on the supposition that large-group identity is always a weak phenomenon, but this is only a half-understanding of the identity debate. If a position on identity is adopted a priori – whether it is viewed as strong (in the era of nationalism) *or* weak (in the currently emerging consensus) – then evidence to the contrary will be ignored or argued away. To my mind, it is important to be willing to re-examine the evidence for migration in the first millennium without assuming that the population groups involved will necessarily have been bound together so weakly as some of the current half-understandings of the group identity issue would suppose.

The second problem emerges when the virulent rejection of migration as a possible agent of past change among some English-speaking archaeologists is set against the kinds of archaeological reflection of migration that is likely to turn up in practice. It is not usual in the modern world for entire social groups to move in a block, and, as we shall see in the chapters that follow, this was also true of the period being explored in this study. There is in fact little or no evidence of first-millennium ethnic cleansing. First-millennium migration almost always consisted, therefore, of moving part of a population from point A to point B, with at least some of the latter's indigenous population remaining in situ, the only exception being

Iceland which was unoccupied when the Norse arrived there in the ninth century. This being so, you can never expect to find the complete transfer of an entire material culture. Rather, only certain elements of the old material culture would be likely to be brought to point B: those invested with particular meaning, perhaps, for the subgroup of the migrant population actually involved in the migration process. At the same time, some or much of the indigenous material culture of point B would probably continue, and some entirely new items or practices might be generated by the interaction of the migratory and host populations. The archaeological reflections of many first-millennium migratory processes, in other words, will often be straightforwardly ambiguous in the sense that you could not be absolutely certain, just on the basis of the archaeology alone, that migration had occurred.[24]

So far so good: if the only archaeological evidence for a possible migration is ambiguous rather than definitive, so be it. Better that than populate European history with a series of phantom invasions. Where this does become a problem, however, is when migration is viewed as 'always simplistic' and 'usually groundless'. If you approach the issue in this frame of mind, then the ambiguity of the evidence will not be treated in an even-handed fashion. Where you're looking at some archaeological transformation which might or might not represent the correlates of a migratory process, then it is important to say exactly that – no more and no less. But because archaeologists have just gone through such a nasty divorce from migration, some have a strong tendency (at least in Britain and North America) to want to write it out of their accounts of the past entirely.[25] It is now enough in some quarters to show that an observable transformation *might* have been generated without migration for this to be taken as a proven fact. But since the archaeological reflections of many migration processes will only ever be ambiguous, the basic fact that just about every kind of archaeological transformation can, with sufficient intellectual ingenuity, be explained in terms other than of migration, doesn't mean that it *should* be. The right answer is not to say that, because there is ambiguity, migration has been disproved, but to accept the ambiguity and see if anything else – especially historical evidence where appropriate – helps resolve it.

It is not safe, then, either to build your estimate of the potential scale of first-millennium migration on the presumption that group identities were always weak, or to dismiss its existence and importance

if you find only ambiguous archaeological evidence. These two observations in turn generate the third problem. The concept of a migration
topos – the idea that Mediterranean writers were led by a cultural
reflex to see any barbarians on the move as a 'people' – has sometimes
been used to dismiss historical evidence for large, compact and mixed
migration groups. Up to this point, however, its supposed prevalence
is based on assertion rather than on any properly argued demonstration
that it really existed. As a concept, it has gained a priori plausibility
from the idea that group identities could never have been strong
enough to generate the kind of large-group migration that the sources
seem to be reporting, and from the fact that, as already noted, the
archaeological reflections of migration are often ambiguous. But if
archaeological ambiguity is only to be expected, and it is unsafe just to
assume that all first-millennium group identities were necessarily weak,
this obviously undermines the support these points have been supposed to provide for the supposed existence of a migration topos. So it
will be necessary in what follows to examine on a case by case basis
whether the historical accounts of large-group migration can really be
dismissed so easily.

Even by themselves, these three problems would be sufficient to
warrant a re-examination of migration in the first millennium. But
there is also a fourth, and much broader, reason why current treat-
ments of the topic require a thorough overhaul.

## Migration and Development

The comparative study of human migration has a lengthy pedigree.
Like many other fields, it has proceeded from originally simple models
to more complex and interesting ones, particularly in the last scholarly
generation or so. Interest originally focused upon economic motives
as the paramount factor in explaining population movements, with a
landmark study arguing pretty successfully that immigration to the
United States was positively correlated with its business cycles.[26] The
quest to understand first-millennium migration has seen some engagement with this rapidly developing field. When thinking about
causation, for instance, the concept of 'push' and 'pull' factors – things
that were bad about a point of departure and attractive about the
destination – has long been part of the scholarly vocabulary. The

importance of accurate information in shaping migration flows, and the fact that larger-scale migration is sometimes preceded by pioneering individuals ('scouts') whose experiences add momentum to what follows, are likewise part of the landscape. But these ideas are no more than the tip of the comparative-migration iceberg and, in general terms, the literature has been little explored by those studying migration in the first millennium.[27]

This is a strange omission because the comparative literature offers a wide range of well-documented case studies against which to compare the first-millennium evidence, with an obvious potential to expand the range of possible migration models beyond the limits of wave-of-advance and elite-transfer. Amongst other examples, more recent history gives us economically driven flows of migrants, who are unorganized in the sense that all are making individual decisions. Nonetheless, they can over time, and especially when allied with population increase among those who have already reached the point of destination, fill an entire landscape: even one as big as the United States. The twentieth century has also underlined the importance of another basic cause of migration: political conflict. Individual refugees fleeing persecuting regimes are extremely common, but political disturbances can also generate much more concentrated migration flows. The most horrific example from recent years is Rwanda, where this chapter began. But there are many others: ethnic cleansing in the former Yugoslavia, the expulsion in just three months of eighty-eight thousand foreigners from Saudi Arabia in 1973, the movement of twenty-five million refugees in central and eastern Europe at the end of the Second World War, the flight and continued plight of Palestinian refugees.

Aside from expanding the underlying intellectual frame of reference, the comparative literature also indicates that it is necessary to ask more detailed questions of any migratory process than has customarily been done in first-millennium studies. Early modern and modern case studies have thrown up no instance where the entire population of place A has moved en masse to place B. Migration has always turned out to be an activity confined to certain subgroups, and a particularly fruitful line of questioning has stemmed from this observation. What leads some individuals to stay at home, when their fellows in more or less identical circumstances move? Work directed at understanding this phenomenon has identified some interesting patterns. Economic migrants tend – certainly in the first instance, at least – to be younger, often male and, in terms of their own societies, relatively better educated. Migration also tends to be undertaken by the already mobile. On closer inspection, half of the Dutch migrants to what became New York turn out to be people who had already migrated once before, from other parts of Europe to the Netherlands. Likewise, many of the 'Irish' participating in the early stages of the colonization of North America came from Scottish families, which, just a generation before, had moved to Ireland.[28] Longer-distance migration flows have always to be understood, therefore, against established patterns of internal demographic dislocation. Participants in the latter will have a greater than average likelihood of providing manpower for the former.

Even within these variegated patterns of participation, however, the decision to migrate does not turn simply upon what you might term rational economic calculation. Other factors complicate the individual's thought process. Information about both projected destinations and the routes to them is one key variable. Large-scale migration flows to a new destination only begin once the pros and cons of the route, and of the potential new home, become generally understood. Before that stage, 'channelled' migration is correspondingly common. Under this pattern, population groups from relatively restricted departure areas end up clustered together again in specific areas at the point of destination. This seems to be caused both by limitations on the amount of available information, and by the kind of social support that can be provided by a host population from the migrants' point of departure. Transport costs, not surprisingly, also intrude into a potential migrant's calculations, and psychological costs are important too. The strangeness of life in a new place and the disruption to emotional ties binding the individual to family and friends affect decisions to move, as well as subsequent decisions about whether to remain. A substantial flow of return migration is thus a significant feature of all well-documented population displacements.[29]

Over and above all these factors, potential migration flows can be interfered with by the political structures in existence at either the point of departure or that of arrival, or both. Since the 1970s, Western European countries have more or less brought to a halt the flows of legal migrant labour from particular parts of the Third World, which had been a regular feature of life since the Second World War. This decision was motivated by political rather than economic considerations, since industry still wanted the relatively cheap labour that migrants provide, but governments were concerned to pacify the hostility towards migrant communities that had grown up in some quarters of their own societies. Migration flows from the old sources have continued, in fact, but in the greatly modified form of family reunification, not new migrant workers, and there has followed a corresponding shift in gender and age patterns among the migrants. Flows of women and the relatively elderly, wives and dependent parents of the original migrants, have replaced the procession of young men. This is but one example of the general rule that political structures will always dictate the framework of available options within which potential migrants make their decisions.[30]

Migration studies also offer new ways of thinking about the effects of migration, of how to form some estimate of whether to rate it a more or less important phenomenon in any particular case. Thanks to the legacy of the invasion hypothesis, these kinds of argument in the first-millennium context are now often wrapped up with the issue of migrant numbers. Are we looking at 'mass migration' or at a smaller phenomenon, something more like elite transfer? – with estimates of a migration flow's importance being adjusted up or down according to the numbers involved. But since first-millennium sources never provide unquestionable data on numbers, even when there's any at all, it is hardly surprising that such arguments often become deadlocked. Of potentially wide application, therefore, is the relative, rather than statistical, definition of mass migration generally adopted in the comparative-migration literature. For what, in fact, constitutes a 'mass' migration? Is it the arrival of an immigrant group that numbers 10 per cent of the population at the point of destination? – 20 per cent? – 40 per cent? – or what? And a migration flow needs in any case to be considered from the viewpoint of all its participants. Theoretically, a flow of migrants might amount to a small percentage of the population at its point of destination, but represent a large percentage of the population at its point of departure. What is elite transfer from the host population's perspective, therefore, could be a more substantial demographic phenomenon for the immigrants themselves. To encompass this variety of situations and avoid numerical quibbling, migration studies have come to define 'mass' migration as a flow of human beings (whatever the numbers involved) which changes the spatial distribution of population at either or both the sending and the receiving ends, or

one 'which gives a shock to the political or social system', again at
either end or both.[31]

This is not just to assume that information and insights from more
modern eras are automatically applicable to the first millennium.
Migration studies have generally been working with twentieth-century
examples, observed more or less contemporaneously, or with the European settlement of the Americas, either North and South in the first
phase from the sixteenth to the eighteenth century, or just the North
in the case of the huge immigration waves of the later nineteenth and
early twentieth.[32] There are major structural differences between any
of these worlds and first-millennium Europe. The latter's economy
was overwhelmingly agricultural in nature, and at subsistence, or not
far above, in its levels of output. It had no mass production, so that
nineteenth- and twentieth-century patterns of migrant labour being
sucked first from agricultural to industrial Europe and then from outside Europe altogether simply do not apply.[33] The population of first-
millennium Europe was also smaller than its modern counterpart to a
quite astonishing degree, and even as late as 1800 governments of
European countries tended to control emigration much more than
immigration. The governmental and bureaucratic capacities, likewise,
of first-millennium states (to the extent that there were any) were also
much less developed, so that they clearly did not have the same
capacity to make and enforce immigration policies as their more modern counterparts.

Similarly with transport and the availability of information. Both
existed in the first millennium, but transport costs were huge compared
with the modern world. Perhaps the most famous economic statistic
from the ancient world is the report in the Emperor Diocletian's *Edict
on Prices* (from c.300 AD) – that the cost of a wagon of wheat doubled
for every fifty miles it was carried. Where transport remained expensive, as it did down to the later nineteenth century, this posed
substantial problems to would-be migrants, although these could
sometimes be obviated by state assistance.[34] Information in a pre- or
non-literate world also circulates over very different (that is, shorter)
distances, and in an entirely different fashion from a world with mass
media, again making it more difficult for would-be migrants to gather
information about possible destinations. In the high Middle Ages, this
was sometimes countered by designated agents mounting recruiting
drives, but the limitations that would have affected information flows

in the first millennium are obvious.[35] Nonetheless, and at the very least, modern migration studies generate a fresh range of issues and more detailed questions to move the study of first-millennium migration well beyond the old invasion-hypothesis model and even beyond current responses to that model.

It is on the issue of what causes migration, however, that the modern world has most to teach those of us who grapple with the first millennium. On the level of the individual migrant, comparative analysis has moved far beyond drawing up lists of push-and-pull factors. There are two basic drivers behind migration: more voluntary economically motivated migration, and less voluntary political migration. But a hard and fast distinction between economic and political migration is usually impossible to maintain. Political reasons may come into a decision that appears economic, since political discrimination may underlie an unequal access to resources and jobs. The opposite is also true – that economic motives can be bound up in an apparently political decision to move, if not quite to the extent that a sequence of British Home Secretaries have sought to maintain. In any case, economic pressures can be as constraining as political ones. Is watching your family starve to death because you have no access to land or a job an economic or a political issue? These complexities mean that a potential migrant's decision-making process now tends not to be analysed in terms of push-and-pull factors, but modelled as a matrix whose defining points are on one axis economic and political, and on the other voluntary and involuntary, with each individual's motivation usually a complex combination of all four elements.[36] In general terms, would-be migrants can be understood as facing a kind of investment choice. The decision to migrate involves various initial costs – of transport, of lost income while employment is sought, of the psychological stress of leaving the loved and familiar – which have to be weighed against possible longer-term gains available at the projected destination. Depending upon personal calculation, the individual might choose to leave or to stay, or to leave temporarily with a view to making enough of a gain to render a return life in the home country much more comfortable (another major cause of return migration).

All this is enlightening and challenging in pretty much equal measure, but at the macro level, migration studies have a still more profound lesson to offer. Not least because politics cannot be easily separated from economics anyway, economic factors remain one of the fundamental triggers of migration. Disparities in levels of economic development between two areas, or in the availability of natural resources, have been shown repeatedly to make a migration flow between them likely, so long, of course, as the immigrant population also values the commodity which is more available at the point of destination. This is a fundamental conclusion of so-called 'world systems theories', which study relations between economically more developed centres and less developed peripheries, where some migration between the two often proves to be a major component of the relationship.[37]

This key observation tells us two things. First, a satisfactory study of migration in any era will require a combination of more general analysis (such as the basic economic contexts making migration likely) with the answers to a series of precise questions: who exactly participated in the flow of migration, why, and how exactly the process began and developed?[38] Second, and even more important, it emphasizes that there is a profound connection between migration and patterns of economic development. Because of the legacy of the invasion hypothesis, it is traditional in first-millennium studies to draw a clear dividing line between internal engines of social transformation, such as economic and political development, and the external effects of migration. For a generation and more of archaeologists since the 1960s, internal transformation has been seen as locked in a death struggle with migration when it comes to explaining observable changes in the unearthed record of the past. Given this particular intellectual context, the most fundamental lesson to be drawn from migration studies is that such a clear dividing line is misconceived. Patterns of migration are caused above all by prevailing inequalities in patterns of development, and will vary with them, being both cause and effect of their further transformation. In this light, migration and internal transformation cease to be competing lines of explanation, but two sides of the same coin.

Old ways of thinking about the first millennium generated one Grand Narrative of how a more or less recognizable Europe emerged from the ancient world order of Mediterranean domination on the back of a thousand years of invasion and ethnic cleansing. New information and, not least, new understandings of both group identity and migration have effectively demolished that vision, and it is time to replace it with something new. It is this central challenge that *Empires and Barbarians* will attempt to take up, arguing above all that migration and development need to be considered together, not kept apart as competing lines of explanation. They are interconnected phenomena, which only together can satisfactorily explain how Mediterranean domination of the barbarian north and east came to be broken, and a recognizable Europe emerged from the wreck of the ancient world order.

# 2

# GLOBALIZATION AND THE GERMANI

IN THE SUMMER OF 357 AD, a huge army of Germani, led by various
kings of the Alamanni, collected itself on the western, Roman, side of
the River Rhine near the modern city of Strasbourg. As Ammianus
Marcellinus, in the most detailed narrative history to survive from the
later Roman period (c.275 onwards), reports it:

> All these warlike and savage tribes were led by Chnodomarius
> and Serapio, kings higher than all the rest in authority. And
> Chnodomarius, who was in fact the infamous instigator of the
> whole disturbance, rode before the left wing with a flame-
> coloured plume on his helmet . . . a doughty soldier and a skilful
> general beyond all the rest. But the right wing was led by Serapio
> . . . he was the son of Mederichus, Chnodomarius' brother . . .
> who had for a long time been kept as a hostage in Gaul . . . These
> were then followed by the kings next in power, five in number,
> by ten princes [regales], with a long train of nobles [optimates], and
> 35,000 troops levied from various nations, partly for pay and
> partly under agreement to return the service.

Ammianus' description beautifully captures the absence of unified
kingship among the Germanic Alamanni who dominated the southern
sector of Rome's Rhine frontier in the late imperial period. On the
basis of it, indeed, historians have sometimes argued that little had
changed in the Germanic world since the first century AD, when
Cornelius Tacitus wrote his famous gazetteer. One of the central
points brought home by even the quickest read of Tacitus' *Germania* is
just how fragmented, in political terms, the Germanic world was at
that date. His work – and in this it is well supported by the slightly
later, second-century, *Geography* of Ptolemy – records far too many
primary political units to list by name: well over fifty. The best thing
to do is place them on a map, which, even if the geographical
placements are approximate, gives an excellent sense of first-century

Germanic political fragmentation (Map 2).[1] A closer look suggests, however, that it is a mistake to suppose that, just because the Alamanni had plenty of kings in the fourth century, nothing important had changed since the first.


# THE TRANSFORMATION OF GERMANIC EUROPE


A first indication of the extent of the change emerges from a quick glance at a situation map for Germanic Europe in the mid-fourth century, which looks very different from its counterpart in the time of Tacitus (Map 3). The south-east has a completely different complexion, with the rise to dominance of various Gothic groups in, around and to the east of the Carpathian Mountains. In the west, too, much had changed. In place of the multiplicity of smaller units known to Tacitus and Ptolemy, four larger groupings dominated the landscape on and just behind Rome's Rhine frontier: Alamanni and Franks on the frontier line, Saxons and Burgundians just behind. In trying to understand the workings of these fourth-century entities, we are, as usual, struggling against the general lack of interest in things 'barbarian' among Roman authors, but, thanks overwhelmingly to Ammianus, we have much more evidence for the Alamanni than for the rest. And, as Ammianus' narrative makes clear, politics among the Alamanni were complex.


## Politics Transformed

In the surviving books of his history, which cover the years 354 to 378 in considerable detail, Ammianus never offers us an analytical account of how politics worked among the Alamanni, or of the institutional structures that sustained rulers in power. What he does provide is a more or less connected narrative of a quarter-century of the Alamannic confederation, as it can best be called, in action, from which it emerges clearly that Germanic politics in this part of the Rhine frontier region had seen two fundamental transformations since the time of Tacitus.

First – and this much is uncontroversial – leadership within the different groups that made up the Alamanni, those headed by the various kings and princes who showed up for Strasbourg and who feature elsewhere in Ammianus' narrative, was more solidly constructed than had been the case in the first century. Tacitus' works – not only his *Germania*, but also the narratives of his *Annals* and *Histories* – give us a fair amount of information about pretty much the same regions of Germania in the first century. At that date, some Germanic groups, such as the Usipii and Tenchteri, functioned entirely happily without any kings at all: group policy, where necessary, being decided by an oligarchy of leading men (Latin, *principes*) discussing matters together in council. And even where royal authority was achieved by a single individual over a particular group, this was never accepted without resistance and usually proved transient, power not passing on to a designated son or heir. In the second decade of the first century AD, the two dominant monarchical figures of contemporary Germanic politics were Arminius among the Cherusci and Maroboduus among the Marcomanni. Arminius' dominance was extremely brief. It was based on leading the famous revolt that had destroyed Varus' three legions at the Teutoburger Wald in 9 AD, but he was only one of several leading figures among the Cherusci. Victory gave him a brief pre-eminence, but it was always contested, not least by Segestes, a second leader of the Cherusci who even aided the Romans. Arminius' power was already ebbing away, in fact, before his death in 19 AD at the hands of a faction of his own countrymen. Maroboduus' dominance had deeper roots, but was eventually undermined both by Rome and by internal rivals, so that in the time of Tacitus, at the turn of the second century, the Marcomanni were no longer ruled by Maroboduus' heirs.[2]

Political life among the fourth-century Alamanni, by contrast, was all about kings (*reges*) and princes. The evidence we have suggests that the region called Alamannia by Ammianus was divided into a series of cantons or sub-regions (the Germanic for which was probably already *gau*), each of which (or all that we know of) was ruled by a *rex* or *regalis*. This royal power seems also to have been at least partly hereditary, if not necessarily in a simple pattern from father to son, then through royal clans. Chnodomarius and Serapio, the dominant leaders at Strasbourg, were uncle and nephew, and Serapio's father Mederichus had been important enough to enjoy a lengthy spell as hostage among the Romans, during which time he developed a penchant for the cult of the Egyptian god Serapis, which led to his son's strikingly non-Germanic name. In Ammianus, we also come across a father and son, Vadomarius and Vithicabius, each of whom was king in turn. It is important not to generalize unwisely. Alamannic kings could be overthrown. One Gundomadus was killed by his own followers because he wouldn't join the army that fought at Strasbourg. Likewise, some people other than kings remained important in Alamannic society. Ammianus, again, picks out the *optimates* who were present at the battle. Nonetheless, kings are a much bigger and more stable presence among the fourth-century Alamanni than they had been in the early Roman period.[3]

Second, the Alamannic confederation as a whole operated as a much more solid political entity than its first-century counterparts. This is a more controversial point because, as we have seen, the Alamanni did not function as a centralized entity, with a single, unchallenged ruler. There never was just a single king of the Alamanni at any point in the fourth century. And first-century Germania had itself been perfectly capable of throwing up larger confederations, incorporating a number of the small primary political units. For some scholars, therefore, the evidence does not suggest substantial change. But the supratribal confederations of the first century were either longer-lived (though not unchanging) and primarily religious in function, or else, where they were political, highly transient. Tacitus mentions three 'cult leagues' (groups of tribes who shared an attachment to a common religious cult in addition to their own individual ones): the Ingvaeones, nearest the sea, the Herminones of the interior and the Istvaeones of the west. We don't know all that much about them, and I would not want to underestimate their overall importance to the early Germanic world, since Ptolemy knew of them too, meaning that they persisted on through the first century into the second. But the narratives of attempted and actual Roman conquests in the region demonstrate that the cult leagues never operated as the basis for political or military response to outside assault. Whatever their significance – and it might well have been substantial in other areas of life – the cult leagues were not political organizations of importance. When resistance to Rome or – at a slightly earlier period – attempted Germanic expansion into the Celtic-dominated world took a confederative political form, it was organized around dominant individuals: Ariovistus in the time of Caesar, Arminius and Maroboduus at the time of projected Roman conquest of the area between the Rhine and the Elbe; or, later, the great revolt organized by the Batavian leader Julius Civilis. These leaders all knitted together – using a mixture of attraction, persuasion and intimidation – large confederations, which drew on a warrior base from across extensive reaches of the Germanic world; that is, from many of the small political units listed by Tacitus and, later, Ptolemy. In every instance, however, these confederations crashed with the defeat of their leaders, and are never heard of again. That of Maroboduus lasted a little longer than the others, but even that unravelled quickly after his death.[4]

It is on this level, the stability of the overall confederation, that a comparison between the first century and the fourth is so telling. The outcome of the battle of Strasbourg was a thumping defeat for the Alamanni:

> There fell in this battle on the Roman side two hundred and forty-three soldiers and four senior officers ... But of the Alamanni there were counted six thousand corpses lying on the field, and heaps of dead, impossible to reckon, were carried off by the waters of the river [Rhine].

Chnodomarius himself was captured as he tried to flee back across the river. The Caesar Julian, ruling in the west in the name of his cousin Augustus Constantius II, then exploited victory to impose terms of his own choosing on the various Alamannic kings who survived the engagement; and, in fact, Chnodomarius had only been able to assemble his forces with such freedom because a Roman civil war had generated a power vacuum in the Rhine frontier region in the first place. Nonetheless, and this is where the fourth century is completely different from the first, the defeat of Chnodomarius did not mean the total destruction of the alliance at whose head he had stood, as the defeats of his first-century counterparts such as Arminius and Maroboduus had done three centuries before. Not only were many of the lesser Alamannic kings who had participated in the battle left in place by Julian's diplomacy, but, within a decade of the battle, a new pre-eminent leader, Vadomarius, was worrying the Romans. He was skilfully removed by assassination, but then a third appeared in his place: Macrianus. Ammianus records three separate attempts by one of Julian's successors, Valentinian I, to eliminate Macrianus by capture and/or assassination, but eventually, pressed by events further east, the emperor gave in. Roman and Alamann met in the middle of the Rhine for a water-borne summit, where the emperor acknowledged Macrianus' pre-eminence among the Alamanni.[5] Unlike in the first century, even major military defeat was not enough to destroy the larger, Alamannic confederation.

This suggests that the confederation had a political identity that was much more firmly rooted than its first-century counterparts, in the sense that it did not rise and fall with the careers of single individuals. As circumstances changed, one canton king or another might rise to pre-eminence, but the confederation as a whole could survive the vagaries of individual political careers more or less intact. The strength of these ties is also suggested by some of the nuggets of information Ammianus preserves, not least about the canton king Gundomadus who was overthrown by a faction of his own followers for not participating in the larger group action that led up to Strasbourg. For these men, at least, group identity could at times be a more powerful determinant of political behaviour than loyalty to their local king. How this group identity worked, Ammianus does not tell us. He does report that the kings of the Alamanni feasted each other, and that ties of mutual support bound together at least some of the kings who fought at Strasbourg. In the details of such agreements and of royal feastings would lie the information we would require to understand the fourth-century Alamanni properly, but Ammianus, unfortunately, does not tell us what we need to know.

Like many late antique and early medieval confederative entities, the Alamanni had, I suspect, an established repertoire of political and diplomatic conventions which defined and bound together their various kings in positions of overking and underking, the latter owing allegiance and some duties to the former, while still retaining direct day-to-day control of their own cantons. In these kinds of systems, political continuity could never be absolute. No overking exactly replicated, nor could he usually directly inherit, the patterns of power enjoyed by a predecessor; but, once a new pecking order had been established, there was an accepted type of relationship between kings of varying statuses that could be used to orchestrate and define the rights of both parties – senior and junior – to any new agreement. Such a system was clearly operating, in my view, among the fourth-century Alamanni, and a visible sign of its overall importance is the

general 'shape' of Roman diplomatic policy on this part of the frontier.
Whenever Roman attention was distracted, usually by events on the
Empire's Persian front in Ammianus' time, an Alammanic overking
would duly emerge, and Roman policy on the Rhine was largely
directed towards removing the succession of such figures who
appeared in the course of the period he covers.[6]

Unfortunately, again, Ammianus does not give us any indication
whether similar systems operated among the other large entities of the
Rhine frontier – Franks, Saxons and Burgundians. Like their Alamannic
neighbours, the fourth-century Franks certainly had a plethora of
kings, but we simply do not see them in action often enough to know
whether a Frankish political identity could, likewise, act as the basis
of collective action even after the shock of heavy defeat. And there is
no reason to suppose that all fourth-century Germanic groups had to
operate on exactly the same basis, any more than their predecessors of
three hundred years earlier had done, when, as Tacitus records, some
groups had kings and others did not. Confirmation that broader and
politically more solid group identities were not confined merely to the
Alamanni in the fourth century is provided by the Tervingi, a Goth-
dominated confederation which operated at the other, eastern extreme
of Rome's European frontiers in the foothills of the Carpathians. The
Tervingi are the one other group amongst Rome's Germanic neighbours, apart from the Alamanni, about whom the sources preserve a
substantial amount of information.

In its political operations and durability, the confederation of
the Tervingi shows three characteristics which strongly resemble the
Alamanni and firmly distance it from any first-century ancestor. First,
central control of the Tervingi seems to have been handed down
through at least three generations of the same dynasty between c.330
and c.370, and their official title was 'judge'. As was the case with the
kings of individual cantons among the Alamanni, therefore, power in
this eastern Germanic world had become much more hereditary.
Second, also like the Alamanni, the judges of the Tervingi ruled a
confederation, which involved a number of kings and princes. And
third, the Tervingi confederation was bound together by ties strong
enough to survive even heavy defeat. We first encounter the coalition
in the early 330s, when a massive defeat was inflicted upon it by the
Emperor Constantine. Not only did it survive that defeat, but the same
dynasty retained power and, a generation later, plotted to overthrow

the most burdensome aspects of the terms that Constantine had imposed.[7] It is important to stress that the Alamanni and Tervingi are the only two fourth-century Germanic entities about whom we are at all informed, and that you cannot just assume that every large Germanic grouping of the period worked the same way. Between them, however, the two cases provide excellent evidence that larger and more coherent group identities had emerged in fourth-century Germania than could have been found anywhere within its limits three hundred years before.

How had this come about?

## The Rise of Military Kingship

This is not a story that can be told directly. No major narrative sources survive between the first and fourth centuries to give a detailed account of any aspect of Romano-German relations in the crucial intervening period. Even such a major convulsion as the second-century Marcomannic War has to be reconstructed from fragmentary evidence. In any case, it is doubtful that any – even lost – Roman historian would have covered a broad enough time frame to be able to chart the long-term transformation that culminated in the Alamanni and their contemporaries the Tervingi. The first-century sources document plenty of power struggles between tribes. We even hear of whole tribes being created and destroyed. The Batavi, for instance, were originally an offshoot of the Chatti, while Roman observers witnessed the destruction of the Bructeri, and Tacitus tells us about a fight to the death between the Chatti and the Hermenduri and the eventual destruction of the exiled and unfortunately landless Ampsivarii.[8] Sometimes, too, if less frequently, we even hear of power struggles within tribes, not least that between Arminius and Segestes for control of the Cherusci. But there's nothing in these bits and pieces of information that would lead you to think that Germanic political structures were heading off on a journey towards greater size and coherence. The most dramatic clue as to the kinds of process that really underlay their appearance emerged from one of the least likely places imaginable.

In 1955, a group of Danish workmen were cutting a drainage ditch at Haderslev in the northern Schleswig region of southern Jutland.

Their work quickly came to a halt, however, when one small stretch of their ditch produced an astonishing haul of six hundred metallic objects, many datable to the Roman period. The low-lying meadow where they were working had in ancient times been a lake, if not a particularly deep one. Over the next nine years 1,700 square metres of meadow were carefully excavated, the site producing a whole series of startling finds, not least the remains of a boat. All of these materials had been dumped in the lake at different points in the Roman period, the clustering of objects showing that, on occasion, literally mounds of them were deposited at one go, emptied out from bags or baskets. This was by no means the first Germanic dumping-ground to be excavated. In the later nineteenth century a whole series of north European, particularly Danish, bogs had produced similar clusters of material. But Ejsbøl Mose, to give the Haderslev site its proper name, was the first of these sites to be excavated using modern archaeological methods. This made it possible to answer the big question left unanswered by the earlier digs. Had these dumping-grounds been created by successive small deposits, or a few much bigger ones?

With careful attention to stratigraphic detail, the answer emerged loud and clear. The items found at Ejsbøl Mose had been deposited at several different moments, but, occasionally, huge amounts of material had been sunk at one time. In particular, the excavators were able to identify as a single, unitary deposit, the entire military equipment of a small army of about two hundred men, which had been submerged in the waters at one go somewhere around the year 300 AD. Amounting to many hundreds of individual items, the equipment turned out to belong to a coherent, well-organized force with a clear leadership hierarchy. It comprised close to two hundred spearmen, each armed with a barbed throwing javelin and a lance for thrusting; the excavators found 193 barbed spearheads and another 187 barbless ones. Something like a third of the men also had side-arms. The excavators found 63 belt buckle sets, with 60 of the swords and 62 of the knives that the belts had originally housed. The military force had been led by ten or more commanders on horseback. Ten bridles and seven sets of spurs were all part of the swag.

Interestingly, all of this equipment had been ritually destroyed before being sunk in the lake. The swords had all been bent out of shape, and many fragments of wood came from smashed spear hafts.

The obvious violence of the process makes it impossible not to associate the remains with the kinds of ritual act occasionally reported in the historical sources, whereby the weapons of an enemy were offered as a sacrifice to the gods.[9] One or two horsemen may have escaped on foot, or maybe the missing spurs were just lost. Essentially, though, the excavators had found the last material remains of a military force wiped out in some long-forgotten, entirely unrecorded *Vernichtungsschlacht* (battle of annihilation) from the turn of the fourth century.

As an archaeological set-piece, Ejsbøl Mose is fantastic, but the finds have a broader significance. The clear image that emerges from them – of a professional, well-organized force with a well-structured hierarchy – coincides with a considerable body of literary evidence that, by the fourth century, Germanic leaders of royal rank – kings – had personal and permanent establishments of household warriors, on precisely this scale of magnitude. When the Romans eventually cornered him after Strasbourg, Chnodomarius' retinue surrendered as well as their leader himself. Coincidentally, it also numbered two hundred men. These retinues had an obvious military function, but a few precious indications confirm what you would otherwise have to suppose, that they were also employed more generally as an instrument of social power. When the leaders of the Tervingi decided that they would attempt to enforce uniformity of belief among their subjects in the early 370s, retinue members were sent round to Gothic villages to demand compliance. The key point here is that Tacitus reports the existence of no institution of this kind for the first century. Retinues and warbands existed at that time, but they were not permanent, and prominent individual leaders received only occasional voluntary donations of food for the upkeep of the men in their service. Archaeological material from this earlier era has also thrown up nothing like the professional, variegated weaponry uncovered at Ejsbol Mose. In the intervening two centuries, Germanic kings had begun to dispose of an entirely new level of permanent military muscle.[10] This immediately explains, of course, why they themselves should appear in our fourth-century sources as a much more permanent and prevalent fixture of Germanic society than their counterparts from the time of Tacitus.

Further striking testimony to the importance of this development has also emerged from a totally different quarter. One of the more exotic and demanding disciplines within the field of humanities is comparative philology – the study of the linguistic origins of words and meanings, together with their transfer between different language groups. As a recent study has demonstrated, all Germanic languages derived their terms for 'king' or 'leader' from just three root words: *thiudans* ('ruler of a people'), *truthin* and *kuning*. Of these, *thiudans* is certainly the oldest, being the only one with parallels in other Indo-European languages, but the pattern of its distribution across the different branches of the German language family also shows that it was falling, or had fallen, out of use by the late Roman period, when it was being replaced by *truthin*. *Kuning* came into currency only later. The striking point is that *truthin* originally meant 'leader of a warband', but by the late Roman period had come into use as the main term for 'king' or 'leader' right across the Germanic world. There is much more to this than merely a change of name. *Thiudans* meant ruler of a people, for whom any military function was only part of the job profile, and perhaps only a relatively small part. Famously, Tacitus remarks of Germanic societies of the first century that 'they chose kings for their nobility, war leaders for their courage', which seems to imply as much. By the fourth century, the new leadership terminology indicates that this distinction had disappeared, and that military command had become the primary function of contemporary Germanic leaders. It is hard to think of better testimony to the overwhelming importance of the rise, by the late Roman period, of a new kind of leader, who owed the strength of his position to having at his beck and call a permanent body of warriors.[11] Archaeology, literary sources and philology all come together to bring to light the roots of the more solidly founded form of kingship that we meet in the fourth century.

What transpired between the first and fourth centuries, then, was broadly this: a class of military leaders developed a new kind of military muscle, and used it to put greater distance, in terms of social power, between themselves and everyone else. It doesn't take more than a moment's reflection to realize that this could never have been an entirely consensual process, since a small elite was busy asserting its dominance over everybody else. And this, of course, provides one possible context for the events that culminated in the weapons deposition at Ejsbøl Mose. What the archaeologists found there was the weaponry of an entire military retinue. And since the weapons themselves had been so thoroughly destroyed, it's a pretty safe bet that this fate was shared by the men who had wielded them. In establishing their social dominance, the new military kings were playing for high stakes, and Ejsbøl Mose serves as a reminder that for every group that succeeded, another, or several others, failed. Two possible scenarios for this failure immediately suggest themselves. The warrior group unintentionally immortalized there may have been destroyed by another, rival warrior band, or by a group of ordinary, less military Germani, who didn't appreciate the kind of dominance that the warriors' leader had in mind. In Hollywood terms, we might be thinking *Godfather* – the ancient lake having been used by a dominant king to send to any rivals the message that they were likely to end up sleeping with the (in this case freshwater) fishes; or *Magnificent Seven* – a band of peasants having found enough military effectiveness to rid themselves of at least one predatory warband. There's no way to be sure, although the fury of the destruction might suggest Yul Brynner rather than Al Pacino, since in some later instances we know of, victorious warband leaders tended to absorb the troops of a defeated rival to increase their own power.[12] But this is a detail. The fundamental point is that the rise of the military kings can only have come about through a periodically violent process whereby rivalries both between different warband leaders and between that class of leader and those they sought to dominate, slowly worked themselves out.

## Expansion and Development

But this is only part of the story. The kind of military retinue destroyed at Ejsbøl Mose, or employed by Chnodomarius, was a high-maintenance item. Not producing their own foodstuffs, professional warriors required feeding, and all the evidence evocative of Germanic warbands at play – mostly deriving, admittedly, from later heroic poetry, but bolstered by hints in Ammianus and anthropological parallels from better-documented but analogous contexts – suggests that we are talking about feeding literally on a heroic scale: lots of roasted meat and alcohol as brought to the big screen recently in Hollywood's *Beowulf*. Military equipment was also not cheap. Admittedly, there is no sign of any body armour in the Ejsbøl Mose finds, and that was the single most expensive item of personal military hardware in the ancient and medieval worlds. Ammianus comments, for instance, that Chnodomarius was easily distinguishable on the battlefield because of his armour, suggesting that even in the fourth century it was not generally being worn by Germanic warriors. Nonetheless, swords were possessed by maybe one-third of the Ejsbøl Mose force. Most of the rest of a warrior's distinguishing equipment was also made by highly skilled craftsmen from expensive raw materials.[13] In other words, the retinues that made the new military kings such a powerful feature of the fourth-century Germanic land-scape could not come into being without two preconditions. First, there had to be surpluses of foodstuffs and/or other forms of negotia-ble wealth being produced by the economy around them, and second, the kings had to be able to turn these surpluses, or a significant portion of them, to their own purposes.

This straightforward observation draws real historical bite from the fact that, up to the birth of Christ, substantial food surpluses and other forms of negotiable wealth were in short supply right across Germanic Europe. The place to start unravelling this story is agricultural produc-tion. The economy of Germanic Europe – as indeed that of Roman and every other kind of Europe in the first millennium – was fundamentally agricultural. There are, however, more and less produc-tive types of agricultural economy. Archaeological research undertaken since the Second World War has demonstrated that Germanic Europe went through its own agricultural revolution during the four hundred years when the Roman Empire was its closest western and southern neighbour.

At the start of the period, agricultural practice east of the Rhine was generally 'extensive': 'extensive', that is, as opposed to 'intensive'. This meant that a relatively large area was required to support a given population unit, because yields were low. It was entirely characteristic of this kind of farming regime that settlements tended to be small, widely dispersed, and to last for no more than a generation or two on any one site. Essentially, the populations of Germanic Europe did not, or did not have to, maintain the fertility of their fields so as to maximize crop production in any given year, or keep the same field in use over anything but the short to medium term. Once yields began to decline below a level that they found acceptable, they would move on to a new area. The evidence underpinning this interpretation comes in many and varied forms.

In large parts of central-northern Europe, the boundaries of the then widely prevalent 'Celtic field' system are still visible in the form of stone walls constructed out of debris cleared from the fields in the course of cultivating them. The fields are extremely large, reflecting the sheer amount of land that was required to keep a single family in business. Known settlement patterns confirm the point. Before 1945, few Germanic settlements belonging to the first two centuries AD had been identified; the early Germani were largely studied, in archaeological terms, from their cemeteries. That situation has now been reversed, with the ratio of settlements to cemeteries standing at 7:1 and growing fast, but the reason for the earlier imbalance has also become evident. All of the settlements now known from these early centuries were small and short-lived. Knowing that any settlement had only a limited life expectancy, in no instance did the inhabitants invest much time or effort in their construction. Therefore, the settlements were both large in overall number and were originally difficult to find. The little direct evidence of prevailing agricultural techniques that happens to survive confirms the point. The well-excavated Germanic-period cemetery at Odry in modern Poland, for instance, was established right on top of an old 'Celtic field'. From underneath one of the excavated barrows emerged evidence of the ploughing and fertilization regimes employed. Both were rudimentary. Ploughing took the form of narrow, criss-crossed scrapings. This means that the soil was not being turned over, and hence that weeds and crop residues were not rotting back into the soil to restore its vital nutrients, particularly nitrogen. The only form of additional fertilization in evidence was some ash. Employing these kinds of techniques, arable fertility could not long be maintained.[14]

Conclusive evidence that something changed dramatically in Germanic agricultural practice over the course of the Roman period has emerged since the 1950s, starting in the muddy fields of coastal areas of modern Holland and Germany. By this time, when Ejsbøl Mose was being excavated to such good purpose, archaeological interest was turning generally to settlement, and techniques had advanced to such an extent that really useful results could be obtained. The first major excavations of early Germanic settlements focused on the characteristic manmade mounds of these coastal areas – called *terpen* in Dutch and *Wierde* in German – formed by many years of sequential settlement on the same, originally low-lying, site. Over the years rotted refuse, house timbers and other human debris caused the ground level of the settled area to rise. This made these sites an obvious target for archaeological excavation, but local farmers had also long realized that the mounds were piled high with fertile topsoil, so many had been fully or partially grubbed out before the archaeologists got there.

The most detailed work was done at a site that has become celebrated in the field, if little known outside it: Feddersen Wierde. Careful stratigraphic excavation over the best part of a decade, from 1955 to 1963, allowed the full evolution of the settlement to be established. It began in the middle of the first century AD, when five families established themselves there. They comprised a total of maybe fifty people at maximum and practised a mixed agriculture, with much effort put into the rearing of cattle. From the number of animal stalls constructed in the first phase, the five initial families possessed about a hundred cows. But this was only the beginning. The settlement prospered over the next three centuries, reaching its maximum extent in the later third century AD, by which time it numbered as many as three hundred inhabitants who, between them, possessed upwards of four hundred and fifty cows. Many detailed studies have been done of myriad aspects of daily life there, but, for our purposes, the key point is the settlement's size and longevity. What these indirectly reflect is a revolution in agricultural practice. Under the old extensive agricultural regimes of the early Germanic world, this many people living in such close proximity for over three hundred years would have been inconceivable. Production could never have been that intense, nor fertility maintained for so long. Feddersen Wierde was only possible because its population had adopted a much more intensive agricultural regime, which allowed them to maximize the fertility of their fields to a much greater extent, and permitted a much greater concentration of population to thrive over many generations. The full details of the revolution are beyond reconstruction, but it certainly involved using the manure from all the cattle in a more integrated fashion to maintain the fertility of arable fields.[15]

It would be rash to generalize from this one example, nor is there any reason to suppose that Feddersen Wierde – based on a greater integration of pastoral and arable agriculture – provides the only possible model of Germanic agricultural intensification. A substantial number of other excavations of Roman-period settlements have made it clear, however, that it was by no means an isolated example of rural development. Nearly as famous as Feddersen Wierde is Wijster, also in north-western Germania. There, originally a single family began to farm in the middle of the first century BC. Grubbing-out by modern farmers meant that large parts of this site were too damaged to excavate properly, but by the fourth century the one family farm had grown into an extensive settlement housing between at least fifty and sixty families, who were busy exploiting the easily worked sandy soils overlooking the mouth of the nearby River Drenthe. Other large settlements of the Roman period excavated in this area beyond the Rhine frontier include Hodde, Vorbasse, Ginderup, Mariesminde and Norre Fjand.

Elsewhere, the picture is not so comprehensive, nor is the precise mode of agricultural intensification so well understood, but enough is known to document the fact that Germanic rural development was a general phenomenon of the Roman period. In what is now central Germany, and the eastern and south-eastern reaches of ancient Germania beyond the Carpathians, the evolving settlement pattern is known in much less detail, and there is no reason, of course, why agricultural practice had to have changed everywhere at the same time. Nonetheless, enough big settlements are known from all these regions – Barhorst, fifty kilometres west of Berlin with thirty families, for instance, or, in the far south-east, the many large settlements of the Goth-dominated Cernjachov system of the fourth century – to show that more intensive agricultural regimes had evolved right across Germanic-dominated Europe in the course of the Roman centuries. Some isolated finds of agricultural equipment indicate the same, iron ploughshares and coulters showing that the soil was being more effectively turned over by the fourth century. The greater size and longevity of settlements, combined with all the evidence for more effective ploughing equipment, document a major transformation of agricultural practice in Germanic Europe in the early centuries AD, even if its techniques remained considerably less specialized than on the other, Roman side of the frontier.[16]

Two observations follow. First, the massive increase in food production that this revolution in agricultural production must have generated goes a long way towards explaining how the new military kings could support their retinues. Before it unfolded, it must be doubtful that there was enough surplus food in the undeveloped Germanic agricultural economy to support permanent specialist warriors on the fourth-century scale. Second, and this is a much broader

point, the vast increase in food production also implies that the
population of Germanic Europe increased exponentially during the
same period. There is no way to put a figure on the increase, but, as
the demographers teach us, one of the key limits on the size of any
human population is always the availability of food. The Germanic
agricultural revolution, with its vast increase in food supplies, meant
that the population must have grown accordingly. Demographic expansion also shows up in other evidence. In Germanic cemeteries occupied
throughout the Roman period and excavated with due attention to
stratigraphy, larger numbers of people are found interred in those
areas in use in the third and fourth centuries compared with the
preceding two hundred years. Pollen studies, likewise, provide an
alternative view of the same development. Over the first four centuries
AD, the proportion of pollen produced by cereal crops increased at the
expense of grass and tree pollen, a further indication of agricultural
intensification.[17]

This major increase in agricultural output not only explains how
retinues were fed, but must also have been one basic source of the
new wealth in Germanic society of this period, visible most obviously
in the form of the retinues' expensive military equipment. Food
surpluses could be exchanged for other desirable items. But while
perhaps of central importance, agriculture was not the only source of
new wealth. Evidence has emerged in recent years to show that, over
the first four centuries, the overall economic wealth of Germanic
Europe was being increased dramatically by a marked diversification
of production and an associated increase in the exchange of a whole
series of other goods besides food.

The evidence for both metal production and its subsequent working is highly suggestive of a similar pattern of expansion in that sector
of the economy. In particular, two major centres of production in the
territory of modern Poland – in the Świętokrzyskie Mountains and in
southern Mazovia – are between them estimated to have produced
upwards of 8,000,000 kilograms of raw iron in the Roman period, with
exploitation increasing dramatically in the later centuries. For metalworking, the evidence is more fragmentary, but equally suggestive.
When they were first excavated, it was thought that the sixty swords
from Ejsbøl Mose represented the greatest find of Roman swords ever
discovered in one cache. More detailed analysis has shown, however,
that, though based on Roman models, the swords were actually copies

forged in Germanic Europe. By c.300 AD, therefore, at least one centre was turning out standardized military equipment on a reasonably large scale, whereas the Germanic swords known from earlier eras were all individual products.[18]

Evidence for the working of precious metals is equally striking. A hoard of exquisite gold and silver vessels was found at Pietroasa in Romania in the later nineteenth century. Much of it dates to the fifth century, but at least one of the silver dishes was produced in the fourth century and outside the Roman Empire, in Germanic Europe. Moulds for making these kinds of item have been discovered in fourth-century Germanic contexts, and the general level of personal adornments made from precious metals increases over the Roman period. By the fourth century, intricately worked silver *fibulae* – safety-pins – by which the Germani customarily fastened their clothes, had become reasonably common, and the remains of workshops for producing them have been found at at least one royal seat among the Alamanni. In the first two centuries AD, *fibulae* had usually been made of bronze or iron. From the mid-third century, Germanic pottery began to change its modes of production. In the third and fourth centuries, Germanic potters for the first time – if not everywhere, and not at the same moment – started to use the wheel to form their wares. This development was combined with much improved kiln technology, allowing the pots to be fired at far higher temperatures, and led to a considerably higher quality of pottery becoming widely available across Germanic Europe. Switching to wheel-made pottery not only generates a higher-quality product but is closely associated with larger-scale, more commercial production. In some areas the transformation was total. In the Goth-dominated Cernjachov world north of the Black Sea in the fourth century, wheel-made tablewares, largely indistinguishable from their provincial Roman counterparts, became the norm (although cooking pots were still made by hand). Among the contemporary Alamanni, by contrast, several local experiments in wheel-made wares never managed to achieve either longevity or widespread distribution – in face, perhaps, of stiffer and nearer Roman competition than their Gothic counterparts. But before the late Roman era, all high-quality wheel-made wares found in Germanic contexts were, without exception, Roman imports, so even this much economic development represents a major transformation.[19]

Metalworking and pottery production are obviously major areas of the non-agricultural economy, producing both more expensive and cheaper, more widely consumed items. Increasingly professional production methods are visible in other sectors of the later Germanic economy as well, some of them again entirely new. One of the most dramatic is glass production. Before the fourth century, all the glass found in non-Roman Europe was Roman, imported across the frontier. But sometime after 300 AD, a glass production centre opened at Komarov in the hinterland of the Carpathians. Its products came to be distributed widely across central and eastern Europe (Map 3). The various contexts in which the glass has been found indicate that it was an elite item, often used as a mark of status. Though hardly a major employer, its production would certainly have represented a highly valuable addition to someone's economy. An equally fascinating, though entirely different, example has turned up in an excavated village within the lands dominated by Goths in the fourth century. At Birlad-Valea Seaca in modern Romania, investigators found no less than sixteen huts devoted to the production of one item characteristically found in graves of this period: combs constructed from deer antler. Hairstyles were used by some Germanic groups to express political affiliations, and also to express status. The most famous example is the so-called Suebic knot described by Tacitus and beautifully preserved on one early Germanic skull (Plate 4). In this context, it is hardly surprising that combs were a significant personal possession. Within the huts, parts of combs in every stage of production were discovered, shedding light on the whole process. In this case, it would seem, an entire settlement was devoted to the production of one key item.[20]

Not only agricultural production, then, but other areas of the economy of Germanic Europe had begun to blossom – in relative terms – by the late Roman period. Right across the region, the early centuries AD witnessed an explosion of development and wealth generation. And like globalization now, at least as important a historical phenomenon as the new wealth itself was the much less comfortable fact that it was not being shared remotely equally. Development in the Germanic world generated clear winners but also clear losers, and it is at this point that military kings, their retainers, and economic development converge still more closely. Many of the items being produced, not just the food, were being consumed by the new military kings and their armed retinues. The iron was necessary for steel weaponry, obviously, but some at least of the glass, precious metal objects and even the higher-quality pottery was aimed in their direction. All of these items have turned up in burials, which careful analysis can show to have belonged to the Germanic social elite of the late Roman period.[21] Just how big a social and political revolution had been set in motion?

## WARRIORS, KINGS AND ECONOMICS

Romantic nineteenth-century conceptions of early Germanic society, framed at the height of nationalist fervour, propounded the notion of early German *Freiheit*, 'freedom': the idea that Germania before the birth of Christ was a world of free and equal noble savages, with no intermediate nobility but with kings who were directly answerable to assemblies of freemen. This was mistaken. Even in the time of Tacitus, Germanic societies had slaves, though the slaves ran their own farms and handed over part of the produce rather than living under closer domination as unfree labour on someone else's estate. And although the material remains of the Germanic world in the last few centuries BC show no obvious distinctions of status, this does not mean that there weren't any. Even in a materially simple culture – and in the third century BC about the greatest sign of social distinction available among the Germani of north-central Europe was to keep your clothes on with a slightly fancier safety-pin – differences of status can still make a huge difference to quality of life. If higher status translated merely into eating more, doing less hard manual labour and having a better chance of passing on your genes successfully, it was nonetheless extremely real, even if it could not be expressed in the possession of much in the way of fancy material goods. I doubt very much, in fact, that the status distinctions we find in Tacitus were new to the Germanic world of the first century AD, even if they can't be measured easily in archaeologically visible material items over the preceding centuries.[22]

That said, the evidence is entirely compelling that pre-existing inequalities grew dramatically during the Roman period. We have met some of this already. The new military kings and their retinues, those at least who prospered, were one set of beneficiaries from the new wealth. Archaeologically, their rise is reflected in two ways: burial practice and settlement remains. There is no simple correlation between wealth of gravegoods and status in life. Really rich graves (called *Fürstengräber*, 'princely burials', in the germanophone literature) cluster chronologically with, broadly speaking, one group at the end of the first century and another at the end of the third: the so-called Lübsow and Leuna Hassleben types respectively. It is not credible, though, that a dominant social elite existed only at these limited moments, and it has been suggested that their appearance may mark periods of social stress, when new claims to high status were being made – claims by the individuals running the funeral, of course, rather than the dead persons themselves. Nonetheless, over the long term, changing burial practices certainly reflect the impact of new wealth. Before the last few centuries BC, Germanic funerary rites seem to have been pretty much identical for all, a little handmade pottery and the occasional personal item being all that the cremation burials of the period characteristically contained. In the Roman period, by contrast, not only are there the clusters of extremely rich princely burials, but also a substantial minority of the other burials started to contain increasing numbers of gravegoods, often including weapons with males and jewellery with women. Monumentalizing graves was another strategy for claiming status in some parts of Germanic Europe, particularly Poland, where groups of burials were marked out as special by piling up stones to create barrows, and individual graves by erecting standing stones (*stelae*). The Wielbark cemetery at Odry, for instance, turned up five hundred flat burials and twenty-nine barrows.[23]

Settlement archaeology, too, generally reflects the kinds of change under way. At the top end of society, the elite dwellings inhabited by the kings and princes of the Alamanni have been quite extensively investigated. One of the best-known is the Runder Berg at Urach, within the territory of the Alamanni. Here in the late third or early fourth century a hill-top area, with maximum dimensions of 70 metres by 50, was surrounded by a stout timber rampart. Inside were a number of timber buildings, including what looks suspiciously like a substantial hall for feasting retainers and/or fellow kings. The lower slopes housed other buildings, including workshops for craftsmen and possibly dwellings for other servants, and the site as a whole has produced higher concentrations of imported Roman pottery and other elite items than the more run-of-the-mill rural sites. No large dwellings dating to the pre-Roman period have ever been thrown up within the bounds of Germania, but in the early centuries AD they started to become reasonably common. At a lower level of grandeur, at Feddersen Wierde again, one particular house within the village was marked out from all the others in the early second century. It was substantially larger and surrounded by a wooden palisade. The excavators interpreted it as the dwelling of a local headman. Similar examples of particularly large dwellings are known from a number of other sites as well, such as Haldern near Wesel and Kablow, thirty kilometres southeast of Berlin; all date to the Roman period. Within the particularly well-studied territories of the Alamanni, no less than sixty-two elite dwellings of one kind or another, dating to the fourth and fifth centuries, have been identified, of which ten have been excavated; and other similar sites, though less thoroughly studied, have turned up right across Germanic Europe, even as far east as the Gothic-dominated territories north of the Black Sea.[24]

The general picture, then, is clear enough. Settlements and grave-goods show up an increasing social inequality, and it doesn't take much thought to see how possession of military might allowed kings and, through them, their retainers to gain privileged access to a more than equal share of the new wealth. By the fourth century, as a direct result, we are faced with a Germanic world that was marked by more social stratification than its first-century counterpart and, in some places at least, greater structural stability in its political organization. It is, in fact, entirely natural that these two phenomena should have gone together. Class definition and state formation have long proved inseparable bedfellows when patterns in the evolution of human social organization have been subjected to comparative study. But how far-reaching had this inequality become by the fourth century, and how should we understand the new political entities that dominated the landscape? Were they 'states' in any meaningful sense of the word?

Categorizing human societies and their political systems is a subject with a long and complex history stretching back to Aristotle and beyond. In the modern era, it received a whole new impetus from the significance that Marx and Engels ascribed to the state and its evolution. In classic Marxist analysis, the state is the sum and guarantor of the social, political and legal structures by which the dominant class in any given era perpetuates its control over the prime means of producing wealth at that time: whether we're talking land in the ancient world, heavy industry in the recent past, or computer software and hardware now. This brute reality is always hidden behind some kind of ideological cloak whereby the elite tells everyone else that the state exists for the benefit of them all, but if you look hard enough, according to the Marxist perspective, it always turns out to be about maintaining the power of the privileged. More recent work has moved well beyond this kind of simple Marxist agenda, with a complex literature devoted to analysing early state forms along a spectrum of size and sophistication marked out by terms such as 'tribe', 'simple chiefdom', 'complex chiefdom' and 'early state'. Rather than worrying too much about where to place the fourth-century Alamannic and Gothic confederations along this sliding scale, though, we can make better use of this literature in a more general way by identifying four key areas to investigate when seeking to understand the operations of any political system.[25]

The first, straightforwardly, is scale. What magnitude of human population is being brought together by the political system under discussion? Second, what kind of governmental systems does it employ? Are there any bureaucrats or governmental functionaries, and what kind of powers do they deploy, using what technologies? The third area is the level of economic development and associated social stratification generally at play. Whether you accept the Marxist diagnosis of why this is so or not, it is simply the case that particular types of political system tend to be associated with particular types of economic organization. Large, centralized governmental systems cannot be supported by economies that do not produce an economic surplus of the appropriate size to pay for the existence of the functionaries not engaged in primary agricultural production.[26] Fourth and finally, we must look hard at a society's political relationships. How are rulers chosen and legitimized, and by what mechanisms do they create and sustain their authority? In particular, this area is concerned with the balance between force and consent, and the extent to which rulers need to give something to their subjects – whatever that might be – in return and in justification for the economic and other support that they themselves receive.[27]

Investigating fourth-century Germania under any of these headings is not straightforward, given the nature of the available evidence. There is generally little of it, and what there is refers primarily to the

Alamanni and the Gothic Tervingi, adding the further complication of how far we might legitimately generalize from these cases. But, at the very least, these entities document the limits of the possible among the fourth-century Germani, and there are enough points of conjunction between the two (and with what wider evidence there is) to suggest that it is not unreasonable to draw more general conclusions from their capacities and modes of operation.

## Power and the King

On questions of scale, the evidence is far from ideal. But the Alamanni and the Tervingi certainly each had a military capacity – young men of military age – amounting to more than ten thousand individuals. Ammianus tells us that Chnodomarius gathered an army of 35,000 for the battle of Strasbourg. Not all of these were Alamanni, and Roman reporting of barbarian numbers is always questionable, even if, as in this case, not obviously outrageous. But the Roman army numbered 12,000, and that figure – which is more secure – confirms an order of magnitude well over 10,000 for Chnodomarius' force. The Romans still enjoyed a considerable tactical advantage over the Germani in the fourth century, not least because, as we have seen, the latter did not usually possess defensive armour, so that Chnodomarius would probably not have given battle without at least some superiority in numbers. The figures for the Tervingi are less straightforward, but on at least three occasions the confederation sent contingents of three thousand men to serve in Rome's wars against Persia, and this is unlikely to have represented anything like one-third of its total military manpower. The Tervingi were also powerful enough to evade the hostile attentions of the Emperor Valens for the three years between 367 and 369, and I would read Ammianus to imply that, even after a split within the confederation, its larger fragment could put at least 10,000 fighting men in the field. All of this suggests that both Alamanni and Tervingi could field well over 10,000 warriors, and perhaps as many as 20,000. Estimates for the size of the overall population of these confederations depend, of course, upon what proportion of the total group you think likely to have borne arms. The minimum multiplier commonly used is something like four or five to one, implying total group sizes in the 50–100,000 range, but I think this is likely, if anything, to underestimate the total population that formed part of these confederations in some capacity or another.[28]

Nor was any of our Roman sources sufficiently interested to provide a run-down of the governmental structures that made these confederations tick. As will pretty much always be the case throughout this study, therefore, their governmental capacity will have to be deduced largely from the kinds of administrative acts of which the system was capable. In some areas, the Alamanni and Tervingi show an impressive capacity. The least that can be said is that in the face of Roman power, both upheld some concept of their own territorial space. When they were in a position to avoid the most intrusive levels of Roman intervention in their territories, leaders of both the Alamanni and the Tervingi met Roman emperors in summit meetings on boats in the middle of the Rivers Rhine and Danube respectively, meetings which symbolically asserted that the river lines marked clear boundaries between themselves and the Empire. Whether their other boundaries, between themselves and their fellow Germani, were so well defined, in both perception and reality, is less clear but perfectly possible. The River Dniester, for instance, seems to have functioned as a marker between the Tervingi and an adjacent group of Goths, the Greuthungi, and there was enough hostility between the Alamanni and their Burgundian neighbours to suppose that both sides – as Ammianus reports – would have carefully defined their territories. According to him, they used some conveniently placed former Roman boundary markers to define the limits of their territories.[29]

Within these territorial spaces, at least in response to Roman pressure again, Germanic leaderships were sometimes ambitious enough to impose a degree of cultural uniformity upon their populations. Roman cultural hegemony on the Danube in the fourth century, for instance, occasionally took the form of an interest in spreading Christianity to adjacent lands. On at least two occasions, when they were in a position to act, the leadership of the Tervingi resisted this with determination. In 348, Christian Roman missionaries were expelled and then a second time, after 369, Gothic Christians were actively persecuted to the point of execution, creating in the process a not insignificant number of martyrs. This suggests that the Gothic Tervingi's sense of their own space, at least, had come to take a fairly active cultural as well as economic and military form.[30]

The actions of various leaders, moreover, show us that certain institutional powers were in place. Particularly impressive, to my mind, is the evidence for a defined military obligation among the Tervingi. On three occasions, as we have seen, the confederation sent military contingents to Rome's Persian wars. The individuals who went received some financial compensation from the Roman state, but overall the evidence suggests that this kind of service – on a frontier over fifteen hundred kilometres away, it should be remembered – was a generally resented imposition. Such service was certainly one of the terms of client status which the Goths' leaders sought to strike out when they were in a position to. Nonetheless, the leadership of the Tervingi was able to make these contingents actually appear, which means that it could both identify individuals liable for military service *and* force them to show up. The Alamanni, likewise, provided contingents for Roman service on occasion, but we have few details and the distances involved were much smaller. Interestingly, the word generally in use in Germanic languages for 'doing military service' is a loan word from Latin, which perhaps suggests that this kind of transferred demand from the Roman state may have been responsible for generating a new kind of compulsory military service among those Germani forced to provide such contingents.[31]

The leaderships of both Alamanni and Tervingi also had defined rights to basic economic support in the form, presumably, of taxation levied on agricultural production. Rights in this area were necessary to support the kings' military retinues. By the fourth century, no king with a full-time professional retinue could afford to rely on purely voluntary donations of foodstuffs for their support, as had apparently been the practice in the first century. The extent of Roman imports, not least of wine amphorae found on elite sites in the fourth century, likewise suggests that kings were creaming off a proportion of basic production to exchange for Roman goods for their own consumption. Quite likely, though, Germanic leaders had at least one other major form of economic support. As we have seen, cross-border trade with the Roman Empire had become a substantial phenomenon by the fourth century. For their part, the Roman authorities certainly imposed customs dues on all this economic activity, and it is overwhelmingly likely that Germanic kings did too. We have no explicit evidence to this effect for the Alamanni or the Tervingi, but other Germanic kings of the frontier region were doing this as early as the first century, when the wealth of Vannius king of the Marcomanni was

incontrovertibly associated with the presence of Roman merchants at
his court, and it is extremely unlikely that their fourth-century counterparts would have failed to do the same. It is hard, otherwise, to explain
why trade and its regulation should have figured so prominently in
diplomatic negotiations between the leadership of the Tervingi and the
eastern Roman Empire; and something made Chnodomarius wealthy
enough to buy in mercenary support in addition to the other forces he
lined up at Strasbourg.[32]

Both confederations also had the right to impose labour services
on at least parts of their population. Kings of the Alamanni could
mobilize labour both for constructing their own defended elite sites,
such as the Runder Berg, and when forced to pay off diplomatic
obligations by providing labour for Roman state purposes, as in the
treaties imposed on them by the Emperor Julian after Strasbourg.
Among the Tervingi, likewise, the then judge attempted to fend off
Hunnic aggression in the 370s by constructing a substantial set of
fortifications – what Ammianus calls the 'wall' of Athanaric. This was
most likely an attempt to renovate an old Roman fortified line on the
River Alutanus, and in the end it came to naught. But the fact that
such a project could even be attempted shows that the right to extract
labour service was established, as does other physical evidence from
the Gothic realms for elite sites similar to the Runder Berg.[33] In the
Roman world, and later in that of the largely Germanic-dominated
successor states to the western Roman Empire, labour service was
imposed usually only on the more servile element of the population,
meaning that part of it which did not do military service. We have no
evidence that this was also the case among the Alamanni and Tervingi,
but it seems likely enough.

In certain key areas, then, fourth-century Germanic leaders had
well-developed rights. They could define and extract – perhaps from
different elements of their populations – military service, labour dues
and a percentage of agricultural production. Almost certainly, too,
although none of our sources is sufficiently interested to tell us about
this, they had rights to be involved in what we would term legal-
dispute settlement – in the case of their more important subjects
anyway. No leader known in any other context, whose powers can
be elaborated in any detail, lacked this kind of authority, so it is
probably safe enough to ascribe it to the leadership of the Tervingi
and Alamanni as well.[34] As to how these various rights were actually

administered, neither confederation ran, as far as we can see, to any kind of articulated bureaucracy. No source mentions bureaucrats in the fourth-century Germanic world, though kings certainly had their functionaries, and the rights were possibly exacted with little or no use of any formal literate administration. Writing of various kinds was known to the fourth-century Germani. Runes were in use, some Germani were able to operate successfully in Latin, and, in the mid-fourth century, Gothic was busily being turned into a written language – the first Germanic tongue to be so – for the purposes of Christian missionaries. There is no evidence, however, that any of these literacies was being applied to the exaction and disbursement of revenues in the form of agricultural produce.

But this need not mean, it is worth stressing, that exaction was an essentially random process. How it might have worked on a regular but essentially paperless basis is illustrated by some of the earliest evidence for administration from Anglo-Saxon England. Here the seventh-century agricultural economy was harnessed by dividing the country up into largish revenue-producing districts, each of which had to contribute a given quantity of agricultural produce annually in the form of food renders. The system required an exhaustive surveying process at the beginning, to divide the countryside up; storage space for the goods, and some kind of tallying system to keep track of deliveries; but not that many officials and no great degree, if any, of literacy. It is, in fact, a straightforward mechanism for extracting revenues from a rural economy that is found in various contexts, and there is absolutely no reason to suppose that something of this kind was beyond the capacities of the Tervingi and Alamanni.[35] Alamannic territory, as we have seen, was already divided into districts (*Gaue*, in German), and it is probable that one of their functions was fiscal. In the Alamannic case, of course, we are dealing with multiple kings, many of whom controlled their own cantons. Any revenue collection in this context, presumably, was in the first instance by and for these canton-level kings, although they may then have had to pass on a portion of their take to an overking.

In Anglo-Saxon England and many other early medieval contexts where fiscal systems mainly produced food rather than some more negotiable form of wealth, what is known in the scholarly literature as 'royal itineration' was central to their operation. This meant that instead of running a fixed royal court, the king, his leading advisers and his professional retinue moved around the kingdom in a regular cycle, stopping at a series of designated points. These stopping points were also the local collection centres for the food renders, thus greatly reducing the inherent logistic problems of a tax regime based on bulky, heavy food rather than, say, comparatively light and mobile coinage. Instead of the food mountains going to the king, the king went to the mountains. We have no explicit evidence for itineration among fourth-century kings of the Germani, but since the consumption of food renders is so much easier on this basis, it must be a priori likely. It is perhaps a reflection of the intineration process that the Romans could not simply predict where a targeted Alamannic king might be, and an observable correlate of such systems is, obviously enough, the existence of many royal centres, which might also explain why there were quite so many such centres, seemingly, among the Alamanni. There were no more than about twenty-five cantons, implying a maximum of twenty-five kings, but sixty-two elite sites have been identified, and these are all hill forts, while the written sources mention others (so far unidentified) in the lowlands as well.[36]

## State and Society

The consequences of all this economic development for the spread of social power among the Germani are difficult to estimate in their entirety, but two initial observations are straighforward. The overall population of Germanic Europe will have increased markedly over the Roman centuries, as agricultural production grew in intensity and the rest of the economy – at least moderately – diversified, but kings and warbands benefited disproportionately from the extra wealth. The difficulty comes when you try to get a sense of the consequent redistribution of social power. A whole host of evidence suggests, in fact, that the degree of overall change must not be overstated. Both literary and archaeological evidence indicate that other people, apart from kings and their retinues, still mattered in Germanic society of the fourth century.

Some of the relevant evidence consists of narratives of Germanic politics in action. As the famous historian of Rome's barbarians Edward Thompson observed, Ammianus' descriptions imply that kings could not simply order warriors about, but had to 'urge' and 'persuade' them to follow their policies. Also, we have already encountered the Alamannic king who was overthrown by his own followers for not attaching himself to Chnodomarius' banner. Ammianus explicitly states that this was the result of action by the 'people' – *plebs, populus* – of his canton. This could just about be referring to a restricted political world of royal retinues, although Ammianus' wording implies not, but Strasbourg involved a military-political community that extended well beyond such limited social circles. The Alamannic army gathered there numbered reportedly thirty-five thousand, as we have seen, and certainly well over ten thousand fighting men. Royal retinues, even of chief kings, numbered just a few hundred. Ammianus refers to sixteen kings and princes assembled for Strasbourg, and even if for the sake of argument we allow each of them a retinue of two hundred (although most will, by definition, have been smaller since Chnodomarius was the most powerful king), that still only amounts to 3,200 fighting men. Military participation was clearly not limited just to kings and small specialist retinues. Nor, it seems, was some kind of elevated social status. Archaeologically, the increase in the quantity of material deposited with the Germanic dead, seen over the Roman period, was not confined to a very small number of rich *Fürstengräber*. Alongside these highly exceptional burials are found both large numbers of graves with absolutely nothing in them at all, and a fairly numerous category containing a moderate number of personal items: usually pottery and, as mentioned earlier, weapons of some kind for men and jewellery for women. The striking increase in weapons burials in the late Roman period, though not found right across Germania, does lend further weight to the idea that the period saw a substantial increase in the importance of the martial side of male life, consonant with the rise of the retinues, but the total number of such burials indicates that others, apart from kings and retinues, were also treading this path to retained or increased social prominence.[37]

A large quantity of legal evidence from the sixth and seventh centuries suggests who these others may have been. These texts, or codes, composed in the successor states to the western Roman Empire, provide us with the first full description of the social categories operating in a Germanic-dominated society. Given the date of the texts' composition, they all reflect Germanic societies that had been through a further stage of interaction with what remained of old Roman imperial economic, governmental and social institutions after the collapse of the western Roman Empire, so there is an obvious difficulty in trying to use them to elucidate the fourth-century Germani. But if anything – and this would be the general consensus, not just my own view – these later interactions will only have increased inequalities of wealth and status in the Germanic world, because the process of taking over former Roman territories led to further unequal acquisitions of wealth on the part of kings and their immediate supporters. That being so, this later legal evidence will tend to underestimate the sociopolitical importance of other social groups not immediately in royal service. It can be used as a guide, therefore, to the *maximum* level of inequality likely to have been prevalent in the fourth century.

The descriptions of status groups found in these legal materials are strikingly uniform. Kings had a special status, obviously, and being in royal service usually increased status as well. In addition, the codes often referred to a noble class. All of these groups can reasonably be thought of as belonging to worlds analogous to those of the fourth-century kings and retinues. But all the codes (and we do have law codes from a large number of the successor kingdoms) also referred to a class, beneath the nobility, of freemen, who still had considerable rights and responsibilities. These freemen stood above two further classes: permanent freedmen and slaves. Characteristically, freemen did military service (as, in fact, often did freedmen, but not slaves); they could also give trustworthy testimony in cases of legal dispute; and their status was ringed about by safeguards to prevent slaves and freedmen from crossing the boundary without permission.[38]

The importance of this free class was overemphasized in romanticizing nineteenth-century accounts of Germanic society. Nothing indicates, for instance, that they formed a numerical majority of the male population; and given their obviously privileged position, I would be willing to bet quite a lot of money that they did not. Privileges are enjoyed by minorities, not majorities. Some not very good Ostrogothic and Lombard evidence might suggest that the freemen amounted to something like a quarter or a fifth of weapon-bearing males of these groups in the sixth century (and slaves are excluded from the equation because they did not bear arms). This of course makes freemen a still smaller percentage of the total population. But neither were they a figment of the law-writers' imaginations. Freemen are encountered in practice right across the post-Roman west as an important group of social actors at the local level in the evidence of legal practice, and also in some of the narrative evidence for warfare between Germanic-dominated groupings and the east Roman state.[39] If this was true of the successor states, when a further influx of Roman wealth had increased inequalities again, then it is overwhelmingly likely that freemen were still more important among the fourth-century Germani, before this later process unfolded. We should not imagine, in other words, that increased social stratification in the Roman period had reduced the sociopolitically important stratum of Germanic society to a tiny group of kings and retainers. A broader world of freemen maintained – or had developed – in the changing economic circumstances its range of social and economic privileges. They perhaps show up archaeologically as the owners of the big and prosperous longhouses found in some of the new villages of third- and fourth-century Germania, and as the occupants of the large number of endowed but not massively rich burials.

This fairly complex account of social stratification among the fourth-century Germani has obvious implications for the final key area of analysis: the balance between constraint and consent in Germanic politics.

Evidence for some degree of constraint is straightforward. Kings had warrior retinues. By use of these retinues, they had established a hereditary element to their position. The retinues could also be used more broadly as social enforcers, as we saw among the Tervingi when it came to persecuting Christians. There, in the incident described, the persecution policy went against the general wishes of the village community.[40] The leadership of the Tervingi could also, as we have seen, levy military contingents to make the onerous and dangerous trek to fight in Rome's Persian wars. And what could be a clearer sign that the rise of military kings was not always a consensual process than the weapons find at Ejsbøl Mose?

But just as kings and retinues had not completely eclipsed a broader privileged (freeman?) class, so the political process also had – sometimes, at least – to take account of, and win the broad consent for, their policies from this larger privileged group within the total population. As we have seen, kings could even be overthrown if their policies proved unpopular. The Alamannic king who wouldn't join Chnodomarius may possibly have been eliminated by his own retinue, but more likely by the broader freeman class of his canton; and similarly, the last member of the old ruling dynasty of the Tervingi, Athanaric, was overthrown in the midst of his fortification work when resistance to his ideas of how to combat the Hunnic menace over-flowed into political dissent.[41] Both events emphasize that there were marked limits to the powers of the new military kings.

It is not possible to explore the subject in any great detail, but the sources do suggest a few of the mechanisms by which these limits were orchestrated and imposed. To start with, we should probably not draw too distinct a line between freemen and royal retinues. There is considerable evidence that Germanic society operated in age sets for both men and women, with rites of passage marking certain clear stages in an individual's life, and each stage having its own rights and responsibilities. Older men, even high-status ones, were never buried with weapons, for instance, suggesting that there was an upper age limit to military obligation; and for women, the legal evidence indicates that within each status group child-bearing years were associated with maximum social worth. Pre-pubescent children, likewise, seem rarely to have been buried in cemeteries alongside adults, again suggesting that age and status went hand in hand.[42] This is not something that the available source materials will allow us to explore very thoroughly, but it is far from unlikely that at least some males of freeman status customarily served, when younger, in the warrior retinues of kings.

There may also have been other links between the worlds of freemen farmers and royal retinues of which we are not properly informed. Villages certainly provided kings and their retainers with economic support, but kings may well have been expected to hold regular feasts for a broader spectrum of the free class as well as for their immediate retinues. If such feasting remained habitual, then some genuinely reciprocal relations continued between kings and freemen into the fourth century. Again, in places these kinds of behaviour survived into later, still less equal Germanic-dominated successor states, which strengthens the likelihood that they were in evidence in the late Roman period. In early Anglo-Saxon England, itinerating kings were sometimes expected to give the benefit of their presence at more communal feasts, in return for the food supplies they were offered, and these events provided a context for many important social and political exchanges. Looking just at scale, for instance, Alamannic cantons were small enough that their kings can hardly have been isolated figures, cut off from the rest of the population, and I would suspect that feasting and other such interaction would have been unavoidable, and had probably long been a feature of the Germanic world, as they have been found to be in many potentially analogous contexts.[43]

Assemblies, too, may have played an important limiting role. Germanic political units of the early Roman period customarily worked through councils, at which group policy was debated and decided. Tacitus' works put a huge emphasis on this institution, and it was clearly much more than a figment of his ever fertile imagination. Particularly striking to my mind is the evidence – several separate occasions being recorded in our highly fragmentary records for the first and second centuries – of the fact that in order to punish a grouping for a revolt, or to prevent one from taking place, assemblies were either prohibited by the Roman authorities, or allowed to proceed only with Roman observers. The fourth-century evidence does not shed much light on the degree to which such assemblies continued, but there certainly seem to have been village gatherings; and the decision of the Gothic Tervingi to seek asylum in the Roman Empire in 376 emerged only after long debate, presumably at a much larger assembly of the socially important. The dispute-settlement procedures envisaged in the successor-state law codes also indicate that regular assemblies were necessary for legal purposes. For all these reasons, I would suppose that an assembly structure continued within the fourth-century confederations, acting as a further brake on the arbitrary powers of kings.[44]

There is also no evidence that Germanic kings were able to deploy self-justificatory ideologies of sufficient strength to entrench an over-arching domination. It has sometimes been suggested, for instance, that they surrounded themselves with a powerful aura of sacrality, which distinguished certain clans as marked out by the special favour of the gods and made resistance to their royal pretensions extremely difficult. But there is actually little evidence of this. None of the three main words used in Germanic languages for 'king' carry sacral conno-tations. They are all, as we have seen, deeply pragmatic: 'ruler of a people', 'ruler of a warband', 'ruler of a confederation'. Germanic kings certainly drew on a concept of divine favour – *heilag* and its various derivatives in the different Germanic language branches – but it was a post de facto kind of concept, which identified itself through practice. If you won battles and therefore power, then you had shown yourself to be *heilag*, but there is no sign that claiming to be *heilag* automatically brought you to power, or prevented anybody else from mounting a challenge to your authority – often to devastating effect, as the narrative evidence again suggests. And if a usurper was successful, then he had proved that he was now *heilag*.

The one context in which we find a heavy emphasis on the manifest destiny of one particular dynastic line for divinely ordained rule comes in the propaganda produced at the court of Theoderic, the Amal leader of the Ostrogoths in early sixth-century Italy and ruler of one of the first-generation successor states to the Roman west. Such a view of his dynasty is directly written up in the *Variae* of Cassiodorus and reflected indirectly in the *Getica* of Jordanes. But when this claim is measured against the actual history of the Amal dynasty, the results are highly instructive. The dynasty had won extensive power in the Gothic world only in the generation or so before Theoderic himself (as we shall see in more detail in Chapter 5), and as soon as it failed to produce suitable male heirs after his death, it was quickly disposed of. Theoderic proved himself to be *heilag* with a succession of stunning conquests, not least that of Italy itself, but that was not enough to protect the dynasty against incompetent heirs. All the propaganda, produced when Theoderic was trying to secure the succession for his under-age grandson,[45] was precisely that – propaganda.

The evidence for age sets, feasting obligations, councils and limited royal ideologies is all very fragmentary, and can only hint at the realities of political life among the Germani. The bottom line, however, is clear enough. While a new elite exploited the economic development of the Roman period to entrench its social prominence, and, in the process, made it possible to build, at least in some areas of Germanic Europe, the larger and more stable political units of the fourth century, we mustn't overstate its powers. A broader social group outside the nexus of kings and retinues remained important, both socially and economically, and had to be involved in the political process. Not least, it continued to outnumber the royal retinues massively, so that its support remained crucial to larger military enterprises. And in any case, as we have seen, freemen and warrior retinues may well have been interconnected in a variety of ways.

More generally, this broader social group must also have given some kind of consent to the creation of the new and much larger confederations of the late Roman period. Ammianus provides an illustration of this in his account of the attempt of one Alamannic king to distance himself from the confederation before Strasbourg, which led to his own demise. The same is suggested by the fact that not all of the old political associations of the first century were destroyed in creating the new ones of the third and fourth. We have explicit evidence only for the Franks, into which confederation late Roman sources indicate that some of the old units – specifically the Chatti, Batavi, Bructeri and Ampsivarii – had been incorporated. This process, obviously, was never as simple as the old units voting to join a new regional association, since some new units were created as well, the Salii already being mentioned by Ammianus; but nor was there total discontinuity either.[46]

Looked at against the comparative literature, the fourth-century confederations fall somewhere in the nexus between 'early states' and 'complex chiefdoms'. According to the normal criteria employed, they were too large and too stable, and encompassed too substantial a degree of marked social differentiation, to be categorized as either 'tribes' or 'simple chiefdoms'. And, looked at closely, the differences between early states and complex chiefdoms are essentially ones of degree, where the former have slightly more organization, stability, power and so forth than the latter. The shortage of evidence about the fourth-century confederations makes it extremely difficult to make more precise judgements, and what evidence there is sometimes prompts contrasting conclusions. The extent of their governmental capacities and, especially among the Tervingi, the establishment of dynastic power look quite state-like, for instance, but the lack of specialized royal functionaries and of any evidence for the survival of a relatively broad (freeman?) social elite suggests a complex chiefdom. This is not, however, an issue to become overly fixated on. The important point is that economic and social transformation had generated a new confederative element in Germanic society, or at least in some of those parts of it closest to the Roman frontier, which was capable of combining, for certain functions anyway, many tens of thousands of people. Politically, these new structures built on the past, incorporating sometimes pre-existing social units, but their powers and solidity represented a decisive break with the Germanic past.

One big question, however, remains unaddressed. What kick-started the economic transformations that underlay the confederations, and how precisely did economic development feed through into new political structures?

# THE ROMAN CONNECTION

In 30 AD or thereabouts, a Roman merchant called Gargilius Secundus purchased a cow from a man called Stelus, a non-Roman who lived near the modern Dutch town of Franeker across the River Rhine. A record of this transaction, which cost 115 silver *nummi* and was witnessed by two Roman centurions, just happens to survive. One modern commentator has called it 'banal', and so it was: small-scale and entirely unremarkable. If it happened once on Rome's European frontier, it happened a thousand times. The reason for thinking so is straightforward. Especially in the early period, but also later on, large numbers of Roman soldiers were stationed right on the imperial frontier. They represented a huge source of economic demand. In the first century AD some 22,000 Roman soldiers, a mixture of legionaries and auxiliaries, were established on the territory of only 14,000 or so indigenous Cananifates in the northern Rhine region alone. The latter could not possibly supply the soldiers' demands for foodstuffs, forage, and natural materials such as wood for construction and cooking, or leather. A legion of 5,000 men required approximately 7,500 kilos of grain and 450 kilos of fodder per day, or 225 and 13.5 tonnes, respectively, per month. Some of the soldiers' needs were supplied directly from the imperial centre, but this was cumbersome and logistically problematic. Where they could, the imperial authorities preferred to pay cash and let local suppliers meet the troops' demands.[47]

## Trade and Control

Throughout the Roman period, therefore, the frontier zone of the Empire had a huge requirement for primary agricultural products of all kinds and there is every reason to suppose that non-Roman sup-

pliers played a major role in meeting it. This was still the case in the
fourth century, where the pages Ammianus devotes to the Alamanni
again make interesting reading. After his victory at Strasbourg, the
Emperor Julian was in a position to impose virtually whatever terms
he wanted on the defeated Alamannic kings. All the treaties differed in
detail, but they had in common demands for foodstuffs, for raw
materials such as wood for construction purposes, for wagons and for
physical labour to carry out rebuilding projects. On the back of his
victory, Julian could simply requisition these items, but even in less
favourable circumstances they were still required by the Roman army,
and presumably had to be paid for. Whether paying or not, the Roman
army was a constant source of economic demand for any neighbouring
Germani.

None of the items mentioned in Julian's treaties is archaeologically
visible. You can't identify – because they couldn't survive – traces of
Germanic-grown wheat, Germanic-felled timber, leather cured by the
Germani, or items constructed by Germanic labour. They were all,
however, real enough, and show up in more indirect fashion in the
huge expansion of agricultural production that we have observed in
Germanic Europe in the Roman period. Some of this extra food was
consumed by the new kings and their retinues, and some by Germania's own expanding population, but a further – perhaps even the
original – stimulus to production was provided by the Roman army.
For one thing, there is close chronological coincidence between the
arrival of Roman demand on the fringes of Germania and the rural
intensification. The earliest of the new villages, such as Feddersen
Wierde and Wijster, also grew up in regions from which it was
relatively easy to ship agricultural products by water to the mouth of
the Rhine and then upstream to the river's military installations. As
much recent literature has rightly emphasized, and as has been shown
to be the case along all of Rome's borders, the frontier acted in some
ways more as a zone of contact than, as you might initially expect, a
line of demarcation dividing the Empire from its immediate neighbours.[48]

In the case of the Germani, Rome may have acted as a source not
only of extra economic demand, but also possibly for some of the
ideas and technology that made agricultural intensification possible. At
Wijster and Feddersen Wierde, higher yields seem to have resulted
from a more systematic integration of arable and pastoral agriculture,

using animal manure to sustain the fertility of the wheat fields. More generally, it involved the adoption of more sophisticated ploughing techniques and equipment. Where and how, exactly, these ideas spread remains to be studied, but both the more efficient ploughs and the better-integrated farming regimes were well known in Roman and La Tène Europe, much of which the Empire swallowed up in the first century BC (Chapter 1), long before they spread into Germania, and these areas may have inspired the Germanic agricultural revolution.

Other goods produced in Germania were also in demand in the Roman world. The occasional loan word and literary reference identify some specific products. Goose feathers for stuffing pillows and particular kinds of red hair dye were two such items. Much more important than any of these, though, was the demand certainly for two, and probably three, other raw materials. The one that is not so certain is iron. There is no specific evidence that pig iron was shipped in large quantities south and west across the frontier from Germanic Europe. But the vast quantities of iron produced at the two main Polish sites far outstripped any amount that can have been required for local use. Possibly, this iron was being circulated within just the Germanic world, but it is entirely conceivable that it was also being processed to satisfy Roman demand. Of the other two materials, there is no doubt. The first is amber: solidified sap from submerged trees washed up on the Baltic Sea coast. Amber is one of few loan words taken over from Germanic languages into Latin, and we know that the Romans took a huge interest in this product for making jewellery. In the time of Nero, a senatorial mission even went north to investigate its origins, and the amber route from the Baltic – in both its main branches, one striking south to the middle Danube at the legionary fortress of Carnuntum, the other going east of the Carpathians to arrive at the Black Sea ports (Map 2) – was well known to Roman authors.[49]

At least as important, though less discussed in our sources, was the demand for Germanic manpower. This took two main forms. First, recruits were always needed for the Roman army. The so-called barbarization of the Roman army used to be one of the main reasons given for the decline of the Empire. The point is at best partly mistaken. From the time of Augustus, at least half of the total army – all its auxiliary formations – was always composed of non-Romans, a substantial number of whom were recruited from the Germanic world. All that happened in the late Empire was a recategorization of military units, which saw the distinction between citizen legionaries and non-citizen auxiliaries partly collapse. Nothing suggests, either, that there were more Germani in percentage terms serving in the Roman army in the fourth century than before, or that the army was any less reliable for their presence – it is normally considered likely, anyway, that legionary recruiters had, in practice, been ignoring for some time the requirement that only citizens should be drafted. Throughout the Roman period, therefore, there was a huge demand for Germanic recruits, and many turn up in the epigraphic record. From narrative sources we know that these men were recruited in two ways. Some were individual volunteers, deciding to follow a potentially lucrative career path in the Roman army. Many others, however, had no choice. Again Ammianus is explicit. A forced draft of recruits was part of most of the peace treaties he records between the Empire and different barbarian groups. Not only did you have to supply labour and foodstuffs to buy your way back into the Empire's good graces after a defeat, but you also had to give over a portion of your young men for service in the Roman army.[50]

Manpower from Germania also entered the Empire in another form: slaves. We have no detailed account of the operation of the slave trade in the Roman era, such as we get from Arab authors for its counterpart of the ninth and tenth centuries (Chapter 10). So there is no information on the identity of the main traders, on the areas from which they tended to take victims, and on whether, as later, there were any major slave markets inside Germania, where slaves could be traded on to middle-men or directly to Roman merchants. But the slave trade was a constant phenomenon of the Roman era, and there is one powerful testimony to its importance. Germanic languages have as one of their basic word-stems for trade and merchants a series of terms deriving from the Latin *mango*. But in Latin *mango* meant not a merchant in general, but very precisely a slave trader. The Roman merchants first and perhaps most often encountered by Europe's Germanic-speaking populations, therefore, were probably traders in human flesh.[51]

Overall, an excellent case can be made that the new opportunities for trading with the much wealthier Roman Empire, which suddenly opened up around the birth of Christ with the expansion of Rome's European frontiers northwards, played a major role in stimulating the evident economic development of Germania in the early centuries AD.

According to Caesar in the mid-first century BC, the Germani of his day had little interest in trading with Roman merchants, and only allowed them into their territories at all in the hope that they could sell them captured war booty. If that had really been the case in the middle of the first century BC, the situation evolved rapidly. By the end of the first century AD, trade was so common across the Rhine frontier that Roman silver *denarii* were being used as a medium of exchange by the Germanic tribes on the east side of the river. It is likely enough, indeed, that much of the silver found in Germania in Roman times – in the form, for instance, of intricate *fibulae* – represents the reworking of metal from such coins, many of which remained in circulation right down to the fourth century. And while (for reasons we will return to in a moment) it is not the case that every frontier grouping was trading so heavily with the Empire as to be using Roman coins, this certainly happened periodically, throughout the Empire's existence. As a phenomenon, it shows up in the presence of relatively dense concentrations of low-value Roman coins from particular periods in areas fairly close to the frontier, such as those of the fourth century found along some of the old Roman roads east of the Rhine which still existed in the *Agri Decumates* – a triangle of territory between the Upper Rhine and Upper Danube – then under Alamannic control; or, further east along the Danube, within regions bordering the Roman province of Moesia Superior.[52]

Equally striking is the fact that throughout the Roman period the Empire's immediate neighbours were interested in obtaining trading privileges with the imperial merchants, privileges which Rome usually kept under tight control. Even when the fourth-century Gothic Tervingi wanted to sever most of their ties with the Empire, it was part of the resulting agreement that two designated trade centres continued to operate. A huge amount of archaeological evidence confirms the impression given by the literary sources. Roman goods of all kinds have been found in large quantities in most of the major excavations conducted on Germanic sites from the first four centuries AD.

There are distinct chronological and geographical patterns to the finds. The first two centuries AD, for instance, saw a huge explosion in the quantity of Roman goods present within Germania in many areas of the immediate frontier zone, up to about a hundred kilometres from the defended line, both on settlement sites and deposited in graves. Fine pottery (*terra sigillata*), bronze ornaments and glass have all been unearthed in substantial amounts, alongside the Roman coins we have already mentioned. In the first- and second-century levels of the site of Westrich, for instance, which is far from untypical, Roman manufactures account for about a third each of the excavated pottery and metalwork. But while common in some places, this pattern does not apply to the regions of the northern Rhine frontier, between the Rhine and the Weser, where Roman materials of this date are much less plentiful. Moving beyond the immediate frontier zone to the area up to the River Elbe, the pattern is again slightly different. Here Roman goods are present in large quantities, but they tend to concentrate in particular areas. The region of the River Saale in modern Thuringia, for instance, has produced one striking concentration. Others have been identified around the tributaries of the Upper Elbe in Bohemia (heartland of the Czech Republic), and south of the Lower Elbe and the Middle and Lower Weser (both in Lower Saxony). The other identified concentration is along the North Sea coast. Moving still further away from the frontier, Roman goods are present only in smaller quantities, but there are still a few identifiable concentrations such as Jakuszowice in southern Poland, the Gudme/Lundeburg complex in Scandinavia, and in eastern Denmark.[53] In general terms, there is more than enough material to show that the Germanic economy was mobilized in the early centuries AD in part to pay for large quantities of attractive Roman imports. But how are we to explain these concentrations?

Part of the answer lies in logistics. The fact that a wagon of wheat doubled in price for every fifty Roman miles travelled emphasizes how difficult and expensive land transport was in pre-modern times. Hence relatively low-value items – such as pottery, bronze and glass – were only ever likely to move comparatively short distances unless water transport or some other mitigating factor intervened. The fact that even spreads of Roman goods have been unearthed only within the immediate frontier zone, then, is not surprising. Transport may also explain some more particular phenomena. The possibility of water shipment probably allowed relatively distant places like Feddersen Wierde to be involved in supplying the Roman army of the frontier, and as the coin distributions suggest, the old Roman road networks of the Agri Decumates perhaps still facilitated trade in the fourth century, even after the area had fallen under Alamannic control. Logistics, however, will not explain everything.

A second line of explanation requires us to look more closely at the mechanics of trade in the Germanic world, and the role played in Germanic society by the Roman goods received in return. If Caesar is to be believed, there was originally some Germanic resistance to trade with the Empire. But this was quickly and entirely overcome to a point where possession of Roman goods came to be associated with high social status. Analyses of the types of goods found together in richer burials have demonstrated a powerful correlation from the late first century AD between the presence of large numbers of everyday items of local manufacture, clearly expensive items of local manufacture (such as weapons and jewellery), and Roman imports. Thus Roman imports quickly came to be part and parcel of demonstrating social pre-eminence. Again, this is not surprising. Roman imports were exotic and had to be paid for by giving something in return to a Roman merchant. They were bound, therefore, to possess a certain cachet. It is also a further dimension of the phenomenon we have already observed. As in modern globalization, the benefits of ancient Germanic economic development were not enjoyed evenly, but concentrated in the hands of kings and their retainers; so, as one might expect, more Roman imports ended up in their hands.

This point is worth dwelling on, because while it might again seem entirely natural from a modern perspective, it is also telling us something important about how the new exchange networks operated. As soon as you stop to think about it, such an outcome can only be reflecting the fact that kings and their entourage were organizing the profits accruing from economic development for their own benefit. On one level, possession of military muscle enabled kings to exact a percentage of the new agricultural surplus now being generated. They could then use this not only to feed their retinues but also to trade on to the Roman world, getting precious metal coins, or wine and olive oil, or whatever else they desired, in return.

But military muscle was also crucial to securing the lion's share of the profits from some of the other new trade flows. Think about the slave trade. Slaves do not volunteer. Someone was rounding them up in Germanic society to sell them on to the Roman traders, and this will not have been a peaceful process. This line of thought also suggests, incidentally, a further possible context for the massacred retinue unearthed at Ejsbøl Mose. If they were a slave-trading outfit, you can quite see why such methodical fury was vented upon them.

And even the amber trade was no gentle process of wandering along the Baltic shore picking up whatever had washed up overnight. One of the most startling finds to emerge from northern Poland in recent years has been a series of wooden causeways, many kilometres long, establishing a network of routes across boggy territory near the Baltic Sea. Carbon-14 and dendrochronology have established that these were laid down around the birth of Christ and then maintained for the best part of two hundred years. They have been interpreted, surely correctly, as servicing the northern end of the Amber Route. But all this took a huge effort. In other words, it must have been enormously worth someone's while to go to this much trouble. In return for their effort, they were clearly receiving a substantial cut of the profits from the trade, presumably in the forms of tolls of one kind or another. Interestingly, 'toll' in Germanic languages is another loan word from Latin, suggesting that the concept did not exist among the Germani before the Empire became their immediate neighbour. And, of course, where taking this kind of percentage from a trade flow was so obviously profitable, others would have been interested in a share of the action. Here again, military strength counted. You could employ it to force those of lesser status to do the physical work of building and maintaining the causeways, and also to prevent any other armed group from taking over what was clearly such a nice little earner.[54]

Contrary to the bland neo-classical platitudes of 1980s-style trickle-down theories, economic development is not always or not straightforwardly, at least, a good thing. Increasing wealth in Germanic society during the Roman period set off major and in some cases seriously violent struggles for its disproportionate control. In some developing areas of the economy, the adverse effects were perhaps not so bad. It is notoriously hard to tax agricultural production, and higher outputs were anyway dependent upon having plenty of labour available, at least for arable agriculture, so that the demands of kings and their warbands, some of whom may anyway have been recruited from the wealthier farmers, perhaps did not impinge too heavily. Other aspects of economic development, however, were much nastier for those caught up on the wrong side: slaves obviously, but I wonder too about iron-mining since, in the Roman world at least, being condemned to the mines was a form of capital punishment. And even at the top end of society, the struggle to control the new wealth could have serious consequences. Ejsbøl Mose is one of over thirty weapons deposits known from the bogs of northern Europe, most of which were laid down between 200 and 400 AD – explicit testimony to the level of violence set loose in the Germanic world for control of all this burgeoning wealth. Moreover, there is no reason to suppose that these struggles were limited to just those areas that happened to have convenient bogs and lakes available for disposing of the defeated. Tacitus refers to a first-century votive ritual which involved hanging the dead and their weaponry from trees. Weapons deposits of this kind would not survive to be excavated by archaeologists, and I am inclined to think that accident of survival is the reason for the direct evidence of violent competition being confined to areas around the North Sea, rather than that the proximity of water made the Germani of this area particularly quarrelsome.[55]

It is not a new idea to discuss trade with the Roman Empire when trying to understand the transformation of Germanic society in the early centuries AD. But, as has reasonably been pointed out, trade on its own never looked like a powerful enough explanatory mechanism, since large quantities of Roman goods have not turned up everywhere. The case for the importance of such trade becomes much more convincing, however, when you factor in not just the new wealth flows themselves, but the consequent struggles for their control. It was this knock-on effect, rather than the mere existence of the new wealth, that had the really transformative effect. Various groups within the Germanic world responded dynamically to the fact that the new wealth existed by seizing control of its profits, and, in doing so, helped remake the sociopolitical structures of the world around them.

This extra dimension of argument belongs alongside those which in the area of post-colonial studies have attracted the general label 'agency'. The point here is that earlier analyses ('colonial' rather than 'post-colonial' ones, as it were) tended to explore the effects that more developed societies have upon less developed ones in too passive a fashion. The fundamental point of 'agency' (although much ink has been spilled over more precise definitions) is to stress that indigenous groups respond to outside stimuli by taking hold of certain possibilities (and not others) for their own reasons and according to their own priorities. In this instance, we see exposure to the economic opportunities presented by contact with Rome taking a number of forms, and being seized on in different ways by different groups. Some learned to expand agricultural production, some exported iron or amber, and still others set up slave-trading operations. Not only did the consequent increase in inequality provide the economic basis for larger political confederations by the fourth century, but this is also reflected in the patchy distribution of Roman goods observable in the archaeological record. The particular concentrations of goods in the intermediate zone up to the Elbe were presumably created by Germanic groups able to dominate some specific new flow of wealth out of the Roman Empire, which they used to pay for the items found by archaeologists. The beneficiaries of the slave trade of the ninth and tenth centuries, for instance, are certainly visible archaeologically through the fruits of their trade, as well as being identified in the historical texts (not true of the Roman era), so it is not unreasonable to apply the same principle to the Germani around the Roman Empire.[56] But even adding in a dynamic indigenous response to the existence of the new wealth flows doesn't come close, in my view, to establishing the full extent of Rome's role in the transformation of the Germanic world. For that, we also need to explore how the Empire set about maintaining long-term stability along its frontiers.

## The Art of Client Management

In 1967 some gravel-digging in the River Rhine itself, close to the old Roman city of Civitas Nemetum (modern Speyer), led to the discovery of loot from a Roman villa. Careful excavation over the next sixteen years reconstructed the full story. The finds were there because late in the third century some Alamannic raiders had been trying to get their booty back home across the Rhine when their boats were ambushed and sunk by Roman river patrol ships. Called *lusoriae*, the latter were light, oar-driven warships equipped with rams and a well armed crew. An everyday kind of frontier story, except for what the raiders were trying to get home. They had with them an extraordinary seven hundred kilograms' worth of booty packed into three or four carts which they were rafting across to the east bank of the Rhine. On close inspection, the loot proved to be the entire contents of probably a single Roman villa, and the raiders were interested in every piece of metalwork they could find. The only items missing from the hoard were rich solid silverware and high-value personal jewellery. Either the lord and lady of the house got away before the attack, or else the very high-value loot was transported separately. In the carts, however, was a vast mound of silver-plate from the dining room, the entire equipment from the kitchen (including 51 cauldrons, 25 bowls and basins and 20 iron ladles), enough agricultural implements – everything from pruning hooks to anvils – to run a substantial farm, some votive objects from the villa's shrine, and 39 good-quality silver coins.[57]

The nature of this extraordinary hoard makes clear the depth of the problem facing the Empire in one dimension of frontier relations. We naturally think of barbarian raiders being interested in gold and silver, and plenty of rich plundered objects have turned up over the years from various hoards of the Roman era. But the total range of desirable goods was massively wider. Because the economy of the Germanic world was so much less developed than its Roman counterpart, all of these goods were directly useful to the raiders, or could be sold on to someone else, whether Alamannic farmer or housewife, or even to an Alamannic smith for reworking. This is just about the most vivid illustration of the kind of booty your average raider targeted ever to be unearthed, but historical sources make it clear that banditry, perhaps often on a smaller scale than this amazingly comprehensive house-clearing exercise, was endemic all along Rome's frontiers.

The fact that the legions' advance had halted at different moments in the first century, broadly along the line of the Rivers Rhine and Danube, did not mean, therefore, that lands beyond the frontier could be left to their own devices. On the contrary, there was a huge propensity for cross-border raiding, the natural result of two very different levels of economic development sitting side by side. Nor, as has sometimes been argued, did the Empire go suddenly from attack to defence. Frontier security demanded a much more proactive response, and throughout most of its history Rome maintained a general military superiority all along its European frontiers, backed up by aggressive diplomacy. These policies turned its closest neighbours effectively into client states.[58]

The methods used remained pretty constant throughout the life of the Empire, and had profound effects upon patterns of sociopolitical development within the Germanic world. For an excellent case study from the fourth century, we can turn to Ammianus' account of the response of the Emperor Constantius II to trouble on the Middle Danube in the years 358/9. Constantius' first step, like every emperor before him, was to establish military superiority. Starting just after the spring equinox, when the opposition thought they were still safe, he threw a pontoon bridge over the Danube and came upon the Sarmatians unexpectedly. The results were nasty:

> The greater number, since fear clogged their steps, were cut down; if speed saved any from death, they hid in the obscure mountain gorges and saw their country perishing by the sword.

In the following weeks, the campaign was quickly extended to the neighbouring Quadi and all the other frontier groups of the region. The Emperor then used this military superiority to dictate what he hoped would be a lasting diplomatic settlement. One by one, the groups and their leaders came, or were forced to come, to hear the Emperor's judgement.

Not all groups were treated in the same way. To some Constantius =showed favour. One prince of the Sarmatians, Zizais, had mastered the script:

> On seeing the emperor, he threw aside his weapons and fell flat on his breast as if lying lifeless. And since the use of his voice failed him from fear at the very time when he should have made his plea, he excited all the greater compassion; but, after several attempts, interrupted by sobbing, he was able to set forth only a little of what he tried to ask.

Barbarians were expected to show subservience to the divinely ordained might of Rome, as Zizais was perfectly well aware, and as the iconography of barbarians on Roman coins and monuments emphasized. Barbarians were always presented lying down in submission at the bottom of any pictorial scene, often literally under an emperor's feet (Plate 7). The Sarmatian's approach may well have been calculated, therefore, and it produced the desired result. Constantius decided to restore the political independence of Zizais' followers, who had been held as junior partners in an unequal coalition, and raised the prince himself to the status of independent king. Rearranging the political alliance systems currently in operation on this part of the frontier after the fashion that best suited Rome's interests was, in fact, was one of Constantius' chief preoccupations. This meant breaking up over-large and therefore – from a Roman perspective – potentially dangerous alliances. Where Zizais gained, others lost. Araharius, a king of the Quadi, was denuded, despite his protests, of the services of his

Sarmatian underking Usafer, who, like Zizais, was restored to independence. Sometimes the interference could be much more violent. Another tactic, which occurs three times in the twenty-four years covered by Ammianus' narrative, was to invite potentially problematic frontier dynasts to dinner and then either murder or kidnap them.[59]

Aside from political restructuring, various other measures were enacted: securing economic returns for the Empire on the military effort it had just expended, combined with strictures to enforce the new settlement once the legions had withdrawn. Some measures were standard, such as extracting drafts of young men from the groups submitting to him to serve as military recruits. This, as we have seen, was one of several ways in which young Germani had entered Roman armies throughout the Empire's existence. Hostages were also extracted from each of group, usually young men of high status. They were not treated as prisoners, exactly, once on Roman soil, but were sometimes executed when agreements broke down. Any Roman captives were also returned to imperial soil. In other respects, the details of agreements differed. According to the amount of blame the emperor decided to allocate to any particular group for the original trouble, it might have to supply labour, raw materials and food; or it might, on the other hand, be granted privileged trading status. Diplomatic subsidies were, in addition, a standard feature of Rome's diplomatic armoury. In the past, some historians have doubted this, supposing payments to barbarian leaders to be a sign of Rome's military weakness in the late period. This is mistaken. We would call such subsidies 'foreign aid', and they were utilized throughout Rome's history, even after major Roman victories. After he crushed the Alamanni at Strasbourg, for instance, Julian granted the defeated kings annual subsidies. The reason is simple. Subsidies helped keep in power the kings with whom Rome had just made its agreements. As such, they were an excellent investment.[60]

Apart from all this diplomatic detail, one further preoccupation emerges from Constantius' intervention. The Empire did not want the immediate hinterland of its frontier to become too crowded, for two reasons. First, this would mean that there were too many groups with an opportunity to raid Roman territory. Second, as the establishment and reorganization of all the over- and underkingships shows, frontier groups were always in political competition with one another, and their jockeying for position stood more chance of spilling over into violence on Roman soil when there were more groups playing the game. In this instance, Constantius and his advisers eventually decided that a key part of the new settlement was to make one group of Sarmatians, the Limigantes (again, a coalition), move away from the immediate frontier zone. This was not something the Limigantes wished to do, so further military intimidation was required and duly delivered. After two of their subgroups, the Amicenses and Picenses, had been brutalized, the rest surrendered and agreed to depart. The region seemed set for peace – but not quite yet. A year later, in 359, some of the Limigantes returned, saying that they would prefer to move into the Empire itself, as tax-paying tributaries, rather than continue to occupy their assigned lands so far from the frontier.

What happened next is rather mysterious. Ammianus blames it all on the Limigantes' bad faith, but then he would. An agreement in principle seems to have been reached. The Sarmatians were to be allowed across the river and to enter the imperial presence, Constantius having returned to the region with his army. Then, at the crucial moment, something went wrong. Instead of surrendering, the Sarmatians attacked the Emperor, or so Ammianus says, and the Romans responded:

> So eagerly did our forces rush forth in their desire to ... vent their wrath on the treacherous foe, that they butchered everything in their way, trampling under foot without mercy the living, as well as those dying or dead; and before their hands were sated with slaughter of the savages, the dead lay piled in heaps.

Perhaps the Limigantes did act in bad faith, or Constantius maybe wanted to put down a clear marker that his orders had to be obeyed – or, just as likely, the tragedy resulted from mistrust and confusion. But throughout its history, the Empire did on occasions use the acquisition of outside population groups as one technique for managing the frontier. While the consequent gain to the Empire in terms of taxpayers and potential soldiers was part of the calculation, so too was a concern to prevent potentially dangerous overcrowding.[61]

This portfolio of methods was applied very generally. Occasional major military interventions made it possible to construct region-wide diplomatic settlements, which broke up dangerous coalitions, identified and rewarded friends and punished enemies, while a mixture of stick and carrot – the fear engendered by punishing campaigns and

hostage-taking combined with targeted foreign aid and trading privileges – was used to make sure that the new settlement held beyond
the short term. The methods were effective, but not, of course, perfect.
From a Roman perspective, their success can be measured in terms of
the life expectancy of the settlements. By my reckoning, the average
fourth-century diplomatic settlement on the Rhine and Danube frontiers lasted about twenty to twenty-five years – one generation, in
other words – per major military intervention. This was probably a
fair return on the amount of force expended, and about as much as
could reasonably be expected. It is important to understand, however,
that the whole system was sustained by occasional but decisive Roman
campaigning. The frontier groups were part of a Roman world system,
but terms and conditions were not arrived at by free, mutual agreement. Rome consistently used military force to maintain its prepon-
derance.

The methods of Roman diplomacy are fascinating in themselves
and have their own scholarly literature. They also advanced the
transformation of Germanic society. To understand why this was so,
we must again reckon with populations on the far side of the Roman
frontier as active agents in the story. Roman diplomacy certainly had
some important direct effects, but that is not the whole story. Groups
and individuals within Germania responded in a variety of ways to the
stimuli applied by the totality of Roman foreign policy over four
centuries, and this response is just as important as the original imperial
interference.

The transformative potential of one aspect of Roman diplomacy
has received due attention over the years: annual subsidies. These
could take the form not just of cash or bullion, but also of highly
valued Roman commodities, such as intricate jewellery or richly woven
cloths. In the Byzantine era, foodstuffs unavailable in the target
economy were sometimes used, and this may have been the case in
earlier eras. The point of the subsidies, as we have seen, was to
reinforce the power of a reasonably compliant frontier king, so that he
would have a real stake in maintaining peace on the frontier. Subsidies
tended to strengthen existing monarchies. But it is important to realize
that, like the amber or slave trades, diplomatic subsidies represented a
major flow of new wealth into the Germanic world, and, as was also
the case with the profits of trade, the appearance of new wealth

sparked off competition among potential recipients. Losing their subsidy may have been one element in the Limigantes' unwillingness to
be resettled further away from the frontier, an extra downside in being
demoted (in Rome's eyes) from overkingdom to underkingdom status.
Certainly, any diminution in the size or quality of the annual gifts
could cause crisis, as it did when Valentinian unilaterally reduced those
of the Alamanni in 364, and we have specific examples of groups
moving into the frontier region precisely to overwhelm the current
recipients of any subsidies and receive them in their place. Competition
for the control of the flow of subsidies thus multiplied its transformative effect, and meant that Rome was sometimes left awarding gifts to
the victors in struggles beyond its capacity to control.[62]

But subsidies were only part of an overall Roman diplomatic strategy
whose other aspects also had powerful effects. Take, for instance, the
periodic military interventions, which seem to have averaged out in the
fourth century at about one substantial campaign per generation in each
sector of the frontier. These interventions classically took the form of
burning down everything you could find until the local kings came into
the imperial presence to make their submission, when all the diplomatic
manoeuvring and subsidy reallocation would begin. The economic
effects of these burnt-earth interventions are worth careful consideration. We have no precise information from the fourth century, of
course, but an interesting analogy is provided by medieval estate records
from areas subject to similar levels of terrorism. Those of the Archbishop
of York's lands, subject to cross-border raiding from Scotland in the
fourteenth century, for instance, show that it took revenues – a decent
proxy for 'output' – a full generation to recover. This was because
raiders, alongside grabbing moveable goods that might be easily replaced, also targeted the capital items of agriculture such as ploughing
animals (approximating, in the medieval context, to tractors), which
were very expensive, not to mention housing and other major items.
The costs of replacing all this meant that revenues were reduced for
twenty or more years.

If you factor this kind of economic effect back into the pattern of
Roman frontier strategy, then, particularly in periods and areas where
conflict was fairly constant, living next to the Roman Empire would
be a substantial hindrance to economic development, and this is again
suggested by the archaeological record. Alongside the other frontier

areas where Roman imports became plentiful in the early Roman centuries, for instance, the Rhine/Weser region stands out as an exception. Few Roman imports have been found there and settlement remained much less dense until the later second century. This reflects the particular hostility between many of the groups of this region and the Empire, the Rhine/Weser being the heartland of the Cherusci and of Arminius' rebellion which destroyed Varus' legions in the Teutoburger Wald in 9 AD. The one area in the fifth-century west that seems to have enjoyed economic expansion at a time when the wheels were otherwise generally coming off the west Roman economy was the territory of the Alamanni, where there is good evidence of deforestation and of the expansion of agriculture and settlement, and hence by implication of population expansion as well. To my mind this is not surprising, since the contemporary reduction in the power of the west Roman state meant that it had stopped burning down Alamannic villages once per generation and regularly stealing agricultural surpluses. It was also in the fifth century that the observable tendency towards political unification among the Alamanni reached its climax, with the emergence finally of a single, unchallenged king. Again, this is not so surprising given that Rome's countervailing interference, bent, as we have seen, on regularly removing emergent dominant figures, had ceased to be effective.[63]

It is also worth thinking about this and all the other aspects of Roman diplomatic strategy from an Alamannic – or general frontier-client – perspective. The regular destruction of villages could only have caused huge resentment, and Ammianus often refers to ill-feeling towards Rome on the other side of the frontier. In fact, even the less violent aspects of Roman intrusion, creating as it did winners and losers, must have been highly resented by the losers. The kind of grovelling expected in public ceremonies and so well mastered by Zizais can't exactly have been welcome to those from whom it was required. And while Zizais may have been happy to have his political independence established, his former overking, who lost command of established rights over Zizais' followers, can only have been hugely irritated. Ammianus records, likewise, that another former overking, Araharius, was angered when he was denuded of his subjects. Additionally, the Empire would occasionally decide – as in the case of the Limigantes – that particular barbarian groups could no longer carry on living where they had long been established, and, as we have seen, was happy to use terror to enforce that decision. This is only one of a series of high-handed actions on the part of the Romans that appear in Ammianus' narrative. Valentinian I, for instance, altered agreements unilaterally when it suited him, both lowering, without consultation, the value of annual gifts made to Alamannic leaders, as we have seen, and constructing fortifications where it had previously been agreed that none would be placed. There are also hints in the sources that emperors would arbitrarily swap around 'favoured ally' status in a region so as to ensure the requisite level of subservience. Most ferociously, emperors were happy to authorize the elimination of frontier kings who posed too great a threat. The picture of Roman frontier management which emerges from all this is clear enough. The regular burning of neighbouring villages was backed up by a repertoire of aggressive diplomatic manoeuvres, which did not stop short of assassination.

If you consider all this from a non-Roman viewpoint, it becomes apparent that we need to factor into the equation a weight of oppressive Roman domination. The resentment among the many on the receiving end shows up in several different ways in the historical narratives. At the lowest level, it is evident in the willingness with which frontier groups engaged in petty and grander larceny. Raiding across the frontier was very general, and of course represented yet another Rome-emanating flow of new wealth to be squabbled over, and whose control might have transformative political effects in the Germanic world. More strikingly, resentment lay at the heart of the willingness of would-be dynasts to mount larger-scale rebellions, whether that of Arminius in the first century (whose explicit cause was taxation demands) or that of Chnodomarius in the fourth, where feelings ran high enough, as we have seen, for a sitting king, Gundomadus, to be ousted for refusing to participate.

A major factor to take into account when trying to understand the transformation of Germanic societies in this period, therefore, is four centuries' worth of ill-feeling caused by Rome's heavy-handed military and diplomatic aggression.

Two lines of explanation have recently been offered for the militarization of the Germani in the Roman period, evident in the increasing deposition of weapons: one, that the Germani were serving in increasing numbers as Roman auxiliary soldiers; second, that Roman campaigning east of the Rhine increased the status of warriors. As has rightly been observed, though representative of opposite reactions to Roman power – the first to its opportunities, the second to its threat – the two explanations are not remotely incompatible. Different elements among the Germanic population surely did respond along each of these lines, perhaps even the same persons at different points in their lives.[64] I would only stress that the negative reaction to Roman power must be taken seriously, and its role in political consolidation acknowledged.

For militarization, as we have seen, went far beyond burying the dead with weapons. A whole new language for political leadership evolved in the Roman period, which stressed the importance of war. Rulers became war leaders literally by definition and this transformation wasn't just achieved by force. The Germanic political community in the late Roman period still involved many others beyond kings and their immediate retinues, and the consent of this (freeman?) community to the process of political consolidation represented by the rise of military kingship was required. Here again, positive and negative worked happily side by side. A militarily effective king, as many have argued, was one more likely to win Roman recognition as a good partner to do frontier business with, and hence attract worthwhile subsidies and gifts. But he was also someone – like Athanaric and Macrianus – who was inherently more capable of resisting the more outrageous demands and intrusions of Roman imperial power. These two figures, it seems to me, show both the importance of anti-Roman sentiment and the limits to its expression by the fourth century. Both gained esteem and power in their own societies by resisting Roman intrusion, but both were willing enough to do deals when the Empire – for whatever reason – backed off and offered more acceptable terms.[65] They vividly illustrate the tightrope that even the prime beneficiaries of the unfolding processes of political centralization among the Germani had to tread.

# GLOBALIZATION

Contact with Rome on many levels, all operating simultaneously and often in overlapping fashion, drove the transformation of the Germanic world. The economic demands of the frontier, combined possibly with transfers of technique and technology, stimulated the intensification of agricultural production upon which all the other changes rested. Many individuals served as auxiliary troops in the Roman army and brought their pay or their retirement bonuses home with them, while, at least at times and places enjoying settled relations, Roman coins were adopted as an efficient mechanism for encouraging exchange. New trade networks grew up, carrying perhaps a substantial trade in iron ore and certainly significant ones in slaves and amber. And just as important as all the new wealth rolling around in the Germanic world was the fact that these latter two trades required much more complex forms of organization. It wasn't simply a case of Roman buyer meets Germanic producer. The northern Amber Route and the violent networks of the slave trade both emphasize that the new wealth did not gently wash over Germanic society in an all-embracing fashion. Particular groups organized themselves, often militarily, to extract disproportionate advantage from the new opportunities presented by the legionaries' advance to the Rhine and the Danube. Diplomatic and political contacts generated new wealth flows, too, and kings organized military power through their retinues so as to benefit disproportionately from the extra trading rights and annual subsidies that came their way.

At the same time, a range of other contacts with the Empire were also driving change forward. Annual subsidies came with a price tag attached, being one strand in a much broader repertoire of Roman techniques for managing the frontier. As well as receiving subsidies, sometimes frontier groups of Germani came under heavy military assault from the Empire. They also felt the weight of intrusive manipulation, which dictated where they lived, who they could be allied with and ruled by, and regularly demanded goods, services and even people. Their public life was required to operate within a framework of overt and demeaning subservience to Roman authority. The resentment of these client states showed itself in endemic small-scale raiding across the frontier. In my view, it also had the more profound effect of legitimizing the new type of military kingship that came to the fore among the Germani at this period, and which provided the bedrock of the greater political consolidation observable in the new confederations. Military kings had the muscle to demand more resources from their own societies, and to take greater benefits from the new wealth flows, but they also offered greater protection for their followers from the excesses of imperial intrusion.

In other words, the 'positive' and the 'negative' types of contact that grew up between the Germanic world and its imperial neighbour – although the use of such words always begs the question: positive or negative for whom? – had the same overall effect. As relations intensified, both pushed forward the process of political consolidation. What we're observing, in effect, is an early example of globalization. A thoroughly undeveloped, essentially subsistence agricultural economy with little diversification of production, trade or social stratification suddenly found itself alongside the highly developed economy and powerful state structures of the Roman Empire. Both the new wealth, and the struggles to control its flows and to limit Roman aggression, then, produced the more stratified social structures upon which the new political entities could come into existence. Between them, Empire and indigenous response generated the new Germania of the late Roman period.

Not, of course, that pre-Roman Germanic society had existed in some state of primeval bliss. As we have seen, there already existed a great differential in development between largely Germanic-dominated Jastorf north-central Europe and largely Celtic-dominated La Tène western Europe long before the legions pushed out from the Mediterranean rim. And, as we have also seen, relatively undeveloped Jastorf societies had already begun to reorganize themselves to gain a greater share of the wealth of their more developed La Tène neighbours even before the legions arrived on their doorstep. The figure of Ariovistus nicely illustrates the transformative effects that tend to follow when neighbouring societies are marked by very different levels of wealth, and these were already beginning to work themselves out before Rome came to the party. But in the early centuries AD, La Tène Europe was replaced by the still richer, politically more monolithic and militarily much more powerful Roman Empire. As a result, the power both of the original outside stimuli, and the resulting internal responses to those stimuli ('agency'), increased dramatically.

It is likely that prevailing disparities amongst the Germani themselves would have eventually generated larger, more consolidated political units even without the arrival of Rome. But the dynamic interaction with the Empire accelerated that process by many centuries. Even this much, however, tells less than the full story of how contact with the Empire transformed ancient Germania. We also need to explore the migratory phenomena that were unfolding simultaneously in some corners of Germanic society, alongside social and political transformation.

# 3

# ALL ROADS LEAD TO ROME?

IN THE SUMMER OF 172 AD, the Emperor Marcus Aurelius found himself in dire straits. The fires of war had been blazing all along Rome's European frontiers since 166, especially in the Middle Danubian sector where Marcus was now embroiled. One of his key commanders, the praetorian prefect Vindex, had already been killed north of the Danube, fighting the Germanic Marcomanni of Bohemia. The Emperor was himself leading a second Roman thrust against the Quadi of Slovakia. It was a burning-hot summer and the Romans, advancing through hostile territory, had no choice but to endure full battle order in heavy armour. The Quadi knew the country and knew that the Romans were coming. Rather than giving battle, they lured them up country, ever further from their supply train. Then they sprang the trap. The Romans were caught without supplies, and without water too; the Quadi were all around them, with no need to fight:

> They were expecting to capture [the Romans] easily because of their heat and thirst. So they posted guards all about and hemmed them in to prevent their getting water anywhere; for the barbarians were far superior in numbers. The Romans as a result were in a terrible plight from fatigue, wounds, the heat of the sun and thirst, and so could neither fight nor retreat, but were standing in the line . . . scorched by the heat.

The situation looked set for disaster

> [w]hen suddenly many clouds gathered and a mighty rain, not without divine intervention, burst upon them . . . At first all turned their faces upwards and received the water in their mouths; then some held out their shields and some their helmets to catch it, and they not only took deep draughts themselves, but also gave their horses to drink. And when the barbarians now charged upon them, they drank and fought at the same time.

The water energized the Romans and forced the Quadi to fight, since it ruined any hope of capitulation from thirst and heat exhaustion. Thunder and lightning – some of the bolts reportedly hitting the barbarians – completed the scene and Marcus emerged from the trap, with his army intact and a famous victory under his belt.

The rain miracle of Marcus Aurelius, as this moment of deliverance has been known ever since, was taken in antiquity as yet another proof that divine power sustained the Roman Empire. It was also squabbled over. Dio Cassius, our main source, attributes the divine intervention to the efforts of Arnuphis, an Egyptian mage, but Christian writers claimed that the prayers of a Christian legion from Syria had worked the trick. Whoever was responsible, the thunderstorm got the Emperor out of jail, and he was duly grateful. He went on to win the war and restore order on Rome's European frontiers, though it did take pretty much the rest of the decade. The rain miracle, along with other events of the war, was immortalized on the carvings of the celebratory column raised by the Emperor in the imperial capital (Plate 5).[1] But why did Marcus Aurelius find himself locked in this death struggle in the first place?

## FROM THE BALTIC TO THE BLACK SEA

Rome's expansion into largely Germanic-dominated temperate Europe ground to a halt in the first century AD more or less along a line marked by the Rivers Rhine and Danube, but this did not mean that the Empire had moved into purely defensive mode. As we saw in the last chapter, Rome's general military superiority was backed by an aggressive diplomacy, which turned the political entities closest to the frontier into Roman client states. Raiding, threats, military demonstrations and barbarian submissions were standard items in the repertoire, but head-on confrontation highly unusual. Harsh experience reinforced the lesson that open conflict with technically superior Roman armies usually ended in disaster. By the mid-second century, the Marcomanni and Quadi had both belonged to this class of frontier clients for over a century, which makes the war in which Marcus

Aurelius so nearly lost his life all the more puzzling. Why were long-standing clients, after a hundred years of fairly minor squabbling, now trying to destroy the Emperor and his army in a full-scale military encounter?

The rain miracle occurred in the middle of a sequence of disturbances which are collectively known as the Marcomannic War. But they involved many groups other than the Marcomanni of Bohemia, even if the latter did star in some of the war's most notorious episodes. Reconstructing the war is also far from straightforward. The historian Dio Cassius originally wrote a full account of the action, including a considerable amount of circumstantial detail, but his narrative survives only in fragments, and our other sources are very limited. The result is a series of episodic moments of action, whose relationship to one another is often unclear. Above all, the related issues of the scale of these wars and their underlying causation are particularly puzzling. Our Roman sources naturally concentrate on violence in the frontier zone and the ways in which it spilled over into the Empire itself. Historical and archaeological sources make it clear, however, that one of the factors destabilizing the frontier zone was the arrival there of new groups of Germanic outsiders.

## The Marcomannic War

Marcus Aurelius came to power in 161 AD, and the early years of his reign were spent dealing with the Parthian menace on Rome's Mesopotamian frontier. Amongst other measures, during these years he had to transfer to the east three full legions – notionally 18,000 men – from the Rhine and Danube, but by the middle of the decade trouble was brewing in the west. In winter 166/7, reportedly six thousand Langobardi and Ubii raided the Roman province of Pannonia – modern Hungary, south of the River Danube, and south and west of the Carpathian Mountains. These raiders were defeated, but trouble continued in this same Middle Danubian region. In 168 the Marcomanni and the Victuali, long-time Roman clients on this part of the frontier, demanded admission into the Empire. As we saw in the last chapter, it was not unheard-of for outside groups to ask to be admitted into the Empire, and sometimes these requests were granted. This time, however, Marcus refused. Perhaps he was not militarily in control of the situation. He was determined, however, to become so.

In 170, the Emperor gathered his forces in Pannonia. There are hints in the sources that he had it in mind formally to annex the territories of the Marcomanni and Quadi at this point. But the resulting campaign was disastrous. The Roman army was outflanked by the Marcomanni and, since many intermediate strongpoints had been stripped of troops for the projected assault, the rampant barbarians were able to break through into Italy itself. Uderzo was sacked and Aquileia besieged. Roman Italy suffered its worst disaster since the third century BC, and the invaders were not fully repelled until the end of 171. Meanwhile, unrest spread the full length of the Danube. Nomadic Sarmatian Iazyges and the Germanic Quadi were causing trouble on the Middle Danube plain west of the Carpathians, while two Vandal groups, the Astingi and the Lacringi, menaced the northern frontiers of Transylvanian Dacia (Map 4). The Costoboci, from the north-east of Dacia, also raided Thrace, Macedonia and Greece, having presumably moved south along the eastern rather than the western slopes of the Carpathians. At the same time, serious raiding was affecting the northern Rhine frontier. Countering all these different threats delayed the Emperor's plans for retribution, and it was not until 172 that Marcus could return to the offensive. Two years of intense campaigning on the Middle Danube, punctuated by the rain miracle, brought the Marcomanni, the Quadi and the Iazyges to heel. Bohemia, Slovakia and the Great Hungarian Plain had been pacified, but much of the rest of the decade was taken up with a complex mix of military and diplomatic countermeasures, designed, as ever, to turn immediate military victory into a longer-lasting peace.[2]

The surviving fragments of Dio give something of their flavour, but are not comprehensive. Nonetheless, the parallels with the stratagems pursued in the same region two centuries later by Constantius II are striking. Hostile kings were replaced with more pliant ones, particularly among the Quadi and Sarmatians, where the removal of the Emperor's previous nominees (Furtius and Zanticus, respectively) had marked the adoption of an openly hostile policy towards the Empire. The Marcomanni and Quadi were forced to accept the stationing of twenty thousand Roman soldiers in a series of forts upon their lands. All this, of course, is a further reminder that, for all the subsidies and blandishments that might accompany the status, becoming a Roman client was often not a freely chosen position. Some groups were allowed to move into new territories (the Asdingi), others prevented from doing so (the Quadi), and some were even received into the Empire (the 3,000-strong Naristi). All this was done according to the Emperor's wishes and his assessment of what would best serve the Empire's interests. The Naristi were a much smaller group than the Marcomanni, and Marcus Aurelius was now dictating terms on the back of a military victory, so that, this time, he was happy enough to receive them. Trading privileges, likewise, were granted or removed according to the Emperor's estimation of a group's loyalty, and neutral zones of differing sizes re-established. The dangerous Sarmatian Iazyges, like the Limigantes in 358, for instance, were forced to move twice as far away from the river as before. Where the Emperor was particularly suspicious, Roman garrisons were established and the normal assemblies by which tribes conducted political business were banned. As order was restored, and more pliant kings firmed up their authority, conditions were relaxed. The Iazyges were eventually allowed to return to the old neutral zone and to pass through the province of Roman Dacia to resume their normal relations with their fellow Sarmatians, the Roxolani. The far-reaching military campaigns of Marcus Aurelius thus underpinned a complex web of diplomatic settlements and alliances, which resonated to long-established rhythms of Roman client management. As Dio commented, such had been the scale of the problem – much greater than that faced by Constantius in 358 – that the work was still not finished on the emperor's death in 181.[3]

But we are still left with the most fundamental question of all. What caused the trouble in the first place?

According to one of our major sources, the underlying cause was a bout of expansionary activity – involving some migration – on the part of several Germanic groups from north-central Europe:

> Not only were the Victuali and Marcomanni throwing everything into confusion, but other tribes, who had been driven on by the more distant barbarians and had retreated before them, were ready to attack Italy if not peaceably received.

In the old Grand Narrative, this passage was naturally seized on as evidence that the Marcommanic War marked the first stage of a large-scale migration out of Germania that would eventually destroy the Roman Empire. But the extract is from the *Historia Augusta*, whose testimony is always problematic. Although it contains much historical information, particularly when dealing with the more distant, second-century, past, the text is in overall terms a fake: a creation of c.400 AD, written in Rome probably by someone of senatorial rank, masquerading as one of c.300. It is impossible to know how much weight to give its testimony at any particular point, since it is difficult to tell what is based on authentic information and what the author has just made up. And an author writing at that time, as we shall see in the next chapter, would have had in front of him an excellent contemporary example of Gothic barbarian immigrants who had entered the Empire in large numbers, on the run from 'more distant barbarians' in the form of the Huns. It is entirely reasonable, therefore, to be highly sceptical of the *Historia Augusta*'s account of the origins of Marcus' difficulties, and one recent commentator has argued that its large-scale vision of the causes and broader significance of the war needs to be rejected entirely. In this view, all thoughts of the fourth century should be put to one side. The Marcomannic War should not be seen as the first onrush of a rising Germanic tsunami which would eventually deluge the Roman world. On the contrary, having just wrapped up the Parthian War, Marcus Aurelius wanted to re-establish Rome's authority on its European frontiers, where the removal of troops to the east had allowed some increase in raiding, but nothing beyond the spectrum of the ordinary. In this view, it was the ferocious nature of the Emperor's projected counterstroke – Roman aggression, in other words – that inflamed the frontier. Panic caused the Marcomanni and Quadi to get their retaliation in first.[4]

Some aspects of this reconstruction are fair enough. It is necessary to be wary of possible anachronisms, but fear of Roman aggression would certainly have been an element in barbarian calculations. Rome expected to dictate matters on its frontiers on the back of military domination, and its barbarian clients can have been under few illusions that the Empire's take on any deserved retribution would be 'fair' or 'proportionate'. Emperors needed to be seen to be tough on barbarians and tough on the causes of barbarism. But, all that said, I do not find at all convincing the argument that there was nothing out of the ordinary going on in the 160s and 170s. It is important not to veer from one simple vision of the war – that it was the start of the great

Germanic counterstroke against Roman imperialism – to another: namely, that it was just a normal frontier tiff. Even putting possibly misleading parallels with the fourth century aside, the war involved frontier conflict on an unprecedented scale, and what we can reconstruct of its causation does suggest that major forces were at play.

First of all: scale. The geographical range of the attacks was extraordinary. By the early 170s, there was serious trouble afoot on the northern Rhine frontier, the Middle Danubian plain, and both the northern and eastern fringes of Dacia – pretty much the entire length of Rome's European frontiers. Even the most serious of first-century revolts had never simultaneously disturbed more than the Rhine and Middle Danube, and this is obviously a very different kind of crisis, again, from that generated by Chnodomarius' ambitions in the fourth century, which, as we saw in the last chapter, disturbed only one sector of the frontier. Also, the war lasted the best part of fifteen years. In the fourth century, most of the well documented frontier conflicts never took longer than two or three years to work themselves out, and even that involving Chnodomarius no more than about five. Geography and chronology are both enough, then, to indicate that something serious was under way.

The hardest aspect of the war to grasp is its numerical scale. Just how many people became involved in it over this decade and a half? The direct evidence is minimal. The only figure we have is Dio's report that six thousand Langobardi and Ubii were involved in the initial attack on Pannonia. If at all correct, this would represent a large but not massive force (judged, say, against the numbers mustered by the Alamanni at Strasbourg). Otherwise the evidence is implicit and/or impressionistic. The number of Roman troops involved in some at least of the Middle Danubian campaigns was clearly substantial; for the start of his major counteroffensive, for instance, Marcus Aurelius raised two entirely new legions (twelve thousand men).

Some of the damage done was serious, too, not only in Italy but also west of the Lower Rhine frontier, from the Belgian coast to the Somme, where Roman cities such as Tarvenna (Thérouanne), Bagacum (Bavay) and Samarobriva (Amiens) were reduced to ashes. The involvement of enough Marcomanni and Quadi to kill a prefect and pose a serious threat to the Emperor's life, likewise, indicates major warfare, as does the fact that Marcus Aurelius could plausibly put up a huge monument to himself in Rome as its victor. The self-aggrandizing propaganda of the column is unmistakable, but previous columns, such as Trajan's, had been used to publicize victories in major wars (in his case, the conquest of Dacia). The fact that Marcus could put up such a major monument to himself without attracting ridicule is again significant. If you are really determined to play down the scale of the action, it is possible to explain your way past these pieces of evidence individually, but collectively they do make the conclusion inescapable that the Marcomannic War represented something entirely out of the ordinary in relations between Rome and its barbarian neighbours.[5]

The same is also suggested by the element of geographical displacement – sometimes clearly in the form of migration – that forms such a striking sub-theme of the war. Here again, it differs markedly from frontier conflicts of the first century. The Langobardi and Ubii whose attack on Pannonia opened proceedings, for instance, apparently moved about eight hundred kilometres south from the Lower Elbe, where both are located by Tacitus at the end of the first century and by Ptolemy in the middle of the second, only half a generation before the war began. Their journey south is undocumented, but the most natural route would have taken them down the Elbe, one of central Europe's main north–south arteries, to Bohemia, before passing through the Morava valley and on to the Middle Danube plain (Map 4). If so, they followed one of central Europe's great thoroughfares, and the same path trodden two hundred and fifty years earlier by the Cimbri and Teutones. We don't know whether these Langobardi and Ubii were raiders who always intended to return home with their booty, or whether they intended to resettle more permanently in the frontier region. For some other groups, the desire for a permanent move is much clearer. This is certainly true of the Vandal groups who also moved south in the course of the war, in this case over a shorter distance from central Poland, and who attempted, with a degree of Roman collusion this time, to seize the territory of the Costoboci on the fringes of Dacia. As a move towards defusing the crisis, as we have seen, the Romans likewise received the Naristi into the Empire, and the Marcomanni and Victuali had earlier asked for similar treatment. Not that all the projected resettlement had the Roman frontier region in mind. Marcus moved decisively at one point to prevent the Quadi from moving as a body northwards into the territory of the Semnones on the Middle Elbe.[6]

It is important not to go overboard here. None of this suggests that there was some unstoppable tide of barbarian migration blowing in from the north, and the Marcomanni, Quadi and Iazyges surely did exploit the advent of trouble to pursue their own wealth-gathering agendas. Some of the outsiders who moved into the frontier zone also came only to raid. Even so, there is enough here to indicate that the Germanic groups of the frontier region, for the most part semi-subdued client kingdoms of the Empire rather than its sworn enemies, became caught up in the war at least in part because of the appearance of intrusive population groups, and to some extent did actually require – as they claimed – Roman assistance. Ballomarius, king of the Marcomanni, at one point stood up before the Emperor Marcus Aurelius as spokesman for delegations from a total of eleven frontier groups whose accustomed haunts were being threatened by pressure from the north.[7] If we had to leave the Marcomannic War at this point, and up to about 1970 we would have, it would all be very intriguing, but ultimately frustrating. By themselves the historical sources cannot give us any real sense of the scale of the bigger picture of which Marcus' quarrels with the Marcomanni and Quadi formed just a part. In the last scholarly generation or so, however, a vast new body of archaeological evidence has come to light, which has added dramatically to our knowledge of what was afoot in northern Germania in the second century.

The fact that this evidence exists at all is a fascinating by-product of the Cold War. Numerous sites had been excavated in central and eastern Europe before 1939, but so many of the finds were lost in the conflagration of war that scholarship more or less began again from scratch afterwards, when much of the impetus, manpower and funding came from a particular quarter: the eastern bloc states that emerged under Soviet hegemony. These states managed to combine two interests, which, on the face of it, should have been incompatible. On the one hand, they were vigorously nationalistic. This expressed itself archaeologically in the desire to prove that the present inhabitants were the latest descendants of an indigenous population that had continuously occupied the same piece of territory with distinction far back into the distant past. This was combined with a healthy interest in demonstrating the truth of the processes of ancient historical development as outlined in the nineteenth century by Messrs Marx and Engels, despite the fact, as we have already seen, that for Marxists any kind of national identity could only be a false consciousness. For both these reasons, investigating the deep past was regarded as the height of chic behind the Iron Curtain, and the result was a huge state-sponsored growth industry. When you read them now, the ideological overtones of some of the publications generated by all this work, particularly those from the 1950s and 1960s, make your hair stand on end. But there were many scholars who steadfastly refused to surrender to the extraordinary weight of the official Marxist-nationalist expectations of the past, and, whether by just paying lip-service to official lines or by ignoring them entirely, pursued their research with integrity. Some tremendously important work was already being done on the basis of all the new finds, even in the Stalinist era, and by the 1970s and 1980s many East European academic communities had won almost complete intellectual freedom.[8]

One direct result is a much clearer picture of the major material cultural systems of Germanic-dominated Europe in the Roman period, and in particular the identification of the Wielbark culture of northern Poland as an entity recognizably distinct from its immediate Przeworsk neighbour to the south, which had been identified and relatively fully investigated between the wars. There are many similarities between the two, but differences both in detail – for example, pot decoration, weapon construction – and on a larger scale distinguish them. Wielbark males were never buried with weapons, whereas Przeworsk males often were, and Wielbark cemeteries often produce a mixture of cremation and inhumation rites, whereas Przeworsk populations only ever cremated. Such differences indicate substantially different beliefs about any afterlife.

What makes these identifications so important for the Marcomannic War is that the plethora of new finds has also made it possible to evolve much more reliable archaeological dating systems for the remains. Kossinna – dread founder of culture history – had started the job using the intersection of two elements. First, he and his peers established the principle of using stylistic development to establish relative dates within a particular 'culture'. The appearance of more developed designs of a particular object, or more sophisticated forms of the same kind of decoration, was – reasonably, as it turns out – presumed to be subsequent to simpler, therefore earlier, forms. In principle, this approach can be taken with any type of object, but the method was originally applied largely to pottery. Early researchers then attempted to use occasional finds of more precisely datable objects, often Roman coins in Germanic remains, to calibrate the stylistic sequences against a more absolute chronology. If a coin of 169 AD was found with a particular type of pottery, then that type was clearly being made after that date. This was fine as far as it went, but the time lag between the production and final deposition of datable objects was always guesswork, and could generate deeply erroneous conclusions, since we now know good-quality first- and second-century Roman silver coins were still circulating widely in barbarian Europe, for instance, in the fourth century.

Applying this basic approach to the much larger body of material that had become available by 1970, scholars were able to establish sequences of stylistic development for a much wider range of items: weapons, buckles, jewellery and combs, amongst others. This put the dating of finds on a much firmer footing, since it could be based on all the materials in a given cache, not just on one item, and, as a result, the chronology of these major Germanic-dominated cultural systems can now be broken down into distinct phases, each typically defined as consisting of an association of particular weapon types with certain forms of brooch, buckle, pot and comb. In particular, this has made it infinitely easier to spot the occasional rogue item that had continued in use from an earlier period and whose inclusion in a later burial would previously have thrown dating estimates out.[9]

All this is relevant to the Marcomannic War because it emerged from the new work that dramatic transformations began to unfold in the configuration of Germanic, or Germanic-dominated, material cultural systems on the territory of what is now Poland from about the middle of the second century AD. In particular, the Wielbark cultural system started to spread southwards from Pomerania into the north of Greater Poland (between the Rivers Notec and Warta), and south-eastwards across the Vistula into Masovia (Map 4). In the past, the identity of the population groups behind this set of remains generated acrimonious debate because of their potential relevance to the highly vexed question of Slavic origins, but it is now generally accepted that the Wielbark culture incorporated areas that, in the first two centuries AD, were dominated by Goths, Rugi and other Germani, even if its population had not originally been (or still was not) entirely Germanic-speaking. The new territories into which Wielbark remains began to spread from c.150, however, had previously been occupied by a population whose material remains belonged to the Przeworsk system. This has traditionally been associated with the Vandals, but certainly encompassed other population groups besides. Like most of these cultural areas, it was so large that it must have included several of the small first- and second-century Germanic groupings mentioned by Tacitus and Ptolemy.

What really matter, however, are not the detailed identifications, but the brute fact of Wielbark expansion. The chronological coincidence here is much too striking to be dismissed. Wielbark expansion – indicating a major upheaval of some kind in northern Poland – occurred at more or less the same time as the Marcomannic War. It must have been connected with it in some way, and shows that the frontier disturbances that appear in the Roman sources were linked to a wider set of convulsions affecting a broader tranche of Germanic-dominated Europe. What the archaeological evidence cannot make clear at this point is whether this link was one of cause or effect. Even the improved stylistic chronologies cannot date remains more closely than phases of twenty-five years or so, and there are always considerable chronological overlaps between adjacent phases. In this case, a twenty-five-year window is large enough for Wielbark expansion to have been either cause *or* effect of the Marcomannic War. More precise carbon-14 or dendrochronological dates will be needed for greater clarity on this point, and will no doubt become available, but for the moment we have to leave the issue open.[10]

It is also unclear how we should envisage the human history behind the expansion of the Wielbark system. Archaeological zones are the material remains of systems, not things, so an expansion in the geographical area of one system at the expense of another need not represent an act of conquest, as Kossinna would automatically have assumed. In principle, expansion might be the effect of a number of different kinds of development: conquest or annexation certainly, but also extensions of trading patterns, belief structures and so forth. In this instance, it does seem clear that Wielbark expansion to an extent represented the acculturation of existing Przeworsk populations to new Wielbark cultural norms, rather than their complete replacement by Wielbark immigrants. As Map 4 shows, at some cemeteries Wielbark-type remains replaced Przeworsk predecessors with no intervening gap, and no obvious signs of discontinuity in use. Here we may well be dealing, therefore, with a Przeworsk population taking on new

Wielbark burial habits with regard to weaponry and inhumation, and presumably also, therefore, the particular patterns of belief that underlay them. But even this much change did not occur in a vacuum. Something must have led these Przeworsk populations to change some long-established life – or rather, death – habits. What this may have been, the archaeological evidence does not say. In my view, some new degree of political influence is much the likeliest answer, since even cultural imitation usually follows political prestige.

Equally important, and operating alongside any acculturation, Wielbark expansion also involved some population displacement southwards from northern Poland. This is reflected in the historical sources. By c.200 AD, for instance, the Roman army was able to recruit into its ranks Goths – one of the old Wielbark groups – from the fringes of Dacia. A hundred years before, Gothic territories had been too remote from the frontier for this to happen. But the archaeological material is itself also highly suggestive. The general density of Wielbark sites had been growing apace since the start of the millennium. Individual settlements were short-lived, falling in and out of use relatively quickly in the first and second centuries, reflecting the population's inability to maintain the fertility of its fields in anything but the short term. But there is also a broader pattern. Within each twenty-five-year period after the birth of Christ, there was a larger total number of settlements in use in Wielbark areas. On the face of it, this suggests population growth, which would help explain both the displacement southwards to the Carpathians, which allowed the Romans to pick up Gothic recruits, and the general Wielbark pressure being applied on its more immediate Przeworsk neighbours in central Poland. As we have seen, the evidence on agricultural production from Germanic Europe does indeed suggest that its population grew substantially in the Roman period, so that this picture is far from implausible. If so, a growing Wielbark population was perhaps posing some of its Przeworsk neighbours a stark choice – between being absorbed into the Wielbark system and finding alternative domains.[11]

There is much more, of course, that we would ideally want to know, and it's particularly frustrating that we cannot be sure whether Wielbark expansion preceded or followed Marcus Aurelius' woes on the frontier. Nonetheless, history and archaeology combine well enough here both to show that the war was highly unusual in its scale and duration and to suggest that one of the causes of this was the role being played by intrusive population groups moving into the frontier region from further afield. It is not just the rather ropy evidence of the *Historia Augusta* that suggest that the events of the Marcomannic War involved large numbers of people on the move. Some of the much more trustworthy fragments of Dio's History suggest the same, with Wielbark expansion adding a further dimension to our understanding of what was afoot. All of this is enough to show that the Marcomannic War cannot be understood as a slightly more violent than usual frontier spat. And the case for seeing it as a watershed is only strengthened when we turn our attention to the third century, when Wielbark expansion increased in momentum and further Germanic migration entirely remade Rome's frontier world.

## To the Black Sea and Beyond

The countermeasures of Marcus Aurelius defused the immediate crisis of the 160s effectively enough, and peace returned to Rome's European frontiers for the best part of two generations. The third century, however, was to witness trouble on a still greater scale. The problems were made all the worse by the fact that the same era saw the rise to prominence of the Sasanian dynasty, which turned the Near East, largely equivalent to modern Iraq and Iran, into a superpower to rival Rome. The Sasanians were much the greatest threat, destroying the armies of three Roman emperors – even capturing the last of them, Valerian, and leading him in chains behind Shapur I, Sasanian Shah-an-shah, 'King of kings'. When Valerian died, they flayed his corpse and pickled his skin as a victory trophy. This new threat naturally forced Roman military resources eastwards, and events on the Rhine and the Danube have to be seen in this context. If the Sasanians had not exploded into history simultaneously, Rome's third-century European antagonists would never have enjoyed such freedom of action.[12]

In western Europe, on the Rhine and the Upper Danubian frontiers, the third-century crisis involved a moderate amount of migration and a larger dose of political reorganization. This was precisely the era in which the new Germanic confederations we examined in the last chapter began to appear. The Alamanni appear as enemies of Rome for the first time in 213, when the Emperor Caracalla launched a punitive or pre-emptive campaign against them. The Alamanni were presumably already posing some kind of threat at that point, but our sources, limited as they are, indicate that it increased dramatically from the 230s. One particularly large Alamannic attack occurred in 242, and such raids were then apparently more or less continuous through the 240s and 250s, although this picture emerges from a scatter of fragmentary historical, archaeological and above all coin-hoard evidence, since no continuous narrative sources survive. But by about 260, at the very latest, the Alamanni and other groups in the region were causing seriously substantial difficulties. Some were already receiving Roman subsidies, and a famous votive altar, recovered from Mainz, records a Roman counterstrike in which thousands of prisoners taken in a raid on Italy were recovered. Most arresting of all, in 261 or thereabouts (the Roman state never trumpeted its defeats) the so-called *Agri Decumates*, land that had been occupied since early in the first century (Map 5), was abandoned.

As far as we can tell, this wasn't exactly an Alamannic conquest. It was more a question of the then Emperor in the west, Postumus, deciding to withdraw much-needed troops from the region for the defence of strategically more important areas. It is testimony, nonetheless, to the level of pressure being exerted on the frontier, and the withdrawal failed to solve the problem. More Alamannic assaults are recorded in the late 260s and mid-270s, vivid evidence of which has come to light in the form of the unlucky thirteen individuals who were brutally killed, dismembered and partly scalped before the remains were thrown down the well of their farm at Regensburg-Harting. The situation on the new frontier was finally stabilized by further Roman campaigning in the late third and early fourth centuries under the Tetrarchs and the Emperor Constantine, which initiated the more stable pattern of fourth-century client-state relations that we observed in Chapter 2.[13]

Although much of this crisis was clearly stimulated by the extra military power that was one result of overall Germanic development and the new political confederations it generated, two bouts of migration also played a significant role. First, following the Roman withdrawal, the Alamanni moved into the Agri Decumates, which is where they were happily ensconced in the fourth century. They had not come from far. What exactly it meant to be an Alamann in the third century is much disputed, and we will return to the issue later in the chapter. But all the physical evidence from the Agri Decumates –

of jewellery, ceramic types and modes of burial – indicates that its new Germanic masters had their origins not very far to the east, in the lands of the so-called Elbe-Germanic triangle, west of the River Elbe from Bohemia in the south to Mecklenburg in the north (Map 5).

Second, established just to the rear of the Alamanni in the fourth century, but still within occasional reach of Roman diplomacy, lay the territory of the Burgundians. Unlike the Alamanni, who were an entirely new political formation of the late Roman period, Burgundians were already known to Tacitus and Ptolemy in the first and second centuries. At that point, they held lands much further to the east (now occupied by modern Poland). They were one-time members of the Vandalic world, living somewhere between the Oder and the Vistula. Thus, by the fourth century some Burgundians had moved around five hundred kilometres westwards. The historical evidence indicates that at this point they were established somewhere on the middle stretches of the River Main, and there is some archaeological confirmation. Materials are not plentiful, but a cluster of sword burials have been excavated in broadly the same area. The materials found in these graves resemble items found earlier in east Germanic territories, and are quite distinct from materials associated with groups from the Elbe-Germanic triangle. It is important, though, to acknowledge the limitations of the evidence. Up to the third century and indeed beyond, east Germanic populations universally cremated their dead, and the Main sword burials are inhumations. The historical evidence also locates fourth-century Burgundians most firmly in the Kocher valley, but no east Germanic materials have been unearthed there. Some migration is clear enough, then, on the part of both Alamanni and Burgundians, but its nature, scale and causation need to be examined with care.[14]

If the third-century crisis was serious enough on the Rhine, the action was much more explosive further east. Where the Marcomannic War had unfolded largely on the Middle Danube plain, this time the worst of the fighting occurred to the east of the Carpathians, in the wide stretches of territory bordering the northern shores of the Black Sea. It began in 238, with a recorded attack by some Goths on the city of Histria, close to the point where the River Danube runs into the Black Sea (Map 6). This inaugurated an initial run of largely Gothic attacks upon the Roman Empire, all launched across its Lower Danube frontier between the Carpathians and the Black Sea. It's impossible to reconstruct anything like a full narrative of these assaults, but they peaked around the year 250. In 249, the east Balkan city of Marcianople was ransacked by the Gothic followers of two leaders – Argaith and Guntheric – and the violence escalated quickly.

In the spring of 250, another Gothic leader by the name of Cniva broke through the Roman frontier and crossed the Danube at the old legionary fortress of Oescus, which guarded one of the river's easiest crossings. He then marched into the heart of the Balkans, capturing the city of Philippopolis (modern Plovdiv in Bulgaria) south of the Haemus Mountains, where he overwintered. The following year, the Emperor Decius attempted to intercept the then retreating Goths, but was himself defeated and killed at Abrittus.[15] This was a huge disaster. On one level, it was even worse than the more famous defeat in the Teutoburger Wald. For the first time, a reigning emperor had been cut down in a battle with barbarians. On another, however, the situation was less serious than it might appear. At the time of Decius' death, the Empire was in the midst of immense internal political upheaval, one knock-on effect from the huge crisis stimulated within the Roman system by the emergence of the rival Sasanian super-power. Decius was the ruler of only part of Roman Europe and North Africa, and had led into battle only a relatively small percentage of the imperial army. It was a major defeat, but troop losses were not so huge as to pose a structural threat to imperial integrity. This shows up clearly in subsequent events. Some further attacks followed across the Danube in 253 and 254, but they achieved little, and the Goths then abandoned the Danubian line of attack. The natural conclusion is that Decius' successors had effectively closed it off.

Shortly afterwards, mixed groups of raiders exploited a second line of attack, crossing the Black Sea to Asia Minor by ship in three successive years, 255–7.[16] The first expedition, unsuccessful, was directed at Pityus on the south-eastern shore of the Black Sea. The second successfully sacked both the previous year's target and the city of Trapezus (modern Trabzon). These initial raids were undertaken by what our main source calls 'Boranoi', a name that perhaps just means 'northerners'. The third, seemingly much more substantial, expedition of 257, this one explicitly including Goths, caused widespread devastation in Bithynia and the Propontis, inflicting damage on the cities of Chalcedon, Nicomedia, Nicaea, Apamea and Prusa. There is then a gap in our sources – which, for all their problems, again probably reflects a cessation or lessening in the intensity of the attacks – until 268, when an enormous maritime expedition left the northern shores of the Black Sea. It was composed again partly of Goths but also of some other Germani, notably Heruli. The new expedition did not sail straight across the Black Sea but moved along its northern and western coasts, keeping within sight of land and raiding some coastal cities, such as Anchialus, as it went. Other assaults on Tomi, Marcianople, Cyzicus and Byzantium were beaten off. The raiders then forced the Dardanelles, and spilled out into the Aegean. For the first time, northern sea raiders had broken into Rome's Mediterranean lake. There the expedition divided into three main groups. These attacked, respectively, the northern Balkans around Thessalonica, Attica, and the coastal hinterland of Asia Minor. The Emperor Gallienus began the counterattack in the Balkans, but it was his successor Claudius who inflicted a massive defeat on the Balkan groups in 269, winning the sobriquet 'Gothicus' – 'victor over the Goths' – for his efforts. The struggle against the Heruli around Athens was led amongst others by the historian Dexippus, while the third group, led by the chieftains Respa, Veduc and Thuruar, was eventually driven back into the Black Sea in 269, but not before it had wreaked havoc. The islands of Rhodes and Cyprus were devastated, as were the cities of Side and Ilium on the mainland. The raid's most dramatic casualty was perhaps the legendary temple of Diana at Ephesus.[17]

The Roman response was fierce. Not only was each of the individual groups defeated, but no major raid ever again broke through the Dardanelles. As with the Danube after the defeat of Decius, one can only presume that effective countermeasures were put in place to seal off the line of attack. Not that this was the end of the Gothic problem. A further attack across the Danube occurred in 270, when Anchialus and Nicopolis were sacked, but the new Emperor Aurelian then led his forces north of the river in 271 and thoroughly defeated a Gothic leader called Cannabaudes, who had presumably been responsible for the latest outrages. Aurelian's counterattack nipped the new threat in the bud. The mid-270s saw some further sea-borne raids, which plundered the Pontus in particular, but no further assaults over the Danube into the Roman Balkans. Not only had the Emperor's defeat of the Goths brought some relief, but he had also organized, more or less simultaneously, a planned evacuation of Transylvanian Dacia.[18]

As with the parallel withdrawal from the *Agri Decumates* in the
west, our information about the abandonment of Dacia is limited. But
both narrative evidence and the coin hoards indicate that most of the
attacks of the third century had skirted Dacia's frontiers and entered
the Balkans proper, or crossed the Black Sea into Asia Minor, rather
than directly affecting the province itself. This withdrawal would again
appear to have been more by strategic design, therefore, than a
headlong retreat from direct military disaster. On one level, Aurelian
probably had it in mind to shorten his frontier lines. Dacia was a
projecting salient north of the Danube, which needed defending on
three sides. By evacuating it, the Roman frontier in south-eastern
Europe could be reduced by something like eight hundred kilometres.
It also gave the troublesome outsiders a new prize to squabble over,
diverting them from making further attacks on Roman territory.
Writing in the fourth century, Eutropius notes that Dacia was 'now'
(369) divided between the Taifali, Victohali and Tervingi. Aurelian's
combination of military success and strategic withdrawal took much of
the steam out of the cross-border attacks, but it was to be another
generation before order was fully restored on Rome's Danube frontier.[19] As on the Rhine, further campaigns by the Tetrarchs and
Constantine were required fully to force the Goths and others into the
semi-client status in which we encountered them in the last chapter.

But who exactly were the Goths who feature so strongly in the
third-century action, and what underlay these two or three generations
of large-scale disturbance on the east European frontiers of the Roman
Empire?

There is no doubt at all that the emergence of Gothic domination
represented a complete revolution in the nature of the threat facing
the Roman Empire across its Lower Danube frontier. In the first and
second centuries, Rome had mostly faced a mixture of nomadic
Iranian-speaking Sarmatians and settled Dacian-speakers in this
theatre of operations. By the fourth century, groups labelled 'Goth'
had become the main focus of Roman campaigning and diplomacy in
the region. The Gothic Tervingi, as we saw in Chapter 2, became the
Empire's main client beyond the Lower Danube, and as the events we
have just summarized demonstrate so clearly, the intervening century
had seen a huge increase in the military threat posed to the Empire
across both its land and its water frontiers. There had been no attacks

via Dacia, across the Black Sea or through the Dardanelles on anything like a similar scale in the first and second centuries.

The traditional response to these observations has always been to suppose that Germanic migration was a key ingredient of this strategic revolution. 'Goths' were nowhere a presence north of the Black Sea in the first and second centuries AD, when Sarmatians and Dacians are the only two groups to be mentioned in the region. The only Goths we hear about at this time were established in northern Poland. So, game, set and match, you might think, to migration? Well, not exactly. It has recently been argued by Michael Kulikowski that the traditional view of the developing situation north of the Black Sea is a 'text-hindered' fantasy. This is a term borrowed from the jargon of archaeologists (although Kulikowski is himself not one), and is used to describe a situation where the interpretation of archaeological evidence has been bent out of shape by a determination to make it conform to the available historical evidence. In this instance, among the range of far from wonderful historical materials available to us for the third century is a sixth-century Gothic history, written by a man called Jordanes, which records the migration of Goths to the Black Sea under a certain King Filimer. This account, Kulikowski argues, not only has little credibility in itself, but has also unduly influenced how historians and archaeologists have looked at the other evidence. Without it, in his view, the other archaeological and historical evidence would not make anyone think in terms of migration. What really underlay the troubles of the third century, and the emergence of Gothic domination in the fourth, was not migration at all but sociopolitical reorganization among the region's existing population: in fact, of broadly the same kind that produced the new Germanic confederations of the late Roman west.[20] Is he correct?

Two elements of the argument are convincing. First, there's not the slightest doubt that socioeconomic and political reorganization – 'development' – were an important dimension of the story. The Gothic Tervingi of the fourth century had a complex, confederative political structure, developed social hierarchies, and an economic profile both in production and exchange that went far beyond the norms of first-century Germania. Their political structures were based on hereditary power, and robust enough both to survive major defeats and to develop coherent strategies for overturning their worst consequences.

Second, Kulikowski is right enough that little reliance can be placed on
Jordanes. Jordanes was writing three hundred years after the event,
and can be shown to have produced a completely anachronistic view
of the Gothic world of the fourth century, on which more in a
moment.[21] If he can be so wrong about fourth-century Gothic history,
this must call his account of the third century into question, even if
we don't have enough contemporary sources to be able to check it
systematically. Even conceding these points, however, there is still
more than enough good-quality evidence to establish that Germanic
migration from the north was a major factor in the strategic revolution
of the third century.

It does need to be emphasized, first of all, that the change in the
nature of the forces Rome was facing across its Lower Danube frontier
was much more profound than a mere change in labels. In the first
two centuries AD, the eastern foothills of the Carpathian range –
modern Moldavia and Wallachia – were occupied by a number of
Dacian groups who had not been brought under direct Roman rule at
the time of Trajan's conquest of Transylvania. In the course of the
third century, they generated a new degree of political unity among
themselves and came to be known collectively as the Carpi. The main
Sarmatian group immediately north of the Black Sea was the Roxolani,
who, together with the Iazyges, had dismantled the dominance of the
Germanic-speaking Bastarnae in the region at the start of the first
century AD. Where the Iazyges had subsequently moved on to the
Great Hungarian Plain, west of the Carpathians, the Roxolani stayed
east, exercising hegemony over the ancient Greek cities of the Pontus,
which retained some independence into the third century. Both Sarmatians and Dacians became at least semi-subdued Roman clients after
Trajan's conquest of Transylvanian Dacia, even though they were not
formally incorporated into the Empire. The sudden dominance of
Goths and other Germanic-speakers in the region represented, therefore, a major cultural shift. And there is no doubt that the new Gothic
masters of the landscape were Germanic-speakers. The Gothic Bible
translation was produced for some of them by Ulfila, the descendant
of Roman prisoners captured by the Goths from Asia Minor, and its
Germanic credentials are irrefutable. The appearance of the Goths thus
represents a massive change in the complexion and identity of the
forces lined up on Rome's north-eastern frontier.[22]

This, of course, was not the first time that Germanic-speakers had provided the dominant population stratum in the region. The Bastarnae, subdued by the Sarmatians around the beginning of the first millennium, had also been Germanic. So in theory it might be possible to explain the rise of Gothic domination north of the Black Sea in the third century as the re-emergence of those Germanic groups who had been subordinated here in the first. However, a pretty extensive range of evidence suggests, on the contrary, that the immigration of new Germanic-speakers played a critical role in the action.

In the period of Dacian and Sarmatian dominance, groups known as Goths – or perhaps 'Gothones' or 'Guthones' – inhabited lands far to the north-west, beside the Baltic. Tacitus placed them there at the end of the first century AD, and Ptolemy did likewise in the middle of the second, the latter explicitly among a number of groups said to inhabit the mouth of the River Vistula. Philologists have no doubt, despite the varying transliterations into Greek and Latin, that it is the same group name that suddenly shifted its epicentre from northern Poland to the Black Sea in the third century. Nor was it the only group name to do so at this time. Goths get pride of place in our sources and in scholarly discussion, but other Germanic groups participated in the action too. We have already encountered the Heruli, and late third- and early fourth-century sources record the presence in and around the Carpathians, in addition, of Germanic-speaking Gepids, Vandals, Taifali and Rugi. The Rugi, like the Goths, had occupied part of the Baltic littoral in the time of Tacitus, and the likeliest location for Vandals in the same period is north-central Poland, to the south of the Goths and Rugi. The presence of Vandals and Rugi in the Carpathian region, alongside Goths, represents a major relocation of some kind on their part, and all were moving south and east from Poland towards the Pontus. The Heruli are not mentioned by Tacitus, but in the fourth and fifth centuries a second, non-Danubian, group of Heruli again lived far to the north-west, suggesting, again, that our Danubian Heruli may have got there via some kind of migration. The Gepids and Taifali, like the Heruli, are first encountered at the end of the third century, and we will return to the significance of these 'new' Germanic-speaking groups later in the chapter.

There is, of course, more that we would like to know, but despite obvious deficiencies the historical evidence in its entirety strongly indicates that a wave of Germanic expansion – moving broadly north-west to south-east – underlay the strategic shift that led Aurelian to abandon upland Transylvania. This has to be deduced. There is no explicit description of Germanic migration in contemporary Roman sources, which confine themselves to accounts of its effects – attacks by these new groups across the Roman frontier. If 'Goth' was the only Germanic group name from north-central Europe to shift its location in these years, you might get away with the argument that it's a case of accidental resemblance, but, as we have just seen, it isn't only 'Goth'. This being so, there is no reason not to accept what the historical evidence is prima facie telling us. In a reversal of the effects of the arrival of the Sarmatian nomads in the first century AD, the hegemony of Germanic-speakers east of the Carpathians, lost in the overthrow of the Bastarnae and their allies, was restored by the migration of Goths, Rugi, Heruli and other Germanic-speaking groups in the third century.[23]

This interim conclusion is only strengthened by two broader aspects of the historical evidence. First, the rise of Gothic power north of the Black Sea eventually led some indigenous groups to evacuate the region entirely. As we shall soon see in more detail, large numbers of Dacian-speaking Carpi (but not all of them) from the Carpathian foothills were admitted into the Roman Empire in the twenty-five years or so after 290 AD. An increased level of competition between groups already indigenous to the region might conceivably have generated such an exodus, but it is much more consistent with the after-effects of substantial Germanic immigration. Second, the new Gothic populations of the region remained highly mobile, even after moving into the plains south and east of the Carpathians following the exodus of the Carpi. In the 330s, the Gothic Tervingi contemplated moving lock, stock and barrel to the Middle Danubian region, and from the 370s, as we will explore in the next chapter, relocated along with their fellow Gothic Greuthungi to new homes in the Roman Empire. This later mobility is relevant, because, as we have seen, comparative studies have consistently shown that migration is a cultural habit that builds up in particular population groups. Finding Gothic populations mobile in the fourth century provides a further reason for accepting the evidence that they – or their ancestors – had been so in the third. Neither of these points would be conclusive by itself, but both reinforce the historical evidence that Gothic migration played a large role in recasting the strategic situation north of the Black Sea in the third century.[24]

The archaeological legacy of the Cold War, moreover, again allows us to expand the discussion beyond the limits of the historical sources. Between c.150 and c.220/230 AD, there occurred a further large-scale south-eastern expansion of the Wielbark cultural system into Polesie and Podlachia first of all, and then on into Volhynia and northern Ukraine. This entirely dwarfed in its geographical scale the earlier Wielbark expansion from around the time of the Marcomannic War. At the same time, Wielbark sites and cemeteries in western Pomerania were falling out of use, so the shift in the Wielbark centre of gravity was huge (Map 6). Given that certainly the Goths and probably at least the Rugi, too, among the newly dominant Germanic groups of the Black Sea region had their origins within the Wielbark system in the first and second centuries, these finds are highly suggestive, in fact, of the route followed by some of the Germanic-speakers who ended up by the Black Sea. A ribbon of Wielbark cemeteries of more or less the right date has been traced south along the upper reaches of the River Vistula, and then on to the Upper Dniester (Map 6). These certainly tie in chronologically with the sudden appearance of Gothic attackers outside the walls of the city of Histria in 238.[25]

The really striking development in the north Pontic archaeology of this period, however, was not the further spread of the Wielbark system per se, but the generation of a series of new cultural systems incorporating some Wielbark features. The most important of these was the Cernjachov, which by the middle of the fourth century had spread over a huge area between the Danube and the Don (Map 6). This is another case where the date and identity of the system used to be much fought over, but its basic characteristics are now well established. Over five thousand settlements have been identified, and many large bi-ritual cemeteries excavated, the remains showing beyond doubt that the system flourished from the second half of the third century down to the year 400, or just a bit later. Chronologically, as well as geographically, its remains coincide with Gothic dominion in the late Roman period as described in trustworthy contemporary sources, and it is now universally accepted that the system can be taken to reflect the world created by the Goths – and probably our other Germanic-speakers too – north of the Black Sea.

Some elements of the new system strongly recall, or are identical to, their counterparts in the Wielbark system to the north-west, but it is important to recognize that the latter did continue on in its own right; there was nothing like a total evacuation of northern Poland. Some of the pottery is identical, with handmade bowl-shaped Wielbark ceramics being particularly prevalent in early Cernjachov levels. Otherwise, many of the *fibula* brooch types, and the style of female costume (brooches worn as a pair on each shoulder), are identical with those found in Wielbark areas. Some house-types, particularly the longhouses shared by both humans and animals (German *Wohnstallhäuser*), are likewise common to certain areas, at least, of both systems. It is also striking, although at present a full comparative study is lacking, that the two customs which distinguish Wielbark cemeteries from those found in surrounding areas of north-central Europe are also found in Cernjachov territories. In cemeteries of both systems, two types of burial ritual coexisted: inhumation and cremation. Likewise, the population of Wielbark areas did not bury weapons (or any other iron objects) with their male dead, and the absence of this habit was also a feature of Cernjachov burial ritual.

Other features of the Cernjachov system had different origins. While handmade Wielbark ceramics were commonly used early on, a more sophisticated wheel-made pottery, broadly analogous to provincial Roman types, quickly became characteristic of the system. And if the longhouse certainly had its origins in the Germanic-dominated cultures of north-central Europe, another characteristic dwelling in many Cernjachov areas was the sunken or semi-sunken hut (in German, *Grübenhaus*). These, by contrast, had long been indigenous to the eastern foothills of the Carpathians and beyond, and are not found in Wielbark or any other northern Germanic settlements of the first and second centuries. Excavators have also found occasional examples within Cernjachov cemeteries of a distinctive Sarmatian burial practice: placing possessions on a shelf cut within the grave. A Sarmatian population group thus apparently continued to play its part in the new mix generated by northern Germanic immigration towards the Black Sea.[26]

The interpretation of these remains was for a long time contentious. As soon as the first Cernjachov materials were recovered in 1906, their obvious similarities to characteristically Germanic materials from north-central Europe, especially in terms of metalwork, were duly spotted, long before the Wielbark system had been identified. They were quickly linked to the migration of Goths known from historical sources, and in the Nazi era cited in grotesque justification of territorial demands in Eastern Europe. Nazi bureaucrats went so far as to rename towns of the Black Sea region after great Gothic heroes, Theoderichshafen – 'the harbour of Theoderic' (a great Gothic leader of the fifth and sixth centuries, Chapter 7) – being suggested for Sevastopol in the Crimea. In short, the 'invasion hypothesis' was applied to the material with unadulterated vigour. Metalwork of the same type had been found beside both the Baltic and the Black Seas, so population groups from the former must have taken over the latter, driving out the indigenous population – a view that found some support, to be fair, in records of the departure of the Carpi.

But, even aside from the politics, this was much too simple a response to the complexities of the evidence. Although its imprint is clear enough, the remains of the Cernjachov system contain many non-Wielbark elements as well, and objects and customs can certainly be transferred from one area to another without the need for a substantial movement of population – migration – as the mechanism. Objects can be traded, and technologies and habits adopted or even evolved separately. The creation of the Cernjachov system, despite the obvious similarities to its Wielbark neighbour, cannot, therefore, by itself *prove* that that there had been any migration. And, as we have seen, it is a key element in the anti-migration argument that the identified parallels between Wielbark and Cernjachov remains would not be strong enough to make anyone think in terms of migration, if Jordanes' account of the Goths' trek in particular did not exist.

In my view, however, not only is the historical evidence – even apart from Jordanes – more than strong enough to support the idea that migration was a key factor in the refashioning of the Pontic littoral, but the archaeological evidence is more compelling than the anti-migrationist reading suggests. Before looking at the material, it is important first of all to remember what we might expect to find. Unless you're dealing with the rare situation of an intrusive population driving out the existing one more or less in its entirety, or where land is being colonized for the first time, then the archaeological traces left by migration are unlikely to be that impressive. Where migrants were mixing with an indigenous population it will only be a few, possibly very few, elements of their material culture – those consciously or unconsciously linked to deeply encoded belief or behavioural patterns – that will necessarily be transferred. In other areas of life, migrants are likely enough to adopt convenient elements of indigenous cultural origin (as many modern migrants do), or become an unidentifiable component in new cultural amalgams created by the collision of migrant and host populations. In short, you're never likely to get more than an ambiguous reflection of migration from archaeological evidence, so that archaeological ambiguity can itself never disprove the possibility of a migration having occurred.

But in the case under discussion, in fact, the archaeological evidence suggesting migration is far from insubstantial. This is not just my opinion, I hasten to add, but also the unanimous verdict of the experts who have been working in detail on the materials in the last generation. It is also worth emphasizing that these experts have no ideological axes to grind. The two most influential figures here are Kazimierz Godlowski and Mark Shchukin, the former Polish, the latter Russian. Both had to fight hard battles in their early years against one-party intellectual establishments that were deeply committed to points of view different from their own. Godlowski's work was instrumental in undermining an old orthodoxy (which we will return to in Chapter 8), that 'submerged' Slavs had always occupied Polish territory. And it was Shchukin who conclusively redated the Cernjachov system to the late third and fourth centuries and established thereby its link to the Goths, against entrenched Soviet establishment opinion which also for a long time was determined to appropriate its relatively advanced remains for early Slavs. In the aftermath of the Second World War, likewise, neither Poles nor Russians have had the slightest ideological interest in exaggerating the role of Germanic-speakers in central and south-eastern Europe, so neither can reasonably be accused of playing intellectual games for the purposes of self-advancement. The reasons behind their unanimity in asserting deep links between the Wielbark and Cernjachov systems are not, in fact, difficult to find.

When the developing Wielbark system of the first and second centuries AD is compared with the new systems generated east of the Carpathians and north of the Black Sea in the third century, the similarities that emerge are striking. We are dealing not with the transfer of isolated objects or technologies but with much more distinctive cultural traits, comprising customs expressive of social norms (female costume), socioeconomic life strategies (longhouses) and even deeply held belief systems (burial rites). It is also striking that Wielbark ceramics are prevalent in the early stages of Cernjachov development, and that the Wielbark system had been expanding dramatically in a south-easterly direction in the preceding generations, right up to the boundaries of the region where its Cernjachov counterpart would come into existence.[27]

None of this is to say that there isn't more to do here. A full-scale monograph comparing the prevalence of cremation with that of inhumation in the cemeteries of the two systems, with proper emphasis on regional variation, would be nice; not to mention, eventually, a detailed regionally based discussion of varying farming strategies within the huge territories of the Cernjachov system. Where do we find longhouses, and where do sunken huts prevail? Given the way that migration tends to operate only in channelled form until a large body of information builds up among potential migrations, my suspicion is that both of these lines of inquiry might help identify the denser concentrations of immigrants, and hence, by inference, other areas where indigenous populations were in the majority. Even with the current state of our knowledge, however, the parallels are strong enough, and run deeply enough, to conclude that the archaeological material does indeed support the historical evidence in indicating that migration from the north-west played a major role in the third-century revolution north of the Black Sea.

As with the Marcomannic War, the evidence base for the third-century migrations is not everything you would like it to be, and the validity of some of the individual items can certainly be challenged. Nonetheless, an entirely anti-migrationist reading smacks of special pleading, given the weight of both historical and archaeological indications that migration played a key role in the action. There is more than enough, overall, to establish that Germanic migration in the general direction of Rome's riverine frontiers began to play a role in disturbing the status quo in barbarian Europe from the mid-second century, and gathered still further momentum in the third. There was some migration in the west, and more in the east, and in both cases migratory phenomena were operating alongside the other political and socioeconomic transformations that generated the new confederations of fourth-century Germania. But to accept this is merely to open the inquiry. Migration can take many forms and have many and interlocking causes. What was the nature and scale of this third-century Germanic migration, how did the minutiae of its processes work themselves out, and what, ultimately, generated it?

# MIGRATION AND THE GERMANI

No surviving contemporary source describes the population movements associated with the Marcomannic War in any detail, but we do
have one account of third-century Gothic migration preserved in the
sixth-century Gothic history of Jordanes, himself partly of Gothic
origins. He describes the move of the Goths to the Black Sea:

> When the number of the people increased greatly and Filimer,
> son of Gadaric, reigned as king . . . he decided that the army of
> the Goths with their families should move from that region
> [beside the Baltic]. In search of suitable homes and pleasant places
> they came to the land of Scythia, called Oium in that tongue.
> Here they were delighted with the great richness of the country,
> and it is said that when half the army had been brought over, the
> bridge whereby they had crossed the river fell in utter ruin, nor
> could anyone thereafter pass to or fro. For the place is said to be
> surrounded by quaking bogs and an encircling abyss, so that by
> this double obstacle nature has made it inaccessible. And even
> today one may hear in the neighbourhood the lowing of cattle
> and may find traces of men, if we are to believe the stories of
> travellers, although we must grant that they hear these things
> from afar. This part of the Goths, which is said to have crossed
> the river and entered with Filimer into the country of Oium,
> came into possession of the desired land, and there they soon
> came upon the race of the Spali, joined battle with them and won
> the victory. Thence the victors hastened to the farthest part of
> Scythia, which is near the Black Sea.[28]

Jordanes is reporting here pretty much a textbook example of the
invasion hypothesis in action. One king and one people move en
masse to a new home, defeat the indigenous occupants and take
possession of the land. How much of this, written down nearly three
hundred years later, bears any relationship to third-century realities?

## The Flow of Migration

Enough information survives in more contemporary sources to demonstrate that the migration processes of the time were far more complicated than Jordanes' much later account suggests. For one thing, a whole series of Germanic groups, not just Goths, were involved in the action. More interestingly – and this is a much more substantial departure from his vision – the Goths and other participants in the migration flow did not operate as united, compact entities along the lines of Jordanes' one king/one people model. This point is best illustrated, in fact, from the Goths, where the more contemporary evidence is fullest. In these sources, Gothic groups are found operating in different ways over a wide geographical area: by land and sea everywhere from the mouth of the Danube, where the Emperor Decius was killed, to the Crimea (a distance of nearly a thousand kilometres) and beyond. Consonant with this highly dispersed action, a whole series of individual Gothic leaders feature: Cniva, Argaith, Guntheric, Respa, Veduc, Thuruar and Cannabaudes. Some appear in alliance with one another, but no overall king of the Goths is ever referred to in reliable contemporary sources, and emphatically not Jordanes' Filimer.[29]

The end result of all this disparate third-century activity was also the creation not of one fourth-century Gothic kingdom, which would be the natural consequence of a single well-organized land-grabbing exercise, but several. It is often supposed, again on the strength of Jordanes, that the events we were discussing generated two major Gothic political entities north of the Black Sea: the Visigoths and the Ostrogoths. But Jordanes has retrospectively imposed the Gothic political patterns of his own sixth century on the fourth-century past. Visigoths and Ostrogoths, groupings who formed successor states to the west Roman Empire in the fifth century, were both demonstrably new creations of that century, formed under Roman eyes and on Roman soil, as we will see in due course. No contemporary source gives us a complete survey of the Gothic-dominated north Pontic world of the fourth century; life is never that convenient. But, in the fifty years or so after c.375, at least six major concentrations of Goths appear as independent actors in entirely contemporary historical sources. Each of these is likely to have derived from a politically independent Gothic unit of the fourth century, suggesting that we should be thinking of half a dozen or even more Gothic political entities rather than just two. This is entirely in line with what you would expect from the highly diverse nature of Gothic activity in the third century. And while this point is best documented for the Goths, it applies to the other groups as well. In the great sea raid of 268/9, the participating Heruli divided in two separate groups – one operating with Goths in Attica, the other besieging Thessalonica in Macedonia. Third-century migration was not remotely as simple as Jordanes' formula – one king, one people, one move – might suggest.[30]

Third-century patterns also departed from the invasion-hypothesis model on another level, with previously unknown Germanic groups appearing in our sources for the first time. Heruli, Gepids and Taifali all make their historical debuts in third- or very early fourth-century sources. It is possible that they had previously existed and just been overlooked, but, on the simple level of naming names, the first- and second-century listings of Tacitus and Ptolemy seem pretty comprehensive, so that there is some reason to think their silence here significant. Nor is it surprising to find new Germanic groups being created in the course of these tumultuous events. New groups – the Alamanni and Iuthungi – were appearing in the west at precisely this time, and we do know that Germanic groups came and went. Like any human organization, they could be created and destroyed, and the information we have would seem to indicate that the political patterns of Roman-period Germania were pretty fluid. For the first century, for instance, Tacitus describes the creation of the Batavi. Originally a part of the Chatti, they broke away from the main group, acquired their own name and subsequently pursued a separate historical course. His work also recounts the effective extermination at different times of three other groups: the Ampsivarii, the Chatti (showing how sensible it was of the Batavi to have broken away) and the Bructeri. All of this makes it entirely plausible that Gepids, Heruli and Taifali were new units of the third century.[31]

Even Jordanes, in fact, preserves an echo of this more complex reality. All his accounts of Gothic migration incorporate a strong motif of sociopolitical fragmentation. In the Filimer migration a bridge falls down, parting some of the Goths from the main body. Elsewhere, he tells the story of a previous Gothic migration in three ships from Scandinavia. In that case too, one of the ships lags behind, and out of this separation, so Jordanes tells us, were born the Gepids. Despite the extreme scepticism in vogue in some quarters, there is actually a good chance that both of these stories echo, if at some remove, Gothic oral histories. If so, those histories, while tending to describe migration in terms of kings and peoples, nonetheless preserved something of the deeper reality – that political discontinuity, rather than the uncomplicated transfer of entire pre-existing social units from point A to point B, was a central feature of the action.[32]

On one very simple level, the archaeological evidence also reflects this basic fact. Although the extensive similarities between the Wielbark and Cernjachov systems can reasonably be taken to reflect a substantial transfer of population between the two, the Wielbark system itself did not disappear but continued to exist down to the fifth century in broadly its old haunts to the north-west of what became Cernjachov territory. Archaeologists have also begun to identify a number of intermediate material cultural systems, placed geographically between the two. Discussion continues as to whether to view these as entirely separate from the two main systems, or as local variants of one or the other, and any temptation to identify them instantly with any of the groups named in third- and fourth-century sources needs to be resisted. Material cultural boundaries might reflect political boundaries, but, as we have seen, it cannot just be assumed that they do. However interpreted – and it may be that, under closer scrutiny, the whole Cernjachov system will eventually be recategorized into a series of interrelated regional groupings – the Masłomecz group (generated c.180–220 AD) and the Ruzycankan and Volhynian groups (generated c.220–60) make it very clear that the material culture generated by the migrants, echoing the new political order, was distinctly non-monolithic. Not all the Wielbark groups involved in the general move south shared in the same outcome. Some followed one historical trajectory which led to their involvement in the creation of the Cernjachov system and the other new groupings, others continued more or less as before but in a new environment, and some chose not to move at all.[33]

The third-century migrations were carried out, therefore, not by total population groups but by a series of subgroups, each operating to some extent independently of one another, very much replicating the pattern of many modern migration flows (Chapter 1). Some of the movements associated with the Marcomannic War were probably similar. The attack on Pannonia which opened the war proper clearly did not involve all the Langobardi. Langobardi in large numbers moved definitively into the same Middle Danubian region only some three hundred and fifty years later, in c.500 AD, and most had probably continued to live in the northern Elbe region in between. The same was substantially true of Germanic migrations in the third-century west. Here we have even less narrative evidence, but the archaeology shows very clearly that the *Agri Decumates* were not occupied in one fell swoop. As we saw in the last chapter, political power remained devolved among the fourth-century Alamanni, and this probably reflects this earlier period when groups moved into the new landscape piecemeal. Some, it seems, moved in soon after the Romans abandoned the territory in c.260, but elsewhere the process was much slower. Elbe–Germanic materials superseded Rhine–Weser materials on the Middle Main, for instance, only in the early fourth century, the best part of two generations later.[34] In both east and west, therefore, the third century saw fragmented, diverse flows of migration rather than massive land seizures by 'whole' peoples. But how exactly should we envisage the population groups who undertook the migrations?

Some of the migrating subgroups were warbands – relatively small groups of a few hundred young men under the leadership of a particularly renowned warrior – on the make. The creation of small organized armed groups (such as that immortalized at Ejsbøl Mose) was a characteristic feature of Germanic society in the Roman period, some led by kings and some of them more egalitarian associations. Hence it is no great surprise that some of the archaeological remains hint at the participation of these kinds of group in the third-century action. East of the Carpathians, a few cemeteries have been unearthed from the early Cernjachov era – Cozia–Iasi, Todireni and Braniste – where, contrary to normal Cernjachov and Wielbark practice, the dead were buried with weapons. All the other equipment found would suggest that the groups interred in these cemeteries were Germanic intruders from the north. The presence of weapons, however, suggests that they originated somewhere outside the Wielbark system, probably from within Przeworsk areas further to the south. The cemeteries are not large, and would be entirely in accord with a picture of small armed Przeworsk groups seeking their fortune.[35] It would be very interesting to have a full study of the age and gender of the populations found in the ribbon of Wielbark cemeteries that stretch along the

Upper Vistula and Dniester. These too might reflect small migratory subgroups similarly skewed in age and gender, rather than a more normal cross-section of humanity. Much of the action in the west is also compatible with this kind of picture, especially since the Agri Decumates were not occupied at one go.

But not all third-century activity is explicable in terms of small groups of a few hundred. The Gothic leader Cniva could not have defeated the Emperor Decius, however restricted the area of his imperial rule, had not the king's armed following numbered thousands rather than hundreds. The Goths and Heruli defeated around Thessalonica by Claudius are said to have lost several thousand men in the battle. You can obviously doubt the precise accuracy of these figures, but Claudius clearly had a major fight on his hands, and the great sea raid of 268–71, of which this encounter was a part, could not have done so much damage had its component forces been appreciably smaller than losses in the thousands would suggest.[36] The evidence from the Marcomannic War is similar. Some of the action can be explained in terms of warbands, but not all of it. There is Dio's report, for instance, that the Langobardi and Ubii between them mustered six thousand men for their initial attack on Pannonia, and there was a moment when the Quadi, seeking to escape from Marcus Aurelius' punitive restrictions, were preparing to 'migrate in a body to the land of the Semnones' which lay further north between the Elbe and the Oder.[37] The Romans prevented this projected move with countermeasures of their own, and we cannot be sure that every single member of the group was about to head off north, but the evidence certainly suggests that Germanic groups numbering several thousand could contemplate hitting the road.

That some groups of migrating Germani, at least, were substantial in number is also indicated by the unfolding pattern of events at their points of destination. The Goths and others who made the trek to the Black Sea, for instance, did not operate there in a vacuum. In 238, after their assault on Histria, the Romans granted the attacking Goths an annual subsidy on condition that they withdrew from the city and returned prisoners. This provoked a howl of protest from the local Carpi, who claimed to be 'more powerful' than the Goths. The Carpi, as we have seen, were a group of so-called free Dacians established in the Moldavian hinterland of the Carpathians, semi-subdued clients who had not been brought under formal imperial rule. The expansion into the frontier zone of Goths and other Germanic-speakers brought the migrants into competition with these Dacian groups. And, over time, Gothic power in the region grew directly at the Carpi's expense. In the end, the Carpi lost out completely. Their political independence was totally dismantled, with large numbers – hundreds of thousands of them, according to Roman sources – being resettled inside the Empire either side of the year 300.[38] Again, precise figures can be doubted, but not the overall picture. The Carpi disappear as an independent political force from the early fourth century, and we have explicit evidence that they were resettled south of the Danube. Likewise, there is not the slightest doubt that Germanic-speaking Goths replaced native Dacian-speakers as the dominant force around the Carpathian system.

It was, as we have seen, a well-established imperial response to competition in the frontier zone to thin it out by taking some suitably cowed immigrants into the Empire. The reception of the Naristi had been part of the solution to the Marcomannic War, Constantius had been ready to do the same with some Limigantes in 359, and there is no reason to doubt the reports that clearing out large numbers of Carpi from the frontier zone about the year 300 was part of the solution to the new problems of the third century. Nor were the Carpi the only losers. Further east, Germanic immigrants subdued the Sarmatian kingdoms and the old Greek cities of the Pontus, and an additional effect of their arrival was to make the Empire evacuate upland Transylvania.[39] Not all the Carpi were transferred south of the Danube, and much of the indigenous population of Transylvania and the Pontic littoral remained in place. Nonetheless, large-scale resettlements and a total reshaping of the strategic situation in the region are clear signs that Rome's existing arrangements for frontier security had been undermined by what was a major intrusion into the region on the part of a non-indigenous, Germanic-speaking population. For all of this, we do have to be talking of Germanic-speaking groups who could put several thousand fighting men in the field at any one time. Groups numbering just a few hundreds could never have achieved so much.

The pattern in the west was not quite the same. There are no records of conflict on such a large scale, and because the Alamanni were taking possession of abandoned territory in the Agri Decumates, they did not face the same imperative of having to oust sitting tenants. But that still doesn't mean that all the action was very small-scale. Outside the Agri Decumates, the Alamanni did impose themselves over other indigenous Germani, such as the Rhine–Weser groups who eventually lost out to them on the Middle Main. This may well have required more consolidated group action. Likewise, as we will explore in more detail in a moment, the Burgundians came in sufficient numbers to preserve their own, distinct east Germanic dialect. Additionally, Burgundians and Alamanni periodically competed with one another in the fourth century, and this could easily have begun already in the third. If so, it will have been another factor pushing the Alamanni into more concerted, group, action – something that is entirely in line with the evidence we have for the whole emergence of their group dynamic.

On the one hand, the Alamannic confederation was the result of a long-drawn-out political process. When we first meet Alamanni in the third century, for instance, the Iuthungi were not part of the confederation. But by the mid-fourth, they were: one among the several cantons among whom protocols of under- and overkingship seem periodically to have operated (Chapter 2). This process had begun early in the third century. At one point, it was trendy to argue that the first convincing mention of the Alamannic confederation could not be dated before the 290s. It was then natural to argue that the third-century raiding and land-grabbing on this sector of the Rhine had been conducted by independent warbands, who started to form larger group structures only after seizing the *Agri Decumates*. But this dating was much too late. The Emperor Caracalla was already fighting Alamanni as early as 213. And while the Alamannic confederation did not at this point incorporate all the subgroups who would be part of it in the fourth century, this does suggest that major political reconfiguration was already under way right at the beginning of the third century, which in turn makes it necessary to think of the Alamanni as more than a collection of warbands even at this point.[40] This being so, the action in the west was probably quite similar to that unfolding simultaneously east of the Carpathians, involving some larger-scale groups as well, certainly, as warbands.

There is probably a more general logic, in fact, to how such patterns of armed expansion tend to unfold, because the eastern evidence is reminiscent in some key respects of the better-documented flow of Norse expansion into western Europe in the ninth century. Here too, the action started small. The earliest recorded incident involved just three boatloads of Norwegians causing trouble on the south coast of England around the year 790. It stayed small-scale for about a generation and a half, but then grew as larger confederate bands began to operate in western waters from the 830s, some of them led by 'kings' or 'jarls', men who were already important in Norse society. The confederative tendency then reached a climax from the 860s in the great army era, when several of the larger groupings began to combine in new ways to achieve ends that required the application of still greater levels of force. In the case of the Vikings, the end in sight was defeating the armies of Anglo-Saxon and Frankish kingdoms. All this strongly recalls the patterns of Germanic expansion visible in the third century. It may well have begun with small-scale raiding, but sacking Roman cities, defeating Roman emperors and appropriating the assets of existing frontier clients all required a much greater level of force, leading, as in the Viking case, to the evolution of new confederations among the migrants so as to generate forces of appropriate size for the new ventures.[41]

The extent to which groups of Germanic immigrants incorporated women and children at different stages of the expansionary process still requires detailed study. But one striking contribution of the Wielbark system to the Cernjachov was precisely in the field of female costume (at least, female burial costume). As noted earlier, in both, women's clothes were held with two brooches (*fibulae*) of similar style, one on each shoulder, and the same styles of necklaces and belts appear too. This mode of dress is not found among Dacian-speaking groups of the Carpathians before the third century. It is hard to believe that such a striking transfer could have occurred without substantial numbers of women – and therefore children too – having trodden the road south. The point is confirmed by the fact that the Goths, at least, among these migrants maintained their Germanic language over several generations from the mid-third to the later fourth century. If, as with the Scandinavian intrusion into Russia in the ninth and particularly the tenth centuries, we were looking at a phenomenon accomplished largely by small groups of armed men, as this latter example clearly was, then we would expect, as happened in Viking Russia, that the immigrants would quickly take on the language of their indigenous hosts. But as Ulfila's Gothic Bible so spectacularly demonstrates, this was not the case following the third-century migrations. Ulfila was working among the Gothic Tervingi in the mid-fourth century, up to a hundred years after the immigrations to the Black Sea began, and the immigrants' language remained at that point unambiguously Germanic.[42] Without Gothic mothers to teach the language to their children, this could never have happened.

The evidence for the other migration flows is more sparse. Even for the Marcomannic War era, however, there is a limited amount of evidence that some of the migrant groups included women and children. It comes, fortunately, from Dio rather than from the *Historia Augusta*, and is therefore that much more credible. The blocked attempted move of the Marcomanni and Quadi into the land of the Semnones, for instance, specifically included the people as a whole (Greek, *pandemei*). Even more explicit, the Hasding Vandals negotiated at one point to leave their women and children in the safe keeping of a local Roman commander, while they attempted to take control of lands which had previously belonged to a free Dacian group called the Costoboci. This latter piece of evidence, in particular, makes it impossible to believe that the action of the Marcomannic War was carried forward entirely by young men on the make.[43]

The historical evidence for the third-century west, unfortunately, is entirely non-explicit on this front, leading one recent commentator to assert that it is 'commonsense' that the action there was carried forward by small male warbands. But some early female and child burials from the *Agri Decumates* incorporate intrusive Elbe–Germanic materials, and I would be cautious about making such assertions. It is not clear either that warbands would have been able to exert a sufficient level of force, or, even early on, that we shouldn't be reading any appearance of the label 'Alamanni' as itself significant of a confederative political entity. More positively, the Burgundians showed a similar capacity to the Goths to hold on to the particularities of their language over the long term. The evidence for the east Germanic nature of their dialect is unequivocal, but actually dates from the very end of the fifth century, from the independent Burgundian kingdom that emerged in the Rhône valley out of the process of west Roman imperial collapse. Hence the Burgundians managed to retain their distinctive dialect despite two hundred years of living in the west. Like the linguistic patterns of the Gothic Tervingi, this is inconceivable without at least some 'complete' social groups, involving women and children, having made their way to the Main from east of the Oder.[44] It is only reasonable to be more guarded when responding to the general dearth of migration descriptions from the third-century west.

To say that it is 'commonsense' to think in terms only of warbands, however, is as much an assertion as always applying the invasion hypothesis, especially given the clear evidence from the contemporary east of more diverse patterns of migratory activity. In their different ways, the Vandal, Burgundian and Gothic evidence all give us excellent reason to think that second- and third-century groups of migrant Germani sometimes included women and children. That being so, I would hesitate to assert the contrary in the case of the Alamanni.

As to the total number of migrants involved, it is impossible to say. We have few figures for this, and anyway could make only a wild guess at the size of the various indigenous populations affected by the Marcomannic War and third-century Germanic expansions. But it is precisely when faced with this kind of evidential impasse that the qualitative definition of mass migration used in comparative studies becomes helpful. The 'shock to the political systems' at the receiving end of each of the migration flows could hardly be clearer. Especially in the third century, the Roman Empire abandoned Transylvanian Dacia, many of the Carpi were pushed out of long-established homes into the Empire, and whatever remained of them, together with the independent Sarmatian kingdoms and Greek cities of the north Pontic littoral, were all eventually subdued into a new political system created by incoming Germanic-speaking immigrants. The domination of this region by Germanic-speakers, so evident from c.300 AD, was the result of an armed migration flow certainly to be numbered in thousands, and very probably tens of thousands. Using a qualitative rather than a numerical type of definition now commonly adopted in migration studies, this was straightforwardly a 'mass' migration. So too, of course, in the west. The arrival of Alamanni and Burgundians, the evacuation of the *Agri Decumates*, the overturning of the domination of Rhine–Weser groups, and even the earlier emigration of the Naristi, cannot be thought of as anything other than serious events for the areas affected.[45]

They were also significant for the migrants themselves, amongst whom were generated in the course of migration both new political structures and even some entirely new groupings. Roman sources naturally concentrate on the violence that spilled over on to Roman soil: sackings of cities, raids over the Black Sea and displacements of groups like the Carpi. But even once the old indigenous groups had been overcome, another, periodically violent, process was let loose, as the various immigrants set about establishing a new political order among themselves. Roman sources from around the year 300 refer in passing to competition between the immigrant groups now established in Dacia.[46] One of the fruits of this process was probably the confederation of the Tervingi in which, as we saw in the last chapter, a series of kings were subordinate to a ruling 'judge'. I suspect that these kings were the descendants of originally separate migrant groups who came, by whatever means and for whatever reasons, to accept the domination of the Tervingi ruling dynasty. Jordanes' simple picture of the transfer of a whole people from the Baltic to the Black Sea entirely fails to capture these different levels of complexity.

There is, of course, much we will never know about these second- and third-century migrations. They clearly were flows of population, not the single pulses envisaged by the invasion-hypothesis model, and some of the action, especially in the early phases, was probably carried forward by warbands. But much larger forces than this were required for the more ambitious activities that were also a documented part of the process, such as permanent land annexations and fighting the bigger battles against the Roman Empire. The fact that the migrations also in some cases led to such substantial transfers of linguistic and material cultural patterns indicates that some of these larger groups consisted not just of men, but of women and children too. In part, then, the action does show some characteristics reminiscent of the old invasion hypothesis, especially in the extension of the domination of Germanic-speakers over the Black Sea region. Their armed arrival also eventually caused the exodus of not insignificant numbers of the indigenous population. Not as simple as the old invasion hypothesis, and not as antiseptic as an elite transfer, the Germanic takeover of the Black Sea region hovers somewhere between the two. It could perhaps be seen as a modified invasion-hypothesis model, where the migrants came in a flow that built momentum over time rather than in a block, where much of the indigenous population remained in place, but where large and mixed groups of migrants asserted themselves vigorously as the new political masters of the landscape.

This much, however, is only an interim conclusion. We need to ask further questions if we are going to arrive at any real understanding of the action. Why did these migration flows occur when they did, and why did they all tend in the direction of the Roman frontier? The conclusion that they consisted on occasion of mixed population groups raises another question of huge importance. Some modern migration flows do consist of large mixed groups, when political motives predominate. But these take the form of unorganized floods of refugees, without political leadership or direction. Before the evidence for large, mixed and, above all, *organized* migrant groups can be accepted, it is also necessary to counter the 'commonsense' objection that expansionary activity was usually undertaken just by all-male warbands. Is there a cogent reason why some of the Germanic migration flows should have included women and children alongside armed men when it came to asserting their domination over a new landscape?

## Inner and Outer Peripheries

The direction of the migration flow – broadly towards the Roman frontier, but with a much more dramatic outcome in the east in terms of how much territory the migrants took over – begins to make sense if we think about it in the light of two factors that play a central role in all modern migration flows: 'fields of information' and the general context created by political structures. The field of information operating in the west doesn't require much comment because the Alamanni were moving over such a short distance into the *Agri Decumates*. We can take for granted that they knew or could quickly come to know about their destination. But the epic treks of the eastern Germani need much more explanation. How much did the migrants actually know about the northern Pontus?

The most direct route from the Wielbark and Przeworsk areas of central and northern Poland to the Black Sea ran around the outer arc of the Carpathians, making use of the Upper Vistula and Dniester valleys. As we have seen, a ribbon of Wielbark cemeteries of the right date suggests that this was the route taken. Not only is this one of central-eastern Europe's natural thoroughfares, but traffic along it had been particularly busy in the few centuries either side of the birth of Christ, when it was being exploited as one of the two main axes of the Amber Route uniting the Mediterranean world with the amber-producing shores of the Baltic Sea. As mentioned earlier, the solidified gum of submerged trees was highly prized for jewellery in the Mediterranean world, and one of the chief exports out of Germania. Substantial numbers of merchants were thus regularly treading the Goths' main migration route during this era, and some Wielbark populations were actually involved in the trade, constructing and maintaining a complex series of wooden bridges and causeways close to the Baltic.[47] Late second- and third-century Germanic-speaking migrants from north-central Europe could thus draw on substantial reservoirs of information about lands south and east of the Carpathians, and possible routes towards them. Thanks to the amber trade, they knew the route well and had some understanding of the societies and contexts that lay at the other end. I strongly suspect, though, that a closer analysis of the archaeological evidence would show that this east Germanic migration flow initially operated in a channelled fashion, the migrants clustering at only a relatively few destinations within the north Pontic zone, until the full regional situation became better known to them.

Once in the Black Sea region, further fields of information quickly came into play. The migrants soon learned of the attractive possibilities for gain presented by raiding the economically more developed Roman Empire, and the different routes by which such raids might be mounted. Some of these may have been partly known already, since Gothic troops were serving with Roman armies against Persia even before the attack on Histria in 238. An inscription dated thirty years before that attack records the presence of what were probably Gothic soldiers in the Roman army of Arabia. But before they arrived, the immigrants can have had no knowledge of the geography of the eastern Mediterranean and its hinterland, or that the rich coastlands of northern Asia Minor lay just across the Black Sea. That information soon became available. From the mid-250s they were mounting sea-borne raids across the Black Sea, and there is no doubt where the necessary intelligence came from. Historical sources are explicit that the maritime expertise of the populations of the Greek cities on the northern shores of the Black Sea provided ships and sailors for these expeditions. It is no stretch to suppose they were also the source of the information that lucrative raiding possibilities awaited anyone who could find some way to cross the two hundred kilometres and more of open sea that separate the northern and southern shores of the Pontus.[48]

But if the choices of third-century migrants were being influenced by information flowing along the Amber Route, they were also shaped, perhaps more decisively, by the political structures of the world around them. In the modern world, migration flows are interfered with by states who attempt to channel, encourage, or limit them by means of passports, border controls and immigration policies. Ancient state structures were much less sophisticated, but the Roman Empire did operate immigration policies when it came to group admissions, and its broader effect on the Germanic migration flows of the third century is obvious.

Expansion out of Germanic north-central Europe from the middle of the second century was not just limited to Wielbark groups. Langobardi and Ubii from the mouth of the Elbe, further west, delivered the wake-up call that marked the onset of the Marcomannic War. And non-Wielbark Germania, as we have seen, remained active into the third century. The migration both of Alamanni from the Elbe triangle and of Burgundians from further east played a major role in reconfiguring the political geography of the Rhine frontier region at exactly the same moment as other assorted Germani were expanding east of the Carpathians. In the course of the third century, therefore, the strategic situation was being restructured in broadly similar ways all along Rome's Germanic-dominated European frontiers. And in both east and west, Rome's strategic position was altered for the worse. In both, an element of migration was operating alongside broader political transformations. In the west, political restructuring predominated and is the element which most immediately catches the eye: its result, the new Frankish and Alamannic confederations. In the east, by contrast, migration predominated, because Germanic expansion took in such huge tracts of territory and effected major cultural changes. In their new world north of the Black Sea, the migrants created larger and more complex political structures than anything that had existed among them in north-central Europe.

But if the broad mix of components was similar, the overall effect was entirely different as between east and west. East of the Carpathians, vast new territories were brought under the control, or at least hegemony, of Germanic-speakers, and a large number of new political units came into being, as the migrants spread out over the landscape. In the west, the geographical expansion of Germanic-dominated territory was limited merely to the *Agri Decumates*, and political transformation ran more straightforwardly towards confederation than the greater diversity of political process visible north of the Black Sea. The explanation for these fundamentally different outcomes lies in the fact that Germanic expansion in the west ran head-on into the military and political structures of the Roman Empire. These were at times during the third century in considerable disarray, mostly because of the rise of Sasanian Persia, which stretched Roman resources and demanded substantial redeployments to the east. This presented expansion-minded Germanic groups with many opportunities for short-term profit in mid-century, but in the long run Roman imperial structures proved durable. After a long period of modification (not least a substantial increase in taxation), enough resources were found both to parry the Persian threat and to limit the possibility of large-scale Germanic expansion to the west. Put simply, because of the strength of the Roman army and its fortifications, Germanic expansion in the west was confined to small amounts of new territory, and most of the energy was channelled into internal political restructuring and short cross-border attacks. There could be no repeat in the west of events north of the Black Sea, where the more fragmented power structure of Rome's clients allowed the Germanic migrants to create a new hegemony over vast tracts. The Roman Empire may not have had the bureaucratic capacity to issue passports, but its frontier structures played a major role in shaping the contrasting outcomes in eastern and western Europe of exactly the same explosive mixture of migration and political reorganization.[49]

Looked at closely, then, the routes and varying results of these migrations make perfect sense in the light of modern migration studies. But two big issues remain. What caused such a substantial number of Europe's Germanic-speakers to take to the road at precisely this time? And how are we to account for the apparently anomalous nature of the migration flow, involving, as the evidence suggests it did, some large mixed social groups?

More than anything else, the lack of first-hand information hampers our understanding of migrant motivations. The discussion cannot be conducted on the basis of individual case studies, as any more recent analogue would be, because none exist. Nonetheless, as we have seen, migrants' motivation is nowadays generally modelled using a matrix with economic and political motives on one set of axes, correlating with voluntary and involuntary movement on the other. The general expectation is that all four parameters will apply in virtually all cases, if in dramatically varying combinations, so that for some migrants voluntary economic motivations will predominate, whereas for others involuntary political ones. And even if we can't do the job in the kind of detail we would like to, adopting this kind of approach remains a highly productive way forward.

Looked at in the round, the evidence strongly suggests that there was an involuntary political element to at least part of the migration flow. We're clearly not talking in terms of a politically motivated flood of refugees on anything like the scale of Rwanda in the early 1990s. But a striking feature of late second- and third-century Germania, as we saw in the last chapter, is the evidence for an increase in violent political competition, as shown by the relatively dense cluster of weapons deposits turning up in Danish and other bogs. And there is no reason to suppose that the proto-Danes of the third century were particularly quarrelsome. The smart money must be on the bogs having allowed both more and better evidence of increased violence to be preserved there than elsewhere. At least, the contemporaneous emergence of the new political confederations, with their growing martial ideologies of leadership, are hard to envisage without the same kind of increased violence. Against this backdrop, it would be odd, in fact, if migration into new areas had not come into the equation as one response to the heightened dangers of living in old Germania. Growing competition for control of the same assets has always been one major cause of relocation.[50] But if escalating political competition partly helps explain why so many Germani were on the move in the first place, a much more positive economic motivation helps explain its main geographical direction.

Occasional Mediterranean imports aside, archaeological investigation has uncovered, as we saw in Chapter 1, a Germanic world at the dawn of the Roman era possessed of only a simple material culture: handmade ceramics, little in the way of precious metals, and relatively few mechanisms for expressing status in material form. Much of this changed over the next few centuries, as the Germanic world opened itself to contacts with the more developed economies of the Mediterranean. The result was to generate many new flows of wealth across the frontier – from the profits of new trade links, diplomatic subsidies and cross-border raiding. A key point about all this new wealth, however, was that the profits were not evenly distributed in social terms: particular classes benefited disproportionately. And nor were they equally distributed geographically. Most of the wealth-generating contacts with the Roman Empire distinctly favoured Germanic groups established in the immediate frontier zone.

Diplomatic subsidies were paid only to groups established close to the frontier. It's hard to tell, for instance, exactly how far beyond the frontier Constantius' rearrangement of frontier politics, examined in the last chapter, would have stretched: certainly more than just a few kilometres, but probably no more than two or three days' march for his legions, so maybe a hundred kilometres. Cross-border raiding, while not confined to those right on the frontier, was certainly also much easier for them. The same is true of trade in agricultural produce and other raw materials. Transport logistics made it much easier for those in the frontier zone to supply their products to the Roman soldiers – the basic source of demand. The point should not be overstated. Villages such as Feddersen Wierde could profit from Roman demand because of easy water transport, and some high-value exchange networks, like those of slaves or amber, stretched far into the interior of Germania. It was presumably predatory interior Germani, for example, who did the initial raiding for slaves, and the Wielbark causeways show that someone in northern Poland was benefiting hugely from the Amber Route. Nonetheless, most of the wealth flows benefited, solely or unequally, the frontier zone, and even longer-distance trade had to work its way eventually through middle-men – kings taking tolls, if nothing else – right on the border. It can't have been only Vannius king of the Marcomanni who saw the wealth-generating potential of making Germanic traders bring their goods to Roman merchants on his soil, so that he could charge tolls. Monopoly is such a beautiful way to make money, and it was in order to achieve precisely this, presumably, that trading arrangements figured so strongly in diplomatic agreements between client states and the Roman Empire.

As much recent work on frontiers in general, and the Roman frontier in particular, has underlined, it is important to view installations like Hadrian's Wall as the centre of a zone of cultural and economic contact stretching out for some distance either side of it, rather than as a preclusive defensive line. One result of this has been a tendency in recent analysis to underestimate the amount of violence and confrontation that we should be expecting along and across the frontier line. There is a significant element of truth in this, but it is not the whole truth about the frontier situation. For all that populations either side of it engaged in a whole range of contacts with one another, they were not just sitting in their own little frontier comfort zone, blithely unaffected by the wider world.

The rhythms of frontier coexistence could be undermined from one direction, for instance, by a Roman emperor's need for prestige. In the later 360s, Valentinian I wanted to show his landowning taxpayers that he was tough on barbarians. He therefore reduced the annual gifts to the kings of the Alamanni – with disastrous results. They recycled these gifts to their followers in order to sustain their own prestige, so that Valentinian's economies threatened their authority. The result was a wave of violence that destabilized the Alamannic sector of the Rhine frontier.[51] Much more fundamental in my view, however, was the inherent tendency of the frontier zone to be destabilized from the non-Roman side. The reason why this was so follows on directly from what we have just observed. Its intense contacts with the more developed Roman world opened up the frontier to a whole series of new wealth flows. Their overall effect was to create a two-speed Germania whose economy and society worked at higher and more intense levels of development the closer you got to the Roman frontier, and vice versa. As a result, marked differences in wealth quickly built up between this frontier zone and the Germanic interior. In my opinion, this inequality was a crucial further component in the motivation behind the migration flows of the second and third centuries. They are an entirely logical consequence of the broader phenomenon of unequal development. Armed groups from the less rich outer regions were looking to seize by force a share of the attractive opportunities available closer to the Rhine and the Danube.

Such a tendency had begun to manifest itself as early as the first century. We have already encountered the first-century client king Vannius who prospered long and happily in the first half of the century on the basis of Roman subsidies and the wealth he derived from Roman merchants residing in his kingdom. This happy state of affairs eventually came to an end in 50 AD, however, when his wealth was ransacked by a group of Germani from outside the frontier zone, who put together an expedition of sufficient strength to seize his assets.[52] This same basic motive – to seize the wealth available in the frontier zone – is evident or deducible in all the events of the third century. The Black Sea region, for instance, was rich in visible and highly moveable potential booty. Fabulously wealthy individual burials, full of precious metals, are characteristic of the archaeology of the Sarmatian kingdoms of the north Pontic shore in the early centuries AD. There is every reason to suppose that so much wealth acted as a magnet to Goths and others who had got wind of it through the regular passage of people and information up and down the Amber Route. And once they had moved in, the Germanic immigrants acted in other ways that were all designed to maximize their access to its riches.[53]

The first armed Goths to appear in the Black Sea zone not only sacked one of its cities, Histria, in 238, but also promised to keep the peace if they were granted an annual Roman subsidy.[54] This group clearly grasped what kind of regular income could be forthcoming from a more intimate relationship with the Roman world. So too with the raiding: the motive, whether in the Balkans or across the Black Sea, was to acquire moveable wealth in all its available forms, human and otherwise. The remains of the new Germanic-dominated kingdoms established there, visible in the Cernjachov cultural system, illustrate the point succinctly, especially when compared with Wielbark remains. Precious metals are much more often found. In Cernjachov remains of the late third and fourth centuries, silver *fibulae* are reasonably common; they are rarely found in Wielbark burials of the first and second. Roman pottery is also extremely common in Cernjachov settlements and burials, both fine dinner services and the remains of amphorae that originally held wine or olive oil. Despite the absence of any internal or private Gothic account of the immigrants' motives, I am confident, therefore, that they organized themselves into armed groups precisely to gain access to the wealth of the frontier zone. Its wider range of contacts with the Roman world had not only made the frontier much richer than outer Germania, but by the same token had made it a natural target for groups from the interior, who organized themselves to seize their own shares.

The largely voluntary economic motivation of our third-century migrants thus also had a strongly political dimension. This was not the negative political motivation that underlies modern trails of refugees, but a predatory motivation of a more (for want of a better word) 'positive' kind. The wealth building up among the mainly Germanic societies on the fringes of the Roman world could not be tapped into by individuals just turning up and requesting a share of it, in the way that migrant labour might seek employment in the industrial or service sectors of a modern economy. The new wealth was not being generated in factories which needed large quantities of labour. On the contrary, it was located at the courts of client kings, who redistributed the profits derived from their various transactions with the Roman state to their key supporters. It was these kings who initially received the subsidies, toll income, payments for military service and, quite probably, a cut from the cross-border raids as well. A few individual immigrants presumably managed to work their way into royal retinues, but this represented no mass demand for immigrant labour. Retinues were not very numerous and required only military specialists anyway. For larger groups of immigrants, the only way to liberate any of the new wealth was to turn up armed and in sufficient numbers to replace a client king and take control of his income. In the third century many immigrants grasped the opportunity, in both east and west, and client kings were replaced in such numbers as to rearrange the political geography all along Rome's European frontiers.

## Germanic Voortrekkers?

This important point explains why, although mainly economic and voluntary in nature, Germanic population flows in the later second and third centuries sometimes involved large migration units. This stands in stark contrast to similarly voluntary flows in the modern world, where the units of migration tend to be tiny: the individual or a few companions. What seems to be a contradiction is explained by fundamental differences in the economic context. Modern migration flows are actually dictated by the type of economic opportunity available – a mass demand for individual workers. The same principle applied in the Roman period, but the nature of the economic opportunity was different. In the modern world an immigrant can access a reasonable share of the wealth being generated by economic development by getting work in factories or service industries. In the second and third centuries, the path to success lay in being the leader, or part of the military elite, of a client state occupying a profitable corner of the Roman frontier world. Here, the appropriate migration unit – even though the population flow was voluntary and largely economically motivated – sometimes had to be large to succeed. From the days of Rome's earliest advance to the Rhine and Danube, no attractive spot along the frontier was ever unoccupied. If you were an outsider wanting to become part of the profitable frontier system, your only option was to move in with sufficient force to oust a sitting tenant.

Predatory activity from outside the frontier zone may have begun with smallish-scale raids such as the first-century attack on Vannius (although even that looks pretty substantial), but if you wanted to move into a region permanently, military manpower in the thousands, not hundreds, was called for.[55]

This explains, if in slightly paradoxical fashion, the other apparent anomaly in these ancient migration flows: that women and children sometimes made their way towards the frontier zone alongside their warrior menfolk. Why this was so follows on from the scale of military force required to take over one of the revenue-generating positions close to the frontier. In Roman-era Germania it was easy enough, as we saw in the last chapter, to put together warbands of a few hundred men, but forces of this size, while fine for raiding, could never have effected the kind of structural change we see happening right along Rome's European frontiers in the third century – everywhere new sets of immigrant clients were replacing the incumbents. If we consider this problem in the light of the degree of development then prevalent in Germania, in order to assemble forces of the necessary size for higher-order military activities such as conquest, kings would need to convince not just their retainers but also large numbers of armed freemen to take part in the expedition. As we have seen, society was not yet so dominated by kings and their retainers that mobilizing these latter alone would provide enough men for the task in hand, any more than assembling just Alamannic kings and their retinues would have given Chnodomarius a chance at Strasbourg.

This observation is central to the seeming peculiarity of third-century Germanic migration. Retinue sizes were structurally delimited by the scale of available economic surplus. So large numbers of freemen had to be involved, and this greatly increased the likelihood that at least some families would also participate in any given expedition. When these expeditions were long-distance, one-way trips, as were those of the Goths and other Germani from Poland to the Black Sea, this was unavoidable, as with the Vandals in the Marcomannic War.[56] Because of the massive overuse of the invasion hypothesis in the past, there is great resistance now, particularly among archaeologists, to the idea that mixed groups might ever move in force, deliberately to take over a new landscape. This negative reaction – that such a vision of any past events must be a myth, even if it is reported in contemporary and generally reliable sources – is so well entrenched that it is worth pointing out that analogous phenomena have been observed in the modern world.

By about 1800 AD, there were around forty thousand Boer settler families farming within the confines of the original Dutch settlement in the hinterland of the Cape of Good Hope, first established in 1652. Most of them were interconnected by marriage. But as the fiscal and cultural pressure of British imperialism started to build up in the early nineteenth century, they began to look for new lands. The Boers' group organization did not run to a state structure but was sufficiently established for a commission (the *Commissie*) to send out scouting parties to check out the agricultural potential of neighbouring territories. One party brought back disappointing news of what is now Namibia, but a second – consisting of twenty-one men and one woman – made its way over the Zoutspansberg Mountains and found that the northern Transvaal and Natal offered more promising opportunities. As a result, individual parties began to assemble and make their way north at a rate of ten to fifteen kilometres a day, at first in groups of about fifty to a hundred families, each accompanied by their livestock and with all their worldly goods crammed into a wagon pulled by oxen. In February 1836, Hendrik Potgieter set out with two hundred people and sixty wagons, closely followed by other groups of similar size: Johannes van Rensburg with nineteen families, Louis Tregardt with seven (including the eighty-seven-year-old Daniel Pfeffer to teach the thirty-four children in the group), Andries Pretorius with sixty wagons, and Gert Maritz and Piet Retief with one hundred each. All of these groups consisted of men, women and children of all ages.

Aside from the quality of the grazing, the Boers had been attracted by the scouts' reports that unclaimed land was plentiful. This proved mistaken. There were two militarily powerful kingships in the target areas, the Matabele of Mzilikazi and the Zulu of Dingane, who were not about to let the Boers take whatever they wanted. After initial attempts at negotiation, one of which led to the famous death of Piet Retief at the hands of Dingane clutching a supposed agreement over land grants, and the deaths in a subsequent night raid of five hundred trekkers including fifty-six women and one hundred and eighty-five children, the Boer leaders decided that the power of these kings had to be broken. So they reorganized themselves to create larger striking forces, which ruthlessly smashed the power of their enemies. The trekkers enjoyed a major technological advantage: five-foot-long flintlocks they could fire several times a minute from horseback. Hence relatively small Boer forces could wreak havoc. Even when attacking Mzilikazi's main political centre, a few hundred men killed three thousand Matabele at no cost to themselves and burned the king's kraal to the ground. Dingane's Zulus, too, proved powerless in the face of firearms. These military successes encouraged more trekkers to move away from British rule, and twelve thousand of them eventually headed away from the Cape.

Apart from their technological superiority, which meant that relatively few Boers were required to fight even major battles, what happened here is identical to that suggested by reports of what went on north of the Black Sea in the third century (and, indeed, in the Viking west in the ninth). Small groups of wealth-seeking intruders reorganized themselves into larger groups when it became apparent that the acquisition of capital wealth – control of the land – required the destruction of major political obstacles. The way that an initially peaceful migration flow quickly turned itself into deliberate armed predation is also a salutary reminder. *Homo sapiens sapiens* is perfectly capable of organizing itself into armed groups with sufficient capacity to seize the assets of others, and does sometimes do so using migration as the vehicle. Equally important, and despite the overtly military element to their activities, the Boer migration units always contained women and children as well as men, just as the third-century materials indicate was the case with at least some of the Germani. This not only shows that armed mixed groups are an a priori possibility (which – so strong is the rejection of the invasion hypothesis – some have come to doubt), but also reinforces the reason why this will tend to happen. Where the military capacity of a land-grabbing group depends either only partly or not at all upon professional soldiery, but rather on owner-farmers who also fight, then any of those farmers who join the migration stream will bring their families with them. Young Boers were taught to ride and shoot from an early age – so, too, the women, who were far from helpless in battle even without their men – and it was this military capacity that subdued the Matabele and the Zulus. As we know, second- and third-century Germania had some military retinues, but they were not huge, and since they did not have a massive military advantage such as firearms over the Carpi and Sarmatians, the Germanic groups who forced their way into the northern Pontus needed to be much larger than a Boer commando.

They had to draw, therefore, on the larger cross-section of freemen fighter-farmers in Germanic society, and these men naturally brought their families with them.

To have a chance of success, would-be expedition leaders had to couch their recruiting drives in broad enough terms to attract freeman warriors. No description of one survives from this early era, but these few words depicting the Gothic leader Theoderic putting together his first major military expedition in c.470 AD nicely evoke the likely process:

> Now Theoderic had reached man's estate, for he was eighteen years of age and his boyhood was ended. So he summoned certain of his father's adherents and took to himself his friends from the people, and his retainers almost six thousand men.[57]

This expedition wasn't a one-way trip, so there was no reason to take families, but it shows that, even in the fifth century, mobilizing a sizeable force meant looking beyond the retinues and towards a broader tranche of Germanic society. For a complete explanation of the second- and third-century phenomena, however, and particularly of what made freemen and their wives open to persuasion that joining an armed expedition to the Black Sea was a good idea, we also need to bring in one further factor, which again figures strongly in modern case studies of migration: inherent mobility.

The populations of both the Przeworsk and the Wielbark zones – like the inhabitants of the rest of Germania in our period – practised a mixed agriculture. Cows, as Tacitus reports and as is borne out in some of the settlement archaeology, were a status item by which wealth was measured, but grain was the staple diet, and its production the cornerstone of economic activity. The Germani were not nomads in any real sense of the word; they did not cycle their herds between designated blocks of summer and winter pasture, as some contemporary steppe nomads did. But in the early centuries AD many Germanic societies, and certainly those of Wielbark areas, lacked the necessary agricultural expertise to maintain the fertility of their arable fields over more than a generation or so. Viewed in anything but the short term, therefore, their settlements tended to be mobile. As the fertility of one set of lands was exhausted, the population would move on, constructing new settlements as they went. Consonant with this, in the Wielbark world cemeteries seem to have provided a much more stable focal point for life as well as for death. They were much longer-lived – that at Odry remained in use for the best part of two hundred years, during which time many settlements came and went – and perhaps even functioned as centres of communal life. A striking characteristic of Wielbark cemeteries before 200 AD, for instance, is a large stone circle, containing no burials but sometimes equipped with a post in the middle. Archaeologists have plausibly suggested that these circles may have marked out communal space for meetings. Be that as it may, the Wielbark population clearly expected regularly to relocate itself.[58]

This is highly relevant because comparative studies have repeatedly demonstrated that migration is a life strategy more readily adopted by populations who are already mobile. The point even applies across generations. Statistically, the children and grandchildren of immigrants are much more likely than the average to move on. Another reason why population groups comprising men, women and children were ready to trek from the Wielbark and Przeworsk areas to the Black Sea is that their inability to maintain long-term agricultural fertility meant that they were already pre-programmed to use relocation as a strategy for achieving greater prosperity. In one sense, to direct that strategy in a coherent move over a relatively long distance represented no more radical a departure, say, than the seventeenth-century English peasant who, having made it out of the countryside and into the town, then decided to take ship for the Americas. In another, of course, it was.

Up to about 200 AD, perhaps on the strength of a slight population increase – to judge by the number of settlements in use in each generation – relocation on the part of Wielbark groups took the form of a steady if unspectacular drift southwards into previously Przeworsk areas. This phase of Wielbark expansion corresponds quite well with what we might expect from a wave-of-advance model, the drift south being the product of random individual choice as the population slowly increased, rather than a large-scale flow of directed migration. Movement north was constrained by the Baltic Sea, and in any case soils improved as you moved away from the sandy, rocky deposits left on its southern shores by ancient glaciers. The subsequent trek to the Black Sea was a totally different kind of enterprise. The distances involved were much greater, and the moves took place over a shorter time. Second-century expansion spread out three hundred kilometres or so in a south-easterly direction over something like fifty to seventy-five years. Its third-century counterpart covered well over a thousand kilometres in an equivalent time. So this second flow, or second stage of the same flow, was obviously much more directed, and it had to be.

Steady settlement drift from a perhaps slightly expanding population had now become deliberate armed intrusion, for financial gain, into an alien political locale. And, again, the parallels with the history of the Boers are striking. Between the first settlement of 1652 and 1800, individual settler families drifted outwards from the Cape over the eight hundred kilometres separating it from the Orange River, which marked its original boundary, as population expanded (Louis Tregardt, for instance, had seventeen children by four wives). This, too, would fit a wave-of-advance model. Movement across the river in response to the negative political, economic and cultural impetus provided by the British was built on the back of this tradition of movement, but directed and accelerated into a quite different phenomenon. Migration units became larger, and, as we have seen, the population flow rapidly evolved into military predation when it was resisted. Likewise, too, in the case of the third-century Germani: their shift in destination with regard to the northern Pontus required careful planning. Individual Germanic families from the north drifting into the Black Sea region would have got precisely nowhere, assuming that they had it in mind to annex land. Establishing military hegemony in a new world required careful planning and a mass of population, even if this mass was organized in a number of separate expeditionary forces rather than the one 'people' envisaged by the old invasion hypothesis.

## FLOWS OF PREDATION

There is much about these second- and third-century migration flows that will always remain beyond our grasp. The available evidence does not allow us to explore precise trigger factors in detail, nor to ask which individuals were ready to participate, and why, when many of their neighbours stayed at home. But the evidence is good enough to establish that migration was a major factor in the reconstruction of the frontiers of Roman Europe. 'Development' – processes of sociopolitical and economic transformation resulting in the new confederations of the late imperial period – was also central to the action. But an anti-migrationist reading of the evidence has to discount too much archaeological and historical evidence, and spectacularly fails to explain the cultural shift in the nature of Rome's main partners across the Lower Danube and Black Sea frontiers. Further west, the migration element was less dramatic, but perfectly distinct nonetheless in the Alamannic occupation of the Agri Decumates and the arrival of substantial numbers of Burgundians on the River Main.

The evidence also establishes the interconnections here between migration and development. The two are not alternative lines of explanation, as they have sometimes been portrayed, but essentially intertwined in the unfolding of events, and on many levels. First, the process of development in Germanic society was itself a fundamental cause of the migration flows, both negatively – by making its internal workings so violently competitive that some may have sought safer homes elsewhere – and positively, in the sense that the new wealth of the immediate frontier zone encouraged groups from the outer periphery to move in and displace the sitting tenants. Contact with the Roman Empire was generating considerable but geographically disparate development in Germania, and, as in the modern world, marked differences in wealth acted as a spur to migration. Second, the mechanism by which this new wealth had largely been generated – being Rome's preferred partner on a particular section of the frontier – also explains part of the seeming oddity of the resulting migration flow. These centuries saw nothing so simple as the old invasion hypothesis at work. Numerous separate expeditions, only some of which were substantial, carried the action forward. Large sections of the indigenous population at both the Baltic and the Black Sea ends remained in place after the migration process had worked itself out. We are not looking, then, at the transfer of an entire population unit from point A to point B, with added ethnic cleansing. But to gain access to the new wealth of the frontier zone by making Rome shift your group into preferred-partner status in place of another, you did sometimes have to assemble large military forces in order to overturn the existing political order. Unlike today, therefore, migration units had to be both large and heavily armed.

Third, the fact that ambitious kings who wanted to move from the periphery into the frontier zone could not put together forces of sufficient size just from their military retinues explains the other peculiarity of the larger groups involved in the flow: the participation of women and children. The result was a migration flow that took the form neither of wave of advance nor of elite transfer. Small familial groups moving randomly over the landscape would have been mopped up piecemeal by the Carpi, Sarmatians or Rhine–Weser Germani, and kings with their warband-sized retinues could not have won the big battles that needed to be fought.

Aside from offering us an additional migration model that emphasizes the fundamental links between migration and development, the changes that took place in Germanic society in the early Roman era have another dimension: we can discern in them the first glimmers of the overarching process that would eventually even out the massive regional disparities in development characteristic of the European landscape at the beginning of the first millennium. Well beyond those regions that had fallen under direct Roman control, contact with the Empire on every level unleashed forces whose cumulative effect was to transform Germanic society. The result by the fourth century, as we have seen, was that much more substantial political structures had come to hold sway over a much larger population. These forces were felt most intensely close to the frontier, but they had some effects beyond, most obviously because some of the economic networks – those producing amber and slaves, for instance – extended long tendrils. Of still greater importance was the appearance of a richer inner periphery, surrounding the Roman Empire proper, which generated a tendency towards predatory migration into it from the regions beyond. Thus, much more than a thin client strip around Rome's European frontiers now fell within range of wider-ranging processes of transformation that would eventually undermine the Mediterranean's dominion. Even by the late Roman period, however, vast areas of east-central and eastern Europe remained unaffected. This would change when the new political order of client states created by the second- and third-century migration flows was thrown into tumult in the later fourth century. And if migration had so far played a secondary role to development that too was about to change. The era of the Huns had begun.

# 4

# MIGRATION AND
# FRONTIER COLLAPSE

PROBABLY LATE IN THE summer of 376, the majority of the Gothic
Tervingi, the Empire's main clients on the Lower Danube frontier for
most of the fourth century, turned up on the northern banks of the
river asking for asylum. They were led by Alavivus and Fritigern, who
had broken away from the confederation's overall ruler Athanaric. The
equally Gothic Greuthungi, who had previously lived further from the
frontier, east of the River Dniester, soon followed them. Both Tervingi
and Greuthungi had been established south and east of the Carpathian
Mountains for at least three generations, so it is not surprising that
their sudden displacement towards the Danube was associated with a
broader wave of regional unrest. After some thought, the east Roman
Emperor Valens decided to admit the Tervingi into the Empire,
offering them assistance across the Danube, but to exclude the Greuthungi. The latter, however, soon found an opportunity to cross the
river without help or permission, and were quickly joined by other
uninvited guests: Taifali plus some Huns and Alans in 377, more Alans
in 378, and some of Rome's Middle Danubian Sarmatian clients in
379. Long-established inner clients like the Tervingi, Taifali and Sarmatians, outer clients such as the Greuthungi and Alans, and previously
unknown Hunnic intruders were battling it out for control of the zone
north of Rome's east European frontier, and the struggle had spilled
over on to imperial territory.

About a generation after 376, the established order beyond
Rome's central European frontier – the Middle Danube basin west
of the Carpathians – suffered an equally spectacular collapse. There
were probably many smaller-scale participants as well, but four major
groupings of barbarians figured in the action. A largely Gothic group,
first of all, led by a certain Radagaisus, crossed the Alps into Italy
in 405/6. These were followed at the end of 406 by a mixed force of

Vandals, Alans and Sueves, who crossed the Rhine into Gaul and cut a swathe of destruction through to Spain. Shortly afterwards, a mixed force of Huns and Sciri crossed into the east Roman Balkans, capturing the fortress of Castra Martis in the province of Dacia. Finally, Burgundians elbowed their way past their western neighbours, the Alamanni, to establish themselves on and over the River Rhine around Speyer and Worms. We don't know when the Burgundians did this, exactly, but it was sometime between 406 and 413. In fourth-century terms, this again represented a mixture of established frontier clients (Sueves), groups who were occasionally part of Rome's diplomatic web (Burgundians and Vandals), and complete outsiders to the Middle Danubian region (Alans).[1]

Nor, from a Roman perspective, was this sequential collapse of its eastern and central European frontiers the end of the misery. The Tervingi and Greuthungi who crossed the Danube in 376 had eventually made a kind of peace with the Roman state in 382, after six years of warfare which, famously, had seen them destroy the Emperor Valens and two-thirds of his field army on 9 August 378. Some of them – how many is a question we must return to – from 395 gathered round the leadership of Alaric and his successors. This force moved first around the Balkans, then into Italy – twice – and finally on to Gaul, where another agreement rooted them more firmly this time, in Aquitaine, from 418. From this settlement eventually emerged the Visigothic kingdom: a first-generation successor state to the western Roman Empire. A similar capacity for continued movement was shown by some of the groups bound up in the central European frontier collapse. Most famously, some of the Vandals and Alans who had ended up in Spain from 409 took ship, twenty years later, for North Africa, where they too eventually established an independent kingdom. And in the meantime the Burgundians too moved on, if in less dramatic fashion. After a heavy defeat at the hands of the Huns, many were resettled by the Roman state around Lake Geneva in the later 430s. From this settlement eventually emerged a third successor state to the old Roman west.

Some of the distances here are extraordinary. The extended trek of the Tervingi and Greuthungi from the north-west corner of the Black Sea to Aquitaine totalled about two and a half thousand kilometres, even just as the crow flies (and as the Goths didn't). The Vandals went from Slovakia or thereabouts to Tunisia, via Spain and Morocco, not far short of four thousand kilometres, and the Alans who accompanied them even further. Before 376, the River Don marked the western boundary of Alanic territory north of the Black Sea, and from there to Carthage it was a – perhaps literally – staggering five thousand kilometres.

In traditional accounts of the first millennium, these tumultuous events on Rome's European frontiers and beyond were heralded as the beginning of the great Germanic *Völkerwanderung*: literally, 'the movement of peoples' (even if not all of those involved were Germanic-speakers). The Goths, Vandals, Burgundians and many others who feature in the two chapters that follow were thought of as complete populations of both genders and all ages who had long-standing group identities and deliberately moved in compact groups from one piece of territory to the next. In the process, they destroyed the power of the Roman state in western Europe, and in some accounts of the action this represented the dénouement of a struggle that had begun as long ago as 9 AD when Arminius' coalition destroyed Varus and his three legions in the Teutoburger Wald. And if this were not a big enough story, the events associated with Roman frontier collapse had, as we have seen, a still bigger role to play in understandings of the creation of Europe. The model they seemed to provide – of entire peoples on the move – was applied wholesale to European pre-history, which was all explained in terms of migration, invasion and 'ethnic cleansing'. The frontier intrusions of the late Roman period thus provide a crucial test case. Were they undertaken by large population aggregates, mixed in age and gender, or were they not?

## 'A SOLDIER ONCE'

Several contemporary sources mention the arrival of the Goths on the Danube in 376. All share the same basic view that its ultimate cause was the emergence of a new force on the fringes of Europe: the mysterious Huns (of whom more in a moment). One even puts a figure on the number of refugee Goths gathered on the riverbank: two hundred thousand people of all ages and both genders. Fundamentally, though, our understanding of what was happening depends on one Roman historian in particular: Ammianus Marcellinus. Only Ammianus provides any circumstantial detail at all about the Goths' defeats and subsequent departure for the Roman frontier. He and he alone, for instance, tells us that at one point there were three separate concentrations of Goths on the Danube's banks, and that non-Gothic groups were involved in the action too. Likewise, it is only Ammianus' account that explains how the Greuthungi made their decision to move after the deaths of two kings and how the confederation of the Tervingi split as different factions advocated and won support for alternative responses to the Hunnic menace. Beyond these details, Ammianus, like the other sources, is entirely explicit on two points. First, the Goths came to the river in very large numbers. He never gives a total figure (in fact he says there were too many to count), but he does record that the Emperor Valens gave battle at Hadrianople on the intelligence that he was facing ten thousand opponents, which he understood to represent only part of the total Gothic military force loose in the Balkans at that point. Second, these warriors had come with their wives and children.[2]

No late Roman commentator ever sat down to draw up a precise description of any migrant group of barbarians – stating that eight out of ten migrant males, say, came with their families – but Ammianus clearly understood the action as being driven by armed migrant males moving with families, their belongings carried in a wagon train, which features at several points as a mobile fortress that could be pulled (like that of the Boers) into a defensive laager, and must have been of enormous size. As noted earlier, historians have often used a multiplier of 5:1 for the ratio of total population to warriors, but that is a guess. But whatever ratio you choose, up to twenty thousand warriors or perhaps even more, plus their families, has to mean many tens of thousands of people in total on the move. And while making it quite clear that not every migrant belonged to one of the major Gothic concentrations, Ammianus does report a striking degree of political coherence among the two main groups of Goths – Tervingi and Greuthungi – who crossed into the Empire in 376. They each negotiated as a body with the Roman state from the banks of the Danube, and continued to act together, for the most part, afterwards.

If we take these main features of Ammianus' report for 376 together – the Gothic groups' mixed gender/age makeup, the fact that we are dealing with several tens of thousands of people, that they were on the run from the Huns, and the coherent way in which the immigrants dealt with the Roman state – then you can see what makes modern commentators hesitate. It all adds up to something that looks worryingly like the old invasion hypothesis: one people, one leadership, and one clearly directed move or set of moves with invasion and flight playing a major role. We have seen too that this kind of phenomenon – different again from the flows of predatory migration of the third century and the Viking period – is strikingly absent from modern, better-documented case studies of migration. In the face of both of these problems, can we believe the picture drawn with such clarity by Ammianus?

Establishing the credibility of an ancient historian operating in the classical tradition is never straightforward. Back then history was a branch of rhetoric, and although it aimed at truthfulness, truth did not have to be merely literal. A high degree of artistry was expected, partly for the audience's entertainment, but this might again be harnessed in the service of bringing out a deeper truth about persons or situations. What we know about Ammianus in particular is deeply intriguing. He closed his History with a memorable and essentially accurate, if limited, one-line self-description: 'a soldier once and a Greek' (*miles quondam et Graecus*). He was born in Antioch in the largely Greek-speaking eastern Empire, and clearly received an excellent education in Greek and Latin language and literature before entering the army, where he rose to mid-staff officer rank as a general's aide. He faced battle many times and undertook secret missions – behind Persian lines on one occasion and to assassinate a usurper on another – but, as far as we can tell, he never commanded a unit in action. He left the army in the mid-360s on the death of the last pagan Roman emperor, Julian the Apostate, and was himself a non-Christian. Otherwise he doesn't tell us much about himself or his purposes in writing history, except to mention in passing a few places that he'd visited between leaving the army and eventually moving to Rome in the late 380s, where his History was brought to completion in the early 390s.

There is a huge and growing literature on the historian and his work, from which two points emerge clearly. First, while claiming to be interested in the truth, Ammianus was not averse to deploying literary artistry in the service of what he considered to be true, and sometimes even evasion. The big cultural story unfolding around him in his own lifetime was the progressive Christianization of the Empire, but he deliberately minimized its appearance in his text, and may even have attempted to conceal a personal aversion to it in the guise of favouring religious toleration. And what is true of his treatment of religion may be equally true of his treatment of other matters, where a lack of candour is less obvious.[3] But all that said, Gibbon regarded Ammianus as a 'most faithful guide'. Gibbon was no fool, and the second point reinforces the quality of this judgement. By an extremely wide margin, Ammianus provides the most detailed and informative narrative to survive from the late Roman period (or pretty much any other Roman period, for that matter). What we've already seen of his Gothic narrative is true at many other points, as well: the level of circumstantial detail included in his text simply overwhelms, where they overlap, other sources of surviving information. This vast body of knowledge was acquired partly from his own experience (his secret missions get extensive and entertaining coverage, for instance, and Ammianus was also on Julian's failed Persian campaign), partly from talking to informed participants such as the retired palace eunuch Eucherius, but also from consulting documentary archives. He refers at one point to a 'more secret' archive he wasn't allowed a glimpse of, which makes it plain that there were others that he did see, and at another he lets slip that it was his normal practice to look up the official records of their careers when writing about military functionaries. A French historian has also successfully demonstrated the substantial extent to which Ammianus' narratives are constructed on his reading of the original dispatches that had gone back and forth between Roman generals and their subordinate commanders.[4] In other words, alongside literary artistry and calculated evasion, you have to reckon with Ammianus having engaged in something analogous to modern historical research, without which the degree of detail in his narrative would have been impossible. No simple blanket answer to the question of Ammianus' reliability is possible, therefore, and passages have to be considered case by case.

In relation to the events of 376, Ammianus' credibility has recently been attacked on two counts, one profound, the other only slightly less so. Most important, it has been suggested that his account of the events of 376 looks a bit like the old invasion hypothesis because he (and the other authors who write in less detail) couldn't help but portray the action in that fashion. It was so ingrained in classically educated authors that 'barbarians' moved as 'peoples' – interrelated 'communities of descent' – that they automatically wrote up any example of outsiders on the march on Roman soil along these lines. Deeply ingrained in their heads, in other words, was a migration topos, which made it impossible for them to give an accurate characterization of barbarians on the move. Second, it has been argued that Ammianus' emphasis on the Huns as the root cause of the Goths' arrival on the Danube is misplaced. It was in fact Roman action that had destabilized the Gothic client world, allowing the Huns to move into new territories, so that the latter were not quite the ferocious outside invaders that our sources portray.[5] These are important critiques, but are they convincing? Has Ammianus misunderstood the significance of the Huns' role, and did he describe the events of 376 as a mass movement of men, women and children because he lacked the conceptual machinery to do otherwise?

Sometimes, as we have seen, our sources do give good reason for thinking that a migration topos was in operation in their authors' heads. The sixth-century Jordanes describes third-century Gothic migrations into the Black Sea region as one 'people' on the move, when the reality portrayed in more contemporary sources was much more complex. In due course we will encounter another excellent example in ninth-century accounts of fourth- and fifth-century Lombard migrations. But what about Ammianus on the events of 376?

In this case, falling back on the migration topos argument looks deeply unconvincing. To start with, though this is just a footnote, it is entirely unclear to me that Ammianus does envisage either the Tervingi or the Greuthungi as 'peoples' in the sense of 'communities of descent' in some ideologically reflexive manner. In fact, he does not analyse them at all. What interests him, and this is generally true of 'imperial' accounts of barbarians, is the power of these groupings as military and political collectives, and hence any threat they might pose to Roman security. How they worked in detail was not his concern. The Tervingi surely were not a 'people' in the classic sense of the word: a closed biologically self-reproducing group whose members all shared pretty much equally in a distinct cultural identity. Social differentiation already existed in the Germanic world at the start of the Roman period, and had grown apace over the subsequent three centuries (Chapter 2). All the Germanic groups of the late Roman period that we know anything about went into battle with two hierarchically arranged groups of fighters, whose investment in their group identities was substantially different. These groups quite probably also incorporated slaves, who were not allowed to fight. That Ammianus does not explore any of this certainly limits our capacity to understand the Tervingi, but that is not the same as saying that he had one simple model for all groups of outsiders on the move. In fact – and this is much the more important point – it emerges clearly from his History that he was perfectly capable of differentiating between different types of mobile barbarian.

In different chapters of his History, for instance, we meet barbarian warbands on Roman soil, engaging in their usual pastime of wealth collection. These groups are always identified as such, their numbers sometimes given in the few hundreds, and Ammianus clearly had no problem in telling a warband from a large mixed body of population. This is perhaps not surprising, given the huge difference in scale between a warband and the Gothic forces in action in 376. For that reason, his account of the battle of Strasbourg, which we encountered in Chapter 2, is still more pertinent. This involved, in Ammianus' view at least, over thirty thousand Alamanni and their allies, gathered under the leadership of Chnodomarius – and all of them on Roman soil. Despite the size of the opposing force, Ammianus is perfectly clear that this was a military action that had the continued annexation of Roman territory in mind and was undertaken only by males. He also distinguishes clearly the range of recruitment methods that had been used to gather Chnodomarius' army. Many were the followers of various Alamannic kings present at the battle, but some had overthrown their king to be present, and others were mercenaries hired for the occasion.[6] Thus although the action involved very large numbers of barbarians, Ammianus did not suffer from any 'barbarian army equals people on the move' reflex.

The point is reinforced if you look more closely at his account of what was going on north of the Danube around the time of the Goths' appearance on the frontier. Not even all the outsiders who crossed the Danube in the run-up to Hadrianople, for instance, are presented as on the move with families. In the autumn of 377, the Goths found themselves in a difficult situation, trapped in the northern Balkans with food supplies running out. To help lever out the Roman garrisons who were holding the passes of the Haemus Mountains against them, the Goths recruited the help of a mixed force of Huns and Alans, promising

them a large amount of booty. The stratagem did the trick. The point
here is that, first, Ammianus can identify a force as politically mixed
(not a 'people') when it was so – this one composed of Huns and
Alans – and, second, that although they were mobile barbarians on
Roman soil, he made no reference to women and children. For
Ammianus, this was merely a mixed mercenary warrior band useful to
the Goths in a tight situation.[7]

Indeed, he does not describe even the Tervingi as a whole 'people'
moving in untroubled fashion from their old homelands on to the
Roman frontier. The Tervingi arrived on the Danube in two separate
concentrations in 376 because there had been a split among them. The
larger group led by Alavivus and Fritigern was composed of those who
had decided to reject the leadership of Athanaric, from the established
ruling house, and seek asylum inside the Roman Empire. A second
and smaller, though still quite substantial, group later followed them
to the river under the command of the old leadership. There, having
initially thought of seeking asylum too, Athanaric took an alternative
option. Ammianus explicitly describes the Tervingi as a political
confederation in crisis, not a 'people' taking seamlessly to the road.[8]
The range of different types even of very large barbarian forces that
he was able to describe, and the details of his account of the Goths in
crisis, both lead to the same conclusion. Our Greek soldier was both
sophisticated enough and well enough informed to describe events on
the Danube specifically and accurately. When he tells us that concentrations of Goths came in large numbers, and with their families, this
does not look remotely like a cultural topos. In other parts of his
History, he described even very large barbarian groups on the move
on Roman soil in quite different ways. He chose to present the events
of 376 in the way he did quite deliberately, and not because it was the
only model in his head. This much now, it seems, is more or less
accepted. Even among scholars generally rather suspicious of large-
scale migration, only one has tried to discount Ammianus' account of
the numbers involved, and that by asserting the existence of a general
migration topos rather than by any more detailed argument.[9] On
balance, it is highly probable, therefore, that Ammianus knew what he
was talking about.

As for the other line of attack on Ammianus' credibility – the
emphasis he placed on the Huns as the first cause of these population
displacements – this derives from a report in the *Church History* of one

Socrates Scholasticus that Athanaric's confederation split not in 376 in the face of Hunnic attack, but immediately after Valens' earlier war against the Tervingi which ended in 369. It was after this, according to Socrates, that Fritigern broke with the leadership of Athanaric. On the basis of this, Guy Halsall has recently argued that Valens, not the Huns, was ultimately responsible for the arrival of the Goths on the Danube, in the sense that Valens' campaigns inflicted defeats on Athanaric and the Greuthungi, thereby destabilizing Rome's Lower Danubian client states. It was this dislocation that allowed the Huns to move into Gothic territory, and accepting this point undermines the traditional picture of the Huns as outsiders of enormous military power whose migratory intrusion destroyed an existing political order north of the Black Sea.[10]

Obviously enough, Socrates' report cannot be seamlessly folded into Ammianus' picture. The two historians have completely different understandings of when and how the confederation of the Tervingi split. And this, in the end, is the fundamental problem with Halsall's line of argument. The title of Socrates' work is accurate, in that most of his work concerns itself with the development of the Christian Church. Only occasionally and tangentially do other events intrude, and then never in very much detail, so that Socrates' overall knowledge of the fourth-century Goths is much less than that of Ammianus. Furthermore, Socrates was writing in Constantinople in the mid-fifth century, so was not contemporary with the events he was describing. When it comes to politics and military matters, it would be unsound methodologically to correct the contemporary and very specific account of Ammianus on the strength of an isolated report by Socrates, unless there was some compelling reason to do so – which there is not. And in fact, while it is easy on closer inspection to understand Socrates' as a confused version of Ammianus' account of Gotho-Roman relations (some of the events are in the wrong order), the opposite is not true, since Ammianus includes much extra material that is not in Socrates' text. Valens' war against Athanaric, it is also worth noting, had ended in a stalemate that would arguably have strengthened the Gothic leader's prestige, since he was invited to a summit meeting on the river with the Emperor and treated with great respect. The conflict would certainly have had much less of a destabilizing effect north of the Danube than the Emperor Constantine's total victory over the Tervingi in the early 330s, when no Huns appeared.[11]

So neither of the critiques of Ammianus' credibility are convincing, and we can reasonably proceed from the premise that large, mixed population groups of Goths were set on the move in the summer of 376 by the aggression of Hunnic outsiders.

That being so, how are we to relate the migratory phenomena Ammianus described to patterns of mass human movement observed in the more modern world? In one sense, the scale and character of the migration flows of 376 are not out of step with modern case studies. For, as Ammianus and all our sources unanimously report, the underlying cause of the Goths' move to the river was political and negative. The Huns were undermining the stability of the entire north Pontic region, and the Goths were looking to remove themselves to a safer locale. As Ammianus puts it:

> [The Goths] thought that Thrace offered them a convenient refuge, for two reasons: both because it has a very fertile soil, and because it is separated by the mighty flood of the Danube from the fields that were already exposed to the thunderbolts of a foreign war.[12]

In Ammianus' formulation, the Goths had two motives in mind: the attractions of Roman territory and a desire to escape the insecurity of life north of the Danube.

Taking the second motive first, it is, of course, politically generated migration – in other words, fear – that characteristically sets large, mixed groups of human beings on the move: 250,000 in one month of 1994 in Rwanda, and over a million in another. Given its strongly political motivation, the scale of Gothic migration in 376 is not a problem. Where the action does depart from modern analogies, however, is in the degree of organization shown by at least the three major concentrations of Goths. This is not to deny – quite the opposite, in fact – that much human flotsam and jetsam was at large north of the Danube, but in the midst of it all, the Romans were faced with three fairly coherent groupings: both parts of the now split Tervingi, and the Greuthungi. This is quite different from all modern analogies. Whether one is talking central Europe at the end of the Second World War or Rwanda and Kosovo more recently, floods of political refugees have been precisely that: many unorganized streams of people running for their lives. If the migrants then found themselves in camps, leadership structures and organization have sometimes emerged, but the modern world has never thrown up an example of the kind of ordered evacuation described by Ammianus. Should we believe him?

Again, I think broadly that we should. The observable contrasts between the events of 376 and modern mass migrations do make sense in the light of some of the basic differences in context. Part of the explanation for the oddity of the action, for instance, lies in the nature of the Hunnic threat facing the Goths in 376. The Goths have generally been portrayed in modern accounts as panic-stricken refugees desperately fleeing masses of Huns who were hot on their trail. The primary authorities provide plenty of justification for this view, since they surround the Goths' arrival on the Danube with an aura of panic and defeat. The historian Zosimus can stand for many others:

> By wheeling, charging, retreating in good time and shooting from their horses, [the Huns] wrought immense slaughter. By doing this continually, they reduced the [Goths] to such a plight that the survivors left their homes which they surrendered to the Huns, and fleeing to the far bank of the Danube begged to be received by the emperor.[13]

Narrative details preserved by Ammianus, however, suggest a significantly different picture. The Huns first attacked the Alans, Iranian-speaking nomads, who lived to the east of the Goths beyond the River Don. Having joined some of the Alans to themselves, they then attacked the Greuthungi. After a considerable struggle and the death in battle of two Greuthungi leaders – Ermenaric and Vithimer – the group decided to retreat westwards. This brought them into the territory of the Tervingi confederation. Its leader Athanaric advanced to the River Dniester, alarmed no doubt in equal measure by reports of the Huns and the fact that a large body of alien Goths was now camped on his borders. A surprise Hunnic raid then forced him back towards the Carpathians, where he attempted to create a defensive line to protect his domains. From Ammianus' geographically elusive description it is possible to deduce that this may have been improvised out of an abandoned line of Roman fortifications that had been used to protect old Roman Dacia north of the Danube, the *limes transalutanus*. But more Hunnic raids undermined the collective confidence of the Tervingi in Athanaric's leadership, and caused the 'majority' of them both to abandon him and to seek refuge inside the Roman Empire. They were joined in this enterprise by the still retreating Greuthungi, who seem to have adopted the asylum idea from the Tervingi.[14]

How long had this all taken to unfold? The Huns' attack on the Goths is usually written up as 'sudden', and, implicitly or explicitly, the events compressed into a timeframe of little more than a year. But some of the narrative details suggest otherwise. Of the two kings of the Greuthungi, Ermenaric resisted the Huns for 'a long time' (*diu*), and Vithimer 'for some time' (*aliquantisper*), a resistance which included 'many engagements' (*multas clades*). These are indefinite chronological indicators, but a 'long' resistance is more likely to be measured in years than months. Moreover, the Huns were still not breathing down the Goths' necks even when the latter reached the Danube. They were able to sit patiently by the river, while an embassy was sent to the Emperor Valens to transmit the request for asylum in person. But Valens was about fifteen hundred kilometres away in Antioch, and, travelling by land, the embassy will have taken well over a month. None of this suggests that Huns were present in large numbers close to the Danube in 376, even if the Tervingi had just suffered from two substantial raids at their hands.

The point finds general confirmation in subsequent events, which show that many Huns were still operating well to the north-east of the Black Sea as late as 400 AD. Most modern reconstructions have tended to picture them sweeping as far west as the Carpathians and even beyond, in 376 or immediately afterwards. In 395, however, when the Huns mounted a huge raid on the Roman Empire, their first on anything like such a scale, they went through the Caucasus Mountains, not across the Danube. This has been seen as a cunning plan, with the Huns dragging their horses thousands of kilometres around the northern shores of the Black Sea from Danubian bases – but this is absurd. Horses and men would have been exhausted even before the attack began. What this raid really shows is that, as late as 395, most of the Huns were still well to the east of the Carpathians, perhaps located in the region between the Volga and the Don (Map 7). This is confirmed by other reliable evidence, namely that more Goths (other than the Tervingi and Greuthungi of 376) and other non-Huns provided the main opposition to the Roman Empire across its Lower Danube frontier certainly as late as 386, ten years after the initial Gothic emigration, and quite probably beyond.[15] Although the Huns certainly started the revolution north of the Black Sea which manifested itself in the arrival of the Goths on the Danube in 376, they did not themselves come so far west in large numbers at that point. In other words, the Tervingi were not facing an immediate deluge of Hunnic arrows and did have the opportunity to make a more measured response to the mayhem unfolding around them than is generally envisaged.[16]

But if the Tervingi had the time to organize the kind of orderly evacuation Ammianus describes, is it plausible to suppose that they did? This would imply that they possessed a decision-making body of sufficient strength and coherence to formulate and push through such a plan, raising related issues about political capacity and about the strength of their group identity. That the leadership of the Tervingi could formulate 'big' decisions is clear enough from other evidence. As we saw in Chapter 2, the confederation managed to sustain coherent policies towards the Roman state, and, in particular, with regard to the degree of subjection that they, as clients, were willing to tolerate. This even stretched to the ambitious policy of organizing the persecution of Gothic Christians, because the new religion was associated with the Empire's cultural domination. There is nothing implausible per se, then, in the idea that the Tervingi might have had sufficient strength of identity to respond as a group to the new threat posed by the Huns.

How exactly these decisions were taken, and by whom, depends on the spread of social power in Gothic society at this date. In particular, the degree of social stratification and the extent of the 'gaps' between strata would dictate who was involved – and in what ways – in the decision-making process. At the top of the social scale, leaders such as Athanaric, Alavivus and Fritigern – called 'judges' and 'kings' in our texts – would have been actively advocating particular policies, but, as emerged in Chapter 2, a broader (freeman?) group would have enjoyed some kind of collective veto on suggestions made by their superiors, and hence would have played at least a passive part in the process. Elements of Ammianus' narrative do indicate that this was so. The discussion about the decision to enter the Roman Empire was drawn out. Ammianus' comment is *diuque deliberans*: they were 'considering for a long time'. And I strongly suspect it was a heated exchange, too. Likewise, once south of the Danube, the new leadership of the Tervingi is repeatedly found 'urging' and 'persuading' its rank and file towards specific lines of policy, not simply issuing orders.[17]

This does not mean, of course, that the entire population of the zones dominated by the Tervingi was involved in the decision-making. The archaeological remains and historical sources both tell us that this was a culturally complex world. It had been created by the military power of Germanic-speaking immigrants, who remained its dominant force. But, despite the evacuations of the Carpi on to Roman soil around the year 300, substantial elements of the old indigenous populations – Dacian-speakers, Sarmatians and others – remained in place under Gothic domination. The hardest question of all to answer, in fact, is what was the relationship between the incoming Germanic-speaking elites brought there by the migration processes of the third century and the residual indigenous population? Largely because you cannot easily tell them apart in the archaeological evidence, the current assumption seems to be that the two groups quickly mingled in sociopolitical terms as well as geographically. But this is neither a necessary assumption, nor even likely. Given that identity is fundamentally subjective, located internally in the self-consciousness of individuals and their relationships with one another, then material cultural similarities are neither here nor there. The idea that material culture might reflect group identity has found some support from comparative studies, but all the reported cases have involved a specific item or two ascribed symbolic significance, not broad regional assemblages of artefacts. And to know for certain which particular items are significant, you need precise ethnographic information.[18] The fact that the remains of the Cernjachov system are broadly similar right across the board does not mean that there were not distinct group identities within it.

It is extremely important, moreover, not to forget the general historical context. The Goths and other third-century Germanic immigrants into the Black Sea region won their place by right of conquest, and had come to enjoy the riches of the frontier zone. Given that background, it is unlikely that differences in identity between themselves and those they subdued would have broken down quickly, even if there weren't the same differences in physical characteristics that helped keep Boers and their new neighbours apart in an analogous situation after the Great Trek. Germanic identity, because of the conquest, meant higher status, and letting indigenous groups across that status divide potentially threatened the immigrant's privileged position. We are, in short, looking at a quasi-colonial context, where the intrusive elite had real reason to protect their privileges against indigenous groups who might wish to erode them. That the fourth-century Gothic world did indeed operate in this fashion is suggested by the way in which Roman prisoners captured in the previous century seem to have been treated. From among their number came Ulfila, and a Christian Church was clearly allowed to operate amongst the prisoners' descendants over several generations. When Ulfila was expelled from Gothic territory in 347/8, furthermore, many of these descendants went with him, implying very strongly that they formed a distinct, and presumably inferior (or they would not have left), community within the Gothic realm.[19] This kind of subjugated autonomy is found, as we shall see in the next chapter, in other complex barbarian state formations of this era.

This is not to say that no indigenous individuals or even groups of individuals managed the leap to a more integrated higher status among the incoming Goths. The need to recruit military manpower might well have led to some alliances that were more equal, like that made between the Goths and some Huns and Alans on Roman soil in 377. It is also possible that some indigenous groups would have been allowed access to the intermediate status of lower-grade fighter (freedmen?), where individuals were allowed to fight, and had considerable advantages over slaves, while being nonetheless personally dependent upon particular freemen. Overall, however, since identity was linked to status, integration could never have been automatic.

Thinking about the events of 376 in this light, Tervingi decision-making would certainly have involved the freeman class, since the advocates of particular policies needed to win its support. The evacuation presumably encompassed both freemen and freedmen, since, between them, these social classes provided the military capacity of the group, and lower-grade warriors are encountered in other Gothic groups on the march.[20] Even so, this would still leave many indigenous groups on the outside, I suspect, who were involved in neither process, and such, it seems, is suggested by both the literary and the archaeological evidence. One historical source refers to 'Carpo-Dacians' north of the Danube after 376, when the Tervingi who dominated the Carpathian region had already left, and there is no sign that all Cernjachov settlements and cemeteries came to a grinding halt at that date.[21] My own best guess is that the complex sociopolitical world of the Tervingi comprised a dominant Germanic-speaking Gothic elite, most of them able to trace their origins back to third-century immigrants, with dependent freedmen and slaves of various origins closely tied in with them. Alongside this world of the Goths 'proper', as it were, also existed many communities descended from the older indigenous populations of the region. They had certainly been subdued by the Goths, and may well have paid various kinds of tributes, but were probably largely autonomous on a day-to-day basis, and that much less likely to have participated in the evacuation of 376.

In short, what we can reconstruct of the confederation of the Tervingi – in particular its military, political and cultural capacity to sustain itself in the face of Roman power – is broadly consonant with the idea that its leading political groups – 'kings' playing to an audience of militarized freemen and perhaps also, to a lesser extent, freedmen – could have engaged in a decision-making process of the kind Ammianus reports. Given the circumstantial detail he reports, and the fact that there is nothing inherently implausible in the action as he describes it, then his account should broadly be accepted. There is certainly not a big enough problem here to justify setting his narrative aside because of a priori assumptions about the limitations of group identity in the Germanic world. These doubts are based in part upon a one-sided reading of recent debates about group identity, and the broader run of evidence does generally indicate that the top echelons of the Tervingi shared at least a strong enough sense of political identity to make Ammianus' account of their decision-making perfectly plausible.

Even a brief glance at the discipline of migration studies requires us to ask a more precise range of questions, however, if we are really going to understand the action. Why did the Tervingi and Greuthungi of 376 respond to the crisis generated by the Huns, first, by moving at all, and second, by deciding to move across the Roman frontier? Ammianus gives us no further details, so that we cannot hope to recover everything discussed in that highly charged meeting north of the Danube. But what can be learned from migration studies about the kinds of factors that play upon migrant decision-making, suggest a few observations of importance.

The fact that the Tervingi should have responded by moving is not in itself that surprising. We knew that its dominant political class was largely descended from Germanic-speaking migrants who had carved out their position in the Black Sea region as recently as the third century. Comparative migration studies have demonstrated repeatedly that a migration habit tends to build up within population groups. As noted earlier, older generations who have themselves moved pass on to their offspring the expectation that, if necessary, one might move in search of better conditions. And the ructions chiefly associated from a Roman perspective with the third century had carried on well into the fourth in lands beyond the frontier. Only after 300 AD, did the Tervingi take full control of the territories between the Carpathians and the Danube that had previously been the preserve of Carpic groups. Several such groups were transported south of the Danube by the Romans between c.290 and 310, and it was this that had allowed the Tervingi to move in. But even as late as the 330s, the Tervingi were still on the move. In 332, they started to move west of the Carpathians into the territory of some neighbouring Sarmatians, but Roman military action forced them to return to the Lower Danube region. Some of those who had participated in the events of the early 330s will still have been alive in 376, so that the possibility that one might solve life's big problems by migrating was certainly a living tradition amongst the Tervingi elite.[22]

Another recurrent theme of migration studies, the importance of an active field of information, also played a central role in the decision to seek out the new territory they wanted inside the Empire rather than anywhere else. The Tervingi, of course, knew a great deal about their powerful neighbour; they had been semi-subdued Roman clients since the 320s. This must have influenced their choice of destination, once they had decided that they needed to up sticks.[23] The advantages they perceived in this Roman option require, though, a bit more thought. Ostensibly, the Goths presented themselves to the Empire as refugees, offering it military service in return for sanctuary. But the Empire had well-established policies for the settlement of would-be immigrants, and of these the Tervingi were, again, well aware. They had witnessed at first hand the resettlements of Carpi around the year 300, and further resettlements of Sarmatians in the 330s. The terms of these resettlements were not necessarily punitive – they could range from the seriously unpleasant to the generous – but all resettlements were made in the context of overt Roman military domination. This precondition did not apply, however, in 376. When the Tervingi requested asylum, the Emperor Valens found himself in the middle of a long and complicated dispute with Persia, which he had initiated, and all his striking forces were tied up in the east.

This makes the issue of motivation on both sides, Roman and

Gothic, significantly more complicated. A variety of sources are unanimous that Valens was extremely happy to see the arrival of the Goths on the Danube, viewing them as a ready source of military recruits. But it was a key feature of Roman imperial propaganda that no emperor should ever have policy dictated to him by barbarians, and this reported joy has to be seen as the propaganda it undoubtedly was. Only an idiot would be happy to see the total breakdown of political stability on one of his two major frontiers when he was already engaged in hostilities on the other, and, though many things, Valens was no idiot.[24] Indeed, absence of overwhelming joy is confirmed by the careful policy he formulated. Rather than letting in all the unsubdued Goths requesting asylum, he admitted only the Tervingi of Alavivus and Fritigern, while posting all available troops in the Balkans to exclude the Greuthungi of Alatheus and Saphrax. Faced with not having enough troops to exclude all the Goths, he was making the best of a bad job.[25]

As for the Tervingi, it is a fair presumption that they were well aware of Valens' situation. Frontier clients were adept at interpreting Roman troop redeployments – from the Danube to the Euphrates in preparation for the hostilities with Persia, for instance – and one basic fact of life in the frontier contact zone was that information leaked through it like a sieve. Ammianus tells one famous story of the Alamanni, who first began to suspect that trouble was brewing further east on the Danube in 376 because troops were being moved away from their front, then had their suspicions confirmed by a Roman guardsman of Alamannic origins returning home on retirement.[26] But even if it seems unlikely that the Tervingi were second-guessing Valens from the start, we have two strong indications that they had something a bit more ambitious in mind than accepting the submissive role they knew the Empire usually assigned to immigrants. As Ammianus tells us, first, their request was for 'part of Thrace' not just as an escape route from the Huns, but also because its fields were fertile. Immigrants into the Roman world, as we have seen, were usually broken up into small groups and went wherever the Roman state chose. The Tervingi, however, had a more proactive choice in mind.

In seeking to understand this, it is important to factor in the general patterns of economic development operating in and around the Roman world. The Goths and other Germanic migrants of the third century had moved into the Black Sea region because it was part of a more developed inner periphery around the Roman Empire, with many economic attractions. And while these migrants were benefiting from that greater wealth, the Roman Empire was operating at a still higher level of development, with still greater economic surpluses. This wealth was immediately visible to outsiders in the Empire's frontier zones in the form of towns, fortifications, armies, even villas, all of which, as we have seen, regularly attracted cross-border raiders. Ammianus' account of Gothic motives – that Roman wealth had entered their calculations – makes perfect sense, therefore, and also recalls modern case studies, where it is rare for economic motivations to be absent from immigrants' calculations, even when their thinking has a strong element of the political and involuntary about it. It also meant, of course, that the Goths were not just refugees in 376, since any ambition to share in Roman wealth was bound to bring them into conflict, in the longer term, with the Roman state, even if Valens was currently too preoccupied with Persia to put up much of an argument.

The second indication that the leadership of the Tervingi had higher-order ambitions in mind, and was well aware of the likely consequences, emerges in their reaction to Valens' eventual decision to admit them, but not the Greuthungi. Instead of just rejoicing at their own good fortune, they continued, as Ammianus tells us, to maintain contact with the Greuthungi, with a view to joint action.[27] This strongly suggests that the Tervingi's leaders had formulated a more ambitious agenda, one that might well require concerted action on the part of both groups to realize. As to the precise nature of these ambitions, one can only guess. But the elite of the Tervingi were directly descended from third-century migrants who had witnessed a Roman withdrawal, under pressure, from the old province of Transylvanian Dacia. This deeper perspective, drawing on a longer-term field of information, as well as their own more immediate experience of Roman clientship, may have powered the hopes that made them turn their eyes towards the Empire in the summer of 376. Behind their self-presentation as refugees may well have lain the hope that they could make the Empire withdraw in due course from part of Thrace as well, and thus gain possession of a fertile landscape whose economic development was generally higher even than that of the inner periphery.

No wonder the discussions were lengthy . . . Moving on to the territory of the Roman state, especially if your ambitions strayed beyond the bounds of total submission, was a manoeuvre fraught with danger. Valens' army may have been fully occupied in the summer of 376, but it was not going to be so for ever, and the Tervingi had first-hand knowledge of its power – from the 330s when it had forced them out of the lands of their Sarmatian neighbours, from the service of their own auxiliary forces within it between times; and from the 360s, when their only mechanism for avoiding outright defeat at its hands had been to run away. What all this emphasizes, of course, is that seeking asylum inside the Empire, despite its obvious economic attractions, was a stratagem that could only work if the migrants were able to field a significant military force. Without it, they would have not the slightest hope of fending off the Roman military counteraction, which was bound to follow in due course. The power of the Roman state supplied, therefore, a fundamental reason why the migration unit had to take the form it did, and this is entirely in line with another key point underlined by comparative migration studies.

Existing political structures are always a key determinant of the nature of migratory activity. Because of their relatively low economic development, fourth-century Germanic kings could support specialist military forces numbering only in the few hundreds. Forces of that magnitude stood no chance of facing up to a Roman emperor complete with a field army intent upon restoring 'normal' patterns of immigration. The best a small immigrant military force might hope for was to find employment as a reasonably well-treated auxiliary unit in the Roman army, and some Gothic groups of this kind who had entered the Empire at other times, it seems, followed precisely this trajectory.[28] But for the Goths' more ambitious enterprise of 376 to stand a chance of success, the leadership of the Tervingi needed to involve the broader militarized element of Gothic society: its freemen with their dependent freedmen – if my identification of the two warrior status groups is correct. The exact terminological identifications do not really matter, though. The key point is that large numbers of warriors were required, and just as in the third century, this meant that recruitment had to look beyond the world of specialist military retinues.

As a result, and again as in the third century, it was entirely natural that the migration units should encompass women and children alongside the warriors. The Goths of 376, like the third-century immigrants from Poland to the Black Sea, were set on a one-way trip, and the option of leaving families behind them on a what-if? basis did

not exist. Families left at home would have been much too vulnerable
to predation from the Huns. And as already noted, the women as
much as the men had had the migration habit firmly entrenched
among them by the remembered life choices of their immediate
ancestors. On the immediate everyday level, Germanic economic
development could not support enough unencumbered specialist warriors to take on the Roman state unaided.

Looked at closely, then, the move of the Tervingi in 376 becomes
less like the old invasion hypothesis in action than it might at first
appear. The decision to move split the confederation, and, given the
patterns of third-century history that had established their domination of their corner of the Black Sea region, a decision on the part of
the Germanic-speaking elite to move on would not have emptied the
landscape. As we have seen, this was a society with a considerable
degree of social stratification, distinguishing between maybe four
different social levels: free, freed, slaves integrated into 'Gothic' households, and, perhaps, largely autonomous tribute-payers as well. The
kings and the broader (freeman?) elite were the dominant group within
this culturally complex world, and many elements of its total population were not necessarily tied closely enough into their sociopolitical
structures to be caught up in the migratory tide.[29] But neither, all that
said, is there any reason to doubt Ammianus' basic premise that this
Tervingi elite amounted to a large mass of individuals, numbering
several tens of thousands. Not only is the account coherent in itself
and confirmed by other sources, but it also makes sense in the light of
the principles that underlie observable patterns of human migration.

This conclusion is important in itself, but there is a bigger point
here too. Given the higher level of documentation provided by
Ammianus Marcellinus, the events of 376 provide an important test
case, illustrating what might also have been possible in other less well-
documented instances involving Germanic groups of the late Roman
period. It cannot just be assumed that all migratory phenomena of this
era took the same form, and some certainly did not. But if we think of
376 as round one of the traditional *Völkerwanderung*, then it is reasonable to think that it saw a large-scale movement being undertaken
not by a single 'people', but by a coherent mass of population. And
the picture is drawn for us by a well-informed contemporary who
was evidently not slave to an ideological blindness about barbarians
on the move. It also makes good sense given both the broader history

of the Gothic world as itself the product of a migration into the Black Sea region, and the spread of political power and military capacity in contemporary Germanic society. To the predatory migration flow building up from small-scale activities into much larger forces, which was characteristic of the third century, we can add a second form of predatory (or, in the Goths' case partly predatory) migration: the massed, mixed group. This is an important interim conclusion to keep in mind when considering the second stage of Roman frontier collapse.

## MOVEMENT OF THE PEOPLES

About thirty years after the knock-on effects of Hunnic invasion destroyed Roman frontier security in eastern Europe, its frontiers in central Europe were plunged into similar turmoil. And unlike 376, when there was only one major frontier crossing, this second crisis had several distinct components. First, in 405/6, the Germanic King Radagaisus led a large and again, seemingly, mostly Gothic force into Italy. The sources are fragmentary, but these intruders came from west rather than east of the Carpathians, since they crossed into Italy via its eastern Alpine routes without passing through the Balkans. Also unlike the Tervingi and Greuthungi, Radagaisus did not stop to ask permission. His was a totally uninvited intrusion.[30]

Second, at more or less the same time, a large and disparate grouping of barbarians left broadly the same region as Radagaisus' force, but moved west along the line of the Upper Danube rather than following the latter south across the Alps. This group consisted for the most part of Vandals, Alans and Sueves, although there were numerous smaller population fragments attached to it as well. The Vandals (in two separate groups – the Hasdings and the Silings) had already appeared west of the Carpathians opposite the Roman province of Raetia (part of modern Switzerland) in 401/2. The Iranian-speaking Alans, originally steppe nomads, had occupied lands east of the River Don as recently as c.370. The identity of the Sueves, however, is more problematic. This term appears in Roman sources of the early imperial period, but not between about c.150 and 400. It most likely designates

some of the Marcomanni and Quadi, who had formed part of the old
Suevic confederation and who had been settled in the Middle Danubian
region, again west of the Carpathians, since the early Roman period.
More Sueves certainly occupied this same region in the fifth century,
and, as Constantius II discovered in 358, the various kings of these
peoples were in the habit of forming temporary political alliances
amongst themselves. Drawing on these highly disparate sources of
manpower, this combined unit eventually forced its way across the
Upper Rhine frontier on to Roman territory. The traditionally accepted
date is 31 December 406.[31]

Third, the same era also saw two rather less dramatic incursions.
In 407/8, shortly after the Rhine crossing, a force of Huns and Sciri led
by a Hunnic leader called Uldin invaded east Roman territory in the
Lower Danubian frontier zone. Formerly a Roman ally, Uldin had
been established north of the river in this region since c.400. Then
fourth, by 413, the Burgundians had moved a significant, if shorter,
distance west to the River Rhine. In the third and fourth centuries they
had built a power base in the Main region, east of the Alamanni.
Somewhere between 405/6 and 413, they leap-frogged their old
neighbours and established themselves both on and beyond the Roman
frontier line in the area of modern Worms and Speyer. This represented a displacement of about one hundred and fifty kilometres from
their fourth-century abodes (Map 8).[32]

The surviving information about this second bout of frontier
collapse is much less illuminating than that for the first (c.376–80)
because we lack a surviving historical source of the calibre of Ammianus Marcellinus. Had it survived in full, the History of Olympiodorus
of Thebes, a diplomat in the employ of Constantinople, would probably have told us much of what we want to know, but unfortunately
we have only his account of events from c.408 to the sack of Rome in
August 410 (though this bit *is* more or less complete).[33] It gives great
insight into some of the consequences of frontier collapse, but not into
its origins. Hence it is no accident that historical debate has focused
largely on the initial events on the frontier. Recent discussion, though,
has allowed some common ground to be established between all
parties, and brought into sharper focus the points of disagreement.

Traditionally, all of these invasions were seen as part of the
*Völkerwanderung*, the 'movement of peoples'. The Vandals, Alans and
Sueves were each whole 'peoples', large groups of men, women and

children. How large, exactly, was always a bit mysterious, but certainly several tens of thousands of individuals. The Hasding Vandals are reported to have lost 20,000 warriors in a hard fight against some Franks even before they got across the Rhine. And given that the ratio of warriors to total population was generally reckoned at something like 1:5, this implied a total force for just the Hasding Vandals of well over 100,000 (since they clearly weren't wiped out by the Franks). Two sources also give figures of seventy and eighty thousand respectively for the number of warriors that could be fielded by the Vandal/Alan coalition and the Burgundians, while Radagaisus is given a total following in the hundreds of thousands.[34]

No one now believes that the size of forces implied by these figures can be correct. The Burgundians proved in practice never more than a second-rate power, whereas an army of eighty thousand would have made them overwhelmingly strong, and another source anyway gives the same figure as the size of their total population.[35] But there is substantial consensus that the military forces deployed by these invading groups had to be significant, with several of them individually fielding warrior groups in the ten-thousand-plus range, just like the two main concentrations of Goths in 376. The scale of the destruction they wrought within the Roman system makes no sense otherwise, and the more specific figures confirm it.

On the Roman side, the cumulative effect of fighting all these invaders shows up in an army listing (the *distributio numerorum*) of c.420. As A. H. M. Jones has demonstrated, this document shows that something like eighty regiments – close to 50 per cent – of the west Roman field army were ground into the dust between 395 and 410. Some of this damage surely occurred in fighting civil wars, on which more in a moment, but much of it was inflicted in the heavy fighting with the different invaders that followed after 405/6. More specifically, Stilicho, commanding general and effective ruler of the western Empire, had to put together a force of thirty regiments (*numeri*), plausibly fifteen thousand-plus men, just to attack Radagaisus. One of the few fragments from the earlier part of Olympiodorus' History also records that, on defeating Radagaisus, Stilicho drafted twelve thousand of the better warriors in the Gothic leader's following into the Roman army, confirming that this intrusion mustered well over ten thousand warriors, or quite plausibly twice that number and more.[36]

For the coalition that crossed the Rhine, the one figure worth worrying about is provided by Victor of Vita, who records that when the Vandals and Alans among them crossed to North Africa they were mustered into seventy groups of notionally one thousand people (not warriors) each, making a total population size of seventy thousand – except that Victor also notes that this was a ruse designed by its leader, the Hasding Vandal King Geiseric, to make outsiders think the group larger than it was. Victor was a North African bishop writing a few decades after Geiseric captured Carthage in 439, but he was working primarily for a North African audience that had had to live with the Vandals and Alans. There is a reasonable case for thinking, therefore, both that he knew what he was talking about and that he had to remain on this point within the bounds of contemporary plausibility. A total Vandal/Alan population of something over fifty thousand – allowing for the exaggeration – would imply again well over ten thousand warriors, and the move to North Africa had been preceded by heavy losses in Spain. When it crossed the Rhine in 406, then, the group is likely to have been considerably larger, not least because the Sueves then formed part of it.[37] The possibility for argument is endless, but the narrative of the groups' activities, and the indications we have both of Roman counterforces and of group size, are all pretty consistent with one another. At least two of the units caught up in the central European frontier collapse could field anything up to twenty thousand warriors, perhaps a few more, and this does seem now to be widely accepted.[38]

Although large, it is evident that the nature of the forces on the move was not so simple as the traditional characterization of them as 'peoples' would suggest. The Vandal Alans and Sueves were a brand-new alliance, not a people, and the same is true of the Sueves as a group, while the Vandals originally came in two distinct sub-units: Silings and Hasdings. And Silings, Hasdings, Alans and Sueves each originally came with their own separate kings. Radagaisus' force may have been, similarly, a new alliance, although he seems to have been its only king, while the Huns and Sciri led into the Empire by Uldin were also a new political unit of the post-376 era.[39]

Women and children are mentioned just explicitly and often enough, and in a wide enough range of sources, to suggest their presence. The wives and children of some of the followers of Radagaisus, who eventually found themselves drafted into the Roman army, were, we are told, quartered as hostages in a number of Italian cities.

For the Vandals, Alans and Sueves we have no evidence contemporary with their initial moves across the Rhine, but a group of Alans operating in Gaul by the early 410s had its women and children in tow. And when the Vandals and Alans moved on to North Africa in 429, they were certainly then moving in a mixed body. The women (and hence their children) could have been acquired since 406, and some probably were; but this seems an unlikely and unnecessarily complicated way to account for them all, especially since we have explicit evidence elsewhere, not least in relation to the events of 376 where the phenomenon is now generally accepted, that Germanic and Alanic groups did on occasion move with families. This makes it likely enough that women and children were already present in 406. The fact that different sources can squabble over whether eighty thousand represents a total figure for the Burgundians or a count of just the warriors implies the same thing about this group. Even if they were not ancient 'peoples', the evidence very strongly indicates that we must still figure on them as mixed groups of tens of thousands.[40]

Two more points have also won general acceptance. First, despite the varied trajectories of their intrusions into the Roman world – Radagaisus into Italy, the Vandals, Alans, Sueves and Burgundians up to and across the Upper Rhine, and Uldin into the northern Balkans – it is right to regard the participants as a clustered group. For although they went in different directions, all were to be found, just before they attacked, on or around the fringes of the Middle Danubian plain of modern Hungary, west of the Carpathians.

Second, it was shortly after these departures that Huns in large numbers first moved into the same Middle Danubian region. It used to be thought that the *Hunnensturm* had swept west of the Carpathians as early as 376. But this was based on a misreading of the Roman poet Claudian who reports Hunnic attacks only through the Caucasus and not over the Danube in 395 (contrary to what has sometimes been thought), and on a miscasting of the Hunnic leader Uldin caught up in the events of 405–8. He was clearly a relatively minor figure, not a conqueror in the class of Attila the Hun. Between them, these observations indicate that the main body of Huns remained north and east of the Black Sea up to c.400 AD, and yet by 411/12 at the latest, and quite possibly 410, many had established themselves west of the Carpathians.[41] Together these points of agreement nicely define the historical problem posed for us by the collapse of Rome's central

European frontiers in the first decade of the fifth century. Everyone accepts the large scale of the intrusive military forces involved in the action, most agree that there were women and children along too, that the crisis had its epicentre on the Great Hungarian Plain and that the Huns moved on to the plain shortly afterwards. But if this much is generally agreed, the underlying causes of the invasions remain hotly disputed.

In 1995, having identified the Middle Danubian origins of most of the barbarian groups caught up in the crisis of 405–8 and established that Huns are first found there in large numbers soon afterwards, I argued that the collapse of Rome's central European frontiers was best understood as as a rerun of 376, as it were, this time played out west rather than east of the Carpathians. Similarities in the nature of the migration units and the precise chronology of the Huns' advance into Europe suggested to me that the crisis of 405–8 was caused by a number of Rome's other barbarian neighbours having decided that they would prefer to take their chances in the Roman Empire rather than face the uncertainties of dealing with the Huns, echoing the choice made by the Gothic Tervingi and Greuthungi in 376. In other words, the crisis had fundamentally non-Roman origins and was caused by developments in Barbaricum.[42]

Two recent studies have taken an alternative approach, locating the key causes of the crisis inside the Roman world, in a combination of evolving Roman policies towards outsiders and the politically dislocating effects of the division of the Empire into eastern and western halves. In his *Barbarian Tides*, Walter Goffart considers it possible that Constantinople may have encouraged Radagaisus' invasion of Italy so as to distract Stilicho from his immediate ambition to take back from the eastern Empire control of parts of the Balkans (Roman east Illyricum) which had traditionally belonged to the west but were currently being ruled by the east. More generally, however, he argues that changes to barbarian perceptions of Roman policy and to the actual power of the Roman state, rather than the Huns, were the prime cause of the crisis. On the one hand, the continued authorized survival on Roman soil of the Goths who crossed the Danube in 376 as semi-autonomous political communities decisively increased the range of ambitions at play in Barbaricum. It raised the prospect for other frontier groups that they might enter economically more developed imperial territory without having to give up their group identity and cohesion. They were encouraged in this idea, the argument continues, because, at the same time, the west was – or was perceived to be – growing weaker. Both the actual and perceived weakness stemmed from the fact that, after the death of the Emperor Theodosius I in 395, a real separation grew up between the two halves of the Empire, ruled by different advisers in the names of Theodosius' two minor sons, Arcadius in the east and Honorius in the west (ruled by Stilicho). This offered outside groups the prospect of being able to exploit imperial disunity to increase their chances of prosperity and survival on Roman soil.[43]

A related line of argument has been put forward by Guy Halsall, who contends that two usurping western emperors of the late fourth century, Magnus Maximus (383–7) and Eugenius (392–4), stripped the north-western Rhine frontier of Roman troops so as to deploy them for their – ultimately failed – civil wars with the eastern Emperor Theodosius. Western troop losses in these conflicts were heavy, especially at the battle of the Frigidus in 394, and after 395 when he was in effective control of the west, the generalissimo Stilicho did little to restore the situation north of the Roman Alps because he was much more interested in pursuing his quarrels with rivals in Constantinople for control of the entire Empire. By the early fifth century, therefore, defence on the Rhine was largely dependent upon the goodwill of local barbarian client kings; and this was only one aspect of a more general withdrawal of Roman state control which also manifested itself in the closing of the Trier mint after the fall of Eugenius in 394, and the transfer of the capital of the Gallic prefecture from Trier south to Arles. For Halsall, this withdrawal had a further effect of particular relevance to the crisis of 405–8. Coin flows to some sites in the Roman north-west were disrupted from the time of Eugenius onwards, and Halsall suggests that this extended into a decline or even interruption in the normal diplomatic payments that had been flowing across the frontier to the Empire's semi-subdued clients for centuries. With their own political power structures thus threatened, these leaders instead moved their followers directly into Roman territory from 405 onwards, to seize the wealth that they needed to keep themselves in power. For both Goffart and Halsall, developments within the Empire thus prompted the Middle Danubian barbarians to move on to Roman soil, and the Huns then moved into the power vacuum they left behind.[44]

Some of the factors identified in these arguments certainly had a major influence on how the crisis played itself out. There is a distinct strand of evidence that the advantageous terms granted to the Tervingi and Greuthungi in 382 were responsible for changing perceptions of what kind of deal it might be possible to negotiate from the Roman state. In the late 390s, the revolt in Asia Minor of some allied Gothic troops under a leader called Tribigild seems to have drawn initially upon resentments of other barbarians in Roman employ that they had not been granted such good terms. Synesius of Cyrene was already claiming in 399, likewise, that the treaty of 382 (specifically as modified in further negotiations between Alaric and Eutropius in 397) had led at least one other group of outsiders to ask for admission into the Empire on similar terms.[45] Divisions between the eastern and western halves of the Empire hindered any coordinated Roman response. From autumn 405, Stilicho, effective ruler of the west, was, as we have seen, in dispute with Constantinople over the control of Illyricum, even threatening war over the issue. In these circumstances, there was no prospect of any eastern assistance for the west as its central European frontier began to collapse – not, at least, until after Stilicho fell from power in the summer of 408. Some military and financial assistance then followed, but by this stage the barbarians were well established on west Roman soil.[46]

But there is no evidence, in fact, that Constantinople encouraged Radagaisus' attack on Italy, and divisions between east and west Rome help explain only the subsequent course of the crisis, specifically why no eastern assistance was forthcoming until 409, not why the barbarians crossed the frontier in the first place. Nor do the changing perceptions of the barbarians provide sufficient explanation. The Vandals, Alans and Sueves still crossed the Rhine on 31 December 406, despite the disasters that had befallen Radagaisus' force the previous summer. It took a while, but Stilicho had eventually put together a Roman army large enough to confront Radagaisus, and the result was a total Roman victory. As we saw, Radagaisus himself was captured and executed, large numbers (reportedly twelve thousand) of the higher-status warriors were recruited as auxiliaries into the Roman army, and so many of their lesser and less fortunate peers were sold into slavery that the bottom fell out of the slave market.[47] Quite clearly, then, no deal analogous to that offered the Goths in 382 was on the table in the Roman west in the first decade of the fifth century. The fact that the Vandals, Alans and Sueves decided nonetheless to cross the Rhine suggests that some other factor was also at play in their thinking.

Whatever else it was, I'm pretty confident that Halsall's proposed Roman withdrawal from the north-west does not provide the answer. For one thing, the evidence that there really was such an evacuation is not compelling, being largely an argument from silence. Many commentators date the transfer of the Gallic prefecture to Arles after 405, seeing it not as cause but as consequence of the Rhine invasion.[48] Furthermore, there were enough Roman troops left in the north-west for yet another western usurper, Constantine III, to launch a putsch which took him from Britain in early 406 to the Alps and the brink of total rule of the west in 409. It was also the wrong barbarians who invaded, if interrupted diplomatic subsidies really had anything much to do with it (and we don't actually know that the subsidies *were* interrupted: this too is an argument from silence). Roman diplomatic payments, as we know, went above all to the major barbarian groupings right on the frontier: namely, working our way round the frontiers of the western Empire – Franks, Alamanni, Marcomanni, Quadi and Sarmatians. The invasions of 405–8 did not for the most part draw on these frontier barbarians. The Sueves of the Rhine coalition probably fell into this category – if they really were Marcomanni and Quadi by another name – but all the others were either from the east, far beyond the western Empire's diplomatic network (Radagaisus' Goths and the Alans of the Rhine coalition), or from the regions behind the main frontier clientele (Burgundians and both groups of Vandals). Interrupted subsidy payments should have affected Franks and Alamanni most of all, but these groups conspicuously stayed put.[49]

This argument could be taken further, but there is yet another decisive problem in supposing a withdrawal of Roman power from the north-west to have triggered the frontier collapse of 405–8. The first of the invasions, the attack of Radagaisus (405/6), didn't actually affect the north-west. It powered its way across the Alps into northern Italy, where it is not possible to argue there had been any reduction of central imperial power. In fact, any troop withdrawals from the north-west would only have strengthened imperial military capacity in Italy. If a reduction in Roman power in the north-west was the prime cause of the invasions of 405–8, why did the first invasion go in a different direction?

More revealing, in my view, is a closer look at the identity of the barbarians caught up in the crisis. The available sources are not good enough to allow us to reconstruct a detailed situation map for the fourth-century Middle Danube, but we can sketch in the basic outlines: Marcomanni and Quadi north and west of the Danube bend, Sarmatians from different groups (Limigantes and Argaragantes) either side of the River Tisza. Further north were to be found Vandals and other Germanic groups, but they did not impinge directly on the frontier action in the fourth century.[50] When this distribution is compared with the invaders who emerged from the region after 405, it becomes clear that the Middle Danube had already seen a huge political-cum-demographic convulsion *before* the outpourings across Rome's central European frontiers.

Vandals first appeared on Stilicho's radar a few years before 405–8, in the winter of 401/2, when their presence nearby posed something of a threat to the peace of Raetia, more or less Roman Switzerland. This neighbourhood had emphatically not been their home in the mid-fourth century, when they were to be found the best part of six hundred kilometres further north-west, in the northern Tisza region and Slovakia, right out on the fringes of the Middle Danubian plain and old Roman Dacia.[51] Their initial relocation to the fringes of Raetia, while nothing compared with subsequent marches to Spain and North Africa, was nonetheless a substantial move in itself.

That Radagaisus' coalition, which certainly included some Goths, should have invaded Italy from west of the Carpathians reinforces the point. One or several of the many Gothic groups known from the fourth century were presumably drawn upon to make up the Gothic contingent in Radagaisus' following. But no Goths inhabited land west of the Carpathians at that time. Likewise, the Alans: historical sources are entirely unambiguous that when they crossed the Rhine, they were the largest single component of the mixed invasion force. In other words, many Alans had come to occupy territory west of the Carpathians by about 405. But again, no Alans inhabited this region in the fourth century. Up to c.370, their westernmost stamping grounds were located around fifteen hundred kilometres further east, on the far side of the River Don.[52] Different Alanic subgroups (their political structure seems to have encompassed many largely autonomous units) had begun to move west on the tails of the retreating Tervingi and Greuthungi from the mid-370s. One group of Alans, in alliance with some Huns, joined the Goths in the Roman Balkans in the autumn of

377 and even fought at Hadrianople. More Alans were encountered by the Emperor Gratian in the north-west Balkans in the summer of 378, who incorporated the same or yet more Alans into the western field army in 380.[53] Things then quietened down, at least in our sources, but Alans on the move to the west were a major part of the first frontier crisis in the years after 376, and some continuation of this phenomenon is necessary to explain why there were so many Alans west of the Carpathians by 406. The observation is only reinforced by the fact that Uldin's mixed power base, which also crossed into Dacia from somewhere on the fringes of the Middle Danube, consisted of Huns and Sciri.[54] Neither of these groups shows up in the fourth century, even on the eastern fringes of the Middle Danube. The Burgundians and the Sueves, if the latter were indeed Marcomanni and Quadi, were hugely in the minority, therefore, in becoming involved in the crisis of 405–8 as long-established inhabitants of the Middle Danube and its environs.

Such a degree of population displacement was entirely abnormal in the hinterland of Rome's frontiers. Group movements in the frontier region were usually controlled by the Romans extremely tightly. As we saw in Chapter 3, when members of just one Sarmatian subgroup, the Limigantes, returned in 359 to the sector of the Middle Danube frontier from which they had been expelled the previous year, Constantius II reacted decisively because of the propensity for disturbances beyond the frontier to spill over on to Roman territory.[55] The arrival of so many newcomers in the Middle Danubian region immediately before the crisis of 405–8 completely dwarfs the amount of disruption faced by Constantius fifty years previously. Two substantial groups of Vandals, very large numbers of Alans, at least the Gothic element of Radagaisus' coalition, and the Huns and Sciri of Uldin were all newcomers to the Middle Danube. So the frontier penetrations faced by the western Empire in 405–8 were the product of an equally large, if not actually bigger, crisis beyond the frontier itself. Something profound must have been going on there to cause all these groups to relocate themselves west of the Carpathians, even before they made their better-documented moves on to Roman soil.

So what was it? None of the factors relating to developments internal to the Roman Empire satisfactorily account for this major concentration of armed groups and their dependants in the Middle Danube region before 405–8, though they certainly help explain what happened next – why the west received no eastern help before 409/10, and why attacking through Gaul proved a better option than invading Italy. In 1995, I argued that it was the second stage of Hunnic movement into Europe that had prompted this gathering of the clans west of the Carpathians, and to my mind this still provides much the likeliest explanation. Not only does the chronological correlation between their advance to the heart of Europe and the departure of our invaders from the Middle Danube plain suggest it, but, as we will explore in the next chapter, a close look at the migratory patterns of the Huns themselves provides two strong planks of further support. First, the Huns had pressing reasons of their own to want to move into central Europe, making it highly unlikely that they were merely exploiting a power vacuum that had already been created there by the departure of the Vandals and others. Second, the Huns' treatment of neighbouring populations who got in their way made it reasonable for those neighbours to want to escape. It is thus entirely comprehensible that a second westward shift in the centre of Hunnic operations from the Black Sea to the Middle Danube, which clearly did occur in the early fifth century, should have had the effect we observe in the run-up to 405–8: causing potential new subjects to move out of its way. Not only is this the simplest explanation for the build-up of immigrants west of the Carpathians, it is also the most cogent and compelling. The proposed alternatives utterly fail to explain what the bulk of the invaders of 405–8 were doing west of the Carpathians in the first place.

Given such a strong likelihood that this crisis was a rerun of that of 376, only this time west rather than east of the Carpathians, we should not be surprised that the sources suggest some similar observations about the detailed operation of the migration processes involved in the later case. Many of this second wave of migrants, like the fourth-century Goths before them, had an established history of relocation. The one exception, it would seem, were the Sueves (assuming, again, that this term does designate various subgroups of the Marcomanni and Quadi), who had not moved anywhere before participating in the Rhine crossing. The Alans, on the other hand, were originally nomads – but this needs a bit more comment. Nomads, contrary to the received images of random movement over vast distances, typically make relatively restricted and cyclical moves between well-established blocks of summer and winter pasture. This is an entirely different phenomenon from the geographical dislocation witnessed in the late fourth and early fifth centuries, when families and flocks were moved hundreds of kilometres from long-established haunts. As with the late second- and third-century Goths, an inherent capacity for movement, engendered by the less rigid attachment of their agricultural economy to any particular territory than we are generally used to in the modern world, will also have been a factor in making this relocation possible. And in any case, by the time the various Alanic subgroups involved in the Rhine crossing had reached the Middle Danube, the jumping-off point for the events of 406, they had recently made one long trek from east of the River Don, so that a properly migratory – rather than merely nomadic – habit had already gathered momentum amongst them.[56]

The same is also true of Radagaisus' Goths. They will have shared some of the past experiences of the Tervingi, being another of those concentrations of Germanic-dominated military power generated by the third-century migrations to the Black Sea. Since Goths are not found west of the Carpathians in the fourth century, the Gothic followers of Radagaisus must have made at least one move in the recent past from the Pontus to the Middle Danube, on the eve of what was to prove their ill-fated journey to Italy. The Vandals had not moved as far as the Goths in the third century, but did extend their control, from the time of the Marcomannic War onwards, south from northern and central Poland to parts of former Roman Dacia in upland Transylvania. They, again, must also have made an initial move west from this region to the fringes of the Alps, where their presence was noted in 402. In large measure, therefore, round two of the *Völkerwanderung* encompassed population groups with firmly entrenched migration habits, who were more likely to respond to major threats and opportunities by moving again.

The range of motivations in play among these later migrants, likewise, was probably similar to those of the Goths of 376. What we cannot reconstruct, since the date of the Huns' entry en masse into the Middle Danubian region is uncertain, is how immediate a threat they faced. Whether they needed to leave their old abodes in more of a hurry than had the Tervingi in 376 is unclear, but this doesn't change the fact that their motives for moving were substantially political and negative. They too were looking for new and safer homes. The influx of substantial numbers of Goths, Alans and Vandals on to the Middle

Danubian plain would have been enough in itself, of course, quite apart from any Hunnic pressure, to generate political problems within the region itself. If the return of one relatively small Sarmatian subgroup to the frontier area was enough to destabilize the situation in 359, a mass influx of outsiders can only have caused political chaos.

But, as was also the case in 376, this does not deny that the immigrants also had their eye on the potential economic and other gains that might come their way from a well-organized relocation on to Roman soil. If increased pressure from the Huns made it imperative to move somewhere, then, as in 376, perceptions of its likely advantages turned the migrants' thoughts towards the Empire. Two further observations are also worth making. First, finding a new home outside the Empire would not have been easy. The smaller concentration of Tervingi who retreated from the Danube in 376 rather than pursue their Roman visa applications further, for instance, relocated themselves in upland Transylvania or its western fringes. But to secure this new territory, they had to expel some Sarmatians already in residence. These latter, in turn, spilled on to Roman soil.[57] Similarly, while en route for the Rhine in 406, the Vandals, as we have seen, had a bruising encounter with some Franks, in which they are said to have lost the unbelievable figure of twenty thousand dead – which we can reasonably take as representing a genuine memory of a hard fight. Germania was not full of fertile land ready for the taking, and given that you would have to fight for a new home wherever you went, at least Roman territory had the attraction of greater economic development. And, like the Tervingi in 376, most of the second wave of migrants had enough knowledge of the Empire to be well aware of these potential advantages. An active field of information, in other words, may have turned the discussions of our later migrants towards an imperial option, just as, even in 376, hopes of economic predation were operating alongside the Goths' genuine fear of the Huns. Second, there is every reason, as we have seen, to suppose that the survival of the Goths of 376 as a semi-autonomous unit on Roman soil provided a further incentive for the displaced groups of the early fifth century to try the Roman option.

None of these immigrants should have been in any doubt, though, that their ambitions for a place in the Roman sun would meet with heavy resistance. If doubt there was, the fate of Radagaisus' force must have quickly defused it. Given that their migration was an attempt to force the Roman Empire into making concessions in their direction, then each group needed to field a powerful military force. This meant, again as in 376, that freemen (or their Alanic equivalents)[58] had to be recruited. For the same reasons as in 376 (and in the later stages of the third-century Germanic and the ninth-century Viking expansions), the only possible migration unit was the large grouping of ten thousand-plus warriors, many accompanied by their families. The immigrants' clear perception of the dangers of their enterprise is also visible in some of the alliances they put together for the purpose. The Sciri footsoldiers sold as slaves and distributed as *coloni* (farmers) in the aftermath of Uldin's defeat probably had no choice, and the sources on Radagaisus' following are not good enough to make comment worthwhile.[59] But the massive alliance of Vandals, Alans and Sueves was an entirely new combination of groups that had not even been near-neighbours in the fourth century. At this point it was clearly still a loose alliance, but even this much cooperation must have taken a great deal of brokering. And not everyone seems to have been persuaded that it was the right move. It has been suggested that enough Siling Vandals stayed put to give their name to modern Silesia, and, more convincingly, that Sueves in large numbers still inhabited the Middle Danube region long after the migrant Suevi of 406 had reach north-west Spain.

So determined and so thoroughgoing was the Empire's resistance to these new migrants that some of them altered their initial strategies. Uldin's force was picked apart by diplomacy, when the east Roman negotiators managed to win over some of his key supporters without a fight. These were offered attractive positions in the Roman military, one presumes, while many of the less fortunate Sciri were consigned to servitude on Roman landed estates. The fate of Radagaisus' force was similar. Again, some of his higher-status supporters abandoned ship, doing a deal whereby they were drafted into the Roman army. This time, however, the scale was different. The twelve thousand 'of the best' of Radagaisus' warriors who were drafted into Stilicho's army may have had it in mind from the beginning that being part of a larger migrating group might be a useful means of eventually cutting their own deals with the Roman authorities. But, just as likely, side-swapping was a stratagem employed only when the brute reality of overarching Roman military power became clear, as Stilicho and his field army approached.[60]

Like the Danube crossing of 376, the demographic displacement associated with the collapse of Rome's central European frontier only partially fits the image of the traditional Germanic *Völkerwanderung*. The crisis of 405–8 did see massive mixed groupings cross the frontier for reasons that had more to do with factors external to the Empire than anything happening within it. And even if some of these groups were too well organized to resemble the floods of refugees sometimes seen in the modern world, their activities are often explicable in terms of the principles behind modern migration patterns, not least the web of negative and positive motivations driving the migrants, and the massive influence of existing political structures and flows of information. That said, the groupings were complex political associations, not 'peoples' in the traditional sense of the term. Some of the groups caught up in the action do seem to have had long histories. Hasding Vandals, for instance, figured in the second-century Marcomannic War. But like all Germanic groups of the late Roman period, they had been through several centuries of dynamic transformation generated by intense interaction with each other and with the Roman state, which meant that they encompassed a wide range of social classes and rights. This internal group complexity was then increased by the inter-group alliances that were forged, such as that between two separate Vandal groups, and Alans and Sueves in order to increase their chances of survival on Roman soil. This added to the picture much greater size, new political ties, and sometimes massive cultural disparity (in the case of the nomadic Iranian-speaking Alans). Even if some of their component units had well-established links, therefore, the entities that crossed the frontier were improvised political alliances, not long-standing aggregates of population.

We should not wonder, then, that the Roman authorities were able to destroy some of them precisely by targeting the joins in their fabric, notably by attracting away elite military followers of both Radagaisus and Uldin at the expense of the group leader and the less favoured rank and file. But the internal disunity that might naturally be generated by social complexity and improvised alliances is only part of the story. Another striking characteristic of those groups that managed to survive their initial encounters with the Roman state was an apparent capacity to repeat the migratory process.

# FIGHTING FOR SURVIVAL

The histories of all the major groups who crossed into the Empire at the two moments of frontier collapse followed a similar course. Their initial – overwhelmingly uninvited[61] – penetrations of Roman territory were followed by periods of armed struggle. They had to force the Empire to accept that they could not be defeated, and that its normal policies for the subjugation and integration of immigrants could not be imposed upon them. For the Tervingi and Greuthungi, these initial struggles lasted for about six years until the negotiation of a compromise peace agreement with the Roman state, which came into force on 3 October 382. That the Empire was willing to agree to such a deal was entirely due to the Goths' military capacity, in particular their successive defeats of two Roman emperors – Valens, most famously, at Hadrianople on 9 August 378, then Theodosius in Macedonia in the summer of 380. Other, smaller migrant groups of the period – Taifali, Sarmatians and isolated Gothic subgroups – who failed this initial military test received much harsher treatment, their defeats being followed by total loss of identity, as group members were distributed as unfree labour to Roman landowners.[62]

The history of the migrants involved in the crisis of 405–8 is similar. Again uninvited, they had to fight, initially, to carve out new homes for themselves. Some failed. Many of the followers of Uldin and Radagaisus, as we have seen, met with disaster, killed or distributed again as unfree labour, though some elements of each group managed to do a deal with the Roman authorities. Initially at least, the Vandals, Alans and Sueves were more fortunate. After a career of wild violence in Gaul, in 409 or 410 they forced their way over the Pyrenees into Roman Spain, which offered them new opportunities. In 412, six years after their initial crossing, they divided up the bulk of its provinces between them. The Siling Vandals took Baetica, the Hasdings most of Gallaecia, the Sueves north-western Gallaecia, and the Alans, underlining that they were the largest component of the force at this stage, the richer provinces of Lusitania and Carthaginensis (Map 9). There is no evidence that this partition was authorized by the central Roman authorities, but it would seem to represent a more ordered exploitation of economic assets, beyond mere looting.[63] The time lag between invasion and eventual settlement, whether we're talking 376 or 406, is entirely understandable. No large surge of armed, unexpected immigration could ever have come to an immediate modus vivendi with the populations at its point of destination.

What does need explanation, however, is that some time after these initial settlements – 382 and 412 respectively – both sets of immigrants apparently took to the road again. The Goths settled in the Balkans in 382, as the story traditionally goes, broke into open revolt under the leadership of Alaric in 395 and spent much of the next two years in a Greek odyssey, accompanied by their families and a vast wagon train, which took them as far south as Athens, round the Peloponnesus and then back north again to Epirus beside the Adriatic. After a brief rest, they moved into Italy in 401/2 before returning to the Balkans until 408, when they headed west, spending 408 to 411 in Italy again before taking off for Gaul, where they finally settled down. Likewise, the Vandals and Alans: after a Hispanic interlude which lasted until 429, they took ship across the Straits of Gibraltar and moved east, in two stages, towards the richest provinces of Roman North Africa. They briefly acquired land by treaty in Mauretania and Numidia in 437, before establishing two years later a more permanent home for themselves by capturing Carthage and the cluster of provinces around it.

Looked at in this longer term, the immigration pattern of those who fled the Huns thus takes on a distinctly stop-start character. In the past, these narrative gaps were never seen as an obstacle to viewing the secondary migrations as the further history of the same groups that had made the original crossing. More recently, however, it has been suggested that the secondary migrations look much more like the activities of mobile armies than of the mixed population groups that made the original frontier crossings, and were indeed undertaken by what were essentially different groups – warbands on the make – who drew only marginally on manpower from the original migrants. This suggestion has been particularly well received among those sharing the conviction that ancient social units such as the invaders of 376 and 405–8 could never have had a strong enough sense of group identity to hold together through repeated upheavals, over such a long time-scale.[64]

So, armies or peoples? And can migration studies help us compre-
hend the renewable mobility of Vandals, Goths and others?

The fact that major disagreement can exist on such a basic point
of interpretation will tell you instantly that, once more, the sources
are not all they might be. They are, however, much fuller for the post-
382 history of the Goths, at least for certain years, and they make the
better test case. In the Gothic instance, the key initial question is
whether those who rebelled under Alaric in 395 really did represent
further movement on the part of all or most of the Goths settled
under the treaty of 382. This was never doubted in the past, but new
expectations that barbarian identity will always have been fluid have
fuelled demands in recent years that the correspondence between the
Goths who made peace with the Roman state in 382 and Alaric's
rebellious following should be proved. Can it be?

In simple terms, the answer has to be no. No Roman commentator
lists in detail the manpower resources drawn upon by Alaric in 395, or
describes exactly how he mobilized support. On the other hand, we
are talking about the middle of the first millennium, so this is not
surprising, and it is important not to use unsatisfiable demands for an
inappropriate degree of certainty as an excuse for denying what is in
fact the very reasonable probability that in 395 Alaric did indeed lead a
major revolt on the part of the treaty Goths of 382. The argument is
not that all those settled under the treaty necessarily participated in
the revolt, but rather that there was sufficient overlap in manpower
between those Goths settled under the agreement of 382 and Alaric's
initial followers for the basic point to hold.

The first plank of the argument is that the better source material
indicates strongly that this was in fact the case. Our two earliest, least
problematic, entirely contemporary and independent Roman commentators on the rebellion, Claudian in the west and Synesius in
Constantinople, describe Alaric's following precisely as the 382 Goths
in revolt. To discredit their testimony, convincing reasons would need
to be found for both commentators – writing in separate halves of
the Empire, for different audiences and for different purposes – substantially to have misrepresented the action, and none has yet been
offered.[65] Moreover, this basic observation – powerful in itself – can be
strengthened. Synesius and Claudian have sometimes been rejected in
recent years on the basis of a passage in the Greek historian Zosimus
that reports Alaric as having originally revolted during the Eugenius

campaign because Theodosius had only given him the command of some barbarian auxiliaries, rather than a proper Roman command. From this it has been supposed that his ambitions, and hence his revolt in 395, did not originally encompass the mass of the Goths of 382. There are three major problems here.

First, what was originally the historian Eunapius' contemporary account of Alaric has become demonstrably mangled at the hands of the sixth-century Zosimus. To put the contemporary Claudian and Synesius to one side on the strength of three lines (literally) of the much later Zosimus, whose account is anyway problematic, with no further argument about why they should both have distorted the action in the same way, is simply unsound methodology.[66] Second, rewriting Alaric as having purely Roman ambitions runs into the problem that, just four years after his revolt began, an east Roman general of barbarian origins, one Gainas, took the opportunity of the revolt of some Gothic auxiliary troops to lever himself into power in Constantinople. Alaric à la Zosimus would be an analogous figure, as those who take that route acknowledge, but of the two authors Synesius had no problem in describing Gainas accurately (Claudian doesn't even mention him).[67] Why would either be likely to have misrepresented Alaric when, if certainly hostile to Gainas, he could describe his activities straightforwardly? Third, we can be certain that from the beginning Alaric's following amounted to a major military force, surely ten thousand-plus warriors, since already in 395 it was able to face down a full Roman field army. If we don't accept what Claudian and Synesius tell us, that it was the treaty Goths in rebellion that Alaric was leading, we also have to find a large alternative source of military manpower for him. This is not easy, given that the western generalissimo Stilicho had both eastern and western field armies under his command at this point.[68]

The second plank of the argument, quite simply, is that it is entirely plausible that the Goths of 382 had maintained sufficient continuity of political identity over the intervening period to mount such a revolt. We are talking only thirteen years. Another generation will have matured in that time, but many adults active in 382 will still have been so in 395. And though woefully ignorant of many of its details, the point of the 382 treaty – for contemporary supporters and critics alike – was that it allowed an unprecedented degree of autonomy to continue among the Goths concerned. Although guilty of rebellion and the death of an emperor, they had not been broken up and widely distributed across the Empire, which is why Themistius, spokesman and propagandist for the Emperor Theodosius, had to work so hard to sell the peace to the Senate of Constantinople. This makes it entirely plausible that the same Goths could have acted in concert again, just thirteen years later.[69]

That original treaty had also left unresolved two big issues in Gotho-Roman relations, and it was these that came to a head in Alaric's revolt of 395. First, the Romans had recognized no overall Gothic leader in the peace of 382. This was in line with established Roman policies for limiting the political cohesion of groups they perceived as potential threats – it was standard policy towards Alamannic overkings, as we have seen, in the fourth century. Also, it was facilitated by developments within the confederations of the Tervingi and Greuthungi themselves. In both, the decision to move into Roman territory had been accompanied by political turmoil at the top and the removal of established leaderships, whether by death in battle or political overthrow.[70] In the run-up to the battle of Hadrianople, Fritigern had tried to fill the gap, and there is good evidence both that the struggle had continued after 382 and that Alaric, too, had had to overcome rivals for the overall leadership of the Goths. It is certainly possible that his position was evolving in 394/5. Although attributable more to Zosimus' garblings of Eunapius' original, it may be the case that Alaric originally had ambitions for a more Roman career. But in the event he chose the Gothic option, and there is one excellent – if indirect – piece of evidence that he elbowed at least one rival out of the way to do so. Alaric's later career, and that of his brother-in-law and successor Athaulf, were dogged by the interventions of a Roman general of Gothic origins by the name of Sarus, who waged a one-man war with a view to undermining any peace deal the two were looking to negotiate with the west Roman state, into whose service Sarus had moved. What's so interesting here is that Sarus' brother Sergeric eventually organized the coup in which Athaulf and his immediate family were killed, and made himself – briefly – ruler of Alaric's Goths. So Sarus clearly came from a family grand enough to compete for the overall leadership of the Goths, and his unrelenting hostility suggests that Alaric's rise was responsible for his departure for Roman service.[71]

Alaric's broader political success among the Goths, moreover, was intimately linked with the line he took on the second unresolved issue of the treaty of 382: the military obligations owed by the semi-autonomous Goths to the Roman state. As noted earlier, it was normal Roman policy in peace agreements imposed upon outsiders to extract drafts of young males for its armies. This may well have happened in 382, creating Gothic auxiliary units in the regular Roman army. But as had previously been the case with the Tervingi north of the Danube from 332, the treaty stipulated in addition that the Goths should provide irregular military service in the form of larger, autonomously led contingents for specific campaigns. Contingents from the Tervingi had fought on four occasions for Rome against Persia, between 332 and 360, and similar demands of the treaty Goths were made by the east Roman Emperor Theodosius I for his two civil wars against the western usurpers Maximus and Eugenius.[72]

There is compelling evidence that this military service was resented by the Goths. On each of the campaigns against the usurpers, the participation of the treaty Goths was accompanied by revolts of some kind. Theodosius' decision to seek assistance on the second occasion prompted a vicious quarrel among the Gothic leadership over how they should respond to his request.[73] The fate of the Gothic forces on the second expedition also shows precisely why it was problematic. At the battle of the Frigidus in September 394, they found themselves in the front line on the first day and suffered heavy casualties. One contemporary Roman historian commented that the battle saw two victories for Theodosius: one over the usurper Eugenius and a second over the Goths. Given that the Goths' semi-autonomy was tolerated by the Roman state only because they couldn't be properly defeated, there was a real danger that such casualties would change the balance of power sufficiently to allow the Romans to rewrite the terms of the treaty. It is not in the least surprising, therefore, that almost as soon as they got home from the Frigidus campaign, sometime in winter 394/ 5, the treaty Goths rose in revolt under a leader committed to rewriting the terms of 382.[74]

Much of what we would like to know about the treaty, and the pattern of Gotho-Roman relations it dictated, is beyond recovery. But as with so many diplomatic agreements, it was clearly a working compromise that left some of the more contentious issues to be resolved later. But it is entirely reasonable to suppose that Alaric's revolt of 395 was of the nature that our two contemporary commentators describe. He was the leader of the bulk of the 382 Goths in revolt, the treaty having left them autonomous enough to be capable of rewriting their terms of agreement by collective action, and losses at the Frigidus had given them a real reason for discontent. This interim conclusion then prompts another set of questions. Why did the Goths' rebellion in search of better terms involve further migration? It is, after all, perfectly possible to revolt without picking up the family and taking to the road again, lock, stock, and two smoking barrels.[75]

The fact that they had an established migration habit has to be one element in the explanation. As its history shows, this was a population grouping prone to solving its difficulties by moving on to pastures new. The descendants of those who had moved from Poland to the Black Sea in the third century and into Wallachia in the early fourth, who had attempted to migrate west of the Carpathians in the 330s and who eventually crossed the Danube in 376, were a population group that knew a great deal about the practicalities of large-scale, long-distance movement, and had shown themselves ready to use it as a strategy for solving their problems. And, of course, some of those who crossed the Danube in 376, would certainly still have been alive in 395. But even groups with well-established migration habits do not move without excellent reason, and the travels of Alaric's Goths, after the revolt, played a specific role in an unfolding strategy aimed at rewriting the unsatisfactory elements of the treaty of 382.

One of the motives was simply to plunder Roman communities en route. In 395, Alaric was a new Gothic leader and had to secure his power base. Putting his followers in the way of funds answered this need, and we have no reason to suppose that our sources are lying when they describe the Goths' slow trot south into and around Greece as an extended booty raid.[76] But that was only part of its purpose. Alaric also needed to force the Roman state into accepting revisions to the treaty in the Goths' favour. Mostly we hear little of the substance of these negotiations, but where the sources are more detailed, as they are for Alaric's second sojourn in Italy between 408 and 410, it emerges that the key issues were full recognition of his leadership, possibly symbolized by granting him some kind of Roman office, the degree of economic support that the Goths would receive from the Roman state, and the finding of a suitable settlement area. Underlying this was a concern to extract a truly unconditional acceptance of the Goths' basic right to exist as a semi-independent entity on Roman soil. In 382, the Roman authorities clearly had at least one pair of fingers crossed behind their backs. When the imperial spokesman Themistius rose to justify the treaty in front of the Senate in January 383, he closed his speech by looking forward to the time when all signs of separate Gothic identity would disappear.[77]

All of these Gothic prerequisites for a lasting peace agreement had to be dragged unwillingly from a Roman state that, for centuries, had enjoyed sufficient military hegemony never to have to accept long-term coexistence with a barbarian power on its own soil. Winning concessions was never easy, therefore, as the better-documented episodes of diplomatic exchange again show. Repeatedly between 408 and 410 Alaric appeared on the verge of a settlement, only to see it torpedoed by imperial intransigence. He showed enormous patience, famously reducing his demands to an absolute minimum before allowing his forces to sack Rome when even these lesser demands were rejected. This time, migration had the purpose both of inflicting damage on imperial assets so as to pressure the Empire into an agreement, and of moving the Goths to the location that offered the best chance for longer-term diplomatic success. The Grecian holiday that Alaric took in 395–7 was an attempt to force the eastern Empire to negotiate, and eventually he succeeded. In 397, the ruling regime in Constantinople, headed by the eunuch Eutropius, cut him a suitable deal. But making these concessions was extremely unpopular in some elite imperial circles, and one of the issues that contributed to Eutropius' own downfall in 399. A sequence of regimes followed that had in common the determination not to negotiate with Alaric, whose concessions were withdrawn.[78] This closing-off of the east sparked Alaric's next migratory venture: the Goths' first intrusion into Italy, in 401/2. This used further migration as a means of pressuring the western half of the Empire into doing a deal. But Stilicho was able to fend off Alaric's advances militarily, and the Goths, caught in limbo, returned to the Balkans with neither half of the Empire willing to negotiate.

The situation was changed only by the intrusion of outside factors. The impending collapse of his central European frontier left the western generalissimo Stilicho desperately in need of military man-power. Having already confronted a Vandal threat to Raetia in the winter of 401/2, he was aware that a highly explosive situation was building up in the Middle Danube, as Goths, Vandals, Alans and other refugees from the Huns moved west of the Carpathians. This made him turn towards Alaric's Goths as possible allies.[79] When Stilicho was eventually deposed in the summer of 408, essentially because of his failure to deal with the mixture of invasion and usurpation that from 405 had ripped the western Empire apart, Alaric had already negotiated an understanding with him, and now pushed his followers back on the road to Italy, ostensibly to collect what he was owed. More fundamentally, the current disarray in the west made it much more likely that he would be able to extract a suitable deal there than in the east.

The Goths stayed in Italy for the next three years, and got close to agreement at certain points. In the end, however, imperial intransigence starved them out, and now under Alaric's brother-in-law and successor Athaulf they headed off to Gaul, again in search of the right combination of circumstances to force a lasting settlement. There, finally, between 416 and 418, the bare bones of a new agreement emerged. The Goths were given a prosperous area for farming and settlement in the Garonne valley of Aquitaine, much richer than any part of the Balkans but more distant from the imperial centres of power in northern Italy, and their leader received full Roman recognition. But they were given none of the gold payments or appointments to high office within the political structure of the Roman state that had featured in Alaric's most ambitious proposals between 408 and 410. Physically and politically they had been banished to the fringes of the Roman world. The Goths agreed to fight on occasion, as before, for the Roman state, and were employed in Spain against the Rhine invaders.[80]

Strange as such behaviour might appear from a modern perspective, the punctuated migrations of Alaric's followers after 395 had their own logic. There is nothing in any of this – and certainly not the final form of the 418 agreement – that requires us to see the core of his support as having been drawn other than from the 382 Goths. They had been attempting to force the Roman state, or one half of it, into a lasting agreement, and their relocations were designed to manoeuvre them into the kind of political and geographical context from which a suitable settlement could be negotiated. What we are witnessing again, in fact, is the inescapable influence exercised by Roman state structures on the Goths' migratory process. Throughout this long period of movement, lasting for nearly twenty years, they were twisting and turning in an attempt to gain sufficient leverage to force the Empire to change centuries-old policies. In the end, it took the crisis of 405–8, and above all the Rhine invaders' annexations in Spain, to make the west Roman authorities receptive to the Goths' advances.

In the emergence of this agreement, one development in particular played a role of special importance. Within the Goths' extended odyssey, stretching from the Balkans to Aquitaine, there were some lengthy periods of relative stability: during 397–401 and again during 402–7 in the Balkans, during 408–11 in Italy, and during 412–15 in southern Gaul. In total, then, maybe only about five and a half of the twenty-odd years from original revolt to settlement in the Garonne were spent in long-distance relocation. Nevertheless, this was an extraordinarily testing and stressful period, and, as you might expect, Alaric's force did not just proceed unchanged from point of departure to final destination. With the benefit of hindsight, we know that this extended odyssey ended satisfactorily enough. But facing hard marches and food shortages – especially in Italy in 410/11 and again in Gaul in 414/15 – and the constant threat of Roman counterattack (not least in confrontations with its field armies in 395, 397, and twice in 402) the Goths did not know that the end result was all going to be worth such a huge effort.

Whereas older narratives took the existence of Alaric's original force for granted, more recent accounts have emphasized, rightly, that its membership changed substantially between 395 and 418. The idea that it rose and fell according to his followers' estimates of Alaric's likelihood of success, indeed, has now become something of a commonplace. In reality, the evidence for a steadily increasing membership is much better than that for its supposed decline. A trawl through the sources throws up a handful of individuals of high status who switched their allegiance to Rome, probably accompanied by their personal military retinues, on being defeated in the ongoing struggles for political pre-eminence that periodically preoccupied the Goths. Sarus and Fravittas, whom we have already met, fall into this category, as, seemingly, does a certain Modares. These men belong to a very specific category, however, providing no evidence that the substantial membership of the group ebbed and flowed. Otherwise, the only reference we have to Alaric losing support is from a Roman spin doctor working for Stilicho, desperate to find some way of salvaging his employer's reputation when the latter had failed to defeat the Goths in battle in 402. His airy claim that Alaric's followers were abandoning him in droves can carry little weight.[81]

Even so, the evidence for renegotiated identity is incontrovertible. To start with, the immigrants of 376 had come across the Danube in two separate groups: Tervingi and Greuthungi. This distinction disappeared, in my view by 395, in another by 408. But the date is a matter of detail. North of the Danube, the Greuthungi and Tervingi had been entirely separate political entities. Within a generation of crossing the Danube, the distinction disappeared.[82] Two had become one, and further additions of manpower followed. Outside Rome in 409 Alaric received two major reinforcements. After the overthrow of Stilicho, a major body of barbarian soldiery from the Roman army of Italy, closely allied to the generalissimo, threw in their lot with Alaric when their families, quartered in various Italian cities, were massacred in a pogrom. It is overwhelmingly likely that these were in large part the men who had, just four years before, followed Radagaisus to Italy before swapping sides in the diplomatic coup that led to their former leader's downfall and death. Alaric's Goths were also joined outside Rome by a very large number of slaves. I suspect many of these had the same origin, given that so many of Radagaisus' less fortunate followers had been sold into slavery in 406. But no doubt there were others, from a variety of origins, besides.[83] We are a very long way here from the old billiard-ball view of Gothic migration explored in Chapter 1.

In the course of Alaric's career, then, a new and much larger political unit was created on the hoof in the years of renewed movement after 395. Why this happened is straightforward, I think, even if the negotiations behind the process are nowhere reported for us. The former military allies of Stilicho joined Alaric simply because of Roman hostility. They had been prepared to contemplate a long-term future as Roman allies, having abandoned Radagaisus with this in mind. Stilicho had offered them an attractive deal, perhaps something like the terms Eutropius had granted Alaric in 397. But on Stilicho's fall, inherent Roman hostility towards 'barbarians', manifested in the attacks on their families, led to a change of mind. The necessary preconditions for the unification of the Tervingi and Greuthungi, likewise, were created by their joint campaigns against the Roman state from 376. Again, the process was not a smooth one. After their joint victory at Hadrianople, the groups split up again in the winter of 379/80, not least because feeding the united force was proving problematic, but probably also because each had its own leadership that was not about to give way to the other – which any definitive unification would necessarily have entailed.[84] But as the narrative makes clear, this new and much bigger military-political entity was primarily created to fend off Roman power, and without imperial pressure would surely never have emerged. Not only did the cracks in Roman political structures direct the precise moves made by the Goths between 395 and 418, but the pressure of Roman military power had the effect of pushing a number of originally separate immigrant groups together just to survive. There are many complementary examples of those who failed to learn the lesson, and suffered as a consequence. Isolated Gothic raiding parties were destroyed in the course of the Hadrianople campaign, while whole breakaway subgroups were subdued and resettled on more normal Roman terms.[85] The only way to prosper on Roman territory was to hang together in sufficient numbers and with sufficient political cohesion to prevent the Roman state from hanging you individually.

Alaric's Goths provide us, therefore, with an excellent example of contingent group identity in action. Most of the constituent elements of the force seem to have been Gothic, but a shared Gothic cultural identity, if this really existed in the fourth century – and it may have – was not a prerequisite for group membership. We know at least of some Huns whose membership of the new group appears to have been permanent, and the origins of the slaves who joined Alaric outside Rome is a thoroughly moot point.[86] But none even of the Gothic contingents had formed part of the same political unit before their entry on to Roman soil. It was Roman military pressure that had brought the Tervingi and Greuthungi together at Hadrianople, and that made Radagaisus' more fortunate followers conclude that their initial choice of a Roman option was a mistaken one so that their interests would be better served by attaching themselves to Alaric's command. On the other side of the imperial frontier, Roman aggression was not so fierce nor so sustained as to cause such a large group to form, but on Roman soil all these Goths had to unite so as to survive as an independent entity. This is, in fact, a classic pattern. Outside pressure often provides the necessary catalyst for active group identities to form.

We have no information on the negotiations between the groups that preceded their unification, but given their previously separate political histories these can't always have been easy, as the number of high-status Goths forced out of the group and into Roman service confirms. But this, of course, is why outside pressure was required to make it happen at all, and doesn't mean that the resulting group identity, forged in the fires of war, was fundamentally weak. If it had been, the Roman state would have been able to prise it apart (as it did with the forces of Uldin and Radagaisus); but even the subsequent diplomatic setback, then famine, and the extinction of its initial leadership line were not enough to cause the new group's unity to collapse. And in this crucial point we find a second reason why the Roman state was willing in the end to do a deal. The Gothic force assembled in Gaul in the 410s was much larger, and, thanks to continued conflict with the Roman state, more cohesive than any Gothic political unit previously seen.[87] The Romans were forced to accept by 418 that a deal had to be done, therefore, not least because the force Alaric had created was now too large to be destroyed.

For all the problems of the evidence, then, the action that unfolded from the outbreak of Alaric's revolt down to the settlement in Aquitaine in 418 is best understood as the immigrants of 376 taking to the road again in search of a better future and picking up en route reinforcements from some of the migrants of 405–8. As we have seen before when discussing Germanic society in this era, army versus people is a false dichotomy. In a world whose economic and political structures could support only restricted numbers of specialist warriors, recruiting for any enterprise that required large armed forces automatically brought freemen and their families into the picture. To have any chance of success, Alaric had to convince large numbers of Goths that it was in their interests to up sticks and move again. But, as we have also seen, the immigrants' aims were destined to be fulfilled only when they were able to recruit from a still wider body of support. The new political identity thereby created may have drawn in part on pre-existing cultural similarities among the various Gothic groups who joined the new enterprise, but cultural similarity was by no means crucial. The Vandal–Alan alliance shows that entities with a strong political identity could be built out of constituent groups with utterly different backgrounds. Much more important than cultural similarity was the hostile presence of the Roman state.

The analysis offered above satisfactorily explains, I think, all the oddities of the action, which the alternative proposition simply cannot. The sophisticated political agendas on display and, above all, Alaric's need for a settlement area do not sit well with the mercenary-band model. Adopting it would also raise the question of where Alaric might have found such a massive reservoir of specialist warriors.

Many of these points also apply to those other great practitioners of repeat migration: the Rhine invaders of 406. You'll be relieved to know that there's no need to rehearse the army-versus-people argument again in relation to their history after their initial settlement in Spain in 412. This would be trying the reader's patience, and the sources are anyway less informative. Whatever view you form of Alaric's Goths, therefore, will tend to spill over into your understanding of the Vandals, Alans and Sueves. Suffice to say that the one detailed, broadly contemporary source with any claim to authority that we have does picture the Vandals and Alans moving on to North Africa with wives and families in tow.[88] And, for similar reasons to those explored in the case of the Goths, there really are no good grounds for doubting it.

In other more precise respects, however, the migration processes of both Goths and Rhine invaders correspond more closely with what comparative migration studies might lead us to expect. Logistics, naturally enough, played a key role in shaping the individual moves. Alaric's Goths hit the road with a huge wagon train. This meant that they were confined to land routes and the Roman road network, which, particularly in the Balkans, greatly restricted the choices of route and helped dictate, for instance, the Goths' circulatory itinerary between 395 and 397. An inability to secure sea transport also nipped in the bud Alaric's plans to ship his force to North Africa after the sack of Rome in the autumn of 410, and eventually made it possible for the Romans to blockade his people in southern Gaul and cut them off from food supplies. The Vandals and Alans also moved with wagons while on land, but fared better than Alaric's Goths in their eventual bid to cross to North Africa. Part of the reason for this lay in the fact that they had had longer to prepare. Alaric considered moving to North Africa only when his sieges of Rome failed to bear fruit in the form of a diplomatic settlement. But he dropped the plan within just a few months, in the late summer and autumn of 410. The Vandals and Alans, by contrast, had been mounting wide-ranging campaigns right across the Iberian peninsula for over a decade before taking ship to North Africa. This gave them plenty of time to organize the necessary shipping, and, again unlike Alaric in 410, in 429 they were not facing the imminent possibility of an imperial counterattack. This meant that they could afford to move themselves across the straits of Gibraltar piecemeal, and hence needed fewer ships, since there was no danger of those left behind being attacked while waiting to be transported.

Fields of information, too, played their part. Participating in the two campaigns against western usurpers made possible the Goths' later intrusions into the western Empire. Hitherto, their understanding of European geography and of the proximity to their Balkan holdings of relatively rich and vulnerable lands in northern Italy would have been minimal. No doubt, too, their three years in Italy around the sack of Rome in 410 also made it possible for them to contemplate moving on to Gaul. The same must have been even more true for the Vandals and Alans. They clearly knew where Rome's Rhine frontier was located in 406, but can have had only the haziest understanding of where Spain might be found; and perhaps no sense at all, at that point, that from the southern tip of Spain it was a short hop to Morocco. Their extended stay in Spain made it possible not only for them to arrange shipping, no doubt from local Roman traders, but also to gather the basic intelligence, likely from the same quarter, that made the move to North Africa possible. As preparation for that fateful crossing, indeed, they had experimented with a few maritime adventures, not least a sea-borne raid on the Balearic Islands in 425.[89]

On a broader canvas, likewise, the motivations underlying the Vandals' and Alans' repeat migrations make sense from a comparative perspective. The combined group made their way out of Spain and on to North Africa for many of the same of reasons that brought Alaric's Goths out of the Balkans and into the west. They were certainly interested in the region's wealth. The central provinces of Roman North Africa – Numidia, Byzacena and Proconsularis – were the bread basket of the city of Rome, and North African traders spread their wares far and wide across the Mediterranean, not least to Spain (as distribution patterns of North African pottery show), where the Vandals' interest in this prize would have been aroused. At the same time, North Africa offered them the hope of much greater security. Whereas the Goths engaged in repeat migration as part of a strategy to extract diplomatic concessions, before they left Spain the Vandals and Alans had never had a treaty with the central western Roman authorities at all. This did not matter much in 409, since the west was busy dealing with Alaric and a succession of usurpers. By the mid-410s, however, stability had returned to the western Empire; the usurpers had been suppressed and the Goths brought on board via their new treaty. At this point, the Rhine invaders became public enemy number one, and a series of punishing campaigns were launched against them in Spain, mounted by imperial and Gothic forces in combination – this being the particular form of military assistance that the Roman state was looking for from the Goths. Between 416 and 418, the Siling Vandals and Alans were savaged to such an extent that they gave up their independent provinces, the survivors attaching themselves to the leadership of the Hasding Vandals. Central political stability collapsed again in the west in the 420s and the pressure eased once more, but the respite was always likely to be only temporary.

Alongside its wealth, then, North Africa offered hopes of much greater security for surviving Vandals and Alans. Once settled there, any future imperial attacks on them would have to come by sea, which was an exponentially more difficult type of military operation, as subsequent events would show. The Empire mounted three large expeditions against them in North Africa from the early 440s to the late 460s, all of which failed.[90] Like the Goths, the Rhine invaders were operating with mixed political and economic motives, and, again like the Goths, used repeat migration to manoeuvre their way to safety and prosperity between the cracks in the Roman Empire's political and military structures. Repeat large-scale migration was of the essence of continued existence for barbarian groups on Roman territory, and attempts to minimize its importance are thoroughly unconvincing.

For the Rhine invaders, as with Alaric's Goths, revisionist views on evolving group identities contain much more mileage. The force of Vandals and Alans who captured Carthage in 439 had not made it there from the Rhine without a major renegotiation of their respective identities, as its individual members struggled for survival on Roman soil. In this case, the restructuring went still further. Whereas Alaric's force was assembled from components that, at elite levels at least, seem to have been mostly Gothic, the Rhine invaders were of a very different composition. The two groups of Vandals, the Hasdings and Silings, may have shared some cultural similarities, but the Sueves were Germanic-speakers from a different region; and the Alans, who had provided the largest block of manpower in 406, were Iranian-speaking nomads with an entirely different economy and social structure from the Germanic agriculturalists with whom they were now allied. In 406, this force had still been held together by only the loosest of alliances, as is shown by the great Spanish share-out of 412, when the groups took separate provinces under their own leaders.

The much tighter unification that followed had the same basic cause as the unification of Alaric's Goths. Once again, the hostile power of the Roman state made it clear to many of the invaders that their best interests would be served by operating together. And again, they were brought to this realization by force: the brute reality of the joint Gotho-Roman campaigns which destroyed the Siling Vandals (whose king was hauled off to Ravenna in the aftermath of defeat) and smashed the independence of the Alans, who, after the death in battle of their king, threw their remaining strength behind Hasding leadership. Without this application of Roman force, there is no sign that the unification would have occurred at all, and even in the face of Roman pressure not all the invaders signed up to the new confederation. The Sueves resisted subsequent attempts by the Hasding monarchy to bring them under its control by force, and some Alans preferred to stay put and accept Roman domination, being settled eventually in Gaul.[91]

The hostility of Roman state power, then, forced those who wished to preserve their independence to renegotiate their original group identities so as to create a larger and more cohesive force that stood some chance of survival on Roman soil. Alongside migration, therefore, a particular kind of group-identity evolution played a key role in the ability of immigrant barbarians to survive.

As for many of the protagonists themselves, reconstructing the story of the migrants of 376 and 405–8 involves an extensive journey. Fortunately for us, these migrants, reasonably well documented for parts of their history, provide a key test case, and some fundamental points have already been established that will not require such lengthy exploration again. Their history shows that migrants into the Roman Empire could – and did on occasion – come in large blocks of organized military manpower with their families in tow. If they entertained ambitions that went beyond mere integration into the Roman system as military cannon fodder or agricultural labour, this kind of migratory unit was essential. Only by recruiting well outside military retinues could enough military manpower be put together for expeditions likely to stand any chance of success. Equally important, the better evidence indicates that the immigrants could and did engage in repeat migrations. The vast majority had a well-established tradition of movement even before they crossed into Roman territory, and repeat migration, alongside a renegotiation, under Roman pressure, of group identity which steadily increased overall numbers, provided a two-pronged strategy for long-term survival on Roman soil.

But if organized block migration does need to be retrieved from the revisionist dustbin as a major theme of the thirty years after 376 and placed alongside the population flow of increasing momentum observed in the last chapter as an important migratory phenomenon of the first millennium, it did not take the form traditionally envisaged. The groups who crossed into the Empire derived from a barbarian world that was already politically, economically and culturally complex. They were not 'peoples', at least not in the sense of culturally homogeneous, more or less equal population groups whose departure emptied the landscape from which they came. Nonetheless, we are still looking at mass migrations in two senses of the term. Even if they still encompassed only an elite, the inclusion of freemen warriors and their social and familial dependants made for major migrant groups numbering several tens of thousands of individuals. The migrations were also mass in the qualitative sense used in migration studies, in that the flow administered a distinct political shock at its points of departure or arrival, or indeed both. The migrants who brought down Rome's east and central European frontiers quickly stacked up between them one emperor dead on a battlefield along with his army, a forced reversal of standard imperial policies towards migrants, and the extraction of some key provinces from full imperial control. The shock in the lands they left behind is equally marked. It is to this subject, the age of the *Völkerwanderung* beyond the Roman frontier, that we must now turn our attention.

# 5

# HUNS ON THE RUN

IN 453, AFTER A DECADE of mayhem stretching from Constantinople to Paris, Attila the Hun died from the after-effects of one too many wedding nights. Following the odd drink or two, the great conqueror retired to bed, burst a blood vessel and died. In the morning, his terrified bride was found cowering beside the corpse. This sudden demise fired the starting gun on a frenzied race for power among his sons, which quickly degenerated into outright civil war. Events then took a yet more dangerous turn. Attila's Empire consisted not just of Huns but large numbers of non-Hunnic subjects besides. The civil war was quickly exploited by some of them as an opportunity to throw off Hunnic control. The lead in the revolt was taken by a king of the Gepids called Arderic – the result, a huge battle in 454 on the (unidentified) River Nedao in the old Roman province of Pannonia.

> There an encounter took place between the various nations Attila had held under his sway. Kingdoms with their peoples were divided, and out of one body were made many members not responding to a common impulse. Being deprived of their head, they madly strove against each other ... And so the bravest nations tore themselves to pieces ... One might see the Goths fighting with pikes, the Gepids raging with the sword, the Rugi breaking off the spears in their own wounds, the Suevi fighting on foot, the Huns with bows, the Alans drawing up a battle-line of heavy-armed and the Herules of light-armed warriors.[1]

It's a famous description, and, even if rhetorical rather than properly descriptive, neatly introduces the issue central to this chapter.

We have already seen that the rise of Hunnic power was responsible for two bouts of mass migration into the Roman Empire. On the face of it, it also prompted major population displacements beyond the frontier. To start with, there are the Huns themselves. In the run-up to the collapse of Rome's east European frontier in 376, they were operating to the north-east of the Black Sea, somewhere opposite the Caucasus. But Roman Pannonia, where the battle of the Nedao took place, encompassed the south-eastern fringes of the Great Hungarian Plain west of the Carpathians, and the Empire of Attila was centred primarily in the Middle Danubian region, thousands of kilometres from the Caucasus. At the same time, as the battle narrative again under-lines, Huns never fought alone. In the 370s, during their first attacks on the Goths north of the Black Sea, Iranian-speaking Alan nomads were also involved, Uldin's following contained Germanic-speaking Sciri, and after driving other Huns out of Pannonia in 427 east Roman forces were left with large numbers of their Gothic allies to resettle. A generation later, Attila's Empire incorporated at least three more clusters of Goths, together with Germanic-speaking Gepids, Rugi, Sueves (those left behind, presumably, in 406), Sciri and Heruli, not to mention Iranian-speaking Alans and Sarmatians.[2] The vast majority of these non-Huns, like the Huns themselves, were living in and around the Middle Danube c.450 AD. But many of them had not occupied land in the Middle Danube in the fourth century, and neither would they in the sixth. Not only did the Huns themselves move west into the heart of Europe, but they seem to have been responsible in some way for gathering many other groups together on the Great Hungarian Plain, most of whom subsequently left as Attila's Empire collapsed.

The migration issues raised by even this bare outline of the Hunnic period in central Europe are clear. What, first of all, brought the Huns to the heart of Europe, and what form did their own migratory process take? And how are we to conceive of the demographic displacements involving the other peoples of Attila's Empire? Was this a case of elite transfer, or something larger-scale?


# 'THE ORIGIN AND SEEDBED OF ALL EVILS'


Of all the migrants featured in this book, the Huns are perhaps the most mysterious. They wrote absolutely nothing themselves, but that's pretty much par for the first-millennium course. More problematic is the fact that very little appears about them even in Roman sources until the time of Attila, or perhaps half a generation before: the later 420s onwards, but above all the 440s. By that date, profound transformations had distanced the Hunnic world from its counterpart of c.370, when the region north of the Black Sea first felt the weight of Hunnic assault. The reason for this dearth of information is not hard to deduce. From a Roman perspective, the crises of 376–80 and 405–8 both saw the Huns push other groups across the imperial frontier. These migrants then proceeded to generate huge disruption on Roman territory. It was only natural for Roman commentators to concentrate on them rather than on the Huns who had caused the initial problem.

As a result, our ignorance of the Huns is astounding. It is not even clear what language they spoke. Most of the linguistic evidence we have comes in the form of personal names – Hunnic rulers and their henchmen – from the time of Attila. But by then (for reasons that will become apparent later in the chapter), Germanic had become the lingua franca of the Hunnic Empire and many of the recorded names are either certainly or probably Germanic – so no help there. Iranian, Turkish and Finno-Ugrian (like the later Magyars) have all had their proponents, but the truth is that we do not know what language the Huns spoke, and probably never will.[3] The direct evidence we have for the motivations and forms of Hunnic migration is equally limited. According to Ammianus, there was nothing to explain: 'The origin and seedbed of all evils . . . I find to be this. The people of the Huns . . . who dwell beyond the Sea of Azov near the frozen ocean, are quite abnormally savage.' They were just so fierce that it was natural for them to go around hitting people. Similar images of Hunnic ferocity are found in other sources. Zosimus, drawing on the contemporary historian Eunapius, records the panic generated by the Huns' first attacks on the Goths, while the sixth-century Jordanes portrays them as the offspring of expelled Gothic witches and evil spirits.[4] Tempting as it is to leave the issue there, we do need to be just a touch more analytical if we're going to find a convincing explanation of the migratory processes at work among the Huns in the late fourth and early fifth centuries.

What we can say is that, originally, the Huns were nomadic pastoralists from the Great Eurasian Steppe. This vast landscape runs for thousands of kilometres from the fringes of Europe to the western borders of China. Summer rainfall is sparse and the characteristic vegetation is grass, so that its populations tended to depend more on herding than their neighbours; but, contrary to received images, they did do some arable agriculture and depended on economic exchanges with more settled populations to make up for any shortfalls in grain, which still provided much of their staple diet. That the Huns were nomads is suggested both by their geographical location when they are first encountered – east of the River Don, which marks the boundary where average rainfall drops below the levels that make widespread arable agriculture possible without irrigation – and by the famous description that Ammianus provides of them. Gibbon loved it, and the words are hugely evocative:[5]

> Their way of life is so rough that they have no use for fire or seasoned food, but live on the roots of wild plants and the half-raw flesh of any sort of animal, which they warm a little by placing it between their thighs and the backs of their horses. They have no buildings to shelter them ... not so much as a hut thatched with reeds is to be found among them. They roam at large over mountains and forests and are inured from the cradle to cold, hunger and thirst ... .Once they have put their necks into some dingy shirt they never take it off or change it till it rots and falls to pieces from incessant wear ... None of them ploughs or ever touches a plough-handle. They have no fixed abode, no home or law or settled manner of life, but wander like refugees with the wagons in which they live. In these their wives weave their filthy clothing, mate with their husbands, give birth to their children, and rear them to the age of puberty. No one if asked can tell where he comes from, having been conceived in one place, born somewhere else, and reared even further off.

Sadly – because the image has a certain romance – its basic implication that the Huns were constantly and randomly on the move is deeply mistaken.

You could work out that there is some kind of problem, in fact, just from the description itself. It was Ammianus' standard practice, and one generally required of those working in the classical historical genre, to introduce interesting new protagonists with some kind of digression, and by the fourth century AD such moments were loaded with high expectation. The audience was looking for highly coloured descriptive rhetoric and extensive reference to well-known classical authors. Ammianus' Hunnic digression did not disappoint. But not only is it full of rhetoric and quotation, there is another still more obvious problem. In the surviving books of his History, Ammianus had cause to introduce to his readers three sets of nomads – Alans and Saracen Arabs, alongside the Huns – and in each case the digression is more or less identical, with just a few details altered. Essentially, Ammianus had at his disposal nomad digression 101, and just hit the recall button whenever he needed to employ it. This raises the issue of what status to accord the details that are specific to each version. In the case of the Huns, Ammianus has some interesting things to say about their political leadership, which we will return to shortly, and records that they kept meat under their saddles as part of a curing process. This used to be discounted as a misunderstood treatment for saddle sores until a modern anthropologist-cum-historian found Mongols doing the same in the 1920s, so perhaps we do need to take seriously at least something of what Ammianus says. On the other hand, one of the few details he recorded of the Saracens is that both men and women enjoyed sex enormously, and you can't help wondering how he knew. But in general, the fact that desert Arabs from the fringes of the Fertile Crescent as well as Iranian-speaking Alans and Turkic or Finno-Ugrian Huns from the Great Eurasian Steppe are described in extremely similar terms should have been enough to set the alarm bells ringing, and for some it did.[6]

These suspicions have been confirmed by the comparative evidence about nomadic lifestyles gathered more recently by anthropologists. There are of course almost as many differences between different nomad groups as there are nomad groups in the first place. According to the types of grazing and animals available, practices and organization vary enormously. But there are nonetheless some important features in common, and one of the key ones is that nomads do not usually either move at random, or that far – long-distance treks being punishing for both humans and animals. Eurasian groups observed at first hand in the twentieth century, for instance, tended to move a limited distance twice a year between designated blocks of summer and winter grazing. In the case of the Khazaks, before Stalin sedentarized them, this distance was about seventy-five kilometres. Stock-raising subgroups then slowly cycled their herds around within the pasture blocks, keeping their distance from one another so that the grass had time to grow after each subgroup's visit. Other parts of the population, in the meantime, occupied fixed camps and some even grew crops.

The purpose of the longer-distance moves in this regime is to connect two blocks of grazing land, neither of which could provide year-round support. Summer pasture, typically, might be up in the hills where it was too cold for grass in winter; winter pasture in reasonably adjacent lowlands where heat and the lack of rainfall limited grazing in the summer months. Essentially, nomadism builds two landscapes into a complete grazing portfolio. In this set-up, movement fulfils a designated function and could never just be random. A nomadic existence is potentially fragile anyway, highly dependent upon rainfall in what are by definition marginal landscapes; but setting off into the wild blue yonder without knowledge of a potential destination's carrying capacity or, equally important, established rights to graze there, would have been to invite economic disaster.[7]

What this means, of course, is that the intrusions of Huns into the Alanic-dominated world north-east of the Black Sea, and then subsequently into the heart of Europe, cannot be viewed – as J. B. Bury did, for instance, in a famous set of lectures given in the 1920s – as a natural extension of their nomad economy. The Huns did not just meander around the Great Eurasian Steppe until they happened to come across its western edge north of the Black Sea and take a liking to it. The decisions to switch their centres of operation westwards – in two distinct stages separated by about a generation – must have been taken for specific reasons, and carefully calculated. The potential gains of these moves had always to be balanced against the dangers of failing to find, or – more likely – establish, rights over sufficient grazing for their flocks at the new destinations.[8]

As to what reason or reasons led the Huns to move westwards, no easy answers are available. Roman sources are of little use. Ammianus' view that attacking other barbarians was just something that came naturally to Hunnic megabarbarians does not get us very far. The available evidence does suggest three factors, however, two possible and the other more certain, that made it generally likely that Hunnic groups would want to move west. One of the possible factors is climate change. Around the year 400 AD, western Europe was basking in a climatic optimum, with long hot summers and plenty of sunshine. But what was good for western Europeans was less good for the world beyond the Don, where the same climatic optimum meant that there was less summer rainfall to make the grass grow. Given these conditions, it would be only natural to expect greater competition for grazing among steppe nomads, and the modern world provides us with a nasty parallel for what can happen. At the heart of the Darfur conflict are Sudanese nomad populations driven out of their old homelands as global warming turns pasture into desert. The trouble with applying this argument to the fourth century, however, is that, for the moment at least, it is impossible to know how severe or, indeed, limited the effects of fourth-century climate change actually were. There are no precise data. And in their absence, the chances are that any effects were fairly marginal. But as we shall see in subsequent chapters, a sequence of nomadic groups exploded out of this same steppe in the mid-to-late first millennium, and more were to follow, which strongly suggests that Eurasian nomadism was not facing any fundamental ecological challenge. And in any case, like the Tervingi and Greuthungi when faced with the Hunnic menace, Huns under ecological pressure could have moved in any of several directions, and adducing climate change would still leave us having to explain why they moved westwards.

The other possible factor is political revolution. At least two of the nomadic groups that followed the Huns out of the steppe into Europe in the later first millennium did so, in part, because they were under political and military pressure from other nomadic groups to their east. The sixth-century Avars were on the run from the Empire of the Western Turks, while the ninth-century Magyars moved from north of the Black Sea to the Great Hungarian Plain because of the attacks of Petchenegs. In the absence of specific information about the western steppe in the fourth century, it would be foolish to rule out the possibility that the Huns too were facing this kind of pressure.[9]

But even if we allow the Huns a negative element to their motivation deriving from a combination of potential climatic and political factors, there is no doubting that this coexisted, as has proved to be the case in so many flows of migration, with some very positive reasons for moving west. Roman sources describing the Huns' initial impact on the outer fringes of the Empire offer no substantial explanation of what was going on, but later materials are highly suggestive. From c.390 and particularly the 420s onwards, we find Huns engaged in a variety of activities in relation to the Roman world. Sometimes they raided it. A huge raiding party targeting both the east Roman and Persian Empires passed through the Caucasus in 395, before the Hunnic main body had moved on to central Europe, and there are

indications of other smaller raids in this era besides. Sometimes Huns
served the Empire as mercenaries. As early as the 380s, the activities
of a body of Huns and Alans led to diplomatic confrontation between
the western Emperor Valentinian II and the usurper Maximus. In
the 400s, likewise, Uldin provided military support for Stilicho, before
his ill-advised incursion into east Roman Dacia. With the arrival of
Huns in large numbers in central Europe from c.410 onwards, however, mercenary service reached its apogee. They were possibly already
providing major military support to the de facto ruler of the western
Empire, Flavius Constantius, in the 410s, but it was in the time of
Aetius, from the 420s, that they became a crucial bulwark of the
western Empire. Not only did Aetius use their support to keep himself
in power against Roman rivals, but they were also deployed to keep
in check the aggressive ambitions of the other barbarian groups now
well established on western imperial territory: most notably in major
campaigns against the Visigoths and the Burgundians in the 430s.
Then, finally, as Hunnic power grew in the time of Attila, the Huns
turned from raiding and mercenary service to large-scale invasion.
Two massive attacks on the east Roman Balkans, in 442 and 447, were
followed by invasions of Gaul and Italy in 451 and 452.[10]

What all of these activities had in common was that they were
different methods of tapping into the greater wealth available within
the more developed economy of the Mediterranean-based Roman
world. Raiding, obviously enough, was all about movable shiny stuff
and other forms of negotiable booty, and this too was the point of
mercenary service. For all his Hunnic connections – and Aetius had
spent three years among them as a hostage – they did not fight for
him without receiving generous payment. And even Attila's invasions
were undertaken with cash in mind. We have very detailed accounts
of the diplomatic contacts that preceded and followed these attacks,
and Attila's central concern was always the size of the diplomatic
subsidy he could secure. Extra territory and other types of gain were
of only marginal interest.[11] If it is legitimate to import this vision of
the Huns' basic attitude towards the Roman Mediterranean back to
the 370s, and there is no obvious reason why not, then the Huns'
decisions to move westwards in two stages make complete sense.
Increased proximity to the political centres of the Roman world in
northern Italy and Constantinople meant greater opportunities for
extracting a share of Roman wealth. In other words, the Huns were

acting like the Goths and the other largely Germanic-speaking preda-
tors of the third century AD: their migrations were a response to
fundamental inequalities of wealth. Like the Goths, they were moving
from the less developed outer periphery of the Empire, and perhaps
from beyond even that, into richer inner zones where there was a
wide variety of wealth-generating opportunities available to groups
able, like themselves, to deploy military force of sufficient potency.

It is also possible to say something useful about the developing
nature of the Hunnic migration flow. No source gives us figures for
the size of Hunnic migration units, but all the contemporary evidence
indicates that the initial expansion into the northern Pontus was carried
forward essentially by warbands: small groups of all-male warriors.
Vithimer, the king of the Greuthungi whose death sparked the move
of the Goths to the Danube in 376, fought many skirmishes – *multas
clades* – against the Alans whom the Huns had displaced into his realm.
This strongly implies that, while hugely destabilizing in aggregate, no
individual engagement at this point was that large. Ammianus also
records that Vithimer was able to hire some Huns to help him fight
off the Alans. This has sometimes been discounted as a copying error,
but there is no good reason to believe so. The report fits into a context
where multiple small-scale warbands were operating on a more or less
individual basis. The fact that Vithimer's predecessor Ermenaric was
able to resist the Huns 'for a long time' (*diu*) also suggests a sequence
of smaller engagements rather than a set-piece confrontation. In similar
vein, we find Huns operating in a variety of places and employing a
variety of strategies for self-advancement as Rome's eastern European
frontiers collapsed.

Aside from the Huns who fought for Vithimer, others are recorded
raiding the lands of the Tervingi (twice), signing up as mercenaries
with some Alans to fight with the Tervingi and Greuthungi against
Rome south of the Danube in 377, and raiding the Empire off their
own bat from north of the Danube with Carpo-Dacians in tow in the
early 380s.[12] There is every reason to suppose that these were all
independent groups of Huns, not the same one popping up in different
places, and none of the recorded action requires military forces of any
great size. One of the specific things Ammianus says about the Huns
of this era in his digression, in fact, is that they were not governed by
kings but by 'improvised leaders'. This is a slightly slippery phrase
whose meaning has been much debated, but again it fits well with a

picture of small independent Hunnic units. It is also striking that this era threw up no Hunnic leaders who were individually significant enough to be mentioned by name.[13] This recalls the first small-scale phases of Slavic and Viking raiding in, respectively, the sixth and ninth centuries. In both of these cases, it was only as raiding groups increased in scale that individual leaders came to be named.

But if the Hunnic expansion behind the crisis of 376–80 was being powered by warbands, the collapse of Rome's central European frontier a generation later saw migration on a much larger scale. A hint that the size of Hunnic groups operating on the fringes of the Empire was growing is already there in the sources before this second crisis. Around the year 400, contemporary Roman sources finally mention a Hunnic leader by name: Uldin. He was powerful enough to provide useful military assistance to the Empire on occasion, with a following composed of Huns and Sciri. But although given to the occasional boast that his power stretched from where the sun rose to where it set, events put him firmly in perspective. His attempt to seize east Roman territory was defused without military action when his leading followers abandoned him, and at that point he disappears from our sources to where the sun of history doesn't shine. This is not the career profile of a genuine predecessor of Attila. To my mind, Uldin's sudden and otherwise inexplicable switch from ally to invader strongly suggests that his power base was not strong enough for him to hold his own in the face of the new Hunnic groups who became dominant there from c.410 onwards, almost certainly because these newcomers were turning up in larger and more organized bodies.[14]

The evidence for this is straightforward. When the east Roman diplomat and historian Olympiodorus visited the newly arrived Huns in the Middle Danube region in 411/12, he found them ruled by multiple kings ranged in order of precedence. At the time of the visit, the Huns had been in central Europe for only a handful of years, with no time for such a complex political order to emerge from a mass of independent warbands, and, in fact, a similar system is documented among another group of fifth-century steppe nomads, the Akatziri. It is overwhelmingly likely, therefore, that the second stage of Hunnic migration westward was actually led by the kings that Olympiodorus encountered. Indeed, given the numbers of Germani and others that the Huns displaced from the Middle Danube in the process – many tens of thousands, as we have seen – it is doubtful that a series of independent warbands could have mustered enough force to take over this new landscape. The kings' presence makes it apparent that the move from north-east of the Black Sea to the Great Hungarian Plain had been accomplished by much larger and more organized social units than the warband activity that underlay the earlier crisis of 376–80.[15]

Overall, therefore, the evidence suggests that Hunnic migration into Europe took a form we have encountered before, in the third century, and will encounter again in the ninth. The initial impulse came from warbands on the make, without their having had, at this early date, any necessary intention to migrate. But when the warband activity proved highly profitable, larger and more organized groups became involved, probably aiming to maximize the amount of wealth that could be extracted by actually seizing total control of the landscape. In this case, the Huns' later actions suggest that the attraction was not the land of the Middle Danube in terms of its agricultural potential (the attraction of England, eventually, for ninth-century Danes or eleventh-century Normans), but the fact that it was conveniently placed for maximizing profits via closer ties of various kinds with the Roman world. As a result, small-scale raiding north of the Black Sea elided into a population flow of steadily increasing momentum, until large-scale group migration emerged as the logical mechanism for maximizing profits by seizing control of the Great Hungarian Plain.

The exact size of the Hunnic groups involved in these two main phases of migration is unknowable. The kind of Gothic political unit whose stability was undermined by the aggregate action of Hunnic warbands and displaced Alans in the first phase of c.370 AD could field perhaps ten thousand warriors in total. But it is hard to extrapolate from this to the size of any attacking Hunnic force, and for two reasons. First, the Hunnic assault was indirect. Political stability north of the Black Sea was undermined over a long period by multiple raids and small-scale attacks, not head-on confrontation, and in the end it was Hun-generated upheavals among the Alans, rather than the Huns themselves, that led the Gothic Greuthungi to take their momentous decision to move in 375/6. So we don't have to be thinking of anywhere near enough Huns to defeat ten thousand Goths in a set-piece battle. Second, like the nineteenth-century Boers, the Huns enjoyed a telling advantage in military hardware. One of their characteristic weapons was the composite reflex bow, long known on the steppe. Now, however, they employed a longer bow – up to 150 centimetres rather than the usual 100 – than had previously been seen on the western steppe. This gave them longer-range hitting power whose effects are visible in the rhetoric of Roman sources. These report Huns able to devastate the ranks of their Gothic opponents while themselves staying safely out of range. The Huns' other characteristic weapon was a long cavalry sabre, which could do an excellent job of mopping up at closer quarters once the opposition ranks had broken.[16] But exactly how big an advantage the bow gave them is uncertain. Flintlock rifles allowed the Voortrekkers to operate highly effectively against odds of about 10 to 1. Commandos numbering in their hundreds could rout Zulu and Matabele forces in their thousands at almost no cost to themselves. With this much advantage, an entire Gothic client state could have been defeated by groupings of no more than about a thousand Huns. But even the Huns' longer bow was probably not as big an advantage as a rifle.

There is no direct evidence, either, for the size of the larger forces that Hunnic kings led on to the Great Hungarian Plain. To judge by Mongol analogies, each Hunnic warrior required many ponies to remain fully mobile. This perhaps provides an indirect indication of the total possible size of Hunnic forces, since it has been calculated that the Great Hungarian Plain could provide grazing for no more than about a hundred and fifty thousand horses. Extrapolating backwards, this number of horse could serve somewhere between fifteen and thirty thousand Hunnic warriors, which is perfectly plausible, but obviously no more than a guess. Lacking better information, I would suspect that the expansionary raiding of c.370, which did not take on the full might of the Gothic client states directly, of course, was undertaken by war parties of a few hundred, and the large-scale group move into central Europe of the early fifth century by a force somewhere in the region, again, of ten to twenty thousand warriors. But this too is only a best guess, and others could legitimately produce very different estimates.

If we can't get very far with numbers, the comparative migration literature does prompt several more general observations about the Hunnic expansion into central Europe. The first stage of activity recalls the way in which many better-documented migration flows build up on the back on the activities of 'scouts', which demonstrate to a broader population the benefits of relocation. And although not something observed in the modern world, even the en bloc migration of large Hunnic groups in phase two is in accord with the fundamental principle that migration units will be of a size and nature that are appropriate to the task of accessing wealth in the particular context in which the migrant flow is operating. For the same reasons we have met before, the kind of large-scale predatory migration eventually undertaken by the Huns also necessarily involved women and children. The numerous dependants of large military forces assembled from non-professional sources cannot be left behind in safety when the military activity encompasses any intent to migrate. As with so many of the other immigrants we have encountered, moreover, the Huns had established traditions of mobility which, all the comparative evidence again emphasizes, must have greatly facilitated their decision to respond to potential gains to be had from the Roman world by upping sticks and moving closer towards it. The biannual migrations common to the nomadic lifestyle meant that the Huns had a greater than usual capacity to organize large-group movement.

As with the Goths, Vandals and Alans on Roman soil, another major reason why there was a substantial chronological gap between the two main phases of Hunnic intrusion into Europe must have been the need to build up geographical knowledge about the new possibilities that opened up for them after they had displaced Goths and Alans from regions north of the Black Sea. From this perspective, the massive Hunnic raid launched into the Roman and Persian Empires through the Caucasus in 395 can be seen as part of a learning curve. This caused huge disruption and attracted a great deal of coverage in Roman sources, not least because one group of raiders even got close to the Holy Land. But the raiders suffered heavy losses, and the experiment was never repeated.[17] This does not suggest that the Huns themselves viewed the raid as a major success, and its relative failure may well have played a role in their eventual decision to move further west on to the Hungarian Plain rather than in any other direction. The knowledge of European geography necessary to make this move was no doubt also built up from feedback from the activities of smaller Hunnic groups we find west of the Carpathians before 405 – some of the mercenaries employed there in the 380s, for instance, or indeed the Huns of Uldin.

As has been observed in so many other cases, moreover, the

process of migration triggered major sociopolitical restructuring among the Huns. When Olympiodorus visited them in 411/12 he encountered, as we have just seen, a political structure based on a series of ranked kings, which was highly appropriate for a nomadic society. Economic logistics require nomad populations to be relatively dispersed. Bunched populations with herds would quickly lead to exhausted grazing and economic disaster. At the same time, subgroups need their own organization for matters such as settling disputes, and the larger group has to be able to act decisively as one on occasion, above all to protect the grazing rights upon which all depend. Well-organized devolution rather than centralized rule is a natural political form for nomadic societies, therefore, and a kingly hierarchy fits the bill nicely.[18]

But when a second east Roman historian and diplomat – the famous Priscus – visited the Huns in the mid-440s in the time of Attila, the system of ranked kings had disappeared. Attila was surrounded by many great men, and although he had originally shared power with his brother, there were no other individuals of royal rank to be seen. No source records how the system of ranked kings was swept away, but one major bone of diplomatic contention between Attila and Constantinople was the protection it accorded to Hunnic fugitives of prominence.[19] I take it, therefore, that Attila's line, at the latest in the time of his uncle Rua who was active in the 430s, had ousted and/or demoted the other kings – a political process we have already observed among Alaric's Goths, and will observe again among the Ostrogoths and Merovingian Franks.

This all relates to migration, and for the following reasons. What went on in these cases, in broad terms, was that one leader came to monopolize the political support that used to be divided between several. This requires the successful leader to have access to unprecedented wealth so as to outbid his rivals in the patronage stakes and win over enough of their supporters, in the process forcing them either to leave the group or to accept more junior, non-royal positions. In the case of the Huns, the source of that new wealth was the profits that flowed from the new relationships they were able to develop with the Roman Empire. Putting yourself by hook or by crook in charge of distributing the combined profits flowing from a potent mixture of raiding, mercenary service and diplomatic subsidy was the shortest path to political triumph. Although this was surely not one of its envisaged aims, Hunnic migration to the Middle Danube naturally brought political revolution in its wake.

In the qualitative sense used in migration studies, therefore, there is not the slightest doubt that the Huns' intrusion into Europe in the later fourth and early fifth centuries must be considered mass migration. It was a flow of gradually increasing momentum, not a sudden, single migratory pulse, but the political shocks the Huns inflicted north of the Black Sea, and then in central Europe, could not be more obvious. Just as powerful, indeed, was the shock that eventually swept away their own political structures. Further analysis is limited by our inability to identify the precise trigger that set the Huns in motion. Roman sources highlight random chance, telling a charming story of wandering hunters who blundered though marshes, then to emerge into a land of plenty, but this is only a story and one based – again, like most of Ammianus' digressions – on classical antecedent.[20] In the absence of any other information, though, it may well be correct in suggesting that it was the wealth of the Roman Empire's periphery that first sucked in the Hunnic raiders, and that migration momentum built up slowly from that point. New information on climate change or on political developments may transform this view in due course, making us redistribute the emphases we presently place on the various factors involved, but for the moment, the attractions of the wealthy imperial periphery seem the best option.

Hunnic-era migration affected not just the Huns themselves, however, but also the many and varied peoples who made up Attila's Empire. Everything suggests that the migratory motivations and processes that brought so many others to the Middle Danube in the period of Hunnic domination were very different from those of the Huns themselves.

## TRIBAL GATHERING

Among Attila's non-Hunnic subjects, Gepids, Sueves and Sarmatians had already occupied lands in the Middle Danube in the fourth century, long before the Huns arrived in Europe. Sueves and Sarmatians appear in Ammianus' account of the Emperor Constantius II's intervention in the region in 358, and Gepids are mentioned in other sources as inhabiting lands to the north-west of the old Roman province of Dacia (modern Romania) on the region's eastern fringes. Their presence in the Middle Danube in the time of Attila is entirely unremarkable. The same is not true, however, of most of the other non-Hunnic components of Attila's Empire. The fourth-century territories of Goths and Alans certainly lay east, not west, of the Carpathians, as probably did those of the Heruli, Rugi and Sciri. The best geographical fix we have for any of these latter three concerns the Heruli, who, though unmentioned in fourth-century sources, certainly occupied land north of the Black Sea in the third. The evidence for the Sciri is not so explicit, but in c.380, when the group name first appears in Roman sources, Sciri mixed with Huns attacked across Rome's Lower – not Middle – Danubian frontier, which implicitly places them to the east of the Carpathians. We have no explicit information for the Rugi from the third or fourth centuries, but they had, like the Goths, formed part of the Wielbark system in the first and second. When we find them, again alongside Goths, in the Middle Danube region in the fifth century, this raises the distinct possibility that they ended up there via a Gothic-style trajectory heading south-east to the Black Sea in the third.[21] So like the Goths and Alans, Sciri, Rugi and Heruli had probably all moved west of the Carpathians into the Middle Danube basin only at some point in the late fourth or early fifth century.

We have rather more information, in fact, about the Gothic contingent within Attila's Empire. It came in a number of separate groups. One was dominated by the Amal family and their rivals, and rose to prominent independence in contemporary sources from the early 460s. A second was led in the mid-460s by a man called Bigelis, while a third remained under the tight control of Attila's son Dengizich until the later 460s. Some of these Gothic groups may, like that of Radagaisus in 405, have moved into the Middle Danube region before the Huns established their dominance there in c.410. Others may have been moved there by the Huns at the height of their power. Still others perhaps followed a different trajectory. According to Jordanes, the Amal-led Goths moved west of the Carpathians only after the death of Attila in the mid- to late 450s, although they had acknowledged his overlordship in the 440s.[22] Aside from all the migration implicit in the story, the Gothic evidence thus has a further dimension of importance. It warns us that each of the Hunnic subjects named in the sources may in fact have operated in a number of independent contingents, and that the history of their transfer west into the Middle Danube region may have been correspondingly complex.

If the rise of Hunnic power, on the face of it, involved a great deal of human displacement into the Middle Danube, its unravelling generated an even longer procession of comings and goings. Prominent among the early departures was that of the Huns themselves. As more and more of Attila's former subjects established their independence after the victory of the Gepids at the battle of the Nedao, where the chapter began, the military potential of the Hunnic Empire declined drastically and suddenly, to the extent that by the later 460s the two surviving sons of Attila – Dengizich and Hernac – concluded that life north of the Danube had become too precarious. They therefore sought new lands inside the eastern Roman Empire. Hernac was well received, obtaining land for himself and his followers in Scythia Minor, but Dengizich was defeated and killed by an east Roman army in 469, and his head put on display in Constantinople. By 470, within seventeen years of Attila's death, the Huns had ceased to exist as an independent force in the trans-Danubian world: an astonishingly dramatic passage of history. And, in fact, the decisions of Dengizich and Hernac to move south of the Danube had been prefigured by some other refugees just a little earlier. Different sources record the intrusions on to east Roman soil, in or around 466, of another Hunnic group led by a certain Hormidac, and a Gothic one led by Bigelis.[23] The circumstances are not known in any detail, but these moves clearly belong to that period when different population fragments originating from Attila's Empire were looking to escape the fighting in the Middle Danube region.

Not that the demographic history of the Middle Danube after Attila's death was all about emigration. According to our one connected account of the action, provided by Jordanes writing in Constantinople in c.550 AD, it was only at this point – in the mid-450s – that the Amal-led Gothic group moved west of the Carpathians, under the leadership of a certain Valamer. The story was probably first written down at the court of Valamer's nephew, Theoderic, King of Ostrogothic Italy in the 520s, however, and Theoderic, born in the mid-450s was over seventy at this point, which does increase the story's credibility. But Jordanes shows some uncertainty about Valamer's early career (which we will come to later), so a degree of doubt must remain.[24] But if the Amal-led Goths were new arrivals, this might explain why the struggles of the 460s seem to have taken the form of the other occupants of the Middle Danubian region – particularly Sciri, Sueves, Rugi and Gepids – all allying against them. Be that as it may, the net outcome of the struggle was more emigration. Not only was their failure to control this competitive conflict the fundamental cause of the Huns' decision to seek asylum in the Roman Empire, but, very much in the same spirit, substantial numbers of Sciri, most famously Odovacar son of their defeated king Edeco, made their way into the west Roman Empire in the aftermath of a second major defeat by the Amal-led Goths in 469/70. Next to leave the region were the Goths themselves. Having – again according to Jordanes – defeated a coalition of their rivals in a bloody battle beside yet another unknown river in Pannonia, the Bolia, the Amal-led Goths moved into the east Roman Balkans in 473/4. This inaugurated a fifteen-year Balkan interlude during which Theoderic came to power. He succeeded his father Thiudimer, who had inherited control of the group when his brother Valamer was killed in an earlier battle against the Sciri. The Goths' Balkan sojourn eventually came to an end in the autumn of 488, when Theoderic's followers marched into Italy to create the Ostrogothic kingdom.[25]

Not even the eclipse of the Huns, the destruction of the Sciri and the departure of the Goths were enough to end the struggle for mastery in the Middle Danube. By 473/4, three main powers were left in the region: the Rugi, Heruli and Gepids. The next major casualty was the kingdom of the Rugi. Settled north of the Danube opposite the former Roman province of Noricum in what is now lower Austria, the Rugi incurred the wrath of Odovacar, ruler of Italy from 476. In 486, he sent a major expedition north of the Danube which heavily defeated them and killed their king, Feletheus. This was the end of an independent Rugi kingdom, though a body of survivors under Feletheus' son Frederic fled south into the Balkans to attach themselves to the following of Theoderic the Amal in 487/8. They subsequently joined in the Ostrogothic trek to Italy.[26]

The demise of the kingdom of the Rugi left the Heruli and Gepids as the major powers in the Middle Danube, but now Lombard groups from Bohemia and the Middle Elbe began to move south into the region, initially into the lands previously dominated by the Rugi. In the first century AD, the heartlands of the Lombards were located in the Lower Elbe region, just south of the Jutland peninsula. The surviving written accounts of the intervening trek, which brought them to Lower Austria by the later fifth (Map 10), were written down only in the ninth century (hundreds of years afterwards) and are full of the kind of fanciful details that make it clear that no authoritative intermediate historical record underlies them. The first secure date we have for the Lombards' progress south is provided by Roman sources, and comes with their entry into Lower Austria in 488/9 to take advantage of the power vacuum created by Odovacar's destruction of the Rugi. Once there, Lombard power increased in two perceptible stages. In 508, first of all, their forces crushed the Heruli. The same late literary sources also report that the remnants of the Sueves were defeated and forced out of the Middle Danubian region at much the same time. The second extension of Lombard power came with the occupation of the old Roman province of Pannonia, south of the Danube. We are so badly informed that this may have occurred as early as the 520s or as late as the 540s, but the overall pattern is clear enough. Trickling in from regions along the Elbe, and most immediately from Bohemia, the Lombards made themselves the dominant power in the western half of the Middle Danube region by the second quarter of the sixth century.[27] The Gepids, established further east, were now their great rivals.

As for the Heruli, defeat in 508 caused an immediate split in their ranks. One subgroup moved away from the Danube altogether, ending up far to the north, in Scandinavia. A second sought refuge first among the Gepids. But the demands placed upon them by their hosts proved too heavy, and they quickly found an alternative sanctuary inside the eastern Empire, where the Emperor Anastasius granted them land on the Danube, sometime early in the 510s. There they stayed until the 540s, when the last surviving member of their royal clan died. Somehow they knew that the other group of Heruli had ended up in Scandinavia, and sent a mission there to find a suitable prince. It took so long to return, however, not least because the first-choice candidate died en route back to the Danube, that the Emperor Justinian had picked out, at their own request, a new ruler for the remainder in the meantime. Civil war broke out when the Scandinavian mission finally returned, and the Danubian Heruli split again. One force remained inside the eastern Empire, the other returned to the Gepids. And in a subsequent war between the Lombards and Gepids, the Byzantines sent some of their remaining Heruli as military support for the Lombards. At that point, they found themselves up against their former comrades, who were fighting for the Gepids.[28]

The fate of the Heruli, however, is no more than an appendix. With the rise of Lombard power, the revolution in the Middle Danube set in train by the rise of Hunnic power had finally worked itself out. An extremely complicated process in detail, it stretched out over pretty much a century, from the first arrival of the Huns west of the Carpathians in perhaps 410 AD to the defeat of the Heruli in 508. There is, however, an apparent logic to these events as they are reported in our various sources, which saw, first, a massing of militarized manpower on the Middle Danubian Plain orchestrated by the Huns, followed by an extended struggle for pre-eminence amongst their subject peoples after Attila's death. Several of the combatant powers left the region as these struggles unfolded, so that the pattern of Middle Danubian affairs in the Hunnic era – many powers in close proximity to one another – eventually gave way in the sixth century to a division between Lombard and Gepid spheres of influence. Our primary interest, however, is in the migratory activity associated with these processes: largely, immigration into the region as Hunnic power increased, followed by emigration after Attila's death, although the Amal-led Goths (possibly) and the Lombards (certainly) provide significant exceptions.[29] That there was some movement of population would be denied by no one. Its nature and scale, however, are hotly contested.

In traditional accounts of these events, the labels used in our sources – Goths, Rugi, Heruli, Sciri and so forth – were conceived of as belonging to 'peoples': as noted earlier, by this was meant compact masses of humanity comprising men, women and children, all of whom shared distinct cultural norms and who were, by and large, closed to outsiders, generally reproducing themselves by marriage within the group. The different phases of migratory activity associated with the rise and fall of Attila's Hunnic Empire could thus be characterized, literally, as part of the *Völkerwanderung*: the 'movement of peoples'. The historical evidence for most of these moves, however, is quite pathetic. Roman historians' accounts of barbarian migration leave much to be desired, as we have seen, even when those migrations directly affected the Roman world. Most of the population movements associated with the Hunnic Empire unfolded outside Rome's borders, and detailed evidence is correspondingly sparse. Often we have nothing more than a bare indication that group A moved from point X to point Y, and sometimes even this much is implicit, with no account at all of the composition of the population unit involved.

In the face of so much resounding silence, any estimate of the scale and nature of the action involved in these population moves – or, to be absolutely precise for a minute, recorded shifts in *names* – is going to depend on your general understanding of the nature of the groups behind the labels. This means in turn that the issue of migration within the Hunnic Empire is intimately linked to the hotly contested issue of barbarian group identity. If you think labels hide population units each with a substantial sense of group identity, then your estimate of the amount of migration flowing on to and out of the Great Hungarian Plain between c.410 and 508 will be correspondingly large. If group identities are perceived, on the contrary, as no more than a set of labels which barbarian populations could adopt or jettison according to short-term convenience, then the movement of these labels around the map of Europe need mean very little in demographic terms. Probably not nothing, since somebody has to move for a label to shift. But there would be no need to envisage large numbers of people on the move. If the label 'worked' (that is, performed a function that people found useful), new recruits could quickly be assembled at their point of destination by the few who did move. What, then, does the evidence suggest about the solidity or otherwise of group identities in the age of Attila?

## EMPIRE AND IDENTITY

In his eyewitness account of an embassy to the Huns, the historian Priscus tells how, in Attila's camp, he was suddenly hailed in Greek by someone who looked like a prosperous Hun 'with good clothing and his hair clipped all around'. On further inquiry, the man told Priscus his life story:

He was a Greek-speaking Roman merchant from Viminacium, a city on the river Danube . . .

When the city was captured by the barbarians, he was deprived of his prosperity and . . . assigned to Onegesius [one of Attila's leading henchmen], for after Attila the leading men . . . chose their captives from the well-to-do. Having proven his valour in later battles against the Romans and the Akatziri and having, according to [Hunnic] law, given his booty to his master, he had won his freedom. He had married a barbarian wife and had children, and, as a sharer of the table of Onegesius, he now enjoyed a better life than he had before.

This Roman merchant turned Hunnic warrior provides a textbook illustration of a major trend in current thinking about group identities in Attila's Empire: they were highly malleable. There is another important individual case history suggesting much the same. Odovacar's father Edeco (if, as seems likely, the two Edecos are the same man) is first met as another of Attila's chief henchmen, alongside the Onegesius whose patronage was so important to the ex-Greek merchant. What's so exciting about Edeco is that he became king of the Sciri after Attila's death, even though he himself was not one. He probably owed his claim to the throne to having married a high-born Scirian lady, since his children, Odovacar and Onoulphous, are said to have had a Scirian mother. But Edeco himself is dubbed variously a Hun or a Thuringian. What these two case histories suggest, of course, is that Attila's Empire was a melting-pot for pre-existing group identities, and the argument can be bolstered with more general evidence. Many of Attila's leading henchmen had in fact Germanic not Hunnic names. Onegesius and Edeco certainly did, while two others, Berichus and Scottas, probably did. The recorded names for Attila and his brother Bleda are also Germanic, which, we know, operated as the lingua franca of Attila's Empire because so many Germani were included within the numbers of its subjects that they massively outnumbered any Hunnic core.[30] All the historical evidence thus suggests that the Middle Danubian world of the Huns was deeply multicultural.

Its archaeological remains tell a similar story. Nearly two generations of work since 1945 have unearthed a vast mass of material dating to the period of Hunnic domination, largely from cemetery excavations on the Great Hungarian Plain. There are some treasure hoards as well. But in this material, 'proper' Huns have proved highly elusive. In total – and this includes the Volga steppe north of the Black Sea – archaeologists have identified no more than two hundred burials as plausibly Hunnic. These are distinguished by some combination of bows, a non-standard European mode of dress, some cranial deformation (some Huns bound the heads of babies, before the skull set into shape, to give a distinctive elongated shape to the head), and the presence of a particular type of cauldron. The number of such burials is tiny. Either the Huns generally disposed of their dead in ways that left no archaeological trace, or some other explanation is required for the profound scarcity of Hunnic material. What these fifth-century Middle Danubian cemeteries have produced in abundance, however, are the remains – or what *look* like the remains – of the Huns' Germanic subjects. The reasons for labelling the material Germanic are as follows. Its characteristic features all have close antecedents in norms operating among Gothic- and other Germanic-dominated areas in central and eastern Europe in the late Roman period, before the Huns arrived. These fifth-century finds belong to a sequence of dated chronological horizons, which, between them, mark the emergence of what has been christened the 'Danubian style' of Germanic burial.[31]

The funerary pattern was inhumation rather than cremation,[32] its characteristic objects being deposited in large quantities in a relatively restricted number of rich burials. Many other individuals were buried with few or no gravegoods. The range of objects included items of personal adornment: particularly large semicircular brooches, plate buckles, earrings with polyhedric pendants, and gold necklaces. Weapons and military equipment are also quite common: saddles with metal appliqués, long straight swords suitable for cavalry use, and arrows. The remains also show up some odd ritual quirks. It became fairly common, for instance, to bury broken metallic mirrors with the dead. The kinds of items found in the graves, the ways in which people were buried and, perhaps above all, the way in which particularly women wore their clothes (gathered with a safety pin – *fibula* – on each shoulder, and another closing their outer garment in front), all follow on directly from general patterns observable in Germanic remains of the fourth century. These traits were then pooled and developed further in the fifth among the massed ranks of Attila's subjects. As a result, it is not possible to tell the Huns' different Germanic subjects apart on the basis of archaeological remains alone.[33] Like the personal histories of the merchant and Edeco, the broadly spread, individually indistinguishable material culture of the Germanic component to Attila's Empire suggests that we are looking at a cultural melting-pot. The melting may even have gone one stage further. One *possible* answer to the lack of Hunnic burials in the fifth century is that they had begun to dress like their Germanic subject peoples, just as they obviously learned their language.

There is no doubt, then, that within Attila's Empire individuals, probably in large numbers, were busy renegotiating their identities as part of their attempt to navigate their way to prosperity, as political conditions and opportunities changed around them. For some scholars, indeed, the historical and archaeological evidence has suggested that group identities within this multicultural Empire were infinitely malleable. Essentially, everyone drawn into the Hunnic orbit in the late fourth and early fifth centuries became fully fledged Huns. The original nomad core and the largely Germanic-speaking contingents who bulked out the manpower of Attila's Empire all came to share fully in the same Hunnic group identity and then, after Attila's death, they renegotiated their identities a second time to form the various groups who emerged to independence in the 450s and 460s.[34] I have no doubt that this model works in the case of some individuals and groups, but it completely ignores a substantial body of historical evidence showing that the structures of the Hunnic Empire imposed distinct limits on the extent to which individuals could adopt the group identity of their choice, which might have given them the greatest material prosperity available to them.

To start with, it's worth thinking a bit more about Priscus' Greek merchant. His route to success came through serving his new master successfully in battle, using the booty he won to buy his freedom. And although plenty of booty was certainly being won during Attila's successful campaigns of the 440s, you do have to wonder how many Roman prisoners are likely to have done so well. The answer surely has to be not that many. Unless Onegesius kept a truly enormous table, there cannot have been room at it for many favoured ex-prisoners, and how many martially inexperienced Roman prisoners are likely to have been skilful and lucky enough to thrive in battle? Much less quoted is another of Priscus' anecdotes. This concerns the fate of two other prisoners, likewise drafted into military service under the Huns, who took the opportunity of the chaos of battle to settle some old scores by killing their master. They were gibbeted.[35] I suspect this less harmonious state of affairs is more likely to have prevailed among the majority of master–slave relationships than the happy outcome enjoyed by Priscus' merchant.

All these anecdotes, moreover, concern Romans taken as individual prisoners. Most of Attila's non-Hunnic contingents were incorporated into the Empire in rather larger population blocks. A large body of historical evidence indicates that, for these, the prevailing pattern of relations was much less conducive to easy, large-scale changes of identity. First, the Hunnic Empire was not something that people joined voluntarily. Evidence for this is plentiful and consistent. Non-Huns became part of the Empire through conquest and intimidation. This was certainly true of the Akatziri, for instance, who became the Huns' latest victims in the time of Attila. There was some diplomatic manoeuvring, but the bottom line was unequivocal: 'Attila without delay sent a large force, destroyed some, and forced the rest to submit.' It was to avoid a similar fate, of course, that the Tervingi and Greuthungi had come to the Danube in the summer of 376. Indeed, all of our evidence indicates that the ranks of Attila's subjects were filled not with volunteers, but with those who had failed to get out of the way in time.[36] This immediately suggests that relations between the Huns and their subjects are unlikely to have been that harmonious. The point is confirmed by the broader run of evidence.

Crucial to any understanding of the Hunnic Empire is the fact that it was inherently unstable. This tends to receive little scholarly attention because most of our descriptive source material is provided by Priscus, writing about its apogee under Attila in the 440s. If you cast your net a little wider, however, the evidence for instability mounts quickly. Because so many of the Huns' subjects were unwilling participants in the Hunnic Empire, the Romans were able consistently to reduce its power by detaching subject peoples from it, many of whom were more than ready to take the opportunity to escape. By losing some of his subjects, of course, was precisely how Uldin had been defeated in 408/9, but in that case we don't know whether it was the fault-line between Hunnic masters and non-Hunnic subjects that was being exploited.

Other evidence is much clearer. In the 420s, for instance, the east Romans stripped away a large body of Goths from Hunnic control when they expelled the Huns from parts of Pannonia. The Goths were transferred to Thrace and seem to have served loyally thereafter in the east Roman military.[37] On other occasions, the subjects took the initiative themselves:

> When Rua was king of the Huns, the Amilzuri, Itimari, Tounsoures, Boisci and other tribes who were living near to the Danube were fleeing to fight on the side of the Romans.[38]

These events date to the later 430s, after Rua, Attila's uncle, had already achieved considerable success, but even that success and their shares in all the booty that followed in its wake were insufficient inducement to guarantee the subjects' quiescence. As might anyway be expected, the beginning of a new reign was a moment of particular stress:

> When [at the start of their reign c.440] they had made peace with the Romans, Attila, Bleda and their forces marched through Scythia subduing the tribes there and also made war on the Sorogsi.[39]

Reasserting your overlordship over subject groups, once you had established yourself as number one Hun, was probably a basic necessity for any new ruler. So much so, in fact, that, when they could, Hunnic leaders tried to ensure that no Romans would be able to stir up trouble for them. In the first treaty they made with Constantinople, Attila and Bleda forced the east Romans to agree that '[they] should make no alliance with a barbarian people against the Huns when the latter were preparing for war against them'.[40]

The massive internal conflicts let loose after Attila's death between the Huns and their subject peoples were not a one-off exception, therefore, but illustrative of a much deeper structural problem within the Hunnic Empire. The picture of internal peace and quiet you get from Priscus' embassy to Attila is deeply misleading. The Empire was created by conquest, maintained by intimidation, and the only way to leave it, as the narrative of events after Attila's death makes clear, was to fight your way out.

Much of the explanation of why there should have been this enduring hostility between rulers and ruled emerges from a further fragment of Priscus' History dealing with Dengizich's last attack on the east Roman Empire in 467/8, almost twenty years after the historian visited the court of Attila. This records how the separate contingents in a mixed force of Goths and Huns was brought to blows by a Roman agent provocateur. He did so by reminding the Gothic contingent of exactly how the Huns generally behaved towards them:

> These men have no concern for agriculture, but, like wolves, attack and steal the Goths' food supplies, with the result that the latter remain in the position of slaves and themselves suffer food shortages.[41]

Taking their food supplies was, of course, only part of the story. The subject peoples were also used to fight the Huns' wars. While Priscus' merchant-turned-Hun certainly prospered, his is likely to have been a minority story. As noted already, few civilian Roman prisoners are likely to have been much use when it came to fighting, and their casualties when they were used for Hunnic campaigns are likely to have been frightful. For most people, the reality of becoming part of the Hunnic Empire was a nasty experience of military conquest followed by economic exploitation, spiced up from time to time by being marched out to fight Attila's wars.

Equally to the point – and this is where it differed so markedly from the Roman Empire – the Hunnic Empire lacked the governmental capacity to run the affairs of its subject peoples at all closely. Famously, the Hunnic bureaucracy consisted of one Roman secretary supplied by Aetius, the de facto ruler of the western Empire, and a Roman prisoner who could write letters in Latin and Greek. What this meant in practice is that, once conquered, subject groups still had to be left largely to run their own day-to-day affairs themselves. This does not mean that everything carried on absolutely as before. For instance, after conquering the Akatziri, Attila appointed one of his own sons to oversee their surviving chiefs, having eliminated several who resisted him. Likewise, while the Goths who provided part of Dengizich's invasion force in 467/8 – referred to in the fragment quoted above – still had their own chiefs; they possessed no overall ruler. Given that all the independent Gothic groups we know of between the third and the fifth centuries had a pre-eminent ruler, even where power was shared between, for instance, brothers (as with, initially, the Amal-led Goths), this strongly suggests that Hunnic supervision often involved preventing the emergence of overall rulers among the larger concentrations of their defeated subjects.[42] The point of such a stratagem would have been exactly the same for the Huns as it had earlier been for the Romans, when they operated it against the Alamanni outside the

Empire, or in the 382 treaty against the Goths within. If you suppress an overall leader, you stimulate political competition within a group, and lessen the possibility of it mounting effective resistance.

Similar conclusions are also suggested by the political history of the Amal-led Goths. Stories preserved by Jordanes suggest that Valamer did not inherit his pre-eminence over them, but had positively to create it by suppressing rival warband leaders, and attaching, where possible, the followings of those whom he had defeated to his own power base. The stories are undated, but it seems more likely that this happened after Attila's death than before it, since it created precisely the problem that Hunnic management strategies seem designed to avoid: a Gothic group powerful enough to act with independence. It was only after such a unification that these Goths had sufficient power either to invade the Middle Danube region or ask Constantinople to recognize their independence.[43] And if what was true of the Goths was the case more generally among the Huns' subjects, this would also explain why the Sciri had to find themselves a king from among Attila's leading henchmen as Hunnic power collapsed.

Looking past the image of Attila in all his pomp, then, we can begin to understand the inherent instability of his Empire. Unlike that of Rome, which spent centuries turning subjects – or at least their landowning elites – into fully fledged Roman citizens, dissipating thereby the original tensions of conquest, the Huns lacked the bureaucratic capacity to run their subjects directly. I suspect, in fact, that the actual extent of Hunnic dominion and interference varied substantially between groups. The Gepids seem already to have had an overall leader at the time of Attila's death, for instance, which probably explains why they were the first to assert independence. Other groups, like the Amal-led Goths, had to throw up an overall leader in the mid- to late 450s before they could begin to challenge Hunnic hegemony; and still others, like the Goths still dominated by Dengizich in 468, never managed to do so.[44]

If the sources were better, the narrative progression would probably show the Hunnic Empire peeling apart like an onion after 453, with different layers of subject groups asserting their independence at different moments, in an inverse relationship to the level of domination the Huns had previously been exercising over their lives. Two key variables – and they may well have been related – were probably, first, the extent to which the subjects' political structure had been left intact, and, second, the distance separating them from the heartland of the Empire, where Attila maintained the camps at which he was visited by Priscus' embassy. Some groups, settled in close proximity to the camps, were kept under tight rein, with any propensity to unified leadership among them strongly suppressed. Others, settled at a greater distance, preserved more of their own political structures and were much less closely controlled. By the time of Attila, Franks and Akatziri defined the geographical extremes. We hear of Attila attempting to interfere in one Frankish succession dispute, so that even the northern Rhine was not completely beyond his compass, and the Akatziri were established somewhere north of the Black Sea. In between, various groups of Thuringians, Goths, Gepids, Suevi, Sciri, Heruli, Sarmatians and Alans were all, if to differing degrees, dancing to Attila's tune.[45]

One other possible complicating factor is worth raising. We have no detailed information for the Empire of Attila, but a trustworthy Byzantine source gives us interesting information about some of the gradations of status that operated in the analogous Empire of the nomadic Avars, two centuries later. This tells the story of a group of east Roman prisoners who were originally dragged north from their homes and resettled as Avar slaves around the old Roman city of Sirmium. Over time, they were raised to free, but still subordinate, status within the Empire and granted their own political leadership.[46] It is important not to narrow unduly the range of allowed possibility just because we lack sources of similar quality. Attila's Empire may have been articulated in a similar way, with intermediate statuses between fully fledged Hun and Hunnic slave. It should be emphasized, however, that even their subsequent promotion did not give the captives and their descendants enough of a stake in the Avar enterprise to want to remain part of it unconditionally. When the opportunity to break away from Avar control arose, they took it.

All of this has strong implications for the operation of group identities within the Hunnic Empire. They were not unchanging. Priscus' former Greek merchant shows that it was possible for particularly successful individual slaves to rise to full free status among the Huns – that is, to pass across pre-existing divides in status and identity. But the original Hunnic core was itself at this time experiencing substantial changes in group identity. I mentioned earlier that as far as we can tell, its original identity was based on immediate loyalty to a series of ranked kings, whose association created the larger group, but

these lower-level identities were swept away by the political restructuring that came with the rise of the dynasty of Rua and Attila. This
kind of process affected other, better-documented nomad groups as
they too worked their way to the western edge of the Eurasian steppe
and beyond. The so-called Seljuk Turks of the eleventh century, for
instance, were not a long-standing political entity, but a large body of
nomadic Turkic-speakers united – temporarily – behind the astonishingly successful Seljuk leadership clan, who eclipsed potential rivals
while conquering much of the Near East.[47] But while dramatic, such a
political process has a strong tendency to generate winners and losers
even within its core supporters, which perhaps explains why we have
indications that some Hunnic groups preferred, as the Empire began
to collapse, to throw in their lot with leaders other than the sons of
Attila.

Even more dramatic was the restructuring experienced by at least
some of the Huns' subjects. Their new overlords interfered pretty
consistently at the top end of the political spectrum, suppressing the
overall leadership structures of some of their more tightly governed
subjects. Attila seems to have recruited aides from a variety of
backgrounds, part of whose job may well have been to supervise the
subject groups – whose status, as we have seen, is likely to have
varied, although we lack detailed evidence from the time of the Huns
themselves. This sort of approach was only sensible. Running an
empire composed largely of more or less autonomous subjects, Attila
needed loyal subordinates to run their affairs or to supervise those
doing the running. The same kind of strategy is suggested by finds
of gold in the archaeological horizons associated with the Empire at
its height. Gold has been found in relatively vast quantities, but even
this probably represents only a fraction of what was originally deposited. How much has been found and recycled over the centuries by
intervening occupants of the Hungarian Plain is impossible to know.
Gold, it should be stressed, is a rare find in Germanic archaeological
remains before the Hunnic period, so the amount of new wealth that
became available as Attila ransacked the Roman world can hardly be
overstressed. Alongside military domination, then, he clearly also used
the distribution of booty captured in his campaigns against the Romans
to give subject leaders a further incentive to consent to his rule, just as
the Romans granted annual gifts even to barbarian leaders they had
just defeated or otherwise subdued.[48]

But while the dense concentrations of military manpower gathered there from all corners of the barbarian, especially the Germanic-speaking, world turned the Great Hungarian Plain into a cultural crucible, it also put barriers in the way of a total dissolution of larger-scale group identities. The whole point for the Huns in conquering Goths, Gepids, Heruli and others was to turn them into subjects whose military and economic potential could be harnessed and exploited. If they were all allowed to become fully fledged free Huns like the former Roman merchant, then the treatment meted out to them, as they acquired such privileges, would have had to change for the better, just as his did. And as it did so, the overall benefit to the Huns from their initial conquests would have been lost. The Hunnic Empire was certainly multicultural, but, as is often the case in multicultural societies, this did not mean that group identities within it were either infinitely malleable or easily eroded. Because being a Hun meant higher status, the Empire's multicultural character effectively erected barriers around Hunnic identity. The Huns' lack of bureaucratic capacity left their subjects with at least their intermediate leaderships intact, thereby perpetuating the structures around which their existing sense of group identity might survive. At the same time, the exploitation they had to endure gave them the incentive to maintain these identities, since they were the only vehicle through which they might be able to overthrow Hunnic domination, either by escaping into the Roman Empire or at some point regaining their political independence by force. Neither of these options would be possible for a group that fragmented and lost all capacity for group action. There is every reason, then, why old identities should not have slipped easily away under Hunnic rule.

Nor, it must be stressed, is the view of the Hunnic Empire which emerges from the historical evidence – one riven with internal tension between ruler and ruled – remotely contradicted by the archaeological evidence, even if you do take the view that the Huns' invisibility stems from their having started to bury their dead in ways previously associated with their Germanic subjects. When it comes to archaeological evidence, in fact, a degree of methodological confusion sometimes prevails. Everyone is now clear, in an intellectual world that has moved on from culture history, that individual groups cannot be assumed to have each had their own distinctive material cultures. But it is sometimes assumed that if a regionally distributed material culture does not show up any very clear differences, then there can't have been any clear distinctions of identity within it. This, however, is just an inverse application of the old mistaken assumption behind culture history: that distinct groups should have distinct material cultures. If you can't use differences within a regional pattern of material culture necessarily to talk about separate political identities, then equally you cannot use the lack of them to deny the possible existence of political distinctions. Identity is about mental and political structures – claims made by individuals and the willingness of groups to recognize those claims – not material cultural structures. This seriously limits the capacity of archaeological evidence to speak to identity debates, except in unusual circumstances, often when there is other information available about particular material items endowed with special significance. The fact that everyone within Hunnic Europe used broadly the same material culture does not mean that there were no crucial status divides or group identities operating within it.[49]

## Collapsing Identities

The narrative of the Hunnic Empire's collapse – complimenting the evidence for its creation and maintenance – confirms just how important these internal identities were, even if further reconfigurations were again part of the process. The Empire was destroyed from within, when its various subject peoples reasserted their independence militarily after Attila's death. If they had all been subsumed voluntarily into an equal Hunnic identity, why should this have happened? Acting collectively, they had been able to extract from the Roman Empire the huge sums of gold that show up in the Middle Danubian burials. This was a level of predation which, separately, they were quite unable to match, as is underlined both by the general absence of gold in earlier Germanic remains and the capacity of the east Roman Empire to rebuild its control of the Balkans in the later fifth century after Hun-inspired unity had collapsed.[50] Indeed, the energy the non-Huns put into escaping from Hunnic rule demonstrates beyond reasonable doubt that the lower status and the scope for exploitation inherent in their position meant that the costs for them of being part of the Empire were not generally compensated for by the gains flowing to some of them because of the greater predatory capacity generated by its exist-

1. The North European Plain is in extent the largest physical expanse of the European landmass. At the start of the first millennium, it was densely wooded and its heavy clay soils made life difficult for farmers lacking the right technology. By the year 1000, its massive economic potential was beginning to be realized for the first time.

2. The Great Eurasian Steppe reaching as far west as the east bank of the river Don, and in part beyond, marks the easternmost limit of where there is sufficient rainfall to make conventional farming possible without irrigation.

3. The Finnish Taiga forest marks the limit of conventional agriculture in north-eastern Europe. Winter cold and the poverty of a soil, not enriched by the build up of humus from deciduous plant life, make normal arable farming impossible.

4. One fourth-century village within the domain of the Tervingi was entirely devoted to the production of combs, and hairstyles sometimes played a key role in contemporary society. Frankish kings left their hair uncut as a sign of royal status and Tacitus tells us that some of the Suebi signalled their group identity by a knotted hairstyle, of which this extraordinary example has survived the intervening centuries.

5. The rain miracle of Marcus Aurelius. The emperor won a big enough victory over the disturbed tribes of central Europe in the so-called Marcomannic War to raise a column to mark his own success. Predatory expansion from the outer periphery towards the Roman frontier underlay these disturbances.

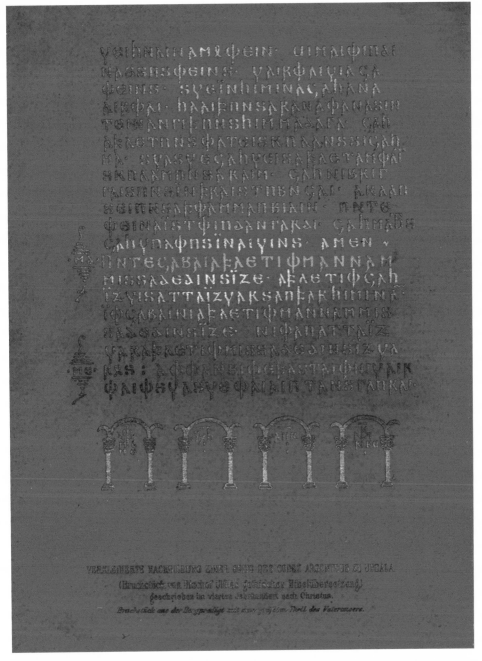

6. Ulfilas produced the first written form of a Germanic language in the fourth century to translate the Bible for Gothic converts. This stunning manuscript in purple, silver and gold was produced in sixth-century Italy at the court of Theoderic the Ostrogoth, but the translation remained substantially that of Ulfilas.

7. Even friendly barbarian kings were expected to prostrate themselves in the imperial presence, and prone barbarians were often portrayed visually, as here, to emphasize the majesty of a reigning emperor, protector of divinely ordained civilization against the barbarian menace.

8. Nothing better symbolizes the heightened threat of the revivified Persian Empire of the third century than this stunning rock relief of the captive Roman Emperor Valerian humiliated in the presence of Shapur I, Sasanian King of Kings. Persia's new power sucked resources eastwards and facilitated Germanic expansion around and across Rome's European frontiers.

9. In the 1830s Boer farmers, complete with families, possessions and animals, moved north from the Cape to escape British imperial control. When they encountered opposition, they reorganised themselves into groups large enough to destroy resistance, illustrating a form of predatory migration flow that is highly applicable to the first millennium AD.

10. The remarkably beautiful triple walls of Constantinople were constructed in the early 410s in response to the relocation of the Huns from north of the Black Sea to the heart of central Europe. The Huns were equally intimidating to many of those more directly in their path, who chose to move onto Roman soil in the period 405–8.

11. Unearthed in 1837, the Pietroasa treasure originally consisted of twenty-two items, but now only twelve survive. Shown here is the famous *patera*, a round sacrificial dish, modelled with Orphic figures surrounding a seated three-dimensional goddess in the centre. Originally attributed to Athanaric, leader of the fourth century Tervingi, it actually reflects the wealth ransacked by Attila from the Mediterranean world.

12. Hunnic treasures from the mid-fifth century Middle Danube. For the first time in this era, large amounts of gold appear regularly in burials from barbaricum. Shown here are items in the characteristic cloisonné style, with garnets (conveniently the colour of imperial purple) set individually in gold 'cells'. The wealth and art styles of Hunnic central Europe set new standards of display for Europe's barbarian elites.

13. Excavations in 1939 uncovered the probable burial ground of the Wuffingas: seventh-century kings of East Anglia. Though unrepresentative in the stunning quality of their craftmanship, the items from the famous ship burial are characteristic of the furnished burial habit which swept through central and eastern England in the fifth and sixth centuries.

14. Descended from a Carolingian copy of a late Roman bureaucratic manual, this page of the Bodleian library's beautiful copy of the *Notitia Dignitatum* illustrates some of the resources at the disposal of the Count of the Saxon shore for fending off the raiding threat to eastern Britain and the channel region posed by Saxons from across the North Sea in the fourth century.

ence. When the chance presented itself on Attila's death, a scramble for independence quickly followed.

Like their initial incorporation, the process of breaking away from Hunnic control involved further renegotiation of group identities. If all, or even many, of the denser concentrations of subjects had had their overall leaderships suppressed as part of their incorporation into the Hunnic Empire, then a rush for position and power of the kind that brought Edeco and the Sciri together would have ensued right across Attila's domain. And certainly, Valamer, as we have seen, had to unite what became the Amal-led Goths by defeating other dynasts, and may well have been recruiting non-Gothic manpower in addition. Aside from the large named population units that emerge as successor states to the Hunnic Empire in the later 450s and early 460s, many smaller groupings also figure fleetingly in our sources, like the Sorosgsi, Amilzuri, Itimari, Tounsoures and Boisci mentioned in different fragments of Priscus' history. Several of these found their way on to Roman soil as the Hunnic Empire collapsed, and something of the chaotic nature of the action as they were resettled by the Roman state is reflected in their subsequent line-up, as reported by Jordanes:

> The Sarmatians and the Cemandri and certain of the Huns dwelt in Castra Martis ... The Sciri together with the Sadagarii and certain of the Alani ... received Scythia Minor and Lower Moesia ... The Rugi, however, and some other races asked that they might inhabit Bizye and Arcadiopolis. Hernac, the younger son of Attila, with his followers, chose a home in the farthest reaches of Scythia Minor. Emnetzur and Ultzindur, kinsmen of his, won Oescus, Utus and Almus in Dacia.[51]

These groups were each assigned to just one or to a few Byzantine military bases in the northern Balkans, so none of them can have been particularly large. Similar groups, presumably, were also being subsumed into the bigger kingships which began to emerge from Hunnic imperial collapse. Among the descendants of Theoderic the Amal's following in Italy in the late 540s, for instance, were Bittigure Huns. These had previously been commandeered by the sons of Attila in the 460s to fight Theoderic's uncle Valamer, and must have renegotiated their political allegiance at some point in the meantime.[52] This could have happened on any number of occasions, of course, but the reshuffling of the Hunnic imperial pack in the aftermath of Attila's death is an obvious possibility.

In the slightly longer term and larger scale, this was very much the fate of the Rugi. They formed one of the initial successor kingdoms to the Hunnic Empire, but then threw in their lot with Theoderic after Odovacar had destroyed their independence. The Gepids and Lombards carried on this tradition of gathering fragments under their wing. Defeated Heruli joined the former (although, at first at least, they didn't like the terms they were offered), and by the time the Lombards left for Italy in the late 560s they took with them, according to Paul the Deacon, Sueves, Heruli, Gepids, Bavarians, Bulgars, Avars, Saxons, Goths and Thuringians. The first three names on this list, at least, represent human flotsam and jetsam from the post-Hunnic Middle Danube.[53] The adjustments in political identity involved in creating the successor kingdoms after Attila's death should not be underestimated. Some, perhaps all of them, were not culturally homogeneous groupings, closed to outsiders and replicating themselves over time through in-marriage, but new kingships stitched together out of a variety of remnants who shared a basic interest in breaking away from Hunnic control. Even the Gepids, who were seemingly less under the Hunnic cosh in Attila's lifetime and already had their own king, may have been picking up new recruits as the Empire collapsed. But this was all the more true of groups like the Sciri and Amal-led Goths, who found – or refound – their unity at this point, and it is entirely likely that others about whom we have no information – such as the Rugi, Sueves and Heruli – had equally messy origins.

Nor were these kingships 'peoples' in a second important sense of the term as it has traditionally been used. As we have seen, three hundred years of growing economic complexity had created, or greatly reinforced, social inequalities in the Germanic world. For the Amal-led Goths among Attila's former subjects, we have explicit evidence that this meant that their populations contained warriors of two unequal statuses, probably to be equated with freemen and freedmen. The same is true of the Lombards who intruded themselves into the Middle Danubian region in force only after Attila's sons had given up the struggle. When it comes to understanding group identity, this adds an important extra dimension. Only higher-status warriors benefited fully from the existence of the group to which they belonged, via the rights and privileges it conferred upon them, and only they can be supposed to have been completely committed to that group's identity. The significance of this shows up in the historical narratives. At one point, in the course of the Byzantine conquest of Ostrogothic Italy, all the higher-status warriors in a Gothic force in Dalmatia were killed. The remaining, lower-status, warriors immediately surrendered. And throughout Procopius' narrative of that war, losses among the higher-status group were a particular cause of alarm and despondency among the Goths.[54]

At least the bigger entities to emerge from the Hunnic Empire, then, were not 'peoples' in the traditional sense of the word. Neither culturally nor hierarchically homogeneous, they were a complex of political alliances and statuses that, as well as the two strands of militarized manpower, probably incorporated unarmed slaves. That said, it would not be right to go from one simplistic extreme to another: from the old view of these entities as entirely closed population groups, to the opposite – that they were mere flags of convenience with no internal structure or stability. This is not the place for a full discussion, but two important observations are worth making. First, group identities were not dependent on royal families, which, in one line of research, have been seen as providing social cement for highly disparate improvised groupings in the form of a mere pretence of ethnic belonging. The Lombards took kings from a variety of dynastic lines, not from one uniquely royal one, and even managed to continue to exist as Lombards without any kings at all in certain periods. This is a well-known point, but it has sometimes not been recognized that the Gothic evidence is much more similar than it initially appears to be. In the 520s, when he was seeking to secure the Italian throne for his minor grandson against a series of rivals – some from within the dynasty, some from without – Theoderic the Amal, Valamer's long-lived nephew, issued a huge amount of propaganda stressing that his was a uniquely royal line, the only one fitted to rule these Goths. Cassiodorus also helped him 'prove' the point from Gothic history, by producing a genealogy which showed that the grandson was the seventeenth generation of kingship within the family. But kings are always saying this kind of thing, and should not be believed, especially when, in this case, Theoderic's claims about the past do not hold up when compared with what can be learned from more contemporary sources. Cassiodorus' Amal genealogy, likewise, was cobbled together from a mixture of Gothic oral history and Roman written history, with touches of biblical inspiration thrown in. Amal domination had in fact been built up over these Goths in stages from as recently as c.450. Hence it ceases to surprise that, when Theoderic's line failed to produce a suitable male heir, it was simply axed: almost literally, when his nephew Theodahad was murdered for his leadership failings in 536, just a decade after the great king's death.[55]

Second, for all the messiness of the post-Attilan political process from which they emerged, some of these larger group identities were not so easy to destroy. Despite becoming part of Theoderic's following in 487/8, for instance, the Rugi maintained their independence over two further generations down to c.540, when they were still a recognizable entity in the Italian landscape. For all their travails and splits, likewise, the Heruli retained a significant sense of their group identity for another forty-odd years after their defeat at the hands of the Lombards in 508. Without it, they would never have sought a leader of the traditional ruling house from among those of their number who had moved north to Scandinavia.[56] To judge by their histories, both the Rugi and Heruli were 'medium-sized' entities. They were clearly not as militarily powerful, say, as the Gothic, Lombard or Gepid confederations which generated much longer-lived political entities, and into which elements of the Rugi and Heruli were eventually absorbed. In both cases, the evidence has been questioned. The mission of the Heruli to Scandinavia has been labelled a 'fairy story', and the resurfacing of the Rugi in 540 no more than an invention of the historian Procopius, who had – it is claimed – such a strong tendency to view any barbarian grouping as a 'people' that he ought not to believed. Both are stories recounted in detail in only the one source, and where that is the case, it is always possible to deny their validity. But is there any real substance to these arguments?

In my view, there isn't. In the case of the Heruli, the Scandinavian mission is told in great circumstantial detail in the middle of what adds up to a full account of their fortunes after their defeat by the Lombards. Other parts of this story are confirmed in other sources, and what Procopius describes, in total, is the effective destruction of Herulic identity. When two contingents of Heruli end up fighting each other, as they did in 549 when one was fighting for the Gepids and the other (via the east Roman Empire) for the Lombards, then you have to conclude that the Herule label had ceased to mean much as a determinant of human behaviour. The account is entirely plausible, there are no inconsistencies or obvious errors. There are of course other things one would like to know, but the narrative satisfies all the normal criteria for basic credibility that ancient and medieval historians usually employ. In the case of the Rugi, likewise, different sources record the extent to which they played an independent hand during Theoderic's conquest of Italy in the early 490s. They swapped sides twice in fact, first to join Odovacar and then going back to the Goths. So we should not wonder at finding them – or some of them – with their identity preserved for a further generation or so after the conquest of Italy.

The only reason to doubt either of these stories is that they fail to fit in with the preconceptions about identity held by the modern scholars doing the doubting. Heavily influenced by the ideas of Barth, both are proponents of the idea that Germanic groups of the mid-first millennium could not have had strong group identities. But Barth, as we have seen, represents only one strand in modern research into identity, which lends no overwhelming support to the preconception that group identities ought always to be highly malleable. According to circumstances – the precise nature of any individual situational construct – group identity can be weaker or stronger, and, in the case of the Rugi, Procopius even offers a mechanism as to how identity was maintained: namely, by a voluntary ban on marriage outside the group.[57] Given its coherence and detail, I am happy to accept what the evidence is telling us. The Heruli and Rugi probably were not 'peoples' in the classic nineteenth-century sense of the term. There is no evidence that either possessed within them strong cultural commonalities (though none either, to be fair, that they didn't), and they may have incorporated outsiders through various alliance systems as Attila's Empire broke up. They surely also, like all the other Germanic groups known from the period, incorporated strong status divides. But nonetheless they were bound by group identities capable of exercising a strong hold over significant numbers of their constituent populations.

And although you can more easily conceive of this being true among such smaller and less diverse groupings, it seems to have been true even of some of the larger group identities as well. When the Byzantines decided to conquer the Ostrogothic kingdom of Italy in 536, their arrival sparked a sequence of defections from subgroups who preferred to make their peace with the invaders rather than continue

with their independent Gothic allegiance. One surviving papyrus
beautifully illustrates the plight of a Gothic estate owner called
Gundilas, who twisted and turned, swapping sides repeatedly in a
desperate attempt to hold on to his land, as the fortunes of war
fluctuated around him over the next twenty years. But neither the
defectors nor Gundilas can have reflected the majority response to
Byzantine invasion among Theoderic's supporters and their descendants. If they had, those twenty years of warfare would not have
followed in which the Goths attempted to maintain their political
independence, especially since the Byzantines offered them a peace
deal that would have allowed them to keep their lands in return for
political submission. What really emerges from both Procopius' narrative and a wider range of evidence is that a core body of higher-status
warriors who had the most invested in Gothic group identity was
slowly destroyed in the war years as more and more of them fell in
battle.[58] These were the men who had most to gain from maintaining
the group identity that gave them their high social status, and these
were the men most willing to fight for its continuance. My best guess
is that such higher-status warriors, both among the Goths and among
other Germanic groups of this era, were the real building blocks of
group identity, and that the relative robustness – or otherwise – of any
particular group depended upon their allegiances and attitudes. That
does not mean, of course, that even among these higher-status
individuals all felt the same degree of group allegiance. This doesn't
happen in the modern world, and it's hard to see why it should have
been any different in the ancient.

## MIGRATION AND EMPIRE

There is not the slightest doubt that even at elite-warrior level the rise
and fall of the Hunnic Empire forced major renegotiations of group
identity. One bout was stimulated by conquest, and the mechanisms
of control this brought in its wake: particularly the suppression of
dangerous larger-scale lordships. A second followed Attila's death,
sparking a rush towards reorganization, as concentrations of military

manpower formed among those subject groups powerful enough to throw off Hunnic control. But there is no reason to suppose that either of these processes substantially eroded the distinction between Huns and their subjects. The Huns themselves had a clear interest in maintaining this divide in broad terms, even if Attila, by targeted blandishments, was careful to cultivate a compliant or semi-compliant set of subject rulers. Without such demarcation, the benefits of having conquered all these subjects in the first place would have been lost, and, in any case, some probably more peripheral groups, like the Gepids, do seem to have been left with their kingships intact. Here was a structure, therefore, in which there were clear barriers to wholesale changes of group identity. But if as a result the successor kingdoms start to look more like alliances than 'peoples', and the kinds of identity they created were more obviously political than cultural, they nonetheless managed to create firm group identities among large cores of supporters, to judge by the fact that extensive military counteraction would be required to dismantle them and that, even after major defeats, these identities would sustain themselves for another couple of generations.

That at least is the conclusion suggested by the historical evidence, and there is no good reason to disbelieve it. The evidence on which this narrative is based passes all the normal tests of credibility, and the only reason to reject it would be an a priori assumption that identity in the fifth century could not have worked like this. But modern understandings of group identity do not sustain that assumption; in fact, it fits perfectly well with a vision of group identities operating in layers, and with individuals having some freedom to alter their allegiances according to circumstance. Even if they did not belong to culturally homogeneous 'peoples', the names need to be taken seriously as considerable concentrations of human beings. This in turn suggests that when these groups moved into and out of the Middle Danube region as the Hunnic Empire rose and fell, it should have generated substantial migratory activity. The limited amount of detailed contemporary evidence available to us confirms this suggestion.

## Attila's Peoples

Most of the best historical evidence for barbarians on the move again concerns Goths, this time the Amal-led Goths who burst into Middle Danubian history under the leadership of Valamer, eldest of three brothers, soon after the death of Attila. It's worth exploring the evidence for these Goths in some detail because it provides a reasonably solid benchmark against which to think about other migratory moments which are referred to much more briefly. The case is still open, in fact, on whether they arrived west of the Carpathians only after the death of Attila, or whether their sudden pre-eminence in the mid- to late 450s was due to Valamer's unification of several separate Gothic warbands who were already settled in the Middle Danube region as Hunnic control collapsed. Either way, in 473, soon after their great victory at the battle of the Bolia, they left Pannonia for the Balkan provinces of the eastern Roman Empire, now led by Thiudimer, the second of the brothers. There followed a number of long-distance treks as a series of complicated political manoeuvres worked themselves out over the next six years. Initially, the group moved about a thousand kilometres from the Lake Balaton area to the canton of Eordaia, just west of Thessalonica. At this point Thiudimer died and leadership devolved on his son Theoderic. In 475/6 they moved on another 600 kilometres to Novae on the Danube, followed by another 800-kilometre trek from the Danube via Constantinople, which in 479 resulted in the seizure of the fortified port of Dyrrhachium on the Adriatic coast.

The negotiations that followed between Theoderic and the east Roman Empire are reported in detail by the contemporary historian Malchus of Philadelphia, who gives us some sense of this group that had covered two and a half thousand kilometres in six years since its departure from Pannonia. In the course of those negotiations, the Goths' leader offered six thousand picked warriors to Adamantius, Constantinople's ambassador, to participate in a number of possible enterprises. This clearly wasn't the sum total of his armed forces, since the non-combatants were to be left in Dyrrhachium, which required a garrison of at least two thousand. In the case of the Amal-led Goths, therefore, we must be dealing with a fighting force of around or perhaps slightly over ten thousand men. In the same negotiations,

Theoderic referred to the 'large number of non-combatants among his forces', and women and children formed an integral part of this force when it subsequently made its way to Italy. If not a people in the nineteenth-century sense of the word, the Amals led a large mixed group of several tens of thousands into the Balkans, analogous to those earlier Gothic groups that crossed the Danube in 376 or the large groups participating in the Rhine crossing of 406.[59]

This central point has been denied by one major study of Gothic identity in Italy (the kingdom that Theoderic's Goths went on to create after their Balkan adventures). This claims that the presence of women and children among the group is reported by only one east Roman historian, Procopius, and that his evidence is tainted by a classical migration topos. Theoderic's force was not a cohesive group of refugees fleeing from the chaos of the post-Hunnic Middle Danube, but a new group that snowballed in the Balkans, composed largely of disparate elements of the east Roman military and very largely of warrior males. That Theoderic's highly mobile force included substantial numbers of women and children is mentioned, however, in a range of sources: not just Procopius, but also a contemporary panegyrist of Theoderic, speaking in 507 to some of those who had made the trek just eighteen years before, and in an Italian saint's life, again composed in Italy under Theoderic's rule.[60] The accusation against Procopius is as unconvincing, therefore, as it was when levelled against Ammianus Marcellinus' account of the events of 376. And in fact, again like Ammianus, Procopius was demonstrably capable of describing a range of barbarian activities. Not all the barbarians found on the move in his histories are described as migrating 'peoples'. Slavic and other raiding all-male warbands for instance, are found there aplenty. We also know that, like the Goths of 376, the Amal-led Goths trailed behind them a huge wagon train. While Theoderic and Adamantius were negotiating, a Roman force surprised this slower-moving tail, which had not yet reached the safety of Dyrrhachium, and captured two thousand wagons. It was presumably in this extraordinary appendage that the group transported its women and children, its possessions, and apparently also its seed grain and agricultural equipment. For it was expected by all the Byzantine negotiators who dealt with Theoderic in the Balkans that any political settlement with him would involve granting his Goths unpopulated agricultural land.[61] Though not a 'people', these Goths formed a large, mixed population, which could plausibly be expected to farm as well as fight. The idea that one group of men might engage in both activities has again been questioned in some recent studies, but, as we have seen before, it makes perfect sense in the light of the limited number of specialist warriors that prevailing levels of economic development in Germanic society could actually support. Any large-scale military enterprise undertaken by Germanic groups in this era had no choice but to recruit from a broader social range than military retinues, among men who held land and had families, as well as among more rootless youngsters. Farmer-fighters, as among the Boers, are a natural corollary of any agricultural society that cannot support a large professional military.

Even this, however, fails to capture the full scale of the following Theoderic led to Italy. During his stay in the Balkans, he added to his entourage a large contingent of new recruits, taken from a second and entirely distinct Gothic force that had been established in Thrace for some time before the Amal-led Goths arrived in the Roman Balkans in 473. How long is a moot point. The origins of these Thracian Goths are obscure, and they could easily have been the product of several separate bouts of immigration into the Roman Balkans. One major influx occurred as early as the 420s, when Roman military action, as we saw earlier, removed many Goths from Hunnic rule in the Middle Danube. These Goths were then resettled in Thrace, which is precisely where we find the second Gothic force well established in c.470. This means, of course, that there is pretty much a two-generation gap between the initial settlement and the point where the Thracian Goths are mentioned as a separate force in contemporary historical sources.

This raises an obvious issue. Linking the two would require the settled Goths to have maintained some kind of group identity in the intervening period, during which time they appear not to have had their own king. The first king of the Thracian Goths we know of established his authority only in the early 470s, when the group revolted following the murder of its patron in Constantinople, the general Aspar. But before Aspar's murder, they had enjoyed a special status, that of *foederati*. The significance of this term seems to have been that it was given only to groups so favoured that their internal cohesion was not destroyed when they were incorporated into the east Roman military. And enough Goths and Gothic-named generals, likewise, turn up among Roman forces in the Balkans between the 420s and c.470 to suggest that the Thracian Goths of the 470s really can be traced back in some way to the earlier settlement. That said, Attila's Empire contained other Gothic groups besides, and its collapse prompted some to move into the eastern Empire. Bigelis led his Gothic force to defeat on east Roman territory in the mid-460s, and its survivors (together, possibly, with others who don't happen to be mentioned) could easily have been incorporated into an existing body of Gothic soldiery. Nor is it necessary to suppose that all the Thracian 'Goths' were indeed Goths, even if contemporary sources describe them as such.[62]

Whatever their origins, by the early 470s the Thracian Goths formed a distinct element within the Balkan military establishment, one again complete with its own women and children. At this date, they too numbered well over ten thousand fighting men. In 478, their leader – also, unfortunately, called Theoderic, but usually known by his nickname Strabo, 'the squinter' – extracted from Constantinople pay and rations for thirteen thousand men. The force was also cohesive enough to elect its own leader to conduct negotiations with the Roman state, and had been its trusted ally. In receipt of large subsidies (nine hundred and ten kilos of gold per annum), they were settled quite near to the imperial capital, with close ties to some important political figures there. The *magister militum* and patrician Aspar, their political patron up to 471, was a power broker and kingmaker who had been responsible for the election of the Emperor Leo in 457. Aspar continued to wield much of the real power in Constantinople, to the extent that Leo – known as 'the butcher' because of it – organized his assassination in 471 so as to claim his political independence. Their closeness to a figure of this stature demonstrates that the Thracian Goths were a major force in the eastern Empire, and they revolted, presumably, because the murder raised questions about the continuation of their privileged status. But even after Aspar's death, Strabo retained ties to the extended imperial family, and other supporters in Constantinople kept him informed of events at court. The Thracians' evident integration into the east Roman body politic also reinforces the idea that some of them had been established there as a privileged body of soldiery since the 420s.[63]

Initially, the arrival of the Amal-led Goths in the Balkans set up a three-way conflict, as the two Gothic groups manoeuvred for position around the eastern imperial court. It was partly resolved when Theoderic the Amal organized the assassination of Strabo's son Recitach in

483/4. He was then the newly elected leader of the Thracian Goths, his father having met an equally grisly end when a rearing horse threw him on to a spear rack. On Recitach's demise, most of the Thracian Goths threw in their lot with Theoderic. No source says this out loud – the east Roman history covering the period survives only in extracts made in the Middle Ages, and the relevant fragment records only the assassination and not its consequences – but, at this exact moment the Thracian Goths suddenly disappear from the historical record as a distinct group, and only a few dissenting individuals, who refused to join the Amal, remained in the east in the sixth century. There was also a logic pushing the two groups to unite, since together they could operate more effectively against Constantinople, whose policy had been to get them to fight each other and then mop up the remains. And the results were momentous. To judge by the separate indications we have for the size of the two forces, this added another 10,000 men to his own, thereby approximately doubling the Gothic military manpower at Theoderic's disposal; and 20,000-plus does seem more or less the order of magnitude of later Gothic forces in Italy.[64]

Recitach's assassination thus completed an astonishing process of amalgamation. Theoderic's uncle Valamer had probably been the first member of the family to achieve an unusual pre-eminence by killing, subduing and forcing out rival Gothic warband leaders in order to unite the Amal-led Goths: manoeuvrings that occurred either in Ukraine before the Goths' move to Pannonia, or in the Middle Danube after Attila's death (if these Goths were already established there). None of these warbands can have numbered much more than a thousand fighting men, and perhaps even only several hundreds. Within two lifetimes, therefore, uncle and nephew had taken the Amal line from one among a set of warband leaders to pre-eminent Gothic kings commanding in excess of twenty thousand warriors. It was this much larger force, complete with women, children and wagon train and amounting to between fifty and a hundred thousand souls, that took the road for Italy in the autumn of 488.

There's more you'd like to know, of course, but for the mid-first millennium this is pretty decent evidence. It also gives us some parameters for considering the other forces that came and went from the Middle Danube as the Hunnic Empire rose and fell, and it's instantly clear that none of the other population groups on the move in this period was quite as big as this truly monstrous force. No source gives us figures for any of those smaller groups of former Hunnic manpower that entered the Roman Empire in the 460s – the forces of Hormidac, Bigelis, and of the two surviving sons of Attila. But none could establish the kind of independent position enjoyed by Theoderic's Goths, and many ended up scattered in small clusters along the Danube frontier. It is hard to envisage that any could have fielded more than a thousand or two fighting men, and most perhaps mustered only a few hundreds.[65]

Somewhat larger, though still nowhere near as big as Theoderic's force, were the population clusters set in motion by the defeats of the Heruli and Rugi. The one other plausible-looking figure we have from the events that followed the death of Attila is from as late as 549. When the Herule allies of the Gepids and of Byzantium faced each other in battle that year, the two contingents numbered, respectively, fifteen hundred and three thousand men. This postdated a second split among the group, the first of which, you will recall, had sent an unspecified number of Heruli spinning off to Scandinavia. It also seems unlikely that either of the remaining concentrations of Heruli left in the Danube area would have been willing to commit its entire military manpower to war on someone else's behalf. Before the splits occurred, and before their heavy defeat at the hands of the Lombards, therefore, the Heruli may have been able to field somewhere between five and ten thousand warriors, making them just a touch less powerful, perhaps, than the Amal-led Goths before Theoderic recruited the Thracian Goths into his following. We have no figures at all for the Rugi, but the fact that they could be defeated so thoroughly by Odovacar indicates that they amounted to no more than a medium-rank power in the Danubian scheme of things, so again perhaps a force of a similar size to or slightly smaller than the Heruli.[66]

The most difficult to envisage of all the comings and goings during this era are those of the Lombards. That Lombard power eventually became dominant in the Middle Danube is clear enough, but the historical process behind this development is opaque. Late Lombard sources report that the seizure of Rugiland and the subsequent occupation of Pannonia, not to mention the earlier moves that had brought them that far from the mouth of the Elbe, were all invasions led by individual kings – the invasion hypothesis trundled out once more. On the other hand, all the contemporary evidence suggests that Lombard royal authority was not a very powerful phenomenon.

After the move to Italy, second-rank leaders murdered the king and operated without central royal authority for a decade. It is quite possible, therefore, that independent initiatives on the part of intermediate leaders played an important part in the action, particularly in its earlier stages. Like Jordanes' account of third-century Gothic expansion, later Lombard accounts have surely become infected with a migration topos that recasts the action in the form of one king, one people, one move.[67]

On the other hand, migrant Lombards were never moving into a complete power vacuum as they came south down the Elbe, and by the time they got to the lands of the Heruli they were taking on a not inconsiderable power in head-to-head confrontation. Lombard expansion into the Middle Danubian region may well have been analogous, therefore, to third-century Germanic expansion towards the Black Sea (Chapter 3). While some of the action was carried forward by separate groups, some or many of which may have been small, especially at the beginning, the migration flow also had the capacity to generate larger groups at crunch moments to fight major battles. It looks like another example, in other words, of the classic pattern widely observable in groups from third-century Goths to ninth-century Scandinavians to nineteenth-century Boers, where the successes of initial intruders into a landscape encourage others, and eventually higher-status leaders enter the fray with larger followings. The lack of historical sources means that we have no indication of the overall numbers involved in these moves, or even whether they were primarily all-male warbands or groups encompassing women and children as well. By the time of the move to Italy in the 560s, whole families were certainly involved, and, since at least from the defeat of the Heruli in 508 large military forces were being assembled, the presumption must again be that militarized manpower beyond the scale of that available in specialist warrior retinues was required. If so, mixed social groups will have played a substantial part in the action in all but the very earliest phases of Lombard expansion.

The archaeological evidence relevant to Lombard migration is not much more informative. The characteristic funerary ritual in Bohemia by the late Roman period was inhumation. In the late fourth and earlier fifth centuries, however, some cremation cemeteries started to appear there which bear strong similarities to those found further north where the Lombards originated (the northern Elbe, northern

Harz, Altmark and Mecklenburg regions). These intrusive funerary rites could be the result of some indigenous Bohemians deciding to cremate their dead, but given that Lombards had certainly made their way to the Middle Danube in some numbers by the end of the fifth century, the cemeteries probably provide us with an indication of their route[68] – hardly overwhelming evidence, but, as we have seen, archaeological finds will almost never provide entirely unambiguous evidence of migration. The material cultures of the populations of the northern Elbe were too similar to one another for shorter-distance population flows within the region to show up with any clarity, so that it is not possible to say where, precisely, the first northern intruders into Bohemia came from. And, in any case, the migrating groups may well have recruited from right across the region.

The archaeological evidence from the Middle Danube after the Lombards took power there, likewise, is in one sense clear enough: in the course of the sixth century, a coherent set of well-dated remains centred on old Roman Pannonia spread over those territories where historical sources report Lombard domination. These without doubt reflect the Lombard kingdom. On the other hand, there is nothing very distinctive about them compared with other Middle Danubian remains, especially those stemming from areas which, the historical sources tell us, were dominated by Gepids. This does not mean that the differences between the Lombard kingdom and its Gepid rival were insignificant. What the resemblance really shows is that sixth-century Lombard material culture followed a similar trajectory to that of the Huns in the fifth. Over time, it lost its original distinctiveness and firmly adapted itself to Middle Danubian norms, which reinforces the idea, perhaps, that the Huns of Attila's time are archaeologically invisible because they too had adopted new material cultural norms. In the case of the Lombards, their original cremation rite was replaced with a new habit of burying unburnt bodies in cemeteries laid out approximately in rows, oriented broadly east–west (German: *Reihengräber*). Lombard women wore their clothes – at least those they were buried in – in the same Danubian fashion as everyone else, with a pair of brooches one on each shoulder. Handmade ceramics with idiosyncratic designs of the kind marking out different northern Elbe groups in the early Roman period made way for wheel-made pottery of a fairly uniform Middle Danubian design. The most that can be argued, and this is in line with modern ethnographic parallels, is that particular *fibula* designs became symbolic of Lombard and Gepid allegiance, since two entirely different designs are found, with their distribution patterns confined to each half of the Middle Danubian plain.[69]

A range of migratory phenomena can be seen intertwined in the rise and fall of the Hunnic Empire. Some of the moves were made by large, concentrated groups, notably those of the Amal-led Goths. In 473 several tens of thousands of people left Hungary for the Balkans, possibly the same group that had moved to Hungary from Ukraine about twenty years before; and in 488 an even larger group, close to a hundred thousand souls if you add in the Thracian Goths and the refugee Rugi, set off from the Balkans for Italy. Other moves were made by smaller population groups, refugees from the military defeats that had dismantled old hegemonies, notably the Huns and Sciri in the 460s, the Rugi in the 480s and the various groups of Heruli after 508. And to complete the picture, the period also saw one predatory flow of migration of the kind we have met before, in the form of the Lombards.

Even though the historical sources give us few decent figures, many of these movements of armed immigrants into and out of the Middle Danubian region represented mass migration at least in the qualitative terms used in comparative migration analysis. The overall 'shock' of Attila's tribal gathering in the first half of the fifth century is visible archaeologically in the so-called Danubian style, and, in narrative terms, in the attacks the Huns launched into the Mediterranean using their unprecedented concentration of military manpower. New political and social relations were generated in the region under Hunnic domination, representing a further level of shock. The whole creaky structure relied on a flow of Roman gold, extracted by war and intimidation, to lubricate its operations. War and its profits kept the mass of the Huns' armed subject groups in line via a potent mixture of intimidation and reward, and intense political and indeed cultural dislocation are visible in all of this.

Much of the undocumented, or insufficiently documented, population displacement of the era of Hunnic collapse, likewise, amounted to mass migration in qualitative terms. Odovacar's intervention came as a huge political shock for the Rugi, since it destroyed their kingdom and set survivors off on two forced treks, each of several hundred kilometres, first to join Theoderic in the Roman Balkans and then on, in his train, to Italy. The intervention of the Amal-led Goths had earlier had similar effects upon the Sciri. That all the Sciri and Rugi left the Middle Danube region following these defeats is unlikely, but their independence was extinguished and enough Sciri left for the army of Italy to contribute to a changing balance of forces there. Hence, in due course, Odovacar became the effective ruler of the first post-Roman successor state on Italian soil. The Lombards' arrival in the Middle Danube, likewise, was a shock for the Heruli, who also saw their independence and their unity destroyed, and many of them felt forced to move on. In pretty much every case, then, though there are few figures worth a damn, we are dealing with groups possessing substantial military power whose migratory responses to the rise and fall of the Hunnic Empire generated substantial restructuring of the political systems operating not only in the Middle Danubian region itself, but also in adjacent and not so adjacent areas of the Balkans, the northern shores of the Black Sea, and even within Italy itself. The detailed narrative evidence available to us thus broadly confirms the picture that emerged from the analysis of the operation of group identities in the Hunnic Empire. The group labels we encounter in our sources belonged to functioning concentrations of human beings, some of them tens of thousands strong, whose lives were wrenched out of shape by the tumultuous events of the rise and fall of Hunnic domination in central Europe, and who often took to the road as a result.

Several different types of migration can be observed, from concentrated mass pulses to more extended flows, but many clearly went far beyond the bounds circumscribed by wave-of-advance or elite-transfer models. Though not all are covered in the same detail as the Amal-led Gothic diaspora, it is clear that many of these moves were hugely traumatic, whether measured in terms of distance, violence or loss of political independence. Viewed from the migrants' perspective, much of the action was 'mass' in a more absolute sense as well. For many of the migrant groups, as we have seen, there is either good (Amal-led Goths, Rugi), or reasonable (Heruli, Huns, Lombards), evidence that they comprised men, women and children. In some cases, such as the Amal-led Goths, these groups numbered several tens of thousands of people, and in many cases, as in 376 and 405/6, they moved in compact masses.[70] None of the participating groups was a 'people' in the old sense of the word, and there is much evidence that the process of migration, as any reading of the comparative literature would lead us to expect, caused splits among the migrants, who were faced with enormously difficult decisions. Some of the Amal-led Goths refused to move south into the Roman Balkans in 473, for instance, preferring the leadership of Thiudimer's younger brother Vidimer. They moved west instead, where they were eventually absorbed into the Visigothic kingdom. Not all the Goths in the Balkans, likewise, were ready to move with Theoderic to Italy in 489. Some preferred a Byzantine allegiance. And the repeated splitting of the Heruli is eloquent testimony to just how difficult these decisions to move actually were, leading some to Scandinavia and others to subordination to the Gepids or east Rome, depending on the outcome of wars and the conditions offered by potential hosts.[71] But despite all the problems with the evidence, the only reasonable conclusion to derive from the rise and fall of the Hunnic Empire is that the migratory phenomena outside the Roman Empire were just as substantial as those that characterized the crises of 376–80 and 405–8.

## Ways and Means

The reasons why some of the migratory processes should have taken this form, so different from any encountered in the modern world, are similar to those that explain its appearance in other first-millennium contexts, and don't need extensive discussion again. Take, for example, the two moves of the Amal-led Goths, first into the east Roman Balkans in 473, then on into Italy in 488/9. Both were underpinned by a substantially economic and hence voluntary motivation. The first was undertaken with the aim of supplanting the Thracian Goths as Constantinople's favoured allies, in order to lay hands on the benefits they enjoyed. Amongst other perks, the Thracian Goths received subsidies measured in thousands of kilos of gold per annum, whereas those of the Amal-led Goths out in Pannonia amounted to just a few hundreds. In the move to Italy, likewise, Theoderic had it in mind to enrich himself and his followers at the expense of Odovacar and such Roman fiscal structures as remained in operation. Theoderic's extant building works at Ravenna, and his many other known monuments besides, bear eloquent testimony to just how much disposable income continued to be delivered to Italy's early-sixth-century ruler. He also recycled some of the tax income to invent salaried posts for his more important Gothic followers: a device surely designed to ensure their

political support. Both of these strategies for economic advance were
entirely dependent, however, on having sufficient military muscle to
transform an existing political situation – to persuade the Emperor Leo
to choose a new set of Gothic allies in the first instance, to defeat
Odovacar's army in the second. And certainly in the second case there
was an extra political dimension, since relations between Theoderic
the Amal and the Emperor Zeno had reached deadlock. Neither trusted
the other, and a series of confrontations had shown that neither could
easily rid himself of the other.[72] In these migrations, economic and
political motivations cannot easily be separated, and, to have any
chance of success, Theoderic had to field a substantial army. As we
have seen before, the number of specialist warriors that could be
supported by the non-Roman European economy in this era was not
sufficient for large-scale campaigning. Freemen and their families thus
became integral to the enterprise.

The play of motivations behind Lombard expansion looks very
similar. As far as we can tell, their move into the Middle Danube was
not made in response to any kind of threat, but inspired by the region's
attractions. The Middle Danube had long formed part of the inner
periphery around the Roman Empire, and over the first four centuries
AD had steadily built up levels of wealth and development far beyond
anything to be found at the mouth of the Elbe. The apogee of Attila
hugely accentuated this imbalance. The amount of gold stashed away
in Middle Danubian burials of the Hunnic period is without precedent
in the Germanic world. And this can only be a fraction of the total
amount, much of which was stored, presumably, in the treasuries of
the kings who now ruled in the region. Even if we lack explicit
evidence, it's much more than a guess that Lombard migration had in
mind a share of this booty, still being reinforced by the smaller
diplomatic subsidies that continued to be paid by Constantinople after
Attila's death. But acquiring any part of this wealth required, as usual,
the application of main force to alter existing political configurations –
in other words, the Heruli needed to be defeated. While Lombard
expansion may have started with warband-size groupings seeping
south, both the Lombards and other immigrants caught up in the flow
had to reform themselves into a more cohesive group, at the latest by
the time they left Rugiland, whence they proceeded to destroy the
kingdom of the Heruli.[73] Even where largely economic, and hence
voluntary, these kinds of migration always had a political dimension.

Did the migrants pack sufficient military punch to succeed in the
enterprise they were about to undertake or did they not?

Some other bouts of migration, by contrast, were pretty much
entirely political. The Sciri, Rugi, Heruli and Huns all faced, at different moments, a powerfully negative and thoroughly political impetus
pushing them out of their existing territories: defeats, respectively, at
the hands of the Amal-led Goths, Odovacar and the Lombards, and,
in the case of the Huns, the steady erosion of an original position
of advantage until their situation became unsustainable. In each case,
military defeat destroyed the group's ability to maintain its independence, even if its victims responded to disaster in a variety of ways.
Whereas the Rugi and Heruli (or large numbers of them) moved en
masse to different areas, the Sciri seem to have broken down into
small groups and negotiated their future piecemeal. The *Life of St
Severinus* refers to a small group of Sciri, not a major force, on its way
to Italy. It was remarkable only for the fact that Odovacar was a
member of the party.[74] The post-Attilan history of the Huns may have
combined both types of activity. As we have noted, the mid-460s
saw both small groups of Hunnic manpower and two larger concentrations, under the surviving sons of Attila, seek asylum in the east
Roman Empire. Economic factors contributed to their choice of
direction, but not to the fact that they were on the move in the first
place.

The pay and other rewards still available to Roman soldiers were
presumably the main reason why so many Sciri and others eventually
headed south of the Alps. Larger concentrations of Rugi, Heruli and
Huns, likewise (sometimes in more than one group), were forced in
the aftermath of defeat either to leave the Middle Danube region
or establish dependent relationships with other powers. The nature of
these relationships is not made clear in the sources, but again influenced their choice of direction. The Heruli found Gepid hegemony
so burdensome that they moved on to a Byzantine allegiance, until
the civil war over succession further divided them, leading some
back to the Gepids. These refugees were clearly expected to fight for
their hosts (whether east Roman or Gepid) and were happy enough,
it seems, to do that much, suggesting that this can't have been at the
root of the Heruli's problem with the Gepids. The refugees may have
been expected to provide some kind of economic tribute as well,
therefore, but perhaps not as much as they had previously paid to the

Huns. The Rugi, perhaps, procured better terms from Theoderic the Amal. Although they swapped sides to Odovacar at one point during the conquest of Italy, they quickly returned to him, and seem to have been content to be part of the Ostrogothic kingdom until 540, a record suggestive of greater contentment than the Heruli enjoyed.[75]

Unfortunately, we don't know what terms Dengizich and Hernac, the sons of Attila, sought from Constantinople. Their move on to east Roman territory was preceded by a demand that the Emperor Leo grant them access to markets. The Huns' declining political hegemony had presumably had economic consequences by the mid-460s, in terms of lost tribute as different subject peoples established their independence, and this erosion of position eventually made accommodation with Constantinople an attractive option. For one of the sons but not the other, the move led to disaster. It is unclear why. The Byzantines presumably perceived a threat in the forces of Dengizich that they did not perceive in Hernac's. It is noticeable, however, that Hernac appears to have been content with only a very limited territory on Roman soil, right on the frontier in the north of the Dobruja, so perhaps Dengizich was too demanding.[76] For all these groups, however, defeat had major consequences. It turned them into political refugees, and forced them to accept sometimes burdensome terms from senior partners. At the very least, it cost them any revenues that had previously accrued to them as the dominant local force, as well as, at least in the case of those Heruli attached to the Gepids, extra tribute that they now had to pay to their 'hosts'. They were also expected to perform military service. Even though it is impossible to study motivation in detail, the intertwining of economic and political factors in the motivations of all our migrants is clear, with economics having the edge, as you might expect, among the more voluntary migrants, and politics among the involuntary. But because even the voluntary had of necessity to remake political circumstances to their benefit in order to enjoy the wealth they were targeting, they had to operate in large and cohesive groupings. If the size and nature of these migrant groups was not in line with modern examples, the complex nature of their motivation was.

Other aspects of the migration process observable across the span of the Hunnic era recall modern exemplars more closely. The degree to which migration was adopted as a strategy in this era by population groups who already had an established propensity for mobility is striking. The Amal-led Goths who eventually moved on to Italy had, at some point in the recent past, moved from east to west of the Carpathians, then south into the east Roman Balkans, where they remained highly mobile. There the group covered another fifteen hundred kilometres and more, as Theoderic the Amal twisted and turned geographically and politically in his attempt to supplant the Thracian Goths as imperial allies. Although we have much less specific information, the same was seemingly true of the Lombard groups who ended up in the Middle Danube. We have little grasp of the chronology, but somehow they got there from the northern Elbe, almost certainly via a number of intermediary moves – or pauses in a flow, perhaps – that had led to an immediate jumping-off point in Bohemia. The point equally applies to the main losers in the fallout from the Hunnic Empire: the Huns themselves, together with the Rugi, Sciri and Heruli. Again, even if the details are not recoverable in every case, all of these groups first made their way to the Middle Danubian region at some point in the late fourth or early fifth century, and their departures followed within two or, in the case of the Heruli, at most three generations. For the populations of all these groups, migration had become an entrenched strategy, a reflex stored in the collective memory that might be drawn upon in appropriate circumstances; for them it was a possible response to a much wider range of stimuli than to groups without an established history of migration.

The importance of fields of information in influencing the directions of these migrations is also apparent. Information clearly played a critical role in shaping the individual moves of the Amal-led Goths. Theoderic the Amal's ten-year spell as a hostage in Constantinople finished when he was eighteen, in 472 or thereabouts. This was precisely the right moment for him to return with news both of the much greater wealth accruing to the Thracian Goths as a result of their court connections, and of the fact that these Goths were currently in rebellion against the Emperor Leo because he had assassinated their patron Aspar. That within the year the Amal-led Goths had moved south to attempt to supplant them as Constantinople's favoured Gothic allies can't be coincidence. That Theoderic's Goths had sufficient geographic and political knowledge to understand, later on, that Italy represented another possible destination is equally apparent, but perhaps requires less explanation. Their old home in Pannonia lay on the fringes of the eastern Alpine passes that gave access to northern Italy, and Odovacar, its ruler, was the son of an ancient enemy of the Amal dynasty. As early as 479, a full decade before his forces moved there en masse, Theoderic was already suggesting to Constantinople's ambassador Adamantius, as they negotiated outside Dyrrhachium, that he might lead some of his troops to Italy on a joint expedition to overthrow him.[77]

Most of the other migrations stimulated by the collapse of Hunnic power operated within discernibly active fields of information too. It is no surprise, for instance, that groups of Lombards settled in adjacent Bohemia should have realized that Odovacar's destruction of the kingdom of the Rugi had created a power vacuum into which they might now move. The Sciri, likewise, had formed part of Attila's army that had raided Italy in 451, and like Theoderic's Goths were settled close to the routes that led into it. The Heruli who accepted Gepid hegemony and then that of Byzantium remained, of course, within the region where they had been established for at least fifty years, so it is safe to assume that they too understood the implications of the moves they decided to make. This leaves two more interesting cases: the Rugi and the wider Herulic diaspora. Somehow or other, the Rugi knew where to find Theoderic after their kingdom had been destroyed by Odovacar in 487. But Theoderic's career in the east Roman Empire had been spectacularly successful, culminating in a consulship in 484, so it is perhaps no wonder that his not too distant neighbours should have had accurate knowledge of his whereabouts within the Balkans. More arresting is the case of those Heruli who made their way to Scandinavia. In Procopius' account it is unclear whether they had any idea of where they were going when they first headed north in the aftermath of defeat. You would think not, except for the fact that those Heruli who remained by the Danube were able to find them again, twenty odd years later, when they needed a prince of the royal clan, despite the eighteen hundred or so kilometres that now separated them. The Heruli who moved north perhaps already had contacts or knowledge that suggested Scandinavia as a possible destination, information shared by those who remained close to the Danube. Alternatively, the two groups may have maintained some contact in the meantime. A case in point is the Scandinavian king, Rodulf of the Rani, who later sought refuge at Theoderic's court in Italy. Vignettes like this make it apparent that you underestimate the circulation of knowledge beyond the old Roman *limes* at your peril.[78]

Knowledge could translate into actual movement, however, only where large-scale transfers of population were a practical possibility. Often the ancient sources give us little relevant information, but some migrations were shaped by transport logistics. Like their Gothic predecessors under Alaric from the 390s, the Amal-led Goths travelled with a massive wagon train. The two thousand Gothic wagons captured by the east Romans in 479 were probably not even its full complement. The ambush occurred before Theoderic integrated the Thracian Goths into his command, so that the wagon train of the united Goths (together with the Rugi) who set off for Italy will have been an even more imposing sight. In single file, two thousand wagons will have stretched over perhaps fifteen kilometres. With this monster at their heels, the Amal-led Goths were naturally limited to the Roman road network in the mountainous Balkans. We happen to know that their initial trek in 473 made use of both of the available branches of the great military road from Naissus to Thessalonica; in their later retreat west from the outskirts of Constantinople in 478/9 they plodded along the Via Egnatia. Presumably all their intervening and subsequent moves, likewise, followed the main Roman arteries of communication. It seems extremely unlikely, moreover, that only the Goths made use of wagon trains for transporting possessions and non-combatants. In fact, there are enough references to suggest that they were the characteristic mode of transport of all these migrant groups.[79]

Perhaps above all, as modern examples would lead us to expect, the 'shape' of existing political structures is firmly imprinted upon the action. It was the rising power of the Huns that caused such a gathering of militarily powerful groups in the Middle Danube region in the first place, as they were either brought there by the Huns or were seeking – in vain – to escape their attentions. Nor, without the Huns' constraining influence, could so many militarized groups have existed in such close proximity to one another, as the violent competition sparked off among them by Attila's death underlines. The continuing survival of the east Roman Empire as a cohesive state was likewise central to the action. It prompted, for instance, the decision of the Amal-led Goths to head south into its Balkan territories. This landscape was not naturally rich – not nearly as agriculturally productive, for instance, as the old province of Pannonia which the Goths had left behind. The rugged Balkans were an attractive destination, though, because they were close enough to Constantinople to allow the Goths to exert pressure on the authorities there, and hence to try to make them hand over some of the wealth they accrued in tax revenues from their much richer territories of Egypt and the Near East. These Goths' ultimate choice of destination was also dictated by political structures. If the western Roman Empire had not ceased in the meantime to exist, they could have had no hope of establishing an independent kingdom in the Italian peninsula, nor would the eastern Emperor Zeno have encouraged Theoderic in the enterprise. Similarly with the Lombards: they could not have moved into the Middle Danube in force, had the Hunnic Empire continued to exist.

As mentioned earlier, in the last decade or so it has become fashionable in some quarters to argue that the rise and fall of the Hunnic Empire shows that group identity in the period was highly malleable, and that the process involved little in the way of migration. This is certainly an area where the evidence base is less than we would like it to be. There are enough solid pointers, however, to indicate that both of these stands require modification. The historical evidence, first of all, makes it clear that becoming part of the Hunnic Empire did not mean that one became a Hun. The Empire was an essentially unequal, involuntary confederation. All the participating non-Huns we know about were forced to join, were systematically exploited under its auspices, and eventually fought their way free of its domination. In light of this, it becomes less surprising that larger group identities were not broken apart by participation in its structures. The Huns themselves had a basic interest in maintaining these identities, since being a Hun was to occupy a position of privilege over others, while from the subjects' perspective holding on to a larger group identity offered the likeliest route, when opportunity arose, of throwing off Hunnic domination.

For many of the groups mentioned in our sources, the information available to us is not good, and for some, particularly the Lombards, seriously deficient; but these observations on identiy sit entirely comfortably alongside the better information, such as there is, about the migratory processes involved in the Empire's creation and destruction. The Amal-led Goths are consistently described as a large, mixed population, comprising ten thousand-plus warriors on the move with dependent women and children and a wagon train several thousand strong. This description is derived from a variety of contemporary historical sources whose reports are consistent, detailed and circumstantial. It is also the image of these Goths on the move given at the court of their king in Italy. Any evidence can be disputed, but the grounds have to be reasonable, and in this case objections are largely based on only a partial reading of the modern scientific literature on the workings of group identity. In broadest terms, the demographic effect of the Hunnic Empire was to suck large numbers of militarized groups into the heart of central Europe, whether as part of its build-up of power or to take advantage of the chaos of its collapse. Once the constraining influence of Hunnic power had disappeared, such a concentration of military potential could not but generate intense competition in which some of the smaller entities lost their independence, but which, overall, prompted many of the groups to leave the region quite as quickly as they had entered it.

At first sight, the role played by different degrees of development in all this action is not so obvious as, say, in the third-century Germanic expansions. Most of the migratory action examined in this chapter looks initially very political, associated either with Hunnic empire-building or the fallout from that Empire's collapse. But first impressions can be misleading. The Huns built their war machine in the Middle Danube region precisely because of unequal degrees of development. It was a conveniently situated base from which to launch the raids and protection rackets that would give them a share of the wealth of the Mediterranean as mobilized by the taxation structures of the Roman Empire. And Attila's demands, recorded for us in detail by Priscus, really were all about cash. Holding the Huns' war machine together at all, moreover, would have been quite impossible without Roman wealth to lubricate its mechanisms. Variations in the prevailing levels of economic development also dictated, after Attila's death, the general directions of the moves made by the various groups who wanted to opt out of the competition. The vast majority, as we have seen, moved south, attracted, again, by the wealth of the Mediterranean; but political structures then again enter the frame. Only if a group was content to be broken up and lose its political independence, following the path trodden by the last son of Attila and some of the smaller former satellites, could it move permanently south and east towards the Byzantine Empire, whose military strength remained largely intact. Theoderic's Amal-led Goths were numerous enough to survive there in the short term, but not numerous enough to force Constantinople into a lasting agreement, so that this seeming exception in fact reinforces the point.

For those with grander ambitions, then, south and west were the directions to take. The obstacle posed to western migration in previous eras by west Roman frontier fortifications and the troops that manned them had been removed, and there was no repeat of third-century patterns of expansion, which had seen Germanic groups spill eastwards to become dominant in areas north of the Black Sea (Chapter 4). During the Hunnic imperial period, central and southern Europe periodically witnessed great concentrations of warriors and their families clogging the roads of the region. At more or less the same time, different kinds of migration were affecting the north-western fringes of the Roman Empire. To complete our survey of the traditional *Völkerwanderung*, we need now to turn the spotlight on the Anglo-Saxons and the Franks.

# 6

# FRANKS AND ANGLO-SAXONS: ELITE TRANSFER OR *VÖLKERWANDERUNG?*

THE PROVINCES OF BRITAIN fell out of the Roman system round about the year 410. They then largely disappear from view for the next two hundred years, one modern historian rightly calling these the 'lost centuries' of British history.[1] When they came back into view in c.600 AD, much of the rich farmland of lowland Britain (the area covered essentially by modern England, the heartland of the old Roman province) had on the face of it fallen into the hands of outside invaders. Germanic-speaking Anglo-Saxons had replaced indigenous Celtic- and Latin-speakers as the dominant social elite. Two hundred years before, Angles and Saxons had been roaming lands the other side of the North Sea. Within the same timeframe, the provinces of Roman Gaul suffered a similar fate, falling under the political domination of intrusive Germanic-speaking Franks, whose previous haunts had been east of the Rhine. The degree of cultural change in Gaul was nothing like so complete as north of the Channel. South of the River Loire, many of the sixth-century descendants of the old Roman elites of the region were still enjoying the landed estates accumulated by their ancestors under imperial rule, and much of their material and non-material culture retained a distinctly sub-Roman flavour. Even in Gaul, however, things were very different north of the Paris basin. There, the use of Germanic languages spread westwards at the expense of Latin and Celtic, and neither historical nor archaeological evidence gives much sign that the Roman gentry and aristocracy of this region was still recognizably in place by 600 AD.

The Frankish takeover of northern Gaul poses many of the same questions as the Anglo-Saxon seizure of lowland Britain. How central was migration to the political and cultural changes observable in these north-western corners of the Roman world? And what form did that migration take? In the past, Anglo-Saxon and Frankish expansions have both been seen as western expressions of the great and pan-Germanic phenomenon of *Völkerwanderung* which burst into action at the end of the Roman imperial period. More recently, they have been recast as examples of the more limited migration model known as elite transfer. The classic archetype of elite transfer, as we saw in Chapter 1, is the eleventh-century Norman conquest of England. Its outlines are comprehensively documented in *Doomsday Book*, which tells us who owned what land in the country both before the Normans arrived – on 5 January 1066, to be precise: 'the day that King Edward [the Confessor] lived and died', in its own evocative language – and twenty years later. Its evidence leaves us in no doubt that the incoming Normans in small but politically significant numbers had inserted themselves as the new landowning class of England in between. Can the same limited form of migration satisfactorily explain the transformations that unfolded in lowland Britain and northern Gaul in the fifth and sixth centuries? A more comparative approach suggests that they can't, and taking the Frankish and Anglo-Saxon cases together, instead of separately, as is usual, helps explain exactly why not.

## ELITES AND MASSES

It can't seriously be doubted that migration played some part in transforming Roman Britain into Anglo-Saxon England, but visions of its extent have varied dramatically. In the nineteenth century, it was generally thought that large numbers of immigrants had, in England at least, more or less entirely displaced the indigenous Romano-British population of Celtic origin, driving any survivors westwards into Wales, Devon and Cornwall, or across the sea to Brittany. Victorian, Edwardian and even later schoolchildren were brought up to believe in an Anglo-Saxon invasion which started with Hengist and Horsa in Kent and rolled triumphantly onwards. This vision of the past rested substantially on surviving narrative sources, particularly Gildas' *Ruin of Britain* and the *Anglo-Saxon Chronicle*. These were always recognized as a touch on the thin side, but could be mined for a story of unremitting hostility between Anglo-Saxon invader and indigenous Celt, and of the invader's eventual success. By 1900, it rested on much larger blocks of evidence too: language and place names. The overwhelming majority of the place names of modern England were by then known to descend from the Germanic tongue of the Anglo-Saxons, not the Celtic of the Romano-British, and the latter had also left little obvious trace on the modern English language. Celtic roots could be detected only in the names of some main rivers. The great age of Victorian railway-building had added a third plank to the argument. A whole series of cemeteries excavated in the later nineteenth century, as branch lines multiplied, provided plentiful evidence of a post-Roman material culture brought by the invaders from the continent, and very little of any surviving Romano-British population. The term hadn't yet been coined, but, in traditional views, the Anglo-Saxons were considered to have engaged in a highly effective process of 'ethnic cleansing'.

Since the 1960s, broad consensus has broken down into sometimes vitriolic disagreement. No one now believes in mass ethnic cleansing, and no one believes that there was absolutely no migration, either. The range of opinions in between is vast, but two broad clusters can be identified. Many historians and some archaeologists perceive the evident Anglo-Saxonization of lowland Britain in the fifth and sixth centuries to have been brought about through a hostile takeover, which involved large numbers of migrants from northern Germany and the Low Countries. A second group of opinion, on the other hand, sees the process as having been effected by many fewer continental European immigrants, whose cultural norms then spread broadly and essentially voluntarily through the existing population: elite transfer followed by cultural emulation. This is subscribed to by some histor-ians but many more archaeologists, and is obviously heavily influenced by the general rejection of the old mass-migration models inherent to culture history.[2] Why is there so much disagreement?

## Sources of Controversy

Here again, as with so many of the subject areas tackled in this book, the escape from nationalist visions of the past has had a profoundly liberating effect. No one would now suppose that Celts and Anglo-

Saxons must have been hostile to one another simply because they were Celts and Anglo-Saxons. And, in fact, after 600 AD, historical sources show that the different kingdoms of Anglo-Saxon England were just as likely to fight each other as their surviving sub-Romano-British counterparts, and would sometimes even ally with the latter against their fellow Anglo-Saxons. The post-Roman world of largely western and northern Britain also varied enormously within itself. One of the most exciting discoveries of recent years has been the revelation, from close analysis of the language used in inscribed standing stones, that there survived in western Britain in the fifth and sixth centuries a Romance-speaking substantially Roman elite, while their more northern British counterparts were always Celtic-speaking.[3]

But if shifting world views have allowed existing evidence to be read in new ways, reinterpretation has also been driven forward by real gains in knowledge. Another great advance of the last fifty years has been an increased understanding of exactly how developed Roman Britain actually was. The study of pottery sherds gathered by surface collection has combined with strategically placed excavation to show that the population of late Roman Britain was in fact extremely large. An absolute figure cannot be generated (recent estimates run between 3 and 7 million, a massive margin for error), but it is now generally accepted that the English countryside was being exploited with greater intensity in the fourth century than at any subsequent point before the fourteenth. Roman Britain was no backwater, as Victorian scholars tended to suppose, but a thriving part of the Roman world. The idea that virtually its entire population could be driven westwards by invaders is thus much more difficult to sustain than when H. R. Loyn wrote, 'The story of Anglo-Saxon settlement, when looked at in depth, yields more of the saga of man against forest than of Saxon against Celt.'[4]

The fact that modern English place names are so overwhelmingly of Anglo-Saxon origin has also been reinterpreted. Most of them – it has emerged – were formed only several centuries after the initial Anglo-Saxon takeover, when rural settlement structures finally became more permanent. The crucial moment was the linked emergence of stable landed estates – manors – and villages, a development that gathered pace only after c.800 AD and lasted through to the eleventh century. By that date, Anglo-Saxon had long been the dominant tongue of the landowning class, so it was hardly surprising that its new estates received Anglo-Saxon names. By the same token, however, since this naming process began two to three hundred years after the initial Anglo-Saxon settlement, place names have become much less good evidence that their Celtic and Roman antecedents had been swept away by a deluge of Germanic settlers. More than two centuries of intervening history is plenty of time, potentially, for the Germanic language to spread through an indigenous population by processes of cultural assimilation.[5]

Pretty well everyone would accept these three basic shifts in understanding. The beginning and end points of the process of Anglo-Saxonization are also clear enough. Lowland Britain (much of what is now England) was a highly developed part of the Roman world in c.350 AD, but by 600 was dominated by Germanic-speaking elites who thought of themselves as having come from continental Europe in the intervening period. What role migration had played in all this, and how the indigenous population had fared, however, are matters of fierce debate.

That this much disagreement is possible tells you instantly that the available evidence suffers from serious limitations. A first key issue is what, exactly, was the state of Roman Britain by c.400 AD? Few doubt that it had been flourishing fifty years earlier. Its towns, admittedly, were not showing the same degree of private investment in public monuments as they had in previous centuries. But this was a common phenomenon right across the late Roman world, and needs to be understood against shifting patterns of local elite life, and not as a simple economic phenomenon, as it tended to be in the past.

It is worth pausing a moment to explore the argument. In the fourth century, patterns of Roman landowning elite life shifted decisively away from their local home towns towards imperial service. The whole point of the private investments they had previously made in the public urban monuments of their local towns had been to win power there. But, by the fourth century, this was no longer such an attractive game to play. To deal with a series of problems collectively known as the Third-Century Crisis, above all the rise of Persia to superpower status, the Roman state had confiscated all the local funds that had previously made winning power in your home town such a worthwhile goal for local Roman elites. By the fourth century, exercising power in your home town involved great responsibilities, but much less spending power. The fun of spending taxpayers' money could now be experienced only by those operating in imperial rather than hometown service. Not surprisingly, local Roman elites right across the Empire shifted their spending priorities appropriately. Instead of trying to win power at home, elite investment was increasingly directed towards preparing their children for, and moving further up within, the bureaucratic structures of imperial service. The public face of towns suffered accordingly, but this was fundamentally a cultural and political phenomenon, and not a sign of economic crisis in any straightforward sense.[6]

The evidence from rural Roman Britain fits this broader pattern well. For in the fourth century, Britain's villas were flourishing as never before. They show every sign of great wealth, with much remodelling, which saw, in particular, pictorial colour mosaics replace black and white geometric ones, and the appearance of private Christian chapels. In the old days this used to suggest a nice parallel with the arrival of colour TV, but that was so long ago now that most of my students have no idea that television ever used to be available only in black and white. The really big question, however, is how much of this rural prosperity endured to 400 AD. Of the 135 excavated British villas that have produced some Roman coins, for instance, the sequence came to an end for sixty-five of them in c.360. Does this mean that the villa economy of Britain – a much better indicator of the general health of Roman provincial life than the towns – started to decline at that point, or just that coins – never a very central feature of Roman economic exchange – were not circulating in the same way?

Some have argued the case for major dislocation, a recent historiographical trend being towards what in archaeological jargon is known as 'systems collapse'. This argues that Roman social, economic and hence political systems were all breaking down in Britain by 400, so that the end of properly Roman Britain had internal causes and that subsequent Anglo-Saxon migration wandered more or less into a power vacuum. The argument finds some further support in a seeming withdrawal of the regular Roman army from the Hadrian's Wall line in the 390s. The forts were still occupied, but the kinds of metalwork associated with Roman regulars are confined after this date to lowland Britain, suggesting to some that independent local chieftains had taken over the frontier forts. The evidence from the forts is ambiguous, however, and the general state of Roman Britain in c.400 AD does basically turn on when exactly the villa economy collapsed. Here the lack of precise dates is a problem. If the villa economy was unravelling in the later fourth century, then the end of properly Roman Britain was nothing to do with Anglo-Saxon invasion. But if the villas ended anytime after 410, the Anglo-Saxons start to appear much more likely suspects.[7]

When it comes to working out how things developed from this disputed beginning, the evidence just gets worse. Historical sources are particularly thin on the ground. One alone – *The Ruin of Britain* by the monk Gildas – was composed by a British native who was a more or less contemporary observer. The precise date at which he wrote is much disputed, but it must have been somewhere between the late fifth and the mid-sixth century. The work's big drawback, though, is that Gildas was not trying to write history, but putting together a moral tract for British kings of his own times, in which he occasionally drew on past events to illustrate points he wished to make about the present. A kind of narrative outline of the Anglo-Saxon takeover can be gleaned, but it is sparse and incomplete at best – and, in fact, some very different suggestions have been made as to how it should be read.[8] To supplement Gildas, there are a few more or less contemporary references to events in Britain in continental sources, and some very late, wildly episodic materials gathered together in the *Anglo-Saxon Chronicle*.

Some of the *Chronicle*'s stories may well reflect actual events. Its entries mostly refer to kings and their conquests, and some of this might have been recalled with a degree of outline accuracy. Sometimes, too, the events even make sense against the landscape, notably the battle of Deorham in 577 which is said to have brought Gloucester, Cirencester and Bath under Anglo-Saxon control. A visit to the site, now the grounds of Dyrham Park just outside Bath, is enough to show you why. Set on high ground, it dominates the territory around. But in overall terms, the *Chronicle*'s coverage is both limited and problematic. It really deals only with the three kingdoms – Wessex, Kent and Sussex – which later formed part of the ninth-century realm of King Alfred the Great, under whose auspices the text reached its extant form. Large areas of what became Anglo-Saxon England – from Essex to Northumbria – either receive little (Mercia and Northumbria) or no (Essex) coverage in an annalistic history which is anyway remarkable for its almost total lack of detail. Many years have no events ascribed to them, and those that do rarely get more than a couple of lines. For teaching purposes, the modern English translation of its entire coverage of the fifth and sixth centuries can be conveniently photocopied on to two sides of A4, and even then the text is not exactly crowded. What it contains is a series of disjointed episodes, not a connected narrative. Moreover, the form and the chronological problems of the text both suggest that, at some point, someone had had to guess the dates at which events ascribed to great heroes of the past, probably in oral stories, had actually occurred. Such a process is discernable in some continental sources of the fifth and sixth centuries which were also drawing in part on oral materials, and these guesses were never completely uneducated. Some sense of chronology, for instance, could be deduced from the kinds of family trees and king lists that were the standard paraphernalia of royal dynasties, and could be used to order events of which the memory had survived attached to particular individuals, such as kings who had won various battles.[9] They were guesses, not certain knowledge, however, and that, combined with the sheer paucity of information, makes the *Chronicle* of only limited use.[10] Our general knowledge of Anglo-Saxon history only starts to increase from c.600, with the arrival of the Christian missionaries. This marks the effective limit of detailed historical knowledge in Bede's *Ecclesiastical History*. After this date, Bede preserves a great deal of independent information. Before it, he largely depended on Gildas, and so still do we.

Of archaeological material there is, it seems, a greater mass. The huge amount of information we have about Roman Britain sits alongside some thirty thousand burials which belong to the early Anglo-Saxon period. But these burials were the remains of some ten to fifteen generations, deposited between the mid-fifth and late seventh centuries, a time when even conservative estimates of the population of lowland Britain would reckon its total never less than a million. Even this many burials, therefore, represents no more than a tiny sample of the original population. Two further problems make their interpretation difficult. First, dating is far from precise. No more Roman coins were imported into Britain after c.400 AD. Scientific dates (carbon-14 or dendrochronological) also remain rare since many graves were excavated before these methods had become available. So for the most part, dating has to be based on the stylistic development of the objects buried with the corpses. As we have seen in other contexts, this kind of dating can locate burials to within twenty-five years or so, which is much better than nothing. But when a developing sequence of archaeological materials is being related to known history, such a window is sometimes too imprecise to be sure whether a set of burials preceded or followed a given set of events.[11]

The second problem is more fundamental. These early Anglo-Saxon burials take two basic forms. In central and southern England, archaeologists have uncovered a large number of quite small inhumation cemeteries, some of the burials being richly furnished with gravegoods. Further east, in parts of East Anglia and along the north-east coast, a smaller number of much larger cremation cemeteries have been excavated (Map 11). The cremation cemeteries raise few problems of attribution. A cremation habit was entirely foreign to late Roman Britain, and both the burial form and the identifiable objects that survived the cremation process have direct antecedents in fourth- and early fifth-century materials from south-eastern Jutland. There is not much doubt, then, that Germanic-speaking immigrants from the Jutland region generated the cremation cemeteries of eastern England.[12]

The inhumation cemeteries are more problematic. For one thing, they contain a large number of burials without gravegoods. Who were these people? Were they poorer Anglo-Saxons, left-over Romano-Britains, whose standard burial rite had indeed been unfurnished inhumation, or people who just chose not to bury their dead with gravegoods? Likewise, while there is little doubt that many of the items found in the furnished graves (brooches, sleeve fasteners, weapons and so on) were first made and used by continental Germanic-speaking populations, this is not true of them all, and, more generally, it can be argued that their appearance and spread in England is not a safe guide to the extent of Anglo-Saxon immigration. Unlike the cremation rite of eastern England, the dress items found in the inhumation cemeteries were not lifted lock, stock and barrel from one particular corner of the Germanic-speaking continent. Particular combinations of items eventually became confined to specific corners of England, but many of these items originated in disparate areas of Germania. Sleeve fasteners, for instance, became a distinctive element in the dress of early Anglo-Saxons living just inland from the Wash, but whereas most of what they wore had disparate origins the fasteners themselves had only been found earlier in parts of western Norway.[13] It looks, in other words, as if the process that unfolded in lowland

Britain was similar to that underlying the so-called Danubian style of Attila's Empire (Chapter 5). New and distinct Anglo-Saxon dress combinations coalesced out of a wide variety of sources in lowland Britain in the fifth century.

If dress items and habits were being passed around between different groups of Germanic immigrants, there is no obvious reason why they could not also have been passing from Anglo-Saxon immigrants to Romano-British natives. We are all now comfortable with the idea that under certain conditions new identities can be adopted. This tends to happen particularly when old identities are in flux, which was true both for Anglo-Saxon immigrants and Romano-British natives in the fifth and sixth centuries. The boundaries of the new Anglo-Saxon kingdoms differed from the pre-existing political structures of Britain, and there is no reason to suppose, either, that they had been transposed from the continent. Famously, individuals with British names – Cerdic and Cynric – appear in the ancestry of the ruling house of Wessex, and the late seventh-century law code from this kingdom, known as *Ine's Law*, explicitly mentions the presence within it of substantial landowners of indigenous non-Anglo-Saxon descent. These are strong indications that Wessex may have been created by a complex Anglo-Saxon/Romano-British double act, rather than a simple Germanic conquest. The cemetery of Warperton in Warwickshire also provides a so far unique example of a chronological progression from late Roman to Saxon-style burials within the single graveyard. This too is suggestive of processes of cultural assimilation. Particularly since many of the inhumation cemeteries continued in use for two hundred years, from the fifth into the sixth and seventh centuries, by which time there must have been much intermingling between immigrant and native, it is perfectly reasonable to question whether continental dress accessories can really be used as a guide to the origins of the corpse found displaying them.[14]

Neither the available archaeological nor the available literary evidence answers in any straightforward way, then, the key questions about the extent and nature of Anglo-Saxon immigration. Nor, unfortunately, is there any immediate prospect of new methodologies or sources of information filling the gap. DNA testing and isotope analysis have both come on stream in the last decade or so to offer new paths forward, but neither looks likely to provide easy answers. So far, it is unclear whether ancient DNA can really be extracted from fifth- and sixth-century skeletons preserved in typically damp British conditions. The jury remains firmly out, and while it is deciding, less direct routes have been explored. The most important concerns the distribution of particular gene combinations within the male Y chromosome among modern English males. This is potentially very useful. The Y chromosome is handed down unchanged over time from father to son through the male line, and there is one gene combination which can with some plausibility be linked to an intrusive population group of males moving from northern continental Europe into lowland Britain in the middle of the first millennium AD. This gene combination is now very widely distributed among modern Englishmen, being found in 75 per cent or more of those sampled.

But how should this exciting new evidence be interpreted? The researchers initially argued that their findings confirmed what the Victorians had always thought, that something akin to ethnic cleansing took place during the Anglo-Saxon invasions with the 75 per cent distribution among the modern population reflecting a 75 per cent replacement of males in the fifth and sixth centuries. Given, however, that arriviste Anglo-Saxon males formed – on any estimate – a new elite in the land, and had therefore greater access both to food and to females, you have to figure that they had a bigger chance of passing on their genes to the next generation than the indigenous Romano-British. And more recent mathematical modelling by the same researchers has shown that you don't have to make that breeding advantage very large for the 75 per cent result among the modern English population to have been generated from an intrusive male group that was originally no larger than 10–15 per cent of its fifth- and sixth-century counterpart. Self-evidently, therefore, the modern DNA evidence is not going to settle the quarrel between those favouring mass Anglo-Saxon migration and those persuaded by elite transfer and emulation.[15]

Nor does isotope analysis look any more promising in overall terms, although it generates fascinating individual results. This technique works on the basis that the mineral contents of an individual's teeth carry the signature of where they grew up, transmitted into the chemical composition of dental remains by the water drunk as a child or teenager, depending on whether you're looking at baby or adult teeth. Some of these chemical signatures can be recognized as belonging to particular regions, where those regions are geologically distinct.

Potentially, therefore, you might be able to show whether an individual buried in Anglo-Saxon clothing really came from the continent, or was an identity-swapping Romano-British wolf. The problem, however, is that the technique will work only for first-generation immigrants. The child of two *echt* Jutlanders, if born after they crossed the North Sea, will have grown up with absolutely East Anglian teeth. Much expensive sampling and a lot of very precise chronological identification would be required, therefore, for isotope analysis to produce any broad conclusions. And given that the offspring even of first-generation Anglo-Saxon immigrants will have had British teeth, I doubt that it ever will. For the moment, therefore, neither isotope nor DNA analysis offers us an obvious way past the intellectual impasse between mass migration and elite transfer originally generated by the limitations of the traditional historical and archaeological evidence.[16]

So by themselves, the available bodies of source material set up an intellectual problem, but offer no obvious solution to it. The historical evidence is much too thin to provide a convincing picture of what went on in lowland Britain in the fifth and sixth centuries, while the major transformations in material culture can be explained either in terms of mass invasion or mass cultural emulation. The new understanding of late Roman Britain, likewise, shows that the province's population was much too large to make ethnic cleansing even the remotest possibility, but the linguistic evidence from post-600 AD shows precious little sign of indigenous influence on the Germanic tongue of the Anglo-Saxon world which emerged from Britain's late antique Dark Age. The argument is more than a little stuck, but if we think first about the evidence of the Anglo-Saxon migration flow itself rather than its effects upon Britain, and then reconsider the issue of mass migration versus elite transfer from a more comparative perspective, it does become possible to move the argument past its traditional roadblocks.

### Adventus Saxonum

The historical work of the Venerable Bede, written in his Jarrow monastery in the early eighth century, provides two dates for the *Adventus Saxonum*: the arrival of Saxon invaders in Britain. The first is 446, based on Gildas' record that the British appealed for imperial

assistance to Aetius, de facto ruler of the Roman west in the mid-fifth
century, when he was 'consul for the third time'. Gildas did not date
this appeal, but Bede had access to Roman consular lists which told
him that Aetius' third consulship fell in the year 446. His other date is
c.450–5, derived from a Kentish dynastic tradition of his own time
that its founders had established themselves in that south-eastern
corner of Britain during the joint reign of the Emperors Marcian and
Valentinian III.[17] Among more modern scholars, however, there is
widespread agreement that, whatever its scale, the flow of Anglo-
Saxon migration into lowland Britain was not a one-off event, but a
long-extended process.

The only account of its origins is to be found in Gildas' *Ruin of
Britain*. This tells us that the Anglo-Saxon takeover stemmed from
extensive attacks made by Picts and Scots (from Ireland and Scotland
respectively) upon the British provinces after they had dropped out of
the Roman imperial system. Plenty of controversy surrounds the
details, but other contemporary sources tell us that in 406 or thereabouts the Roman army in Britain had put up the usurper Constantine
III, who shifted his command to Gaul to fight the Rhine invaders.
Eventually, perhaps in 409, the British provinces revolted again,
breaking away – it seems – from the usurper's control. Shortly afterwards, they may or may not have received a letter from the western
Emperor Honorius telling them that they would have to look after
their own defence. At this point, however, such a letter would have
been no more than *de jure* recognition of the *de facto* situation.
Honorius could do nothing to help, and the Britons found themselves
in a decidedly sub- or post-Roman situation.[18]

It is at this point that Gildas apparently picks up the story. The
difficulties facing the Romano-British, now independent, eventually
became so severe, that

> they convened a council to decide the best and soundest way to
> counter the brutal and repeated invasions and plunderings . . .
> Then all the members of the council, together with the proud
> tyrant, were struck blind; the guard . . . they devised for our land
> was . . . the ferocious Saxons . . . A pack of cubs burst forth from
> the lair of the barbarian lioness, coming in three *keels*, as they call
> warships in their language . . . On the orders of the tyrant they
> first of all fixed their dreadful claws on the east side of the island,

ostensibly to fight for our country, in fact to fight against it. The mother lioness learnt that her first contingent had prospered, and she sent a second and larger troop of satellite dogs ... [Eventually the Saxons] complained that their monthly allowance was insufficient ... and swore that they would break their agreement and plunder the whole island unless more lavish payment were heaped upon them. There was no delay, they put their threats into immediate effect ... A fire heaped up and nurtured by the hand of the impious easterners spread from sea to sea. It devastated town and country round about, and, once it was alight, it did not die down until it had burned almost the whole surface of the island and was licking the western ocean with its fierce red tongue.

Despite all these defeats, which caused many British, Gildas tells us, either to surrender themselves into slavery under the invaders, or flee overseas, the Romano-British were not finished. Even when Aetius turned down their final appeal for imperial assistance, they continued to resist. One of their number, the famous Aurelius Ambrosius, historical prototype of the mythical Arthur, organized a counterattack which culminated in a great British victory at the siege of the unidentified Badon Hill. After this, prosperity returned to the island, a happy state of affairs that lasted for the entire and considerable intervening period down to the moment that Gildas wrote.[19]

One major problem with Gildas' account from the modern historian's perspective is chronological imprecision. When did the events he describes begin? Gildas gives no indication at all of when the council might have issued its original and ill-fated invitation to the Saxon mercenaries. Bede clearly supposed that all the action from invitation to revolt and beyond unfolded in quick succession, and hence dated the arrival of the Saxons to 446, on the basis of the appeal made in the middle of the mayhem to Aetius when he was consul for the third time. Most modern scholars would argue that the action was much more drawn out, on the basis of contemporary sources of reasonable quality which record some major Saxon attacks on Britain already in c.410. This makes it likely that the original invitation for mercenary assistance would have been issued a generation or so before Bede supposed, which is compatible with Gildas' actual wording. Gildas' account then becomes a brief summary of a lengthier sequence. A more extended chronology also fits well with the fact that the earliest datable Saxon remains in England belong to the 430s.[20]

As for the Saxon revolt that spread its fire 'from sea to sea', the best chronological fix we have on this part of the action may come from a continental source, the so-called *Gallic Chronicle of 452* (so called in a fit of wild scholarly fancy because it was put together in Gaul in 452), which reports that Britain fell to the Saxons in 441/2. This chronicle was composed only a decade after the reported events, and we know that considerable contact had continued between the Romano-British and Roman Gaul after 409 – on which more in a moment – so that it is actually a pretty decent piece of evidence. There are other possible ways of construing events, certainly, but it seems most natural to associate Gildas' mercenary revolt with the mayhem of the early 440s. And by the 460s, at least one important British leader was operating in northern Gaul, in the Loire region, which would tie in with Gildas' report that some British fled overseas. And even if you were to deny this specific association, one period of major Saxon invasion and British disaster would anyway have to be dated to the mid-fifth century on the basis of the *Chronicle*.[21] That, however, wasn't the end of the story. Gildas closed his historical excursus on a remarkably high note, which is one reason why his text has sometimes been considered a late fake. Thanks to Aurelius Ambrosius, the Romano-Britons were eventually successful, and, while detailed geography is non-existent, the general sense of Gildas' account is that in the forty-year peace that followed Badon Hill the Saxons were confined, at most, to the eastern end of the island. Most historians would date this peace to sometime between 480 and 550 AD.[22]

When Bede's detailed historical narrative begins in earnest, however, with the arrival of the Roman mission in Kent in 597, virtually all of lowland Britain was firmly under Anglo-Saxon control. Either there had been further dramatic Anglo-Saxon advances in the mid- to late sixth century, or the level of Romano-British success implied by Gildas is massively misleading. The available evidence suggests the former. For what it's worth, the *Anglo-Saxon Chronicle* places a major expansionary phase in the history of Wessex in the late sixth century when, under the leadership of one Ceawlin and his nephew Ceolwulf, great tracts of Devon and Somerset first passed into Anglo-Saxon hands. Despite the text's problems, this may preserve echoes of an important later phase of expansion. Most of the royal dynasties that controlled the seventh-century Anglo-Saxon kingdoms which appear in Bede's History, likewise, seem to have descended from an ancestor whose floruit dates to the last quarter of the sixth century rather than earlier.[23] This again suggests that something important happened after Gildas had finished writing.

Continental evidence adds further weight to the argument, showing that Saxon populations remained highly mobile into the sixth century. One substantial group of Saxon migrants, reportedly twenty thousand strong, moved south in its middle years, eventually participating in the Lombard invasion of Italy. Another established an enclave at the mouth of the Loire at more or less the same time (the 560s).[24] Such unimpeachable evidence of continued demographic upheaval in the Saxon homeland makes it entirely plausible to suppose that still more Saxons were at the same time following the route to Britain. Continental influence from a different direction also shows up in some of the later archaeological materials. Contacts of some kind between Scandinavia and East Anglia, quite possibly a new migration flow from Norway in particular, were established from the late fifth century, and there is some reason for thinking that the East Anglian royal dynasty had Scandinavian roots. Bede, in fact, generally agrees with the archaeology. He reports that Germanic immigration into Britain drew upon a very wide range of manpower: not just the Angles, Saxons and Jutes he mentions in the first book of his Ecclesiastical History, but also Frisians, Rugi, Danes and others besides.[25] Burials in the Anglo-Saxon inhumation cemeteries increase in frequency, likewise, from the late fifth century onwards: from one in every four years in c.500 AD to one every two to three years by c.600.[26] This can be explained in several ways: the conversion of Romano-British to Anglo-Saxon cultural norms, or a natural increase in numbers among the immigrants. All the same, something apparently tipped the balance of power established at Badon Hill firmly in favour of the Germanic-speaking immigrants – or at least the dominance of their cultural forms – in the mid- to late sixth century. In all probability, continued immigration from the continent played some part in the process.

Sparse and difficult though it is, then, the evidence strongly suggests that continental migration to Britain in the fifth and sixth centuries took the form of a flow, like that of Germanic-speakers south to the Black Sea in the third century or of Lombards towards the Middle Danube in the fourth and fifth (Chapters 3 and 5), or indeed of the Vikings to the west in the ninth, rather than a single concentrated pulse as was the case, for instance, in 376. Its minimum duration would appear to have been c.410 to 575, although even this might be a substantial underestimate. The movement was probably also not continuous, ebbing and flowing with the lows and highs of the struggle it generated with elements, at least, of the indigenous Romano-British population. Unless Gildas is substantially misrepresenting the career of Aurelius Ambrosius – and there is no reason to think he was, since to do so would have undermined the case he was trying to make to a British political audience who knew these events for themselves – immigration into Britain must have become considerably less attractive after the native victory at Badon Hill. Interestingly, both Gregory of Tours and Procopius note the presence of Germanic-speakers from north of the Channel among the continental Franks in the first half of the sixth century, suggesting that this period, which coincides with the aftermath of Badon Hill in most chronologies, even saw some reverse migration.[27] Furthermore, the flow clearly recruited from a wide geographical area, to judge both by Bede's historical account of the migrants' origins and the geographically diverse origins of the material culture that spread among them.

None of these sources gives you any sense of the overall numbers of immigrants involved in this highly extended flow. Many of the individual migrant groups, especially at the beginning, may well have been small. According to Gildas, the initial force of mercenaries came in just three boats, and could therefore have numbered little more than a hundred men. Three ships is possibly something of a folklore motif, however, and not all the groups need have been that small.[28] On the continent, groups of Saxons up to twenty thousand in number – explicitly including women and children – took to the road in the fifth and sixth centuries, and some larger groups of this type may possibly have come to Britain. The large cremation cemeteries of eastern England, for instance, look like the remains of more unified migrant groups than the smaller inhumation cemeteries of southern England, though they are certainly not the burial sites of groups twenty thousand strong. It is likely enough, too, that the migration flow would have had to respond to the changing nature of British resistance. It is the central drift of Gildas' narrative summary, and the basis of his unflattering comparison with the current state of affairs, that Aurelius Ambrosius had pulled substantial numbers of the native

British together into a reasonably united response to the Saxons, but that this strength was now being dissipated by competition amongst his lesser successors. The immigrants, of course, would necessarily have had to respond in kind to Ambrosius' success, fielding more substantial forces of their own to resist the greater level of British resistance that he organized. Even if the immigrants started out in small parties, therefore, concerted British counterattack would have forced them to reform into larger units.

There is no narrative evidence to support this vision of ebb and flow, but its reality might well be reflected in, and is certainly compatible with, the seemingly late arrival into England of the ruling dynasties of the Anglo-Saxon kingdoms of c.600 and beyond. These were perhaps the leaders who provided the greater unity necessary to turn the tide of war once more in an Anglo-Saxon direction. If accepted in its outlines, such a picture of the migration flow would have many parallels. The evolution of migration flows into new forms to overcome obstacles, or to allow a range of greater ambitions to be fulfilled is, as we have seen, a common thread from the third-century Goths to the ninth-century Vikings, to the nineteenth-century Boers. It is also, of course, an underlying constant in work on group identities, that they form and strengthen in the face of conflict (Chapter 1). Nonetheless, it is important not to overstate the military problem that even a more united Romano-British world presented. The Saxons never faced an opponent with anything like the military power of the western imperial state encountered by continental migrants on to Roman soil. Hence it is not surprising that the end result of the Anglo-Saxon takeover was a multiplicity of smaller kingdoms, certainly at least ten and perhaps many more, in c.600. The new kingdoms of Anglo-Saxon England encompassed military forces which added up to far more than a few boatloads, but the lower degree of danger faced on British soil was insufficient to make them go through the kind of process of political unification that proved necessary to the Visigoths, Vandals, Franks or Ostrogoths, all of whom were operating in contexts requiring military forces in the tens of thousands.[29]

It is also certain that the migration flow included women and children. The first mercenary groups presumably were all-male, but female dress items of continental Germanic origin (again, especially brooches) provide much of the archaeological evidence unearthed from the cemeteries. Some of this material could have arrived without women attached, destined for Saxon invaders' Romano-British brides; but to suggest that there were no women at all looks rather forced, not least since migrant groups of Saxons on the continent certainly took women and children with them. There are two possible reasons why Saxon groups migrating to Britain may have been skewed to the male gender. The first is again the smaller scale of some of the action. Before the era of Aurelius Ambrosius, military retinues numbering in the few hundreds might have been sufficient to carve out niches within Britain for intrusive Saxon leaders. If so, these leaders would have had less or no need to recruit followers more broadly within their home societies, and hence there was less likelihood of men with families becoming involved. The second was logistics. The large-scale land-based migrations of this period – all those documented, at least – moved baggage and the physically less able in huge wagon trains, thousands of vehicles strong. This must have been cumbersome enough, but shifting families, animals and baggage across the Channel or North Sea to Britain represented an entirely different order of logistic difficulty. Shipping non-combatants would not only have meant finding more ships, but would also have incurred many other costs.

Nonetheless, comparative evidence suggests that we should not overstate the likely effect of either factor. There is unimpeachable DNA evidence that the ninth- and tenth-century Norse took Scandinavian women with them to Iceland in substantial numbers, as well as other females they had picked up in the meantime from Scotland, Ireland and the northern and western isles. About one-third of modern Icelandic female DNA is derived from Norwegian ancestry. Even if the immediate forebears of these ancestors had moved over the North Sea first, so that the Norwegian babes journeying to Iceland came only from the islands or mainland of northern Britain, this would stress only that the initial Norse settlements in Britain had involved Norse women in large numbers. And all of these ninth- and tenth-century sea crossings – from Scandinavia to the northern British Isles and from there on to Iceland – were longer, more difficult and more costly than those of the fifth and sixth centuries that brought Anglo-Saxons to southern Britain. It is also the case that a substantial female presence is required to explain the degree of language change that followed in southern Britain. We will return to this issue in more detail in a moment, but the dominance of the immigrants' Germanic language, which was essentially untouched by native British Celtic tongues, could never have occurred, in the absence of Saxon grammar schools, if Germanic mothers had not been teaching it to their children.[30]

If the overall scale of Anglo-Saxon migration into lowland Britain in the fifth and sixth centuries is highly debatable, we can make some headway with its nature: namely, an extended flow of population over time which included women and children. Thanks to the dearth of historical sources, we are again short of explicit information about its causes, but it is a pretty safe bet that an overriding motivation among the migrants was the wealth of the relatively developed Romano-British agricultural economy. Gildas' account indicates as much. In his view, it was the prospect of good pay that brought the original Saxon mercenaries to England, and their subsequent revolt focused on ransacking the island for everything they could find once they couldn't extract any more cash.[31] Having made themselves supreme, they then took control of the landscape – the primary means of wealth production in this fundamentally agricultural world – to ensure their prosperity in the longer term. By 400 AD, the Romano-British economy may or may not have been past its mid-fourth century peak, but either way it was still much more developed than the rural world inhabited by the Anglo-Saxons on the other side of the North Sea. And in fact we have unimpeachable evidence that this greater wealth had long held an attraction for Germanic populations from less developed landscapes over the water.

Saxon pirates had been finding their way across the North Sea to lowland Britain from at least the mid-third century. And although narrative accounts to this effect are lacking – one major sea-borne Saxon raid on northern Gaul is reported in some detail by Ammianus, but none on Britain – we have impressive indirect evidence that Saxon sea raiders had remained a threat to Romano-British landowners throughout the fourth century. From the late third, the central Roman authorities operated a unified military command which encompassed both sides of the Channel and the eastern shoreline of Britain. Its commander disposed of naval flotillas and garrisons, and a string of powerful fortifications some of which survived the Saxon takeover. The massive fortifications of Portchester (just outside modern Portsmouth) were formidable enough, indeed, to fulfil many functions right through the medieval period and down to the Napoleonic War, when it served as a prison camp for French sailors. This whole collection of men and materiel was designated the *litus Saxonum* – 'the Saxon Shore'

– leaving no doubt as to the threat it was designed to counter (Plate 15). That the Romans should have bothered to maintain a military investment on this scale suggests that Saxon sea raids, if usually small, were nevertheless an endemic problem.[32]

In the drawn-out migration flow of the fifth and sixth centuries, there was plenty of time for subsidiary motives to come into play as well. Sea levels were rising in the North Sea, to the extent that some continental communities may have been more ready to move because their traditional way of life was under threat. More than a few long-standing coastal villages – including many of the *terpen* we met in Chapter 2 – came to an end in this period. Abandonment stretched, in fact, over a very wide area: from the Frisian coast to the Elbe–Weser region, all the way to Schleswig-Holstein. In the past, this phenomenon led some to suggest that rising sea levels were the fundamental cause of Anglo-Saxon migration, but this is overstating the case. Eastern England, where many of the migrants ended up, was also affected by rising sea levels, and eventually land was abandoned well beyond the coastal regions of Saxony as the fifth century turned into the sixth. At most, then, rising sea levels can have been only a secondary factor. By the sixth century too, Merovingian Frankish power began to intrude aggressively into the Saxon homeland. It was this political factor that prompted the exodus of those twenty thousand Saxons who eventually joined the Lombards, and there is no reason why Frankish pressure should not have led others to join their peers across the North Sea. Nonetheless, a broadly voluntary, economic motivation was probably the main cause of the Anglo-Saxon migration flow, since it began long before the Franks became a factor. This is also suggested by its basic nature.[33] A drawn-out process, as opposed to a sudden surge of migrants, does more suggest the steady pull of economic attraction than the impact of major political crisis, such as that which propelled the Goths across the Danube in 376.

As the existence of the *litus Saxonum* also shows us, the active field of information necessary for any migration flow already existed between lowland Britain and northern Germania by the year 400. Anglo-Saxon migration was exploiting known routes, and in some ways represented merely an extension of a pre-existing tendency towards Germanic expansion in this direction. The wealth of Roman Britain was well known to Saxon raiders of the third and fourth centuries, whose understanding no doubt included plenty of information about coastal and North Sea waters, and the best routes to take to target areas. This will also have included considerable knowledge of inland areas, since all rivers leading to the interior of Britain will have been part of the zone explored by ship-borne attack. First-millennium boats were small enough to go far inland along the rivers and were not restricted just to immediate coastal hinterlands. Gildas' account suggests that this fund of information continued to expand as the fifth century progressed, very much as a developing knowledge base underpins modern migration flows. The first Saxons may well have been a mercenary outfit, as Gildas reports, hired by former or potential victims of previous predations to help in their defence. Such a move had been prefigured, it seems, at the end of the third century, when a usurping Roman commander in Britain, Carausius, initially appointed to fight Saxon and Frankish pirates, incorporated some of them into his forces. It was also fairly common in the later Viking period. Sea raiders were difficult for land-based forces to combat. News of the mercenaries' prosperity led others to join them on the British side of the North Sea. This need not always have been the deep, dark plot that Gildas supposed. The original mercenaries may have signed up in good faith, but, as the situation developed – in other words as the information field expanded – their ambition increased, perhaps, or new Saxon groups with greater ambitions saw the opportunity for self-enrichment on a grand scale and moved in on the action, just as small-scale raiders in the Viking period were eventually supplanted by more important leaders with larger followings.[34]

It was not new geographical information about lowland Britain, then, that transformed Saxon raiding into Saxon migration as the fifth century progressed, but an increased understanding that the previous political and strategic situation had been transformed out of all recognition. As long as Britain remained part of the Roman Empire, any serious attempts by continental Saxons to annex its landed assets were doomed to failure. The forces of the *litus Saxonum* were more than powerful enough to deal with raiders not smart enough to beat a hasty retreat: exactly the fate suffered by those Saxon raiders who turned up in Gaul in the time of Ammianus. Once Britain fell out of the Roman system, however, much more than the odd hit-and-run raid became possible, and not only for ambitious Saxons. As Gildas reports and other evidence confirms, raiders and even immigrants from Ireland and Scotland – Scots and Picts respectively – were also queuing up to feast on the remains.[35] The pull of a developed, Roman-style economy underlay the entire sequence of events, and, as with the other migration flows we have examined, the intermixing of politics and economics could not be clearer. The wealth of lowland Britain could become available to Saxon migrants only if they took its political control into their own hands, and this only became possible when Britain lost its Roman umbrella. It took perhaps as much as a generation for the continental intruders to realize how vulnerable their preferred British targets now were. Raiding seems to have begun already, as we have seen, in c.410, but it was c.440 before the situation turned really nasty, at least according to continental observers. This is a plausible time lag for the Anglo-Saxons either to come to realize that the old blocks on full-scale expansion had been removed, or to develop a range of new ambitions that went beyond raiding to outright annexation.

Prevailing political structures also shaped the action on another level. Compared with contemporary migratory phenomena on the continent, what's striking about the Anglo-Saxon case is how much evidence there is for small-scale activity. By 600, the end result of the migration flow was, as we have seen, a series of relatively small Anglo-Saxon kingdoms. The same is true of the Romano-British world, which, in the era after Aurelius Ambrosius at least, fragmented in political terms. Looking at this pattern, one recent study has questioned why there were so few examples from fifth-century continental Europe of the kind of local takeover of power evident in the person of Aurelius Ambrosius, or in the quite small kingdoms which dominated Cornwall and Wales in Gildas' day.[36]

In part, this oddity was a result of transport logistics, whose impact went far beyond a possible skewing of gender ratios. Anglo-Saxon migration into Britain had to take the form of an extended flow of population rather than a single pulse of invasion because of the impossibility of transporting large numbers of people across the North Sea at one go. In one respect, the evidence is equivocal. We don't know whether the population of Jutland customarily used ships with sails in the fifth century or not, and oar-powered vessels could have transported large numbers of passengers only on a one-way trip since there was little room in them for other than the rowers themselves. But sail-powered ships were available just a little way down the coast in Roman Channel ports, and there is no reason to suppose that their captains were not being paid to carry Saxons in larger numbers to Britain (as their counterparts elsewhere carried Goths and others across the Black Sea in the third century, and the Vandal–Alan coalition across the Straits of Gibraltar in 429). Other Saxons, as we know, were making their way as far as the Loire at the same time, which would have been one hell of a row. More important than the sail issue, therefore, is the fact that the available ships were all small, and limited in number. Just as more modern migration across the Atlantic was limited to a steady trickle until the advent of transatlantic liners in the later nineteenth century, so it was logistically impossible for large numbers of Anglo-Saxons to arrive en masse on the British coast.[37]

But the political context, too, played a crucial role in shaping the British outcome. On the continent, migrants were forced to operate in large concentrations because they needed to put substantial military forces into the field, whether to survive in the face of Roman imperial power or to escape from Hunnic control. No such constraints operated in Britain. Local government in the Roman provinces, not least the raising of taxes, operated on the basis of the city territory – the *civitas* – and it was thus that sub-Roman Britain seems to have continued. It was the tax revenues of these city units, no longer handed over to the Roman state, which provided, it seems, the Anglo-Saxon mercenaries' pay. The boundaries of some of the easternmost, therefore presumably the earliest, Anglo-Saxon kingdoms – East Anglia, Essex, Lindsey and Kent (Map 11) – roughly correspond to likely *civitas* boundaries, suggesting that they might have been founded by migrants taking over the relevant *civitates* (cities) as still-functioning entities. But these *civitas* territories were not very large, and could never have supported large armed forces. This state of affairs must have evolved in the time of Aurelius Ambrosius. From this point, perhaps, you did have to organize a larger migration force if you wanted to carve out a nice piece of lowland Britain from the now more organized Romano-British. Even so, no sixth-century Romano-British king could field anything like the armies available to the Roman state or Attila the Hun, so the difference in requisite magnitude was still enormous, and any British military-cum-political unity proved only temporary. One of Gildas' main declared motives for writing was precisely the fact that the political leaders of his own generation (and he names five kings) were squandering the Ambrosian inheritance by petty internal squabbling.[38]

As far as we can reconstruct it, therefore, the Anglo-Saxon migration flow was no *Völkerwanderung* and little resembled the old culture-historical model of mass movement combined with ethnic cleansing. It was a long-drawn-out phenomenon, not an event as Bede's single date for the *Adventus Saxonum* might lead you to think. Many of the groups involved were perhaps small, especially at the beginning, but probably increased in scale as obstacles were encountered. Women and children also participated. The motivation was a desire to profit from the wealth of lowland Britain's developed agricultural economy, but secondary factors affected at least the speed of the flow at different moments, and there was also a strong political dimension, since the wealth of Britain could only be accessed fully by seizing control of the land. For all the shortage of information, therefore, the Anglo-Saxon migration into lowland Britain clearly took the form of a predatory population flow. And, as the comparative literature on migration would suggest, it is also fairly easy to work out the profound effect of factors such as the availability of information, logistics, and the evolving political-cum-strategic context in which it was operating.

But what about the question we have so far avoided? Was the Anglo-Saxon migration flow a case of elite transfer, or need we think in terms of a different migration model?

## The Limits of Emulation

It's worth considering what is at stake. In its classic form, the elite-transfer/cultural-emulation model would suggest that incoming Germanic-speakers represented only a small percentage of the total population that either partly or wholly replaced the indigenous Romano-British landowning elite. The bulk of the Romano-British population remained in place and massively outnumbered the immigrants, but, over time, absorbed the latter's material and non-material culture until immigrant and native became indistinguishable. What you essentially see is an overwhelming majority of Romano-British voluntarily exchanging their group identities to become Anglo-Saxons. The underlying purpose of this model is specifically to show that massive material and non-material cultural transformation in a Germanic direction can reasonably be explained by only a limited number of Anglo-Saxon immigrants having come across the North Sea. More generally, it is part of a broader argument downplaying the importance of Anglo-Saxon migration as an agent of major change. For in most of the variants put forward, what happens in Roman Britain before the Anglo-Saxons arrive (for example, the collapse of Roman structures), and the reaction of the natives to their arrival (their voluntary decisions to become Anglo-Saxons), are at least as important as the migration flow itself. As such, the model was originally, and in its variant forms has continued to be, framed in reaction to past overuse of the invasion hypothesis.[39]

The other side of the argument has become harder to define, since no one now believes that the incoming Anglo-Saxons wiped out or expelled virtually all the native population. Anglo-Saxon 'mass' migration just isn't what it used to be. In a very real sense, it is now defined negatively, against the elite-transfer model. Fundamentally, it amounts to the proposition that there were too many Anglo-Saxon migrants for them to be categorized as just an aristocratic elite, and, more generally, that they – rather than the indigenous population by their own free choice – were responsible for the cultural and other transformations that unfolded in lowland Britain. So Anglo-Saxon numbers are at the heart of the argument, along with the overall nature of their relations with the indigenous population. Were the Romano-British free to respond to the arrival of the Anglo-Saxons as they chose, or were the immigrants aggressive and politically dominant? Of these two issues, the question of numbers is at first sight the more problematic, since it is precisely on this issue that none of our sources provides straightforward information. We have only very broad estimates of the native Romano-British population in c.400 AD, and little of substance on the scale of the subsequent Anglo-Saxon migration flow. But if we don't obsess about precise numbers, a more productive way forward begins to emerge.

The place to start is with the revolution in the organization of the countryside which unfolded in the fifth and sixth centuries. Late Roman Britain was divided into a number of large and medium-sized estates, many run from villas: substantial country houses-cum-estate-centres. Land, as in much of the Roman world, was unequally distributed, with large quantities in the hands of a relatively small landowning class. By c.600, this property distribution had been replaced with another, worked out on a very different basis. Not only had all the villa buildings fallen out of use, but the estate boundaries, too, had failed to survive. In only one or two cases has it even been suggested that old Roman estate boundaries were still in use in the Anglo-Saxon period, and none of these has been convincingly proven. In effect, the economic map of the countryside had been totally redrawn. By 600 AD, Anglo-Saxon kings had delineated larger zones for the purposes of taxation, but much of the farming was based on much smaller units than the old Roman villas, and it was not until the ninth century that large centrally organized estates began to re-emerge in the English countryside. These were the first of the manors, which went on to become a dominant feature of the countryside by the time of *Doomsday Book*.[40]

This shows us immediately that the Anglo-Saxon takeover was not a simple case of elite transfer after the classic pattern of the Norman Conquest, half a millennium later. By the time the information recorded in *Doomsday Book* was gathered, twenty years after Hastings, the indigenous Anglo-Saxon aristocracy had been swept away, its lands transferred to William the Conqueror's chief henchmen: the so-called tenants-in-chief. The process reached down to more local elites, the gentry, because the tenants-in-chief in turn enriched their more important followers by granting them economic rights over large amounts of the land that they themselves had received. This secondary process was as much a political necessity as the Conqueror's original gifts to his tenants-in-chief, because it was the loyal service of all these men that had made the conquest possible, and they were consequently expecting a share in the profits of their joint military enterprise. As a result, the Anglo-Saxon gentry as well as the aristocracy lost ownership of their land, even if some still survived as tenants on property they had previously owned.

But a central feature of the process was that none of this property-swapping disturbed existing estate boundaries, or changed the working pattern of the manorial economy. As functioning farming units, the manors continued to operate. There were some alterations in detail, and a convincing argument can be made that elements of the Anglo-Saxon peasantry suffered a considerable demotion. Fundamentally, however, manorial estate boundaries and the general working of the rural economy were left undisturbed by the massive transfer of property rights which resulted from the Normans' great victory. This was the best possible economic outcome for the Norman conquerors. The main activity of a manor was arable agriculture – growing grain –

using a centrally directed labour force, but it still needed its pasture-lands and woods to provide for the animals and people without whom the estate could not function. Any disturbance of these arrangements would have lowered agricultural outputs and the new estate owners' incomes.[41]

The Anglo-Saxon takeover of the fifth and sixth centuries, by contrast, did not see anything like such a straightforward transfer of property. The new Anglo-Saxon landowning elites did not simply take possession of existing villa estates, even though this would, in economic terms, have been much the best option. Like the manors of the eleventh century, Roman villa estates were integrated farming units whose output had provided the wealth for a very prosperous class of rural landowners. Changing villa boundaries meant disturbing the actual functioning of the rural economy, and there is good evidence that this process, as you would expect, led to substantial declines in rural output. While the overall area under cultivation did not change markedly (this is shown by pollen analysis), even if some marginal areas were abandoned, more complicated estate structures fell out of use. Some of the Roman-era drainage mechanisms around the Thames at Dorchester, for instance, were not maintained into the Saxon period, and a less sophisticated 'scratch plough' generally replaced the heavy Roman ploughs previously in use. The latter were expensive items of capital equipment because of the costs incurred in generating enough spare fodder to overwinter the draught animals required to pull them. Presumably the smaller farming units of the early Anglo-Saxon era could not afford to maintain them, even if they had wanted to.[42] This also goes a long way towards explaining why the old towns of Roman Britain lost what was left of their urban character. They had not been centres of industrial production, anyway, but, 'agro-towns', existing to serve certain functions in a relatively developed agricultural economy, in return for which some food surpluses found their way out of the countryside to feed the urban population. If you disturbed the organization of the rural economy, particularly by simplifying its functioning and reducing total output, you would be cutting away at the roots of this kind of urbanism, so that it is not surprising that the towns as such disappeared in the post-Roman period, even if they sometimes retained an administrative importance, with new Anglo-Saxon royal palaces being established within their boundaries.[43] The next question, therefore, is an obvious one. Why did the Anglo-Saxon takeover break up existing Roman estate structures, even though this brought with it substantial economic costs?

One line of approach has located the answer to this conundrum in developments internal to Britain before the Anglo-Saxons arrived. Some have seen the British rebellion of 409 reported by Zosimus as a kind of peasants' revolt which not only threw off central Roman control but overturned the established social domination of the villa landowning class. The villas, of course, would be a natural casualty of such an uprising. More recently, Guy Halsall has argued that the villa estate structure of lowland Britain crumbled as a direct consequence of its separation from the imperial system under whose umbrella it had emerged, but he identifies a different sequence of development. In his view, the position of the villa owners at the top of the social heap depended on the relationships they had forged with the Empire, and when those ties were broken after 410 AD, they had to work much harder to maintain their elite status. The profits from their estates, which they had previously used to build and decorate their elaborate villas and for other forms of conspicuous consumption, or to trade for valuable items of Roman manufacture (Mediterranean foodstuffs, fine pottery and so on), now had to be distributed locally instead, as gifts to establish networks of supporters. These networks replaced the Empire in structural terms, allowing the landowners to maintain their position in the new conditions, but were relatively expensive, leaving little or no surplus for them to invest in the old forms of conspicuous expenditure. As a result, villas and trading patterns quickly disappeared, and a competitive burial ritual – 'furnished inhumation' – grew up among them in lowland Britain as these men staged lavish funerals, depositing much finery with the dead as part of the struggle to maintain their social position.[44]

The plain peasants' revolt version of the argument is not convincing. Despite the prevailing chaos, the contemporary Roman west throws up almost no evidence of this kind of activity, but plenty of local elites taking power into their own hands, and precisely in contexts where central imperial authority had failed to answer local needs. In 409 or thereabouts, Constantine III had long since abandoned his British base and his attention was focused firmly on Italy and Spain, where he was trying simultaneously to supplant the Emperor Honorius and to deal with the Rhine invaders who were now established south of the Pyrenees. To my mind, and here I am in full agreement with Halsall, the British rebellion is much more likely to have been of this standard kind, a response to Constantine's neglect rather than a social revolution that was in any sense anti-Roman. Equally important, the *Life of St Germanus of Auxerre* portrays a distinctly Roman-looking elite of lowland Britain seeking help from a still Roman continent against both invasion and heresy in the 420s and 430s. Romance (simplified Latin) remained the spoken language of lowland British political life well into the fifth century, and I am also inclined to believe that Gildas' famous reference to the British seeking help from the Roman general-issimo Aetius, 'three times consul', rests on something concrete. All this would mean that a Romanized British landed class was still look-ing in a Roman direction, and had held on to some of its Roman structures as late as the 440s. This makes the class-warfare argument unappealing.[45]

Halsall's version of internal systems collapse is a much more possible explanation for two of the central phenomena in the fifth-century transformation of the British lowlands: that the villas disap-peared and that inhumation furnished with graveoods came into fashion. In assessing the argument, however, it is only reasonable to point out why it exists. Halsall is the scholar we met in Chapter 1 who has argued that to sidestep migration in explanations of archaeological change 'is simply to dispose of an always simplistic and usually groundless supposition in order to enable its replacement with a more subtle interpretation of the period'. His explanation of developments in lowland Britain is entirely in line with this world view, since it is fundamentally internalist. The villas disappeared because of a crisis within lowland British society, which prompted hugely expensive competitive funerary display, and Anglo-Saxon immigrants are denuded of any major role in the action. But while the invasion hypothesis was certainly overused in the past, there can be problems with an a priori determination to deny migration any role of importance. The danger is that any argument will command assent among like believers just because it moves the historical spotlight away from migrants, whatever its intellectual and other qualities.[46] And in this case, I would argue that there is a much more straightforward explanation for the disap-pearance of the villas available if you are not worried about being considered a simple-minded migrationist, and the virtues of economy and Occam's razor should not be forgotten. Equally important, the alternative explanation also does a better job of accounting for all the available data.

For one thing, it's not clear that there was scope in the fifth century circumstances for Halsall's vision – of the villas literally crumbling away through a purely British, internal political process – actually to have worked its way through in the decades after 409. According to the *Gallic Chronicle of 452*, Saxon attacks had already begun around the year 410, and the villas – large, isolated country houses of the wealthy – were both highly vulnerable to attack and obvious targets. We have encountered in Chapter 2 the looted contents of one of their number which Alamannic raiders failed – for once – to get back across the Rhine. More generally, whenever Roman frontier security broke down in any region, villas were the first to suffer.[47] There is every reason to expect, therefore, that any increase in outside attack would have affected the villa network immediately. To my mind, this makes it unlikely that a fairly lengthy process of internal erosion would have had time and space after 409 to unfold untouched by outside attack.

Equally important, the collapse of the villa network and the rise of furnished inhumation are not the only phenomena that need to be explained. What Halsall's argument (or any version of internal-systems collapse) doesn't easily explain is the degree of cultural change that accompanied the socioeconomic revolution of the fifth and sixth centuries. Not only did the villa estates of lowland Britain disappear, but by 600 AD the region's Latin-speaking Christian elite had been replaced by Germanic-speaking non-Christians. Halsall of course recognizes this, and accepts that there has to have been a significant degree of Anglo-Saxon migration to account for these shifts even if he provides no real mechanism to explain them, and is trying, overall, to decouple migration from what he sees as the more fundamental process of socioeconomic transformation. The profound nature of these cultural changes, however, needs to be taken fully into account.

For one thing, most of the items buried with the dead in the furnished graves were Germanic, but this is only part of the story of Germanization. What's really striking about the written Anglo-Saxon language, which survives in a variety of texts dating from just after the year 600 all the way down to the Norman Conquest, is how little it was actually influenced by indigenous British Celtic. Loanwords are few and far between, and there is almost no Celtic influence on its grammatical structures. This is telling us something important: that the spoken language in the various local dialects of the new land-owning elite of lowland Britain as it had emerged by 600 AD, the tongue that provided the basis for the extant written form of the language, was not only thoroughly Germanic, but also firmly insulated from contact with the native Celtic tongues of Britain. And in this era, language was transmitted within families, especially through mothers on whom most childcare devolved – one reason, as we have seen, why the Anglo-Saxon flow must have included large numbers of women. Incidentally, this also explains why, in later medieval examples where migration did generate large-scale language change, this occurred only when a peasant population (even an elite one of free, if fairly small-scale, landowners) was involved in the action, and was never generated by very small-scale aristocratic elite transfer along Norman Conquest lines alone.[48]

Similarly intense cultural transformation can be found in other areas too. Roman society was divided in the first instance into free and slave classes, with freemen subdivided further into *honestiores* (higher) and *humiliores* (lower). The *honestiores* were essentially the landowning class. Anglo-Saxon society as it emerges in our sources after c.600 AD shared the categories of free and slave with the Roman system, but added to it a third: the half-free or freed class, a non-slave group which remained in permanent hereditary dependence on particular members of the freeman class. The free class was subdivided into gradations measured by different *wergilds* – social value as expressed in their 'life price', to be discussed in a moment – but all are envisaged as landowners, or at least landholders. This same triple division of society is found among all the continental Germanic groups of the post-Roman period, whereas the permanent freedman concept in particular was quite foreign to Roman society, where the offspring of freedmen became fully free. In all probability, therefore, this categorization of social classes had its origins among the Germanic immigrants. It's not impossible to imagine each of these post-Roman Germanic-dominated societies evolving a tripartite division of society independently, but it seems unlikely.[49]

Taking full account of these cultural transformations allows us to redefine the problem. Clearly we need to explain the break-up of the villa estate network in the fifth and sixth centuries and the appearance of burials containing Germanic clothing accessories and weaponry. But at the same time we need to account for the fact that the new elite of c.600 AD spoke a Germanic language untouched by Celtic, and that society had been reordered along Germanic lines. Given this combination of phenomena, an altogether simpler explanation for the collapse of the villa structure suggests itself, one that raises no chronological problems and accounts for both socioeconomic and cultural revolution.

It starts by thinking a bit harder about that classic case of elite transfer, the Norman Conquest of England. What happened in the eleventh century, as we have seen, was that individual manors changed hands, as *Doomsday Book* graphically illustrates, but the prevailing network of manors was left undisturbed – the best outcome in both overall economic terms and for the individual manor owners. But the Norman Conquest could work in this fashion only because the incoming Norman elite was of the right order of magnitude to be able to take possession of the existing manor network without having to subdivide the estates. Thanks to *Doomsday Book* we can see what happened in some detail. By 1066, there were approximately nine and a half thousand manors in the English countryside, and the Norman settlement redistributed their ownership amongst an incoming elite of about five thousand families. The king, his tenants-in-chief, and various Church institutions each owned many manors by 1086, but this still left enough for each member of the new elite to receive his own estate. But what if William and his henchmen had had too many supporters to reward to give each his own manor? What if there had been fifteen or even ten thousand supporters of sufficient importance in the Conqueror's following each to require a reward in the form of a property stake in the newly conquered kingdom? In that case, the political imperative to reward those supporters who had put William in control of England's agricultural assets would have overriden the economically desirable outcome of leaving the highly productive estate network untouched. Kings and lords who did not satisfy the expectations of their most important supporters did not tend to stay kings and lords for very long. Not for nothing is generosity – measured in gifts of gold but also of land – highlighted as the key virtue of an early medieval lord.[50] Had the incoming Norman elite been too large to be accommodated within the pre-existing estate structure, then the manors would have had to be broken up for political reasons, despite the economic costs of doing so. The Norman Conquest can be seen as a very particular type of situation, where the incoming elite and the available agricultural production units broadly matched each other in scale.

The fact that, by comparison, the equally complex and productive Roman villa network was not left similarly undisturbed by the Anglo-Saxons is highly suggestive. Again, it would have been both much simpler and better in economic terms for the new arrivals to keep existing agricultural production units intact. The new Anglo-Saxon kings of lowland Britain would have had a more productive rural economy to tax, and the new elite would each have received a more valuable landed asset. But both of these considerations could only be secondary to the greater imperative of rewarding loyal supporters. As in the years after the Conquest, rewarding loyal service must have been the process that drove Anglo-Saxon land annexation forward, and in fact a king's ability to find landed rewards remained a crucial dynamic in the longer-term development of the Anglo-Saxon world. As the seventh century progressed, it was the three kingdoms that could expand into open frontiers (Wessex, Mercia and Northumbria), and hence provide land that would attract a greater number of warriors, that eventually emerged as the great powers of the pre-Viking era.[51] The fact that, despite the economic costs of doing so, the countryside was entirely reordered in the fifth century strongly suggests that the number of Anglo-Saxon followers to be accommodated in the landscape was too great for them simply to replace the existing Roman landowning class on a one-for-one basis.

This explanation of the break-up of lowland Britain's villa estates makes excellent sense in the broader context of what we know about the patterns of development prevailing in the Roman and Germanic worlds by the end of the fourth century. Although both were thoroughly agricultural, the two economies were operating at substantially different levels of development. The Roman world, including its British provinces, was dominated by a relatively small, relatively rich elite, whereas the Germanic economy supported a less rich, but numerically broader (freeman?) elite. The Anglo-Saxon migration flow brought this second type of elite into the socioeconomic context that sustained the first, and something had to give. Given the political necessity for Anglo-Saxon leaders to reward the loyal military service of their retainers, it was the old socioeconomic order that had, eventually, to be remade. The detail of when and how this happened is not clear. Some Roman estates seem to have remained active at the beginning of the Saxon period, which is what you might expect. Initially, immigrants may have been willing to live off the distributed production of existing estates. But once they became more numerous and/or developed a sense that their control of the landscape was permanent, prompting them to demand a share of its capital resources, existing estate boundaries had to be redrawn, and overall output headed firmly downwards.[52] The partition of the 'white' farms in Zimbabwe in recent years, where the sum of the parts has proved unequal to the whole, gives something of an analogy here.

Exactly how much larger this new Anglo-Saxon elite was than its Roman predecessor is difficult to say. The proportion of landowners to landless peasants in both the Roman era and the manorialized Middle Ages has been estimated as at most about 1:10, and was probably substantially less. Few would now share Sir Frank Stenton's vision of an early Anglo-Saxon society composed almost entirely of free peasant warriors, but social and economic power was quite widely distributed, as we have seen, among continental Germani of the late Roman period. Manorialization and the generation of a more restricted social elite – recreating something much more like the socioeconomic set-up that had sustained the narrower Roman upper class – unfolded only from the eighth century. One interesting line of argument has suggested that the presence of weapons in graves of the fifth to seventh centuries might actually reflect those making a claim to free status, since it was demonstrably not simply a means of distinguishing warriors. If so, the free class of the early Anglo-Saxon period may have represented something closer to half the male population, since up to half of male graves contain weaponry of some kind. Such evidence as there is from the sixth-century continent, however, suggests that the free class there was perhaps more in the region of one-fifth to one-third of the total population, making a half look rather high. Perhaps social structures among the Anglo-Saxons were more egalitarian, or possibly the intermediate semi-free class, which also had some military obligations, buried its dead with weapons too.[53] Either way, the disparity in scale between Roman and Germanic elites is clear.

This still makes the Anglo-Saxon takeover of lowland Britain a kind of elite transfer. One recent estimate, for instance, calculates the maximum possible ratio of immigrants to natives – even after Romano-

British demographic collapse – at no more than 1:4, and Victorian-style ethnic cleansing out of the question.[54] In numerical terms, substantially fewer immigrants than indigenous natives were caught up in the total genetic mix of the new Anglo-Saxon kingdoms that had come into existence by the year 600. The comparison with the Norman Conquest, however, is highly instructive. Unlike its Norman counterpart, the new Germanic elite of the fifth and sixth centuries was too numerous to be accommodated within the existing socioeconomic framework, so that a fundamental reordering of the basic means of production had to follow. The situations generating these profoundly different outcomes must be carefully distinguished, no matter that the immigrants were in the minority in both. To classify both under the same heading of elite transfer is confusing in analytical terms, as it leads you to miss some key points of particularity and difference.

But what can be said about the other key issue, the kinds of relationship operating between immigrant and native? How free were indigenous Romano-British to choose their own fate, as Anglo-Saxon kings took control of the countryside. No one would now suppose that there had to have been hostility between native Romano-British and incoming Anglo-Saxons simply by virtue of their different ethnic backgrounds, and some voluntary renegotiation of identity on the part of the indigenous population is certainly possible. More specifically, *Ine's Law*, the seventh-century law code, shows that there was a Romano-British component within the landowning elite of the Anglo-Saxon kingdom of Wessex as late as the 690s, as we have seen, and there is no obvious reason why at least some Romano-British landowners should not have become valued members of the entourages of earlier Anglo-Saxon kings as well. When thinking about how much of this went on, though, it is important to bear in mind the basic purpose of the Anglo-Saxon migration flow. Developing from raiding and mercenary service into outright annexation of landed assets, it did, by its very nature, put Anglo-Saxon immigrants into direct competition with the surviving landowning elites of sub-Roman Britain for control of the means of wealth production. We don't have to suppose, necessarily, that all Romano-British landowners were wiped out in an initial apocalypse, but neither is Gildas' image of violence and terror likely to have been pure imagination. Land seizures do not tend to go pleasantly: even that of the Normans, relatively antiseptic in some ways, was thoroughly brutal in places, not least in the infamous

Harrying of the North in winter 1069/70 when food stocks were deliberately destroyed and tens of thousands died.[55]

It is also important to look at the terms under which native landowning elites continued to hold their positions within seventh-century Wessex. Who these non-Saxon landowners were is itself an interesting question. Wessex was expanding westwards into a still British West Country in the seventh century, and some have wondered whether these British landowners were recent additons to the kingdom rather than long-term survival artists from Hampshire or Wiltshire, but there is no way to be certain. Either way, even if their lands had not been taken from them immediately, Ine's law accords these men only half the social value – as expressed in their wergild or life price – of an Anglo-Saxon of equivalent wealth. This was a highly significant proviso. The wergild was a crucial element of social status, the basis on which all kinds of compensations were calculated when it came to resolving disputes. As one recent study has pointed out, the difference in wergild between immigrant and native landowners of equivalent wealth might even provide the key to the eventual disappearance of any non-Anglo-Saxon landowners who did survive the violence of initial contact. Because of the difference in wergilds, then, if a hypo-thetical immigrant and a hypothetical indigenous landowner got into a dispute, and even if a court judged fairly – giving an equal number of verdicts in either direction – the net result over time would still have been a transfer of wealth from native to immigrant. The latter's higher wergild would always mean that the compensation settlements he received were twice as high as he had to pay out for any similar offence.[56]

This more specific evidence is really only confirming what we might anyway deduce from the political context. As the Anglo-Saxon immigrant flow established its dominance over different parts of the landscape of lowland Britain, indigenous landowners will have had every reason to want to cross the political-cum-ethnic divide and become Anglo-Saxons. That was the only way in the longer term that they could hope to hold on to the highly unequal property distribution that had made them so powerful in the Roman era. Just because they wanted to, however, doesn't mean that they were able to. Incoming Anglo-Saxon migrant leaders (in so far as they could control the process)[57] had every reason not to allow them to – not, at least, in large numbers, since they had their own warrior followings to reward.

And these followers were much more politically important to the new kings than any Romano-British landowners, because it was they who had put those same kings in power. As has shown up in so many contexts, unfortunately, *Homo sapiens sapiens* really is predatory enough to want to seize the wealth of others and to organize and perpetrate any violence that might be necessary in the process. And even if, as an indigenous landowner, you did manage not to lose your estates immediately, then as Ine's law emphasizes, you were still not certain of a secure future.

Relations between incoming Anglo-Saxons and the non-landowning elements in Romano-British society, by contrast, would not have been so competitive, since the latter did not own the assets that the immigrants were trying to seize. It is also true (even though I don't believe in a peasants' revolt) that these non-landowning classes will not have had any great community of interest with the villa owners, since the latter formed a highly privileged elite who were living off the fruits of their labours. There is every reason again, therefore, why indigenous non-landowners would have wanted to win acceptance as newly recruited Anglo-Saxons. Whether they would have been likely to succeed in significant numbers, however, is again doubtful. As was true of our Roman merchant in the Hunnic Empire, allowing someone of subordinate status to move into the dominant group necessarily involves treating them better: that is, self-evidently, why people always want to move across such divides. But by the same token, dominant groups lose the capacity to exploit promoted subordinates as thoroughly as before, and this always imposes limits on such promotions. In this instance, having just taken ownership of the excellent arable land of lowland Britain, Anglo-Saxon immigrants had great need of a mass of subordinates to do all the heavy manual labour that arable agriculture always involved before the invention of tractors. While the interests of the non-landowning classes of former Roman Britain were not so diametrically opposed to those of the immigrants as their landowning compatriots, therefore, there were still excellent reasons why the immigrants would not have been ready to allow them wholesale access to the new elite of lowland Britain. Laws and charters demonstrate, in fact, that large numbers of slaves and semi-free were central to the social structure of the new Anglo-Saxon kingdoms that formed, and I would suppose that much of the indigenous non-landowning population of lowland Britain found itself consigned to these subordinate classes, even if there were occasional success stories, similar to that of our Roman merchant turned Hunnic warrior.

Viewed from this perspective, the lack of indigenous influence on the Anglo-Saxon language acquires yet greater significance. Since language was taught within families and not through formal education, the lack of any detectable British influence on the Germanic language of the new dominant elite from c.600 onwards is very suggestive. Had this elite encompassed large numbers of Britons-turned-Saxons, you would expect a fair amount of indigenous linguistic influence to show up in its lingua franca. That there should be so little demonstrates that the new elite was substantially dominated by the immigrant component.[58]

Unless you come to the subject with a predetermination to prove that migration is never an agent of significant change, it is difficult to avoid the overall conclusion that Anglo-Saxon migration played a huge role in remaking the social, political and economic foundations of lowland Britain in the fifth and sixth centuries. Decoupling this landscape from the Roman imperial system, which had profoundly shaped it up to 400 AD, was bound to push its history in new directions. The relatively small, relatively rich class of villa owners owed their prosperity to that system, and became instantly vulnerable once their ties to it were broken. In my view, like their peers elsewhere in the Roman world, they are likely to have had sufficient social power to maintain their position if their only problem had been social subordinates within the British provinces. They were not, however, the only problem. Britain's wealth was well known to its neighbours, who had been raiding it for centuries, and once central Roman protection was withdrawn the villa owners were always going to struggle to hold on to their thoroughly unequal share of its assets, in the face of Picts, Scots or Anglo-Saxons.

Even if better dating evidence for the collapse of villa society were eventually to lead to the conclusion that Roman society fell apart before Saxon assault became significant, moreover, this would only partly alter the picture. For one thing, as we will examine in more detail in the next chapter, Romano-British landowning society was cast adrift by its Roman mother ship only because of the damage inflicted upon central imperial structures by other immigrants into the continental territories of the western Empire after 405. More specifically, it was also the Anglo-Saxon migration flow that dictated what happened afterwards: the fact that a relatively small dominant elite was replaced by a relatively large one, and that major cultural changes, linguistic and others, moved lowland Britain in a decidedly Germanic direction. Everything suggests that the indigenous population had only a limited capacity to decide its own fate in these centuries.

Fundamentally, therefore, a combination of elite transfer followed by cultural emulation cannot satisfactorily explain the transformations observable in lowland Britain between 400 and 600 AD. But nor was the Anglo-Saxon takeover a mass replacement of the existing indigenous population. In deciding how we might usefully recategorize it, it is helpful first to explore the analogous transformations unfolding simultaneously in northern Gaul, where the largely more recent archaeological evidence allows us to look more closely at the response of an indigenous society facing, in circumstances similar to the Romano-British, the arrival of land-grabbing outsiders.

## THE FRANKS AND ROMAN GAUL

The intrusion of Frankish power into Roman Gaul presents us with a similar intellectual problem to that which has generated such different views of the *Adventus Saxonum*. At broadly the same time as historical sources (in this case of slightly better quality) indicate that Frankish power was building up west of the River Rhine, a new burial habit was adopted across wide areas of Gaul north of the River Loire. Roman burial patterns, in Gaul as elsewhere, had evolved over the centuries towards inhumation with no gravegoods. Around the year 500, however, there was a sudden explosion in richly furnished burials right across the region, and it became common for most graves to contain at least something. Males were customarily buried with a range of weapons, together with some personal items, females with rich costume jewellery of kinds not dissimilar to those found in lowland Britain in the early Anglo-Saxon period (Map 12). The big question, as north of the Channel, is this: can elite transfer followed by cultural emulation satisfactorily account for all the observable data?

## The March of the Merovingians

The rise of Frankish power under the Merovingian dynasty was essentially a phenomenon of Roman imperial collapse. The term 'Frank' first appears in contemporary sources right at the end of the third century, like that of the Alamanni, but postdated accounts of the crisis earlier in that century give Franks a major role, and there is no good reason to disbelieve them. It is unclear, as we saw in Chapter 2, whether subgroups given the Frankish label (Ampsivarii, Bructerii, Chattuarii, Chamavi, Salii) in our late Roman sources had any real sense of overall political community. They lived in sufficient physical proximity to make political interrelationships a necessity and may even, like the contemporary Alamanni, have seen moments of real confederation under leaders of pre-eminent power. But the sources do not allow for certainty, essentially because Ammianus tells us much less about them than about the Alamanni. At this point, like so many Germani all along Rome's European frontiers, the different Frankish groups were the Empire's semi-subdued clients. Individual Franks were regularly recruited into the Roman army, some rising to top commands, while whole auxiliary contingents occasionally served on particular campaigns. Yet at the same time, campaigning was periodically required to keep them from raiding the Empire too successfully and too often; or even, when opportunity presented itself, from seeking to annex pieces of Roman territory. After the defeat of Chnodomarius the Alaman, for instance, the Emperor Julian also found himself having to fend off Salian Franks who were trying to move on to Roman territory.[59] With the decline of the western Empire in the fifth century, this balance of power was undermined, and the Frankish cat leapt vigorously out of the bag. Frankish groups figure more prominently, and in a wider range of roles, in the declining western Empire's affairs from around the 460s, when we start to hear in particular of a group of Franks led by one Childeric.

Childeric's father, eponymous founder of the Merovingian dynasty, was called Merovech, but all the sources report of him was that he was the offspring of a sea monster. And even Childeric's career is full of question marks. His grave at Tournai in modern Belgium is one of the great all-time finds of European archaeology (Plate 16). When the mound was opened in May 1653, the excavators found a staggering array of gold and jewellery, including a signet ring which conveniently carried the name of the grave's occupant: *Childeric regis* (King Childeric). Many of the items were subsequently stolen from their display cabinet in 1831, but they had been extensively recorded in great, if sometimes mistaken, detail within two years of their discovery. At that point, famously, the pins of Childeric's brooches were thought to be pens. The sad remnants of the original treasure can now be viewed in the Cabinet des Médailles in Paris. Fascinatingly, a recent re-excavation of the burial site has revealed that, aside from this plethora of gold, Childeric was also buried with the corpses of at least twenty-one horses in three separate pits. Among the gravegoods were some of the unfortunate animals' gold fittings. A few of these, found in the first excavation, had generated another of history's great foul-ups. In the time of Napoleon, according to one of the more imaginative ideas of the excavator, they were interpreted as the remains of a great royal cloak, and the Corsican emperor had one made, embossed with similar designs, for his imperial coronation in 1801.[60]

The grisly magnificence of Childeric's tomb marks him out as a powerful warlord, but still leaves many puzzles, especially when compared with the historical sources. These amount to a tantalizing series of vignettes, including the arresting comment that he was exiled for eight years at one point for seducing too many of his followers' women. Putting the complexities of his personal life to one side, these vignettes show his career to have been immersed in the death throes of Roman imperial power in Gaul in the 460s. By that time, the Empire's central authorities had lost control of much of their tax base, with the result that its power was in terminal decline. In Gaul, this manifested itself in an increasing difficulty in exercising control over both the Empire's own army commanders and the various groups of outsiders (such as Alaric's Visigoths) who had already been settled there. Thus we find Childeric in 463 leading a Frankish contingent serving in the forces of Aegidius, commander of the Roman army in Gaul, who was fighting the Visigoths. Such was the complexity of imperial dissolution by this date, however, that the Visigoths were allied with the central imperial authorities in Italy against Aegidius, who was in rebellion. Whether this shows Childeric as loyal to the Empire or not is a thoroughly moot point. It is also clear that he never ruled more than just one group of Franks, who, even in the next generation, operated in a number of separate warbands.

What the sources don't shed any light on is the original basis of Childeric's power. Was he a prince of the Franks selling the services of his warband to the Roman state, or had he followed a more Roman career, rising though the ranks of the Roman army of the Rhine in the years of its decline? The other large gap in his career profile is how he moved from subordinate ally of Aegidius in the 460s to ruler of a substantial chunk of Roman Gaul by the time of his death. Immediately afterwards, Bishop Remigius of Rheims wrote to Clovis, Childeric's son and heir, in terms that portray him as the ruler of the former Roman province of Belgica Inferior. On the basis of this description, and of his Belgian resting place, the source of Childeric's power has traditionally been placed in the north. But the limited information we have from the 460s places him further south and much more within a Roman military context. It has recently been suggested that the real source of his power was his command of a substantial part of the old imperial field army, after central control over it had finally collapsed. This is certainly possible, but would make his Belgian burial just a little odd. The evidence is equally compatible with seeing him as a Frankish warband leader who played Roman politics while there still seemed real rewards to be won from it, then returned to a more straightforwardly Frankish political context once the Empire had lost all meaning in Gallic political life. The Burgundian king Gundobad, for instance, followed the same kind of career trajectory at exactly the same time. Either way, we have to see Childeric as one of the most successful warrior leaders to emerge from the wreck of Roman power in Gaul, commanding one of the largest remnants of its former forces, and operating alongside those headed by other commanders mentioned in our sources, such as Aegidius' son and heir Syagrius and the Counts Arbogast and Paul.[61]

Although Childeric was highly successful, it was in the reign of his son that Frankish history was really transformed. As you'll find it in the textbooks, Clovis reigned from c.482 to 511, but only the date of his death is certain. His accession has to be worked out from other dating indications in the account of his reign provided by the later sixth-century historian Gregory of Tours. These, however, are not trustworthy.

The outlines of Clovis' career are clear enough, but many question marks hang over the details. Shortly after his accession, Clovis is traditionally held to have extended his territory as far as Paris, well beyond the confines of Belgica Inferior, by defeating Syagrius, who probably inherited what was left of Aegidius' old command. The victory has long been part of the Clovis story, but the source base is extremely thin. The victory is placed in 485/6 by Gregory of Tours, the only author to report it, and has recently been the subject of controversy, particularly over the likely size of the territory under Syagrius' command. But if there is considerable reason to wonder about Gregory's chronology, as we shall see in a moment, the campaign itself was probably historical enough.[62] Less doubt surrounds the overall effects of this and Clovis' other campaigns. By his death in 511, he had taken most of south-western Gaul from the Visigoths, brought the Burgundians under Frankish hegemony, and ranged widely on the eastern bank of the Rhine, with the Alamanni in particular having been brought under his sway. In the process, the Frankish world was turned upside down. Not only did Clovis conquer large tracts of ex-Roman territory, but he also eliminated many rival Frankish kings. Gregory of Tours mentions seven individually: Sigibert and his son Chloderic who were established at Cologne, Chararic and his son, Ragnachar plus his two brothers, Richar and Rignomer, who held power in Cambrai and Le Mans. There is also a reference to 'other relatives', who may or may not have been rulers with independent power bases. A political patchwork, where power had been divided between a number of independent princes, gave way to the undisputed sway of a single monarch. Gregory was careful to note that, on executing each of his rivals, Clovis added their followers and treasure to his own power base.[63]

Precisely when this restructuring of Frankish politics occurred is unclear. Again, our only narrative is provided by Gregory. Writing sixty years and more after Clovis' death, Gregory was clearly stitching together stories about Clovis from a variety of sources, in many cases having to guess at their chronology. The Visigothic campaign is well dated by other sources to 507, but independent confirmation of the other events is lacking, and Gregory's overall vision of Clovis' military progress is deeply suspect, not least because all the major campaigns are placed at convenient five-year intervals through the reign. This could, of course, be correct, but it does look as though Gregory (or even a later interpolator) just spaced them out evenly. There are also more specific reasons for suspicion. Clovis' great victory over the Alamanni is placed by Gregory in the fifteenth year of the reign (496), but contemporary sources record him inflicting a huge defeat on the Alamanni about a decade later. There could have been two campaigns, of course, but if there was only one it will be Gregory who is mistaken. Controversy also surrounds his account of Clovis' conversion to Catholicism. Gregory places it just before the attack on the Arian Christian Visigoths, and was thus able to portray that campaign as a Catholic crusade that God crowned with victory. Another contemporary source puts baptism after the victory, and implies that Clovis had at least toyed with the idea of converting to Arianism.[64]

The elimination of Clovis' Frankish rivals, likewise, is traditionally dated to c.508, because Gregory places all these killings after the defeat of the Visigoths. This is entirely possible, but it is just as likely that the rivals had been eliminated in stages throughout his career. Clovis' reported excuse for eliminating Chararic, for instance, is that the latter had failed to aid him against Syagrius. But Syagrius had been defeated (admittedly only according to Gregory) in c.486 and it seems odd for Clovis to have waited more than twenty years before taking out the defaulter. You also have to wonder how Clovis managed to put together enough military power to defeat the Alamanni and Visigoths in such quick succession, if he had not already increased his power base by incorporating these other warbands, and this would be my own best guess at the true story. Nonetheless, the overall picture is clear enough. In a career analogous in its effects to the combined careers of Valamer and Theoderic among the Ostrogoths (Chapter 5), Clovis created one of the most powerful of the successor states to the western Roman Empire by simultaneously annexing large tracts of Roman territory and uniting a series of previously independent Frankish warbands.[65]

How much Frankish migration was part of this process?

## The Divided Kingdom

Both historical and archaeological sources demonstrate that from within the sixth-century Frankish kingdom there emerged two distinct zones, broadly separated from one another by the River Loire. South of the river there was considerable continuity with the Roman past. Many of the old Roman landowning families retained their estates, along with much of their culture and many of their values. As they appear especially in the writings of Gregory of Tours and Venantius Fortunatus, two generations after Clovis, these people spoke Latin, were conscious of their Roman senatorial heritage, and retained an interest in Roman culture. This is not to say that the new kingdom had left their lives untouched. It was no longer possible for them to follow bureaucratic careers in the imperial administration, for example, and success or failure now had to be fought out at the royal courts of Clovis and his Merovingian successors, the source equally of major secular and Church appointments. There were also important economic developments, with Marseilles replacing Arles, for instance, as the chief entrepôt for Mediterranean trade. Nonetheless, south of the Loire intrusive barbarian settlements seem to have been few in number: one or two have been identified potentially in the Charente, and on the border with the Visigoths in Aquitaine. Otherwise the archaeological landscape continued to resonate to sub-Roman norms in its funerary rites, the dead being buried without gravegoods, and in its general material culture. There is hardly any sign of Frankish immigration at all, not even at the level of Norman conquest-style elite transfer, and the basic Roman unit of local political, social and administrative life – the city (*civitas*) together with its landowners – remained firmly in place.[66]

North of the Loire, the situation could not have been more different. Somewhere between c.400 and c.600 AD, life moved decisively away from the established norms of the Roman era, in ways that were not dissimilar in material cultural terms to what we have already observed in Anglo-Saxon England. As in lowland Britain, the *civitas*, that stalwart of Roman administration, disappeared from view. There is no evidence that military service was organized here in the sixth century on the basis of *civitas* contingents, as it was in the rest of the kingdom. Social and economic structures were likewise transformed. Legal sources portray a society recategorized, again as in Anglo-Saxon England, into three social groups: the free, a class of permanent freedmen, and slaves. The second of these, it is worth remembering, was unknown to the Roman world. There is also much qualitative evidence that a Roman-style restricted aristocracy was replaced with a broader social elite of less entrenched pre-eminence – again, as in Anglo-Saxon England. The legal sources do not differentiate by different wergilds, for instance, between the mass of freemen and a smaller nobility; Gregory of Tours does not refer to any major figure from the north as a 'noble' in the course of his massive narrative of sixth-century events (where many, from old Roman families south of the Loire, are so designated); and large, compact landed estates, the essential building block of socioeconomic dominance for a true aristocracy, only began to re-emerge in this region in the seventh century. Up to that point, the term *villa* simply meant a geographical area, not a centrally run unit of agricultural production.[67]

This does not mean that there weren't significant variations in wealth in these northern territories, or even that their old Roman elites had completely disappeared. Well into the seventh century, leading landowners of the former Roman regional capital at Trier determinedly styled themselves 'senator' in inscriptions. One surviving Roman landowner from the early Merovingian period has even left us a will: no less a figure than Bishop Remigius of Rheims himself, whose congratulatory letter to Clovis on his accession provides us with key information about the rise of the Merovingians. But Trier was clearly exceptional. Over eight hundred, or about a third, of all the post-Roman inscriptions of northern Gaul have been found in its environs, with none of the other old Roman cities of the region producing any comparable cache. And while Remigius' will is decent enough evidence that some kind of Roman elite survived, it does show him to have been only a very modest landowner compared either with his properly Roman ancestors of the fourth century or his later Frankish successors of the seventh and beyond.

None of this evidence fundamentally contradicts the broader picture, then, that the social structure of northern Gaul would not be dominated by a small aristocratic elite until after 600 AD, unlike the regions south of the Loire where descendants of the old Roman aristocrats remained firmly in place. Culturally too, discontinuity was manifest. In wide areas of the north-east, episcopal succession was not continuous from the late Roman period into early medieval times (Map 12). So a period of positive paganism, or at least Christian interruption, must be envisaged in these lands. At the same time, the language line was also on the move. Germanic dialects became prevalent to the west of the old Roman frontier on the Rhine.[68]

Material culture, too, north of the Loire was significantly different from southern areas of the kingdom. In the late fifth and the sixth century, inhumation that was furnished – sometimes spectacularly – became the vogue, replacing Roman-style burial. Men were buried not only with some personal items, but also with weapons: normally a long sword (*spatha*), javelin (*angon*), axe (*francisca*) and shield (of which only the conical boss usually survives). Women were buried fully clothed with their jewellery, their clothing fastened with a brooch at each shoulder. The brooches themselves were often framed in cloisonné work, with semi-precious stones mounted in individual settings. This was a Roman form of decoration in origin, but had become widely popular in barbarian Europe as a characteristic element of the 'Danubian style' that evolved in the Hunnic Empire. Even burial sites changed. In the sixth century, many of these new furnished burials were within new cemeteries well away from old habitation sites, the graves arranged in ordered lines (hence their technical German term *Reihengräber*, 'row-grave cemeteries').[69] These centralized cemeteries presumably reflect some sense of community among an otherwise more dispersed rural population, rather like the large cremation cemeteries of East Anglia. All this firmly indicates that a new, non-Roman social order had come into being, and there is no doubting the degree of discontinuity it represents. What were its causes?

Parts of north-eastern Gaul had suffered heavily in the raids of the later third century, and, unlike most of the Roman west, rural prosperity in some of its zones seems not to have recovered. But this was true only of a relatively restricted area to the west of the Lower Rhine. Throughout the fourth century, by contrast, Trier and the entire Moselle valley remained a hub of prosperous *romanitas*: in town, country and culture. The city itself was an imperial capital for many years. Further to the north-west in Picardy, likewise, an active villa culture seems to have survived the disasters of the third century, while the frontier continued to be heavily and actively defended by extensive fortifications and large numbers of troops. While the third-century crisis had caused some lasting disruption, the region between the Rhine and the Loire as a whole was by no means abandoned by the Empire, and active Roman life continued across much of it.[70] Substantial structures of Roman life remained to be toppled here, therefore, before any new order could emerge.

One body of evidence has sometimes been thought to show that a bout of pre-Merovingian Frankish immigration played a direct role in the process of imperial dissolution in these territories. Excavations of some late Roman cemeteries in the region have thrown up furnished inhumation burials ranging in date from c.350 to 450 AD. Unlike their

Merovingian counterparts, these earlier inhumations are relatively few, just small clusters in cemeteries where the mass of burials entirely lacks any gravegoods. Males – whose graves predominate in these clusters – were buried with weapons and Roman military belt sets; a smaller number of females were buried alongside some of the men, with jewellery and personal items such as glass and pottery. These burials were first identified as a group by Hans-Joachim Werner, who argued that they were the graves of Franks known from historical sources to have been forcibly resettled on Roman territory in the 290s, as so-called *laeti*. He also saw the continued distinctiveness of these men and their descendants as an important contributory factor to the later Frankish conquest of the region in the time of Clovis: a sign that a first phase of Frankish settlement had disrupted the normal patterns of Roman life. As was pointed out by H.-W. Böhme, however, the graves date from a generation or two after the settlements of *laeti* mentioned in written sources, and, more importantly, are the remains of individuals of reasonably high status, whereas *laeti* were not even fully free. Böhme suggested, therefore, that the graves belong to the category of higher-status barbarian immigrant called *foederati*, linking them to a succession of Frankish officers known to have risen to high Roman rank in the fourth century.[71] The graves, he argued, belonged to their slightly less distinguished peers. Nonetheless, Böhme's argument kept the overall connection between the burials and an important group of immigrant Franks.

Recently, however, Guy Halsall has challenged the whole idea that these graves belonged to immigrants at all, on the reasonable grounds that furnished inhumation was not the funerary rite practised by Franks beyond the frontier in the late Roman period. In fact, Frankish burials of the period c.350 to 450 (and, indeed, earlier) are undetectable in the confederation's heartlands between the Rhine and the Weser. Enough work has been done in these areas to suggest that this is not just a gap in the evidence. Almost certainly, Franks in the wild disposed of their dead in an archaeologically invisible manner, quite likely cremation followed by a scattering of the ashes. It is also the case that the belt sets and weaponry contained in the furnished male burials on Roman soil were all of Roman manufacture. The idea that burial with weapons was a Germanic habit, Halsall argues, is an anachronistic back-projection from later Merovingian practice, when furnished inhumation did spread through the Frankish world. Rather than indicating that these graves were occupied by non-Romans, this fourth- and fifth-century group of furnished inhumations shows that a new, competitive burial practice was spreading among the would-be social leaders of the region. As imperial structures offered increasingly less support to those whom they had previously benefited, competition for social superiority began, and a new furnished burial ritual was one element in the process.[72] This is obviously a variant of the same argument used in the case of fifth-century Britain, but in Gaul the new burial rite certainly came in long before there was any large-scale Frankish immigration.

On balance, neither of these interpretations seems entirely convincing. The disparate nature of the find spots of these graves – cemeteries attached to military installations, rural settings, and even some in urban graveyards – indicates that, in life, the people being buried in this fashion were not a unified group, but individuals operating in a variety of contexts. It is certainly very difficult to see them, therefore, as any kind of Frankish fifth column. Both the chronology of the burials and the nature of the male gravegoods also suggest, more generally, that they were individuals working within and not against Roman imperial structures. But nor is the social-stress argument completely convincing either. For one thing, the furnished burials start too early (c.350 AD) to be associated with any major decline in Roman imperial power in the region, which even Halsall would not date before the late 380s, and I and others would actually date to the aftermath of the crisis of 405–8.

The burials are also relatively few. If they were the products of a process of social competition, it was a very low-key one. And that the individuals concerned might just possibly have been Germanic immigrants of some kind (though not necessarily Franks) is suggested by the female graves that accompany some of the males. Not every male has a female counterpart, but in Picardy as many as half do, which is a strikingly healthy proportion. And while the goods buried with the men are undoubtedly Roman-made, their accompanying womenfolk were buried with 'tutulus'-style brooches, which are otherwise found only in a group of rich Germanic burials from the Lower Elbe, far beyond the Rhine in Saxon country. The Elbe brooches are mostly of slightly different types from those found in northern Gaul, and the latter may be earlier in date. In that case, the brooches would not provide any reason for thinking these burials Germanic, since Roman fashions were often adopted by Germanic elites beyond the frontier.

But, for the moment at least, the jury appears still to be out on these more technical matters, and if this brooch type does prove to be basically non-Roman we may still be looking at the burials of migrants who did well in the Roman system. Either way, Halsall is entirely convincing both that the burials have nothing obvious to do with later Merovingian-era burial habits and that, even if Germanic, they would provide no compelling evidence for a large-scale late Roman settlement of Franks between the Rhine and the Loire that facilitated Clovis' later triumphs.[73]

If the north–south divide within the sixth-century Merovingian kingdom cannot be traced back to a preceding Frankish settlement north of the Loire in the late Roman period, part of the explanation lies in the fifth-century political history of the region, in which Franks played a part. Arguments for a large-scale withdrawal of Roman power before the crisis of 405–8 are no more convincing here than they are in the case of Britain.[74] But as the potent mixture of invasion and usurpation began to work havoc with the power base of the western Empire, then parts at least of northern Gaul, like Britain another fringe region of the Empire, began to feel a similar loss of protection. Thus Armorica – north-western Gaul (now Brittany) – revolted at the same time as Britain in 409/10, likewise perhaps from the control of the usurping Emperor Constantine III. But whereas Britain was cut permanently adrift from the Empire at this point, serious efforts were made in the 410s to bring northern Gaul back under the imperial umbrella, when the worst of the initial crisis had been weathered. And throughout the first half of the fifth century, periodic efforts were made to maintain imperial control north of the Loire: a mixture of direct interventions against breakaway groups, maintaining some regular Roman forces in the region, and occasionally implanting irregular ones.[75]

In the longer term, however, these ongoing attempts to project imperial authority in northern Gaul were steadily undermined by the knock-on effects of the crisis of 405–8. As we shall see in the next chapter, the imperial centre progressively lost control of its key revenue-producing districts, and with them its capacity to maintain significant military forces and control its regional commanders. As a direct result, it could no longer protect the key structures of Roman civilian life. This all came to a head in the mid-450s in the additional chaos generated by the collapse of Attila's Empire (Chapter 5) – the context in which Childeric rose to prominence in the 460s. Northern Gaul thus navigated its way from Roman past to Frankish future via a political process that was both long-drawn-out and highly contested. It began with the Rhine crossing of 31 December 406, and didn't really come to an end until Clovis consolidated his power in the decades either side of the year 500. In the meantime, the region had seen many contestants for power: Roman central authorities, local self-help groups (often labelled *Bagaudae* after third-century bandit groups), barbarian invaders and settlers, and, eventually, Frankish military forces. The process was also essentially a violent one. So we should not wonder that the region's Roman landowning elite suffered huge disruption. Their villas were rich and vulnerable, and here, as everywhere else where the capacity of Rome's armies to provide security withered away, the villa network failed to survive the process of imperial collapse.[76]

The role of the Franks themselves in all this would appear to have been substantial, but not primary. As we have seen, Frankish forces become prominent only towards the end of the process, in the 460s. This pattern stands in marked contrast to the history of lowland Britain, where the disappearance of any imperial protection was quickly followed by the arrival of Anglo-Saxon raiders, mercenaries and migrants who displaced sitting Roman landowners in a pretty direct fashion. Unlike those Anglo-Saxons, therefore, the Franks cannot be fingered in any simple way for the destruction of Roman life north of the Loire, which began long before the Franks emerged as a major military power. Indeed, given that Roman interventions in Frankish politics had probably aimed, as with the Alamanni, at preventing the emergence of larger and more dangerous coalitions among them (Chapter 2), the unified Franks should themselves be thought of as basically a post-Roman phenomenon, in the sense that Clovis' career would not have been possible had the Empire maintained its full military and political capacities.[77] But if there is good reason to separate the erosion of Roman life in northern Gaul from the effects there of rising Frankish power, what role did Frankish immigration play there in the Merovingian sixth century?

## Skulls and Sarcophagi

In trying to answer this question, we are pretty much dependent upon archaeological evidence. Gregory of Tours does not deal with the issue of Frankish settlement, and the archaeology poses the same basic methodological problem that we have just encountered in lowland Britain. The new burial habit in northern Gaul coincides chronologically with the rise of Frankish power, but was everyone buried with gravegoods a Frankish immigrant? If so, we would be looking at something like a *Völkerwanderung*, since the new *Reihengräber*, replete with furnished burials, became widespread across northern and eastern Gaul (Map 12).[78]

There have been many attempts to resolve the problem. Nineteenth- and early twentieth-century investigators were convinced that skull shapes could do the trick. Indigenous Celts, they argued, were brachycephalic (round-headed), whereas immigrant Germans were dolichocephalic (long-headed). Other scholars looked at details of burial rite. The use of sarcophagi was thought a uniquely Roman habit, and the same label was attached to burials without gravegoods, of which there are some in most *Reihengräber*. Sadly, none of these older methods works. There are no simple ethnic differences in skull shape, and explicitly documented Franks have been found in sarcophagi. Nor are the burials without gravegoods any more useful. These show a marked tendency to cluster on the edges of the *Reihengräber*, and modern excavation methods have shown that use of these cemeteries started in the middle and worked outwards. The real explanation for the absence of gravegoods is chronological. From the seventh century onwards (as was also the case in longer-lived Anglo-Saxon inhumation cemeteries – if cemeteries can have a long life), there was a marked decline in the use of gravegoods, probably under the influence of Christianity, until funerary rites returned to the unfurnished burial typical of the late Roman period.[79]

If no simple method has yet emerged for telling Romans from Franks, there is some entirely convincing evidence that some of the men buried with weapons in the sixth century were of indigenous Gallo-Roman stock. An excellent case study is the large, carefully excavated cemetery at Krefeld-Gellep on the Lower Rhine in northern Germany. This is one of few burial sites that remained in continuous use from the late Roman into the Merovingian period. In c.500 AD, close to an existing late Roman cemetery, a second cemetery was inaugurated with the interment of one richly furnished burial and subsequently continued in use with a pretty standard collection of Merovingian furnished burials. Opening the second cemetery, however, did not lead the first to close, and what happened there is striking. Furnished inhumation – with standard Merovingian collections of weapons and jewellery for males and females, respectively – quickly became the normal mode there too. The original excavator and secondary commentators have all concluded, surely correctly, that in the first cemetery an existing late- or now post-Roman population adapted itself to the new cultural norms inaugurated by the rich burial in cemetery two: a beautiful case of elite emulation at work. And what happened so demonstrably at Krefeld-Gellep is likely to have been happening right across northern Gaul, in other areas where existing late Roman cemeteries were entirely replaced by *Reihengräber*, and where, consequently, it is not possible to demonstrate a similar cultural evolution. Many of these new *Reihengräber* surely must include populations of Gallo-Roman descent who adapted themselves to the new Merovingian-era norms.[80]

A further body of evidence which seems, in part at least, to reflect this process consists of those cemeteries whose use began with one particularly rich burial, like that second cemetery at Krefeld-Gellep. Thanks to a half-century of careful work on the chronology of Merovingian material culture, this pattern has been documented at a whole string of sites: Mézières in the Ardennes, Lavoye on the Meuse, Pry, Gutlingen, Chaouilley in Lorraine, Rübenach, Héruvillette and Bale Berning. It might be tempting to think of many of the burials in such cemeteries as those of Frankish immigrants, but you can't just assume so. This has been demonstrated at Frénouville in Calvados. Here, a freak genetic marker in the form of a cranial suture shows that substantially the same population remained in place before and after the rise there of furnished inhumation, even though the new rite appears in an entirely new Merovingian cemetery. The furnished-burial habit was imported into Frénouville, it would seem, by just the one elite family responsible for the rich 'founding' burial in the new cemetery, but by the mid-sixth century it had spread right across an indigenous population that now also used the new cemetery.[81] The evidence is unimpeachable, therefore, that, in part, the new habit of furnished inhumation spread so widely over northern Gaul because the indigenous Gallo-Roman population adopted it with enthusiasm.

But what was the origin of this rite, and why was it adopted? One strand within modern archaeological theory tends, as we have seen, to interpret clusters of relatively rich burials as evidence of social insecurity and competition. Because status was not clear, families aimed to put on a competitive show for their neighbours. Such an interpretation is clearly possible in this instance. The rise of the Merovingian kingdom enforced, as we have seen, rules on social status that were new compared with its Roman predecessor, and you can see precisely why this might have sparked off social competition.[82] But this is not the only possible explanation, nor in this case even the most persuasive one. For one thing, the same remaking of the social order happened south of the Loire, but this did not spark off burial competition. You could reasonably counter this with the fact that there the old elites survived with many more of the building blocks of their social distinction intact, so that there was no need for them to compete; but there are other more significant objections to the social-stress theory as well. Above all, the neatly laid-out *Reihengräber* look much more like highly organized communal spaces than arenas of intense social competition. Their carefully ordered lines strongly suggest that burial was being policed in some way. As indeed do the goods put in the burials: particular categories of dead – adult but not elderly males and young women at the height of childbearing – were consistently buried with more goods than others. Again, it has been suggested that this is because these deaths were more stressful, but the law codes tell us that this is when wergild was at its height, and that could just as well be the key point.

In more general terms, the legal evidence does indicate both that there were clearly marked-out status groups in Merovingian society – free, freed and slave (which interlinked with adjustments for age to give the precise value of any individual) – and that some clear functions were attached to the different groups. Free and freed could be called on to fight, for instance, but slaves were excluded from what was seen as a higher-status function. Other legal evidence also calls for public ceremonies to be held when an individual was promoted from one status group to another, and for the most part, these rural social communities were small enough for everyone to know one another.[83] These observations suggest a significantly different interpretation, in which burying males, particularly with weapons, certainly represented an assertion of status, but in which, at the same time, it was far from easy to claim an inappropriate status in small-scale, not to say claustrophobic, rural societies.

By itself, therefore, the social-stress argument is far from self-evidently correct, and the evidence we have for the spread of the furnished habit suggests another line of explanation, if one that retains an element of social stress within it. The richest of all the Merovingian furnished burials is in fact the oldest: that of Childeric himself. His burial (481/2) was followed in close order, perhaps very close order, by a series of rich, but not quite so staggeringly rich burials, known as the Flonheim-Gutlingen group – a name that doesn't exactly trip off the tongue. None of these graves can be dated with absolute precision. In stylistic terms, their gravegoods are so similar to those found with Childeric that the burials must be coincident with his, but they are located outside the limits of the old Roman province of Belgica Inferior, the territory that Childeric is traditionally thought to have bequeathed to Clovis. This suggests, on the face of it, that they followed at least Clovis' initial conquests, but the argument is possibly circular, since, as we have seen, Childeric's territories may have extended beyond Belgica Inferior. Either way, they clearly belong somewhere in the last quarter of the fifth century.[84]

There are no such chronological doubts about the further spread of the new burial habit. Next in line is a set of less rich though still strikingly well-furnished burials, Rainer Christlein's so-called Group C burials – another far from exciting term, but at least easier to say. These burials provide both a chronological and a qualitative link between the small numbers of hugely rich burials dating to the late fifth century and the more numerous, if more modestly furnished, graves that are characteristic of the Merovingian period proper and which date in fact from the sixth century rather than the later fifth, and probably mostly from its second quarter rather than the first.[85] On balance, this chronological progression of the habit suggests that the new burial rite gained general currency by trickle-down effect from the very grand funerals of Childeric and his immediate associates. The new rite represented a huge break from past Frankish practice – cremation followed by the scattering of the ashes – and hence it is perhaps not surprising that it took the best part of fifty years to take general hold.

It makes a kind of intuitive sense that Merovingian inhumation developed as the wider population started to emulate – on a more modest scale – the practices of its leaders. This effect is often seen, of course, but doesn't add up to anything like a full explanation of the phenomenon. In the case of Childeric's himself, the idea of mounting a really grand burial, dripping in gold, was probably a spin-off from the funerary habits of the Danubian style generated in Attila's Empire at its height. The Germanic world had seen occasional clusters of rich burials before the fifth century, though none in properly Frankish areas, but as we saw in Chapter 5 the Hunnic Empire marked a watershed in the deposition of wealth with the important dead. The staggering wealth of the Hunnic and immediately post-Hunnic horizons entirely eclipsed anything seen before in the amount of gold put in the ground. The Franks were not among the Huns' most dominated subjects, but they did fall sufficiently within Attila's orbit for him to have interfered in a succession dispute, and the Danubian style did generally change the norms of barbarian burial.

From that point on, the practice of rich burials for leaders became widely adopted, and lasted well into the sixth century. It would come as no surprise, then, for Frankish leaders of the generation after Attila to have adopted the practices of the greatest Empire that non-Roman Europe had ever seen. It is also true that Childeric and Clovis – it was the latter who presumably organized his father's funeral – were busy changing the nature of Frankish politics. Both had every reason to mobilize Hunnic practice so as to mark out the fact – or claim – that Childeric had been a Frankish ruler quite beyond the ordinary. This certainly means that there was a strong element of competitive display in the revolutionary funeral Clovis arranged for him. Indeed, if the Flonheim-Gutlingen burials were of the same date, rather than a little later as is usually supposed, then the display would have become all the more competitive, since they could even have been the burials of rivals rather than lieutenants.

The subsequent spread of the habit more broadly down the social scale is not so easy to explain. What was powering it, obviously enough, was new wealth that became available within Frankish society thanks to the astonishing conquests particularly in the time of Clovis, but expansion did also carry on into the reigns of his sons. Against this background, it is perhaps reasonable to think of the later, but still comparatively rich, Group C burials as the crucial catalyst. These men were presumably intermediate leaders whose families wanted to show off their high status by burying their dead along the chic new lines pioneered by their kings. This would be linked to a process of social competition, since Clovis' conquests put a lot of new wealth into new hands, and what we are seeing here, it would seem, is the winners showing off. This reflex then worked its way down to a much more everyday social level, where, presumably, similar processes were at work, as the wealth generated by conquest percolated down the scale, generating winners who wanted to show themselves, and perhaps also losers who were desperate not to be seen as such, until the new order eventually solidified and produced the much more stable-looking *Reihengräber* cemeteries of the mid-sixth century.

The process did, though, take a while. The new burial habit really only became established from c.525 onwards, nearly half a century after Childeric's death, and this leaves more than enough time for other factors to have impinged. In Anglo-Saxon England, for instance, cremation quickly disappeared with the coming of Christianity, which clearly regarded it as an illegitimate form of funerary rite. Even though Christianity had only just begun to spread among the Franks in the early sixth century, this may also have helped push funerary habits towards inhumation, even if it had nothing to do with the amount of wealth on show.[86]

The direct progression down the social scale from Childeric's burial to those of the second quarter of the sixth century suggests that we should associate the new rite pretty directly with the rise of Frankish power, and particularly with the way in which the wealth of conquest generated competition. But the fact that a strong element of accultur-ation can be so clearly demonstrated in the spread of furnished inhumation – that indigenous Gallo-Romans clearly bought into the new habit in spades – does not mean that there was little or no actual Frankish immigration into northern Gaul, or that the spread of the new ritual was entirely unconnected to this process. On the contrary, there is every reason to think both that Frankish immigration into northern Gaul was substantial, and that it played a major and direct role in spreading the new burial habit.

The evidence for Frankish migration west of the Rhine veers from the specific to the general. The detailed case study of Krefeld-Gellep again commands attention. If, as seems likely, the original cemetery continued to be patronized by the indigenous population, a key question becomes who was being buried in the second cemetery, from whose foundation the furnished burial habit then spread over to the first? As the excavators suggested: most likely a community of immigrant Franks. The rich founding burials at the heart of some of the other new *Reihengräber*, likewise, look like elite immigrant Franks around whose new social power local rural societies were being remade: hence the relocation of burial sites as well as the adoption of the furnished habit. At first sight, then, the archaeological evidence leads us back to the kind of impasse we have just encountered with the Anglo-Saxons. On the one hand, the new burial habit originated as a trickle-down effect from a new and immigrant Frankish elite. On the other, it was adopted – much more demonstrably in this instance – by considerable numbers of the indigenous population. In the absence of very specific archaeological evidence such as that available in the cases of Krefeld-Gellep or Frénouville, distinguishing between burials of those of Frankish as opposed to Gallo-Roman descent is impossible. Any particular individual might perfectly well be one or the other – or, indeed, both, since intermarriage surely must have occurred. It is possible, however, to take the argument further.

If the only evidence for immigration were the handful of richly furnished burials at the heart of several of the new *Reihengräber* cemeteries, Frankish migration into northern Gaul could very plausibly be considered as elite transfer followed by cultural emulation. But there is excellent evidence, in fact, that a much more substantial migration flow underlay the acculturation process. It is worth thinking for a moment about broader patterns of continuity and change right across the Merovingian kingdom. As we have seen, a few furnished burials have been found south of the Loire. In these areas, however, the new habit did not take hold, and the indigenous population as a whole stuck to established burial norms. Within the overall Frankish kingdom, therefore, adopting the burial rite was not an automatic process. It was not enough just to dump the odd Frank in a Gallic landscape for everyone suddenly to be overcome with the brilliant new idea of burying weapons and other valuables with the dead.

A priori, it is possible to think of several reasons why the new habit should have caught on in the north and not in the south, but there is a correlation between *Reihengräber* and levels of Frankish settlement. As with Anglo-Saxon England, the linguistic evidence is again crucial. In general terms, the overall effect of Frankish immigration was to shift the line of Germanic language use westwards from the Rhine frontier by a width of territory that varied between about 100 and 200 kilometres (Map 12). But this was the end result of a complex process and did not occur all at once around the year 500. In the first instance, Frankish immigration seems to have generated interlocking patterns of linguistic islands. Even within the area where Germanic eventually prevailed, some of the larger former Roman centres remained Romance-speaking down to the ninth century: particularly Aachen, Prüm and the old Roman capital at Trier. At the same time, place-name evidence indicates that Germanic-speaking communities originally spread much further westwards than the current language line. Germanic place names can be found well to the north-west of Paris, in Normandy and Brittany, meaning that, as in England, a Germanic-speaking elite must have survived in these regions for long enough to give their names to the permanent settlements that eventually emerged (Map 12). In northern Gaul, more or less permanent villages and estates evolved a little sooner than in Anglo-Saxon England, from the seventh century rather than the eighth, so that isolated Germanic place names don't necessarily provide evidence for very lengthy language retention – maybe just a century or so.[87] Nonetheless, as in Anglo-Saxon England, these Germanic linguistic islands could only have been created by migrant groups that included women and children as well as men, even if the much more restricted westwards drift of the overall language line provides a broad indication of where Frankish settlement was at its most dense.

Although we lack specific historical evidence, it is most likely that the process that brought these immigrants west across the Rhine was similar in some important respects to that which brought Anglo-Saxons to England. While not by any means the richest of Roman territories, northern Gaul was in the main economically more developed than neighbouring non-Roman territories to the east of the Rhine, and, more simply, the Frankish political dominance created by Clovis' victories meant that more land could be acquired in outright ownership in the newly conquered territories than was easily available at home. This is not to say that lands east of the Rhine were overpopulated, any more than was Normandy in 1065, but just that military victory opened up exciting new possibilities for wealth acquisition, and the expectation among Clovis' followers that some of it would come their way. Especially after the dramatic successes of Clovis' reign, the demand for seriously substantial rewards among his following would have been overwhelming. These expectations are likely to have gone well beyond the distribution of looted movables and on to the level of landed assets – as happened in a variety of ways in the other successor kingdoms to the Roman Empire – and such demands had to be satisfied.[88] In reality, there were always alternative leaders for followers to turn to should expectations *not* be fully satisfied. The spread of the high-status founding burials of the new *Reihengräber* across the land-scape of northern Gaul, in my view, is most likely an archaeological reflection of the allocation of due rewards to Clovis' loyal followers (and possibly those of his successors too).

Like that of lowland Britain for Anglo-Saxons, the land and wealth of northern Gaul had been exercising a magnetic pull on neighbouring Franks long before Roman imperial collapse allowed settlement to proceed. Franks had been raiding across the northern Rhine frontier since the third century, and when political circumstances were favourable, whole groups of them had sometimes attempted to annex particular territories. In a famous incident of the 350s, for instance, the Emperor Julian had to expel Frankish groups who had taken advantage of a Roman civil war to seize control of the city of Cologne and some surrounding areas. Some of these Franks claimed that they were refugees from Saxon attack, so that there may have been an additional political motive, but the attraction of Roman wealth is clear enough from the long history of cross-border raiding.[89] By the same token, a strong enough field of information was already in operation to kick-start a migration flow, and northern Gaul was in no sense *terra incognita* for inbound Franks.

The sources offer us no clear sense of the size of these Frankish migration units. The degree and longevity of linguistic change indicates that many of them included women and presumably also their children. If it is correct to see the migration process as driven by a process of political reward, as broadly it must be, then these migration units will probably have consisted of the warrior to be rewarded and his dependants, familial and otherwise. But, as the later evidence from Viking Danelaw shows, this could still have taken the form of rather more people than a nuclear family. There, whole warbands seem to have been settled together with the followers gathered around their immediate leaders, and this could easily have happened in the Frank-ish case too. The legal evidence suggests, for instance, that freedmen stood in permanent dependence to particular freemen, so a freeman and his semi-free dependants might well have moved as a group. This may also have been true of greater lords and their free retainers (and the free retainers' freedmen too).

The linguistic islands were created, presumably, as these migrant groups established themselves in the landscape. Where these people were more densely packed in, total language change eventually followed; where less so, their linguistic influence shows up now only in Germanic place names. In this case, however, as was not true of the Anglo-Saxons, Frankish migration seems to have begun only after total military victory, and there are no hints of a Gallo-Roman Aurelius Ambrosius. Frankish units of migration could therefore be smaller and, once again, the influence of political structures on the migration process is clear. Parallels with the Norman Conquest would also suggest that this process of land acquisition was unlikely to have been fully under royal control. One of the things that emerges from *Doomsday Book* is how much unlicensed appropriation had gone on in the twenty years since 1066, one plausible motivation for the report's creation being that, on the back of this free-for-all, William was unclear in 1086 about who among his followers held what. Overall, we might see Frankish intrusion into northern Gaul as a non-random form of wave of advance, where the intruders were all looking for a nice piece of Gallo-Roman countryside to make their own.[90]

The available materials can only leave many questions unanswered, but the evidence for large-scale Frankish migration (if in small units) is unimpeachable. And the crucial point for present purposes is that there is also enough to indicate a clear link between migration and the establishment of the furnished burial habit. On one level, this is strongly suggested by the link between rich founding burials and the spread of the furnished habit into particular localities. And more generally, where there was no migration, as south of the Loire, then no *Reihengräber* appeared. Identifying a link between *Reihengräber* and Frankish migration, however, is not a complete contradiction of the social-stress explanation of the new burial habit, in fact more a refinement. From the Frankish perspective (as from the Anglo-Saxon or Norman in parallel circumstances), the fact that migration was about securing new wealth meant that there was a substantial element of social stress inherent in it, on at least two levels.

First, the Frankish followers of Clovis and his sons were competing fiercely among themselves for the largest shares of the spoils of conquest (as William's followers did after 1066). This was an anxious business for all concerned: hence perhaps their original tendency to show off their new wealth by burying large amounts of it with their dead in imitation of the sub-Attilan practices of their leaders. At the same time, the process was stressful for the indigenous population, who found themselves invaded by an intrusive new elite and incorporated into a kingdom that was imposing upon them new duties based on the alternative conception of a triple-tier social order and the rights and responsibilities appropriate to each of those tiers. For the indigenous population, therefore, in the midst of the major reshuffling of the social deck of cards set in train by Frankish victory, the new game in town was to find their way to the best possible outcome. This naturally meant cosying up to a member of the incoming Frankish elite, if one happened to settle in your immediate locality, a process illustrated perhaps at Frénouville; or more generally negotiating recognition of the highest possible status for yourself in the eyes of the new Frankish rulers. Either way, it is immediately apparent both that the process would be inherently stressful – and stressful in spades – and that there would be a powerful tendency to absorb the cultural and other norms currently sweeping through the Franks as they showed off the new wealth of conquest.

Immigration and social stress are not competing explanations for the spread of the furnished burial ritual and the emergence of the new *Reihengräber* cemeteries. The process of Frankish migration itself generated competition and social stress which here took the form of the widespread adoption of burial trends that had their origin in the Danubian style of the Hunnic Empire. That, however, was in the beginning. Once the period of negotiation was complete and it had been decided who was free, freed or slave, then, as the nature of the *Reihengräber* cemeteries and the legal evidence suggest, the new social order acquired a greater stability.

For all the problems that the sources present, it emerges that the creation of the Frankish kingdom involved migration on two or, better, three levels. South of the Loire, there was very little. Only a few garrisons were established, and while elite life there resonated to the new demands of Frankish kings, the amount of cultural and socioeconomic disturbance in the first instance was limited. North of the Loire, the picture is very different, although linguistic evidence indicates that this area requires subdivision. Between the River Rhine and the new Germanic/Romance language border, migration was significantly heavier than further west, where only some place names were affected in the longer term. In both parts of northern Gaul, however, the revolutionary nature of the changes is apparent. This was not a case of elite replacement, but, like the Anglo-Saxon takeover of Roman Britain, a redefinition of the entire meaning of elite status, and the social norms and value structures upon which it rested. The fact that some of those participating even at the upper levels were probably descended from indigenous inhabitants of the region does not make the transformation any less revolutionary, nor hide the fact that it was successful Frankish political expansion, involving a substantial element of migration, that made it all happen.

## MASS MIGRATION AND SOCIAL STRESS

In the literal meaning of the term, neither Frankish expansion into north-eastern Gaul nor the Anglo-Saxon takeover of lowland Britain qualifies as *Völkerwanderung*. Neither were 'peoples' (German, *Völker*) to begin with, so they could hardly go wandering anywhere. And contrary to older conceptions of these processes, which envisaged something close to ethnic cleansing unfolding certainly in Britain and also in some areas north of the Loire, many indigenous Romano-British and Gallo-Romans clearly formed part of the new ethnic mix that had emerged in these former Roman provinces by the year 600 AD. The truth of this statement, however, doesn't deny another. The previous two centuries had seen in both regions the unfolding of migratory phenomena that were substantial enough, whatever the actual numbers involved, to bring about major change on just about every level imaginable: politics, socioeconomic patterning, administrative organization and culture, whether material or non-material.

One advantage of taking the Anglo-Saxon and Frankish case studies together is that, between them, they pinpoint the limits and potential dangers of overusing the elite-transfer concept. It does not make analytical sense to bracket together the Norman Conquest of England, where the incoming migrant elite settled happily within an existing socioeconomic structure of eliteness, with other instances where migrants demanding rewards came in sufficient numbers to cause a major restructuring of the prevailing social and economic order. The fact that the immigrants probably amounted to no more than a minority both north of the Loire and south of Hadrian's Wall makes no difference. In both zones, Anglo-Saxons and Franks were responsible for revolutionary transformations going well beyond a simple process of elite replacement of the kind exemplified by the Norman Conquest.

This raises the (perhaps not hugely important) issue of what might be the most apposite label to attach to each of these situations. Different researchers, I suspect, will take different views, but to my mind 'elite transfer' might be most usefully restricted to the type of encounter in which the domination of new immigrants did not require major socioeconomic restructuring along the lines of the Norman Conquest. And if you make that choice, the obvious term to reserve for alternative instances that did require a complete remaking of the socioeconomic order becomes 'mass migration'. This will have some jumping backwards in alarm, but the fact is that no one believes any more in complete population replacement – the old invasion-hypothesis version of mass migration – so that 'mass' is an available and currently undefined, or imprecisely defined, term. It also has the advantage of tying in very neatly with the qualitative definition of mass migration employed in comparative migration studies. Remaking social and economic orders right down the social scale will always administer a huge shock, whatever the cultural context, and whatever the numbers of migrants involved.

Much more important than particular choices of label, however, is the conclusion that in cases such as the Franks and Anglo-Saxons, migration is not an alternative explanation for major cultural change – even material cultural changes such as the adoption of a new burial rite – to social stress. The supposed equation between furnished burial rites and social stress does not always work, and each case needs to be looked at closely. Neither the odd furnished burial in an otherwise unfurnished cemetery landscape, nor regularly furnished burials in highly regulated contexts such as the *Reihengräber*, look as though they reflect social stress. The great advantage of the Frankish evidence over the Anglo-Saxon comes from the fact that so many of their cemeteries have been dug up more recently (although some of the more recent

Anglo-Saxon cemetery excavations do make the same point). These excavations have also allowed the initial process of electing to bury the dead with a relatively wide array of goods to be more thoroughly explored, and it is this which to my mind puts social stress and migration so firmly on the same page of the explanatory hymn book. Being able to see that the insertion of a rich outsider into a community led the locals to bury both in an entirely new cemetery and according to the outsider's rituals can only prompt the conclusion that adopting the new rite was part of the indigenous response (part-voluntary, part-involuntary, I would imagine) to the problem posed by having a new landowning elite roll into town (or, in fact, into the country).

This of course is only a model, and matters did not everywhere progress in the same fashion. At Krefeld-Gellep, immigrant and native seem to have kept to separate cemeteries, but the general pressure to conform was strong enough to bring the latter culturally into line nonetheless. The fact, too, that the Frankish settlement process happened after the fact of conquest, while that of the Anglo-Saxons occurred in mid-struggle, could have contributed to some substantially different local consequences. Continued conflict with other indigenous groups might well have made it more difficult for conquered natives to achieve good outcomes in the Anglo-Saxon case than in the Frankish, and, as we have seen, the linguistic evidence strongly indicates that the new landowning elite of lowland Britain by c.600 AD was composed overwhelmingly of immigrant elements.

These particular points aside, there are many ways in which Frankish and Anglo-Saxon migration illustrate and develop the main themes of this book. Transport logistics – the Anglo-Saxons providing a first example of sea-borne migration – and active fields of information decisively shaped both, but perhaps above all it is again the interaction of migration and patterns of development, and the huge role played by prevailing political structures, that jump out of the evidence. Frankish and Anglo-Saxon migration can be seen as mechanisms by which unequal patterns of development were renegotiated. Despite its own economic transformations during the Roman era, non-Roman western Europe lagged sufficiently far behind adjacent areas of the Empire for the latter's wealth to exercise a strong pull. Unlike a modern economy, the wealth of this world was generated above all by agricultural activity, and offered migrant labour few high-paying or high-status jobs – being a peasant was no more fun west of the Rhine than it was further east. The main way for most outsiders to access any of this wealth, therefore, was to raid it regularly for movables, apart from a relative few who made it big in the Roman army. Throughout the Roman period, this greater wealth was protected by armies and fortifications. As lowland Britain and north-eastern Gaul fell out of central imperial control at different points in the fifth century, however, the restriction these imperial institutions had imposed upon the capacity of outside populations to seize control of capital assets was removed, and raiding, after a time lag, turned into predatory migration, aiming at the seizure of landed estates.

Unequal development was ultimately responsible, then, for both flows of migration. But both the Frankish and the Anglo-Saxon versions were effect, rather than cause, of central Roman collapse. They played a major role in dismantling such structures of local Roman provincial life as remained upon their arrival in northern Gaul and Britain, respectively, but in both cases it was the failure of the imperial centre's capacity to maintain enough force on its fringes that exposed these provincial Roman societies to immigrant attention.

What, though, of the bigger picture? If we widen the focus to the western Roman Empire as a whole, what role did migration play in its overall collapse? And given that migration and patterns of development ought to be close bedfellows – as indeed we have found them to be again in this chapter – what effects did the collapse of the Empire have upon the prevailing pattern of unequal development that had marked out Rome and its neighbours before the era of the Huns?

# 7

# A NEW EUROPE

IN 476 AD, ONE HUNDRED YEARS after the Goths first asked its ruler for asylum, the eastern half of the Roman Empire was still a going concern, running much of the Balkans, Asia Minor, the Near East, Egypt and Cyrenaica as a unitary state. Some migrants had found their way into its Balkan territories as the Hunnic Empire collapsed, but most were incorporated on the kinds of terms that the Roman Empire had always offered. They may well have retained some low-level autonomy, but after the departure of the Amal-led Goths for Italy in 488 they were made part of the Balkans' military establishment only in such small concentrations that they posed no substantial political or military threat to the integrity of central imperial control.

The situation in the old western Empire was entirely different. In the fourth century, it continued to dominate its traditional territories from Hadrian's Wall to the Atlas Mountains of North Africa, as it had for the past three hundred and fifty years, or, if you leave Britain out of the equation, four hundred and fifty. By 500 this long-standing unity had vanished. In its place stood a series of successor kingdoms, most of which, some small exceptions in the western British Isles apart, were built around military forces whose ancestors had lived beyond the imperial frontier before 376. Vandals and Alans built a kingdom centred on the richest provinces of former Roman North Africa, Sueves another in north-western Spain, Visigoths a third in south-western Gaul and the rest of Spain, while Franks in northern Gaul, Burgundians in south-eastern Gaul, Anglo-Saxons in Britain and the Amal-led Ostrogoths in Italy had all done much the same.

This book is about migration and development, not a fully fledged exploration of the collapse of the western Empire. It is no part of its subject matter to consider the internal evolution of the Roman state over its five hundred-year history, or how this contributed to eventual imperial collapse, which it certainly did. It is to the point, however, to take stock of the migratory phenomena examined in the last three chapters, and their overall contribution to one of the great revolutions in European history. Traditionally these kingdom-forming groups from beyond the frontier were thought of as 'peoples': culturally homogeneous entities, mixed in age and gender and with strong senses of group identity, who reproduced themselves over time largely by endogamy rather than by taking in new recruits from outside. In more romantic visions, the action was also given a strongly nationalist spin. The vast majority of these kingdom-forming groups were Germanic-speaking, and if you crossed your fingers firmly enough behind your back the fifth century could be presented as the culmination of four hundred years of Germanic resistance to Roman oppression, which had begun with Arminius' destruction of Varus and his legions in the Teutoburger Wald in AD 7.

Recent revisionist views have sought to overturn such interpretations in a number of key areas. First, the kingdom-forming groups were not 'peoples', but improvised coalitions of manpower with neither cultural homogeneity nor any strong senses of identity. Second, so the argument goes, their manpower was literally that: manpower. There may have been some women, but not many, and the groups resembled armies much more than peoples. More radical revisionists have even argued that our Roman sources are infected with a migration topos that turned all outsiders on the move in Roman territory into 'peoples'. Less radical ones would prefer that while some barbarians certainly moved, the more important story, given the lack of strong group identities holding these barbarian groups together, was the way in which manpower gathered around new leaderships once a few people had moved. Third, the period was marked by no straightforward hostility between Romans and outsiders; in one influential view, the fall of the western Empire has been characterized as a 'surprisingly peaceful' process, where the Romans showed a marked willingness to come to terms with outsiders, and the outsiders lacked any intention of bringing down the Roman state. Rather than the violent cataclysm traditionally portrayed, the Empire disappeared by mixture of accident and consensus as barbarian outsiders were invited inside it, and some of the greater Roman landowners eventually preferred to come to terms with them rather than continue to pay the amounts of taxation that the imperial state had required to support its armies.[1]

So how do the processes of migration we have been observing in the late fourth and fifth centuries shape up in the light of both traditional and revisionist conceptions of the fall of the Roman west? Equally important, what part did Roman imperial collapse play in transforming patterns of political and economic organization – development, in other words – right across the European landscape?

# EMPIRE FALLS

Some of the revisionist arguments have real substance. There was no barbarian conspiracy to bring down the Roman Empire. The vast majority of the immigrants we have been examining did not cross the frontier and march hundreds of kilometres with that as their express intention. For the most part, too, the different immigrants operated independently of one another, and were just as likely to fight one another as they were the Empire. The Visigoths were happy to be employed by Rome to fight Vandals, Alans and Sueves in Spain in the 410s, and in the 420s Vandals and Alans fought their erstwhile Suevic partners. Later on, Franks fought Visigoths; and in their conquest of Italy, the Amal-led Ostrogoths, the various refugees from the collapse of Attila's Empire who had become incorporated into Odovacar's army. Even as late as 465, most groups south of the Channel still had no idea that the western Empire was about to end. Their political agendas even at this late date were focused on securing a beneficial alliance with the rump west Roman state, while seeking to prevent other groups from doing the same.[2] There is also much evidence of immigrant leaders and Roman elites forming new political bonds that cut across the old divides between Roman and barbarian. As early as the 410s, Alaric's successor at the head of the Visigothic coalition, Athaulf, rallied Roman support to his cause in Gaul, and the Vandals had some Hispano-Romans in tow when they conquered North Africa. This type of alliance continued right down to the deposition of the last western emperor in 476, but perhaps found its archetypical expression in the attempt by Goths, Burgundians and Gallo-Roman aristocrats to construct their own imperial regime behind the figure of Eparchius Avitus in the mid-450s.[3] Other elements of the revisionist case, however, are much less convincing.

## Peace in our Time?

The idea, in the light of such observations, that the transition of the Roman west from unitary Empire to multiple successor states was a largely peaceful process, for one thing, will not stand comparison with the evidence. Its initial premise that the outside groups who eventually founded the successor states had originally been invited across the frontier rests on the flimsiest of bases. There is no shred of evidence that any Roman official invited in Radagaisus' Goths, the Rhine invaders (Vandals, Alans and Sueves), the Burgundians, or Uldin the Hun. In other words, every intrusive outsider involved in the crisis of c.405–8 was an uninvited guest, and all were resisted with might and main. The same is true of all the smaller components of the earlier frontier crisis of c.375–80: the Taifali, Farnobius' Goths, the Sarmatians, and the Huns and Alans who allied with the rebellious Goths in the autumn of 377. And similarly with one of the two major Gothic groups who crossed the Danube in late summer or early autumn 376, the Greuthungi of Alatheus and Saphrax. They were originally excluded by force, but took advantage of an opportunity presented by increasing tension between the Roman state and the Gothic Tervingi to get across the river.

The only outsiders in this entire saga that actually crossed into the Empire with imperial permission were the Gothic Tervingi, and even here it is very likely that Valens had no real choice. The Emperor was fully committed to war with Persia in the summer of 376 when the Goths arrived on the Danube and asked for asylum. You'd have to think him a complete idiot to suppose that he would have been happy to see one major frontier go up in flames when he was already at war – with most of his army – on the other. As one source reports, the decision to admit the Tervingi was taken only after rancorous debate, and it looks, in the circumstances, like damage limitation. The emperor did not have enough troops to hope to exclude both the Tervingi and the Greuthungi, and was looking to divide and rule by letting one in and excluding the other. The point is confirmed by the various contingency plans that were put in place to neutralize any military threat the Tervingi might pose, especially the strategic control of food supplies and orders to attack the Tervingi's leadership in case of trouble. It is true that in the fourth century (and before) emperors had periodically used contingents from their Gothic and other client kingdoms in their wars, even civil ones, but this provided no motive for admitting large groups of armed men permanently on to Roman soil – a much more dangerous proposition than recruiting armed bands from across the frontier and sending them home again once a campaign had finished.[4]

If it is demonstrably not true that the barbarians who made their way across the imperial frontier in the late fourth and fifth centuries did so at Roman invitation, a more sophisticated version of the idea has been proposed for the crisis of 405–8. This argues that the Empire issued a kind of implicit invitation by loosening its hold on the relevant frontier regions. It's a bit like the argument heard at the time of the Falklands War in the early 1980s, in which the British decision to scrap the minesweeper *Endeavour* on financial grounds was read by the Galtieri junta as a sign that Britain would not resist an Argentine takeover. The ship had previously spent its time flying the flag in the South Atlantic. Applying this kind of analogy to 405–8 makes for a much more possible and interesting argument, but not in the end a persuasive one. In particular, the precise triggers of barbarian invasion are argued to have been the withdrawal of Roman military forces from the frontier region of northern Gaul, and the end of, or a substantial reduction in, subsidies paid to its frontier clients. The problem with this, however, is that the invasions of 405–8 were not for the most part mounted by those living on the immediate frontier, the prime recipients of such subsidies, but by other entities from outside the frontier region – sometimes, like the Alans, from far beyond it. There were also enough Roman forces in Britain and northern Gaul to propel the usurper Constantine III to within a cat's whisker of controlling the entire western Empire in the autumn/winter of 409/410, and, in any case, the first attack (that of Radagaisus) didn't target the supposedly semi-evacuated area. In short, there is no reason to think that the unprecedented pulses of barbarian intrusion had anything to do with a Roman invitation, explicit or implicit. The outsiders moved on to Roman soil in acts of violent self-assertion.[5]

What followed on from the original invasions was nothing very different. The hundred years separating the arrival of the Goths on the Danube in 376 from the deposition of Romulus Augustulus in 476 witnessed the working-out of many different political processes, within which there was certainly no underlying aim of bringing down the

Empire. But all of these processes involved periodic violent confrontation, often substantial, between the intruders and the Roman state. Looking at it from the immigrants' perspective, the politics of this century had two main stages. The first consisted of putting up a good enough fight to prevent the Roman authorities from destroying your group's independence at the initial point of contact. The Tervingi and Greuthungi managed this between 376 and 382. Military might and the capacity to run away to North Africa were central to the ability of the groups who crossed the Rhine in 406 to survive their initial clashes with Roman (and Visigothic) forces in Spain. The Burgundians, on the other hand, were resettled further into Roman territory in the 430s by consent, it seems, but only after they had been devastated by the Huns, and the Roman general Aetius seems to have had a role in sponsoring those attacks.

If these groups managed to survive their first encounters with Roman might, many others did not. A number of Gothic subgroups were destroyed piecemeal between 376 and 382, Radagaisus' force was bodily dismantled in 405 and many of its members sold into slavery, though some of the survivors later rejoined Alaric. The Rhine invaders suffered such heavy casualties between 416 and 418, likewise, that, as we saw earlier, three previously separate groups – Hasding Vandals, Siling Vandals and Alans – combined into one. However you look at it, surviving an initial encounter with the Roman state was no cakewalk. On my count, between 376 and their eventual establishment in Gaul in 418, the Goths that combined to create the Visigoths had between them fought eleven major campaigns and a host of smaller ones.[6]

This overall level of violence was central to two specific features of the migratory activity characteristic of this first stage. On the one hand, it helps explain why immigrant groups tended to engage in repeat migration. Continued movement was part of a survival strategy as they either manoeuvred for a compromise with the Roman state (the moves of Alaric's Goths, for instance, from the Balkans via Italy to Gaul), or looked for safer and more prosperous venues from which to continue to defy it (the Vandal coalition's move to North Africa). Second, it is impossible to explain why, without continued large-scale conflict, so many different immigrant groups came to operate together in a smaller number of larger confederations. The new political units formed on Roman soil – the Visigoths, the Vandal–Alan coalition, the

Ostrogoths – all had in common the fact that they represented larger units that were better able to confront the military power of the Roman state, both to ensure their members' survival and to extract from it more advantageous terms.[7]

More violence was central to stage two of migrant political activity: maximizing their position once they had ensured initial survival. These two stages tended to elide into one another, since not even the first Gothic immigrants of 376 entered the Empire without a range of ambitions that went beyond mere survival, but the second is distinct enough to be worth identifying. It can be characterized as the emergence of a framework of Roman–barbarian diplomatic relations, which had moved beyond any possibility of the particular immigrant group's destruction. In the case of Alaric's Visigoths, this stage was reached somewhere between 395 and 418, and is highly visible in the nature of the group's subsequent diplomatic contacts with the Roman state. From 418, diplomacy focused only on how much territory the Visigoths were going to dominate, and on what terms: not, any longer, on whether their existence was going to be tolerated or not. Even so, stage two was still marked by repeated military conflict: first in southern Gaul – where the regional capital at Arles provided an attractive target for the Goths in the 420s and 430s – and then more widely between the Loire and Gibraltar in the late 460s and 470s, when the Goths under Euric (467–84) founded a huge and independent kingdom. The Vandal–Alan coalition, by contrast, only began to reach the second stage from the mid-440s, when the west Roman state was forced to acknowledge its North African conquests, and, in fact, never enjoyed it as securely as the Visigoths. The death throes of the western Empire involved two serious attempts to reconquer the Vandal kingdom in 461 and 468. The Franks and Anglo-Saxons, on the other hand, never had to confront the Roman state head-on, and so in a sense moved direct to stage two. Nonetheless, they still pursued their ambitions by a violence-fuelled mixture of conquest and expropriation.[8]

Switching the perspective now to that of the Roman state, the connection between immigrant violence and the collapse of the western Empire could not be more direct. In simple terms, Rome taxed a comparatively developed agricultural economy in order to fund its armies and other structures. There were other sectors to the economy, but no one thinks that agriculture constituted anything less than 80 per cent of Gross Imperial Product, and many scholars would put that figure higher. In this context, the activities of the immigrants had direct effects on imperial tax revenues, and in so doing materially diminished the state's capacity to survive. Any loss of territory to an immigrant group, such as the Spanish provinces to the Rhine invaders in the 410s, meant that the area concerned was now no longer contributing to central imperial coffers. Additionally, provinces caught up in any fighting, even if not conquered outright, were also much less able to pay their taxes. Nearly a decade after they had been occupied for only two years by Alaric's Goths, the provinces around the city of Rome were still being assessed at only one-seventh of the normal tax rate. A similar rebate was also granted to two North African provinces which were not part of the Vandal–Alan kingdom of the 440s, but had been occupied by them for three years in the mid-430s. A six-sevenths reduction was perhaps generally granted, therefore, to provinces that had been heavily fought over.[9]

Once you start adding up the tally of lost and damaged provinces with the western Empire's landed tax base in mind, the extent of the problem posed by immigrants quickly comes into focus. As early as 420, Britain had been definitively lost to central Roman control, along with the Garonne valley granted to the Visigoths. In addition, most of Spain had been taken or fought over by the Rhine invaders, and much of central and southern Italy damaged in the course of the Visigoths' stay there between 408 and 410. The reduction in tax revenues caused by all these losses shows up beautifully in a late Roman resiger of military and civilian officals called the *Notitia Dignitatum*, which includes a listing of the western Empire's armies dating to the early 420s. By this point, about half of the field army regiments, as constituted in 395, had been destroyed in the intervening quarter-century. But over half of the replacement units now incorporated into that army – 62 out of 97 – were simply old garrison troops upgraded on paper to field army status. Not only had field army losses not been replaced with troops of top quality, but neither is there any sign that the upgraded garrison forces had been replaced at all. Quality and quantity had both declined drastically as a direct effect of the erosion of the Empire's tax base.[10]

Worse was to follow. By 445, the western Empire's richest provinces – Numidia, Byzacena, and Proconsularis in North Africa – had succumbed to the Vandals, and part of Pannonia (modern Hungary) to the Huns, while Burgundians and some other Alans had been granted smaller areas in Gaul in the mid-430s. At this point, something close to 50 per cent of the western Empire's tax base had been eroded, and the money was running out. Not surprisingly, this is the era in which western legislation both complained about the unwillingness of land-owners to pay their taxes and attempted to claw back existing tax breaks. Any disinclination on the part of landowners to pay up is obviously an important phenomenon, especially since there is good reason to suppose that normal tax rates were having to increase at this time. Furthermore, new taxes were being invented. But to argue from this that the unwillingness of the rich to pay their taxes was a central cause of western imperial collapse, as has sometimes been done, is to put the cart before the horse. Tax privileges for the rich and well connected had always been part of imperial politics: enriching your friends was one reason why they backed you to win power. The phenomenon assumed an unwonted importance in the 440s only because so many provinces had already been lost to immigrants, or so damaged by warfare, that the western Empire's revenues had shrunk to dangerously low levels.[11]

This aggregate loss in the state's military and political effective-ness in turn contributed to a new strategic situation that allowed the immigrants further to expand the areas under their control, and dramatically so from the mid-460s. By that date the western army, bled dry by declining tax revenues, was a shadow of its former self and unable to confront with any chance of success the Visigoths, Vandals and others, particularly the Franks, who had just started or were finishing carving out power bases on former western territory. Looked at in terms of its effects upon tax revenues, and hence upon the Empire's military establishment, there is no mistaking the direct line of cause and effect that runs from the immigration of armed outsiders to the collapse of the Roman west.

Against this backdrop, the increasing tendency of local Roman aristocrats to do deals with the various immigrants as the fifth century progressed can only be considered, like aristocratic unwillingness to pay high taxes, a very secondary phenomenon in the story of Roman collapse. Again, it is important to put these deals in context. The local aristocrats involved in them were all essentially landowners, whose estates, the fundamental source of their wealth, were for the most part situated in one locality. These physical assets could not be moved. So if that locality started to fall within the expanding sphere of influence of one of the immigrant groups, the relevant landowners had little choice. They had either to come to some accommodation with the immigrants' leadership, if they could, or risk losing the land that was the source of all their wealth and status. Such accommodations were not automatic. In lowland Britain, as we have seen, the old Roman landowning class completely failed to survive the Anglo-Saxon take-over.[12]

Attempts to make the end of the western Empire into a largely peaceful process, carried forward by the withdrawal of the local elite from continued participation in central state structures, are unconvincing. On the contrary, all the various political processes of the fifth century were implemented by violence. Those elites were caught in the middle, with little choice but to make accommodations with the new powers in their lands, whether they wanted to or not, and if they could. A key distinction sometimes missed here is that between the central Roman state and local Roman landowner. Looking at just the latter, it is possible to document many stories of accommodation. These occurred, however, only after, and because, immigrant groups had fought their way across the frontier, and so stripped the western Empire of its tax base that it no longer had sufficient revenues to keep worthwhile armies in the field, leaving provincial landowners completely exposed.


## Know Your Barbarians

When it comes to the immigrants of the late fourth and fifth centuries, there is again real substance to some of the revisionist arguments. Most of these groups were new political entities, not 'peoples'. Ostrogoths and Visigoths, the Franks of Clovis, the Vandal and Alan alliance, and the Sueves of Spain: all were new entities forged on the march. A new political order was created among Anglo-Saxons, likewise, during their takeover of Britain. Of all the kingdom-forming groups who established successor states to the western Roman Empire, it is only the Burgundians for whom we lack explicit evidence of a major sociopolitical reconfiguration on the move, and even this may be due to a lack of information rather than any smooth continuity in their fifth-century history, which was pretty chequered.[13]

But if the immigrant groups weren't 'peoples', neither does it fit the evidence to take an equally simple, if opposite, point of view and write them off as small-scale will-o'-the-wisp entities of little historical significance. Many were substantial. The few plausible figures we have, confirmed by their capacity to stand up to major Roman field armies, all suggest that the largest groups were able to put into the field forces numbering over ten thousand fighting men and sometimes over twenty thousand, especially after the amalgamation processes of the fifth century had run their course. The group identities operating within these large assemblages were not as straightforward as old nationalist orthodoxies imagined. Not even all the fighting men enjoyed the same status. At least in the larger alliances, there were two distinct status groups among warriors, and quite probably a third, of non-militarized slaves, besides. How many slaves there might have been is impossible to know, but we can't just assume that they were few in number. Some of the kingdom-forming groups even crossed major cultural boundaries, the long-time alliance of Germanic Vandals and originally Iranian-speaking nomadic Alans being the classic case in point. What exactly happened when Vandal met Alan in the Middle Danube in the run-up to 31 December 406 is extraordinary to contemplate.[14]

But to conclude from these undoubted truths that the new group identities meant little is mistaken. Full participation was not allowed to all group members, as the existence of lower-status warriors and slaves within the new group identities makes clear. Neither of these lesser-status groups had as much invested in the identity of the group as its higher-status warriors. But neither was full participation the preserve of just a few individuals. Royal families came and went much too easily for us to characterize group identity as short-term loyalty to a particular dynasty. Even after deposing their last Amal ruler, the Ostrogoths retained their identity. I would argue that the prime carriers of, and beneficiaries from, the group identities being negotiated and renegotiated during this period were precisely the higher-status warrior groups. Some indications suggest that these may have comprised something like a fifth to a third of all armed males. And even if subject to periodic renegotiation – essentially political, perhaps, rather than cultural – nothing suggests that the kinds of group identities these men constructed were easy to destroy. Among the larger groups, the Ostrogoths did not, as has recently been argued, easily fade away into the Italian landscape after 493; while, amongst the smaller, Heruli and

Rugi both showed considerable capacity to survive, in their different ways, even major defeats. Though not 'peoples' in the classic sense of the word, then, the immigrant groups were substantial not only in size but in structural resilience. Here again, the degree of violence characteristic of the era had an important role to play.[15]

When social scientists started thinking about group identity, they generally assumed that human population groups became politically and culturally distinct from one another as a result of physical separation. One major advance since the Second World War is the insight that active group identities are regularly generated out of precisely the opposite scenario: intense contact in the form of competition.

Developing a group identity is often about becoming part of an entity strong enough to protect a particular set of interests. And you don't have to look very far in the events of the later fourth and the fifth century to find violence – the epitome of competitive contact – brokering the renegotiations of identity that produced the new kingdom-forming barbarian alliances. Some of the new identities (particularly those of the Visigoths and the Vandal–Alan coalition) were formed by migrants who needed to operate on Roman soil in larger groupings so as to preserve their independence against traditional imperial policies designed to dismantle threatening concentrations of outsiders. Others were born out of the collapse of Attila's Empire which again generated fierce competition, this time among the many armed groups gathered by the Huns on the Middle Danubian plain. And yet a third was generated among groups looking to take over the landed assets of the collapsing western Empire. The Visigoths and Vandal–Alan coalition were well placed to play this more profitable game, having united originally so as to survive, but new groups formed to participate in the same land-grabbing exercise – particularly the Ostrogoths, Franks and Lombards. On a smaller scale, the Anglo-Saxons moving into lowland Britain also fall into this category.

All of these new group identities were born in violence, and even if recently renegotiated they were reasonably durable, at least among the higher-status warriors who were the prime beneficiaries of the ambitions they had been formed to pursue. That does not mean, of course, that every member of the group, even those higher-status warriors, was equally committed to the new identities, or that they were indestructible. Neither of these is true of any modern group identity, either. But those forged in the later fourth and the fifth century were real political phenomena, not mere ideologies or dynastic fantasy.[16]

The migrations undertaken by these groups were correspondingly substantial. As we have seen, some of the historical evidence for large, mixed population groups taking to the road with massive wagon trains is much too weighty to be dismissed. Ammianus on the Goths of 376, in particular, is too well informed and demonstrably capable of describing a variety of barbarian activities for us to dismiss his account as migration topos. As the revised notions of group identity would suggest, the large kingdom-forming concentrations of population did not move from point A to point B untouched by the process. They recruited extra manpower as they went, which they slotted in, as appropriate, to the various positions available within the group: in Germanic-dominated groups, it would seem, either as higher-status free warrior, freed lower-status warrior or non-militarized slave. But accepting this does not license us to dismiss their migrations as relatively small-scale phenomena. While certainly different from migration units you find today, large mixed population groups do make sense in their own context, given the general level of development of contemporary non-Roman society and the kinds of enterprise being undertaken.

Three principal types of migration emerge from the narrative. The first comprises those mixed groups of outsiders who moved across the imperial frontier because of the direct or indirect threat posed to their existing territories by the build-up of Hunnic power. The Tervingi and Greuthungi of 376 fall into this category, as do, in my view, the Goths of Radagaisus who invaded Italy in 405/6; and the Vandals, Alans and Sueves who moved over the Rhine shortly afterwards. The many different strands within these two pulses of migration eventually reorganized themselves into two large confederations: the Visigoths and the Vandal–Alan coalition, as noted earlier. These could each field something in the region of ten to twenty thousand warriors, and both had women and children along besides, not to mention slaves. The motivation for all these groups was essentially political and negative – fear of the Huns – but they were also busy calculating, increasingly from direct experience, what it would take for them to carve out a profitable niche within Roman territory. The constituent groups behind the Visigothic alliance, moving from Ukraine to southern France via the Balkans and Italy, the others from central Europe (or from much

further east in the case of the Alans) to North Africa via Spain, also
provide the most spectacular examples of long-distance movement.
Their treks took the form of discrete jumps, with considerable pauses
in between, rather than one continuous movement, because migration
was part of a developing survival strategy. The chronological gaps also
reflect the distances involved in these treks, since information had to
be acquired at each jumping-off point about the new options that were
opening up. The Vandals – from modern Hungary or thereabouts –
can have had little sense of how to get to North Africa from Spain
when they first set out, or even perhaps that you could.[17]

The second category consists of those groups, many again involving women and children, who moved out of the Middle Danubian
heartlands of the Hunnic Empire in the chaos following Attila's death.
Again, some of these were substantial. The Amal-led Goths from
Pannonia comprised over ten thousand fighting men, besides women
and children. The Sueves, Heruli and Rugi who made their way into
the army of Italy or joined the Amal bandwagon certainly mustered
at least a few thousand warriors each, and of these the Heruli and
Rugi, at least, were again moving with women and children.[18] These
groups' motivation was, again, partly political and negative: fear of
the other parties involved in the competition unleashed by Hunnic
collapse. At the same time, there was a powerful element of oppor-
tunism. The Amal-led Goths took calculated decisions first to throw
themselves into east Roman territory, and second, having united with
the Thracian Goths, to move on to Italy. In both cases, their decisions
were based not only on the limitations and difficulties of their current
situation but also at least as much on the greater degree of prosperity
potentially available at the projected destinations. This category is
distinguished from the first not only by a greater element of opportun-
ism, but also by the distances involved. The long march of Theoderic's
Goths from Hungary to Thessalonica, to Constantinople, to Albania
and then on to Italy is impressive, but it was not quite of the same
order as the epic trek of the Vandals, or the trials and tribulations of
the Visigoths.

Frankish and Anglo-Saxon migration into north-eastern Gaul and
lowland Britain, respectively, took a third and different form, although
there were some significant variations between the two. Distances
were shorter; and the characteristic migration unit within the flows,
smaller. The archaeological evidence suggests that the most intensive

Frankish settlement happened in areas of Roman Gaul within a radius of only a hundred kilometres or so from the limits of their previous holdings. Anglo-Saxon groups obviously had to cross the Channel and/or the North Sea, but this too was a relatively short hop. The range of motivations in play was also different. The North Sea may at this time have been eroding some continental coastlands, making some long-cultivated areas unusable.

For the most part, however, the motivations behind Frankish and Anglo-Saxon settlement were positive and predatory. Both followed the elimination of effective Roman state power at their respective destinations; for both, previously, the Empire's armies, fleets and fortifications had made it impossible for them to do anything more than raid. Both flows were filling power vacuums in fairly adjacent landscapes, attracted by the relative prosperity of the target area's more developed economy and the fact that landed wealth was easier to access there. Franks and Anglo-Saxons had no need to operate in migration units on anything like the scale of those in the other categories, therefore, although it does seem likely, since conquest and settlement were simultaneous in Britain, that the Anglo-Saxon migration groups were larger than their Frankish counterparts. Both migration flows certainly also included women and children as well as warriors. These positively motivated expansions, carried mostly by smaller units over shorter distances, stand in marked contrast to the more spectacular, longer-distance moves made by larger concentrations of population whose motivations were much more mixed.[19]

## Brave New Worlds

All of these migrants represented minorities in the new kingdoms they created. In those generated by longer-distance migration, the minorities were tiny. The Ostrogoths weighed in at some tens of thousands, but no more than a probably generous maximum of one hundred thousand, though this might be an underestimate if slave numbers were substantial.[20] The population of late Roman Italy is normally reckoned at a few million. If we estimate it for the sake of argument at five million, then the immigrant Ostrogoths would have amounted to no more than 2 per cent of the total. You could fiddle endlessly with these figures, but the basic ratio won't change very much. Ostrogothic immigration generated only a fractional increase in the total population of post-Roman Italy. The same was true of the Vandal–Alan coalition and the Burgundians, both of whom (the latter certainly) seem to have been second-rank powers compared to the Ostrogothic kingdom. From the perspective of the Italian, North African and Gallic populations, these migrations would have been experienced not even as elite replacements but as partial elite replacements. Within the kingdoms the newcomers created, many of the indigenous landowners of Roman descent remained in place, along with much of their Roman culture and even some Roman governmental institutions. The Visigothic kingdom of Gaul and Spain also falls into this category, although its origins were different. On being settled initially in just the Garonne valley in 418, the Goths must have represented a greater addition to the local population, even if still a minority. Within the larger kingdom created by Euric's campaigns, which stretched from the Loire to Gibraltar, Gothic immigrants probably represented an even smaller minority than the Amal-led Goths in Italy.

The Franks in northern, especially north-eastern, Gaul, and especially the Anglo-Saxons in what became England, represented a bigger influx of population in percentage terms, though they were still very much a minority. Even so, it is hard to get their numbers much above 10 per cent of the total population in the areas affected, and, in some places it may have been considerably less. Here, the new landowning elites that had emerged by the second half of the sixth century, and especially in Gaul, may again have included some genetic descendants of the old indigenous Gallo-Roman and Romano-British populations. But this must not obscure the point that north-eastern Gaul and lowland Britain represent an entirely different case from Italy, North Africa, Spain and the rest of Gaul. In the old Roman north-west, the elite class and its cultural norms were completely remade between 400 and 600 AD, and the landed assets upon which elite status was based completely reallocated, as the old villa estates were broken up into different-sized parcels. If the migrations involving Goths, Vandals and Burgundians were experienced at the receiving end as no more than comparatively unrevolutionary partial elite replacements, those of the Franks in north-eastern Gaul and the Anglo-Saxons in lowland Britain represented mass migration with profound social, political and cultural consequences for the areas concerned. If we take these different types of case together with the complete elite replacement represented by the Norman Conquest, there are actually three types of situation that need to be differentiated: partial elite replacement, elite replacement that doesn't disturb major socioeconomic structures, and the mass migration of Franks and Anglo-Saxons.

But even if discussion were to be confined just to the cases of partial elite replacement, there remain levels on which the population movements of the late fourth to the early sixth century would still have to be considered, both individually and in aggregate, as mass migrations. To start with, there is the fact that, between them, the migrants destroyed the long-standing Roman imperial edifice, or at least the western half of it. The Empire was always hampered by its economic, political and administrative limitations, but there is not the slightest evidence that it would have ceased to exist in the fifth century without the new centrifugal forces generated by the arrival within its borders of large, armed immigrant groups. Collectively the immigrants must be 'credited', if that is the correct word, with administering a huge political shock to the Roman world, or at least to the central state, even if some Roman landowners and even some more local and regional Roman institutions were left intact after the state's collapse. This state was a powerful organism that had shaped life within its borders for five hundred years on every level from culture and religion to law and landownership. The point is easily overlooked, because the Roman Empire was large and ramshackle, operating with frankly pathetic communications and bureaucratic technologies, which meant that it could not run its localities with anything approaching close day-to-day control. Nevertheless, its structures had long set the macro conditions within which particular social, economic and cultural patterns evolved. A comprehensive listing would require another book, but the existence of the Pax Romana and state-generated transport systems dictated particular patterns of economic interaction, its legal structures defined property ownership and hence social status, its career structures – demanding a sophisticated elite literacy – underpinned an entire education system, and so on. Even religious institutions were largely dictated by the state. As Christianity matured into a mass religion in the fourth and fifth centuries, its authority structures became closely intertwined with those of the Empire. Given all this, the consequences of imperial extinction could not but be profound, setting local society and culture in western Europe off in quite new directions, some of which we will explore briefly in the second half of

this chapter.[21] In the qualitative sense used in migration studies, the
overall impact of Hunnic-era migration qualifies in all respects as mass
migration.

The impact of the Franks in northern Gaul and of the Anglo-
Saxons in lowland Britain also counts as mass migration, in the same
qualitative terms but at a more local level. Reallocating the landed
resources of these regions from scratch among intrusive elites caused
many more cultural, economic and political transformations, which
again qualify for the 'mass' label. Within the other successor kingdoms
which saw only partial elite replacement, the local shock experienced
was much less, but there was still some transfer of economic assets.
Scholars of earlier generations were pretty much unanimous that this
took the form – as in Britain and northern Gaul – of landed property
passing from its previous Roman owners to at least some of the
immigrants. This is another dimension of the barbarian issue that has
come in for substantial revision in the last scholarly generation, again
as part of the general tendency to downplay the significance of the fall
of the Roman west. In this case, the revisionist view argues that,
initially at least, incoming barbarians were rewarded not with landed
estates taken from their former Roman owners, but with a share of
the tax revenues raised from these estates – a type of exchange that
would have generated much less friction than actual land seizures.[22]
There is no space here for a full discussion of the technical evidence
relating to this issue, but in my view the revisionist case remains
substantially unproven. There were important local variations, and
adjusting the tax regime was probably one measure that sometimes
came into play. Nonetheless, I am confident that a transfer of landed
assets – as the most recent restatement of the revisionist position partly
concedes – was at the heart of paying off the newly dominant
immigrant element in all the major successor kingdoms.

That is not to say that every member of each immigrant group
received the same degree of remuneration, or even, necessarily anything at all. *Doomsday Book*, to draw again on the better-documented
Norman analogy, shows that William's more important supporters
received much bigger payouts than their lesser peers, and that there
were many rank-and-file Norman soldiers who received no land at all.
As this parallel emphasizes, in general terms immigrants will surely
have been rewarded in proportion to their pre-existing importance

within their groups. But even if the big rewards were given at first only to the most aristocratic among them, they will in turn have had their own chief supporters to reward (just as the tenants-in-chief did after 1066). Among the immigrant groups of the late fourth and the fifth century direct landed rewards from the king may well not have gone further down the social scale than leading members of the higher-grade (free?) warrior class, though its lesser members and even some or all of the lower-status warriors are likely, on the Norman Conquest model, to have received something from the higher-status warriors to whom they were attached.[23] The detailed evidence also suggests that land transfers within the kingdoms created by partial elite transfer were restricted to specific localities.

While the Vandal–Alan takeover of the richest provinces of Roman North Africa (Proconsularis, Byzacena and Numidia) represented a substantial shock for the political systems of the entire region, any deeper socioeconomic shock was geographically much more limited. After the conquest, Geiseric expelled some of the larger Roman landowners of the region and appropriated their estates to reward his important followers. This disruption at the local level, however, was confined to the province of Proconsularis. In Byzacena and Numidia, indigenous landowners seem to have been left in place; and any shock there was, limited to the operation of the new kingdom's central political systems. Much of the land in Proconsularis was owned by absentee Italo-Roman senatorial families, so this was probably a good place to find land at minimum cost in terms of political hostility provoked. Strategically, too, Proconsularis faced towards Sicily and Italy, from where any significant Roman counterattack was likely to come.[24]

The Amal-led Ostrogothic takeover of Italy was as much of a political shock as the Vandal–Alan takeover of North Africa, but perhaps less of a social one, since on the whole Theoderic pursued a more conciliatory policy towards the Roman landowners of his new kingdom, although this should not just be taken for granted. At one point during the conquest, he threatened Romans who did not support him with the loss of their lands. After the conquest, though, he devoted much of his reign to establishing good relations with them, and many preserved their elite status under his rule. Like Geiseric, Theoderic – it seems – endowed his important followers with substantial landed estates, together with rights to annual donatives, but this process of enrichment seems to have been accomplished without the kind of expropriations seen in Proconsularis.

Gothic settlement was clustered in three particular areas of the Italian peninsula (Picenum and Samnium on the Adriatic coast and between Ravenna and Rome, in Liguria on the north-west of the north Italian plain, and in the Veneto in the east), and what appears mainly to have been transferred was the ownership of landed estates, quite likely from public as much as from private sources. The tenant farmers who had customarily done the work may well have been left in place. As far as we can tell, these transfers caused no massive socioeconomic dislocation. The size of Theoderic's Italian kingdom perhaps made it easier to find the requisite portfolio of estates, in fact, than would have been the case in a smaller one. Nonetheless, the immigrant Gothic military elites did form a new, politically dominant force. Some Roman elites participated in court politics, but, to judge by our narrative sources, the migrant Gothic contingent remained dominant in such crucial political areas as royal succession and war-making. The Ostrogothic seizure of Italy seems to have had only a limited socioeconomic impact, then, even if its political effects were much larger.[25]

In the Visigothic and Burgundian kingdoms the position was similar, but with one important variation. Laws issued in the Burgundian kingdom indicate that affected Roman landowners had to hand over two-thirds of their estates, whereas the corresponding figure in the Visigothic kingdom was one-third. Again there is much about this evidence that requires careful discussion – too much to engage in here – but one especially relevant factor is that, at its fullest extent from the mid-470s, the Visigothic kingdom ran from the banks of the Loire to the Straits of Gibraltar. It was many times larger, in other words, than the Burgundian kingdom centred on the Rhône valley. If you stop to think about it, it is hardly surprising that more expropriation was required to satisfy the incoming outsiders in a smaller kingdom, where there was a more restricted range of landed assets available. That variation aside, however, the evidence suggests that broadly comparable patterns prevailed everywhere outside of Britain and north-eastern Gaul. In all the successor kingdoms created by partial elite replacement, the immigrants generated a dramatic enough political shock as the given territory passed under new management, but the indigenous population would have experienced these immigrations as 'mass' only in distinct and limited areas, where substantial amounts of land passed into migrant hands: Proconsularis, for instance, and the three clusters of settlement in the Ostrogothic kingdom. For the Visigothic and Burgundian kingdoms, the best we can do is guess as to the areas of densest settlement on the basis of place names and/or archaeological evidence.[26]

From the perspective of the immigrants themselves, moreover, sanitary terms like elite transfer, partial or otherwise, entirely fail to capture the nature of the action. Even where they were ultimately successful in establishing themselves in conditions of prosperity, there is no mistaking the scale of dislocation and trauma that preceded settlement. Between 406 and 439 the Vandal–Alan coalition moved in two stages, first from the Great Hungarian Plain to southern Spain (2,500 kilometres), then a further 1,800 kilometres south and west, before their eventual capture of Carthage, the latter involving crossing the Straits of Gibraltar. The Alans amongst them, of course, had made an earlier, westerly, trek of 2,000 kilometres sometime between c.370 and 406, from east of the River Don to the Great Hungarian Plain. These distances are huge and would have been punishing for the groups' weaker members – the old, the young and the sick – especially since they tended to be covered in great leaps: the Don to Hungary, Hungary to Spain, and – if perhaps less of an ordeal – Spain to North Africa. Each of these leaps was a traumatic event that would have caused substantial loss just in itself. In aggregate, such journeys may even have distorted age profiles within the groups, killing off old and young in disproportionate numbers. Among modern political migrants forced to move long distances, exhaustion combines with the propensity for disease generated by overcrowding to make the experience a deadly one. Close to 10 per cent, or a staggering hundred thouand, of the refugees from Rwanda in 1994 succumbed en route to cholera and dysentery. Most of our first-millennium migrants were making more calculated moves and were probably better prepared, but modern comparisons warn us not to underestimate the degree of loss inherent in movement alone.

These losses were greatly increased by conflict with the Roman state. The initial Rhine crossing, for instance, may have caused more losses to the indigenous populations of Gaul and Spain than to the migrants. But, as we have seen, in the late 410s Roman counterattack destroyed one of the two Vandal groups as an autonomous unit (the Silings), and so savaged the Alans – up to that point the most powerful of the invaders – that they submitted to Hasding leadership. The subsequent Vandal–Alan conquest of North Africa, to judge by the admittedly sparse sources available, probably did not involve losses on the same scale, but in its early stages, at least, was hard fought.[27] Sheer distance and heavy military conflict combined to make the process traumatic in the extreme for the migrants, even if they were ultimately able to insert themselves as a new elite in the richest provinces of Roman North Africa.

Similarly with the Ostrogoths, the Visigoths and the Burgundians. Take particularly the Ostrogoths, who ended up, of course, as conquerors of Italy. This staggering achievement laid open to them the region's wealth, which they proceeded to enjoy. It is not so obvious, at first sight, that their migration involved anything much in the way of trauma, but between 473 and 489 they (or at least the original Amal-led Pannonian group) first had to trek almost a thousand kilometres south, from Hungary to Thessaly. By 476, they had notched up a further 500 kilometres, moving north-east to the banks of the Danube. In 478 and 479 they then moved another 1,200 kilometres, first south to Constantinople, then west again (past Thessalonica) to Dyrrhachium on the Adriatic coast. As part of an agreement with the east Roman state in 482/3, they appear to have been resettled six hundred kilometres to the north-east, on the banks of the Danube again. The mid-480s then saw a contingent of Gothic soldiers campaign for the Emperor Zeno against the usurper Illus in Asia Minor (another 1,100 kilometres each way), before the whole group first besieged Constantinople (400 kilometres from the Danube) and then made its 1,500-kilometre trek to Italy. If Jordanes is to be believed, all of this was prefaced in the mid-450s with the small matter of a 700-kilometre journey from east to west of the Carpathians.

There was also plenty of conflict. The group suffered no defeats on the scale that savaged the Vandal–Alan coalition in Spain, but the Amal-led Goths variously fought the east Romans, the Thracian Goths (initially) and the usurper Illus – in 473/4, 476/8, 478–82 (including, in 479, the loss of a baggage train), 484, 486/7 and 489–91. All in all, the trauma was still severe.

The experiences of the Visigoths were similar, in terms of distances covered, to those of the Ostrogoths (from the eastern Carpathians to south-western Gaul), and they also suffered substantial losses. The moves undertaken by the Burgundians were much more modest: from southern Germany to the Rhine, and then south into the Lake Geneva region and beyond. But this relative absence of geographical drama was more than compensated for by much larger losses, particularly at the hands of the Huns in the 430s. All the migrants suffered huge dislocation to the pattern of their lives, and whatever the view from the Roman side of the fence, their experiences can only be characterized as mass migration.[28]

## Migration and Development

The interconnections between migration and prevailing patterns of development in the period of Roman collapse were multifaceted and profound. Straightforwardly, the greater wealth of Roman provincial economies exercised an enormous pull on both of our main sets of shorter-distance migrants, the Franks and the Anglo-Saxons. To judge by the fortifications already required to keep them out in the fourth century, this wealth disparity had been calling from across the Rhine and the North Sea for some time. And once the power of the central Roman state collapsed, what was in many ways its natural consequence simply worked itself out. Militarized outsiders, previously excluded from Roman territory by force of arms, were able to take possession of the more developed economic zones within their vicinity, and the rest, as they say, is history.

Disparities of development also partly explain the choices of the longer-distance migrants. Their motives were often highly complex, involving a large negative component, since they were regularly moving into territories of which they had little direct knowledge and where the Roman state was still alive and kicking, so that they were facing a much greater military threat. This being so, it took an extraordinary kind of stimulus – that provided by the dramatic events surrounding the rise and fall of the Hunnic Empire – to get them moving. In both of the main initial pulses of Hun-generated migration, 375–80 and 405–8, the motivation was political and negative: the desire to avoid coming under Hunnic domination. Later on, as the Hunnic Empire unwound, motivations remained equally political, if now more positive. The Amal-led Goths in the 470s in particular, but also

Lombard groups slightly later on, moved on to or towards Roman territory to secure a larger share of the greater wealth available there. But even for the initial migrants of 375–80 and 405–8, the pull of Roman wealth had some role to play. Hunnic aggression may have prompted their initial decision to leave their established homelands, but at that moment it was open to them to seek new homes either inside the Roman Empire or somewhere outside of it. The fact that most chose the former again reflects the pulling power of greater Roman wealth. One predominant feature of the period can reasonably be understood as barbarian outsiders from beyond the limits of imperial, developed Europe using immigration as a device by which to access a share – for good and ill – of its greater economic wealth.[29]

Equally important, prevailing levels of development explain what at first appears to be the very peculiar nature of the migration units undertaking at least the longer-distance moves. Because contemporary non-Roman European societies could field specialist warrior retinues only in their hundreds, any migration that involved taking on the Roman state would necessarily include women and children as well. As we have noted for earlier eras, only by recruiting from a broader range of militarized manpower, some of which naturally came with families, could military forces of sufficient size be generated for these ambitious enterprises. The families' participation was itself facilitated by another feature of economic development in barbarian Europe. Prevailing agricultural regimes, at least among Germanic groups east of the River Oder – those falling within the areas of Przeworsk and Cernjachov cultures – meant that central and south-eastern European populations retained an inherent tendency to shift settlement site. Shifting settlement every generation or so in search of more fertile fields was obviously a completely different kind of movement from the major migratory episodes of the fourth and fifth centuries. Comparative migration studies suggest, however, that this would still have made them more open to being persuaded to participate in the large, carefully organized expeditions that were required to move into Roman territory with any hope of success.

There is also, I think, one further level on which an interaction between migration and development profoundly shaped the action. What in the end made it possible for some of the first, longer-distance migrants of 375–80 and 405–8 to succeed on Roman soil was their capacity to renegotiate their group identities quickly enough to create new groupings that were too large for the Roman state easily to destroy. The Tervingi and Greuthungi who appeared on the Danube in the summer of 376 were each substantial in their own right, and they clearly got very lucky at the battle of Hadrianople two years later. No other confrontation of the era produced anything like such a one-sided result, and it bought the Goths breathing space in the form of the semi-autonomy granted them in the treaty of 382. At that point, the Roman state had by no means renounced hopes of renegotiating these terms at the point of the sword sometime in the future, so as to bring them much more into line with its traditional treatment of immigrants. One key element in frustrating these hopes was the unification brokered in Alaric's reign between both of the original Gothic groups of 376 and the survivors of Radagaisus' later attack on Italy – the process that created the Visigoths. In a subsequent treaty negotiated with this enlarged force in 418, the Roman state was forced to acknowledge that it could not seriously hope to destroy it in its present configuration – as a unified and autonomous Gothic grouping on the Roman side of the frontier line. Similar processes of unification, likewise, made it possible for the Vandal–Alan coalition and the Amal-led Ostrogoths to survive and flourish. In all of these cases, had the unifications not happened, the Roman state could have mopped up piecemeal a more motley collection of smaller groups, as was the fate of many smaller groupings even in this era. The capacity of immigrants to reconstitute themselves into entities capable of fielding 10–20,000 warriors, or just a touch more, was critical to survival.[30]

This means that the longer-term transformation of Germanic society examined in Chapter 2 is entirely relevant to the migration processes of the fourth and fifth centuries. If the Huns had arrived in the first century instead of the fourth, and pushed the kinds of Germanic group that then existed across the Roman frontier, the overall result would have been very different. Because of the smaller size of the primary political units that existed in the first-century Germanic world, too many of them would have had to become involved in too complicated a process of political realignment to make the creation of entities capable of mustering twenty thousand or more warriors at all likely. The kingdom-forming groups of the fifth century were created out of no more than half a dozen, sometimes only three or four, constituent units. Precisely because these base units were by this date so much larger, the twenty thousand-plus warriors that long-term survival in the face of Roman power broadly required could be rounded up much more easily. To get that many Germanic warriors facing in the same direction in the first century, you would have had to unite maybe a dozen of the smaller and highly competitive units that then existed, and the political problems would have been correspondingly huge.

Even so, the processes of political unification which unfolded among the immigrants in the late fourth and fifth centuries were anything but plain sailing. Each of the new kingdom-forming super-groups was generated out of something like four or five constituent units, and each had its own pre-existing leadership. This meant that there were always at least four or five potential leaders for these new confederations, all but one of whom had to be eliminated in some way. The threat of Roman violence played a huge role in generating broad acceptance of the need to create the new confederations, and some of the potential contenders were willing, it seems, to resign their claims on that basis. Among the Ostrogoths, Gesimund (or Gense-mund) the son of Hunimund was remembered as an independent Gothic warband leader who decided to support the Amal dynasty from whom Theoderic came, rather than press his own claims. But other contenders were much less amenable and had to be suppressed. Other members of the Hunimund line pressed their own claims with vigour, in addition to which the Amal line had to defeat that of another Gothic king, Vinitharius, before the group entered east Roman air space in 472/3, and the rival Triarius line at the head of the Thracian Goths after that. Clovis' unification of the Franks, likewise, involved elimi-nating at least seven rival kings. It is not possible to explore parallel leadership struggles in the same kind of detail for some of the other new confederations, but they certainly occurred.[31]

Furthermore these struggles for power among the newly united supergroups were themselves interacting with patterns of development, because they too were dependent upon the greater resources that were available in the Roman context. The smaller size of barbarian political units beyond the Roman frontier was not accidental, but structural, reflecting the amount of redistributable wealth available for kings to build up loyalty among their followers; and even much of this, as we have seen, usually came from Roman sources. But the greater wealth available on Roman soil, whether extracted directly or indirectly, changed the parameters of political possibility among the barbarians, enabling their leaders to conciliate and control much larger groups of followers. Even the only seeming counter-example, when you examine it, isn't one. One large supra-regional power was constructed in non-Roman Europe in late antiquity: the fifth-century Empire of Attila the Hun. But even this could not support itself from the resources of the non-Roman economy. Rather, it was dependent on broad flows of Roman wealth in the form of plunder and tribute, and collapsed when these were cut off. Non-Roman levels of economic development by themselves were insufficient to sustain political structures of the scale necessary for carving out a successor state on Roman soil.[32]

Prevailing disparities in development thus dictated both the westerly and southerly directions taken by most of the migrants, once the Huns or the decline of Roman power had set them on the move, and the nature of the migratory units themselves. And all this, of course, is exactly what modern migration studies would lead us to expect. As we have seen, patterns of migration are intimately linked to patterns of unequal development. In the case of the late fourth and the fifth century, however, the migratory processes not only reflected existing inequalities of development across different parts of the European landscape, but also caused their substantial rearrangement. This was true both for the different migrant groups as they coalesced into the new state-forming supergroups, and also right across the European landmass.

# THE NEW ORDER

In 510 or thereabouts, Theoderic the Amal, Ostrogothic King of Italy, wrote to the eastern Emperor Anastasius:

> You [Anastasius] are the fairest ornament of all realms, you are the healthful defence of the whole world, to which all other rulers rightfully look up with reverence: We [Theoderic] above all, who by Divine help learned in your Republic the art of governing Romans with equity. Our royalty is an imitation of yours, modelled on your good purpose, a copy of the only Empire.

This looks like sucking-up in spades, but it wasn't. In 507/8 Anastasius' fleet had been raiding the eastern Italian coastline, and the Emperor had also provided diplomatic support for Frankish attacks on one of Theoderic's main allies, the Visigothic King Alaric II. Against this backdrop, the really significant part of the letter comes in its next few lines:

> And in so far as we follow you do we excel all other nations . . . We think that you will not suffer that any discord should remain between two Republics which are declared to have ever formed one body under their ancient princes, and which ought not to be joined together by a mere sentiment of love, but actively to aid one another with all their powers. Let there be always one will, one purpose in the Roman kingdom.

Theoderic's initial flattery thus leads into a carefully crafted argument, which, in context, amounted to a diplomatic demand note. It can be paraphrased roughly as follows: 'The eastern Empire is the model of complete divinely ordained rectitude, I follow it entirely; therefore I am the only other properly legitimate Roman ruler in the world, and superior – like you – to all the other successor state kings. You should be in alliance with me and not the Franks.' And his pretensions were not greatly misplaced. He eventually came through the crisis of 507/8 with his position greatly enhanced. The Franks smashed the Visigothic kingdom at the battle of Vouillé in 507, but east Roman sea raids didn't prevent Theoderic from picking up the pieces. From 511 he became sole ruler of both the Visigothic and the Ostrogothic kingdoms, comprising Italy, Spain and southern Gaul. He also ruled a chunk of the old Roman Balkans, exercised a degree of diplomatic hegemony over both the Burgundian and the Vandal kingdoms, and ran an alliance system that stretched up into Thuringia in western Germania. At the height of his powers, he dominated the western Mediterranean and ruled over a structure encompassing a good third to a half of the old western Empire. His ruling style – as the letter suggests – was also entirely Roman. He built Roman-style palaces, held Roman-style ceremonies in them, maintained the public amenities and even subsidized the teaching of Latin language and literature. The signals were easy to read. One of his Roman senatorial subjects hailed him in an inscription as 'Augustus', the most imperial title of them all.[33]

Faced with Theoderic in all his intimidating pomp, you could be forgiven for wondering if the fall of the Roman west to intrusive military powers from beyond its frontiers had made any real difference at all. In the second decade of the sixth century, forty years after the deposition of Romulus Augustulus, western Europe was still dominated by a Mediterranean-based imperial power. The fact that the edifice was under new management might seem neither here nor there. But appearances are deceptive. Theoderic's revival of a Mediterranean-based western Empire proved entirely transitory. In the second half of the millennium the centre of imperial power in the west was to be located not in the Mediterranean at all, but much further north.

## Empires of the Franks

First impressions might suggest that the Franks inherited Rome's imperial sceptre through an entirely contingent sequence of events. Theoderic's Gothic Mediterranean Empire failed to survive a succession crisis generated by his own death in 526. At that point, and contrary to the king's wishes, the Ostrogothic and Visigothic parts of his Empire were redivided, each being ruled separately by different grandsons. And any lingering hopes that some future successor might rekindle the flames of the western Empire on the back of a Gothic power base were utterly extinguished in twenty years of warfare, starting in 536, when the east Roman Empire under the rule of Justinian (527–65) destroyed the Ostrogothic kingdom, as it had destroyed that of the Vandals in the early 530s. There was also a strong element of chance in Justinian's decision to launch these western campaigns in the first place, since they were born of defeat in an earlier war against Persia that had left him desperately in need of a victory to shore up his waning prestige. Looked at more closely, however, the failure of Theoderic's Empire reflects much more fundamental adjustments in Europe-wide balances of power – themselves the result of an interaction between half a millennium of development in barbarian Europe and the collapse of the Roman state.

By the late fourth century AD, before the great era of migrations began, the European landscape was marked, as we have seen, by massive inequalities of development. South of the River Danube and west of the Rhine lay the territories of the Empire, characterized by

Europe's highest population densities, the most developed exchange systems capable of supporting towns and considerable short- and long-distance trade, a relatively small and relatively rich landowning elite, and state structures of real power. These could mobilize the resources of the Empire's territories to support such large-scale enterprises as professional armies, major building programmes and a governmental bureaucracy. Roman territory was bordered by its inner periphery of semi-subordinate client kingdoms, which generally received substantial trade privileges and diplomatic subsidies from the Empire but were subject to political interference and notionally owed certain – particularly military and economic – services to the Empire, which it was periodically able to extract.

These client states were part of the broader imperial system, but their relationships with the Empire were never entirely smooth. They often used force, or the threat of it, to attempt to maximize the financial benefits that could follow from a close relationship with the Roman state, and to minimize any accompanying exploitation. As we have seen, the Empire periodically launched campaigns to achieve exactly the opposite outcome. The new wealth that collected in the periphery via interactions with the Empire – trading, raiding and diplomacy – had also played an important role in generating political transformation. Dynasts who wished to control all the new wealth that came from proximity to the Empire had had to build up their military power accordingly, and were enabled to do so by the extra wealth that they came to control. But there was also an element of consent within this process, since the greater power of these leaders meant that they could offer their supporters the best hope of fending off imperial interference. All of these processes pushed political organization in the inner periphery towards the creation of larger and more powerful entities, and their aggregate effects show up in the new confederations that appeared along the entire length of Rome's European frontiers in the third century.

Beyond this inner periphery – still viewing matters from a Roman perspective – lay an outer periphery. Here the populations generally stood in only an indirect relationship with the Empire, but their territories were a source of raw materials and other resources that were shipped into it via the inner periphery. Hence they had received some of the economic benefits that flowed into barbarian Europe from five hundred years of interaction with Rome. The outer periphery also shared in some aspects of the inner periphery's political transformation, not least because elements of its population periodically organized themselves to take control of the greater wealth that was available closer to the frontier. This began to happen through raids in the first century AD, but shows up in more substantial transfers of militarily organized population groups from the outer to the inner periphery in the so-called Marcomannic War of the second century, and above all in the expansions of Goths and others from the outer periphery towards the Roman frontier in the third.

The boundary between the inner and outer peripheries cannot be fixed with precision, and in practice the two probably elided. As well as the periodic population intrusions from outer to inner, Roman diplomatic contacts spread to some extent beyond the innermost ring. In the fourth century we know, for instance, that from time to time the Empire had diplomatic relations with the Burgundians of the Main valley, 'behind' the inner Alamanni on its southern Rhine frontier. The boundary of the outer periphery, however, is reasonably easy to fix. There is no sign of any interaction – direct or indirect – with the Roman world in archaeological remains of the period very far east of the River Vistula or north of the forest steppe zone of southern Russia (Map 2). Down to the late Roman period, the populations of most of this huge territory continued to preserve the very simple Iron Age farming lifestyles that had marked out these landscapes from long before the birth of Christ.

In the broadest of terms, therefore, development in the Roman period had created four bands across the European landscape compared with the three-speed Europe that existed around the start of the millennium. Then, Roman/Celtic Europe west of the Rhine and south of the Danube was generally far more developed than Germanic Europe up to the Vistula, which, in turn, was more developed than the lands further to the east. By the fourth century, the more intense development generated by contact with the Empire had subdivided the old middle band of Germanic Europe into the inner and outer peripheries that we have just examined.[34] The migratory activity associated with the fall of the Roman west not only reflected the four bands of unequal development running across the European landscape, but also transformed them out of all recognition. The profound nature of these changes shows up clearly if we take a close look at the kingdom of the Merovingian Franks north of the Alps and Pyrenees,

and consider why it was left as the only possible centre of supraregional power in the west after the destruction of Theoderic's Empire.

As we saw in the last chapter, the Franks' progression towards
superpower status had accelerated in the reign of Clovis. Not only did
he unite some previously separate Frankish warbands, but he used this
power base to conquer large swathes of territory in what is now
France and western Germany. And once Theoderic's Gothic Empire
fell apart, the way was open for a dramatic escalation in Frankish
expansion. From the early 530s, Clovis' sons and grandsons extended a
mixture of hegemony and conquest over a much wider swathe of
territory. Like Theoderic earlier, they were well aware of their achievements. When Clovis' grandson Theudebert wrote to Justinian in about
540, he declared himself the ruler of many peoples, including Visigoths,
Thuringians, Saxons and Jutes, as well as the lord of Francia, Pannonia
and the northern seaboard of Italy. Theudebert went very close indeed
to claiming the imperial title outright. A prerogative of Roman
emperors was that they alone could issue gold coins. This had been
inherited from the period when many Roman cities had had their own
base-metal coinages, and continued generally to be observed after 476.
Theudebert, however, started to issue his own gold coins, and many
of his Merovingian successors followed suit.[35]

To explain the rise of Frankish imperial power just on the basis
of contingent events, like Justinian's destruction of the Ostrogothic
kingdom, would be to miss much of its real significance. For all
his glory, even Theoderic had had to strain every sinew to hold the
rising Frankish tide in check. His alliance system of the 510s was
designed to contain further Frankish expansion, and the whole edifice
rested on a rickety unification of the Visigothic and Ostrogothic kingdoms, which, for all Theoderic's ambitions, must always have been
odds on to collapse after his death. And once this extraordinary but
improvised Gothic power block fell apart in 526, Frankish expansion
began again, well before Justinian's assault on Ostrogothic Italy. In
the early 530s, the Burgundian and Thuringian kingdoms, deprived
of Gothic support, quickly fell under Merovingian sway, and all this
before the first east Roman troops set foot in Italy.[36] Justinian's campaigns removed any chance that a Gothic counterbalance to the Franks
might re-emerge in the western Mediterranean, but that had been
looking unlikely anyway. The main point to emerge from all this is
that in the post-Roman world the most likely source of supraregional

power in western Europe lay not in the Mediterranean, but north of the Alps and Pyrenees.

This was an unprecedented development, which must not be taken for granted, as it easily can be if you view events just from a modern perspective. It is not that odd, given everything that's happened since, to find France, Benelux and western Germany providing the basis of a militarily and politically powerful entity. But when this first happened in the sixth century AD, it represented a huge break with the past. The ancient world order in western Eurasia was one where the resources of the Mediterranean reached such a precocious level of development that states based upon them had always been more powerful than anything further north.[37] In the sixth century, for the first time in recorded history, an imperial power emerged that was based on the exploitation of more northern European resources. This very signifcant phenomenon was a direct result of the processes of development that had been operating on the fringes of the Empire during the Roman period. The social, economic and political transformations under way on its periphery had all tended to generate ever stronger economies and political societies, and the rise of the Franks exploited this new strength to the utmost.

As first Roman control and then Gothic influence evaporated from north of the Alps, Childeric, Clovis and their descendants swallowed up both Roman territory west of the Rhine and large parts of the Empire's old inner and outer peripheries on the other side of the river. East of the Rhine other, so-called Ripuarian, Franks were quickly incorporated into the new enterprise, as were the Alamanni, again in Clovis' own lifetime, after the huge defeat they suffered in 505/6. In subsequent generations, a mixture of conquest and domination established different degrees of Merovingian control and hegemony over more easterly neighbours – Frisians, Saxons, Thuringians and Bavarians. Some kind of Frankish superiority was even acknowledged, it seems, in parts of Anglo-Saxon England. This new supraregional power base ran from the Atlantic in the west more or less up to the River Elbe in the east (Map 13). It combined, therefore, both a substantial portion of former Roman territory west of the Rhine, and large portions of the old Empire's inner and outer peripheries to the east.[38]

The ancient world had seen Mediterranean-based supraregional powers of several shapes and sizes, and in this sense the successor states created there by longer-distance migrants such as Theoderic's Ostrogoths were just a new variation on a long-established theme. But a brand-new phenomenon now emerged in the European landscape, and the existence of the Frankish superpower firmly reflected the five centuries of transformation effected in the north by the diplomatic, economic and other workings of the Roman state. Without the increased socioeconomic and political development that its existence stimulated in the inner and outer peripheries east of the Rhine and north of the Danube, these lands could never have provided the basis for a truly imperial power. By sponsoring the emergence of the new Frankish-dominated northerly power block, therefore, these earlier transformations set the developing pattern of European history off on a new trajectory in the second half of the first millennium. And from the sixth century onwards, the new superpower was itself to become a major factor in the further development of the European landscape.

That said, the path of Empire north of the Alps in the second half of the millennium did not run so smoothly as it had for its Mediterranean counterpart in the first. Roman emperors had come and gone, and a few peripheral territories had been lost in the third century. The Empire's modes of government, likewise, were transformed over time. But this was largely a process of organic, internal evolution, at least up to the third century. Essentially, the Roman Empire remained the same state ruling over broadly the same territories for the best part of five hundred years.[39] The same was not remotely true of imperial western Europe in the second half of the millennium. Merovingian greatness peaked in the sixth century, and by the second half of the seventh, much of the real power had fallen into the hands of regionally dominant blocks of local landowning elites, in Neustria, Austrasia and Burgundy (Map 13). This in turn allowed peripheral areas to reassert their independence. The Thuringians seem to have been independent from the revolt of Radulf in 639, the Saxons and Bavarians soon after 650. Even the long-subdued Alamanni reasserted their independence by the early eighth century.[40]

Later Merovingian political fragmentation was followed by a dramatic resurgence of Empire in the same century at the hands of a second Frankish dynasty, the Carolingians. The new dynasty originally came to prominence as Merovingian loyalists with lands between Cologne and Metz, more or less modern Belgium, where the Merovingians too had first burst on to the historical stage. Those who study the first millennium AD have a distinct advantage when it comes to the age-old game of Name Five Famous Belgians. There is no need to tell the Carolingian story in any detail here, but in the late seventh century the first really prominent member of the dynasty, Pippin, made himself dominant in northern Francia, over both Austrasia and Neustria, after the battle of Tertry in 687. Ruling at first through a Merovingian frontman, in the next generation Pippin's son Charles Martel success-fully reunited to this northern Frankish heartland all the old territories of Gaul controlled by the Merovingians at their height. By 733 he was moving his supporters into Burgundy to establish his control in the south-east. After a lengthy struggle, Aquitaine in the south-west was conquered in 735. Charles Martel also campaigned east of the Rhine, forcing the Frisians, and notably the Saxons in 738, to start paying him tribute again.[41]

Imperial momentum had been established, and his sons and grandsons did more than maintain it. First, they ditched the Merovin-gians. After securing his own position, Charles's son, another Pippin, made the final leap to royal lightspeed, deposing the last Merovingian, Childeric III, and having himself crowned king in 752. Now royal, the Carolingians quickly expanded the area under their control, the second half of the century being consumed in an orgy of conquest, initially under Pippin, but more particularly under his son and heir Charles, better known as Charlemagne: 'Charles the Great' (*Karolus Magnus*, 768–814). East of the Rhine, direct Frankish rule was asserted for the first time over peoples who had been periodically subordinate to the Merovingians, but often autonomous and sometimes entirely independ-ent. By 780, self-assertive ducal lines in Alamannia, Thuringia and Bavaria had all been extinguished, and further north, Frisia had been subdued. Saxony, too, was eventually conquered outright, for the first time, but only in the early ninth century after two decades of punishing campaigning that had included forced baptisms, population transfers and wholesale massacres. On the back of these successes, Charlemagne directed his attentions further afield. The independent kingdom of the Lombards was crushed in the mid-770s, and in campaigns that culmi-nated in 796 he destroyed the central European Empire of the Avars. The plunder taken on this expedition became proverbial.[42]

Charlemagne's conquests thus united Gaul, the territory between the Rhine and the Elbe, northern Italy and much of the Middle Danube region, together with parts of northern Spain, into one vast imperial state (Map 13). The Merovingians had at times exercised influence over large parts of this territory, but not everywhere in the form of direct rule, and their domination had never extended into Italy or the Middle Danube. Consonant with this, Charlemagne was much less shy in asserting that he had created an empire. From about 790 onwards, a consistent thread appeared in the writings of his team of resident royal intellectuals, extolling his success and his piety and declaring that both showed him to be a (or even 'the') true Christian emperor. There is not the slightest doubt, therefore, that Charlemagne's imperial coronation on Christmas Day 800 in St Peter's basilica in Rome happened not by accident but by design. Three hundred and twenty-four years after the deposition of Romulus Augustulus, full-blown Empire in the west was reborn.[43]

For all its grandeur and the lasting importance of some of its cultural legacies, however, the Carolingian Empire proved no more stable than its Merovingian predecessor. By the later ninth century there were still Carolingian kings, but their effective power was confined to a limited block of territory around Paris. Elsewhere in west Francia, authority had devolved once again to a constellation of local princes who each exercised within his own domain the kinds of powers (over justice, the minting of coins, ecclesiastical appointments and so forth) that Charlemagne had previously wielded over the entire Empire. Sometimes these rights had been formally granted, sometimes merely usurped. As one contemporary chronicler, Regino of Prüm, put it in a charming phrase, after the death of Charlemagne's grandson Charles the Bald in 871, each area had made a prince 'out of its own bowels'. In the west, the Carolingian Empire had come and gone within a century of Charlemagne's coronation.[44]

In east Francia, beyond the Rhine, greater unity prevailed, providing – eventually – the third Frankish imperial moment of the second half of the millennium. Here, another of Charlemagne's grandsons, Louis the German, enjoyed an unusually long reign, providing a greater heritage of political cohesion for the constituent duchies of east Francia – originally Saxony, Thuringia, Franconia, Suabia and Bavaria, to which Louis added Lotharingia and Alsace (Map 14). East Francia's cohesive tendency survived the extinction of Louis's line at the turn of the tenth century, and the region was brought to still tighter unity first by Conrad (King of east Francia during 911–18), originally Duke of Franconia; and then by Henry, son of Otto son of Liudolf, the Duke of Saxony from 912, then King of the east Franks from 919 until his death in 936. Within three years of his accession, Henry had forced the Suabians and Bavarians to recognize him as King of the east Franks. He then provided effective war leadership against the pagan Magyar nomads, who had moved into the Middle Danube region from the western steppe around the year 900. They rapidly made themselves public enemy number one, raiding far and wide across northern Italy and southern France and defeating no fewer than three major east Frankish armies between 907 and 910. On the basis of a carefully crafted programme of military reforms in the late 920s, Henry was able finally to defeat them at the battle of Riade (in northern Thuringia) in 933. This victory secured Henry's position as king, but it was his son Otto I who took the dynasty's authority to a new level.

Not that this was easy. It took Otto until 950 finally to subdue different combinations of rebellious dukes and familial rivals. He also effectively continued another of his father's key policies: expansion in the east. Otto then launched a powerful expedition into Italy in 951, taking control of most of its northern and central regions. This demonstrated that he was now the most powerful ruler of Latin Christendom, a status he confirmed by inflicting a crushing defeat on the still pagan Magyars at the battle of the Lech in 955. This gave him an irresistible combination of overt power and ideological legitimacy, since it was clearly God who had allowed him to defeat the pagans where so many other Christian rulers had failed. So armed, Otto was able to browbeat the papacy into another imperial coronation. A second Italian expedition was mounted in 961, after which he was crowned Emperor in 962. The third Empire of the second half of the first millennium had come into being. Although based ultimately on Otto's inherited position in Saxony, the Ottonian Empire was a distinctly sub-Carolingian entity, a reasonably direct descendant of the east Frankish kingdom of the ninth century.[45]

A succession of Frankish empires based firmly in northern Europe thus dominated large parts of western and west-central Europe between about 500 and 1000. They were never as stable as their Roman predecessor, the exercise of imperial power being punctuated by two periods of considerable political chaos, c.650–720 and c.850–920. This was because all three were based on a weaker type of state structure. In the Roman Empire, much day-to-day control was in the hands of local communities, but the the central authorities had always retained some key levers of power. They had the right systematically to tax the largest sector of the economy – agriculture – in order to generate substantial annual revenues. These were used to support a large professional army, a governmental machine and state legal structures (both laws themselves and the courts), which were the font of legitimacy in the Roman world. For all its limitations, and there were many, the Roman Empire thus operated a relatively big state structure in pre-modern terms. The three Frankish Empires of the second half of the millennium differed considerably in detail from one another, but none taxed agricultural production systematically to maintain large professional armies. They all drew the bulk of their armed might from the militarized landowners in the localities under their control. Sometimes this support could just be extorted, but usually it had to be attracted via reward. And since these later rulers were not renewing their revenues annually through large-scale taxation, this meant that wealth tended to flow outwards from the imperial centre to the more local landowning elites.

As has been well observed, the three Frankish imperial moments of the later first millennium all occurred when circumstances favoured expansionary, predatory warfare. Profits from this activity allowed the imperial dynasts, whether Merovingians, Carolingians or Ottonians, to reward their militarized landowning supporters without having to impoverish themselves. But when expansion stopped, political fragmentation quickly returned, as rewards flowed outwards again from a now fixed body of resources.[46] As we shall see, this particular aspect of later first-millennium imperialism would play an important role in the further transformation of barbarian Europe, as well as providing much of the explanation for the rather stop–start character of Frankish imperialism. Even so, for most of the second half of the period, the view from outside would have identified a predominant western European power whose influence encompassed large parts of the continent. And it is, of course, precisely the view from outside – that of the barbarians in the rest of Europe – that will concern us in the chapters that follow. Before we can properly examine how the rest of European society responded to the stimulus provided by this entirely new north European imperial power, and the patterns of expansion inherent to it, we must take account of two further major reconfigurations of the ancient world order.

## The Strange Death of Germanic Europe

The first unfolded more or less simultaneously with the rise of the first of the Frankish imperial dynasties: the Merovingians. Their Empire, as we have just seen, stretched from the Atlantic to the Elbe, and comparing this area with prevailing patterns of development across the European landscape as they stood in the sixth century, it quickly becomes apparent that its extent east of the River Rhine coincided closely with those parts of the old Roman periphery – inner and outer – that had maintained a considerable continuity in their long-standing Germanic-type material cultures and associated levels of socio-political organization during the period of Roman collapse. This is a point of critical importance that is easily lost because it concerns areas of Europe whose history finds little or no coverage in the surviving historical sources. Its importance emerges immediately, even from a quick overview of the archaeological evidence.

In the late Roman era, the largely Germanic-dominated inner and outer peripheries of the Roman Empire comprised huge swathes of territory running broadly north-west to south-east across the map of Europe. Its breadth in the north was approximately 1,000 kilometres, from the east bank of the Rhine to just beyond the Vistula. In the south, it was broader – more like 1,300 kilometres from the Iron Gates of the Danube to the west bank of the River Don (Map 15). Societies within this block of territory had relatively dense and increasing populations, relatively developed agricultures, relations of some kind with the Roman Empire, and material cultures that characteristically included substantial amounts of carefully crafted metalwork and pottery. By the sixth century, culture collapse had engulfed most of the area. In Ukraine and southern Poland, this occurred when the Cernjachov and southern Przeworsk systems disintegrated, not long after 400 AD. In middle Poland, collapse can be dated to c.500, and in Pomerania by the Baltic to c.500–25. In the Elbe–Saale region, complete collapse came right at the end of the sixth century; between the Elbe and the Oder, there is no sign of any Germanic continuity into the seventh. To the south of this zone, in Bohemia and Moravia, a thinning-out of Germanic-type remains is once more observable in the fifth and sixth centuries, followed by the total disappearance of such material between the mid-sixth and early seventh. By c.700, characteristic styles of traditional Germanic material culture were thus confined entirely to areas west of the Elbe (Map 15).[47]

The fact that Merovingian Frankish expansion did not extend into any of the areas affected by Germanic culture collapse was not an accident. Like its Roman counterpart, Frankish expansion was accomplished by military annexation, whose potential benefits had always to be weighed against its many costs. Battles had to be fought, and these were many and fierce even if the historical evidence is not good enough for us to reconstruct them in detail. Sometimes, though, you get lucky. The nature of the Frankish takeover of the Alamannic kingdom, for instance, shows up beautifully in the evidence of widespread and dramatic destruction from the old hillfort sites, which, as we saw in Chapter 2, had emerged in the late Roman period as the centres from which the authority of kings was exercised. About the year 500, when historical sources tell us Clovis won his great victory, they – or all that have been investigated – were taken by storm, and, more generally, huge material-cultural discontinuities show up right across Alamannia. Not only were the hillforts abandoned, but new burial rites appear in the cemeteries, and in some places entirely new cemeteries came into use. The degree of investment of human and other resources required for such an aggressive takeover would only be made when its rewards were going to be commensurately large.[48]

The collapse of long-standing patterns of central European, largely Germanic material culture in the fifth and sixth centuries meant that, east of the Elbe, there were no similarly coherent political structures to confront, and no relatively developed economies with accumulations of movable wealth to ransack. In the centuries either side of the birth of Christ, the Roman Empire had expanded to the limit of that era's profitable warfare, and in the sixth century the Merovingians did the same. The one area of old Germanic Europe that maintained the old cultural patterns and didn't fall under Frankish domination was southern Scandinavia: the Jutland peninsula, the south-western Baltic islands and the southern coast of what are now Norway and Sweden. But Merovingian power was exercised in neighbouring Saxony only in the form of hegemony rather than outright conquest, and this probably insulated Scandinivia from any wider Frankish ambition. This one partial exception doesn't negate the general point, though. Only those areas of Rome's inner and outer periphery where continuity of development had been maintained were worth the effort of Frankish conquest. In this sense, the new trajectories of development from the late Roman period played an important role in defining the limits of the new supraregional power of the post-Roman world.[49] So far so good. But what exactly had happened in those other areas of Germania that saw such a dramatic disruption to well-established material cultural patterns?

Thinking about this phenomenon, it is important to be absolutely clear about its nature. As the Polish archaeologist Kazimierz Godlowski above all demonstrated, culture collapse involved the disappearance, in the fifth and sixth centuries, of long-standing patterns of material-cultural development over vast tracts of central Europe. These patterns often ran back at least to the start of the millennium and sometimes beyond. But when discontinuity hit, it manifested itself in virtually every area of life reflected in the material-cultural remains: everything from the enduring economic links with the Mediterranean world that generated regular flows of Roman imports, to established craft traditions in pottery and metalwork. Technologically, pottery production simplified dramatically, the use of the wheel was abandoned. This was matched by a marked diminution in the range of pot forms and even in the overall quantities being produced. Metallurgical production similarly declined in scale – the range of ornaments being produced (or at least deposited) shrank almost to zero. Settlements also became much smaller.[50] Essentially, the archaeological record shows striking simplification in every category by which the activities of the populations of the region are customarily analysed, compared and dated in the Roman period, and it all adds up to a massive change in lifestyles.

What human history underlay these striking archaeological discontinuities?

According to the interpretation championed by Godlowski, traditional cultural patterns vanished because the population producing them had itself largely disappeared. Where we have relevant literary sources, material-cultural collapse is geographically and chronologically coincident with the known movements of Germanic-speakers on to Roman soil. The Cernjachov and Przeworsk systems collapsed at the same time as Goths, Vandals and their other constituent populations were being displaced by the rise of Hunnic power in central Europe (Chapter 5), while the thinning-out of Germanic material culture along the Elbe in the fifth century has long been associated with the transfer of Angles, Saxons and others to Britain, and the southern movement of Lombard groups into the Middle Danubian region. These flows both continued into the sixth century, as we have seen, not least in response to the extension of Frankish imperial power eastwards, which led a large number of Saxons to join the Lombards in their trek into Italy.[51]

The chronological links are much too tight to be accidental, but the total departure of Germanic populations is not the only possible, nor even the most likely, explanation of this extraordinary phenomenon. Since archaeological cultures must be understood as systems, the disappearance of established cultural forms can a priori have a number of causes. In this case, as other commentators since Godlowski have stressed, what we are dealing with is the disappearance of ornamental metalwork, weaponry and specialized wheel-made pottery, and these were largely produced for a Germanic social elite. The absence of such items from the observable spectrum of archaeological remains could reflect, therefore, the disappearance from these lands only of the political and militarized class for whom they were manufactured. A numerous – possibly very numerous – but archaeologically invisible peasantry, users of a much simpler material culture, might have been left behind.[52] In theory, therefore, it is possible to explain culture collapse by positing anything from a total evacuation of the landscape at one extreme of the spectrum, to what you might term elite departure at the other. Where within this range does the evidence suggest the human history behind Germanic culture collapse fell?

We will need to return to some of the evidence in more detail in the next chapter, when we look at the Slavic populations who eventually took control of these de-Germanized areas of central and eastern Europe. For the moment, a few more general observations can be made. First, Germanic culture collapse surely does not reflect a total evacuation of the affected landscapes. As we have seen in the case of the Goths north of the Black Sea, there is good reason to suppose that many groups among the indigenous population, who had become subordinated to Gothic intruders in the third century, did not form part of the later Gothic migration units that moved on into the Roman Empire from 376. Nor, again in general terms, do the numbers of Germanic migrants moving into the Empire in the late Roman period seem anything like large enough to have created large empty landscapes.

It is obviously not possible to say exactly how many people were caught up in the migratory activity generated by the rise and fall of the Hunnic Empire and the new opportunities for expansion that then became open to Rome's nearer neighbours as it lost the capacity to maintain frontier security. One negative thought experiment, however, is worth running with. This involves considering how many migrants are known to have emerged from the areas that suffered culture collapse. There are reasonable indications, for instance, that both Visigoths and Ostrogoths could field around, or a few more than, twenty thousand fighting men. The armies of the Vandals, Alans and Sueves were between them probably just as large, certainly in 406 before they suffered such heavy losses in Spain, while Burgundian manpower, if probably smaller, was not minimal. We have little conception of how many Middle Danubian refugees were recruited into the army of Italy or east Rome's Balkans military establishment; but to judge by the numbers given for the Heruli, the many different groups we hear of will between them have amounted to at least another 10,000-plus warriors, and quite possibly double that. Migrant Anglo-Saxon numbers are perhaps the most controversial of all, with guesses ranging from 20,000 to 200,000.[53]

If for the moment we take a maximum view of this evidence – for reasons that will become apparent – it would suggest that the largest possible figure you could reasonably calculate for the number of Germanic warriors who departed from the zones suffering culture collapse was something over 100,000 men, but certainly not 200,000. There is much guesswork here, but it is not a vastly inflated figure, and this order of military magnitude really is required to explain how the immigrants were able, between them, to bring down a west Roman state that determinedly resisted their intrusions. I suspect, anyway, that 100,000 is not making sufficient allowance for how many immigrant warriors died in the course of the action. Nonetheless, something over one hundred thousand does give us a ballpark figure to work with. How many people in total were on the move depends on how consistently women and children accompanied these warriors, and on the very murky subject of how many slaves came along for the ride. Here again, let's take a maximum view – and in any case, despite some recent attempts to deny it, there is both a decent amount of evidence that most of the larger groups were mixed in age and gender, and also, further reason to accept that this was so. As we have seen, traditional accounts multiplied the numbers of fighting men by five to get total population figures for mixed groups, but something nearer to four may be more correct. On the other hand, none of this makes any allowance for slaves. Putting all this together, a reasonable maximum estimate might put the total exodus from the areas which suffered culture collapse at something around or perhaps a bit over half a million souls.[54]

The reason for bothering with such calculations is that we do know the size of the territory affected. Germanic culture collapse affected an area defined broadly by the Rivers Elbe and Vistula in the north and the Iron Gates and the Lower Don in the south. At a rough calculation, this weighs in at close to a million square kilometres. For the migrations of the late Roman period to have emptied this area, population densities across it would have to have been in the region of 0.5 per square kilometre. This is an impossibly low figure. Even allowing for the fact that agricultural regimes were not intensive, it is simply impossible for the departure of half a million people to have emptied such a huge area. The figures are only guesstimates, but one recent study has suggested (and reasonably so) that just what it calls the Pontic-Danubian region (Map 15) must have contained between three and four million people in antiquity, and the population of just the Great Hungarian Plain has been put at something like three hundred thousand in the early medieval period. For all that every number cited in the last two paragraphs is an approximation, we can nonetheless safely discount the possibility that culture collapse in central and south-eastern Europe was caused by the complete evacuation of its population.[55]

In general terms, then, Germanic culture collapse was caused by the disappearance only of particular elite groups from the affected areas. But this conclusion needs to be tempered with two further observations. First, for all the transformations of the preceding centuries, Germanic society of the fourth century was not dominated by a very small elite. New distributions of social power did emerge between the first and fourth centuries, but the elite of the Germanic world still represented a larger percentage of the population than the tiny landowning class, say, that had dominated in the Roman world. As we saw in Chapter 2, and as the events of the so-called *Völkerwanderung* confirm, we must think in terms of social and political power (and group identities) shared between fairly broad oligarchies of freemen, numbering between a fifth and a third of the warrior population. Nor was participation in the migrations, at least among the larger groups like the Goths and Lombards, limited just to this dominant oligarchy. At least two social strata of warriors – possibly to be equated with the free and freed classes documented in early medieval law codes – are observable in these intrusive groups, not just a single body of elite soldiery, and sometimes they brought slaves with them as well, not to mention families.[56] Elite departure was thus not a very small-scale phenomenon.

Second, as we shall see in the next chapter, the evidence indicates that population levels did nosedive dramatically in some particular localities. Once again, this suggests that Germanic migration may not have been entirely negligible in demographic terms, and the two points may well be linked. Because the Germanic elites were not so tiny in the first place, and had some dependent social groups (slaves and freedmen) attached to them, then when a concentrated group of migrants left *a particular area*, this may well have created empty districts.[57]

Not only did prevailing patterns of development dictate the working-out of the migratory processes of the late fourth and the fifth century, therefore, but the reverse was also true – the migrations affected patterns of development. One major consequence of this interaction, as we have seen, was the emergence of an unprecedented type of imperial power for western Eurasia, based on north European resources. Because, however, the Roman Empire came to an end in a process that saw substantial armed and organized groups from the periphery relocate themselves in the heart of its former territories, the process of imperial collapse was matched by parallel transformations in large parts of this periphery. Culture collapse caused by the departure of the still fairly broadly based elite of Germanic Europe changed totally the socioeconomic and hence political organization in the old periphery of the Empire, and marks a second major break with the ancient world order – a break quite as important as the rise of the Franks' northern European Empire. It was to have enormous consequences for the emergence of Slavic Europe, as we shall see in Chapter 8, but this process was also profoundly shaped by the third major reconfiguration of the old world order that unfolded in these middle centuries of the first millennium.

# Out of Arabia

Up to about 600 AD the eastern half of the Roman Empire, with its capital at Constantinople, maintained its imperial credentials as the dominant power of the Mediterranean. Strong though his position was in the 510s, Theoderic the Ostrogoth had held back from making his claim to imperial power absolutely explicit, for fear of alienating the rulers of Constantinople. And in the next generation, the astuteness of the king's judgement showed through, when Justinian's forces, in twenty years of brutal warfare from 536, played more than just a walk-on role in the emergence of imperial power north of the Alps by destroying the Ostrogothic Italian kingdom. This military adventure followed an astonishingly successful earlier conquest of the Vandal North African kingdom in 532–4. Then in the early 550s, in Justinian's later years the east Romans established a toehold in southern Spain. Constantinople's domination of the Mediterranean had moved from latent to manifest within the space of about twenty years.

East Rome's collapse in the seventh century from these heights of imperial grandeur was every bit as dramatic as that of its western counterpart in the fifth. In the early 610s, it looked as though it was about to be conquered by its traditional *bête noire*, Sasanian Persia, which took control of many of its key revenue-producing districts: Syria, Palestine and Egypt. By 626, a Persian army was even camped on the south side of the Bosporus, while its nomadic Avar allies besieged Constantinople, just over the water. Astonishingly, the Empire clawed its way back from the jaws of this defeat. Constantinople survived the siege, and the Emperor Heraclius mounted a series of campaigns through Armenia into Mesopotamia which, by autumn 628, had brought Persia to the brink of collapse. The Sasanian King Khusro II, who had launched the war of conquest, was deposed, and most of the conquered territories were restored to Heraclius' rule.

No sooner was the ink beginning to dry on the history of Heraclius' great victory, however (provisional working title: *The Original Comeback Kid*), than it had to be deposited in the nearest waste-papyrus bin. Out of a long-neglected corner of the Near East burst a new enemy – Arab tribes united only within the last decade by Islam and Muhammad – sweeping all before them. Heraclius' triumph turned to dust in his mouth as, before the end of his reign, Syria, Palestine and Egypt were all lost once more, and Asia Minor turned into a battle-ravaged wasteland. By 652, other Arab armies had conquered the entire Persian Empire, and within a further two generations the new Empire of Islam stretched from India to the Atlantic.[58]

The details of this astonishing revolution in world history are not central to this study. Suffice it to say – and this will come as no surprise – that nearly as many reasons have been offered for east Roman imperial collapse as for that of its western counterpart. Traditional lines of explanation have often centred on Justinian's conquests in the western Mediterranean, arguing that they were overambitious and left his successors a poisoned chalice of bankruptcy and imperial overstretch. But if 'a week is a long time in politics', as one British prime minister famously commented, this link looks hard to sustain. Justinian died in the mid-560s, the Arab conquest came seventy years – or pretty much three whole generations – later. The events could still be interrelated in some way, of course, but they don't look like simple cause and effect. More recently, those concentrating on internal reasons for Constantinople's collapse have switched their attention to alternatives: the periodic sequence of plagues that afflicted the Mediterranean world from 540 onwards, and – perhaps related – signs of possible later sixth-century economic decline in the Roman Near East.

These explanations all have something to say, but outside factors also need to be taken into account: not least, the all-in knock-down twenty-five-year war between Constantinople and the Persians that immediately preceded the Arab conquests. Persia and eastern Rome fought one another on and off throughout the sixth century, but for the most part only in limited fashion: through surrogates in Caucasia, or by sieges designed to capture the odd strategic fortress. This restricted pattern of warfare fizzled out in the early seventh century, when the two powers fought each other head on, and ultimately to a standstill. There was a triumphant fightback by Heraclius when all seemed lost, but the terms of the 628 peace treaty show that the end result was actually a draw, through exhaustion. Despite Heraclius' victories, Constantinople failed to get back every piece of territory lost since 602. This, of course, immediately provides part of the explanation for the Arab victories over both empires that quickly followed.[59]

But attention also needs to be paid to the Arab world itself. Here, the galvanizing effect of Muhammad's new religion, creating unity within a previously fragmented population, ranks centre-stage. But, as with the appearance of new confederations capable of forming successor states out of the western Empire's periphery in the late fourth and the fifth century, there is a backstory here of huge importance. Looked at in the round, the evidence demonstrates a steady growth in the size and power of Arab client states on the fringes of the Roman and Persian Empires between the fourth and sixth centuries, just as there had been in those of the western Empire's European peripheries between the first and the fourth.[60] What concern us here, however, are the broader effects of this seventh-century revolution on European-wide patterns of power. Two stand out.

First, the rise of Islam destroyed east Rome as a truly imperial, supraregional power. If you read texts produced in Constantinople after the deluge, this is not immediately obvious, and the city itself was not to fall to a Muslim power until Mehmet the Conqueror's cannon finally blasted a hole through the city's great Theodosian landwalls in 1453, near the modern Topkapi bus station. For most of the preceding seven hundred years, the rulers of the city had called themselves 'Romans' (even while writing in Greek), and maintained all the old Roman ideologies of supremacy: claiming to be god-appointed emperors, whose job it was to bring proper order to the entire human cosmos.

As in so many contexts, though, it is important to look beneath the surface. Then, what really strikes you about Constantinople after the mid-seventh century is how much state power had haemorrhaged away. Islamic conquest deprived Constantinople of many of its richest provinces: Syria, Palestine and Egypt in the first generation, quickly followed by North Africa about forty years later, and eventually Sicily as well. Asia Minor was retained, but became a major battlefield in further conflicts with the new Islamic state, and the archaeological evidence shows how badly its economy was affected. All the great cities of antiquity, where they survived at all (and some didn't), ceased to be major centres of population, manufacture and exchange, being transformed into military fortresses and command posts. Coinage, likewise, became exceedingly scarce, and everything points to a massive simplification of the economy. Before these disasters, the east Roman Empire was quite similar in 'shape' to the Ottoman Empire of the sixteenth century, from which interesting tax records survive. These can be used to gloss the likely extent of Constantinople's losses in the earlier period in terms of state revenue (although the overwhelming nature of the disaster is anyway clear). And if you do the calculations and make some appropriate adjustments, it becomes apparent that the rise of Islam deprived Constantinople of between two-thirds and three-quarters of its revenues; that is, of between two-thirds and three-quarters of its capacity to act.[61]

The consequences of this diminution show up with great clarity in the big picture of European history after 600 AD. From the early seventh century, Constantinople was no longer a pan-Mediterranean power and major player on the broader European stage. Though still important in the eastern Mediterranean, it became in many ways an unwilling satellite state of the Islamic world, no longer substantially in charge of its own fate. Its subsequent periods of prosperity and decline correlate closely and inversely with the history of the new Islamic power block. When Islam was politically united, Constantinople was condemned to decline; when – as sometimes happened – Islam itself fragmented, there was room for modest expansion. In short, the self-proclaimed imperial Romanness of the rulers of post-seventh-century Constantinople is a chimera. The losses suffered at the hands of Islam meant that these emperors were now ruling what was as much a successor state to the Roman Empire as any of the new powers of the Roman west a century earlier. My own preference, in fact, is to use 'Byzantine' rather than 'east Roman' from the mid-seventh century, as a reflection of how great a sea change the rising tide of Islam had created in Mediterranean history.[62]

Second, the reverse of the same coin, Islamic explosion created a new superpower on the south-eastern fringes of Europe. It engulfed not only much of the east Roman Empire, and certainly its richest territories, but its old Sasanian sparring partner too. The result, when some of the dust had settled by the early eighth century, was a gigantic Empire running all the way from Spain to northern India. Ruling such an enormous entity using pre-modern communications was always a logistic nightmare, in addition to which there were major ideological divisions over how the Islamic Empire should be run, and by whom. Not surprisingly, therefore, its internal history was rarely stable. Even if their political control was always a bit arthritic, though, and certainly declined with distance from their respective capitals, both the Umayyad Caliphate centred on Damascus between the 660s and the mid-eighth century, and the Abbasid Caliphate centred on Baghdad from the later eighth to the early tenth, represented huge concentrations of imperial wealth and power, on a scale that surpassed even that of the Roman Empire at its height.[63] This superpower based in the Near Eastern fringes of the European landmass was too far away to intervene directly in the unfolding history of migration and development in barbarian Europe, but its indirect effects on these processes were enormous. Not only did it remove the east Roman Empire from the map of major players in European history, but, as we shall see in the chapters that follow, its diplomatic and economic tentacles stretched up through the Caucasus on to the western steppe, and from there beyond, into eastern and even northern Europe.


# SYSTEMS COLLAPSE AND THE BIRTH OF EUROPE


In part, the fall of west Rome (and that of the Roman east too, for that matter) has to be understood as the playing-out of the full consequences of development processes that had been at work throughout the half-millennium of the Empire's existence. Much of the new strategic pattern that prevailed across the European landscape from around 500 AD was dictated by the emergence of a supraregional power block in northern Europe made possible by the transformations of the previous five hundred years. As we have seen, in the late fifth century the Franks emerged as a new force in the old Empire's inner periphery. They proceeded to combine their original homelands with former imperial territory west of the Rhine and other parts of Rome's inner and outer peripheries. The resulting imperial power block was the first of its kind based on the exploitation of northern, non-Mediterranean, European resources. There is a very real sense, there-fore, in which the Roman Empire, in the long term, sowed the seeds of its own destruction. Its economic, military and diplomatic tentacles transformed adjacent populations until they were strong enough to rip it apart.

But if the nature of Empire after Rome was in one sense almost predictable, the usual dose of historical accident also played its part. Thinking about the patterns of transformation in the round, then what you might have expected to see was fringe pieces of Roman territory falling into the hands of ever more ambitious and aggressive frontier dynasts as, over time, economic and political change increased the power at their disposal and slowly eroded the initial power advantage that had allowed the Empire to establish such widespread dominion in the first place. Indeed, such a sequence of events did begin to unfold in the Roman period. In the third century, Transylvanian Dacia and lands between the Carpathians and the Danube had to be ceded to the Goths and other new powers of the Empire's east European periphery, while in the west Alamanni took possession of the abandoned *Agri Decumates*. In the fourth century, in similar vein, a particularly aggressive king of the Alamanni such as Chnodomarius could extend his control to the western side of the Rhine valley, and Salian Franks made moves on land west of the lower Rhine frontier. At this point, imperial power was still strong enough to keep such ambitions in check, but the tendency is clear enough.

Instead of following anything like this scenario, however, the rise and fall of Hunnic power generated an unprecedented degree of politically motivated migration, which caused a sudden and unpredictable relocation on to Roman soil of militarily powerful groups from parts of its inner and outer peripheries. The first crisis of 375–80 saw Goths, Sarmatians and Taifali enter Roman territory from the inner periphery beyond the Lower Danube frontier region, to be followed in 405–8 by some of their Middle and Upper Danubian counterparts: the Sueves (if they were Marcomanni and Quadi) and Burgundians. Amongst groups from the outer periphery caught up in the same events we can number Alans, different groups of whom entered imperial territory both in 375–80 and again in 405–8, accompanied in the later crisis by Hasding and Siling Vandals, who hovered somewhere between the inner and outer peripheries – their territories were not that far from the frontier, but we know of no diplomatic relations between them and the Empire before the convulsions of the Hunnic era.[64] These migrations caused the western Empire to suffer sudden and catastrophic losses of tax base in its heartlands, which in turn precipitated the total and equally rapid collapse of its military and political systems.

Instead of a new supraregional power emerging gradually in northern Europe as competitive dynasts slowly built up their domain, biting off chunks of imperial territory while outfacing their peers beyond the frontier, the intervention of the Huns dramatically altered both the timing of the process and, at least in part, its nature. In the fourth century, the far boundary of Rome's outer periphery, dominated by largely Germanic-speaking groups and characterized by very particular kinds of material-cultural systems, stretched over a vast expanse of territory. In the sixth century, after the migrations of the Hunnic era and the associated collapse of the Przeworsk, Wielbark and Cernjachov systems, the old patterns of material culture could no longer be found east of the Elbe or outside of the Middle Danube basin. Nor is there any sign in the historical sources of the substantial political structures that had previously existed there in the Roman period. West Roman imperial collapse was thus accompanied by a huge reduction in the extent of Germanic-dominated Europe, and the unification of most of what remained under Frankish hegemony. Both the speed of Roman collapse and the dramatic shrinking of Germanic Europe resulted from migratory processes unleashed by the Huns. In overall terms, this amounts to a dramatic sea change in European history.

When measuring the total effect of the Roman Empire and its fall upon patterns of European development, then, we are faced with some paradoxical conclusions. First, in the Roman period proper – up to, say, 350 AD – interaction with the Empire helped spread more developed political structures and more complex patterns of economic interaction across broad tranches of the European landscape. I have no idea whether this was a 'good' or 'bad' thing overall for human history. The march of civilization is not at all easy to measure. What I am confident about, however, is that it was a phenomenon of huge importance. But, second, the collapse of the Empire dramatically reduced the geographical extent of more developed Europe, as migratory processes – partly predatory in nature, partly more negative in motivation – sucked armed and politically organized groups south and west across the map. The fact that the new Frankish superpower was a weaker type of state to some extent reduced the old differential between developed and non-developed Europe that had existed in the Roman period. Nevertheless, by the sixth century, more developed Europe – counting both Empire and periphery – now encompassed a much smaller area, following the concertina-like effects of Roman imperial collapse.

In the longer term, however, this second factor would prove much less important than the breaking of Mediterranean domination across western Eurasia. The Franks started this process by building the first imperial power that northern Europe had ever seen. It was completed by the rise of Islam, which turned east Rome into the satellite state of Byzantium and broke the political and even, eventually, the cultural unity of the Mediterranean. This freed northern Europe from the long-standing patterns of political interference that had marked the ancient world order. The fall of the Roman Empire saw the birth pains of Europe because Germanic and Arab expansion between them destroyed the domination of the Mediterranean over its northern hinterland. By the end of the millennium, developed Europe and the club of Christian monarchical states would run not just to the Elbe, as 500 AD, but all the way east to the Volga. The interaction of migration and development that created this further astonishing transformation of the European landscape provides the subject matter of the remaining chapters.

# 8

# THE CREATION OF SLAVIC EUROPE

ONE OF THE GREAT LANGUAGE GROUPS of modern Europe, Slavic-speakers currently comprise nearly 270 million individuals, and primarily Slavic-speaking countries account for something like half of the European landmass. This last point, at least, was substantially true by the end of the first millennium AD. Already in the year 900, Slavic-speakers dominated vast tracts of the European landscape east of the River Elbe and even some more limited territories west of it, in the Bohemian basin and around the River Saale. The eastern extent of Slavic control at this date is not completely clear, but it certainly extended to much of European Russia – as far east as the River Volga and as far north as Lake Ilmen. Slavic-speakers also dominated much of the Balkan peninsula (Map 16).

But such a massively Slavic Europe was only a recent creation. In the Roman period, Europe as far east as the River Vistula, the best part of five hundred kilometres further east than the western boundary of later Slavic-dominated territory on the Elbe, had been dominated by Germanic-speakers. In the same period, the Balkans were part of the Roman Empire, home to ethnically disparate populations who spoke Latin and Greek as well as a variety of indigenous dialects and languages. River names (hydronyms) also indicate that much of central European Russia had at one point been dominated by the speakers of Baltic, not Slavic, languages, while its northern zones were in the hands of Finnish populations (Map 16). Even more startling, there is no mention of 'Slavs' in any Roman source – Greek or Latin – written before the deposition of the last western Roman Emperor Romulus Augustulus in 476, and this despite the fact that the knowledge of some Roman geographers ranged widely over northern and eastern Europe. If little discussed in anglophone circles, the rise of Slavic Europe is one of the biggest stories of the entire first millennium. Where did it come from and what role did migration play in its creation?

# IN SEARCH OF THE SLAVS

For all its historical importance, the creation of Slavic Europe is extremely difficult to reconstruct. Some of the reasons for this are straightforward, others a touch more exotic. First and foremost, we have no contemporary account of the process from any Slavic author. Literacy eventually came to the Slavic world with conversion to Christianity. But it was only in mid-ninth-century Moravia (see page 518), where we began, that the Byzantine missionaries Cyril and Methodius created the first written version of a Slavic language to translate the Bible. In the centuries that followed, even Latin and Greek literacy remained largely restricted to religious contexts, and it was not until the early twelfth century that the Slavic world started to generate its own accounts of the past: the *Chronicle* of Cosmas of Prague in Bohemia (written from c.1120), the *Gallus Anonymus* in Poland (c.1115), and the *Russian Primary Chronicle* in Kiev (or *Tale of Bygone Years*, 1116). Nearly half a millennium separates these first Slavic accounts of Slavic history from the period when Slavic domination was becoming established over vast tracts of the European landscape. The focus of these texts was also on the much more immediate history of the states in which they were composed, and of their ruling dynasties, with references to any deeper past few and far between. Hence all of our more or less contemporary information on the rise of the Slavs is provided by east Roman or Byzantine authors in the east, and post-Roman (largely Frankish and Italian) authors in the west. In all of these texts, Graeco-Roman conceptions of the 'barbarian' were alive and kicking. The extent to which any particular report can be relied upon, or represents an ideologically loaded construction of reality brought into line with the preconceived expectations of author and audience, is thus always an open question.

This problem fades into relative insignificance, however, next to a more basic one. Even our outsiders did not write very much about the Slavs. East Roman sources tell something of the Slavicization of the Balkans in the sixth and seventh centuries, western sources add the odd snippet about the western spread of Slavs along the line of

the Carpathians and into the foothills of the Alps, and Viking-era
sources provide some insight into the final push of Slavic groups north-
eastwards towards Lake Ilmen. But the Slavicization of large swathes
of northern Europe between the Rivers Elbe and Volga is covered by
no historical documentation whatsoever. It would be very nice to have
the problem of worrying about the extent to which sources are
presenting their own construction rather than reality, but for the most
part we can't even take the discussion that far. So deficient is the
coverage provided by the written sources that the creation of Slavic
Europe has to be studied as virtually a prehistoric subject, using almost
entirely archaeological evidence.


## Pride and Prejudice

Once again we are indebted to the two scholarly generations after the
Second World War that saw such a huge investment in archaeological
investigation in eastern bloc countries. When I first went to Poland,
there were about two thousand undergraduates at the Institute of
Archaeology in Warsaw alone, each of whom had to be involved in
three digs to qualify for their degree. There were several other
archaeological institutes in the country besides, and the pattern was
similar right across the former Soviet bloc. Consequently, vast amounts
of material became available for the study of prehistoric Europe, not
least the sixth, seventh and eighth centuries that were so crucial to the
rise of the Slavs. In particular, Central and East European archaeologists have successfully identified a specific material-culture assemblage
that occurs often enough at broadly the right times and places for a
plausible association to be made between it and at least some Slavic
groups of the critical period. These 'Korchak'-type remains – and
closely related 'Penkovka' materials – consist of simple assemblages of
pottery, in the form largely of handmade cooking pots, associated with
settlements of huts, usually numbering not more than about ten in a
cluster, which were partly sunk into the ground and whose design
incorporated an oven, often built of stones, in one corner. Occasionally,
small cremation cemeteries have been found alongside the settlements,
where human remains were interred in simple handmade urns. All this
reflects small-scale agricultural communities, practising mixed agricultural regimes of a broadly self-sufficient kind using some iron tools. As

you would expect, they are generally found in areas where fertile land was easily available, in terraces just above the flood plains of nearby rivers. Korchak remains are also remarkable for the more or less complete absence of foreign imports and fancy metalwork of any kind, indigenous or imported.[1]

If a broad association of Korchak remains with some early Slavs seems secure enough, these materials are nonetheless deeply problematic. One immediate issue is chronology. Korchak remains lack the kind of metalwork and more sophisticated pottery whose stylistic changes over time can provide broad dating guides. Germanic remains from the first half of the millennium can usually be located to within a twenty-five-year period, Korchak materials by themselves only to within a two-hundred-year span between about 500 and 700 AD. More technical dating methods, such as carbon-14 or dendrochronology, can be used for greater precision wherever wood or carbon is available, but these are much more expensive and, as yet, are available only for a relatively small number of sites.

An even bigger issue is how precisely we should understand the relationship between Korchak remains and the early Slavs. Exactly how close and how exclusive was the association? Did all Slavic-speaking communities of c.500 live the kind of life that generated Korchak remains? And were Korchak-type remains generated only by Slavic-speaking populations? Some Slavs certainly lived a Korchak type of life, but that does not necessarily mean that all did. Inversely, there is absolutely no reason a priori why a variety of languages might not have been spoken in the kinds of simple farming communities that generated Korchak remains.[2]

Furthermore, early Slavic history has long been complicated by other problems. The nature of these problems emerges clearly from a map of the different original homelands that have been proposed for the Slavs over the last century or so (Map 17). As even a quick glance shows you, these are many and varied, stretching as far west as Bohemia in one version and as far east as the River Don in another. There is, moreover, a deeper pattern underlying these disagreements. First, there has been a marked tendency for scholars to identify original Slavic homelands that coincide with their own place of origin. Running briefly across Map 17, Borkovsky, who identified Bohemia as the Slav homeland, was a Czech; Kostrzewski, who went for Poland, was a Pole; Korosec, who plumped for Pannonia, was a Yugoslav (northern former Yugoslavia encompassed part of old Roman Pannonia); while Tretiakov and Rybakov, who opted for areas further east, were Soviet scholars. There are, of course, exceptions. Kazimierz Godlowski, who argued the case for the outer rim of the Carpathians on the basis of a thorough and dispassionate review of all the evidence unearthed since the Second World War, was a Pole, and I don't believe that his own Romanian origins have anything to do with Florin Curta's more recent championing of the zone between the Carpathians and the Danube.

Overall, however, the impact of nationalist rivalries – actually from two different ideological eras – could not be clearer. As you might expect, inter-Slavic rivalry was a marked feature of the nationalist era of the late nineteenth and early twentieth centuries. Slavic intellectuals were jockeying for position and favour within their own national circles by attempting to tie the earliest Slavs to their own homelands. It was a particularly hot potato in Polish–Russian relations, given the Poles' subordinate position within the Russian Empire up to the end of the First World War. Perhaps more surprisingly, the same old rivalries persisted into the Soviet era. In classic Marxist dogma, as mentioned earlier, any kind of consciousness apart from class-consciousness is by definition 'false' – that is, an ideology generated by an elite to control the masses. You wouldn't have expected the Soviet intellectual establishment to have been much bothered about where exactly a 'false' Slavic ethnic consciousness first emerged, but one of its many paradoxes was the way in which the Soviet era stitched Marxism and nationalism together into a seamless robe. The (at that stage) seemingly obvious fact that destiny had chosen the Slavs to be the first people to bring the new Marxist world order to fruition merely added extra spice to the old national rivalries, and the consequences could be brutal. Before the 1980s, Polish scholars who doubted that Slavic-speakers had always been indigenous to the area between the Oder and the Vistula – that is, the territory of the post-1945 Polish state – were punished for their views.[3]

Sometimes, these competing visions of Slavic history were designed to fight off outsiders. Gustav Kossinna, as we saw in Chapter 1, was ready to mobilize a supposed Germanic past to justify the territorial claims of the modern German state; and in part, Kostrzewski, a student of Kossinna's methods, was replying in kind. His argument that the heartland of the new Polish state – as reconstituted after the First World War – had always been occupied by Slavic-speakers was directed not only against Russian pretensions but also against Kossinna. Making the argument stick posed some tricky intellectual problems. Tacitus' *Germania* records that Germanic-speaking groups – particularly the historically prominent Goths – had occupied territories as far east as the River Vistula in the first century AD. On the face of it, this was difficult to reconcile with the theory of an ancient and continuous Slavic occupation of the same area. Kostrzewski argued, however, that Goths and other Germanic-speakers were no more than a thin layer of population on top of a 'submerged' Slavic-speaking majority. To make his case, Kostrzewski's work set out to trace the history of this majority back through time from the early Middle Ages into the early Roman period (via the Przeworsk culture) and even back to c.1000 BC (via the so-called Pomeranian and Lusatian cultures).[4]

Imparting yet another twist of intellectual intrigue to this web of argument was the natural desire of Slavic intellectuals to associate the early Slavs with the 'best' – in other words, technologically most advanced – sets of possibly relevant ancient remains. On once being shown some supposed early Germanic materials from the Baltic Bronze Age, Hitler became very agitated because, at the same date, Egyptians were already building pyramids. In his mind, this made the jumble of simple handmade pottery that had just been presented to him look just a touch unimpressive. The same kind of reflex has also distorted arguments over Slavic history, with many researchers wanting to associate their supposed ancient forebears with something a bit more presentable than crumbly handmade pottery. Rybakov's identification of an original Slavic homeland in Ukraine, for instance, was based on associating the Slavs with one of the richest sets of remains from Iron Age eastern Europe: the Cernjachov culture. As we have seen, this boasted substantial settlements, iron weapons and tools, wheel-made pottery in a wide variety of designs and interesting jewellery: altogether a more satisfactory set of ancestral Slavs than other contemporary east Europeans living in sunken huts with handmade pottery of one drab design. Likewise Kostrzewski: measured in technological terms, the Przeworsk cultural system was one of the 'best' of Iron Age central Europe.

In the aftermath of the Nazi era, Kostrzewski's retorts instinctively command greater sympathy than Kossinna's original arguments, but both were equally rooted in the demands of contemporary politics. Like so many of the alternative accounts of Slavic history produced

before about 1970, constructing the best possible account of the
pre-history of Central and Eastern Europe was firmly subordinated
to political agendas. But in the last scholarly generation or so, and
particularly since the Berlin Wall came down (although intellectual
revolutions had then already been under way for a decade or more in
parts of the Soviet bloc), these old political imperatives have lost much
of their force. In the 1970s, Mark Shchukin demonstrated that the
chronological coincidence between the rise and fall of the Cernjachov
cultural system north of the Black Sea and that of Gothic power in the
region was much too tight for it to be seen as anything other than
Gothic-dominated. Slavic-speakers may well have lived within its
boundaries, but it was the military power of the Goths that gave it
shape. In Poland, too, Kostrzewski's vision of Slavic continuity was
being challenged, as profound discontinuities were shown to separate
the pre-historic Lusatian and Pomeranian cultures of the first millennium BC from the Wielbark and Przeworsk cultural systems occupying
the same landscape in the Roman period.[5] Arguments in favour of a
Slavic population between the Oder and the Vistula with a continuous
history from at least c.1000 BC have lost much of their credibility, and
the whole subject of early Slavic history is no longer marked by the
same desperate scramble to fight off rival Slavs, minimize the role
played by Germanic-speakers, and identify all the 'best' sets of remains
as Slavic. This does not mean that the fights are going out all over
Central and Eastern Europe, but current arguments are much better-
tempered, and much more about the past for its own sake.

   With so much distracting superstructure stripped away, what do
we now know about the Slavicization of Europe?


## Proto-Slavs


The only possible place to begin is with the first documented appearance of Slavs in European history. Slavs – properly Sclavenes – make
their debut just north of the Lower Danube frontier of the east Roman
Empire in the first half of the sixth century. Writing around the
year 550 AD, the east Roman historian Procopius records numerous
raids by Sclavenes and Antae, whom he reports closely related, across
the Danube and into Constantinople's Balkan provinces. These attacks,
or those of the Antae, to be precise, began in the reign of Justin I

(518–27), although the Antae eventually became east Roman allies. By the 530s and 540s, in fact, the Sclavenes were posing the bigger problem, and Procopius' narrative strongly implies that their attacks had steadily increased in frequency and ferocity. The recorded names of the leaders of these groups indicate that both were Slavic-speaking, and there seems no reason to doubt that Procopius' account here is basically accurate.[6] From around the year 500, then, we first find Slavic-speaking groups active in what is now Wallachia and southern Moldavia, the area between the Carpathians and the Danube.

This region also throws up Korchak-type materials dating to the correct period. By themselves, Korchak remains cannot be dated with any accuracy, but among the Korchak materials of Wallachia and southern Moldavia archaeologists have found some datable imports. A late fifth-century brooch associated with some Korchak pottery was found at Dragosloveni in Wallachia, in a typically Korchak sunken building, and the same region has produced a famous cemetery, Sarata Monteoru, where the burials contain several brooches and belt buckles of the late fourth and early fifth century. In Moldavia, likewise, otherwise typically Korchak material has been found in several contexts alongside imported wheel-made pottery dating to the fifth century or the very beginning of the sixth, and one site near Kishinev produced a mid-fifth-century Hunnic-type mirror in a find of Korchak wares. You never know, of course, how long an item may have remained in circulation before being buried, but enough mid- to late fifth-century items have been found among the region's Korchak materials to confirm that they spread across Moldavia and Wallachia in the later fifth and early sixth century, at the same time as Procopius above all, but also other east Roman historical sources, first record the appearance of Slavs in the same spot.[7] This much is accepted by everyone. But was this Slavic presence south of the Carpathians generated by migration from elsewhere, or had Slavic groups been living here all along?

The traditional answer has always been migration. For one thing, being so close to the Roman frontier and encompassing some territories that had even been part of it in the second and third centuries, the sub-Carpathian region is relatively well documented during the first half of the first millennium. It is not, therefore, your average run-of-the-mill argument from silence, that no source mentions Slavs here before the year 500. Other, non-Slavic-speaking groups occupied it in the Roman period. Equally striking, there is no evidence that Slavs played any significant role in the mid-fifth-century Hunnic Empire of Attila, whose remit certainly encompassed this zone. Many different subject peoples figure at different points in narratives of its rise and fall, as we have seen, but Slavs are notable only for their absence. The best that anyone has ever done in arguing for a Slavic presence in Attila's world is to claim that the word *strava* – which the sixth-century Jordanes says was the term used by the Huns for funeral eulogies of their dead leader – derives from Slavic. It may do, but we know nothing about the language of the Huns, so it may, alternatively, have had its own *echt* Hunnic origin. It is certainly a very slender peg upon which to hang the claim that otherwise undocumented Slavs played a major role in Attila's Empire.

The argument in favour of migration also has its more positive dimensions. Writing in Constantinople at more or less the same time as Procopius, Jordanes gives the following famous account of the Slavs in the mid-sixth century:

> Within these rivers lies Dacia, encircled by the lofty Alps [Carpathians] as by a crown. Near their left ridge, which inclines towards the north, and beginning at the source of the Vistula, the populous race of the Venethi dwell, occupying a great expanse of land. Though their names are now dispersed amid various clans and places, yet they are chiefly called Sclaveni and Antes. The abode of the Sclaveni extends from the city of Noviodunum . . . to the Dniester, and northward as far as the Vistula . . . The Antes, who are the bravest of these peoples . . . spread from the Dniester to the Dnieper, rivers that are many days' journey apart.

Much of this coincides with what Procopius reports, with the extra piece of information that the Sclavenes and Antae had emerged from an earlier group called the Venedi. This is potentially of great importance because, unlike Slavs, the Venedi are mentioned in sources of the Roman period. As we have seen, Tacitus places them geographically east of the Vistula in a broad belt of territory in between the Fenni (Finns) of the arctic north and the Carpathian Mountains. Pliny, a little earlier, had also heard of Venedae, as he named them, but gave no further information. The second-century geographer Ptolemy knew no more about them than a few extra group names. There's no doubt that the Venedi existed and that they lived in eastern Europe in the first half of the millennium, but more than this the Romans didn't know. This part of Europe was slightly less mysterious for them than what lay beyond, where people had 'human faces and features, but the bodies and limbs of beasts', but only just. The key point, of course, is that if you compare these earlier reports with Jordanes', it is only natural to suppose that the appearance of Venedi-derived Slavs in the sub-Carpathian region around or just after the year 500 was the result of migration from the north.[8]

Jordanes' evidence also partly coincides with one of the most famous arguments of them all in early Slavic studies, deriving from the study of linguistics, and with some of the more respectable archaeological ones. All modern Slavic languages have in common an old Slavic name for the hornbeam, whereas the terms for beech, larch and yew are all Germanic loanwords. This must be, so it was argued influentially at the beginning of the twentieth century, because the hornbeam dominated the vegetation in the original 'Slavic homeland'. On investigation, the only suitable geographical locality turned out to be the Pripet marsh area of Polesie, a rather soggy zone some 350 kilometres north of the Carpathians (Map 17). Not surprisingly, this led to much subsequent archaeological effort being expended in the Pripet region, with Irina Rusanova arguing, on the basis of extensive research there in the 1950s and 1960s, that she had unearthed the very earliest Korchak materials. The type-site of Korchak itself was one of her excavations, and led her to change Borkovsky's original 'Prague' label to 'Korchak' for the characteristic combination of sunken huts and handmade cooking pots on the basis of its claimed anteriority.[9]

This once standard vision of early Slavic history has recently been challenged, however, by Florin Curta, who argues that, on the contrary, historical Slavs emerged precisely where they are first mentioned: the south-eastern fringes of the Carpathian system. His reasoning is based on a mixture of history and archaeology. To start with, he denies the veracity of Jordanes' report that the Slavs derived from the Venedi. Jordanes' history can be shown to depend at certain points upon Tacitus' *Germania*, and Curta argues that the Venedi–Slav linkage was Jordanes' own invention on the basis of what Tacitus has to say – a further example of a documented tendency for Roman writers to claim that there were no 'new barbarians', merely old ones by new names. On the archaeological front, Curta also attacks Rusanova's conclusions, arguing that the Korchak materials of the sub-Carpathian region are older than their equivalents in Polesie and hence could not derive from them. More positively, and this is the main focus of his broader study, Curta draws attention to the substantial body of both historical and archaeological evidence showing that those Slavs in contact with the east Roman world in the sixth century were caught up in a dynamic process of sociopolitical and economic transformation. It was, he argues, precisely this process which 'created' the 'first' or Proto-Slavs.[10]

Many of Curta's points are well taken. His demolition of Rusa-nova's chronology is entirely convincing. The Polesian Korchak materials certainly postdate their equivalents south of the Carpathians. It is also very likely that somewhere in the Carpathian system is the correct zone in which to place the origins of at least those Slavs who ended up in an east Roman orbit in the sixth century. Curta himself argues for their origin in its south-eastern approaches. Another recent view, proposed first by Volodymyr Baran and taken further by Polish archaeologists of the so-called Cracow School, suggests that we should perhaps be looking more to the north-east. Here, in modern Podolia, large quantities of early-vintage Korchak materials (much earlier than those of Polesie still further to the north-east) have been unearthed. The fundamental Korchak dating problem remains, but there do seem to be more, slightly earlier, datable imports in Podolia than in Curta's favoured spot to the south-east. Curta's sub-Carpathian Korchak settle-ments also came into being after a century of sparse settlement in that region. For these reasons, it looks likely that the first Slavs explicitly to appear in the historical record had their immediate origins in a population group from north-east of the Carpathians. If so, they spread quickly. The Podolian Korchak materials can predate the Wallachian and Moldavian by at most an archaeological generation (about twenty-five years) or two.[11]

I am not convinced, either, that Curta is right to be so dismissive of Jordanes. By definition, since we don't have Jordanes' own account of his working methods or any real means of cross-checking, the idea that he invented the link to the Venedi on the basis of Tacitus can only be hypothesis. It is not demonstrable fact, and there are some telling points against it. Jordanes started life as the military secretary of an east Roman commander stationed on the Danube frontier at the very same time that Slavic attacks were intensifying. He also provides – again, presumably, drawing on his own knowledge – very precise information on the resettlement south of the Lower Danube frontier line of various population fragments from the wreck of Attila's Empire. This underlines his knowledge of the region, and makes it far from implausible that he had authentic information on what the Slavs of this region themselves understood of their origins. In fact, Jordanes may well also provide the earliest historical reference to a Slavic group in action, making passing reference to a war of the Gothic king Vinitharius against the Antae. Jordanes is chronologically confused here. He thought that Vinitharius lived in the later fourth century, but he was in fact one of those warband leaders that Valamer defeated to create the Amal-led Ostrogoths, probably after the death of Attila. But Jordanes certainly places this war before the Amal-led Goths moved west of the Carpathians to the Great Hungarian Plain, so this does fit with a picture of Slavic-speaking Antae operating on the eastern fringes of the Carpathians in the fifth century. It is also the case that the term 'Wends' – deriving from the old Roman label Venedi – was used from the seventh century onwards by many early medieval western European populations of their new Slavic neighbours; and migration, as we shall see, was a characteristic of documented Slavic-speaking populations from the sixth century onwards. Large numbers of Sclavenes and Antae of Moldavia and Wallachia would end up in the Balkans from the early seventh century, and already in the sixth, other Slavs can be documented moving west through the central European uplands. Given that, as we have seen so often before, real migration habits build up in population groups, this does add further weight to the suggestion that the first Slavic groups found north of the Lower Danube frontier in the early sixth century had moved into the region in the recent past. All this is certainly enough to make Curta's dismissal of Jordanes at best inconclusive, and to my mind it is likely that, for once, the historian actually knew what he was talking about.[12]

But there is also a bigger point here. From about the year 500, as we shall examine more closely in a moment, a huge expansion process unfolded that would make Slavic-speakers the dominant force across vast tracts of the European landscape from the Elbe to the Volga. This process is not well documented, but it does seem inconceivable that all this can have derived from an original population group confined just to Moldavia and Wallachia. Even if you do discount Jordanes on the Venedi and accept that Sclavenes and Antae emerged where they are first mentioned, this still leaves you with the overall phenomenon of Slavicization to explain. Putting tree names to one side, the linguistic evidence provides two broader points of reference.

First, the modern Slavic language groups (east, west and south) are remarkable for how close they have remained to one another: so close in fact that they are mutually comprehensible. Everything suggests that this closeness results not from processes of linguistic convergence in the recent past, but from the fact that they split apart from one another at a comparatively late date. Second, Slavic languages as a whole are most closely related to those of Europe's Baltic-speakers, whom hydronyms show to have been much more widely distributed over eastern Europe in the past than is the case today (Map 16). As we saw with the Anglo-Saxons in England, the names of larger rivers seem to have a fossil-like capacity to survive major cultural transformations. Not so long before the split between the various branches of Slavic, therefore, we must envisage a previous split between Slavic-speakers and Baltic-speakers. They had previously shared the one, older set of closely related Indo-European dialects.[13] Seen in equally broad terms, the archaeological evidence paints a very similar picture. The only possible progenitors of the still extremely simple farming lifestyles visible in Korchak and closely related remains of c.500 are the subsistence-farming communities of Europe east of the Vistula and north of the Carpathians in the Roman period. Both sets of evidence tell the same story. The broader Slavic-speaking population of Europe clearly emerged from somewhere among eastern Europe's non-Germanic-speaking population. Even if Jordanes was making up the link between the Sclavenes and the Antae (which I strongly doubt), the likelihood is that he was correct.


## THE SLAVICIZATION OF EUROPE


Where linguistic evidence can give us very little help, however, is with chronology. We know the Slavic language family emerged relatively recently, but what does that mean? Some experts argue that the split with Baltic-speakers began only in the middle of the first millennium AD, at the precise moment when Slavic-speakers begin to appear in our sources. Others would place it much earlier – by maybe even a thousand or more years. This difference of opinion matters when it comes to trying to understand the Slavicization of Europe which unfolded after c.500 AD. If we should be envisaging very few Slavic-speakers at that date because the linguistic split was just beginning, so that Europe's Slavic-speakers may have amounted to no more than the Sclavenes and Antae of Korchak and Penkovka fame, then the broad Slavic domination of Europe achieved by c.900 AD has to be accounted for from an extremely restricted demographic base. If, on the contrary, the Slavic linguistic family had emerged much earlier, the Sclavenes and Antae might only be two particular subgroups from within a far larger Slavic-speaking population. At this point, there is no way to be certain, but most of the experts would place the emergence of the Slavic language family much further back in time than the mid-first millennium AD, and it does make much better sense of the broader evidence for Slavic expansion to suppose that Slavic-speakers were not just restricted to Moldavia and Wallachia at that point.[14] Nonetheless, it is worth keeping in mind both possibilities when trying to compre-hend the explosion of Slavic dominance along its three main trajector-ies: south into the Balkans, west and north to the Elbe and Baltic, and east and north to the Volga and the fringes of the Arctic tundra.

## The Balkans

For Slavic expansion into the Balkans, there is a relatively full selection of broadly contemporary east Roman and Byzantine historical sources. Until recent archaeological materials came online, they provided much the earliest body of information of any quality about early Slavic history. As a result, and this always happens when too many clever people have been studying a limited amount of information for too long, the subject area came to resemble a famous chess match, each intellectual gambit with its well-rehearsed counter. We have no need, fortunately, to become entangled in these set-pieces, since the broader outlines of Slavic expansion into the Balkans are clear enough.

As we have just seen, Slavic raiding into the Balkans increased in scope and ambition towards the middle of the sixth century. In 547/8, a large raiding party spread south-west from the Danube through Illyricum as far south as the major Adriatic port of Epidamnos

(Dyrrhachium). Procopius reports that these raiders captured many strongholds, a phenomenon not previously witnessed. The success encouraged further attacks. The next year, three thousand Slavs crossed the Danube and advanced on the River Hebrus. There they defeated some local Roman forces and captured the fairly major settlement of Topirus, by luring the city's garrison into an ambush. Some thirteen thousand male inhabitants are said to have been killed in the subsequent sack, with many women and children taken prisoner. The year 550 then saw an unprecedentedly large force move south past Naissus, with the highly ambitious aim of capturing Thessalonica, the heavily fortified regional capital of the western Balkans. Eventually the raiders turned aside, moving through the mountains into Dalmatia and scattering in front of the major Roman army that was on its way north through the Balkans to complete the conquest of Ostrogothic Italy. When the army had passed, the raiders doubled back to the western Balkans, defeating a second, improvised Roman force at Hadrianople. Following this victory, the raiders spread to within a day's march of the imperial capital of Constantinople itself.[15]

There is no good evidence, though, that any of these Slavs were actually settling on a permanent or semi-permanent basis inside the imperial frontier at this point. The Antae were granted the old Roman fortress of Turris by treaty in 540, but this was north of the Danube and the whole point of the arrangement was to block further raiding on the part of the Sclavenes. Some Slavic place names, perhaps, figure in lists Procopius supplies of Balkan forts repaired or built by the Emperor Justinian (527–65), but, if so, the fact they are attached to forts might suggest that they were the outcome of authorized settlements of Slavic recruits into the Roman army rather than any proper migration as such. In any case, Slavs were not operating in sufficient force in these years to attempt a formal conquest of any part of the Balkans, or to capture major centres such as Thessalonica.[16] The overall situation was radically transformed from about 570, however, by the rise of the Avar Empire.

The Avars figure so strongly in what follows that they require some introduction. They were the next major wave of originally nomadic horse warriors, after the Huns, to sweep off the Great Eurasian Steppe and build an empire in central Europe. Thankfully we know rather more about them than about the Huns. The Avars spoke a Turkic language and had previously starred as the dominant force behind a major nomadic confederation on the fringes of China. In the earlier sixth century they had lost this position to a rival force, the so-called Western Turks, and arrived on the outskirts of Europe as political refugees, announcing themselves with an embassy that appeared at Justinian's court in 558. The Emperor saw them as a new pawn in the great diplomatic game of divide and rule by which he sought to prevent really serious trouble in his north-eastern approaches. This, however, proved hopelessly over-optimistic. Not content with the role assigned them, the Avars quickly created an imperial power block of real menace. Attaching Bulgar nomads to their train, by 570 they had relocated to the Great Hungarian Plain, the old stomping ground of Attila, where they added Gepids to a growing list of conquered subject peoples. Their arrival also prompted the Lombards to leave for safer Italian domains on the other side of the Alps.[17] If all this wasn't enough, the arrival of the Avars also marks a watershed in Slavic history.

Like many of their Middle and Lower Danubian neighbours, the Slavs of the Carpathian region found themselves targets of aggressive Avar ambition. The Antae seem to have suffered particularly at their hands in a punishing campaign of 604, which destroyed their political independence. On one level, the rise of the Avars meant that some Slavic groups now sought to move south of the Danube permanently, to escape their domination. In this area, massive Avar attacks on the east Roman Empire, particularly widespread in the 570s and 580s and again in the 610s, also provided such Slavic groups with much greater opportunity to pursue these ambitions free from Roman counterattack. At the same time, the Constantinopolitan authorities were having to defend their eastern territories in Syria, Palestine and Egypt against Persian and then Arab assault. The latter were a much richer source of tax revenues than the war-torn Balkans and always received – naturally enough – a higher priority.

The new era announced itself in the 580s. The Emperor Maurice (582–602) was embroiled in a major war with the Persian Empire in the Near East, which sucked most mobile Roman forces away from the Balkans and allowed the Avars to launch a series of severe and wide-ranging attacks in Thrace. At the same time, Sclavenes mounted successive highly destructive campaigns in Thrace and Illyricum, the first really threatening assault upon Thessalonica, regional capital of Illyricum, occurring in 586. In the same year, 'the fifth year of the

Emperor Maurice', one of the famous texts, the *Chronicle of Monemvasia*, even reports that Slavs took over all the Peloponnese except for an eastern coastal strip that remained in east Roman hands. According to the *Chronicle*, this caused a mass evacuation of 'all the Greeks' from the captured zones: the citizens of Patras went to Rhegia in Calabria (southern Italy), those of Argos to the island of Urok, the Corinthians to Aegina, the Spartans to both Sicily and to Monemvasia itself, a rocky, defensible peninsula in the southern Peloponnese.

The terminal Slavicization of the Peloponnese, however, did not happen so early. The *Chronicle of Monemvasia* is a late text and, although preserving some authentic information, it kaleidoscopes the process of Slavic settlement. In the 590s, with the Persian War successfully won, Maurice was able to counterattack in the Balkans. Diplomatically, he paid the Antae to attack the raiding Sclavenes, while his armies inflicted major defeats on the main Avar host in 593–5 and again from 599. In 602, his forces were even operating north of the Lower Danube, mounting a series of pre-emptive strikes which destroyed some whole Slavic groups. Letters of Pope Gregory I from the same period demonstrate that Church structures were restored in Illyricum generally, and in the Peloponnese in particular. While they certainly occurred, therefore, initial Slavic settlements of the 580s were swallowed up by Maurice's counterattacks.[18]

But this wasn't the end of the story. From 604, repeating the pattern of the 580s, Maurice's successors Phocas and Heraclius found themselves embroiled in a war with Persia, which by the early 610s was going diabolically badly, with control lost of pretty much the whole of Egypt, Palestine and Syria. Every military resource available had to be turned eastwards, opening the way to further Avar and Slav attacks on an unprecedented scale. In 614, disaster struck. Thessalonica avoided capture by a whisker. Salona, on the other hand, the largest Roman centre on the Dalmatian coast, fell into Avar and Slav hands, along with many of the Empire's key cities in the northern Balkans, such as Naissus and Serdica. The action then spread as far south as the Peloponnese, when – amongst other things – Slavic raiders took to coastal waters in vast flotillas of dugout canoes. Constantinople itself eventually came under threat in a week-long Avar siege in 626. Alongside this military assault, Slavic settlement was gathering momentum.[19]

Heraclius eventually won his war with Persia, but was immediately faced with the rise of militant Arab Islam. In contrast to the 590s, there was no opportunity this time to repair any of the damage done to the fabric of Roman life in the Balkans. Consequently, the disasters of 614 marked the definitive collapse of the Danube frontier of the old east Roman Empire, and paved the way for Slavic settlement across most of the Balkans: all the way from the Dobrudja in the north-east to the Peloponnese in the south-west. It is impossible to reconstruct a detailed narrative of this settlement process, but a series of vignettes, provided by various sources, leave us in no doubt as to its scale. In Macedonia in the northern Balkans, the *Miracles of St Demetrius* shows that large-scale Slavic settlement in the region of the Strymon River around Thessalonica was well established by the mid-seventh century. From one of its episodes it emerges that several Slavic groups were settled in the vicinity of the city by about 670, a point confirmed by later events. In the late 680s, the Byzantine Emperor Justinian II was able, if temporarily, to take the offensive in Macedonia, subduing the Slavic tribes of the region and restoring central imperial control. As part of the process he transferred reportedly as many as thirty thousand Slavs to Asia Minor. The reports also find some archaeological reflection. Seventh-century Macedonia and adjacent areas to the north did not see the spread of fully formed Korchak-type cultural systems across their landscapes, but many isolated discoveries of Korchak materials have been made in cemeteries and find-spots across Serbia and Croatia – Bakar Muntjac, Osijek, Stinjevac, Vinkovci.[20]

Further east, in Thrace, Slavic settlement is equally well attested. When the first Bulgar state was established north of the Haemus Mountains in c.680, seven Slavic tribes already inhabited the region. They were resettled in an arc in the uplands around what became the Bulgar heartlands on the Danubian plain. Here the pattern of archaeo-logical remains is different from that in Macedonia. Isolated Slavic ceramics, mixed with indigenous materials, have been discovered in sixth-century levels in cemeteries and rural zones around some of the fortresses of the frontier region, particularly Durostorum and Bononia. But excavations in northern Bulgaria have also uncovered sites such as Popina, where Korchak-type materials appear with no admixture of foreign imports. This and related sites used to be dated to the sixth century, but have now been shown to be later, postdating the definitive collapse of the Danube frontier in 614, which clearly marked the beginning of full-scale Slavic settlement in this part of the Balkans too.

In archaeological as well as historical terms, the situation was then transformed by the arrival of the originally nomadic and Turkic-speaking Bulgars, but these further developments sat on the back of an earlier, large-scale Slavic settlement.[21]

Literary and archaeological evidence also attests to a substantial Slavic presence further south, right in the heart of what is now Greece and the Peloponnese. The *Miracles of St Demetrius* mention in passing more Slavs, the Belegezitae, established near Thessaly and Demetrias. Later texts specifically mention other Slavs in the Peloponnese, not least the Milingas and Ezeritae in the vicinity of Patras, who in the early ninth century revolted against the tribute payments imposed upon them by a (slightly) resurgent Byzantine state. The archaeological echoes of this Slavic presence more closely resembled those of Macedonia in the north-west Balkans than those in Thrace in the north-east. Just a few, relatively isolated, finds of Korchak materials have been made, with no sign that the immigrant Slavs imported with them a complete material-cultural system. And some of the materials that used to be attributed to them probably had other origins anyway. A cemetery at Olympia, for instance, turned up twelve armed cremation burials of individuals interred in Korchak-type funerary urns. These are in all probability east Roman soldiers, if perhaps of Slavic origin, rather than independent immigrant Slavs. More convincing Slavic ceramics have been found at Argos, Messina and Demetrius, and Greece as a whole, like the rest of the Balkans, has thrown up a selection of the 'fingered' style of *fibula* brooch which was often, but not exclusively, sported by Slavs in the early medieval period. There are other possible explanations for this relative lack of Slavic materials. Above all, the first classical archaeologists, who were completely uninterested in medieval remains, ravaged most of the major Greek sites in the late nineteenth and early twentieth centuries and simply threw anything post-classical away. Nonetheless, it does appear that, again, the advance of Slavic groups into Greece proper did not generate entire Korchak-type material-cultural systems.[22]

By the mid-seventh century, Slavic settlement was already affecting more or less the entire Balkans, but this is perhaps not yet the full story. According to one source, the north-west Balkans saw a further distinct wave of Slavic settlement. The *De Administrando Imperio* of Constantine Porphyryogenitus records that a first wave of undifferentiated Slavs originally settled in the lands now largely divided between

Croatia, Serbia, Montenegro and Macedonia as Avar subjects, at the time when Avar rule was establishing itself in central Europe (from c.560 onwards). They were followed somewhat later, but still in the time of Heraclius (610–41), by two, more-organized, Slavic groupings – the Serbs and Croats – who arrived from the north to expel most of the Avars from that region (causing the others to submit) and establish their own rule instead, over Serbia and Dalmatia respectively. In the case of the Croats, the *De Administrando* preserves two versions of the story, one obviously Byzantine, the other Croat. These vary – as you might predict – on whether the Croats were invited to the Balkans or acted on their own initiative, and whether or not they promised to acknowledge Byzantine overlordship as a condition of settlement.

The stories are famous, but it is difficult to know what to make of them. Serb and Croat nationalists have long cherished them as the origin stories of their 'peoples', arriving as fully formed units in the Balkans landscape. The problems they pose, however, are obvious. By virtue of being unique, they lack corroboration. They also occur in a comparatively late source, the *De Administrando* being a mid-tenth-century text, and their telling has a distinctly legendary tone: the Croats are led south by a family of five brothers. Not surprisingly, they have often been rejected outright. On the other hand, tenth-century Arab sources confirm the existence of other Serbs and Croats north of the Carpathians at that point, and there is nothing inherently impossible in the general action outlined. If it is accepted that they possess a kernel of truth, the stories suggest that some more organized Slavic groups asserted their independence from Avar rule by moving south into the Balkans and establishing some kind of a relationship with the Byzantine state before the death of Heraclius. Indeed, the northern Serbs (or Sorbs) themselves threw off Avar domination – if perhaps temporarily – in alliance with an ex-Frankish merchant, Samo, in about 630; that is, precisely in the reign of Heraclius. This was, in fact, a moment of general crisis for the Avar Empire following its huge defeat at the siege of Constantinople in 626, and the consequent loss of prestige for its ruling Khagan. Substantial numbers of its Bulgar subjects also escaped Avar domination by fleeing into Italy at this point, so that the idea that other Slavic groups were doing the same, either with or without a Byzantine invitation, is perfectly plausible.[23]

But if this much is plausible, the seventh-century Serbs and Croats were not whole peoples responsible for the complete repopulation of these parts of the Balkans. As we have seen, the better-documented instances of first-millennium migration have never thrown up a case of total demographic replacement: some indigenous population elements always survive. And there is in fact a possible extra twist to this story. The group names 'Serb' and 'Croat', together with some of the personal names reported of their leaders, might derive from Iranian rather than from the Slavic language group. It has been suggested, therefore, that both groups may have originally been dominated by cores of Iranian nomads.[24] This is not inherently impossible. It could have come about, for instance, by Slavic groups established in the northern Black Sea region becoming part of a military confederation dominated by Iranian nomads. There is not the slightest shred of narrative evidence to support such a view, but this is how nomads like the Huns tended to operate on the fringes of Europe. That the Serbs and Croats asserted their independence at Avar expense in the reign of Heraclius, perhaps around 630 when their Empire was in crisis, and that the Byzantines used them as part of a broader strategy for limiting Avar power in the Balkans, all seems likely enough. Whether we should envisage them as already entirely Slavic at this point, or as a structured confederation with distinct groups of Iranian-speaking nomads at their cores, is entirely unclear. It is also unclear whether their arrival represented a further major wave of Slavic immigration into the north-western Balkans, or whether they functioned essentially as an organizing element for Slavic groups already present there but formerly subject to Avar domination. If the latter, this would make them not unlike the Bulgars of the eastern Balkans.[25]

## Central Europe

Slavic expansion into central Europe between the Elbe and the Vistula was equally thorough. The key proof text is a short and unpretentious document of staggering historical importance: the so-called *Anonymous Bavarian Geographer*. Dating from the 820s, it was written by an anonymous geographer working somewhere in Bavaria. It surveys and names the Frankish Empire's neighbours between the Rivers Elbe and Oder, and even attempts to give some indication of their relative power, each unit being given a rating in terms of the numbers of 'cities' (*civitates*) that it comprised (Map 18). What these cities may have looked like is a point we will return to in Chapter 1. The central point is that all of these units have Slavic names. We know from other sources that some Slavic-speakers had even penetrated west of the Elbe at certain points before the rise of the Carolingians, but these immigrants were never numerous enough in these regions to challenge the dominance of Germanic-speaking Saxons and Thuringians. The *Anonymous* gives out pretty much at the River Oder, and knowledge of areas still further to the east, between the Oder and the Vistula, was perhaps not yet common in Carolingian Europe of the early ninth century.[26]

A fuller picture of the extent of Slavic domination in central Europe had to wait until the Ottonian era of the tenth century, when the third of the Frankish imperial dynasties stretched its tendrils of dominion eastwards from the Elbe. In 962, a nascent Polish state suddenly appears in the historical record, providing unimpeachable evidence of Slavic domination of its territories between the Oder and the Vistula as well, with Arab sources confirming the point. From the mid-tenth century at the latest, then, all of north-central Europe between the Elbe and the Vistula was now the domain of Slavic-speakers. Indeed, the fact that historical documentation for lands east of the Oder is available only for the tenth century surely shouldn't be taken to mean that Poland was Slavicized later than Bohemia or Moravia. What we're looking at are the dates when interaction between these lands and western European imperial power gathered momentum, not the moment when they first came to be occupied by Slavs. The overall revolution in north-central Europe effected by Slavic expansion is plain to see. In the first half of the millennium, all this territory between the Elbe and the Vistula had been dominated by Germanic-speakers.[27]

But if Carolingian and Arab sources between them document the total Slavicization of central Europe by c.900 AD, they provide little insight into the chronology or nature of the historical processes responsible for it. With the end of the western Empire in 476, historical light on north-central Europe – fitful at best, in the Roman period – is pretty much extinguished for the next three hundred years. All that the written sources preserve are a few vignettes that shed a little light on spreading Slavic domination through the uplands of central Europe: the extension of the Carpathians westwards to meet the Alps. The first refers to events of the year 512, when, as we saw in Chapter 5, the unfortunate Heruli began their long march to Scandinavia. According to Procopius, they first passed 'through the land of the Slavs'. Most likely the Heruli left the Middle Danube by the valley of the River Morava, the main natural route north out of the Great Hungarian Plain. If so, Slavs were already then established in what is now Slovakia. This conclusion is supported by a second incident, of 543. In that year, a Lombard prince named Hildegesius attacked east Roman forces with six thousand warriors, most of whom were again Slavs. Since the Lombards were still living at that point in the Middle Danube, before the arrival of the Avars, it seems probable that he recruited his Slavs from the edges of that region – the Morava valley again, or somewhere nearby. Our third marker dates to the end of the sixth century, when Bavarian militias had to fight off Slavic attacks in both 593 and 595. So within half a century of the Hildegesius incident, Slavic groups are documented another 250 kilometres to the west, on the fringes of Bavaria.

A similar vision of the western extent of Slavic expansion by the early seventh century is provided by one of the most famous episodes in early Slavic history, the adventures of Samo, our Frankish merchant turned Slavic prince. In the course of his colourful life, which involved – amongst other feats – siring twenty-two sons and fifteen daughters by his twelve Slavic wives, it emerges that by 630 the Slavic Sorbs were established on the borderlands of Thuringia.[28] This would suggest that they were entrenched somewhere in the southern Elbe region. They had by this date, according to the Frankish chronicler Fredegar, a 'long-standing relationship' with their Thuringian neighbours, which would date the Sorbs' occupation of these lands to c.600 at the latest. From these few references it is possible to get some sense of a westward Slavic penetration through central Europe, working roughly along the line of the northern hinterlands of the Carpathian Mountains and the Alps in the course of the sixth century (Map 18). But this is all the sources give us, and there is nothing here about the northern lowlands or the shores of the Baltic.

The archaeological evidence, such as it is, broadly confirms the picture. As we have seen, Korchak-type material assemblages probably first emerged in the outer arc of the Carpathians in the later fifth century, but then spread over a much wider area. To the west, they diffused right around the outskirts of the Carpathians and on through the central European uplands as far west as Bohemia and adjacent areas of the southern Elbe region. An additional cluster of Korchak remains has also been excavated further to the north-west, in Mecklenburg and Lusatia (Map 18). The archaeological pattern here is rather different from that of most of the Balkans. Instead of a few isolated finds of Korchak ceramics or the odd burial, the central European uplands have thrown up entire Korchak cultural complexes. Not just stray Korchak items, but an entire Korchak way of life – including agricultural production methods and patterns of social connection – came to be reproduced in these areas.

When they were first identified, the Korchak materials of Bohemia and Moravia were dated to the mid-fifth century. But it is now clear that Korchak remains in Bohemia date to no earlier than the second half of the sixth. Brzezno is the oldest Korchak site identified so far, and its remains date from no earlier than c.550. This is entirely in line with the new dating evidence from Moravia, a little further east, where, again, Korchak materials have now been shown to have appeared no sooner than c.550 at the absolute earliest. Dendrochronology has also provided precise dates for the Korchak sites in the Elbe–Saale region, west of Bohemia. Here, too, they have extended the received chronology. The Elbe–Saale remains used to be allocated to the late fifth century or the early sixth; their earliest materials have now been dated to no earlier than the 660s.[29]

The geographical spread of Korchak materials across south-central Europe thus amplifies the picture of Slavic expansion suggested by the stray historical references. The new chronologies have also put paid to older theories that an initial Slavic penetration into the Elbe region in the later fifth or sixth centuries was followed by a second wave of migration in the seventh. This hypothesis had in mind a potential parallel with the Serbs and Croats and the Balkans. It was based, however, on the appearance of brand-new types of pottery in the Elbe region, which were finished on a slow wheel rather than entirely hand-formed. The geographical spread of the subtypes of this pottery broadly coincides with the main tribal confederations known from the Carolingian and Ottonian eras (Map 18): the Wilzi (Feldberg pottery), the Lausitzi (Tornow pottery) and the Sorbs (Leipzig pottery). It used therefore to be thought that the appearance of the new pottery types marked the arrival in the region of these tribal groups. Dendrochronology has shown, however, that the sites containing these wheel-turned pottery types date not from the late sixth and the seventh century, but from the later eighth and ninth. By this date, Carolingian narrative coverage of the region is more than full enough to rule out the possibility of any further large-scale migration. The new pottery types therefore represent the spread of new ceramic technologies among Slavs already indigenous to the Elbe region. The later dating also makes much better sense of the fact that some of the pottery resembles eighth-century Carolingian ceramics, by which they were clearly influenced.[30]

From all these materials, therefore, a clear enough picture emerges of a ribbon of Slavic settlement extending westwards from the northern hinterland of the Carpathian Mountains as far as the northern reaches of Slovakia in or around 500 AD. About fifty years later, a Korchak-type material culture penetrated south into the river valleys around the Middle Danube, and pushed on westwards to Bohemia. Another fifty years further on, and Slavic groups were both threatening the fringes of Bavaria and establishing themselves in the Elbe–Saale region.

So far so good; but we have not yet got to the heart of the Slavic takeover of central Europe. As we have seen, ninth- and tenth-century sources demonstrate that in this era Slavic-speakers dominated the entire North European Plain between the Elbe and the Vistula as far north as the Baltic. But this is a much bigger area than that encompassed by our 'thin' ribbon of Korchak sites along the central European uplands and part of the way up the Elbe, and the historical evidence only comes on stream after Slavs were well established here. So what do the archaeological materials reveal of the process of Slavicization in north-central Europe?

A first stage seems to be reflected in the so-called Mogilany group of sites from the Cracow region of south-eastern Poland. They are probably best viewed as a local variant of the Korchak-type sites found in nearby areas of the Carpathians, which they strongly resemble. Mogilany sites produce a range of similar handmade ceramics, and are marked by the familiar sunken floored huts with stone-built ovens. As yet, and this is the only reason they have been given a different name, no cemeteries have been found alongside Mogilany hamlets. No dendrochronological dates are available for this group, so its dating has at the moment to rely on an older method. This was based on the fact that, in most of central Europe, the largely undatable Korchak-type remains succeed the materially richer and hence chronologically more helpful materials generated by its previously dominant Germanic speakers, before the phenomenon of culture collapse set in. The end date for these Germanic-type cultures in any given area, therefore, can provide a useful earliest possible date for the advent of Slavic settlement there, so long as two conditions apply. First, the immigrant Slavs must not have coexisted with the Germanic-speaking groups responsible for the richer material culture being used to provide the date. But, second, there has to have been no lengthy interval between the disappearance of Germanic materials in the area and the arrival of Slavs.

Both conditions are potentially problematic, but the approach does work reasonably well where it can be tested against dendrochronological information in the south. There is no evidence, for instance, that the previously dominant Germanic cultures of northern and eastern Slovakia, and north-eastern Moravia, continued in existence past the year 500. In southern Slovakia and Moravia, together with Lower Austria (Austria north of the Danube), on the other hand, enough later Germanic materials have been found to suggest that they continued in use there until c.550. Bohemia also continued to generate Germanic-type cultures until a similar date.[31] These chronologies are broadly consistent with the new scientific dates for the earliest Slavic settlements in these regions, suggesting that it is still worth applying the method to regions where more scientific dates are currently lacking.

In the Roman period, Cracow, home of the Mogilany group, fell within the southern expanses of the old Przeworsk system. Its collapse coincided, as we saw in Chapter 5, with the rise of Hunnic power sometime in the first half of the fifth century. An imported *fibula* brooch found at the Mogilany site of Radziejow Kujawski can be dated to the later fifth or the very early sixth century, and the start of a second and distinct cultural phase within the group is marked by the appearance of metalwork datable to c.600 AD excavated at Mogilany pit number 45, providing an earliest possible date of the sixth century for what went before. It seems likely enough, then, that Korchak-type Slavic speakers spread into the power vacuum created by Przeworsk culture collapse in south-eastern Poland in the late fifth or the earlier sixth century, soon after they first became visible in the Carpathian region.[32]

The early medieval period in most of what is now Poland is not marked, however, by the widespread dissemination of such Korchak-type remains. Areas north of Lublin, eventually extending as far west as the Elbe, saw the development of another regionally distinct archaeological system: the so-called Sukow-Dziedzice culture (Map 18). Up to now, a clear boundary has been drawn between this second set of sites and those of the Mogilany type. Although some of the smaller pot-types of each group are identical, the larger pottery is entirely different in shape, and a much wider repertoire of forms was used here than by potters working more directly in the Korchak tradition. Some of the pots even look like handmade imitations of those previously in vogue in the same lands during the period of the Germanic-dominated Przeworsk culture. The sunken log cabins (*Grubenhäuser*) which are such a distinctive feature of Korchak areas have also not generally been found in Sukow-Dziedzice lands. Apart from an isolated group on the fertile loess-type soils of Mazovia, Kuiavia and Celmno, the major house-type identified so far is an above-ground wooden cabin. This different building tradition has provided one of the planks of the argument that Poland became Slavic-speaking via an entirely different trajectory of historical development from that which was working itself out in Moravia, Bohemia and the southern Elbe region. To some scholars, the Sukow-Dziedzice and Korchak cultures look so different that the former must have been generated by an entirely separate Slavic-speaking population. According to different views, this population was either indigenous to Poland – having been long submerged under a Germanic elite – or moved into Poland after 500, and not from the Carpathians but from a second 'Slavic homeland' outside of Korchak-dominated Carpathian areas – perhaps Byelorussia. According to either of these views, the Slavicization of central Europe so evident in Carolingian sources was the product of two simultaneous but independent waves of Slavic expansion: Korchak-type populations from the Carpathians, and Sukow-Dziedzice from Byelorussia or from within Poland itself.[33]

The tail end of old nationalist agendas seems to be lurking behind this determination that Poland should have had its own unique trajectory towards Slavdom. In particular, the idea that house-types can provide a secure means of so absolutely distinguishing two population groups has been undermined by some recent excavations. These unearthed sunken huts in three areas where they had been unknown: at Wyszogrod, Szarlig and Zmijewo. At Wyszogrod, moreover, contemporaneous sunken huts and surface cabins were found on the same site. These discoveries make it likely that continuing investigations will uncover Korchak-type sunken huts more generally within Sukow-Dziedzice territories, eroding the apparently clear line that used to be drawn.[34] That said, because of the uncertainties of the linguistic evidence, it is perfectly likely that Slavic-speakers were more widely dispersed north of the Carpathians and east of the Vistula in the later fifth century, with the Korchak Podolians being no more than one subgroup among them. It is also entirely likely, that this broader Slavic-speaking population, if it existed, would have later become involved in the broader Slavicization of areas such as Poland. The much wider range of pot forms in use in Sukow-Dziedzice areas is very striking, and strongly suggests that, unlike the Mogilany group, Sukow-Dziedzice has to be seen as a more specific phenomenon than merely another local Korchak Polish variant. This could be because its Slavs had different origins, but, as we shall see in a moment, it may have more to do with conditions the immigrants encountered when they arrived in Poland.

How quickly the new Sukow-Dziedzice cultural form spread across the area between the Vistula and the Elbe is difficult to say, since the internal chronology of the system has not yet been established. Germanic culture collapse in more northerly Przeworsk and Wielbark areas had occurred by 500 or shortly afterwards, which is consistent with a stray reference in a work by the east Roman historian, Theophylact Simocatta, which might just about indicate that some Slavs had reached the Baltic Sea by the 590s (or, frankly, might mean nothing at all). On the other hand, scientific dates for Sukow-Dziedzice sites in Lusatia, in the former DDR, indicate that these belong to a rather later period. Scandinavian metalwork found with Sukow-Dziedzice remains at Rostow Karkow provides a terminus post quem for that site of just after 700 AD. Absolute dendrochronological dates from the actual site of Sukow-Dziedzice itself and a number of well holes in the same region have likewise provided eighth-century dates. These dates apply only to the westernmost Sukow-Dziedzice territories, and, since there is good reason to suppose that the Slavic spread worked generally from east to west, do not necessarily contradict a sixth-century date for some of the Polish materials. For the moment, however, that is the best that can be done, although more scientific investiations will certainly provide more information in due course.[35]

In broad outline, therefore, the spread of Slavic-speaking domination across the whole of north-central Europe, documented in the Carolingian era, seems to have converged on the Elbe from two different directions, if not necessarily from two points of departure. One line of advance is marked by the ribbon of Prague-Korchak sites running through the uplands of central Europe into Bohemia – and even onwards, in places, west of the Elbe. This trajectory of advance extended over about a century, between c.500 and 600. A second line of advance is marked by the spread of the Sukow-Dziedzice culture across the North European Plain, which was equally successful. It spread eventually, if more slowly than used to be thought, as far west as the River Elbe, which it had reached apparently by c.700. Much here remains obscure, but a broad outline of the initial Slavicization of Europe west of the Vistula can be sketched in from a mixture of literary and archaeological sources.

## Mother Russia

For the Slavicization of European Russia up to the Volga we have two main reference points. The first comes from historical sources. Thanks to Islamic geographers of the tenth century, we know that territories east of the Vistula that correspond to modern Byelorussia and Volhynia were under the control of so-called 'eastern Slavs' at this time. The most comprehensive picture of the area at the end of the early Middle Ages, however, is provided by a still later source, the *Russian Primary Chronicle*, whose text, as we now have it, was a product of the early twelfth century. According to its account, by about 900 AD a number of separate Slavic-speaking groups had come to occupy a truly vast area of eastern Europe. The text has most to say about Polyanians, the Slavic-speaking group settled around Kiev where the *Chronicle* was composed, but many other groups and their approximate locations are mentioned in passing. It is obviously retrospective, but there is no reason to think that it misrepresents to any significant degree the spread of Slavic-speakers across the East European Plain at the turn of the millennium. Byzantine sources, above all the *De Administrando Imperio* (but this time providing much less problematic, contemporary information), confirm the essential outlines. By the end of the first millennium, Slavic-speaking groups dominated a huge portion of the

East European Plain, taking in territory well to the east of the River Dnieper and, in the case of the Slovenes, stretching their control as far north as Lake Ilmen (Map 19).[36]

From a modern perspective, it's no surprise to find Slavic-speakers distributed so widely across Mother Russia, but our second reference point shows that this had not always been the case. All the major rivers' names across a massive tract of territory between the Vistula and the Volga, north of the confluence of the Pripet and the Dnieper, are in fact derived from Baltic rather than Slavic languages. The conclusion seems inescapable, therefore, that Baltic-speakers had at one point dominated this landscape. The situation observable in the tenth century, when Slavic-speakers were in more or less total control of it, must have been created at some point, therefore, by Slavic expansion. This sets up the fundamental conundrum of Russian prehistory.[37] In the complete absence of historical sources, which of the succession of archaeological cultures observable in the Russian landscape across the eons of the first millennium represents the initial penetration of Slavic-speakers into zones originally dominated by Balts?

This is another subject area that has benefited hugely from the immense archaeological enterprise that unfolded in Communist Europe after 1945, and here, too, many of the old Soviet-era agendas have been subsiding. It is now possible, on one level, to tell a fairly straightforward story, starting again from the certainly Slavic-speaking world of the Korchak Carpathians in c.500 AD. By the mid-sixth century, Korchak-type materials had spread not only westwards and southwards, but also eastwards further into Ukraine. In this period, the type-site – Korchak itself – was first occupied on the River Teterev near Zhitomir, and the spread continued subsequently. In the seventh century, Korchak materials were to be found further north, in Polesie: in the Pripet marsh zone of tree-name fame. At more or less the same time, a second cultural zone of importance to our story, the so-called Penkovka system, was coming into being, which between 550 and 650 took in large expanses of the forest steppe zone of Ukraine.

In many ways, Penkovka materials are indistinguishable from their Korchak counterparts. Both systems generated small clusters of houses on river terraces that were highly convenient for subsistence agriculture. Penkovka houses, likewise, were partly sunk into the ground, and boasted stone-built corner ovens. The only things that distinguish Penkovka remains are the biconical shape of some the larger ceramics, together with the wider variety of iron tools and decorative metalwork often found in Penkovka contexts. To the outsider (and many insiders too, in fact) the similarities are thus massively more impressive than any differences, and most scholars are confident that if Korchak-type materials were generated by Slavic-speakers, then so was the Penkovka system. Indeed, on the basis of Jordanes' report of the relative geographical distributions of the Sclavenes and Antae, Penkovka has often been thought to have been the product of the latter, and Korchak of the former. These precise identifications are questionable, but the basic similarities of the two systems, combined with the geographical coincidence between their spread and where we actually find Slavic-speakers in the sixth century, does make it reasonable to think of Penkovka, like Korchak, as at least Slavic-dominated.[38]

The later seventh century, however, was an era of major change. Across previously Korchak areas and much of the Penkovka zone, together with a substantial area to the north on either side of the Dnieper which had previously fallen beyond the boundary of either system, there arose between 650 and 750 a new culture: Luka Raikov-etskaia. Like its counterparts of the same era in the western reaches of Slavdom (the Tornow, Feldberg and Leipzig systems) the main difference between Luka Raikovetskaia and its predecessors was the fact that much of its pottery was now being finished on a slow wheel. Everything suggests that, in general terms, Luka Raikovetskaia represents the reincarnation of the Korchak and Penkovka systems in an era of technological advance, although debate continues over the extent to which it is correct to identify it as one unified system or to pick out instead a number of local variants.

At the same time, some of the easternmost Penkovka areas underwent a further and very distinctive process of development. This zone, together with other territories, which had previously fallen outside the Penkovka system altogether, saw the development of the so-called Volyntsevo culture. Aside, again, from slightly different ceramics, it is distinguished from the Luka Raikovetskaia by a strikingly greater prevalence of both metalwork and strongholds. Its history began in the seventh century, again, but it continued to spread into the eighth, at which point its development is marked by the acquisition of a new name, Romny-Borshevo. The ceramics of this system stand in a direct line of development from the Volyntsevo, but spread over a much wider area (the main reason for the change of name), and particularly into the basins of the Upper Don and the Oka. Its settlement sites are also characterized by the still more extensive use of fortifications. After the period of initial formation, Luka Raikovetskaia and Romny-Borshevo both continued in unbroken sequences of development, with an ever-widening geographical distribution, through to the tenth century. By this point, they extended over the areas where most of the Slavic groups named in the *Russian Primary Chronicle* were located (Map 19), and there seems no doubt, therefore, that a direct association can be made between tenth-century Slavic-speakers and these two archaeological systems.[39]

The rise and fall of the material-cultural systems of the East European Plain is now easy enough to follow in outline, and two sets of equations – between Korchak and Penkovka and known Slavic-speakers of the sixth century, and between Luka Raikovetskaia and Volyntsevo and Romny-Borshevo and known Slavic-speakers of the tenth – seem secure enough.

But this is not a historical narrative, and should not be confused with one. What can be charted with some security now is the developing sequence of pottery traditions on the East European Plain in the second half of the first millennium. Historical sources also make it clear that the later phases of Volyntsevo and Romny-Borshevo coincide geographically and chronologically with the dominance of Slavic-speakers by the tenth century. But pots aren't people, and trying to understand the human history that underlies these ceramic sequences, and their relationship to broader historical patterns of state formation and migration, raises many further questions.

Two have particular force. First, the introduction of wheel-made pottery makes it difficult to be certain how direct was the line of evolution from Korchak and Penkovka populations to those of Luka Raikovetskaia and Volyntsevo. Did the new systems come into being just because Korchak and Penkovka potters adopted a new ceramic technology? If so, then given that the Korchak and Penkovka were in all probability dominated by Slavic speakers, presumably so too were the Luka Raikovetskaia and Volyntsevo. This is the usual assumption, but the ceramic transformations could be hiding a much more complex human history, and the improved pottery – wheel-made pots are better than their handmade counterparts – might also have been adopted by non-Slavs. Second, what is the human history behind the subsequent spread of the patterns of the Luka Raikovetskaia and Volyntsevo cultural systems further north and east from the eighth to the tenth centuries? Was this an expansion of living human beings, or merely the spread of new habits among existing populations? These are both questions to which we will return.

Underlying both, however, is the still bigger issue that emerges when archaeology is confronted with linguistics. Does the document-able spread north and eastwards of the Korchak and Penkovka systems, a trajectory taken further by their Luka Raikovetskaia and Volyntsevo successors, represent the initial Slavicization of Russia and Ukraine, and the overall removal of these areas from a Baltic-speaking orbit In one view, this is perfectly possible. Some linguists, as we have seen, would date the initial separation of the Slavic and Baltic language families to the middle of the first millennium AD, making it natural to equate the appearance of Korchak-type cultures in the Carpathians rim with this moment of linguistic definition. If so, the subsequent spread north and eastwards of probably related archaeological cultures would in all likelihood represent the initial Slavicization of Mother Russia.

But other linguists would date the Baltic/Slavic split rather earlier, possibly even to the second millennium BC. And, in line with this, other archaeologists would argue, on the basis of the general patterns of life that generated them, that some of the systems to be found on the Baltic side of the hydronym divide in the mid-first millennium – in particular the so-called Kolochin culture – are so similar to those that generated the Korchak system that it is arbitrary to suppose the latter was dominated by Slavic-speakers, and the former not. Again, this is, a priori, a perfectly possible argument. In that view, what we would be seeing in the spread of the Korchak system would be the ability of one particularly successful group of Slavic-speakers to spread their domin-ation over an already broadly Slavic-speaking landscape. The first model – where the political dominance of Slavic-speakers and the arrival of the language go hand in hand – would resemble the broad pattern observed already in the Balkans and central Europe. But the less dramatic possibility – that much of Russia and Ukraine became Slavic-speaking sometime before our period – cannot be ruled out.[40]

# MIGRATION AND THE SLAVS

From the outer foothills of the Carpathian system in the late fifth century, Slavic groups spread decisively south into the Balkans in the seventh, after a period of aggressive raiding that had lasted through most of the sixth. Other Slavic-speaking groups were at the same time spreading into southern Poland (the Mogilany group of the early sixth century) and westwards along the northern foothills of the Carpathians, reaching Moravia sometime in the first half of the sixth century, Bohemia in the second, and the confluences of the Havel, Saale and Elbe in the early seventh. A second line of advance also reached the Elbe perhaps only a little later, having spread north and west from the Vistula, but, as we have seen, the internal chronology of the Sukow-Dziedzice system remains vague. Dynamic sixth-century Slavic expansion towards the west was fully matched in Ukraine on the other side of the Carpathians, where both the Korchak and the closely related Penkovka systems spread over large areas in the sixth century. Even this much expansion, however, does not explain the dominance of Slavic-speaking groups across large areas of previously Baltic-speaking regions visible by the tenth century. The spread subsequently of the Luka Raikovetskaia and Volyntsevo systems over and beyond Korchak and Penkovka areas may reflect this, but, as we have seen, that story may be much more complicated than the simple linear progression of material cultures might suggest.

Without historical evidence, it is impossible to know how dispersed Slavic-speakers already were in eastern Europe in c.500 AD. The geographical range of the action and the number of different forms it took does suggest, though, that there must have been substantially more Slavic-speakers at this point than just the Sclavenes and Antae of Moldavia and Wallachia, but this still makes Slavic expansion, particularly into European Russia, highly problematic. The spread of the Penkovka, Luka Raikovetskaia and Volyntsevo systems over different parts of the East European Plain really could represent either the initial Slavicization of these territories, or the triumph of one particular group of Slavic-speakers over their peers. Even more

fundamentally, none of this does more than sketch in the barest outlines of Slavic expansion.

By what means did Slavic-speakers spread their domination over
such a large part of the European landscape, and what caused this
fundamental revolution in European history?

Trying to understand the human history behind the creation of
Slavic Europe is even more difficult than exploring the migratory
activities of the Germanic groups caught up in the fall of the Roman
Empire, for two main reasons. First and foremost, the historical
evidence has yet more holes in it. The second reason would apply
anyway, even if the literary evidence were fuller. The appearance of
Sclavenes and Antae in the sub-Carpathian region by c.500 AD represented one huge revolution in itself, in that Slavic-speakers are not
previously documented in this area. But other Slavic-speakers then
spread over a vast range of times and places to create Slavic Europe as
it stood at the end of the first millennium: Moravia, Bohemia and
Ukraine in the sixth century, the Balkans in the seventh, the Russian
forest zone as late as the eighth and ninth, and north-central Europe
sometime in between. It is inconceivable that expansionary activities
that were dispersed so widely in time and space could all have taken a
single form.

## Flows of Migration

In the absence of historical sources of good quality, the scale of the
population units involved in Slavic migration is particularly difficult to
estimate. The only decent-looking figures refer to sixth-century raiding
parties, who consistently came in groups of a few thousand. On one
occasion, a mixed group of 1,600 Huns, Antae and Sclavenes burst on
to east Roman territory; on another, 3,000 Slavic raiders had to pay the
Gepids a gold coin apiece to be ferried to safety. Hildegesius' mixed
warband of Gepids and Slavs comprised 6,000 men, and a reportedly
'elite' force of 5,000 Slavs made a surprise attempt to storm the
defences of Thessalonica in 598.[41] These figures are reasonably consistent, but they refer to a different kind of activity from the expansionary
migration that affected the Balkans in the seventh century and the
Carpathians and central European uplands in the sixth. It is not likely
that the same kinds of social group were responsible for both activities.

As its various contexts indicate – ranging from central Europe in the sixth century to Lake Ilmen in the ninth – there were so many different processes involved in the creation of Slavic Europe that it is worth confining the discussion initially to sixth- and seventh-century central Europe and the Balkans, where we have at least some historical documentation. But even just within these spheres, two completely different kinds of outcome are visible in archaeological terms. In some contexts – particularly in the foothills of the Carpathians, Moravia, Bohemia, the Elbe–Saale region, and western and southern Ukraine in the sixth century, together with parts of Thrace shortly after 600 AD – the upshot was the more or less complete transfer to a new area of a Korchak-type material culture in all its measurable expressions: lifestyle, technology and social patterns. The only thing that varies between these areas is the shape of some of the pottery. A very different archaeological result is found in many other areas that we know to have been Slavic-dominated, but where recovered archaeological assemblages have produced only isolated Korchak elements in what is overall a much more varied body of material. This pattern prevailed over much of the former Roman Balkans and much of the North European Plain west of the Vistula from the seventh century, where investigation has thrown up only a few Korchak-type ceramics, not the whole system transferred to a new area. Any account of Slavic expansion must account for both of these consequences.

Despite the lack of narrative sources, the translation of whole Korchak-type socioeconomic systems into entirely new landscapes is suggestive of a particular kind of migration process. The standard settlement unit – therefore, presumably, also the socioeconomic one – prevailing in these areas was small. Korchak hamlets typically consist of groupings of no more than ten to twenty small dwellings, each clearly designed for nuclear families. On reflection, these hamlets also provide an indication of the maximum size of the basic migration unit involved in areas that have produced a 'pure' Korchak result. Korchak Europe was clearly created by the spread of such units outwards from the foothills of the Carpathians, and they were moving either as ready-made communities of this kind (the maximum view) or possibly in even smaller groups that came together only at their destination. Korchak dwellings look large enough for about five people, so we're looking here at migration units of no more than fifty to a hundred. Comparing this phenomenon with the different migration forms we have so far encountered, the likeliest process to have produced it was something along the lines of expansion by wave of advance (see page 22). In about one hundred and fifty years, as we have seen, Korchak remains spread from the fringes of the Carpathians to the Lower Elbe, while retaining much of their basic cultural form. The extended chronology of these remains makes clear that this group of Europe's Slavic-speakers was more conservative than once thought. Older chronologies confined Korchak settlements to the fifth and the earlier sixth century, but we now know that some groups maintained this lifestyle for two centuries or more, spreading slowly in small groups across the European landscape.[42]

One caveat, though, needs to be added. As generally conceived, wave of advance is a model of random movement, whereby the build-up of population at one point leads subgroups from that settlement to move on in the next generation to the nearest available piece of suitable land. One application of this model to the spread of Europe's first farming populations suggested that the mathematics of such a process dictate that a population spreading over a landscape by this means might make an aggregate advance of around a kilometre a year. But Korchak Slavs went from the fringes of the Carpathians to the Elbe–Saale region, a distance of around 900 kilometres, in only a hundred and fifty years. This is a sufficiently faster rate to suggest that some of the assumptions normally inherent in the wave-of-advance model did not apply in this case. One possible explanation is that Slavic movement – like the spread of Frankish settlers in northern Gaul – was not random. A Byzantine military treatise called *The Strategicon of Maurice* reports that some Slavs preferred to inhabit wooded uplands rather than more open plains, and the ribbon of Korchak sites through upland central Europe might be taken as some confirmation of this statement. If true, the choice of destination for each new Korchak generation was limited to similar and particular environments, and in fact this does all make a kind of sense. Most of the open plains of Europe were dominated by larger political powers (whether Byzantines, Franks or Avars), so if you wanted to live independently in the kind of small community characteristic of the Korchak world, lowlands were not an option. For Korchak Slavs, migration was a means to carry on traditional lifestyles, including a very small scale of social organization, quite probably at a time of population expansion.[43]

Seventh-century Slavic settlement in the Balkans, by contrast, was undertaken by considerably larger units: tribes, for want of a better word. Around Thessalonica, a series of larger named Slavic groups were already settled in the valley of the River Strymon in the middle years of the seventh century. Our source here, the *Miracles of St Demetrius*, also tells us that another Slavic group mentioned earlier, the Belegezitae, held land somewhere further south. Further south in the Peloponnese, likewise, named Slavic groups existed in the early ninth century – the Milingas and the Ezeritae. The same pattern is also found in ninth-century Slavic Bohemia, and the wider regions covered by the *Anonymous Bavarian Geographer*. In these central European cases, and possibly also the Peloponnese, the larger named groups probably did not migrate as whole units into the regions where the literary sources later find them, but were later evolutionary creations within that landscape from a much more fragmented, wave-of-advance type of migration. Bohemia, at least, was originally settled by Slavic migrants generating a 'pure' Korchak outcome, so that its more organized structure in the ninth century was apparently a later development. It does not seem possible, however, to explain the size and organization of the seventh-century Belegezitae or the other groups settled around Thessalonica as the products of a post-migration process. These areas have produced no evidence of an initial Korchak outcome, and the historical evidence for the tribes' existence dates from shortly after the initial migration. The text of the *Miracles* is contemporary and local, recording an incident of c.670, while the settlement itself, as we've just seen, cannot have happened before the 610s. In this case, the time lag, barely two generations, seems insufficient for a whole new sociopolitical order to have emerged from a flow of extended family units.[44]

So how should we envisage these larger groups? Historical sources consistently describe the early Slavs as living in small sociopolitical units, but how small was small? Some were very small. The Korchak system was probably being transported about the European landscape in the sixth and seventh centuries by social units less than a hundred strong. As an important recent study has rightly stressed, however, other parts of the Slavic-speaking world underwent a major sociopolitical revolution in the sixth century. In the many pages of his histories devoted to a wide range of Slavic activities in the period c.530–60, our east Roman historian Procopius names no individual Slavic leaders at all. In the last quarter of the sixth century, however, the pattern suddenly changes. In a number of different east Roman sources various Slavic leaders appear, with enough circumstantial detail to show that we are dealing with substantial political figures. The territory ruled by a certain Musocius, for instance, took three days to cross, suggesting that it covered somewhere between 100 and 150 kilometres. The rule of another leader, Ardagastus, was solid enough, likewise, to survive for the best part of a decade between 585 and 593. Perigastes had enough forces under his command to kill a thousand east Roman soldiers, while another named figure, Dabritas, was confident enough of his military strength to kill the diplomatic envoys of the Avar Khagan, boasting with the suave masculine charm typical of the period: 'What man has been born, what man is warmed by the rays of the sun who shall make our might his subject? Others do not conquer our land, we conquer theirs.'

Territories extending over a hundred kilometres, even with relatively low population densities, indicate social units of several thousand individuals, and this is confirmed by the one plausible overall figure to survive. After east Roman assault destroyed the domain of Ardagastus, a quarrel broke out between the Romans and the Avars over who should have control of the prisoners. It was eventually decided in the Avars' favour, and the Romans duly handed over five thousand individuals. This figure is consistent with the new Slavic kings of the late sixth century commanding populations of something like ten thousand, but not several tens of thousands. And while not huge, we are clearly talking here of an entirely different order of magnitude from the kind of social units involved in spreading Korchak culture further north. And if we can estimate from the Ardagastus incident a rough figure for the larger Slavic groups that had coalesced on the fringes of east Roman territory by c.600, this would suggest that the four groups settled in the region of Thessalonica comprised between them several tens of thousands of Slavic immigrants. For what it's worth, this also fits with Byzantine reports that a later pacification of the area, in the 680s, involved transferring thirty thousand Slavs to Asia Minor.[45]

Serbs and Croats might represent yet a third type of migrant group caught up in the Slavic diaspora of the sixth and seventh centuries. There is obviously a huge margin for error built into the tenth-century traditions retold by Constantine Porphyrogenitus, but if there is any truth to them at all, the Serbs and Croats were breakaways from the

Avar Empire which had previously used them in a military capacity. Avar campaigns between 570 and 620 were many and varied, and this would provide a plausible context for a further bout of sociopolitical evolution among those Slavs caught up in this latest nomad war machine to establish itself in central Europe, sufficient to produce this third type of Slavic migrant group that was either large enough or militarily specialized enough to throw off Avar domination. It might be the same kind of force as the five thousand militarily 'elite' Slavs who launched a surprise attack on Thessalonica. If so, Serb and Croat migration might have taken the form of a kind of elite transfer, with a militarily effective force breaking out of the Avar Empire and establishing its own niche in the Balkans.[46] This is speculative, but well within the bounds of possibility, and we do have independent contemporary evidence that the evolution of Slavic society was throwing up military specialists at this time. At the very least, it underlines exactly how many and varied were the migratory processes that get lumped together retrospectively to account for the 'Slavicization of Europe'.

A comparison of the historical and archaeological evidence thus sets up a seeming paradox. Those regions of Europe that saw the complete transfer of a Korchak-type material-cultural system also witnessed a Slavic migration process involving only very small social units. On the other hand, the historical evidence for much larger Slavic social units on the move (whether 'tribal' or military specialists – if such, indeed, were the Serbs and Croats) relates to those areas where archaeologists have not uncovered any large-scale transfer of 'complete' Korchak-type socioeconomic systems. This is at first sight surprising. The larger the migration unit, you might suppose, the greater its capacity to import and maintain its own distinctive way of life. When you think about it, though, the larger Slavic social units were actually very recent creations, generated by processes of rapid sociopolitical and economic development that were unfolding among those Slavs closest to the Roman frontier or who became caught up in the Avar Empire. We will return to these processes in Chapter 10, but there is every reason to suppose that much of the momentum behind them was generated by a dynamic interaction between the groups involved and the opportunities and dangers that came their way from an unprecedented proximity to the bigger and materially rich east Roman and Avar Empires. In other words, it was precisely the larger Slavic groups rather than the small-scale farmers of the Korchak world who would have been more open to the kinds of influences and processes that would have caused their patterns of material culture to evolve away from older Korchak-type norms.

Because of the lack of information, there is no point in spending much time on the issue, but it is worth reflecting on what all this suggests about the kind of Slavic migration units which were operating in those contexts that are entirely undocumented in the surviving historical sources: north-central Europe in the seventh and eighth centuries, and European Russia in the eighth and ninth. In central Europe, between the Vistula and the Elbe, archaeologists have revealed a third kind of outcome. The Sukow-Dziedzice culture certainly saw the absorption by incoming Slavs of some existing patterns of indigenous material culture, notably its repertoire of pottery. But the Mogilany culture, which started the process of Slavicization, is really a Korchak variant, and even the Sukow-Dziedzice culture, in its earliest levels, did not depart far from these norms. In its original 'islands' (Map 18), settlement originally came in the form of small open villages, similar in size to the Korchak norm, but the buildings were usually above ground rather than sunken huts. Although they absorbed more of native culture than elsewhere, the original Slavic migration units probably differed little in size from those that created Korchak Europe. Why they should have departed from Korchak norms as far as they did, is a question we will return to in a moment.

For European Russia, the only evidence we have for the migration process is again archaeological and hence, by its nature, indirect. But some of the settlement patterns, like those from Korchak Europe, are again highly suggestive of the type of social unit engaging in the expansionary process, and hence shed at least some light on that process itself. Take, for instance, the Borshevo-era hilltop site at Novotroitskoe in the Psiol valley in northern Ukraine. Here, the steep sides of the hill form natural defences, and the excavators found clustered together about fifty sunken-floored huts dating from the eighth and ninth centuries. This indicates that the total population of the settlement must have been just a few hundred people. The choice and nature of the site itself are enough to suggest that prevailing conditions were far from peaceful, as does the end of this initial period of its occupation, when it was apparently destroyed by raiders. Novotroitskoe is not an isolated example. Romny-Borshevo settlements were customarily situated in highly defensible situations on hilltops or in swamps, often walled, and they generally hosted a similarly dense clustering of population.

All this suggests two things. Most obviously, the progress of Slavic-speakers over this landscape was far from uncontested. You go to the trouble of building this type of settlement only if you need to, and its eventual fate does suggest that it was necessary. Second, and this follows from the first observation, Slavic expansion in this region was probably being conducted by groups big enough to build and maintain settlements of this type. If expansion was contested, small groups could not just pitch up in a new area. They had to come with sufficient strength to construct a settlement in which they could protect themselves and their families.

Despite the lack of historical description, therefore, it seems that the migration units operating from the eighth century in north-western Russia were considerably larger than those that had earlier spread Korchak culture and its variants across the central European uplands and east of the Carpathians into southern Russia and Ukraine. Their defended settlements stand in marked contrast to the small undefended ones of the Korchak, Penkovka and even Kolochin systems of the sixth and seventh centuries, emphasizing the degree to which the later centuries marked a new era in the nature of Slavic expansion. We are still looking here at an expansion that began with something akin to a wave of advance rather than the sudden occupation of an entire landscape, but it evolved over time, until larger social units were eventually moving into contested areas. Overall, Slavic expansion into European Russia may well have taken a form we've seen in other contexts, ancient and modern, where a flow of small-scale social units builds up momentum and is forced to reorganize itself into larger groups when it eventually encounters serious opposition, as the Goths and others did in the third century, the Vikings in the ninth and the Boers in the nineteenth.[47]

The range of evidence available for the nature and scale of Slavic migration flows bears not the remotest resemblance to anything you might consider an ideal data set. But this is all part of the fun of early medieval history, and in any case, it is still sufficient to show that Slavic expansion took a variety of forms, as we would anyway have to suppose given the wide variety of contexts it encompassed. At one end of the spectrum we have the transfer of replica Korchak-type settlements from the foothills of the Carpathians across wide tracts of

central and eastern Europe from the Elbe to Ukraine. In the Romny-
Borshevo era further to the north and east, by contrast, more substantial settlements were the norm, constructed by Slavic population units
several hundred strong. Different again was the movement of entire
'tribes' into the former Roman Balkans in the seventh century, where
the groups may have been up to ten thousand strong, if it is correct to
think of them as the kind of unit run by an Ardagastes or a Perigastes
taking to the road. With so few sources, the details of all this could be
argued over endlessly, and there is a large margin for error. But the
Slavicization of Europe clearly involved a wide range of migratory
activity, with unit sizes extending from family groupings at one
extreme to social units in the thousands at the other.

## Immigrant and Native

Composed around the year 600 AD, the east Roman military treatise
often attributed to the Emperor Maurice (582–602) includes a fascinating comment on the approach of some early Slavic groups to prisoners
taken on their raids:

> They do not keep those who are in captivity among them in
> perpetual slavery, as do other nations. But they set a definite
> period of time for them and then give them the choice either, if
> they so desire, to return to their own homes with a small
> recompense or to remain there as free men and friends.[48]

This immediately raises the basic intellectual problem involved in
trying to understand the astonishing rise to prominence of Slavic-
speakers all the way from the Elbe to the Volga in the early Middle
Ages. On the one hand, there is no one who supposes that this could
have happened without an element of migration: actual Slavic-speakers
on the move across the landscape. On the other, old culture-historical,
quasi-nationalist visions of the Slavs as a 'people', a single population
group that started from one geographical point and then went forth to
multiply over vast tracts of the European landscape, are not credible.
In similar vein, although they did add up in aggregate to substantial
population movements, the earlier, largely Germanic migrations of the
fourth to the sixth century were certainly not large enough to create
entirely empty landscapes in the vast tracts of Europe that were

affected by Germanic culture collapse. Most of these areas reappear in Carolingian sources under new, Slavic, management, but the original Slavic migrants were mostly interacting with an indigenous population. The two key issues we need to explore, therefore, are, first, just how big a demographic event was Slavic migration itself; and, second, what kinds of relationship did incoming Slavs form with the indigenous populations they found at their various points of destination?

Comprehensive information is not available, but there is good reason to suppose that incoming Slavs did encounter a substantially reduced population in areas affected by Germanic culture collapse, and even, in a few localities, some entirely abandoned landscapes. For just a few areas, general settlement surveys are available. In Bohemia, for instance, there seems to have been a substantial decline in population in the late Roman period. Twenty-four major find-spots (mostly cemeteries) are known from the early Roman period, but this declines to just fourteen in late antiquity. Slavic immigrants into Bohemia encountered not an empty landscape, therefore, but certainly a smaller population than the region had previously carried. Elsewhere, pollen diagrams provide further insights. Pollen is carried in the wind and, on landing, will sink to the bottom of standing water. A core can then be extracted from the bottom, particularly of lakes, allowing changes in the varieties of pollen deposited over time to be charted. Continuous activity from an indigenous farming population shows up as an undisturbed pollen sequence, with no great rise in tree or grass pollen, and no major change in the range of cereals being produced. Pollen diagrams are unavailable for much of eastern Europe, but they do indicate that in some places a substantial indigenous pre-Slavic population was not displaced. Samples from the Baltic island of Rügen and from Saaleland show more or less total continuity from the Roman into the Slavic periods, even though both passed into Slavic control at some point before 800 AD. But in other areas, a different picture has emerged. In large parts of Mecklenburg in the former DDR, the pollen diagrams indicate great disruption to established farming patterns in the same period. Here, at least, it would seem, Slavic-era immigrants more or less started farming the landscape again from scratch. Similar evidence for disruption and forest regeneration has also emerged from Biskupin in modern Poland.[49]

Where the pollen gives out, we are forced back on indications of a more general kind. Some again suggest we should not underestimate the demographic component of Slavicization. In Procopius' account, the unfortunate Heruli evicted from the Middle Danube in 512 (Chapter 5) initially passed north through Slavic territory and then into 'empty lands' before eventually finding their way to Scandinavia. The empty area ought to be north-central Europe, somewhere beyond the Moravian Gap, and, on the face of it this seems to indicate a major population decline in that region, since pretty much everywhere between the Moravian gap and Scandinavia had been substantially populated in the Roman period. There is also good reason to think that the migration process would have prompted a considerable population increase among the immigrant Slavs. One limit on human population is the availability of food supplies. When more food is produced, more children survive, there is better resistance to disease, and couples are often allowed to marry younger, with the outcome that populations can increase surprisingly quickly if extra food supplies are available in abundance. In the case of the Slavs there are no figures, but plenty of reason to think that the overall demographic effect would have been large. For one thing, migration brought Slavic-speakers out of the Russian forest zone and on to the generally better soils of central Europe. In addition, Korchak and Penkovka farmers quickly adopted the more efficient type of plough in use in the Roman world and its peripheries by 400 AD, abandoning their original scratch ploughs. The new ploughs allowed them to turn the soil over so that weeds rotted back into it, allowing fertility to be both increased and maintained and making for much higher yields. Even if we cannot put figures on it, we must reckon with migration having generated a substantial population increase among Slavic-speakers, with obvious knock-on effects for their capacity to colonize new lands in central Europe. Not all Slavs will have scored the threefold personal increase in population achieved by the Frankish merchant Samo, who produced twenty-two sons and fifteen daughters with just a little help, of course, from his twelve wives, but population increase was a genuine phenomenon.[50]

At the same time, other indications reinforce the pollen evidence from Rügen and Saaleland. The Sukow-Dziedzice system, covering much of what is now Poland, has thrown up much pottery of standard Korchak types, but, as we have seen, its remains are really distinctive for their strikingly wide range of pot-types. In addition to the standard Korchak cooking pots (which tend towards wider-mouthed, more open forms than the Korchak norm), Sukow-Dziedzice sites customarily throw up a wide range of plain medium-sized jars, globular bowls and jar-bowls. Much of the non-Korchak pottery looks in fact like hand-made versions of the kind of wheel-made pottery that was being made in the same region by Przeworsk potters in the final century or so of Germanic domination. These resemblances could have been generated by Korchak potters coming across Przeworsk ceramics in abandoned settlements, but this kind of imitation is not found anywhere else. Much more likely, we are looking at the results of an interaction between Korchak Slavs and an indigenous post-Przeworsk population that was still living in situ.[51]

The range of available evidence – some specific, some more general – makes it clear that the demographic significance of Germanic culture collapse and Slavic immigration is not simple to predict. A substantial peasant population remained at work in at least some parts of old Germanic Europe, despite the population movements of the fourth to the sixth century. The Bohemian evidence suggests, however, that we may have to reckon with a general thinning-out of the indigenous population, which, as the pollen diagrams show, could even lead in places to the wholesale abandonment of farming: a pattern that is found in many of the fringes of the Roman Empire in the period after its collapse.[52] When you also add to the picture that the Slavic-speaking populations involved in the migratory process would have been increasing in numbers as they applied more-developed farming techniques to better soils, then it does seem that Slavic immigration must be considered a major demographic event, even if it did not everywhere, or even often, take the form of recolonizing abandoned territories.

It is now such a mantra in some circles that migration never happened in the first millennium on a large enough scale to have a major demographic (as opposed to political or cultural) impact, that it is worth dwelling on this point a little further. It is certainly true, when dealing with hierarchically stratified societies, that the kind of culture collapse associated with the disappearance of a social elite need not represent much of a population exodus. As we saw earlier, according to the *Chronicle of Monemvasia*, the arrival of Slavs in the Peloponnese prompted the total evacuation of its native Greek population. When the Slavs around Patras revolted in the early ninth century, however, there was a native Greek-speaking population living alongside them.

Possibly, the Greek-speakers had all returned from Calabria in the meantime, but this seems unlikely. And logistically, the sea-borne evacuation of an entire region would have been impossible, given the kind of shipping available. In parallel circumstances in the west, only wealthy members of the landowning class, those with some movable wealth, tended to flee.

That similar patterns surely prevailed in the Peloponnese, despite the *Chronicle*'s report to the contrary, is suggested by reactions elsewhere in the Balkans to the build-up of Slavic pressure. Another admittedly late chronicle source, though one usually taken to be drawing on much earlier information, reports that Salona in the northwest fell to the Slavs when panic swept through the city following the discovery that its notables had been moving their goods on to ships in the harbour. In similar vein, Constantine Porphyryogenitus reports that the inhabitants of Ragusa still remembered that their city had been founded by immigrants fleeing from Pitaura. It goes on to list them by name: Gregory, Asclepius, Victorinus, Vitalius, Valentinian the archdeacon and Valentinian the father of Stephen the *protospatharius*. A *protospatharius* was a high-ranking court dignitary, which, together with the mention of an archdeacon, makes this sound like the exodus of a small group of notables – presumably also with their households and retainers – rather than the mass transfer of an entire population.[53] Culture collapse and elite migration in a Roman context, therefore, probably only involved a small percentage of the population, and it is likely that immigrant Slavs within the Balkans were always closely coexisting with a substantial indigenous population.

The socioeconomic patterns of Germanic Europe in the late Roman period, however, were very different. Despite the major transformations of the previous four centuries, it remained nothing like so hierarchically stratified as late Roman or early Byzantine society. New Germanic elites did emerge between the first and fourth century AD, but still represented a much larger percentage of the total population than the tiny landowning class which dominated the Roman world. As we saw in Chapter 2, everything suggests that we must think in terms of social and political power shared between a fairly broad oligarchy of freemen, not a small aristocracy. And participation in the *Völkerwanderung*, likewise, was not limited just to this dominant oligarchy. At least two social strata of warriors appear in some of the intrusive groups alongside an unspecified number of slaves, adding up, on occasion, to groups of ten thousand-plus fighting men, together with women and children.[54] The emigration of this kind of social elite, with its many adherents, would have an entirely different effect upon a region from that of a few Roman notables and their households. None of this denies, however, that much of north-central Europe remained home to an indigenous population at the time of Slavic migratory expansion.

So how does the evidence suggest that we should characterize relations between native and immigrant populations, both here and elsewhere, such as the Balkans and European Russia, where Slavic-speakers came into contact with indigenous societies?

One recent approach to the problem has started with the *Strategi-con*'s report firmly in mind, and taken the argument further on the strength of some general observations about the material-cultural effects of the rise of Slavic domination in central and eastern Europe. Its most striking effect was the replacement (at least in the areas affected by Germanic culture collapse) of the bigger and the more complex with the smaller and simpler, in pretty much every aspect of life from pottery technology to settlement size. This simplification, it is argued, wasn't just an incidental effect of population elements from the woods of eastern Europe – who had very simple lifestyles anyway – taking over large parts of the landscape, but a key reason for their success. What we're observing, in this view, is not so much the takeover of a Slavic population as the spread of an attractive cultural model, energetically seized upon by non-militarized indigenous peasant populations of central Europe left over after the old elites had departed south and west for Roman territory. In effect, the Slavs are recast as the champions of an alternative lifestyle, early medieval hippy travellers who found widespread support, unlike their later counter-parts in Mrs Thatcher's Britain of the 1980s. As Procopius reports, vigorously egalitarian and dramatic, if primitive, ideologies prevailed among the Slavs of his day, and this, it has been argued, was very attractive to peasants who had been labouring hard to provide sur-pluses which the militarized elites of Germanic central Europe had previously exploited.[55] This model is really describing Slavicization as a process of non-elite transfer and cultural emulation, where a few immigrants, but above all a way of life, spread across large parts of central Europe on being adopted by a substantial indigenous popula-tion. How well does this model fit the available data?

At least in some places, the incoming Slavic migrants did treat the indigenous population more generously than would appear to have been the case, for instance, in Anglo-Saxon England. There was certainly some assimilation. The *Strategicon* does suggest that some early Slavic groups were remarkably 'open' in terms of their group identity, being willing, as we have seen, to accept prisoners as full and equal members of their own society. This is remarkable. Many societies are willing to take in outsiders, but it is more usual for the latter to have to adopt, at least initially, relatively inferior social positions. Full equality was clearly not an offer being made, for instance, by Germanic groups of the 'Migration Period'. These came out of the migration process with their well-entrenched social distinctions between the two statuses of warrior and slaves intact – top status had clearly not been on offer to all the new recruits they had picked up on the way. With little, seemingly, in the way of original social hierarchies to protect, however, a willingness to attract recruits seems to have been of higher priority to some early Slavic groups, who erected no substantial barriers to the admission of outsiders. Beyond the *Strategicon*, we have no narrative descriptions of this process in action, but it finds some confirmation in the Samo story. Here was an outsider, a Frankish merchant, who showed the right qualities and ended up as a figure of authority among the Sorbs and other Slavs of the Avar/Frankish frontier region.[56]

The absorption of outsiders surely also operated at less exalted social levels. The population increase generated by better farming methods does not seem remotely enough to account for the immense areas of the European landscape that had come to be dominated by Slavs from c.800 AD. This even remains the case if you also suppose, which I tend to, that the Slavic language family had evolved before the middle of the first millennium AD, and that, consequently, Slavic-speakers were more broadly dispersed in c.500 AD than identifying them exclusively with Korchak remains would suggest. The creation of an almost entirely Slavic Europe from the Elbe to the Volga does seem, therefore, to call for a large element of population absorption. This of course would provide the historical context in which Slavic-speakers acquired more advanced farming technologies from their neighbours, and, in the case of the Sukow-Dziedzice system, more developed ceramic repertoires.[57] This is not to advocate a return to old nationalist ideas of indigenous 'submerged Slavs' between the Oder and the Vistula triumphantly re-emerging from Germanic domination. Far from it: frankly, we have no idea what linguistic and cultural identity the leftover peasantry of this region are likely to have had after Germanic culture collapse – but presumably Germanic, if anything, since they had been under Germanic domination for several hundred years. But whatever it was, their longer-term trajectory was to be absorbed into the evolving norms of a Slavic cultural context. Such a large-scale absorption, it is worth underlining, is perfectly in line with modern studies of ethnicity, which make it clear that, according to circumstance, groups erect stronger or weaker barriers around themselves. The early Slavs – or some of them at least – would be an example of a group erecting only a very porous frontier between themselves and outsiders, and this, of course, is what the report of Maurice's *Strategicon* suggests. It is also worth pointing out that this is a unique comment, not a topos trundled out every time Roman authors discuss barbarians.

That said, however, it is extremely important not just to jump from this evidence to the conclusion that the Slavs took over huge expanses of Europe more or less peacefully. In the former East German Republic in the Soviet era, it was ideologically highly desirable to find cases of Slavs living peacefully alongside a native Germanic-speaking population, and the evidence was manipulated accordingly. During these years a corpus of sites was identified where, so the claim went, Germans and Slavs had lived peacefully side by side for some time. Two were in Berlin (Berlin-Marzahn and Berlin-Hellersdorf), the others spread more widely, Dessau-Mosigkau and Tornow being the most prominent.

The collapse of the Berlin Wall has prompted important revisions. That late Germanic and early Slavic materials had been found on the same sites in these instances was clear enough, but, under reinvestigation, the case for simultaneous occupation has failed to stand up. At Berlin-Hellersdorf, the Germanic and Slavic moments of occupation were separated from one another by a layer of deposited sediment. On the face of it, this denied simultaneous Slavic and Germanic occupation, and carbon-14 datings made since 1989 have confirmed the point. At Berlin-Marzahn, similarly, carbon-14 dates for the Germanic-period materials range from 240 to 400 AD, those for the Slavic from 660 to 780 AD. In this case, the carbon-14 datings merely confirmed an earlier dendrochronological date of the eighth century for some wood from the Slavic phase. Looking to prove coexistence, the original excavator considered this dendrochronological date too 'unlikely' to be worth publishing.[58] The later Slavic expansion in north-western Russia, as we have seen, looks too contested, likewise, for immigrant/native relations in that context to be characterized as fundamentally peaceful. Not all the evidence for peaceful interaction is flawed, but neither is it the only type of interaction documented in our sources.

In the longer term, as the cultural and linguistic transformation that came over central and eastern Europe in the second half of the millennium makes clear, Slavic-speakers became a dominating force right across this landscape. Slavic society may have been open to outsiders, but open to outsiders who were willing to join it and become Slavs in every sense of the word. The world created by Slavic immigration shows no sign of migrants and natives happily agreeing to differ over lifestyles. On the contrary, it generated a monolithic cultural form in which the Slavic contribution was dominant. The Slavs did not just insert themselves into the society of central Europe at the head of structures that already existed, so we are not looking here at some variant of a Norman Conquest model of elite transfer. What they did was redefine social norms along lines dictated by themselves. In other words, longer-term Slavicization was a bit like Romanization: the generation of an all-encompassing new socioeconomic and political order, with powerful cultural overtones, which became the only game in town. In the end, affected populations had no real choice about whether to join in or not, and Slavic became the predominant language right across this huge territory.

You have to wonder, too, how long Slavic societies remained so open to outsiders joining it on equal terms. Certainly by c.800 AD, as we will explore in more detail in Chapter 10, some of these new societies were becoming more stratified, with a distinctly predatory attitude to prisoners. By this date, prisoners were no longer being absorbed as equals but recycled into a highly profitable slave trade. The absence, before the ninth century, of real material cultural differentiation clearly reflecting the existence of an elite might lead you to think that the closing of Slavic society to outsiders was a relatively late phenomenon. But, as we have seen before, elites can exist without consumer goods. Having servile dependants to do all the back-breaking work of farming, while you eat more and enjoy more leisure, can give 'elite' real meaning, even when you don't possess lots of shiny goods.

It is also important to remember that although the first historically documented Slavs operated in small social groups – some of them very small – this did not make them all notably peaceful. Smallish groups of Slavs raided the Roman Balkans almost continuously from the mid-sixth century, and quickly acquired a warlike reputation. Some of the prisoners who fell into their hands received conspicuously ungenerous treatment. The fifteen thousand Roman prisoners impaled outside the city of Topirus in 549, or those others killed in 594 when their Slavic captors were surrounded, would have found the *Strategicon's* comments about Slavic generosity towards captives less than convincing.[59] The more organized Slavic groups of Serbs and Croats, if we may trust the *De Administrando Imperio*, were probably even more formidable, since they were capable of throwing off Avar domination. When thinking about the Slavicization of Europe, then, it is important to see that Slavic expansion was occurring at a point where Slavic society was itself already in the throes of major transformations. One of the results were armed groups of great military competence, and it is extremely unlikely, where these kinds of groups were operating, that Slavicization was being carried forward solely by processes of peaceful absorption.

While accepting that the *Strategicon's* account of ethnic openness did apply to some of them, an overly romantic vision of the early Slavs must be avoided. Slavic expansion was carried forward by a range of groups of very different kinds and with different motivations, and it is likely that they responded to the indigenous populations they encountered in a variety of ways. In some parts of north-central Europe, Slavic immigration generated the recolonization of lands left empty by Germanic migrants of the *Völkerwanderung* era, or the primary exploitation of upland wooded agricultural niches that had previously not proved attractive. Where indigenous populations survived, but not much in the way of state structures, by contrast, Slavic immigration probably amounted to a kind of 'elite re-creation', somewhat along the lines of what happened in early Anglo-Saxon England or north-eastern Gaul. Here new immigrant–native amalgams were eventually generated. But, even if some Slavic groups were particularly open to outsiders, and overall the process was maybe more peaceful than anything seen in Gaul or England, the immigrants did come to dominate – in thoroughly monolithic fashion – the new societies created.[60]

Overall, and despite the lack of figures, there is no doubt that, in the qualitative terms used in modern comparative studies, Slavic expansion must count as an example of mass migration. Politically and culturally, the shock is overwhelmingly clear at the receiving end of the migration flow. Most of the Balkan peninsula, central Europe as far west as the Elbe, much of Ukraine and a huge region of western Russia came to be dominated by Slavic-speakers in the three or four centuries after 500 AD. This was new. Many of these territories had previously been dominated by Germanic- and Baltic-speakers, or formed part of the east Roman Empire. It could be objected – given the gaps in the evidence – that Slavic expansion was much more of a slow process than a genuine 'shock'. And there is something in this argument. Germanic culture collapse indicates that in some of the areas affected by the extension of Slavic power, a first major shock had already happened before the Slavs arrived. Even taking a minimalist view of this phenomenon, the disappearance of a sociopolitical elite and several hundred years' worth of continuous material-cultural tradition was no insignificant event, and certainly paved the way for Slavic expansion in the form of very small migration units. Elsewhere, however, the creation of Slavic power was both sudden, and the product of violent self-assertion. Up to the 610s, east Roman forces had just about held the Danube line against their Slavic antagonists, preventing raiding from turning into settlement. It was at that point that the frontier collapsed, and large-scale settlement quickly followed. And as the fortified settlements of the Romny-Borshevo era also emphasize, there is no reason to suppose that the Balkans was the only area in which Slavic expansion was a hotly contested phenomenon, requiring larger and more aggressive migration units.

The migration process also administered a huge shock – measured in terms of economic and sociopolitical dislocation – for at least some of the Slavs themselves. Our knowledge of the Slavs before their diaspora is limited, except for the fact that they originated somewhere in the eastern stretches of the Great European Plain. As we have seen, the general character of Korchak-type systems bears witness to populations practising a very simple form of mixed farming, with few material possessions, and this broadly corresponds to descriptions of early Slavic society in east Roman literary sources, which again stress its poverty, simplicity and relatively egalitarian nature. Migration eventually changed all this, if at different speeds for different Slavic-speaking groups. One population element affected from a very early date was the specialist warrior class which quickly emerged in the foothills of the Carpathians to take advantage of the raiding opportunities provided by their new proximity to the Balkan provinces of the Roman Empire. In the longer term, these changes were to spread much more widely through Slav-dominated lands.[61] But if there is no real doubt that Slavic expansion must be considered a mass migration, why did it happen at all, and why did its processes unfold as they did?

## Migration, Development and the Slavs

With Slavic expansion encompassing so many types of migration unit, functioning in so many contexts, we should not be surprised that a wide range of motivations operated within them. Some Slavs were on the move for largely voluntary and economic motives. This is true most obviously of the Slavic raiders of the Roman Balkans in the sixth century, whose activities were entirely concerned with siphoning off part of the movable wealth available there. Raiding was one method of doing this, but Slavic auxiliary troops are also found in Roman employ in these years – another means to the same end. The Antae, in particular, seem to have benefited from becoming licensed Roman allies from the 530s. In broad terms, it was the initial moves of the Sclavenes and Antae into Moldavia and Wallachia south and east of the Carpathians that brought them close enough to the east Roman Empire to make these different kinds of money-making activity possible. There is no reason to think that this wasn't one of the aims behind the original move.

The material benefits accruing to certain elements, at least, within the Slavic world from all the migratory activity of the fifth to the eighth century are also obvious if you compare the Slavic material culture at the beginning with that of the end of the era. More sophisticated metalwork, including some in precious metals, a greater range of material goods, and even some differentiated housing – all appeared in these years to the benefit particularly of the warrior classes, who became able to take advantage of the new opportunities that were now available as a consequence of their greater proximity to developed Europe. Obviously, this is to reconstruct motivation not on the basis of direct evidence but from actions and their consequences, but it seems reasonable nonetheless.[62] It also means that Slavic migration – or some of it – falls into a pattern we have encountered before, whereby groups from a less developed periphery moved into contact with imperial Europe or its immediate hinterland, where new opportunities for gathering wealth existed in abundance. It would also put Slavic migration firmly in line with one of the essential conclusions of modern migration studies: inequalities of wealth and development provide one fundamental stimulus to migration.

But as Slavic expansion unfolded, the integration of outermost periphery and imperial Europe reached a new intensity. Slavic-speakers originated somewhere within the very simple farming societies that spread east of the Vistula and north of the Carpathians in the first half of the millennium, as we have seen, whether or not you believe Jordanes' account of them as an offshoot of the Venedi. At that point, they were part of a world that had never come into serious contact with the Roman Empire, even though it lasted for half a millennium. This prompts an extremely important question. If it is fair enough to think of the Slavs as wanting to move out of the periphery in order to expand their wealth-grabbing opportunities, as the historical and archaeological evidence broadly suggests, we still need to explain why this started to happen in the later fifth and sixth centuries, and not before. There had been countless other chances for them to make these kinds of wealth-generating moves over the preceding five hundred years, and yet they didn't. Why did this process start to unfold when it did?

The likeliest answer to this, in my view, has two dimensions. The first is straightforward, bringing us back to the revolution generated by the rise and fall of the Huns on the fringes of the Roman Empire. Arguments will continue over the demographic scale of the Germanic migrations, but their political impact on the previously Germanic-dominated periphery of the Roman world is incontrovertible. The result of two waves of invasion, in 376–80 and 405–8, followed by the knock-on effects of the struggle for control of the Middle Danube after Attila's death, was, as we have seen, dramatically to reduce the number of Germanic-dominated power blocks operating in central and eastern

Europe and the amount of territory that they controlled. Whatever its wider demographic significance, Germanic culture collapse certainly reflected the disappearance from central and eastern Europe of militarily effective, larger-scale political structures. This played a key role in making possible subsequent Slavic expansion into the Roman periphery, because it eliminated many of the intermediate Germanic powers that had previously monopolized the profitable positions to be had just beyond the imperial frontier. Slavic-speakers could now move into that periphery because the organized, armed groups were out of the way.

The point is worth developing just a little further. To benefit from the money-making advantages brought by proximity to the Roman frontier, Slavic groups had to transform themselves into more structured entities with greater military potential. This was, of course, a two-way process, since the movable wealth extracted from the Empire in turn provided the new Slavic leaders of the late sixth century with the powers of patronage they required to be successful. The degree of reorganization that would have been required in the Roman period, when ambitious incoming Slavs would have been competing with the already well-organized, largely Germanic client states who then occupied the frontier zone, would have been much greater, and hence that much more difficult to bring about. Such reorganization would also have had to happen out in the forests of the eastern stretches of the Great European Plain before the Slavic groups concerned could have begun to move into a profitable slot in the periphery. Otherwise, they would not have been able to compete with the sitting Germanic tenants. It is hard to imagine any leader finding sufficient resources in these localities in the first half of the millennium to muster enough followers to mount an effective challenge. The rise and fall of the Hunnic Empire created a relative power vacuum north of the Lower Danube frontier, which allowed the smaller armed Slavic groups to move in.

The second dimension is more hypothetical, but follows on from this. If the initial crystallization zone of those Slavs who were to come into contact with the Roman Balkans in the sixth century has been correctly identified as Polesie, or certainly the foothills of the Carpathians, in the fourth century, it fell within the confines of the largely Gothic-dominated Cernjachov system (Chapter 3). This would suggest that their initial transformation arose as a response to that Gothic domination, as part of a process of reformation designed to throw off or at least minimize its worst effects. Like the Hunnic or Avar Empires, the Černjachov system presumably demanded of indigenous subject peoples that they provide economic support in the form of food supplies, and possibly also military manpower. In this context, it is perhaps significant that the first appearance of any Slavic-speaking group in a late antique historical narrative is in the context of conflict with some Goths. Jordanes reports that one of the great victories of the Gothic leader Vinitharius, who ruled in the mid-fifth century, was over some Antae:

> When [Vinitharius] attacked them, he was beaten in the first encounter. Thereafter he did valiantly and, as a terrible example, crucified their king, named Boz, together with his sons and seventy nobles, and left their bodies hanging to double the fear of those who had surrendered.[63]

One example can't prove that a whole process was under way, but the pattern here is suggestive. As is so often the case with modern examples too, even what appears to be economically motivated migration has significant political dimensions. Without the political changes generated by the Huns, even the new militarily improved Slavic-speaking communities would have had difficulty in acquiring the new economic opportunities of a frontier position that came their way so much more easily once their former Germanic overlords were out of the way.

Moving beyond the first half of the sixth century, the balance between economic and political motives varied substantially between different elements of the Slavic migration flows. The motivation behind the spread of Korchak-type, extended familial settlements across the central European uplands can probably be partly explained in terms of population growth, generated not just by the absorption of outsiders but also by the increased availability of food supplies. But even Korchak-type expansion may have had its political dimension. For one thing, Korchak drift must have been greatly facilitated by the struggles that drove Goths, Heruli, Sueves, Rugi and others out of the Middle Danube region and sucked the Lombards south into it from Bohemia and beyond (Chapter 5). These conflicts were under way in the later fifth and the earlier sixth century, precisely when Korchak Slavic-speakers were spreading westwards from the Carpathians, and must have eased their takeover of Moravia and Bohemia. There may also have been a second political dimension to the motivations of Korchak groups. As we have seen, these migrants, moving as small-scale farming communities, need to be distinguished from the larger and more militarized Slavic entities that were simultaneously evolving further east and south through direct contact with the east Roman Empire. Given this, the Korchak-type migrants may also have been on the move so as to avoid being sucked into the orbits of these new and more powerful Slavic polities. Post-nationalist perspectives apply to Slavs too. You cannot assume a strong sense of community between different Slavic populations just because they all spoke related languages, and the Korchak-type migrants were making very different life choices from their cousins, preoccupied as they were with thoughts of Roman wealth. One incentive behind those choices could have been to avoid the latter's unwelcome and predatory attentions.

The rise of Avar power also added its own momentum to the Slavic migratory process. The Avar Empire operated in broadly similar ways to its Hunnic predecessor, in that its power depended upon subordinated allied groups who provided it with military manpower and economic support. It was, in short, a hegemony, established by military conquest and maintained by intimidation. East Roman historical sources preserve numerous instances of the determined efforts of Avar Khagans not to lose face even in defeat, since any sign of weakness was always a signal for some of their more disaffected subjects to rebel. The historian Menander preserves one particularly beautiful example, in which an Avar leader whose siege of Singidunum (modern Belgrade) was failing asked for a large gift from the city's commander, so that he could retreat with his honour intact. Even more dramatically, in 626 when the Avars' last stratagem for the capture of Constantinople failed and their Slavic footsoldiers began to run away, the Avars began to kill them.[64]

The militarizing Slavs of the Carpathian region thus made potentially useful subjects for the Avars, who quickly attached some of them to their train. In pursuit of this aim, the Avars were willing to be employed by the Roman state to attack Slavic groups in the early 570s and 580s, and at one point were even ferried down the Danube in Roman ships to attack some Slavs who were causing trouble on the frontier (probably in the Banat region and Wallachia) southwest and south respectively of the Carpathians. Slavic groups were not generally brought into this new nomad Empire by peaceful negotiation, and enjoyed, if that's the right word, thoroughly ambivalent relations with their Avar masters. On the one hand, as we have already seen, there is a real sense in which the Avar war machine (with Persian and Arab assistance) blew a hole in the east Roman defences of the Balkans, and made possible the large-scale Slavic settlement there of the seventh century. On the other, Avar domination was itself something that many Slavic groups wanted to avoid – or to throw off, having once fallen foul of it. The Serbs and Croats who settled in the Balkans reportedly did precisely this, as we have seen, as did the Sorbs further west under the leadership of Samo. Fredegar, our source for this incident, is explicit as to the causes of revolt:

> Whenever the [Avars] took the field against another people, they stayed encamped in battle array while the [Slavs] did the fighting . . . Every year the [Avars] wintered with the Slavs, sleeping with their wives and daughters, and in addition the Slavs paid tribute and endured many other burdens.[65]

Avar domination thus provided yet more reasons for Slavic groups to move out of the Carpathian and Middle Danubian regions. First, while the initial spread of Korchak-type communities clearly had other origins, having begun before the Avars became a factor, their further spread from Bohemia towards the Saale and beyond the Elbe after the mid-sixth century will have had the extra motivation of seeking to avoid absorption into the exploitative Avar Empire. This may well have prompted the spread of Slavic-speakers northwards into Poland at more or less the same time.[66] Second, Avars were responsible for the spread of the larger 'tribal' Slavic communities into the Balkans after 610, which would have been impossible if the former had not destroyed Roman frontier security. But these were the same Slavs who had been alternately fighting and serving the Avars over the previous fifty years, so there is every reason to suppose that they also wanted to put themselves, not to mention their wives and children, out of the latter's reach. Third, again like the Huns, the Avars resettled some subject peoples around their core dominions on the Great Hungarian Plain. Historical sources document them doing this, amongst others, with Bulgars and Gepids, and with communities of Roman prisoners taken from the Balkans. The archaeological evidence also suggests that they were doing the same with those Slavic groups that they particularly dominated.[67]

Motivation and context thus go a long way towards explaining the variety of migratory process observable among the Slavs. That Slavic expansion was carried forward sometimes by larger groups and sometimes by smaller, sometimes peacefully and sometimes much more aggressively, should not disconcert us. Sometimes the prevailing motivation was political, sometimes economic. Which of these dominated in the case of the expansion out on to the East European Plain from the seventh century onwards is impossible to say in the absence of historical accounts of the action and of its political contexts. The groups who moved east of the Dnieper in the later period quickly began to profit from the fur and slave trades which began to build up in this region from the eighth century, as we shall see in Chapter 10, but whether this was the reason that brought them into those lands, or an accidental consequence of the move, is impossible to say.


## MIGRATION AND SLAVIC EUROPE


As a response to inequalities of wealth and development, in its complex interplay of economic and political motivations, and in the determinative influence upon its various outcomes exercised by surrounding political structures, Slavic migration flows of the later fifth century and beyond worked themselves out in ways that are analogous to their more modern counterparts. Some of these migration units consisted of 'whole' population groups of men, women and children of all ages, like some of those we have already encountered in the Germanic world. These kinds of unit, as we have seen before, reflect the particularities of first-millennium conditions and are comparatively rare in the modern world. But, in general terms, the comparison works. The nature and direction of Slavic migration flows are in accord with the deeper principles behind modern flows. There are also some particular ways in which Slavic migration strongly resembles better-documented population flows of more recent eras.

It is commonly the case that a few individuals, often younger males, make the first moves into a new area. From these, knowledge of the new opportunities gradually spreads back across the broader population. Slavic raids into the Balkans in the sixth century, the precursor to full settlment after 610, in a sense functioned in this fashion. The young men conducting these raids built up a good knowledge of the routes and possibilities of the region through (sometimes bitter) experience, and this knowledge informed the full-scale migrations of the seventh century. The new and better-grounded chronology for the western spread of Korchak migrants through upland central Europe shows, likewise, that this process of migration took much longer than used to be thought. This means, amongst other things, that participating groups had plenty of time to build up an active knowledge of the next destination in between moves, and this must have been crucial to the process. In modern examples, an active body of (not necessarily accurate) information about the point of destination plays a hugely important role in both stimulating and channelling migration flows. Just as the pattern whereby many of the longer-distance fifth-century Germanic migrants moved in discrete 'jumps', with lengthy breaks in between, must in part be attributed to the need to build up information, so the same seems true of Slavic groups of the sixth and seventh centuries.[68]

Fully in line with modern migration flows, too, is the fact that the same Slavic population groups seem to have participated in not just one, but several moves spread out over a number of generations. As modern studies stress, a migration habit is something that builds up within a given population. When friends and relatives migrate, or are remembered to have done so in the past, this increases the likelihood that migration will be adopted as a life strategy by other members of the same population group. The Slavic migration profile fits this pattern perfectly. The – probable – original move into Moldavia and Wallachia in the late fifth and the early sixth century was followed two or three generations later by a further move by the descendants of many of these original migrants on to the territory of the east Roman Balkans. In the meantime, successive generations were also moving both east and west into Ukraine and the uplands of central Europe, and then both of these strands threw out ribbons of northern expansion as well, all of this taking several generations to unfold. Migration clearly became a well-entrenched life strategy among many Slavic populations, so that, as knowledge of the surrounding districts grew, new migrants were ready to intrude themselves there, with previous successful outcomes adding their own momentum to their migration habit.

A propensity to adopt movement as a life strategy, moreover, was probably pre-programmed into the first Slavic migrants of the later fifth century by the limitations of their agricultural technology. Whoever they were exactly, we know that the first Slavs originated somewhere north of the Carpathians and east of the Vistula. While firmly agriculturalists rather than nomads in any real sense of the word, the populations of this region lacked the farming technology before 500 AD to maintain the fertility of their fields for any length of time, and hence tended to shift settlement site every generation or so. This was still true for a century or more into the second half of the millennium. Recent excavations of the early Slavic village of Dulcinea in Wallachia have shown that this settlement of ten to fifteen houses shifted its site on several occasions in response to the need to open up new arable fields. Like the Germani of the early Roman period who renegotiated small-scale mobility into larger-scale migration, the fact that Slavic-speaking farmers were not so rigidly tied to a particular piece of land surely made them readier to respond to the new opportunities created by the implosion of the old largely Germanic-dominated peripheries of the Roman Empire.[69] This involved movement in a new direction and on a much larger scale, but these were already mobile populations well equipped for the challenge.

Whether Slavic expansion also generated a significant amount of return migration, an ever-present epiphenomenon of modern population flows, is, however, unclear. Apart from raiders returning home after successful expeditions, no return migration is mentioned in any of our historical sources. On the other hand, the archaeological evidence for Korchak expansion north and eastwards from the Carpathians into Russia and northern Ukraine in the seventh century and beyond might represent an analogous process, if the initial impetus towards Slavic migration had come from this direction. Return migration is usually generated by the impact of the emotional and other costs of transporting yourself to a new environment, as well as by any failure to succeed at the point of destination. In this case, the rise of Avar power, with all the demands it made upon the subordinated Slavic populations, as much as any inherent love of the east European forests, might have prompted Korchak migrants to change direction.

But this is highly speculative, and there are other possibilities. The more advanced agricultural techniques picked up from the developed world, combined with their new military capacities, alternatively, might have given those Slavic groups who had initially moved into the sub-Carpathian region a strategic advantage over what had originally been their peer populations of European Russia, which then allowed them to expand over time at the latter's expense.

Transport logistics, finally, do not seem to have played much of a role in shaping Slavic migration. Unlike the Anglo-Saxons they had no seas to cross, although when raiding the Roman Balkans major rivers such as the Danube or the Save could be problematic. As mentioned earlier, in 550/1 three thousand Slavic raiders each had to pay the Gepids a gold coin to be ferried out of Roman territory, but this may reflect a need for speed rather than a basic inability to handle water. In the early 610s, Slavs used dugouts to great effect to raid around the coast of Greece, and a fleet of similar boats was employed, if to no military effect, during the Avar-led siege of Constantinople in 626. The great European river systems probably posed no major problems to migrating Slavs, therefore, especially since, lacking much in the way of material possessions, they seem to have moved without the huge baggage trains that accompanied their Germanic counterparts of the fifth century. At least, no source ever reports that the Slavs used wagons, and this was certainly true of Slavic raiders, who were able to move independently of the Roman road network in the Balkans in a way that the Goths of a Theoderic or an Alaric could not. Whether this was also true of the larger Slavic units who settled in the vicinity of Thessalonica is unclear, but it is perhaps implied by the main line of advance westward through the central European uplands chosen by Korchak groups, where wagons would have been a liability.[70]

It is just possible, indeed, that we should view the whole phenomenon of Korchak-type assemblages as a kind of migration strategy. The usual view of their characteristic combination of sunken huts and plain pottery has been to stress their technological simplicity and, by extension, the relative backwardness of Europe's first documented Slavic-speakers. Recently, however, it has been pointed out that, even if simple, these materials are all well made and would have performed their functions verey effectively. More particularly, it has been suggested that Korchak assemblages represent a pared-down version of contemporary Slavic material culture designed precisely to facilitate movement. The point about Slavic material culture being thoroughly fit for purpose is surely well taken, and a reasonable counterpoint to any tendency to dismiss the historical significance of its bearers. Given the general lifestyle of the European Russian populations from which the Slavs emerged, though, there may be a more straightforward explanation of overall Korchak simplicity: namely, that it reflects the starting point from which subsequent Slavic material complexity developed, rather than a particular form of material culture geared towards migration. But if contemporary and obviously related Slavic sites of greater complexity than the Korchak norm should come to light, the case will obviously acquire greater force.[71]

Any discussion of Slavic migration keeps encountering the limitations of the available source materials. The processes that unfolded from the later fifth century and which underlay the eventual spread of named Slavic groups right across the landscape of European Russia by the end of the millennium are largely hidden from us. Much of the action further west is similarly obscure, especially the human history that underlay the spread of the Sukow-Dziedzice system north and west from central Poland. Even the Slavic occupation of the Balkans, comparatively well documented as it is, poses many puzzles. How exactly did Serbs and Croats overthrow Avar dominion, and what was the precise original nature of these groups? In some areas, we can reasonably hope for further enlightenment. No new historical sources are likely to be discovered, but more archaeological materials will be found, and interpreted in a more sophisticated way. At some point, therefore, we will probably have a clearer idea of the extent to which Slavic migration operated in demographically sparse, as well as politically fragmented, landscapes, and of the extent of any surviving Germanic- or other-speaking indigenous populations in the areas affected. The chronology in particular of the Sukow-Dziedzice system will surely also become much more certain.

For the present, it is the complexity of the overall Slavic migration process that should be stressed: it took a variety of forms, and unfolded at different times and in different places. In some contexts, small population units generated movement patterns resembling those predicted by the wave-of-advance model, although the Korchak passage through upland central Europe was perhaps not so random. In others, the same kind of original flow then seems to have increased in momentum, as resistance increased and the migrants (like their Gothic,

Boer and Viking analogues) were forced to reorganize themselves and move in larger groups. This, at least, is what the larger walled settlement units characteristic of Slavic spread into the more north-easterly reaches of the Great European Plain suggest. Elsewhere, still larger units several thousand strong seem to have operated together in smaller versions of the modified invasion hypothesis that we have already observed among Germanic migrants, particularly when the larger units formed on the fringes of the east Roman Balkans in the later sixth century then started to annex land within it in the seventh. The wave-of-advance-like variants seem to correlate with more voluntary, economically motivated displacement, although the political context was always crucial to their success; the larger-scale 'tribal' movements look less voluntary, more politically motivated.

The other point to stress is that, whatever the size of the migration unit involved, we are dealing with Slavic-speaking migrants who became a dominant cultural force over vast regions of central and eastern Europe. As the size of Slavic Europe makes clear, Slavic migrants were extremely effective at establishing their dominance, and already in the sixth century were known for military effectiveness. Slavicization certainly had its more voluntary component, at least in its early stages, since some Slavic groups were open to indigenous populations willing to adopt the new cultural forms. But it is very unlikely that we can really view the early Slavs as the most successful hippies Europe has ever known. They may have lacked circuses, togas, Latin poetry and central heating, but they were as successful in imposing a new social order across central and eastern Europe as the Romans had been to the west and south. Their military effectiveness makes it extremely improbable that this came about just because indigenous populations thought it would be great to become a Slav.

A generally less pacific view of the early Slavs is also strongly suggested, to my mind, by the nature of the first Slavic states that eventually emerged in the ninth and tenth centuries, and the processes of further transformation that brought them into being. The expansion of the sixth to the ninth centuries was very much part of the same story, and to a great extent the original Slavic migrations and eventual Slavic state formation were generated by the same forces. But the latter can be fully understood only as part of a much wider transformation of northern and eastern Europe, which also manifested itself in the expansionary Scandinavian explosion of the Viking era. Before turning to the processes of Slavic state formation, then, we need to explore this last great indigenous migratory impulse from within first-millennium Europe. And while its link with Slavic state formation means that Norse expansion south and east across the Baltic is in some senses our prime focus, this can itself be understood only in the context of the wider Scandinavian diaspora.

# 9

# VIKING DIASPORAS

To reach Greenland, turn left at the middle of Norway, keep so far north of Shetland that you can only see it if the visibility is very good, and far enough south of the Faroes that the sea appears half way up the mountain slopes. As for Iceland, stay so far to the south that you only see its flocks of birds and whales.

So, ROUGHLY PARAPHRASED, run the navigational directions in an Icelandic manual of the Middle Ages,[1] and it's enough to make your hair stand on end. With detailed instructions like this, how could you fail to hit the target? All you need is the ability to recognize whether the visibility is very good or not around Shetland, and if not (as it often isn't), to guess at the island's whereabouts; an instinctive grasp of the height of the Faroes; and knowledge of how to sail in a straight line using the stars in between. Add to that a deep knowledge of the fauna of the seas around Iceland, the luck not to be blown off course by the notoriously wild Atlantic winds (or the ability to reorient yourself, once you have been), and there you are. And all this in a small open boat made of wood, under sail power, with no radios (and no lifeboat services should you have had one). Given all this, the fact that the Viking who found the eastern seaboard of America did so while looking for Greenland becomes much less surprising. Late in the first millennium, the North Atlantic was clearly full of courageous, skilful, lost Scandinavians blundering around 'discovering' things.

For all these difficulties, between 800 and 1000 AD Scandinavians took to water of different depths with great gusto. Aside from their very well-known voyages of discovery in the North Atlantic, they were also exploring the river routes of western Europe, central Europe and European Russia in boats of all shapes and sizes, and for a wide variety of purposes. In these centuries waterborne Vikings exploded out of the narrow confines of their native Baltic to trade, raid, settle and form political communities all the way from the Pillars of Hercules to the Ural Mountains. The societies they encountered in the course of these journeys, and their own, were completely transformed in the process. The purpose of this chapter is not to discuss the Viking period in general, but to explore the extent to which Scandinavian migration featured in its different phases, and compare its forms, motivations and effects both with modern examples and with the other early medieval case studies examined in this book.

# VIKINGS AND THE WEST[2]

In western Europe, Viking raiding began with a vengeance in the late eighth century. The first really spectacular act of Viking destruction came in 793: the sacking of the famous island monastery of Lindisfarne off the Northumbrian coast of Britain on 8 June (which just happens to be my birthday). Within two years, the raiders had worked their way around the north coast of Scotland and down through the western isles, where they sacked an Irish monastery on Rathlin. These acts of destruction were carried out, it seems, largely by Norwegians, led to the northern coasts of the British Isles by a natural combination of winds and currents. The prevailing easterlies of springtime carried the Norwegian raiders across the North Sea to Shetland, Orkney and north-eastern Scotland. This involved braving the open sea between the coasts of Norway and Shetland, initially out of sight of the land. This was a major undertaking, but not an overwhelming one. Going from Bergen in western Norway to Shetland took no longer than coasting round southern Scandinavia through the Skagerrak and into the Baltic. And once you had reached Shetland, everything else could be done without losing sight of land. Scotland was within easy reach, and straightforward coastal routes then led the Norwegian raiders round its north coast to the Hebrides, the Irish Sea, western Britain, and Ireland itself. Then – very conveniently if they had no wish to stay longer – the prevailing winds of autumn in the North Sea, being by contrast, westerlies, took them home again. If seasonal winds and currents were reversed, we might now be writing about medieval Scottish invasions of Norway.[3]

At the same time as northern Britain and Ireland were coming under attack, there was also trouble along the coasts either side of the English Channel. Sometime between 786 and 802 (the incident cannot be placed more definitely because of the vagaries of the dating system employed by the *Anglo-Saxon Chronicle*), in what is possibly the first recorded raid of the Viking period, three ships containing North-men landed at Portland on the south coast of Britain. The local royal official wanted to take them to his king, but they killed him; it has been argued that he mistook them for traders. The ships were from Horthaland in Norway. Other evidence of trouble is less direct, but clear enough. As early 792, Offa, King of Mercia and overlord of England south of the Humber, allowed a coastal monastery in Kent to prepare a place of refuge for itself further inland, safe inside the still-standing Roman walls of the city of Canterbury. Preparations were also made south of the Channel. In 800, the Emperor Charlemagne strengthened his defences at the mouth of the River Seine. Viking raiders had already sailed much further afield. The previous year, they had made their way round the coast of Brittany to attack the island monastery of Noirmoutier at the mouth of the River Loire in western France. Ten years later, the Emperor decided to establish fleets at Ghent and Boulogne, their purpose again the suppression of sea-borne raids.[4]

Like the sack of Lindisfarne, the Portland incident involved Vikings from Norway. For the most part, however, the action on this southern front in the ninth century would be carried forward by Scandinavians from Denmark. Again, this was due to facts of geographical proximity that made the eastern seaboard of England and the entire Channel zone highly accessible to Danish seafarers. This was, however, only a tendency. 'Norwegian', 'Dane' and even 'Swede' are anachronistic categories in the Viking period. At its opening, none of the three existed as a cohesive political unit, and leaders of note recruited manpower from right across the Baltic.

# Raiding

Some aspects of the violent but smaller-scale raiding characteristic of the first phase of Viking activity in western Europe are better documented than others. The action in northern Britain was both dramatic and early. Already by the mid-ninth century, the island systems of Shetland, Orkney and the Hebrides had not only been raided, but were playing host to large-scale colonization. This story is largely untold in historical sources, but there were already established Norse leaders in the western isles by the year 850, and, for their northern counterparts, place-name and archaeological evidence are both eloquent. In the long run, every older layer of name-giving was wiped out in Shetland and Orkney. Every name for every place in these islands derives from the Old Norse language. The archaeological evidence mirrors the same substantial level of takeover, with Pictish settlement forms being eclipsed by new ones of Scandinavian type. Throughout the northern and western isles, the old circular and figure-of-eight building styles of native Celtic and Pictish traditions were quickly replaced by the Scandinavians' rectilinear houses, off-spring of an alternative cultural tradition. In the Hebrides, Norse-derived names are plentiful if not quite so comprehensively prevalent, and the archaeological evidence is similar. The Isle of Man and possibly also the western fringes of Wales saw both raids and some initial settlement at this point.[5]

Further south, in England and Ireland and on the continent, historical sources help establish some clearer patterns. Odd references to Scandinavian attacks appear in continental and insular sources for the early decades of the ninth century, but then the raiding intensified dramatically. In Irish sources, the first named Viking leaders appear in the *Chronicle of Ireland* for the mid-ninth century: a greater knowledge had been born of more intense contact. And the narrative confirms the point. Monasteries within Ireland, not just coastal establishments, became subject to attack for the first time in 836. To do this, the Vikings had penetrated the island's internal river systems and loughs: another sign of the greater knowledge they were building up of their target. At the same time, Channel ports were being heavily hit. Between 835 and 837, the port of Dorestad in Frisia was attacked in three successive years, while Sheppey in Kent was attacked in 835, and

Wessex in 836. In the same era, Viking raiders forced the monks of Noirmoutier to abandon their monastery and start a prolonged retreat inland. In the next two decades, some Viking raiders ranged still further afield. In 844, one group sailed right across the Bay of Biscay to attack the Christian Spanish kingdom of Galicia in what is now north-western Spain, before moving south into Al-Andalus, the rich lands of Islamic Spain. Perhaps the most spectacular raid of all came in 858, when Spain was rounded, the Straits of Gibraltar penetrated, and the coast of Italy attacked. Overwintering in the Mediterranean, the same group attacked up the River Rhône in 859, and even kidnapped the King of Pamplona in northern Spain on its journey home in 861. He was ransomed for sixty thousand gold pieces.[6]

Such long-distance raids were the exception, however, not the rule. Sustained attack went no further than south-western France, and the Garonne River system of Aquitaine. These assaults were eventually countered by the efforts of the rulers of the region – Charlemagne's grandson Charles the Bald, and his nephew Pippin – but even Aquitaine was a sideshow compared with the increasingly intense raiding unfolding further north, on either side of the Channel. Here, the increase in Viking assault manifested itself in three ways: a growth in the number of Viking groups involved, an increase in the frequency and duration of the individual assaults, and, as in Ireland, the spread of raiding from the coast up through the river systems leading into the interiors. The rich monastery of St Wandrille was sacked in 841, the port of Quentovic in 842, and the city of Nantes in 843. Two years later a Viking leader by the name of Reginharius (as in Ireland, it is a significant moment when chroniclers start to name names) penetrated with his followers up the Seine as far as Paris itself, where he broke into what was probably the richest monastic foundation of western Europe: St Germain. But the monks had been forewarned. The monastery's relics – including St Germain himself – and all its treasures had been evacuated further up the Seine. When the monks returned six weeks later they found only some superficial damage to their church and a couple of burned outbuildings. The real damage was to their wine cellar, which the Vikings had found, and with predictable results. The rest of Paris was not so lucky. All told Reginharius extracted for his trouble over three thousand kilos in weight of gold and silver: a mix of protection money, loot and ransom.

From about 850, the level of assault intensified still further. For the first time, the Vikings began to overwinter in western Europe, reducing the respite that usually came between November and March when the North Sea was too dangerous for navigation. This was also ominous for the degree of detachment it suggested in the attackers' attitudes to their Scandinavian homelands. Raiding groups occupied the isles of Thanet and Sheppey in east Kent in the winters of 850/1 and 854/5, respectively. The Seine region of northern France was subject to virtually continuous attack between 856 and 866. By this stage, Viking raiders were such an established part of the political landscape that they were being hired by opposing sides in internal political disputes. In 862 both the ruler of Brittany, Duke Salomon, and his great rival Duke Robert of Anjou, each hired their own Viking auxiliaries. Vikings were also being hired to fight other Vikings. In 860, Charles the Bald took on a Viking leader by the name of Weland to attack other Vikings who were wreaking havoc along the Seine. A certain amount of haggling delayed matters slightly, but in 861 Weland duly turned up with two hundred ships. Such were the tangled webs being woven by this stage, however, that he was paid off a second time by his intended Viking victims. But they did at least disperse into a number of separate and less threatening groups in the winter of 861/2. Paying chosen Vikings to help defend against the threat posed by their countrymen was by this stage, in fact, a well-established tactic. Charles's father Louis the Pious had done it with a Danish king called Harold in the 820s, and Charles himself had tried it in 841 with Reginharius, who a few years later would so much enjoy his cruise up the Seine to Paris.[7]

In Ireland too, the pressure had increased. Between 830 and 845 the *Chronicle of Ireland* records specific attacks on about fifty monasteries and another nine general assaults on people and churches in larger areas such as Leinster and the kingdom of the Ui Niell. By the mid-ninth century, the larger monastic centres such as Armagh, Kildare and Clonmacnoise represented the largest concentrations of wealth and people to be found anywhere in Ireland, and hence made excellent targets. Faced with this aggression, the kings of Ireland responded with vigour. In 848 Mael Sechnaill, High King of Tara, defeated one group of Vikings in County Meath, killing some seven hundred of them. The same year the Kings of Munster and Leinster achieved even greater success in County Kildare. The Viking Earl Tomrair and twelve hundred of his men were left dead on the battlefield. News of the Irish victories was sent to the courts of Frankish kings, but any sense of triumph was premature. In 849, an ominous new development showed itself. For the first time, the *Chronicle of Ireland* noted the arrival of a Viking leader whom they styled 'king'. At the head of 120 ships, this individual set about subduing those Vikings who had already moved west, as well as extracting further tributes from the unfortunate Irish. By 853 there were two 'kings', identified in some sources as brothers, operating in Irish waters, and they had forced all the Vikings already resident in Ireland to acknowledge their leadership. They stayed in Irish waters until the mid-860s.

The identity of these kings has been much debated, but they were probably brothers – Ivar the Boneless and Olaf the White – who from 866 switched their attentions to England, where, as we shall see in a moment, they started a further dangerous escalation in the level of Viking assault with the help of perhaps a third brother, Healfdan. Although this has been disputed, it is also likely that they came to the British Isles directly from Scandinavia in the 850s, and did not originate in Scotland and/or the Hebrides as has sometimes been claimed. More legendary material, preserved only in much later sources written down over two hundred years after the events, also suggests that the three were sons of Ragnar Lothbrok ('Hairy Breeches'), whose death in the snake pit of King Aelle of Northumbria, after a spectacular career of destruction in which he mistakenly sacked the Italian city of Luni thinking it was Rome, is said to have inaugurated the Viking conquest of England. None of this is at all likely, but the Ragnar of legend may indeed preserve some memory of Reginharius of Paris fame, and the importance of Ivar, Olaf and Healfdan requires them to have been from a very significant family. So they could well have been Reginharius' sons, but the Reginharius of history didn't die in Aelle's snake pit. He met his end at the court of Horik King of Denmark, where St Germain is said to have struck him down in revenge for sacking his monastery.[8] If so, this would ruin the motif of revenge that the sagas used to explain the brothers' assault on Northumbria, but, in the broader scheme of things, even the family ties of Ivar, Olaf and Healfdan are of only passing significance. Their real importance lies in the new era of Viking activity inaugurated by their arrival on the British mainland.

## *Micel Here*

This process of intensification culminated in the 860s when the violent conquest of entire Anglo-Saxon kingdoms was achieved by Viking forces, largely Danish in origin, labelled 'Great Armies' (in Anglo-Saxon, *micel here*). The first Great Army gathered in the kingdom of East Anglia in winter 866/7, extracting horses and supplies from its hosts. In 867, it attacked Northumbria, taking advantage of a succession struggle that had divided the military capacities of the kingdom and set them behind two contenders, Osbert and Aelle. The two kings eventually united, but by then it was too late. The Vikings broke into the city of York and killed them both. In 868, spurred on by this success, the Great Army turned its attentions on Mercia, but were driven back by the combined forces of Mercia and Wessex. This setback did not prevent the conquest of East Anglia in 870, and subsequent long-drawn-out campaigns eventually led to a further victory over Mercia in 874.

Wessex under King Alfred now became the target, but a further four years of war, culminating in his great victory at Edington in 878, saw him preserve its independence – if only just. The critical moment came in winter 877/8 when the Vikings took Alfred by surprise and stormed into the heart of his kingdom. This was when he hid himself on the island of Athelney and famously burned the cakes while deciding how best to retrieve the situation. In spring, cakes notwithstanding, Alfred bounced back, concentrating his forces to win his famous victory. In the aftermath of Edington, the Viking leader Guthrum accepted Christian baptism, then retreated into East Anglia. Alfred's victory drew a boundary around the area of Danish conquest in England, but could not prevent the distribution of the landed spoils won by the earlier victories. Either side of Edington, in separate groups, the Vikings shared parts of Northumbria among themselves in 876, and parts of Mercia in 877. Guthrum's followers did the same with East Anglia in 880. Danelaw was born.[9]

One important factor in Alfred's success lay in the fact that the Viking forces had turned to Wessex last. All the so-called Great Armies were coalitions. This was what made them 'great'. The first, of 865, for instance, was created by an alliance of the kings who may or may not all have been sons of Ragnar, together with more forces, some of them substantial and under independent leaders of second rank, called *jarls* (Norse equivalent of 'earl'). By 878 and the attack on Wessex, some of these constituent elements had either dropped out of the action or were continuing only half-heartedly, since the land-grabbing in Northumbria in 876 and Mercia in 877 meant that some of them – those who had already received land – now had much to lose. But Edington just rang the bell on round one of the Great Army era. Some of the constituent parts of the first Great Army – and there had been plenty of comings and goings since 866 (a subject we will return to shortly) – may have been left out of the land distributions. And more Vikings, encouraged no doubt by the army's successes, soon came to join them. The *Anglo-Saxon Chronicle* notes the arrival of a particularly large new force, which overwintered on the Thames at Fulham – then outside London proper, of course – in 879/80.

All of these new Vikings, together with all those who had not so far satisfied their expectations, were still ready to fight. But with opportunities in England being shut down by a combination of the resurgence of Wessex under King Alfred's leadership, the land distributions themselves, and Guthrum's commitment after Edington to help keep the peace, it is hardly surprising that they had to look elsewhere. Frankish sources record the renewal of large-scale Scandinavian activities on the continent from the spring of 880.

In that year, the Fulham arrivistes departed from England in search of new areas of profit. The political situation on the continent looked particularly promising. Three kingdoms had eventually been carved out of Charlemagne's Frankish Empire for his grandsons: a western kingdom controlled by Charles the Bald, the middle kingdom of the eldest, Lothar (Lotharingia), and the eastern kingdom of Louis the German. Lothar's son had died childless, leaving the middle kingdom without its own ruler; Charles and Louis were quarrelling over the spoils. With a ready eye for an opportunity, the returning Vikings concentrated their attention on the coastal zone of northern Lotharingia, what is now Belgium and Holland, and the extremities of the eastern and western kingdoms. In 880, an initial success went to the Franks. One group of Vikings on the Scheldt was defeated by Louis the German, who inflicted on them losses of more than five thousand dead. Another Viking group further east, in Saxony, was more successful, though, killing two bishops and twelve counts, together with many of their followers. But the main Viking successes in subsequent years were to come in the Low Countries, the old heartlands of Lotharingia.

In 881, despite a defeat said to have cost it nine thousand dead, the Great Army pillaged Cambrai, Utrecht and Charlemagne's great palace at Aachen, as well as burning Cologne and Bonn. Once again, this was a composite force led by three Scandinavian kings – Godfrid, Sigfrid and Gorm. The ageing Louis the German was now too ill to intervene, dying on 20 January 882. Hence it was under Louis's last surviving son, Charles the Fat, that Frankish forces gathered in that same year. Charles decided to echo the policy of Alfred of Wessex, making a treaty with Godfrid which included his conversion to Christianity, presumably hoping to divide and rule the Viking forces. The policy worked well enough for three years, despite Viking attacks up the Scheldt in 883 and up the Somme to Amiens in 884. At that point, the ruler of west Francia was killed while out hunting. This encouraged the Vikings to attack in greater force, and in 885 was enough to make Godfrid break his treaty. Godfrid was quickly disposed of, but Viking forces enjoyed extensive success further west, moving inland in great numbers, beyond Paris and as far as Rheims in 886 and 887. Dissension within the Frankish kingdom prevented any effective response until 891, when Arnulf, the illegitimate grandson of Louis the German and King of east Francia (who had deposed his uncle Charles the Fat in 887), caught a large Danish army in their fortifications on the River Dyle close to Louvain in modern Belgium. The Franks stormed the fortifications and inflicted a massive defeat on their enemy, killing two kings and capturing sixteen royal standards.[10]

Frankish resurgence had the same effect – in reverse – as Alfred's successes a decade earlier. With no more easy pickings on the continent, much of the continental Great Army headed back to England, where the 880s had been quiet apart from one abortive attack on Rochester in 886. But Alfred had always understood that the Viking threat had been parried, rather than defeated. Throughout the 880s, the *Anglo-Saxon Chronicle* noted where the Viking armies were operating in each particular year, giving a strong sense that they were being watched with trepidation. And with huge urgency, Alfred inaugurated a programme of defensive building, which established a series of fortified centres – *burhs* – throughout his kingdom. His policies not only built the refuges, but organized their garrisons and revamped the field army as well. In the 860s and 870s the first Great Army had been able to march unmolested across England, covering large distances in a short space of time. The fortresses changed all this. They were not easy to capture, and could not be left unsubdued in an army's rear, since they contained an armed garrison that could conduct harassing operations. Alfred's plan was clearly to tie up and wear down any attacking Viking force, before fighting a pitched battle with his new field army, if and when he so chose.

It worked pretty much to perfection. Again, as in the 860s and 870s, the returning Viking armies of the 890s came in several groups. One force of over two hundred ships landed in east Kent, fortifying a base at Appledore, while a second force landed not far away in the Thames estuary, establishing itself at Milton Royal near Sittingbourne. Even though some of the Danes of Danelaw made common cause with the newcomers, three years of campaigning brought the Scandinavians little reward, and the contrast with the first Great Army is very striking. Whereas it had marched the length and breadth of England, and could even, as in winter 877/8, penetrate freely into the heart of the Wessex kingdom, the second failed to win the pitched battles against Alfred's revamped field armies, and its attempted raids lost all momentum because of a mixture of counterattack and failed sieges. As a result it was largely confined to the fringes of Wessex – parts of Kent and Essex – and worn down too by shortages of supply. Generals are famous throughout history for coming unstuck by basing their plans for future wars on how to fight the last one, but in Alfred's case the wars were close enough in time and character for the planning to pay off. As the *Anglo-Saxon Chronicle* reports, 'afterwards, in the summer of this year [896], the Danish army divided, one force going into East Anglia, and one into Northumbria; and those that were moneyless got themselves ships and went south across the sea to the Seine'.[11]

The main action then switched back to the continent, where those Vikings who had failed to make enough money to settle in England were joined by further reinforcements. By the late ninth century, the Viking presence in Ireland had evolved into a limited number of fortified coastal enclaves, the major ones being Limerick, Wexford, Waterford and, above all, Dublin. In the last decade of the century, the Irish kings united against even this limited presence. The separate Viking forces of Limerick, Wexford and Waterford were all defeated individually, and in 902 even the Dublin Vikings were thrown out of their stronghold. Some of the refugees settled on the Isle of Man and the west coast of the British Isles, not least in Cumbria and Wales. But the expelled Irish Vikings probably also contributed to the events that now unfolded in northern France.[12]

Unfortunately, the continental sources become much too fragmentary at this point to reconstruct a historical narrative. Even annalistic sources like the *Anglo-Saxon Chronicle* tended to be written as celebratory pieces to preserve the deeds of kings, but the early tenth century was a period of great political fragmentation in western Francia, with the descendants of Charlemagne losing power in the regions to a whole series of more local lords. In this context, no one was writing connected history and the detailed progression of events is lost to us.

We do know, though, that substantial Viking inroads were made. The independent kingdom of Brittany was submerged beneath Viking attack in the 910s, some of its political leadership fleeing to the court of Wessex in search of asylum. Viking control then continued in Brittany for twenty years, until the native dynasty reasserted itself in 936 under Alan II. This Viking interlude had virtually no lasting impact upon place names, but did generate the wonderful pagan ship burial found at Île-de-Groux (Plate 24). Faced with this kind of pressure around the northern and western fringes of his domains, the King of the Franks resorted to an old stratagem. In 911, land in and around the port of Rouen at the mouth of the Seine was granted to a Viking leader by the name of Rollo. From his line and this settlement would eventually evolve the Duchy of Normandy. A second Viking settlement was licensed at Nantes in 921, at the mouth of the Loire, although this one lasted for only sixteen years. Both settlements were designed to establish tame Viking leaders who would help control the greater Viking threat. But such settlements were only part of the story. In the same era, other Viking groups were establishing themselves on the Cotentin peninsula and upper Normandy around Bayeux. What we don't know, and probably never will, is which particular Viking groups from England and Ireland contributed to the settlements at Rouen and Nantes, and whether there were still more Vikings coming directly from Scandinavia at this time.

These, however, are essentially matters of detail. A combination of forced and licensed settlements in England, Ireland and northern France in the first two decades of the tenth century tied down most of the armed drifters from Scandinavia who had arrived in the west at the tail end of the ninth.[13]

The raiding and Great Army eras in the west thus generated a huge Scandinavian diaspora. The northern and western isles of Britain, including probably Man, had been settled in the early ninth century. The Faroe Isles to the north-west were next in line, although the process is undocumented. They had clearly been settled by the mid-ninth century at the latest, and the Great Army era saw still more colonization. Most famously, Scandinavians began to move into Iceland in large numbers in the generation before 900 AD. The 'official' story of this settlement, told by the Icelanders themselves in the twelfth century, was that the outward expression of growing centralized royal power in Norway at this time led both Norwegians and some of the earlier settlers of the northern and western isles to move on. This is probably an anachronistic construct, however, reflecting the reaching-out of Norwegian kings of the twelfth century towards the north, because there's nothing to suggest that their counterparts of the ninth century were anything like so powerful. But the late ninth did see the emergence of an alternative source of centralized authority in the northern and western isles (between 860 and 880): the Earldom of More, based in Orkney. It is this new and demanding authority, it seems, that prompted Scandinavian settlers to move on to Iceland. And from Iceland, or course, Greenland was opened up for settlement from the mid-tenth century. The Earls of More also seem to have been responsible for organizing the campaigns on the northern Scottish mainland that made it possible for yet more Scandinavians to move into Caithness, in particular, which had been wrested from Pictish control at precisely the same era.[14]

The final settlement of the Great Army era was in fact a resettlement. The Irish kings' destruction of the Scandinavians' bases, culminating in their expulsion from Dublin in 902, had contributed Norse manpower to further settlements in the Isle of Man and western Britain. In 914, however, a large Scandinavian fleet anchored off Waterford, having made its way there from Brittany. Three years later it was joined by a certain King Sihtric, descendant of the dynasty of King Ivar that had ruled in Dublin from the mid-ninth century until 902. Mobilizing the fleet, Sihtric re-established himself at Dublin. At the same time, his brother Ragnall made himself King of the Vikings of York, and from the latter's death in 921 Sihtric proceeded to rule a united kingdom of Dublin and York. This strange offspring of the Viking era then proceeded to generate a hugely complicated thirty years of political history, whose details do not concern us here, until the defeat of Eric Bloodaxe in 954 severed the bond and set the two Viking centres off on separate trajectories: York to become part of a united Anglo-Saxon England, and Dublin to play a fascinating bit-part in Irish politics.[15] But the whole western diaspora was itself only one part of a much bigger phenomenon. At the same time as raiders and the Great Armies had been rearranging large parts of western Europe, other Scandinavians were exploring the river routes of western Russia.

# RUSSIA'S VIKINGS

Early in the tenth century, in a major diplomatic coup for the Muslim world, the Volga Bulgars officially declared their conversion to Islam. Between the Bulgars and the central world of Islam – the Caliphates – lay the Khazars, who had occupied territories on the Lower Volga and between the Black and Caspian Seas since the seventh century (Map 20). Relations between Khazars and the Caliphs had long been of a settled nature, and alongside the diplomatic niceties trading relations had grown up. The Bulgars had been drawn into this diplomatically stable world of mutually advantageous exchange in the eighth and ninth centuries, participating in the profitable trading alliance. Their conversion to Islam was a declaration of cultural allegiance, and the logical result of their burgeoning relationship with the Islamic world. Early medieval Islam was at the height of its prosperity and political cohesion. It was a world of extravagant wealth and lavish court life, where scholars had an interest in preserving the ancient traditions of Greek and Roman learning, not least in science and geography, subjects which had largely fallen into abeyance in Christendom.

As the Volga was drawn into this orbit, not only caliphal embassies but merchants, travellers and scholars, interested in the peoples and customs of this obscure corner of the world, journeyed north. In the lands of the Bulgars, in the emporium of Bulgar, one of the great markets of the early medieval world, they encountered a host of strange peoples. They quickly became aware that the most important were the Ar-Rus. Being ethnographers of the best school, these Islamic Dr Livingstones were not content simply to hear about the Ar-Rus and meet some of them in the Bulgar markets, but travelled west and north to inspect their territories at first hand. Here they found something between a state and an association of merchant princes. The Rus had a king who lived on a fortified island. He maintained a military establishment of many warriors, whom he funded by taking 10 per cent of all, the associated merchants' profits. There were also priests, but above all, this powerful mercantile class, who drew up the rules of life around their interests. If you insulted one, it would cost you your life or 50 per cent of your property.[16]

Who were the Rus, and where had they come from?

## The Rus

In the past, the identity of the Rus was hugely controversial. Round one of the battle – as usual – was fought out with the nationalistic fervour that so marked the later nineteenth century. Scandinavian scholars argued that the word 'Rus' was derived from the Finnish name for Swedes, and identified the Rus as Scandinavian Vikings. This meant, they claimed, that medieval Russia, the state based on Kiev which eventually developed from the modest beginnings observed by the Muslims, was a creation of Scandinavians! In the later nineteenth century, this sort of claim was not likely to go unanswered. That some Scandinavians had played a role in the action could not be denied. The Old Norse names for the rapids that punctuated the lower reaches of the River Dnieper, until they were submerged by one of the great hydraulic projects of the Soviet era, have been preserved in the Byzantine source that we encountered in Chapter 8, the *De Adminis-trando Imperio*. Also, the earliest Russian chronicle preserves the texts of two Rus trade treaties negotiated with the Byzantines in the tenth century, and many of the Rus participants had straightfor-wardly Scandinavian names. The scholars who prepared the Slavophile counterblast in the so-called Normannist debate, however, were not daunted. They derived 'Rus' from a small river of the northern Black Sea region – the Rhos – and argued that Scandinavians participated in the action only in small numbers, as merchants and mercenaries. Medieval Russia was, of course, the creation of Slavs.

In the twentieth century, the Russian Revolution added its own twisting entrenchments to the Slavophile position. This, of course, had nothing to do with nationalist pride. As we've already encountered in other contexts, according to Marxist-Leninist dogmas, throughout history major epochal developments have come about through internal socioeconomic transformation. Each of the canonically prescribed sequences of modes of production – ancient (that is, slave) mode, feudal, bourgeois – develops, according to this theoretical model, massive internal contradictions – Marxist-speak for class conflict – which lead to its replacement by the next mode of production in line. According to this construct, the Kievan state represented the arrival of feudalism in the forests of Russia. There were some problems. No one could find any evidence of the slave mode of production, which ought to have preceded feudalism, before the foundation of Kiev. Likewise, the feudal mode of production ought to be characterized by agriculture based on the exploitation of large estates, from which a small thoroughly militarized landowning class primarily benefited. But while a Kievan state of some kind certainly existed in the tenth century, the historical evidence shows no sign of large estates before the eleventh. One problem was solved by inventing the concept of 'state feudalism', where state structures could perform the functions of the landowning class, and the slave problem was quietly dropped. In fact, in one of its many paradoxes, the Soviet state combined adherence to the internationalist vision of Marx – where nationalism was a false consciousness developed by elites to divide and rule workers who would otherwise unite against them – with rampant nationalistic fervour. So the older arguments were at all times interleaved with the new emphasis on the primacy of internally driven socioeconomic development. Both nationalism and Marxism, then, denied that a bunch of Scandinavian adventurers could have had anything much to do with the emergence of the first Russian state.[17]

With the collapse of the Berlin Wall – closely followed by that of the Soviet system – discussion of the Russian past has been relieved of much of the pressure imposed by such intrusive modern agendas. As a result, some consensus has begun to emerge. Most scholars are happy now to acknowledge that the name 'Rus' surely does derive from the

Finnish name for Swedes, and that Scandinavians played a critical role in the historical processes which underlay the emergence of the first Russian state. Some Rus sent on from Constantinople to the court of Charlemagne's son Louis the Pious in 839 were unambiguously identified by the Franks as Scandinavians, and other historical evidence, such as the names in the tenth-century trade treaties, is equally conclusive. The collapse of the Soviet system has also made it possible to recognize (or, at least, to air the recognition in public) that more material of Scandinavian origin has been found in European Russia than used to be acknowledged. Some of the reports of Muslim travellers, likewise, for all their ethnographic distortions, are strongly suggestive of the northern origins of the Rus. Most famously, Ibn Fadlan witnessed in the lands of the Bulgars a Rus boat burial, and his account of it has always made its readers think of the Vikings. Full of gory details of animal and even human sacrifice, it describes how the corpse and all its attendant offerings were placed in a boat and hauled on to land, then set on fire, the remains of the pyre being covered by a mound, in the top of which was set a wooden post.[18]

So the Ar-Rus of northern Russia and their island king were Scandinavians, but what were they doing there, and what was their role in the generation of the first Russian state?

There are no contemporary accounts of the arrival of Scandinavians along the river systems of eastern Europe. The south-eastern hinterland of the Baltic was too far away from any of the European (or, indeed, Muslim) centres of literacy in the eighth century, when it all began, for these events to attract contemporary comment. Of later texts, there are a few references to Viking activity in Russia in some of the Scandinavian saga materials. The most coherent account of the pre-history of medieval Russia, however, is preserved in the so-called *Russian Primary Chronicle* (henceforth *RPC*), a more descriptive title than its proper, more Proustian alternative, *The Tale of Bygone Years*. The surviving manuscripts are no older than the fourteenth century, but the text as we have it was a creation of the early twelfth. We know from archaeological materials that Scandinavians began to penetrate the forests of European Russia from the second half of the eighth century at the latest, so that even the *Tale*'s original compiler was having to cast his mind back over three hundred and fifty years of history, much of which had unfolded before literacy became a feature of the Russian world. The author was probably working in one of the monasteries of Kiev in Ukraine, capital of twelfth-century Russia. But Scandinavians came south to Kiev only at a relatively late date, and for a long time, as we shall see, this riverine axis in Russian history – focused on the Dnieper – was much less important than another that focused on the Volga.

Much of the pre-history of Russia was worked out far to the north and east, therefore, of the area central to the interest of the text recounting it. The author of the *Chronicle* was aware of this in outline, and traces the arrival of the later Riurikid ruling dynasty of Kiev back to northern Russia, where an invitation is said to have been issued to its founder, a Scandinavian by the name of Riurik (surprise), by a group of five tribes who had long been at war with one another: the Chud, the Merja and Ves all of Finnic stock, and the Slavic Krivichi and Slovenes (Map 19). Riurik came in, supposedly with two brothers, Sineus and Truvor, imposed order, and that was that. We will return to the likely historicity of any of this in a moment, but the main point is that the literary tradition has little to tell us about the earliest history of the Rus.[19] Archaeological materials have therefore come to the fore.

Trying to construct anything like a historical narrative from archaeological materials, as we have seen many times before, is an exercise fraught with danger. They are wonderfully evocative of patterns of longer-term change, but not necessarily amenable to documenting the kind of shorter-term exchanges that are the stuff of history. Nevertheless, as with the Slavicization of Europe, the preoccupation of the Soviet state with pre-history means that a huge amount of new material came to light after 1945, and some striking insights have emerged. Above all, it is now certain that in the mid-eighth century, a generation or two before raiding began in the west, Scandinavian adventurers were moving south and east of the Baltic into European Russia. The Baltic had never been a barrier to movement in the first millennium AD. Traces of Scandinavian communities established at more westerly points on its southern shores, in what is now Pomerania, have long been known and can be dated to the fifth and sixth centuries. None of these survived as an identifiably Scandinavian community into the seventh century, the groups concerned either being swallowed up by incoming Slavs or having returned to their homelands. But, after a short break in the mid-seventh century, identifiably Scandinavian materials began to be deposited further east, in Baltic- and in the Estonian-dominated lands, starting at Elblag and

Grobin. In the eighth century, a marked Scandinavian presence grew up at Janow in the Vistula delta, and at more or less the same time increasing Scandinavian exploration of the rivers feeding into the Gulf of Finland manifested itself in the form of a permanent, if small, colony established on the River Volkhov close to Lake Ladoga. Thanks to dendrochronology, we know when it began. The wood used for the earliest houses was cut in the year 737.[20]

What these Scandinavians were doing in the northern forests emerges clearly from the later historical evidence. In the great emporium of Bulgar, Islamic merchants travelled north to meet their Rus counterparts, who were selling above all slaves and furs, but also amber, honey and wax. These same goods were also traded with the Byzantines in the tenth century, and it must be odds on that Scandinavians first came south and east of the Baltic to collect these fruits of the northern forests. Apart from the slaves, this is a classic example of what made long-distance trade profitable in antiquity, despite the great costs and difficulties of transport. The Scandinavians were able to extract goods from one ecological zone – the sub-Arctic north, where the intense cold makes furry animals grow coats of a density and quality that would overheat any of their southern cousins – and then sell them in another at premium prices.

There is no strictly contemporary evidence for how these eighth-century Scandinavian traders procured the items they were trading, but again, later evidence sheds important light. The slave trade, of course, was run through compulsion. Slaves do not usually volunteer their services. Again, the literary sources provide us with important information. The Arab geographers report that the Rus regularly attacked Baltic-speaking Prussian tribes living near the eastern Baltic, and that the less powerful eastern Slavs lived in dread of their more powerful western Slavic neighbours.[21] That this dread was closely related to the operations of the slave trade is suggested by the fact that Arab silver coins are found precisely among the western Slavs, west of the Vistula, and no further east. There is a largely blank area between the zone of operations of the Rus and that of the western Slavs (Map 20). It must have been from this area that most of the unfortunate victims for the Muslim slave markets were taken.

The extraction of the other goods was not necessarily so involuntary. Where the sources refer to the process, the skins and furs produced in the northern forests and sold on by Scandinavian mer-

chants are often referred to as 'tribute'. This word suggests an element
of compulsion, which finds some confirmation. One relevant anecdote
appears in the ninth-century *Life of St Anskar*, a Christian missionary
to Scandinavia, which describes a Swedish raid on the Curs of the
southern Baltic who had ceased to provide their agreed tributes. As
soon as we have any records, likewise, the Scandinavians of Russia
imposed tributes on the Slavic groups that came within their political
orbit. Tribute could be extracted on a micro-economic scale too. An
appendix to the Anglo-Saxon translation of the history of Orosius
produced at the court of, and possibly by, Alfred the Great tells the
story of the king's conversations with a Norwegian trader by the name
of Ottar (Othere). Ottar regularly sailed north up the west coast of
Norway with his companions, and received furs, bird feathers,
whalebone and ship's ropes made from the hide of seals and whales
as tribute from Laplanders there within the Arctic Circle. Ottar was
working northern Norway rather than northern Russia, but there is
every reason to suppose that Scandinavian merchants in that area too
were unafraid to resort to robust persuasion.[22]

The full run of evidence does not suggest, however, that relations
between Scandinavian merchant and indigenous producer were run
solely on this basis. For one thing, even Ottar acquired some of his
trade goods through his own efforts. Again, as he told King Alfred, he
and five friends killed sixty whales in two days. More generally, and
this applies to Ottar too, the whole process of collecting goods clearly
involved small groups of Scandinavians moving among much larger
indigenous populations, who were themselves central to the trading
process. Trapping, for instance, is a highly skilled art, which requires
detailed local knowledge of animal runs, and outside Scandinavians
making occasional visits to an area would have been incapable of
extracting their own furs with any degree of efficiency, so that most
trapping was presumably done by local populations.[23]

This kind of pattern held good into the tenth century, when the
*De Administrando Imperio* describes in some detail the winter circuit
followed by Rus merchants among their Slavic subjects, in the course
of which the next year's trade goods were collected. Indeed, the whole
process of connecting up different patches of Russian forest – each
being worked individually for trade goods – to the broader exchange
system operating up and down Russia's river systems was conducted
by relatively small groups of Scandinavians working more or less

independently of one another. This is implied in the Muslim accounts of the northern king who skimmed a percentage off the top of independent merchants' activities, and in Muslim accounts of merchants at work. Ibn Fadlan, for instance, describes the individual merchants making offerings to their gods of commerce before uttering this entirely apposite prayer:

'I would like you to do me the favour of sending me a merchant with a large number of dinars and dirhams, who will buy from me everything I would wish and will not enter into dispute with me over what I say.' . . . If [the merchant] has difficulty in selling and his stay is prolonged, he returns with another present a second and a third time.[24]

The merchants may have come in groups, but they sold as individuals. The same point is amply documented in the trade treaties the Rus negotiated with Byzantium in the tenth century. These documents show that, while the Grand Prince of Kiev had paramount authority, there were lesser Scandinavian princes operating in the other centres established up and down the river network, men who had their own representatives at the negotiations and were mentioned separately in the final treaties.[25]

The Scandinavian traders worked the forest zone, then, in relatively small and largely separate groups, which would have made them very vulnerable to attack if their relations with indigenous population groups were entirely hostile. Against this backdrop, it is striking that the hoards of Muslim silver coins – the fruits of the trade activity – are widely dispersed across the Russian forest zone (Map 20). This may indicate that the Scandinavian merchants purchased a degree of consent from their Slavic and other indigenous producers by recycling to them a share, if perhaps a lesser one, in the fruits of the trading. Slavs were able to profit from the trade network in other ways too. The *De Administrando Imperio* tells us, for instance, that the Rus brought their goods down the River Dnieper and across the Black Sea to Constantinople in boats purchased from the Slavic Krivichi and Lenzanenes, who spent their winters constructing them.[26] The provision of suitable river boats was not simply demanded, therefore, and this is again suggestive that Scandinavian–Slavic relations were not just about constraint. We have to envisage Scandinavian exploitation of the northern forests in the form of a series of small companies with certain rights negotiated and/or asserted over their own particular goods-producing territories. The locals provided the goods, or many of them, the Scandinavians the organization, the transport and the knowledge to take those goods to distant markets and return with a healthy profit. Such a vision takes us a long way from the sterility of the old Normanist debate, emphasizing as it does the symbiotic relationships that clearly grew up on the local level. The ninth and tenth centuries were not about Scandinavian versus Slav, but about small, and, in economic terms, mutually competitive producers. Each individual trading enterprise, composed of Scandinavians and indigenous population (whether Finns, Balts or Slavs), was selling the same products in the same market.

## The King in the North

The projected market for the goods being collected from Staraia Ladoga was initially western. The colony was established at exactly the same time as trading contacts were building up right across the Baltic and North Sea areas, but long before there is any sign of contact between northern Russia and the Islamic world. The furs and other products being collected by the shores of Lake Ladoga were at this point being shipped west to be sold to the elites of Latin Christendom. In particular, the mid-eighth century was springtime for the Carolingian dynasty and its supporters, and many of the furs collected surely had this market in mind. It did not take long, however, for Scandinavian merchant adventurers to become aware of a particular important fact of east European geography. While some of the rivers of European Russia flow north into the Baltic, others drain south into the Black and Caspian Seas. The whole area is so flat, moreover, that the headwaters of both north- and south-flowing rivers lie extraordinarily close together. By following the River Volkhov south from Lake Ladoga, new and exciting possibilities came into play. A combination of tributaries, especially the west–east flowing River Oka, combined with carefully reconnoitred portages, where ships were dragged usually on rollers from one set of connected river systems to another, allowed access to the Black and Caspian Seas via two major routes, the Dnieper and the Volga.

Of these, it was the Volga that most attracted the Scandinavians, even though the literary material – both Kievan and Byzantine – tells us far more about the Dnieper route, on which Kiev itself was eventually founded. But no Scandinavian material found on sites along the middle reaches of the River Dnieper can be dated before the end of the ninth century, and there is incontrovertible evidence that the Volga route had been opened up long before. This comes in the form of the Islamic silver coins that the Rus merchants received in return for their goods. Many thousands of them have been found in north-west Russia and the general Baltic region. For dating purposes, hoards – rather than single finds – have prime importance. The latest dated coin in any hoard gives some indication as to when the whole assemblage may have been deposited, and where hoards are plentiful there is a good chance that the time lag between issuing and deposition was not too great. In the forests of north-west Russia, the earliest latest coin, so to speak, discovered so far was minted in the year 787. Allowing a margin for time delay, this suggests that the hoard was deposited somewhere around the year 800, and hoards of a similar date have also been found in Scandinavia and the Baltic. Muslim silver was certainly flowing to the north by 800 at the latest, but had perhaps begun a little earlier, in any case a generation or two before the Dnieper route was opened up.[27]

This makes perfect sense. The Volga route led straight to the Caspian Sea and the economically developed world of the Islamic Caliphs, by this date based on the Abbasid capital of Baghdad. There the taxes of a vast empire, stretching from the Atlantic to India, were being consumed at a court of stupendous magnificence. Here was a real centre of demand for merchants with luxury goods to sell. The southern reaches of the Volga route were already well mapped out, moreover, since the Khazars had long since traded for furs as far north as the Middle Volga. The Dnieper route, by contrast, was far more difficult, involving some awkward rapids around which boats had to be carried, and led out into the Black Sea – not the Caspian – near the Crimea. One could still reach the Islamic world by sailing east, but it was less direct, and the more natural trade axis led to Constantinople. But, as we have seen, Byzantium was a sadly reduced power from its glory days under Justinian, and the Islamic Caliphs and their court grandees represented a far richer market for the luxury goods that the Scandinavians had to offer. Whether Scandinavian merchants themselves regularly went as far south as the Caspian is difficult to know. Some certainly did, but the journey was long, and there may have been a whole series of middle-men. In the second half of the eighth century, at least, the numbers of Scandinavians involved remained limited. Apart from Staraia Ladoga, only one other site in north-west Russia, Sarskoe Gorodishche (Sarski Fort), has so far produced both silver coins and Scandinavian materials that date to 800 AD.[28]

In the absence of narrative sources, the full story of what happened next cannot be recovered, but developing Scandinavian contacts with the east may have followed a similar trajectory to the patterns we have already observed further west. One reflection of this is a slow but observable increase in the flow of Arab silver coins into Scandinavia and the Baltic in the ninth century. As the century wore on, increasing numbers of adventurers from the north, whether directly or through middle-men, were using the waterways to sell northern goods to the Islamic market. Theoretically, this could have happened without more Scandinavians actually settling south of the Baltic, but enough evidence has survived to show that they were.

In 839, as we have seen, some Swedish Vikings came to the court of the Carolingian Emperor Louis the Pious. They had been sent on from Constantinople, having reached the city only by a difficult journey past fierce tribes, and were in search of an easier route home. If, as seems likely, they had come down the Dnieper, they had had to carry their boats past its rapids, and the indigenous inhabitants of this region had quickly learned that this was an excellent place for an ambush. In 972, one later prince of the Rus, Sviatoslav, lost his life – and his head – at exactly this point. (The nomadic Pechenegs turned it into a drinking cup.)[29] The envoys reported to the Emperor that they were already sufficiently organized to have their own ruler, called a Khagan, and had indeed been acting on his behalf in attempting to establish friendly relations with Constantinople. This mention of a Khagan of the Rus as early as 839 is tantalizing, but at least a sign that the Scandinavian immigrants to the forests of Russia were beginning to evolve some kind of political organization. As in the west at more or less the same time, however, where the initial political structures that emerged among the Vikings in the Hebrides and Ireland were swamped by the arrival of the more powerful 'kings' around the year 850, so political developments in the east also failed to move in straight lines.

Probably in 860, Vikings from somewhere in Russia launched a first attack on Constantinople. Two hundred boats sailed across the

Black Sea and ravaged the city's outskirts. The Byzantines attributed their survival to the intercession of the Virgin, and, whatever credence one gives the figures, this was clearly a major attack.[30] It was followed by an intense diplomatic effort to head off further incursions. This included sending Christian missionaries away into the Russian forests. But after an initial claim of success from the Byzantine Patriarch in 867, the mission disappeared without trace, and there is no mention of further diplomatic contacts with the north for more than a generation. This suggests that the political authority to whom the mission had been sent was itself not long-lived: something which, as we shall see, was true of most Viking Age Scandinavian monarchies. There are also other clear signs of trouble. At more or less the same time, the settlement on Lake Ladoga was burned down. Dendrochronological evidence dates the disaster to between 863 and 871. It was manmade and deliberate. The original settlement consisted of isolated wooden blockhouses, all of which were destroyed at the same moment. It is highly implausible that an accidental fire could have spread amongst them all so effectively. In the same era, a Persian historian reports that Rus attacked the port of Abaskos on the south-east coast of the Caspian Sea, but the event can be dated no more closely than c.864–83.[31]

Without better historical sources, it is hard to know how to assemble this jigsaw. But the burning of Staraia Ladoga and the attacks on Abaskos and Constantinople indicate that new Scandinavian powers had entered the arena, and it is a striking coincidence that this was happening at exactly the same moment as, further west, kings were arriving and the Great Armies being assembled. I strongly suspect, therefore, that the simultaneous turmoil on the north Russian water-ways and the sudden appearance of an authority large enough to attack Constantinople both reflect the intrusion of certainly more organized, and probably also larger, Scandinavian forces into the eastern as well as the western areas of Viking operation. Like their western counterparts, these more powerful newcomers will have been looking to take over and extend the profitable wealth-extracting operations that already existed. The evolving Viking period in east and west in the ninth century reminds me of nothing so much as Chicago in the prohibition era. First small groups started to make limited amounts of money from smuggling in and producing bootleg alcohol, then the more organized gangs set themselves up, alternatively demanding a cut of all profits or suppressing rival organizations, as circumstances demanded. Once the flow of wealth was up and running, the already powerful stepped in to control it and take their cut: precisely 10 per cent, of course, according to Ibn Fadlan.

In Russia, a second factor ratcheted up the competition. To judge by the deposition of coin hoards, the flow of Arab silver reaching the north slowed considerably between c.870 and 900. The slowdown coincides, in fact, with a period of internal political chaos in the Islamic Caliphate – the 'anarchy at Samarra' – which lasted from 861 to 870 and may well have been caused in the first place by disruption on the demand side of the trade equation. This degree of crisis can only have had an adverse effect on the demand for luxury goods at the caliphal court, and would have increased the competition between different groups of Scandinavian fur and slave producers in northern Russia. This may help explain the struggle for dominance of what was left of the luxury trade from the north and, in turn, why Byzantine diplomatic feelers got nowhere. Eventually, however, some degree of order was restored, not only in the Islamic world but in the north – a process, even given the continued absence of narrative sources, that we can still get some grasp of through less direct evidence.[32]

For one thing, Staraia Ladoga was eventually rebuilt, probably in the early tenth century, this time in stone. Finds of Scandinavian materials dating to c.900 have also been made at a series of other northern sites: Gorodishche (old Novgorod), Timerevo, Mikhailovskoe, Petrovskoe, Pskov, Yaroslavl and Murom. These settlements were all placed at convenient points of access to, and hence to profit from, the main trade route down the River Volga (Map 20). Between them these sites have generated a greater quantity of Scandinavian material than any of their counterparts of the ninth century. Some of it is also women's jewellery, suggesting that a mixed immigrant population, rather than just armed Nordic males, was now occupying at least some of the sites.

This further Scandinavian influx coincided with a renewal of silver flows from the Islamic world, which, from c.900, started to arrive in unprecedented amounts. According to the available hoard evidence, something like 80 per cent of all the Islamic silver that flowed into northern Russia and Scandinavia between c.750 and 1030 (when supplies dwindled virtually to nothing) did so after the year 900. It was also coming by a different route. By the 920s, where we began, the Volga Bulgars had established their control of the Middle Volga and become Muslim. The reports of Islamic travellers show that most Scandinavian Rus were by this stage no longer trading directly with the main Islamic world. Most of the trading was being done in the land of the Volga Bulgars, where Islamic and Viking merchants met to do business. This is reflected in the origin of the tenth-century coins. Whereas the eighth- and ninth-century coins had mostly been minted in the great centres of old Islam, in what are now Iraq and Iran, the tenth-century coin flows had a further eastern origin, being produced for the most part by the newly dominant Samanid dynasty of eastern Iran. At this point, the silver mines of Khurasan, controlled by the dynasty, were at the peak of their production, which has been estimated at between a hundred and twenty and a hundred and fifty tons of silver per annum, or a staggering forty to forty-five million coins. Not surprisingly, the territories of the Samanids were a magnet for anyone with something – or someone – to sell, and well-established trade routes led from their lands east to the Middle Volga. A huge new market, served by much less difficult access routes, was attracting larger numbers of Scandinavians than ever before into Russia's forests.[33]

This provides the context for the greater power among the Rus encountered by Islamic travellers of this era: the island king. Everything we know about this king and the structure he presided over suggests that we should think of him as a *capo di capi*. He took a 10 per cent cut of everyone else's mercantile operations, and enforced his orders via a permanent armed retinue reckoned at four hundred-strong. If the *RPC* is correct, the first of these kings ought to have been Riurik, founder of the dynasty, but that is far from certain. Whatever his identity, his seat was almost certainly Gorodishche. Scandinavian occupation began here in the later ninth century, and as the Muslim travellers describe it, it was an island, strategically placed at the point where the River Volkhov flows out of Lake Ilmen (Map 20). Unlike the other Scandinavian sites of this date, it was also defended by walls, which supports the idea that it was a centre of authority. Anyone who didn't obey the orders emanating from it was liable to the fate of the inhabitants of Staraia Ladoga, just down the Volkhov, whose houses had met with such a nasty accident in the 860s. No doubt some of them had found horses' heads in their beds just before the conflagration.[34]

But this kind of political structure was hardly stable, and for all the

15. Some fortifications survive along the east and south coasts of Britain, not least Portchester castle. Its scale and placement on the Solent emphasises the nature of the Saxon threat it was designed to counter. Within a generation of Roman Britain losing its central imperial protection, predatory Saxon migrants were able to exploit the new strategic situation to take control of the wealthiest farmlands.

16. Few of the original pieces now survive from the grave of the Frankish King Childeric (d. 482), originally opened in 1653. Those that do, and the drawings made of the remainder at the time, show the influence of both the workmanship and overall splendour of mid-fifth century Middle Danubian royal funerals of the Hunnic era.

17. Crowned emperor on Christmas Day 800, Charlemagne's reign reassembled and extended the new northwest European imperial powerbase of the second half of the first millennium which first emerged under the Merovingians.

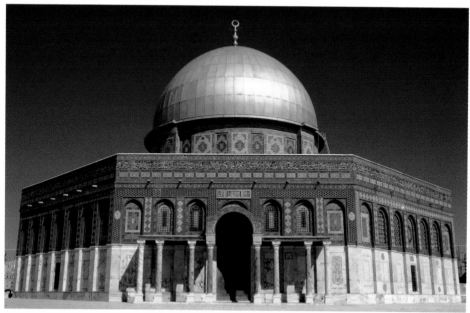

18. Completed in 691, the Dome of the Rock in Jerusalem is the oldest Muslim public building in the world, and the first monument of the new religion which swept out of Arabia to consign the world Empire of East Rome to regional power status in the mid-seventh century.

19. The spread across central and eastern Europe of one type of Slavic migrant –
small-scale communities of subsistence farmers – can be traced in the distributions
of handmade pottery of so-called Korchak (*left*) and Penkovka (*right*) designs and the
settlements they characteristically accompanied. The broader evidence demonstrates
these were not the only type of Slavic group on the move in the sixth and
seventh centuries.

20. This type of early Slavic sunken hut is well-suited to the harsh winters
of central and eastern Europe. It is the characteristic family dwelling of those
Slavic groups who moved in small-scale farming communities and used
Korchak and Penkovka pottery.

21. An unprecedented ability to move over water – both seas and rivers – made possible the Viking era of Scandinavian expansion. Each new stage of the network that was opened required the build up of detailed knowledge, hard won through trial and error, starting, as illustrated here, with mastery of the Baltic sea and its rocky coastlines.

22. All the different Viking activities in east and west – trading, raiding and extortion – led to unprecedented flows of wealth back into Scandinavia, reflected in the vast hoards of silver (of which this is by no means the largest) that are still unearthed in the modern era. As control of this new wealth fell into new hands, old political structures (above all the first known Danish monarchy), saw their power destroyed.

23. There is no evidence that Scandinavians had mastered sea-going naval technology before the eighth century. The evidence both of shipwrecks and of these famous Gotland picture stones indicates that it was only when the growing wealth of the emporia network of the North and Baltic Seas provided the necessary stimulus that keels were made strong enough and sails were added.

24. Buried in c.900 AD and excavated in 1880, the Gokstad ship is a superb example of the Viking warship design which emerged from the experimentation of the eighth century. Carrying thirty odd men it would weather storms at seas and penetrate far up river systems, providing a high-speed link between Scandinavia and the rest of Europe.

25. The third emperor of the same name, Otto III, made a state visit to the tomb of the martyr Adalbert in Gniezno in the year 1000. This state visit marks the culmination of the processes by which Europe as a meaningful historical entity emerged from the barbarian/imperial divide which characterised western Eurasia at the birth of Christ.

26. Vladimir I (c.958–1015) converted his
kingdom definitively to Christianity and
inaugurated a series of building projects
and political transformations which turned
the Rus polity from a 'glorified Hudson Bay
company' into a fully-fledged early medieval
state ready to join the club of Christian
European polities.

27. Constructed by Vladimir I between 989
and 996, the tithe Church of Kiev was the
grandest building ever seen so far
north and east in Europe.

28. King Wenceslas of Bohemia was killed by his brother Bolelas I, in part for threatening to curtail the slave trade on which his Premyslid dynasty's wealth and power squarely rested. Bolelas' son Bolelas II also chose St Wencelas' day in 995 to destroy the dynasty's last remaining rivals within Bohemia, the Slavniks.

29. The famous rune stone of Harold Bluetooth at Jelling – here being studied in considerable detail by persons unknown – proclaimed both the king's conversion to Christianity, and his feat in reuniting the Jutland and its adjacent coastlines. This marked Denmark's claim to join the first European Union which emerged in the ninth and tenth centuries.

wealth flowing through it, northern Russia of the early tenth century was hardly a land of peaceful prosperity, either. For one thing, much of the business being carried on came in the form of a slave trade. By its very nature this was a violent and unpleasant activity, involving armed raids on likely victims and the brutalization of captives as they were transported to market. Armed raids for the extraction of booty or better trading terms were still being conducted too. Both of the trade treaties with Byzantium, for instance, were the result of armed demonstrations which induced the emperor and his advisers to offer better trading terms. Islamic sources, likewise, report a huge raid on the Caspian in the year 912. And there was a further, internal dimension to the turbulence of this world. The mercantile colonization of European Russia was conducted, as we have seen, by a number of independent Scandinavian groups, not one organizing authority. You can bet your life that, originally at least, the required 10 per cent of the merchants' profits was not handed over to the king in the north voluntarily. And such a process always carried within itself the potential for generating new rivals for the current *capo*.

The king in Gorodishche won out, it seems, in the north. But precisely at the moment that Muslim travellers were taking stock of him, the political structure over which he presided was being overturned by the emergence of a second Scandinavian power base at Kiev, much further south, on a natural crossing of the Middle Dnieper. According to the *RPC*, Scandinavians first came to Kiev when two followers of Riurik called Askold and Dir obtained his permission to leave Novgorod (Gorodishche) to journey to Constantinople. On the way, they arrived at Kiev and decided to establish themselves there, from where they later launched an attack on Constantinople with two hundred boats. The *Chronicle* places their arrival in Kiev under the year 862, and the attack on Constantinople during 863–6. About twenty years later, Riurik's successor, a man 'of his kin' by the name of Oleg who was ruling on behalf of Riurik's young son Igor, set off south with a mixed army of Scandinavians, Finns and Slavs. Askold and Dir were tricked and killed, a fortified centre was built, and tribute imposed upon the surrounding Slavic tribes. Oleg had united north and south and the Russian kingdom was born. These events are placed under the years 880–2.

The outline of the story seems reasonably correct. Kiev was a secondary and later centre of Scandinavian operations in western

Russia. It is one of a series of sites along the Dnieper route to have produced Scandinavian materials, but only from about the year 900. Key to all further progress down the Dnieper was the settlement at Gnezdovo, which controlled the passage from Lake Ilmen to the Upper Dnieper and made it possible for Vikings from the northern Ladoga region to move down towards the Black Sea. Scandinavians established themselves at Gnezdovo only towards the end of the ninth century, and then at Kiev and a number of other centres around it: Shestovitskia and Gorodishche, which was near Yaroslavl where archaeological evidence of a Scandinavian presence of around the same date has emerged, and others such as Liubech and Chernigov which are mentioned in historical sources. The presence of Scandinavians is clear enough in the Middle Dnieper region from c.900, but, so far at least, the archaeological excavations would suggest that the Vikings came here in smaller numbers than in the north, where the materials of c.900 and beyond are far more plentiful.[35] If the general chronology of the *RPC* seems correct, other aspects of its story are much less convincing.

For one thing, its specific dates are no more than a later attempt to make sense of oral sources, and are thoroughly unreliable. The attack on Constantinople is the one we've met already, its date taken directly from the Byzantine *Chronicle* of George the Monk, which does not name the Viking leaders involved. At some stage in the compilation of the *RPC*, someone decided that the attack on Constantinople recorded in the Byzantine source was the same as that made by Askold and Dir, and the rest of their story was dated by that decision. This was probably a mistake. Extensive excavations at Kiev have produced no Scandinavian material dated before about 880 (the Podol excavations), so that the attack on Constantinople of the 860s, documented in Byzantine sources, was probably launched from further north.

The *RPC*'s story also poses other problems. Its compilers were obviously a bit puzzled by Oleg's relationship to Riurik. In the main Kievan tradition, he is described as a relative of some kind, but in the northern tradition, in a version of the *Primary Chronicle* which seems to derive from Novgorod, he is Riurik's unrelated commander-in-chief. The idea that Askold and Dir would have bothered to ask Riurik's permission before setting off for the south likewise fails to convince.[36] As we have seen, in the ninth and the earlier tenth century, the Grand Prince of Rus was little more than *primus inter pares*, and Scandinavian expansion was carried forward by a whole series of independent initiatives, with the *capo* moving in only later to claim his percentage. There is no reason to suppose that moves towards Kiev, whoever made them, took any different form. Perhaps above all, there's also the much bigger problem of why Viking Russia came eventually to be dominated by its second and later power centre – Kiev in the south rather than Novgorod in the north – especially since Kiev was situated on the much less rich Byzantine/Dnieper trading axis, where fewer Scandinavians had actually settled. These, however, are puzzles for the next chapter. For now, we must analyse the Viking diaspora in both east and west as a flow of migration.

## FLOWS OF MIGRATION

Questions of scale raise one of the most famous controversies in Viking studies. In the past, there was a strong tendency to interpret the Viking Age in the light of traditional perceptions of the classic Germanic *Völkerwanderung*. Tens if not hundreds of thousands of people were thought to have been on the move, driven on by a lack of resources: a deluge that drowned western Europe in an unprecedented orgy of violence. The old schoolbooks reproduced the famous Anglo-Saxon prayer 'From the fury of the Northmen, Good Lord deliver us', and more scholarly equivalents are easy to find. A textbook of Latin grammar, copied in Ireland in about 845 and eventually brought to the continental monastery of St Gall, has written into its margins this short but wonderfully evocative poem in Old Irish:

> The wind is fierce tonight
> It tosses the sea's white hair
> I fear no wild Viking
> Sailing the quiet main.[37]

Battle with such views was joined with a vengeance in the 1960s by the most prominent of current anglophone historians of the Vikings: Peter Sawyer. He argued that the traditional views were wildly overstating the likely size of Viking forces. Most of the chroniclers who produced the surviving historical accounts of Viking violence were churchmen, if not monks, and, as we have seen, churches and monasteries provided rich, 'soft' targets for predatory Vikings. Hence, he argued, there is an inbuilt tendency for the sources to stress Viking violence, when the Dark Ages were generally pretty violent anyway. The only thing that was perhaps new in the period was that the pagan Vikings attacked Christian religious establishments with a greater sense of freedom than was usual. Equally important, these monastic chroniclers ignored other important kinds of Viking activity, such as trading, which were less or non-violent, and their estimates greatly overstated the numbers involved. In his view, the more specific evidence suggests smaller forces: witness the three ships, maybe ninety or a hundred men, who were involved in that first incident at Portland. There is also, Sawyer argued, precious little evidence of women and children being involved. Viking activity was carried on not by 'whole' migrating peoples, but by warbands, whose manpower should be numbered at most in the hundreds.[38]

This argument was a necessary corrective, and its validity for the early phases of ninth-century Viking activity has been generally accepted. The argument that the Viking period largely involved males in warbands also seems largely, if not without some exceptions, correct. But as Viking activity in the west intensified from the 830s, there is good reason to believe that larger forces than Sawyer originally had in mind became involved in the action. The *Chronicle of Ireland*, for instance, records in the 830s that two Viking fleets of sixty ships each were simultaneously in action in Irish waters. The beautiful ninth-century Gokstad ship excavated in the Norwegian Vestfold in 1880 and now on display in Oslo could have carried thirty men, or just a few more, without a problem. At thirty-plus men per boat, each of these fleets would have fielded over a thousand, and this general order of magnitude is consistent with some convincingly specific casualty figures recorded in the same source. In 848, three engagements were fought by different Irish kings against separate Viking forces, who suffered losses of 700, 1,200 and 500 men. And when the fleets of Scandinavian kings started to hit western waters from c.850, then Irish, English and continental sources all – with great consistency – describe them as leading fleets numbering between one hundred and two hundred ships. This would suggest armed forces of a few thousand men.[39]

The point is only reinforced by the evidence from the Great Army period. These armies were composites, each bringing together several independent Scandinavian kings and their followers, together sometimes with more warriors under the leadership of independent jarls. The original Great Army assembling in East Anglia in winter 866/7 comprised, probably amongst others, the forces of Ivar and Olaf – who disappeared from Irish waters between 863 and 871 (Ivar is probably the 'Ingvar' of the *Anglo-Saxon Chronicle*) – and the Vikings who had been harassing the Frankish world of the River Seine for most of the previous decade. Continental sources indicate a gap in Viking violence between 866 and 880, which corresponds to the first phase of Great Army activity in England, and the Norse departure from Frankish waters was probably hastened by Charles the Bald's construction of fortified bridges across the Seine which made it much more difficult for the Vikings to penetrate inland. Apart from Ivar, the *Anglo-Saxon Chronicle* also mentions by name two further kings, Healfdan (probably a third brother of Ivar and Olaf) and Bagsecg, and five jarls (two called Sidroc, the older and the younger; Osbearn, Fraena and Harold). These kings and jarls led independent contingents within the confederate army. In 875, they were reinforced by three more kings – Guthrum, Oscetel and Anwend – making a grand total of eleven Viking contingents gathered in England. Yet more Vikings arrived just a few years later to overwinter at Fulham in 879/80. The same multiple, composite pattern holds true of the later Great Armies as well.

Not all of these different contingents operated as part of a single army at the one time. Contingents came and went according to their perceptions of the best available opportunities. But five kings, at least five earls (jarls), and other forces besides clearly amounted to a substantial body of warriors. In 878, Healfdan was killed in Devon with 840 (or 860 in another version) of his followers, which suggests that royal contingents may have been somewhere in the region of a thousand men. The *Chronicle* also notes that this force was carried in twenty-three ships, making about thirty-six men per ship, which fits nicely with the carrying capacity of a Gokstad-type ship. Estimating each of the Great Army's main contingents in the high hundreds or roughly one thousand mark is also in line with the kind of forces operating in Ireland after the 830s when raiding intensified. If this reasoning is correct, the Great Armies – each composed of half a dozen or more such contingents – must each have mustered several thousand warriors, though probably not much more than a maximum of about ten thousand. This is an entirely appropriate size for armies able to conquer whole Anglo-Saxon kingdoms.[40] And there were, moreover, several of them. As we have seen, two well-documented Great Armies attacked England: one between 865 and 878, the other from 892 to 896. Encompassing some of the same manpower, there were also another two armies which assaulted the north coast of the continent in the 880s; and the forces operating in Normandy and Brittany, and back and forth to Ireland in the last decade of the ninth century and the first twenty or so years of the tenth. All told, and even allowing for overlaps between the different forces, we must reckon with a minimum of twenty thousand warriors on the move.

This is directly relevant to the scale of Viking migration because, in eastern England and northern Francia, it was the Great Armies who turned victory into settlement. Whether this was part of the original design or not, the first Great Army destroyed three out of the four independent kingdoms of ninth-century Anglo-Saxon England, and reallocated substantial parts of their landed resources to its own members. These original settlements of the 870s were then reinforced by more pulses of settlers from the later Great Armies. One is explicitly recorded in 896, and there may have been others. On the continent, further Great Army activity eventually led, as we have seen, to settlements in Normandy and Brittany, one licensed, others not. What percentage of Scandinavian manpower participating in the Great Army action eventually settled in the west is unknowable, but the numerous different settlements are likely to have involved well over ten thousand individuals, even allowing for the fact that some surely preferred to take their wealth back to the Baltic. This is substantial, but not massive, given that the total population of the areas affected must be reckoned in the high hundreds of thousands at least.[41]

The Great Army settlements took a particular form, however. Highly suggestive is the entry of the *Anglo-Saxon Chronicle* under the year 896, recording the break-up of the second Great Army to attack England: 'In this year, the host dispersed, some to East Anglia, some to Northumbria, and those without wealth got themselves ships there, and sailed south over the sea to the Seine.' This is not without its puzzles. Does the reference to wealth mean that the Vikings had to buy estates in Danelaw rather than just seize them? I strongly doubt it, but either way, the entry makes powerful links between membership of a Great Army, amassing wealth and subsequent settlement. Individual Vikings did not drag themselves overseas to fight a series of thoroughly dangerous engagements far from home, in order then to settle down as moneyless peasants. The point of all the effort, for those who wanted to settle in the west, was to amass sufficient resources to establish themselves in a desirable socioeconomic niche. If they had just wanted to be peasants, there was no need to fight. Anglo-Saxon landlords were always looking for labour.[42]

How relationships within a particular Great Army contingent may then have translated themselves into a settlement pattern, when lands were distributed, is suggested by case studies of the detailed evidence for Scandinavian settlement in the Danelaw county of Lincolnshire. Lincoln itself was one of the five boroughs of central Danelaw, from which some kind of independent political power was exercised; there were kings in Danelaw after 878, but never a king *of* Danelaw. The centre of Lincoln itself perhaps saw some Viking settlement and certainly expanded considerably in the later ninth and tenth centuries. Outside the town, Viking settlement seems to have come in two forms. Some of the greater estates were received intact by leading Vikings. These are marked by place names of the famous Grimston hybrid variety, where a Norse personal name (*Grim-*) is combined with the Anglo-Saxon suffix for a settlement (*-tun*), and are by and large to be found on the best-quality land throughout the Danelaw counties. Other pre-existing estates were then broken up, it seems, to be parcelled out in individual holdings to Vikings of lesser but still free status. The evidence for this is provided by the coincidence between the distributions of Norse place names (ending in *-by* and *-thorp* and, again, very often combined with a Norse personal name) and that of smaller landowners with unusually high status – called *sokemen* – in the official documentation for Lincolnshire generated after the tenth-century Anglo-Saxon state incorporated the county into its territory. The same sokemen also seem to have kept their Norse-derived tastes in the decoration of everyday metalwork well into the tenth century.

If Lincolnshire can be taken as more than a one-off case, as does seem likely, then Great Army contingents seem to have kept something of their social shape upon becoming landed, since settlements were organized by the leaderships for those who had already amassed enough booty to satisfy their aspirations and pick up a small landed estate pretty much like the normans. Those who hadn't, presumably, took their booty and went looking for a new leader to follow. The landed estates used in the settlement had all been confiscated from Anglo-Saxon owners. Some were taken from secular landowners who had been killed or exiled – although there does not seem to have been a complete extinction of the old Anglo-Saxon landowning class in Danelaw – but there is good evidence too that many estates were taken from Church institutions, which by the ninth century may have owned up to one-quarter of England's landed resources.[43]

If Lincolnshire can be taken as a particular example of the general rule, then the following model could be suggested for Danelaw and northern Francia. The basic migration unit was the individual Great Army contingent of up to a thousand men, or just a bit more in the case of kings, less in the case of jarls – not the army as a whole – whose leaders organized the allocation of lands to those who were ready to settle. Some of the relevant issues – who would qualify for any land, and on what scale – were presumably discussed in the original negotiations which brought the Great Armies into being. These settlements took a form analogous to the kind of partial elite replacement we have encountered in some of the fifth-century Germanic settlements in former Roman provinces in Europe, except that the sokemen with their -bys and -thorps may have represented the insertion of a smallholding elite at a lower social scale than anything suggested by the settlements on Roman soil. The main reasons for thinking so are the smallish size of their holdings recorded in *Doomsday Book*, where their descendants survived until 1066, and the fact that they generated a bigger cultural change on the linguistic and other fronts than anything analogous in the post-Roman west.

Certainly in northern Danelaw, at least, Norse became the prevalent language, whereas Germanic languages never replaced Latin and its dialects except in Anglo-Saxon England, where the elite replacement had been more or less complete. When it comes to explaining the linguistic change and all the Scandinavian place names, some have supposed it necessary to envisage that the settlement of Great Army contingents was followed by further – undocumented – settlements of Scandinavian peasants. This seems unnecessary. Given that certainly ten thousand Vikings – and potentially considerably more than that – had to be accommodated in the distribution process, this was enough to generate a Norse-dominated landowning class at a sufficiently local level to explain the cultural changes. In comparison, the Norman Conquest involved accommodating only around five thousand new landowners, and that over the whole – not just part – of England, so there is no doubt that the new dominant Norse class lived much more cheek by jowl with their Anglo-Saxon peasant labourers than the Normans who were to follow.

Great Army contingents were responsible, however, for only one part of Norse migration into the west. In Ireland, settlement took a different form. There Scandinavians never managed – perhaps never tried – to destroy the coherence of whole kingdoms and make possible the large-scale redistribution to themselves of landed assets. Instead, we see only niche settlements, limited to a few coastal towns: Dublin above all. These were quite large, and economically powerful. After its re-establishment, rival tenth-century Irish kings competed with one another to exercise hegemony over Dublin's valuable mercenary and monetary assets. Nonetheless, although the migration unit must again have taken the form of organized warbands, permanent Norse settlement in Ireland can only have amounted to a few thousand individuals at most.[44]

In the northern and western isles and north and western Scotland, the mode of settlement was much more like Danelaw, in the sense that an intrusive Scandinavian population took control of much of the areas' landed assets. We have no documentation here of the numbers involved, nor any narrative of the settlement, but its effects show up in the place-name evidence. In the northern isles – Shetland and Orkney – no pre-Scandinavian place names survive at all. Every older stratum of name-giving has been eclipsed by the cultural effects of Viking-era settlement. In the western isles and affected areas of the Scottish mainland the wipe-out was not so complete, but again there is a dense spread of Scandinavian names. What scale of ninth-century settlement is required to explain this remarkable outcome?

When the place-name evidence was first assessed, the researchers thought that the complete disappearance of any older name-giving stratum had to mean that the indigenous, probably Celtic-speaking, populations of the area had been completely eradicated – early medieval ethnic cleansing. More recent approaches to place names have emphasized, however, that the modern spread of Norse names reflects all the intervening centuries of Norse-speaking domination of the area, not one apocalyptic moment of takeover. Norse settlement was clearly substantial, and the place-name effect could not have been achieved by much less than a complete takeover of land ownership by dominant Norse, who must have intruded themselves into local society on a level of intensity at least similar to that achieved by the sokemen of Danelaw. This would not require ethnic cleansing, though, and some of the recent archaeological evidence has confirmed the point. Even where distinctively Norse house-types replaced earlier Pictish forms, such as at Buckquoy, detailed excavations have shown that many small items of indigenous manufacture continued in use, suggesting that the old populations were living alongside, if subordinate to, the Norse settlers.[45]

In the western isles and Scottish mainland, some continuity of the indigenous population was always supposed, since the place names betray more mixed cultural origins. More than that, the Irish annals record, in a series of entries from the 850s, the activities of *Gallgoidil*: 'Scandinavianized Irish'. These mystery men have been much discussed, but they seem later to have given their name to Galloway and the consensus view places them in the Hebrides, as Celts who quickly reached an accommodation with incoming Norse settlers.[46] DNA patterns among the modern populations of these areas confirm the point. Forty per cent of the modern population of Shetland possess DNA types which show them to have been descended from Norse ancestors. In Orkney, the percentage is 35 per cent, and in Scotland and the western isles about 10.[47] It is dangerous, as we have seen in the case of the Anglo-Saxons, to read modern DNA patterns as fossils from the moment of settlement. There have been too many events in between that might have caused one strand of DNA to spread preferentially. Nonetheless, this evidence does show that while there was a substantial Norse migration flow into these areas, it did not involve the total ethnic cleansing once supposed. A more precise indication of the kind of migration unit operating in these contexts is also provided by evidence from the final area of western Norse settlement: the North Atlantic.

Scandinavian colonization of the Faroes is completely undocumented, but since that of Iceland began in the 870s, and the Faroes are en route, then presumably it was under way by the mid-ninth century at the latest. For Iceland, there is much more information. There, from the early twelfth century and in complete contrast to Viking communities established anywhere else, its Norse colonists began to write down their own history, primarily, it seems, to document claims to landownership. Around the year 1100, the Icelandic Norse traced the settlement of their island back to four hundred main colonists, each of whom established one of the large farming establishments which at that point dominated the island. These four hundred establishments were the centres of larger, interconnected networks of agricultural activity, not single farms, and it has been estimated that there were more like four thousand actual farmsteads of varying sizes in existence at this date. Each farmstead supported a family and some dependants, so that we get a figure in the low tens of thousands for the population of Iceland in c.1100. The Icelandic literature also preserves some sense of the kind of migration units by which the settlement had been made. The costs involved in getting from Scandinavia (or indeed from the British Isles, the intermediate point from which many of the settlers came) to Iceland were prohibitive. The major colonists all seem to have been wealthy men, able to fit out or hire the necessary ships to transport the people and equipment that would be required for a successful farmstead. Poorer men could either not take part at all, or had to attach themselves to the train of one of these grandees. As such observations suggest, we are certainly talking here of extended flows of migration rather than the more distinct moments of settlement that occurred in England and Francia when a Great Army contingent settled down on the land. No numbers are preserved for the aristocrat-led fleets that made their way to Iceland, but one such fleet in the later push on to Greenland consisted of twenty-five ships, thirteen of which in the end failed to make the crossing.[48]

In Iceland, of course, there was no indigenous population to subdue, so the settlers could safely come in dribs and drabs, rather than in the much larger Great Army contingents required to create political *Lebensraum* in Anglo-Saxon England. This was probably also true of the northern and western isles. There, as we have seen, indigenous landholders were certainly subordinated, but any pre-Viking political structures in these areas seem to have been on such a local, small-scale level that large Norse forces were not required to win major battles. It may well have been possible, therefore, for an individual or small groups of aristocrats and their retainers to bite off a piece of territory. Again, in the absence of direct narrative evidence, there remains a strong element of supposition about this, but it is the case that a larger political structure – the Earldom of Orkney –

emerged among the Norse of the northern and western isles only at the end of the ninth century, long after the initial settlement process was complete. The emergence of this earldom was enough to make some of these Norse push on to Iceland where they could re-establish their independence. Both points lend further weight to the argument that the subsequent migration flow onwards to Iceland and Greenland was similar to the one that had created the original Norse domination of the western and northern isles in the earlier ninth century.

Despite many gaps in the evidence, then, it is possible to come to some conclusions about Scandinavian migration flows towards the west in the ninth and the early tenth century. Two very distinct types of unit are evident, each appropriate to its context. Where large indigenous political entities had to be subdued for settlement to proceed, then the typical unit was the major warband, operating with up to a thousand warriors or just a few more. These warbands were also capable of banding together to take on really big targets such as Anglo-Saxon kingdoms. Elsewhere, where there was no indigenous opposition or where it was organized only in small sociopolitical units, much smaller aristocrat-led migration units could achieve adequate domination. All told, the total numbers involved in the different migration flows were substantial. Well over ten thousand Norse warriors, and perhaps double that, were accommodated in the settlements carved out by Great Army activity in England and on the continent. A few thousand more settled in Ireland, and probably rather more in the northern branch of the Scandinavian diaspora which spread over north Britain and the Atlantic islands.

But there is one other important issue we haven't yet addressed. How many of these armed males brought dependent women and children with them from Scandinavia? If an adult male's dependants are to be reckoned at between four and five, the usual convention, the presence or not of dependants could increase your estimate of the total migration flow from a few tens of thousand of people to over a hundred thousand. For the Great Armies we have little information, but, perhaps surprisingly, there is some. Part of the second Great Army to attack England in the 890s left its women and children in Danelaw for safe-keeping while it launched its attacks. What percentage of the army had such dependants is unclear, and also where these dependants originated. Had they come from Scandinavia, or were they picked up en route?

Some information on the latter point has emerged from recent work on the DNA of modern Iceland. Iceland has not seen a huge amount of either immigration or emigration since the Viking Age, so that there is a better than usual chance that modern DNA patterns will reflect those of the original colonists. This work has looked at both Y chromosome patterns transmitted only through the male line, and mitochondrial DNA transmitted only through the female. A fascinating contrast has emerged. Amongst the male population, 75 per cent possess Y chromosomes whose particularities can be traced back to Scandinavia, and only 25 per cent those suggestive of an origin in the British Isles. The mitochondrial evidence, however, is very different. Thirty-six per cent of the modern Icelandic population descends from Norse womenfolk, whereas 62 per cent possess DNA suggestive of female ancestors from the British Isles. Substantial numbers of female colonists, maybe something like one-third, had come all the way from Scandinavia, therefore, but maybe two-thirds were women picked up by Viking males on their travels.

Similar results have been obtained from the Faroes. In Viking Scotland and the northern and western isles, however, the pattern is different again. In these regions, there is no substantial dichotomy between the percentages of Norse male and female DNA among the modern population, suggesting perhaps that, in these zones of earliest Norse colonization, the basic migration unit was familial, with similar numbers of male and female colonists coming from Scandinavia. By the time colonization moved on to the Faroes and Iceland, however, Viking males increasingly obtained women from the British Isles. What the proportion of indigenous to Scandinavian females was among the womenfolk of the Great Army warriors we cannot tell, but the DNA evidence from further north would indicate that there were certainly some of the former present. We clearly shouldn't be multiplying our estimates for Scandinavian males by four or five, therefore, to take account of accompanying dependants, but maybe by two or three.[49]

Viking migration into eastern Europe took substantially different forms. The Norse diaspora into Russia shows no sign at all of conquering armies creating the political *Lebensraum* for subsequent settlement, and little of minor aristocratic farmers setting up independent farmsteads. As it shows up in the archaeology, there were two main phases of Norse intrusion. For the first – the later eighth and the early ninth century – substantial traces have been uncovered at only two sites: the oldest levels of Staraia Ladoga and the fortified site of Sarskoe Gorodishche on the Upper Volga. Only half a hectare of Staraia Ladoga has been excavated, however, so we have no real understanding of its size at this early date, and no estimate at all of the Scandinavian population of Sarskoe Gorodishche. This does not amount to much, and it would be tempting to think that only a very few Scandinavian traders had started to explore the river routes of European Russia at this time, were it not for the fact that the existence of a Norse-dominated Khaganate in northern Russia is reported as early as 839.[50] This could not have come into existence without either substantial numbers of Norse immigrants, or a considerable degree of organization. There may well be more archaeological evidence of eighth- and early ninth-century Scandinavian immigration waiting to be found.

As was also the case in the west, the flow of migrants picked up considerably in the second half of the ninth and the early tenth century. At this point, Scandinavian migration was clustering in three distinct zones (Map 20). The first ran along the River Volkhov between Lakes Ladoga and Ilmen. At the northern end, Staraia Ladoga was rebuilt and grew to its maximum size of ten hectares. Further south lay Gorodishche (the Holmgard of Norse sagas), as we have seen, the main power centre of the region – a fortified site surrounded by stone walls three metres high and three metres thick. Its third known major Scandinavian centre was Izborsk-Pskov. The cemeteries of all three centres have thrown up enough Norse material to suggest that they had real functioning Scandinavian communities of men and women, who had imported much of their way of life with them. The country-side round about – the Priladozhie – has also produced enough stray finds of Scandinavian materials to suggest that this region may have seen some Norse farmers and well as traders.[51]

A second clustered Scandinavian presence is known from sites along the Upper Volga. There, nineteenth-century excavations pro-duced Norse materials from Yaroslavl, Pereslavl and Suzdal-Vladimir. The methods employed were too haphazard to be able to say anything very precise. More recent and more careful work at a number of other sites in the region, however, has confirmed a substantial Scandinavian influx. A late ninth- to early tenth-century settlement at Timerevo, for instance, eventually spread over ten hectares. Excavations there have uncovered over fifty dwellings and a cemetery. This site was eventually occupied by Finns and Slavs as well as Scandinavians, but the Norse were there first. A substantial Scandinavian presence has also been established at Petrovskoe, where there were two settlements, and at Mikhailovskoe, where a cemetery containing four hundred burials (63 per cent of them cremations) has been excavated. Most of the Scandinavian materials here date to the tenth century.

The third zone of settlement was centred on the River Dnieper, although this should perhaps be subdivided in two, for whereas the Upper Dnieper region could still give access to the Volga route, routes from its middle reaches led unambiguously to the Black Sea and Byzantium. The biggest Scandinavian site uncovered so far is Gnezdovo on the Upper Dnieper (probably the Smaleski (Smolensk) of the sagas). In the 920s, it tripled in size and grew fortifications, and its cemetery, now partly damaged, contained a minimum of three thousand graves and perhaps twice that number. The original Soviet investigator claimed that only about a thousand of these were of Scandinavians, but that greatly understates the reality. Gnezdovo was a Norse-founded and Norse-dominated site, which, following its tenth-century expansion, had a population of about a thousand. Further south, on the Middle Dnieper, Kiev – as you would expect – has produced some Scandinavian materials. Three of its hilltops beside the river were occupied by Scandinavians from the early tenth century. Much more plentiful Scandinavian materials have emerged about 100 kilometres to the north, however, at Chernigov and Shestov-itsa, which were, again, substantial tenth-century sites.[52]

These geographical clusters of Scandinavian sites make perfect sense given the nature of Norse activities. The cluster on and around the Volkhov in the north controlled, and had easy access to, the main trade route out into the Baltic; the Upper Volga and Upper Dnieper sites gave settlers easy access to the main trade route to the Islamic world; and the Middle Dnieper led, eventually, to Constantinople. Scandinavian settlements clustered around the major trade routes, therefore, and these excavated sites were presumably all trading centres, from where individual traders established relations with local fur trappers in the surrounding countryside, and set off in the spring either for Bulgar or for Constantinople.

All of this is straightforward enough, but it is not possible to derive any sense of the actual numbers of Scandinavians caught up in these eastern migration flows. For one thing, all the excavated remains relate

to trade centres. Did Scandinavian farmers also establish rural settlements, as they did in Iceland and the northern and western isles?
Stray finds from the Volkhov region might suggest that there at least
they did, in which case we would have to multiply our conception of
immigrant numbers considerably. There is also good reason to doubt
that anything like all the Scandinavian settlements in Russia have been
identified. Staraia Ladoga and Sarskoe Gorodishche would not be
enough to support the reported Khaganate, but they are the only two
sites known so far to have been in existence by 839. Similarly I doubt
very much that even the fourteen or so known Scandinavian sites of
the tenth century are telling the full story. The proportion of women
to men among the immigrants is also unclear, although the presence
of Scandinavian women is evident in all the tenth-century settlements,
except for those of the Middle Dnieper. There are far too many
unknowns to hazard much of a guess, but, by the tenth century we
must be talking again ten thousand-plus male immigrants, and this is
likely to be a gross understatement.

When it comes to understanding the Scandinavian migration units
carrying forward the Russian colonization, there is again an absence of
historical sources. At least some, however, are likely to have taken the
form of small-scale merchant adventurers, like Ottar and his companions, who either owned one boat, or just a share in one – a pattern
recorded on at least one runestone. A famous group of over twenty
runestones, likewise, was put up in Svinnegarn in Uppland in the mid-
eleventh century to commemorate a group of local merchants who
failed to return from an expedition led by a certain Ingvar.[53] This was
obviously later and larger, but, originally, a flow of Ottar-type figures down the Russian river systems was probably a common sight.
At the same time, we must also reckon, at least from the ninth
century, with larger and more organized intrusions: jarls or kings, with
retinues in the hundreds. It would have needed a group more on this
scale to establish the first Khaganate already in the ninth century, and,
as we have seen, coinciding with the Great Army era in the west,
much larger Scandinavian forces began to operate on the Russian
rivers.

Scandinavian migration into Russia thus probably combined a
steady flow of small-scale merchants, some of whom eventually settled
there, with more sporadic intrusions of larger armed forces. As in the
west both types, presumably, sometimes brought their womenfolk

with them, but we have no idea how often. The overall effect of these migration flows, however, was very different from in the west. Scandinavians came to Russia to exploit the wealth that could be generated by trading its natural resources, not to steal its movable wealth and/or to seize farms from existing owners and take control of its landed assets. There is no sign in Russia, therefore, of even a partial elite replacement. In Russia, the Norse formed a new kind of elite, which made its fortune by connecting up areas rich in the requisite raw materials with established centres of consumption in western Europe and the Near East.

While it is important to sift through the evidence, not least to establish the different types of Norse migration flow, the numbers game, as so often in the first millennium, fails to get you very far. Either we have no idea of how many migrants there were, or we don't know their ratio to the indigenous population, or both. But, again, taking a qualitative approach is much more revealing. The flow came in several forms. The land-grabbing in the north-west was led by small-scale local elites who could afford ships and gather small armed retinues, Danelaw and north Francia were settled by kings and jarls at the head of much larger warbands, while a mixture of merchant adventurers and kings or jarls was responsible for different aspects of the diaspora into European Russia. Even where landed assets were being seized, none of this looks at all like the Hun-generated migration into the Roman Empire of the later fourth and the fifth century. Viking migration everywhere came in the form of extended flows, sometimes over a century and a half, rather than one big pulse of mass movement. What some of it most resembles, in my view, is what can be constructed of the spread of northern Germanic groups south and east to the Black Sea region in the second and third centuries, or the Boers among more modern examples. And particularly in the west, we are seeing a flow that changed form and grew in momentum as understanding of the range of opportunities now available grew among Scandinavian populations.

Despite these variations, Viking migration administered a substantial political and often cultural shock, as well, to all the areas it affected. In the northern and western isles, together with Danelaw and Normandy, local political and socioeconomic structures were bent completely out of shape. Local elites were either fully or partially replaced in their control of landed assets, old kingdoms were sometimes destroyed, and new political structures created. The amount of violence here must be properly acknowledged. It is a striking fact of Anglo-Saxon studies that almost no pre-ninth-century charters survive from the old kingdoms of Northumbria and Mercia that fell into the hands of the Vikings as Danelaw. They are not that numerous elsewhere, but some survive. They fail to survive from Danelaw because the monasteries, where they were kept, were burned. We know too that the kingdom of Northumbria, the home of Bede, built up a powerful Christian intellectual tradition in the seventh and eighth centuries. Alcuin, the greatest scholar of the early Middle Ages, was a Northumbrian cleric, and has left a detailed account of the library at York. Again, the Vikings destroyed all the books along with the institutions that housed them. In certain places, even bishoprics – highly durable institutions – were extinguished. Three old English sees never resurfaced after the Viking period.[54]

Some of the settlements of the Great Army era did not last long as politically independent entities. In the early tenth century, Wessex subdued Danelaw to create a united English kingdom. But even this is a sign of the political shock generated by Norse migration. There is no sign, had the Vikings not previously destroyed the power of Mercia and Northumbria – its two main rivals – that the Wessex monarchy would have become so predominant. Equally important, Wessex's conquest did not lead to the return of many of the seized estates to their former owners: the sokemen were still there in 1066. Much the same is also true in Scotland, where the emergence of one united kingdom in place of three previously independent polities – the Dalraida Scots, the Picts and the Strathclyde British – owed a vast amount to the damage inflicted on the latter two by Viking attack.[55]

Elsewhere, the political fruits of the Viking diaspora were longer-lived. Much water would flow past it down the Seine in the meantime, but the settlement at Rouen was destined to become the Duchy of Normandy. The northern and western isles of Britain, together with northern Scotland and the Atlantic isles, likewise, became part of a long-lived Scandinavian commonwealth. And the interrelations of its many different Scandinavian merchants, along with the kings who came to take a percentage of the wealth they generated, would eventually stitch together the first Russian state, to which we will return in the next chapter, and whose history continued its more or less stately progress down to the Mongol invasions. Of all the areas affected by Viking assault, it is only arguably in Wales and Ireland that the effects were less than earth-shattering, but even in these cases it is at least arguable that, because of the Norse, political development took new and complex trajectories.[56] To get too worried about numbers of migrants in the Viking Age is to miss the wood for the trees. In qualitative terms, the 'shock' administered to all the societies that played – usually unwilling – host to Scandinavian migrants is clear enough. In that sense, we are once again looking at a set of migration flows that can only be labelled mass migration. But this is to explore only one dimension of the Scandinavian migration process, and big questions remain. Why did the Scandinavian diaspora occur when it did, and why did it take so many different forms?

## THE VIKING EXPLOSION

The underlying causes of these flows of Scandinavian migration in the ninth and tenth centuries clustered, initially at least, at the positive/economic as opposed to the negative/political corner of the motivation matrix. Such a conclusion would come as a bit of a shock to scholars working before the mid-twentieth century. Then it was generally argued that it was overpopulation that was to blame for a great exodus of men, women and children from Scandinavia. At the time it was thought by many that the Goths had come from Scandinavia, which was, as Jordanes reports, a 'womb of populations'. Also, recent experience included large-scale migration, particularly to the United States in the late nineteenth and early twentieth centuries. In this context, it seemed an inescapable conclusion that the Viking diaspora was just one in a whole series of pulses of migration outwards, each occurring when population levels in Scandinavia reached bursting point.

The kind of detailed investigation of landscape and population made possible by modern archaeological methods have clearly shown, however, that some key corners of the Baltic world – Rogaland, Öland and Gotland – were more heavily populated in the sixth century AD than they were in the ninth. It was also the eleventh century – after

the Viking period had ground to a halt – that witnessed large-scale
clearances of woods and forests to create new arable land right across
Denmark. Again, therefore, the chronology is off. If overpopulation
was a problem in the ninth century, why wasn't new land opened up
then? There remains the possibility that at that point resources were
already tight in western Norway, where fjord and mountain have
always offered narrower ecological niches for farming populations.
This might explain why moderately prosperous Norwegian farmers
and their dependants seem to have been at the forefront of early
settlement in the northern and western isles. But this applies only to a
restricted area of Scandinavia, and even here we are talking possibility,
not demonstrated fact. In general terms, the Viking diaspora cannot be
explained by overpopulation in Scandinavia.[57]

In most cases, Scandinavian settlement in a given locality was
preceded by a lengthy period during which that same place was being
targeted for its movable wealth. And for a time, this wealth was carried
back to Scandinavia, not used to set up its beneficiaries in new
homelands, whether western or eastern. Except, it seems, for the
northern and western isles of Britain there was no substantial Scandinavian migration before the 860s, and a determined seeking after
wealth is really what unites the diverse activities clustered together
under the Viking label. From the east the merchant adventurers
wanted Muslim silver. Astonishingly, well over two hundred thousand
silver dirhams have been recovered just in hoards of five coins or more
from Baltic and northern Russian contexts. And this, of course, is only
those coins that have survived. Silver has never been anything other
than a precious metal, and it is impossible even to guess how many
other dirhams have, in the intervening millennium, been resmelted a
dozen times into everything from personal jewellery to Church plate.
Trade with the east, while eventually dominant in economic terms,
was chronologically secondary to trade with the west. Staraia Ladoga
was founded long before the river routes to the Muslim world had
been reconnoitred, and there was enough wealth being generated by
western trade connections to give rise to other trading stations as well
(a point we will return to in a minute).

In addition to trade, and sometimes actually alongside it, there was
a huge amount to be made in both east and west by raiding. Raiding
produced loot of all kinds, of course, but also slaves, and there is no
doubt, as we shall see in the next chapter, that Vikings played a key

role in what became an international slave trade in these centuries. This is a key point, one which makes some recent attempts to minimize Viking violence by pointing out that they were mere traders look a little silly. When you're trading in slaves, raiding is an essential part of your commercial activities. Raiding also generated higher-status captives who were excellent for ransoms, and it offered the possibility of demanding protection money in order to buy your departure. Between them, the many different types of opportunity for money-making generated by successful raiding brought in huge sums. Just from what happens to have been recorded – and again there is no reason to suppose the records comprehensive – Viking assault on ninth-century Francia extracted 340 kilos of gold and 20,000 of silver.[58]

Even Viking settlement, when it did eventually come, can be thought of as at least partly caused by positive, economic motivations. Since there is no evidence that landed resources were particularly tight in Scandinavia in the Viking era, then where Scandinavians did take land elsewhere it is likely a priori that they did so because more and better land, or better terms and conditions for landholding, were available in the areas to which they migrated. This is generally borne out by the detailed evidence. In the west, Norse migrants settled as dominant landholders. Their estates varied considerably in size. At the top end, the larger ones went to jarls and *godar*, the kind of men whose land seizures in Danelaw are reflected in the Grimston hybrids. But even at the more modest social level of sokemen, Scandinavian migrants were important landholders. Their holdings may have been limited in size, but they were their own, they probably ran them using dependent labour, and they personally retained elevated political rights and social status. Even if the individual farms were not huge, then, there is every reason to suppose that this was a desirable outcome for the individual migrant, and represented a better level of existence than would have been available to him had he not come west. In the east, the bulk of Scandinavian settlement – that, at least, so far visible in either texts or archaeology – was focused on trading opportunities. Scandinavians went to Russia to open up relations with indigenous fur trappers and/or to situate themselves in a more advantageous position on one of the riverine trade arteries. In some areas, such as along the axis of the Volkhov, they established themselves in areas that could be farmed before any Slavic-speaking population got there, so that, as in west, there may have been some taking of landed estates.

But whether this happened or not does not affect the fundamental point. Real Scandinavian migration – with the northern and western isles as a possible partial exception – developed out of previous contacts that were all about Scandinavians extracting new types of wealth.

There was a further reason why migration had to be secondary to trading and raiding. It was these activities that allowed Scandinavians to build up the wealth of detailed knowledge about both east and west without which settlement would have been impossible. The Scandinavian north had never been entirely cut off from the rest of Europe. In the Roman period, the Amber Route led from the southern shores of the Baltic to central Europe and the Black Sea, and this axis had facilitated and maintained considerable contacts between north and south. Some Jutland populations had been involved in the Anglo-Saxon takeover of Roman Britain, the ruling dynasty of East Anglia seems to have had some Norwegian connections, and some Heruli from the Middle Danube responded to defeat by migrating north at the start of the sixth century. Nonetheless, trading and raiding in the later eighth and the early ninth century brought larger numbers of Scandinavians into a much more intimate set of relationships with populations in both western Europe and European Russia than they had ever previously established, and provided the active fields of geographical, economic and even political information that made settlement possible.[59]

The need for geographical understanding is probably the most obvious of these. Without a long period of trial and error, even the terrifyingly vague navigational instructions with which the chapter began could not have existed. The whole North Sea/North Atlantic axis had to be opened up by the intrepid navigators who made the initial jump from western Norway to Orkney, and then made their way round the northern coasts of the British Isles before pressing on out into the Atlantic to open up routes to the Faroes, Iceland, Greenland and, eventually, even North America. There is a chance that the Irish already had some knowledge of the Faroes and Iceland, which may have sparked the Scandinavians' interest in the Atlantic, but reports that the first Norse found some Irish monks already in Iceland have never been confirmed archaeologically.[60] Less challenging, perhaps, but no less important, other Scandinavians were at the same time busy exploring British, Irish and continental river systems. It is easy to take all this for granted, but detailed knowledge had to be gathered before Norse raiders could push upriver and put fleets on to the inland loughs of Ireland, sail up the Trent to sack the Mercian royal centre at Repton, or find their way up the Seine to the riches of St Germain and Paris.

Russian river systems, too, took a huge amount of working out. In the mid-eighth century, it seems, all the Norse were doing was pushing up the rivers that flow into the Baltic in search of more chunks of fur-producing forest. From this it was a huge leap to finding out where their tributaries led, what possible further connections might be made, and how, eventually, you might end up in Baghdad. Rapids had to be avoided, shallows and sandbanks noted, and portages established between the headwaters of the different river systems. All of this required a huge amount of information and organization, not to mention changes of boats. Round about Ladoga it was necessary to change from ocean-going ships to riverboats, and archaeological evidence has shown that some of its inhabitants made their living by servicing this need. Elsewhere, the biggest problem was organizing the labour for portages. Although the requirement that the population of Smolensk pay its dues to medieval Russian kings in portage work is found only in a charter of 1150, this is the earliest charter to survive from the area and may well reflect long-established practice. When you stop to think about all the information that needed to be gathered, the two-generation time lag between establishing Staraia Ladoga to serve western markets, and the first evidence of contact with the Muslim south, becomes entirely explicable. The large amount of detailed geographical knowledge that the Scandinavian adventurers needed to acquire in every geographical quarter in which they operated is reflected in the geographical texts of medieval Scandinavia. These are full of classically and biblically derived knowledge, as you might expect of a learned tradition perpetuated by monks, but they combine with this specific and accurate information reflecting the practical intelligence built up over centuries of voyaging.[61]

Economic information was also critical. Without a detailed understanding of markets and of the almost unlimited demand for northern forest products represented by the Muslim world, trading down the Russian river systems could never have gathered momentum. An entirely different kind of economic information came to be understood early on by western raiders, namely that Christian monasteries were centres for precious metals, and sometimes too, especially in Ireland, for valuable human beings. Also fundamentally economic in nature was the growing appreciation of the value of different areas' landed resources which fed more directly into the later settlement processes.

Political understanding, too, was vital, not least when it came to settlement. Given that Scandinavian migrants were looking to settle as relatively wealthy, socially dominant landholders, they had to understand existing sociopolitical structures at their chosen points of destination. Before setting out, they had to be certain that they could oust the sitting elite, either on their own or with the help of a few retainers – as was the case, it seems, in the northern and western isles. Either that, or they had to work out how much force was required to achieve a similar result in areas of greater social and political cohesion, such as Anglo-Saxon England and northern Francia, and put together sufficient military manpower for the job. Whether this was their intention from the outset is unclear, but one key point about the Great Armies is that they were large enough to destroy the military and political capacity of targeted Anglo-Saxon kingdoms. And without this destruction, the reallocation of estates could not have followed. Sometimes, too, political knowledge of a more specific kind is evident. It would beggar belief to suppose it a coincidence that, having gathered in East Anglia, the Great Army then headed off for Northumbria. Any direction (except east – they would have got wet) was available to them, but they went north. And Northumbria was in the middle of a civil war. In similar vein, the switching of Viking forces in the decades either side of the year 900, backwards and forwards from England and Ireland to the continent, as opportunities arose and then were cut off, similarly reflects the impact of more particular intelligence.

We have, of course, encountered the necessity for active fields of information in every pulse of first-millennium migration. That operating in the Viking era was more complicated, and took much longer to build up than some of the others because of the huge distances and wide variety of locations it encompassed. It is over five thousand kilometres from Reykjavik to Baghdad even as the crow swims, with a hell of a lot of dangerous water, shorelines and riverbanks in between. For the same reasons, the Viking diaspora involved more complicated logistic problems than any other of the migration flows we have so far encountered.[62]

Aside from the prevalent emphasis on wealth generation – or perhaps one should say wealth gathering, since there was not much generation involved in sacking monasteries – the other unifying feature of the Viking diaspora is that all of its many and varied activities were waterborne. Trading, raiding, even settlement: all of these were based on the exploitation of the sea and of river systems. Access to the relevant mode of transport – ships – was of critical importance, therefore, and ships were not cheap. Only with the advent of the transatlantic liner – particularly its capacious steerage class – in the late nineteenth century did it become possible to transport vast masses of humanity overseas at relatively low cost. Before that, sea passages were too expensive to make mass waterborne migration for the poor a practical possibility, unless states decided to provide subsidized transport for their own reasons, whether free passages for workers required in new colonies, or convict fleets bound for Botany Bay. The few pieces of evidence we have all highlight the costs of shipping in the Viking Age. It was for this reason, as the sagas and other Icelandic texts suggest, that colonization of the North Atlantic was led by aristocrats – even if relatively minor ones. Only they could afford the necessary ships, although they brought their less well-off retainers along to provide the military manpower required either for subduing Picts and Scots, or for clearing the land and starting up farms in the Faroes and Iceland. The kings who came later into western waters presumably fitted out, in part, their own fleets, as well as hiring in those who already had their own transport. When an ex-King of the Swedes returned to re-establish himself in Birka, for instance, he had eleven ships of his own and hired in twenty-one others. Serving in the retinue of a king or jarl who could afford an entire fleet must have been one way for poorer men to get overseas, and presumably represented the path to eventual success taken by many a Danelaw sokeman.

An alternative approach for those who were less well off but had *some* wealth was to buy a share in a ship. A runestone from Aarhus records one Asser Saxe, who owned a part share in a merchant ship. The same stone records that he was also a lithsman – a member of the company of a warship – and it may be, too, that some raiding ships were fitted out on a part-share basis. One Frankish source refers to the Viking companies overwintering on the Seine in 861/2 as 'brotherhoods': *sodalitates*. This fascinating word perhaps indicates that each ship represented a small jointly owned raiding company. A similar conclusion is also suggested by the runestones from southern Sweden commemorating those who had failed to return from Ingvar's Russian expedition. That their families – presumably – could afford to raise the stones again suggests that they were not from the poorest stratum of society.[63]

Access to shipping, then, was the key logistic problem, even if the boats required were not all the same. There's a famous passage from *Egil's Saga* that you often see quoted. It records that Egil sometimes went trading and sometimes went raiding. Asser Saxe of runestone fame confirms that the substance of this report, while deriving from an entirely post-Viking source, is not at all inconceivable, and even traders went armed. On his first visit to Denmark, St Anskar hitched a ride with some merchants who had the capacity to fight all day when pirates attacked. But the two activities – trading and raiding – required different types of ship (hence, perhaps, the runestone's noting that Asser Saxe had an interest in both). Warships carried more men to row and fight, and had a shallower draft for penetrating further upstream on river systems. Merchantmen were broader of beam so as to carry more goods. At certain points, too, ships had to be swapped en route for riverboats. In Russia, as we have seen, Slavs provided the rivercraft – *monoxyla*, the word implying that they were constructed from a single tree trunk – used on the Dnieper.[64]

Scandinavian migration in the Viking era was strongly influenced, therefore, by the logistic problems it encompassed. Sheer cost is an important factor in explaining why the migration units involved were smaller than many of their counterparts of the so-called *Völkerwanderung*. Sailing may have been quicker than walking, but it was also much more expensive, and it seems highly unlikely that poorer Scandinavians could have afforded to take up any of the exciting and profitable new opportunities. This, it seems to me, is another reason for not believing in a large-scale migration of Scandinavian peasants into the Danelaw after the Great Army era settlements. Why would anyone have bothered to pay their transport costs, when there was a plentiful and thoroughly subdued Anglo-Saxon labour force already available for nothing? This may also be relevant when considering how many women and dependants are likely to have accompanied the warriors westwards. As we have seen, the explicit evidence isn't good, but, again, if women were available locally, then transport costs may have been one factor that reduced the number of Scandinavian females taking part in the action.

There is, moreover, a second hugely important fact to recognize about the naval technology that lay at the heart of the Viking diaspora. Not only was it expensive – much of it was also new. Sea-going naval technology had existed in the Mediterranean and even the Channel and the North Sea for many centuries by c.800 AD. But while inshore boats of skilful design had long been in use in the Baltic region, sea-going ships were a new phenomenon there at the start of the Viking period. Characteristic of Baltic waterborne transport in the late Roman period is the famous Nydam boat. Constructed in 310/20 AD, it was essentially a war canoe, powered by fourteen pairs of oars. It was found in the mid-nineteenth century, ritually sacrificed along with the equipment of the raiders who had manned it, in the same kind of bog deposit that has given us so much information about military retinues (Chapter 2). Its existence is a sign, presumably, that its former owners made one raid too many. For our purposes, though, the point is that it is an inshore boat. Lacking sails, its range was limited, and its hull design would not have been seaworthy in open waters. Up to the eighth century, moreover, nothing changed. No Scandinavian wrecks designed for sea work dating from earlier than c.700 have been pulled up by underwater archaeologists. A second famous source confirms the point. Amongst its other treasures, the island of Gotland is home to a series of picture stones, some of which portray Baltic shipping. No stone dating before the eighth century pictures a boat with sails.

It is impossible to be certain of the exact chronology, but from c.700 this changed. Pictures, the occasional fabulous burial such as the Gokstad ship as well as wrecks, not least the five Skuldelev ships which, when worn out, were used to block one of the sea lanes into Roskilde Fjord, document the critical revolution in naval technology. The new design had two basic components. First, the hull was made strong enough for the open sea. Clinker-built strakes combined with a one-piece central keel and elevated prow and stern to create a hull with sufficient freeboard, and which was both strong and flexible enough to plough through ocean waves without either foundering or being battered to pieces. Like modern skyscrapers that can sway up to six metres each way at the top in high winds, flexibility meant survival, where a rigid hull would have broken apart. Second, sail technology appeared. This involved learning not just about the sails themselves, how to make them and use them to tack against the wind, but also all about masts and how to fix them to the hulls. By the early eighth

century all of this had come together, and ocean-going ships superseded inshore war canoes. The whole Scandinavian diaspora would
have been impossible without this technological revolution, and it
began to work itself out less than a century before the first Viking
raiders exploded into western waters.[65]

This observation begins to answer some of the key questions about
what precisely triggered the Scandinavian flow of migration in the late
first millennium. In a real sense, the Viking period began when it did,
and not before, because the developing naval technology of the Baltic
made it possible for it to do so. But that is only half the answer. Why
should this technology, readily available nearby for centuries, have
been imported into the Baltic only around the year 700?

No shipwrights' diaries are available, but a broader run of evidence
allows us to make a pretty good guess as to what was going on. The
collapse of the western Roman Empire in the fifth century caused a
huge amount of disruption in established interregional trading structures in northern Europe. By the seventh century, however, trade
flows were strong enough again for kings to establish trading centres.
The deal was straightforward. The king guaranteed protection for
all mercantile activities taking place at the market he established, and
in return charged the merchants a percentage in the form of tolls
and customs dues. A still-growing body of archaeological evidence
has started to document the revolution that followed, as one trading
centre after another – they are generally called *emporia* in the scholarly
literature – sprang up along the Channel and North Sea coasts. The
first to be excavated was Dorestad, already known to have existed
from its coinage, hidden a little way upstream at the mouth of the
Rhine (Map 20). The wood cut for its ship quays shows that it was in
action by 650 AD. It was one among many important trading centres
on the north coast of the continent: Quentovic, upstream from modern
Boulogne, for instance, and the emporium on the Dutch island of
Walcheren. North of the Channel, Hamwih – old Southampton –
came into operation just a touch later than Dorestad, by 675; and
Londonwic, the Middle Saxon trading port upstream of the old Roman
city of London, has been identified as running along the Thames,
behind the line of what is currently the Strand. The new trade network
started in the Channel/North Sea zone, but quickly spread to Jutland
and then on into the Baltic. Ribe, an emporium on the west coast of
Jutland, was in operation by the year 700, and through the eighth

century other markets opened up around the Baltic circle: Birka and Reric earlier on, Hedeby slightly later. It was also precisely to serve the growing western European demand represented by this chain of markets that Staraia Ladoga was founded.[66]

It is just about possible that the chronology is coincidence, but I greatly doubt it. Human beings generally make technological leaps when there is a clear motivation for doing so. There is an overwhelming likelihood that the Scandinavians developed ocean-going naval technology precisely to grab a share of all the new wealth being generated by the burgeoning north European trade network. The chronology works, and the motivation is right too.

The texts suggest that much of this traffic was originally dominated by Frisian traders, but in the longer term they would lose out to their Scandinavian rivals. And it is always the middle-men, not primary producers, who make most of the money from any exchange system. The switch began in the eighth century when Scandinavian merchants started to get hold of ships that would allow them actually to traffic in goods, and not act merely as suppliers of raw materials to others. This marked the beginning of a major reorientation in trading patterns. The Norse raiders and traders of the Viking period not only took the trade into their own hands, but also redirected it through centres under their control. Sacking the old emporia was a game enjoyed by all self-respecting Vikings, and by the tenth century the only ones still in operation, which included Rouen, York and Dublin, were under Scandinavian control. Whether there had been a conscious plan to wipe out the competition represented by the non-Viking trade centres is impossible to prove, but this outcome is deeply eloquent.[67] The whole Viking diaspora of the ninth and tenth centuries must be seen as a consequence of the emporia network of the seventh and eighth. The powerful stimulus provided by the new riches flowing through northern waters made Scandinavian shipbuilders extend their skills dramatically, and eventually lured Scandinavian merchants and adventurers out beyond the inshore waters of the Baltic.

# MIGRATION AND DEVELOPMENT

So far, the evidence has been mounting up for the 'positive' – that is, the economic – motivations underlying the various activities of the Viking diaspora, whether trading, raiding, or actual settlement. In this sense, the migration element within it conforms to the classic pattern whereby major wealth differentials function as one of the prime motors behind human displacement. The word 'positive', of course, is jargonese from modern migration studies, and applies to the perspective of the Vikings themselves, the ones who were making most of the money. Those dispossessed of their lands, those raided, or those dragged away from loved ones to a miserable life of slavery would have had a very different point of view. But even from the perspective of those Scandinavians who were participating, a much more negative, political motivation did underlie some of the activities, often – as in modern migration flows – operating simultaneously with and alongside the positive drives.

A case in point is the settlement of Iceland. As we have seen, the early Icelandic accounts insist that settlers went there from about 870 onwards to escape the growing political power of the Norwegian monarchy. The culprit was probably the Earldom of More on Orkney, but in any event the Icelandic texts can be believed in reporting a negative political element to settlement. There are some very good reasons for thinking that such political motivations in fact applied much more generally to the Viking period, at least from about 850 onwards. In a rightly famous paper, Patrick Wormald suggested some years ago that the armed exodus from Scandinavia, which is such a feature of the period, was a sign of considerable political crisis within the region. The evidence in favour of such a view is compelling. Its origins are more than a little obscure, despite the progress made in recent years, but a powerful 'Danish' monarchy had come into existence in southern Jutland and some of the adjacent islands by c.700 AD. From the middle of the eighth century it commanded enough authority to undertake major public works, erecting a huge ditch and earthwork along its southern boundary – the Danevirke – and cutting a canal through the island of Samsø. In Carolingian texts of c.800 we meet one of its kings, Godfrid, who could assemble ships in the hundreds and warriors in the thousands, and who was capable of relocating – whether they liked it or not – merchants from adjacent Slavic territories to his own newly planned emporium at Hedeby, presumably because he wanted their customs dues.

It would be wrong to overstress the degree of political stability enjoyed by this polity. Godfrid himself was eventually assassinated, and Frankish annals from the first half of the ninth century make it possible to reconstruct some of its subsequently rocky political history, as either members of two branches of the same dynasty, or of two different dynasties, fought for its control. In the mid-ninth century, however, the violence exploded beyond the bounds of the normal. On his second visit to Scandinavia, the missionary St Anskar found King Horic II, and everyone else with whom he'd previously had contact at the court, dead, and from c.850 to 950 there is no sign at all of a unified Danish monarchy. It has sometimes been argued that this is an illusion created by the silence of Frankish sources, but the problem went deeper than that. The first really powerful figure to re-emerge in Jutland and the islands is Harold Bluetooth of the Jelling dynasty in the mid-tenth century. And amongst his famous monuments is a runestone on which he claims that uniting the territories under his rule was his own political achievement. I see no reason to disbelieve him, because the claim fits well with all the other evidence. After about a century of impressively documented activity, between c.750 and 850, then, the centralized Danish monarchy collapsed. As Patrick Wormald pointed out, this fragmentation coincided pretty much exactly with the explosion outwards from Scandinavia – eastwards as well as westwards – of higher-status leaders and their retinues. It was this latter phenomenon, as we have seen, that created the Great Army era, and it surely cannot be a coincidence that it occurred as home political structures were collapsing.[68]

As we have found with every other migration flow of the first millennium, external political structures affected the action. Development is an umbrella concept that is as much about politics as it is about economics. Greater levels of wealth, or the opportunities for acquiring it, attracted the Norse out of the Baltic circle, but the nature of the political structures at the points where this wealth was to be found dictated the means and mechanisms by which Scandinavian populations could get access to it. As we have seen, local political structures firmly dictated the scale of Norse migration units. Where they were small-scale, the settlers did not have to come in compact masses, whether we're talking the northern and western isles of Britain or indeed the North Atlantic. This would also have been true of northern Russia if, indeed, there was some land-grabbing there too. Where political structures were large-scale and robust, however, the Scandinavians had either to access local wealth by less direct means, such as trading with the Islamic world rather than confronting it head-on or developing a more symbiotic relationship with the kings of Ireland. Alternatively, they could come in sufficient numbers to stand some chance of winning the battles that had to be fought, which they did with great gusto in the Great Army era in England and northern Francia. Here, settlement on the kinds of terms Vikings were interested in required the prior destruction of local political structures, and the Great Armies provided the necessary vehicle. More short-term political factors also influenced the precise shape of the action. The Great Army attacked Northumbria first because that kingdom was in the grip of civil war, and over the next thirty years the action ebbed and flowed across the Channel in an inverse relationship to the perceived strength of Frankish and Anglo-Saxon monarchies.

Migration and political development were interacting, however, on yet another level in the Viking era. Returning to Wormald's argument – what was it, exactly, that caused the explosive political crisis in mid-ninth-century Scandinavia? We have no contemporary Scandinavian accounts, and Frankish chroniclers were much too exterior to the action, so there is no circumstantial narrative to illuminate the situation. It is highly pertinent, however, to think in general terms about what had been happening in Scandinavia in the fifty years or so before the murder of Horic II. As we have seen in some detail, the effect of the Viking period as a whole, with its potent mixture of trading and raiding, was to bring a huge flow of wealth into the region from entirely new sources – Muslim silver, precious metals from the west, the returns on slaves and furs traded in east and west. These wealth flows, moreover, were not under the direct control of the Jutland monarchy. When the Carolingians wished to curb the piracy, they had to persuade the Danish kings to act. Even more important, the wealth generated overseas was sometimes used to further political ambitions at home. The *Life of St Anskar* reports the highly revealing case of King

Anoundas, who had been expelled from Birka but then made enough money in the west to hire himself a big enough force to regain control. A Frankish source also tells us – rather cryptically – that Reginharius, the sacker of St Denis, met his end at the court of Horic, perhaps in response to Carolingian prompting. Maybe so, but Horic will have had his own reasons for making the hit, and this takes us straight to the extra dimension I would add to Wormald's original argument.[69]

It was, I would argue, the huge flow of riches into Scandinavia generated by the first fifty years of the Viking diaspora that actually caused the political crisis that destroyed the Danish monarchy and led so many high-status Scandinavian leaders to turn westwards. As the Anoundas anecdote shows us, wealth was power in a straightforward fashion in the ninth-century Baltic. Gold and silver allowed you to recruit and control larger military followings. The Danish monarchy of c.800, however, was a fundamentally pre-Viking era political construction. Although it was certainly deriving some extra wealth from the economic currents – not least from the emporia trade network, as Godfrid's construction of Hedeby demonstrates – it was neither in direct control of, nor the main beneficiary of, all the new wealth flooding into the Baltic from Viking activity. These riches, much of them ending up in other hands, were a direct threat to the Danish monarchy. It needed to be the wealthiest body in the region to command the loyalty of enough warriors to maintain its position. Horic surely appreciated this, and may well have scotched the ambitions of Reginharius with this in mind, but so much new silver and gold was coming in that the old power structure, built essentially on Scandinavian sources of wealth, could not maintain itself. Something very similar is seen in parts of the modern developing world where non-state organizations, particularly drug cartels, can sometimes make so much more money than their home state structures are able to from ordinary taxation that they become the real power in all or parts of the territories affected.[70] More than that, there was now so much movable wealth, in so many different hands, that the main political effect of the Viking era wealth flows can only have been to stimulate significant competition among Scandinavian leaders.

In this view, it was the flow of wealth that stimulated the crisis in Baltic politics. And the flood of leaders outwards that marks the Great Army era was caused by an appreciation of the fact that competition at home was now so heated that prospects for a long and prosperous

career were much better abroad. There were too many would-be
Horics, all so eminently able to buy in warrior support that the
attractions of trying to rule in Jutland and the islands were diminishing
rapidly. Not only did a more negative, political motivation apply to
the settlement of Iceland, therefore, but a good case can be made for
seeing the whole Great Army era as the product of a fascinating
interconnection of economic and political motives, of migration and
development. Certainly the higher-status leaders were coming west in
search of wealth, but one of the reasons they were now inclined to
stay there rather than return to Scandinavia – a tendency documented
in the settlements in Danelaw and Northern Francia – was the fact
that the political competition in Scandinavia was so intense as to make
carving a niche somewhere in the west (or, indeed, in northern Russia)
look comparatively attractive.

The Scandinavian diaspora of the Viking era again shows us
migration and development as two deeply related first-millennium
themes, in this case working themselves out rather differently from
some of the patterns we have observed in earlier contexts. Although
not completely cut off from the rest of Europe, the Baltic had been
something of backwater before the later eighth century when it began
to be drawn into the new north European trading networks – initially,
it seems, as a source of desirable raw materials. But Scandinavian
populations were quick to appreciate the broader opportunities opening up, and the new maritime technology that they developed enabled
them to profit more directly and, as a spin-off, to add new markets in
the rich Muslim world. Also, the more intensive trade links with the
west brought in their wake an appreciation of all the different ways
that were now open for making money out of that part of the world
too, and the Viking period proper, with its characteristic intertwining
of trading, raiding and settlement, got under way.

As we have seen in so many other cases, a basic imbalance of
wealth was the fundamental cause of the human diasporas of the
Viking period, and migration towards that wealth was part and parcel
of the general response to the original inequality.

In this era, however, direct relocation by large, mixed population
groups into the wealthier regions was a less marked response than we
have seen in analogous situations, when groups from the outer
periphery of the Roman Empire moved at different points into the
wealthier inner periphery, or from the inner and outer peripheries into

the Empire itself in the Hunnic period. In the Viking diaspora, at least initially, there was as much removing of wealth back to Scandinavia as there was direct movement to appropriate the assets where they were located. This difference was caused by logistics, which gives the Viking era its particular form.

The Viking diaspora was all about ships, whose expense posed considerable limitations in terms of scale and access. Even when migration occurred, it could not take the form of massive mixed population groups, as some of the displacements of the fourth and fifth centuries did. As we have seen, some of the groups involved in these earlier eras may have numbered as many as a hundred thousand men, women and children. In the ninth and tenth centuries, Scandinavian kings transported warrior retinues, minor aristocrats with their retainers and some farm workers, while lesser men joined together to buy ships for war and/or trade. But not everyone had access to the necessary transport to participate, and it was just too far – or too wet – to walk.

When all is said and done, then, we are led firmly back to the ships, and even if they imposed certain limits it is the ships that made it all possible. What we're seeing here is the full working-out of an early phase of European integration. Moving by land, early medieval populations could hope to manage maybe forty kilometres a day. Viking sailing ships, however, could cover four times that distance or more in twenty-four hours. Measured in human terms, then, the overall effect of importing the new sea-going naval technology into the Baltic in the eighth century was to bring the rest of Europe four times closer to Scandinavia than had previously been the case. It was the Dark Age equivalent of building an airport in or a high-speed rail link to the Baltic. And once the new transport was in place, it didn't take Scandinavians long to appreciate that, compared with societies nearer home, it was the rest of Europe that offered the really exciting opportunities for acquiring wealth. The end results were excellent for those elements of the Norse population able to benefit, but not so good for those left out in the cold. Not every phase of European integration, you might say, has had such positive effects as the determination to avoid any repeat of the Second World War, which has been so evident since 1945.

With the working-out of Norse migration, cultural patterns in central and eastern Europe more or less assumed the shape that would characterize them in the year 1000. Compared with the Roman epoch, Germanic (or rather, Germanic-dominated) Europe had shrunk drastically in the second half of the millennium, being replaced by a truly massive Slavic-dominated periphery. Its extent was itself tempered only slightly by Norse expansion into western Russia, because there is no sign that the Scandinavian immigrants there had any desire to absorb indigenous Slavic and other groups into their culture. But if a powerful combination of migration and absorption had finally replaced the cultural patterns of the Roman era with others more directly ancestral to those of the modern day, there is another dimension to the creation of central and eastern Europe that we need to explore. Not only was this region dominated by Slavic-speakers with a seasoning of Norse by the year 1000, but it was also home to powerful state-like structures that had replaced the very small-scale societies typical of the Roman period. What was the nature of these new entities, and why did they now dominate large expanses where previously human beings had tended to operate in groups of a few hundred?

# 10

# THE FIRST EUROPEAN UNION

In the winter of 999 AD, the Holy Roman Emperor Otto III left the city of Rome. He was a Saxon, not a Roman, and not particularly holy, but such was the draw of the imperial city that he had made his way there both to make a statement about his own importance, and to use its religious prestige to hold a synod in which to slap down an archbishop who had been causing him the odd problem. This much was more or less standard – if you happened to be an emperor. What's really striking, however, and the point at which the third Otto's activities intersect with the focus of this book, is where he went next. Normal imperial activities over the winter might include a spot of hunting, or heading off somewhere pleasant to hold a synod or a council, and/or celebrating one of the major Christian festivals with his great men, ecclesiastical and secular. But Otto did none of these. The emperor had heard of the miracles being performed at the tomb of a recent Christian martyr, the bishop and missionary Adalbert, and had resolved to pay the shrine a visit. Nothing out of the ordinary in that, you might think. First-millennium emperors, Roman or not, all thought they were appointed by God and had a vested interest in manifestations of divine power. But this is where it gets interesting.

Before turning to the brief and ill-fated missionary drive that led to his death, Adalbert had been Bishop of Prague in Bohemia. Otto, however, was not setting off for Prague, nor in fact for Bohemia at all, but Poland. There the latest representative of its ruling Piast dynasty, Boleslaw Chrobry ('the Brave'), had ransomed Adalbert's body and built a magnificent tomb for it at Gniezno. We can pick up the story of what happened next in the words of a contemporary chronicler, Bishop Thietmar of Merseburg.

> [Otto] was led into the church where, weeping profusely, he was moved to ask the grace of Christ's martyr. Without delay, he

established an archbishopric there ... He committed the new foundation to Radim, the martyr's brother, and made subject to him Bishop Reinbern of Kolberg, Bishop Poppo of Krakow, and Bishop John of Wroclaw ... And with great solemnity, he also placed holy relics in an altar which had been established there. After all issues had been settled, the duke [of Poland] honoured Otto with rich presents and, what was even more pleasing, three hundred armoured warriors. When the emperor departed, Boleslav and an illustrious entourage conducted him to Magdeburg, where they celebrated Palm Sunday with great festivity.[1]

For our purposes, it's the backdrop to Otto's imperial progress that is so significant.

At the start of the first millennium, Poland and Bohemia had been dominated by Germanic-speakers, and the basic pattern of life involved clusters of wooden huts – some larger, some smaller – grouped together amidst the prevailing forests. There were still plenty of trees left at the end of the millennium, but the ruling Premyslid and Piast dynasties of Bohemia and Poland were all Slavic-speakers. The wooden huts had been superseded by castles, cathedrals and armoured knights, which, as we shall see in a moment, had become pretty much standard appurtenances of power right across central and eastern Europe. Not only that, but central Poland had become a destination fit for an emperor, and a suitable location for an independent province of the Christian Church, complete with its own archbishop. There could be no greater symbol, if an imperial visit was not itself symbol enough, that Poland had just been welcomed to the club of Europe's Christian states.

Nor was Poland alone. Prague, as we have just seen, had a bishop too, and although Bohemia didn't yet rate an archbishopric, it too had its fair share of castles, cathedrals and knights. Its Premyslid dynasty had definitively converted to Christianity in the person, no less, of Good King Wenceslas – or perhaps just Wenceslas, since we are dealing with his historical incarnation – in the 920s. Subsequent members of the dynasty slipped in and out of Ottonian imperial favour, but this would be true of the rulers of Poland too, and doesn't alter the fact that both these Slavic ruling lines were firmly members of the club. The first Slavic entity to demand and be granted recognition on this higher plane, in fact, had been 'Great' Moravia, which emerged from the wreck of the old Avar Empire in the mid-ninth century. It was the first Slavic state to convert to Christianity, receiving in the 860s, amongst other missionaries, the famous Byzantine Saints Cyril and Methodius, who were responsible for the first written form of a Slavic language, produced to translate key Christian materials for their new converts.[2]

In Scandinavia too, in the aftermath of a chaotic Viking century, matters were moving in a similar direction. From the mid-tenth century, a powerful state structure began to emerge, based on Jutland and the Danish islands and dominated by successive members of the Jelling dynasty, named after the place from which they originated. Originally pagan, the dynasty converted to Christianity in the person of Harold Bluetooth, and while maintaining a larger naval capacity than its continental Slavic counterparts it too was soon putting up castles and cathedrals, and likewise alternately squabbling with or receiving favours from different Holy Roman emperors. Intermarriages between the Danish and Slavic, particularly the Polish, dynasties soon followed, and they were all part of the same broader diplomatic and cultural orbit.[3]

As we saw in the last chapter, moreover, Scandinavian expansion had flowed as much eastwards as westwards, and one of its chief outcomes in this sphere was the Rurikid-dominated Rus state, centred on Kiev. This dynasty held on to its ancestral paganism for a little longer than its western counterparts, and, reflecting the particularities of its origins, took a bit longer to get round to castles and cathedrals. Not, though, that much longer: Prince Vladimir converted his state definitively to Christianity in the late 980s, and shortly after the year 1000 constructed in Kiev the famous Tithe Church dedicated to the Mother of God. Built of brick and stone, it measured twenty-seven metres by eighteen, and could boast three aisles, three apses and a cupola: the greatest structure yet seen so far east and north in the European landscape.[4]

The last two hundred years of the first millennium thus saw new political powers of considerable stature spring up right across central and eastern Europe, in some of the areas that had belonged to the most underdeveloped parts of the western Eurasian landscape. With their emergence, Europe finally took on something of the shape that it has broadly retained down to the present: a network of not entirely dissimilar and culturally interconnected political societies clustering at the western end of the great Eurasian landmass. But what, precisely, was the nature of these new entities, and how had they come into being? What, too, was the nature of their relationship to the patterns of Slavic and Scandinavian expansion we have been examining in the last two chapters. Did they just mean that you ended up with Slavic dynasties in some parts of old barbarian Europe and Scandinavians in another, or was migration central to the whole process of state formation?

## POLITICS AND DEVELOPMENT

As is often the case with the first millennium, it is easier to ask questions than answer them, and for all the usual reasons, though by the end of the period the situation as regards sources is a huge improvement on the era of Slavic expansion. Literacy eventually came to the Slavic world, as we have just seen, with the conversion to Christianity of Moravia in the mid-ninth century. But written Slavic did not acquire any non-religious purposes in this era, and in the centuries either side of the year 1000 even Latin and Greek remained largely restricted to religious uses within the new states. It was not until the early twelfth century that chroniclers around the courts of the new dynasties started to generate homegrown accounts of the past: Cosmas of Prague in Bohemia, the *Gallus Anonymus* in Poland and the *Russian Primary Chronicle* in Kievan Russia. These texts do contain some useful information, but all had at least partly celebratory purposes vis-à-vis their intended dynastic audience and patrons, and their memories of the ninth and tenth centuries tend to verge on the mythical.[5]

Of necessity, then, we are again often forced back on historical texts produced by outsiders: the western and southern European states with whom our new states quickly came into contact. This material poses the usual problems of reliability, although they are, in fact, less pressing than those we faced with Roman writers. For one thing, there is much more information. The Viking revolution in Baltic transportation brought Scandinavia into a much closer relationship with literate Europe, while Moravia, Poland and Bohemia were all its close neighbours. And much more was being written in literate Europe, in any case, thanks to the renewed emphasis on literacy that sprang out of the ninth-century Carolingian renaissance. The Emperor Charlemagne had made determined efforts to improve standards of literacy as part of his broader project of Church reform, and literacy continued to increase after Carolingian imperial collapse. When you also throw into the mix the fact that Islamic Arabic authors transmit some important information from another direction entirely, then you can immediately see why we are better endowed.[6]

A second point is nearly as important as the first. Within pretty short order, all our new entities converted to Christianity. This did not mean that their relations with more developed Europe, from whom they had acquired the religion, proceeded henceforth without conflict. Far from it; but the fact that they adopted Christianity did mean that they could not be viewed as barbarian 'outsiders' in the same unrelenting fashion that classical authors had adopted towards all non-Romans. In 1002, shortly after his Polish progress, Otto III went on another journey, this time to meet his maker. Sonless, he was succeeded by his cousin Henry II, whose arrival on the throne inaugurated over a decade of warfare between the Holy Roman Empire and the Polish state. Much of this is lovingly chronicled for us by Bishop Thietmar of Merseburg, but his narrative is striking for its lack of any real demonization of the Poles, despite the ferocity of much of the fighting. That this was at least in part due to the Poles' Christianity shows up in Thietmar's criticism of Henry for employing still-pagan Elbe Slavs as allies against the Poles.[7]

In addition, the new Scando-Slavic states constitute yet another subject area that has benefited hugely from the Soviet archaeological bonanza of the postwar years. Originally, of course, the usual distorting agendas were firmly in play, but so much information became available that they were fast losing their credibility even before the Berlin Wall came down. And, in overall terms, the Communist years brought into the scholarly domain a vast amount of information that would not otherwise have come to light. All in all, then, both texts and archaeology provide a great deal of information about our new dynasties and the political structures they erected. What does all this material allow us to say about how these new states worked?

## State and Periphery

Like their earlier counterparts on the fringes of the Roman Empire in the fourth century, these new entities in some ways fell short of modern conceptions of the word 'state'. The largely Germanic-dominated polities of the Roman frontier zone had been limited in their capacity to undertake centrally organized action. Politically, they were confederative, which meant that their overall rulers had to coexist with other 'kings', who retained real power, if usually perhaps within one locality rather than over the group as a whole. They were also limited in the quantity of resources – human and economic – that they could redirect for centrally designated purposes. Royal retinues numbered only in the few hundreds, even if the groups as a whole could field total military forces of ten thousand-plus. They have likewise left us few signs of any capacity to erect and maintain fortifications or other types of monument. Nor were these entities particularly large, although Roman counteraction was partly to blame for this, and the realm of the Gothic Tervingi, further east, covered a substantial area from the Danube to the Dniester. On all these counts, the new political entities of northern and eastern Europe in the late first millennium were much more impressive.

Geographically, the new states of the ninth and tenth centuries were huge. The Rus state ran from Kiev to Novgorod in a north–south direction, and east–west from the Dnieper to the Volga. All told, this amounted to a staggering million square kilometres, or near enough. The other states, too, were much bigger than their late Roman counterparts. Bohemia was the most contained, but this name is more than a little misleading since the kingdom usually encompassed most of what is now Slovakia as well (Moravia in ninth- and tenth-century parlance) – a much bigger area than that dominated by any Roman client state. The Piast dynasty of Poland, likewise, customarily governed lands all the way from the Oder to Volhynia and Galicia beyond the River Vistula, again an unimaginably large territory in mid-first-millennium terms. Even Denmark was bigger than modern preconceptions would lead you to think. The Jelling dynasty quickly put together Denmark and the largest of the adjacent islands (Öland, Skåne and Sjaelland), but also made their presence felt in nearly all of the most fertile lands of southern Norway, particularly around Oslo

Fjord and in what is now western Sweden. True to the best Viking traditions and proper first-millennium logistics, water united these different components, giving Harold Bluetooth and his son and grandson, Svein and Cnut, a large enough power base from which to conquer the populous and prosperous Anglo-Saxon kingdom in twenty years of warfare from the mid-990s.[8]

The disparity in profile between these entities and standard client states of the Roman period becomes even more marked if you look at governmental capacity: the kinds of powers they had available and the institutions they used to activate them. Archaeologically, the most striking legacy of these later states consists of castles. These new political authorities were capable of erecting by the score. By the year 1000, the Piast dynasty had dotted its domains with no less than fifty. The Premyslids, likewise, used garrisoned forts to control their central areas. In this, the tenth-century dynasties were following firmly in the footsteps of their ninth-century Moravian predecessors. Piast and Premyslid fortifications were constructed largely in wood (in case 'castle' brings to mind something anachronistically grand, along the lines of Edward I's constructions in Wales), but the Moravians had quickly learned to build in stone, and for good reason. One of our chroniclers notes the dismay felt by Carolingian forces in 869 when they suddenly found themselves faced with the 'insurmountable' – probably stone – fortifications of Rastiz (perhaps Stare Mesto now in the Czech Republic). On previous campaigns, they had been able to burn their way through Moravian obstacles, but not any more. The Moravians also used fortified centres to control landscapes. Their key political centre of Nitra was surrounded by a ring of forts: Devin, Novi Voj, Kolyka and Bratislava.

Individual population centres in Kievan Russia, likewise, were fully fortified, but here the archaeology provides us with a more striking echo of Rurikid power. Running south and east from Kiev for over a hundred kilometres are the 'Snake Walls': ramparts originally three and a half to four metres high, reinforced with a twelve-metre outside ditch. These were constructed in the very early eleventh century (so it's not really cheating to include them in a book that notionally stops at the year 1000) to counter the threat posed by the Pechenegs, the latest nomads to crash into the adjacent steppe north of the Black Sea. And if the new Slavic dynasties were the past masters of castle construction, the habit at least partly rubbed off on to the Scandinavians.

One of the most exciting finds of postwar Danish archaeology was a series of fortified power centres datable, thanks to dendrochronology, to the reign of Harold Bluetooth. Named 'Trelleborg fortresses' after the first of them to be excavated, they vary in size but are all beautifully circular monuments with a symmetrical arrangement of large halls within. Otherwise, being an entity whose constituent parts were linked much more by water than by land routes, its ruling Jelling dynasty was less obsessed with castle-building. Nonetheless, the list of late first-millennium monuments impressively underlines the capacity of these new states to engage in concerted construction. The most any Roman client state could manage was to put the odd wall round a king's hillfort in the case of the Alamanni, or try to repair an existing line of Roman fortifications in the case of the Tervingi, and even this much stretched group loyalty to breaking point. It is also unclear whether what were basically single fortified dwellings, such as those put up among the Alamanni, reflect the public power of a state or state-like entity – as both the regularity and the mass of late first-millennium construction do – or the clout of a particularly important individual.[9]

The capacity of these new states to raise and maintain troops was equally impressive. It had to be, of course, since to build multiple castles and not garrison them would have been a charmingly pointless exercise. We have no detailed evidence for Moravia, although the concerted efforts of various Carolingian rulers to dominate the territory, together with their ultimate failure, are eloquent testimony to the overall military power of the first of the new states. In the case of Poland the evidence is more specific. First, one of the Arab geographers tells us that a Piast king was capable of maintaining an armed retinue of three thousand armoured knights, paid for out of personal funds. The figure may be questionable, but not the nature of the force, since Boleslaw Chrobry had promised to aid the Emperor, whenever needed, with three hundred 'armoured men' as part of the archbishopric deal in the year 1000.

The key word in the original Latin is *loricati*, *lorica* being Latin for 'coat of mail'. The rise to military predominance of soldiers equipped in this expensive manner – the mailcoat being the single most costly item of contemporary military equipment – was a revolutionary development of the late first millennium. The fact that the Piast retinue was so equipped emphasizes that they were fully up to date.

And the promise to send three hundred men when asked is compatible with a total retinue size in the thousands, as Ibn Fadlan reports, since no one would ever agree to send anything like their full force to a foreign war. Equally important, this retinue was only one part of the Piast war machine, which rested on a military obligation imposed more broadly on at least some categories of the wider population. Again, the early eleventh-century sources don't give us the full rundown, but in the campaigns against Otto's successor Henry I we see a Piast army of many thousands which was capable of operating in detached divisions towards a common aim – as in 1003, when a force of three thousand men represented only one out of four Polish divisions engaged in the defensive holding effort against Henry's imperial might. What hits you about all this is the cost. Germanic retinues of the late Roman period numbered only in the few hundreds, and the indications we have suggest that coats of mail were at that point restricted only to a small elite. The Piasts reportedly maintained retinues on ten times this scale and were able to equip them fully with all the latest hardware. We have no contemporary documentation on how the money was raised, but later arrangements give some idea. Areas under Piast control were administered from the nearest castle, and, of the revenues gathered, one-third went to the castle commander, presumably in part to maintain his garrison forces, and two-thirds to the king. There were other, perhaps more important, sources of revenue too, but it is likely enough that the ancestor of this later system was already in place to help the Piasts maintain their forces.[10]

The observable patterns of military power in the other states are similar. They had to be. The Piasts, Premyslids and Rurikids regularly fought one another, the military balance swinging, depending on circumstances (usually which of the states was in the middle of a dynastic crisis), first one way and then the other. This cyclical pattern would not have been possible had not all three been able to deploy military forces that were roughly equal in size and nature. As part of their treaty obligations with the Byzantine Empire, the Kievan Rus agreed to send to the Emperor, when asked, a military force several thousand strong. This was large enough to play a crucial role in keeping the Emperor Basil II on the throne in the face of a major revolt, and again underlines the overall scale of Kievan Rus forces, since this expeditionary force would have represented only a part of the total available. Again, these forces were composed partly of specialist retinues, who figure at many points in our narrative sources, and partly of contingents drawn from the major settlements of the realm. We have no figure for the size of retinues, but the *RPC* gives some detail on two of the territorial contingents. One from Novgorod figures strongly in a civil war of 1015, a second from Chernigov in another of 1068. Both are said to have numbered three thousand men. Retinues likewise appear in our early Bohemian sources, a more general military obligation only in later documents. But, again, I'm confident that retinues alone would never have been sufficient for the rulers of Bohemia to compete so successfully on the international stage.[11]

The Jelling dynasty was rarely involved in these interdynastic struggles, but it did have to fend off the hostile attentions of successive emperors, and, as we have seen, was perfectly capable of sustained aggressive warfare against the Anglo-Saxon kingdom under Svein (986/7–1014) and Cnut. Exactly how they did so is controversial. Did they use retinue and mercenary soldiers and/or forces levied under a more general military obligation to the state? In thirteenth-century Danish documentation, the levied force is called the *leding*, and in that century could produce for the king a fleet of notionally one thousand ships, each manned by forty warriors. At issue is whether any kind of direct ancestor of the *leding* system was used by Svein and Cnut, in addition to the mercenaries (lithsmen), whom they certainly also employed. In my view, it is extremely likely that they did. Assessing and mobilizing a military obligation is one of the basic powers of any ruler, and it's hard to see that the Jelling dynasty's power could have amounted to much if they were not able to do this in at least some of the territories they controlled. It is also suggested by some of the more detailed evidence. The more or less contemporary *Encomium of Queen Emma*, wife successively to Aethelred the Unready and Svein's son Cnut, records that, in gathering his expeditionary force, Svein ordered that it should contain 'no slave, no freedman, no low born'. This sounds like a general mobilization order, and certainly overseas Scandinavian societies, such as those created in the Scottish islands during the Viking period, quickly organized with clearly defined military obligations.[12]

The power of these central political structures was not limited to the waging of war. We've already met Vladimir's Tithe Church in Kiev. Not only was this the Empire State Building of its day – at least as far as the Dnieper region was concerned – but it was just one part of a larger palace complex built by Vladimir on the Starokievskaia Hill. Two-storeyed stone halls, each over forty metres long, were built to the south, west and possibly also the north-west of the church. All were floored with glazed ceramic tiles whose design included the eagle, one of the oldest symbols of empire, and decorated with mosaics and paintings. Nor was this much grander than the best the rest had to offer. The grandest of the Christian basilicas discovered in Great Moravia was constructed at Mikulčiče and covered an area of four hundred square metres, making it very similar in scale to the Tithe Church, although little is known of its decoration. This was one of twenty-five stone-built churches known to have been constructed in ninth-century Moravia, and there were probably many others of wood. Denmark and Bohemia, similarly, quickly acquired a stock of more and less impressive churches, not least their chief cathedrals at, respectively, Roskilde and Prague. As befits so early an independent archbishopric, however, the Piasts trumped their rivals in the religious arms race. The cathedral at Poznan was a monstrous three-aisled basilica covering no less than one thousand square metres, while the tomb of Adalbert at Gniezno was adorned by Boleslaw Chrobry with a solid gold cross said to have been three times his own body weight. It has been estimated that there were, in addition, another thirty to forty churches constructed across the Piasts' Great Polish heartland by the time of Boleslaw's death in 1025.[13]

The capacity of these new states to make things happen also extended to communications. Odd bits and pieces of relevant evidence turn up in the narrative sources: the construction of bridges and roads, for instance, features in the *RPC*. More generally, in the earliest monastic documents from Poland and Bohemia, labour dues owed for bridges and roads feature as royal rights which were never given up when a piece of land was handed over to the Church. The land's labour force, in other words, would periodically be turned out to work on the highways at the ruler's command. Some of what this meant in practice has been elucidated by Danish archaeologists. Another of their great postwar treasures is the Ravning Edge Bridge, dated conclusively, again by dendrochronology, to the reign of Harold Bluetooth. This was a kilometre long, part causeway, part raised bridge over a particularly soggy bit of central Jutland. It required four hundred separate sections and the small matter of seventeen hundred posts to complete. Not exactly the Golden Gate, it was still a magnificent piece of determined construction, typical of the kinds of enterprise required to make the boggier parts of the North European Plain reasonably amenable to land transport.[14]

Looked at under these different headings – and I have chosen only a few examples – the new states of northern and eastern Europe appear potent indeed. They enjoyed considerable powers over their constituent population. More elite elements could be made to turn out and fight, the poorer to build roadways, palaces, churches and fortifications. Economic resources could also be mobilized to support rulers and their extensive retinues, not to mention an associated Christian priesthood, which was growing apace under princely sponsorship. There is not the slightest doubt that their achievements dwarf the political structures that emerged on the fringes of the Roman Empire. Nonetheless, there were still some important ways in which the new states remained profoundly limited.

For one thing, they operated with little in the way of administration or written record-keeping, even if writing played a slightly more important role among them than in Rome's client states of the fourth century. International treaties were on occasion committed to paper. The *RPC* includes the texts of two trade treaties made in 911 and 944 between the rulers of Kiev and the Byzantine Empire. All the internal evidence indicates that these texts are authentic, but the *Chronicle* was put together two hundred years later. The Papal Archives, likewise, contain a short but fascinating text known as the *Dagome Iudex*. A summary of it was copied into a register of Pope Gregory VII in about 1080 AD. Examined closely – the author mistakenly thought that the original was talking about Sardinia! – it turned out to be the last mortal remains of a late first-millennium international manoeuvre whereby in 991 the Piast ruler Miesco I (father of Boleslaw Chrobry) granted some kind of highly notional overlordship over his kingdom to the Pope in return for persuasive lobbying with the Emperor. In this case, the Polish original disappeared at some point; but clearly some of the diplomatic backdrop to Otto's progress of the year 1000 was conducted on paper.[15]

Literacy also played some role in the management of internal resources, but within the period covered by this study, only a marginal one. The oldest written records of land grants from Bohemia date to about the year 1000. They detail royal land grants to favoured monasteries, and provide some insight into how kings shared their existing rights over people and their labour with the new religious foundations. But even in Bohemia such texts are few and far between at this date, and in most of the other new states it is the later eleventh century before such grants took a written form, the twelfth in Kievan Russia. As the physical monuments surviving from these states imply, these early documents show that rulers had well-established rights to produce and services, and like early Anglo-Saxon England these states were capable of assessing the economic potential of populations and landscapes and of recording the fulfilment of the obligations thereby derived, but its scarcity suggests that not much of this was happening on paper.

This picture is confirmed by the other kind of written document to survive from the early years of these states: formal codes of law. From before the year 1000, evidence for the distribution of rules and regulations in written form come only from Church contexts. Among the materials translated into the first written form of Slavic by Cyril and Methodius in Moravia, for instance, were two Byzantine texts of Church law: the *Nomokanon*. Canon law texts in written form put in a similarly early appearance in Bohemia: surviving examples date to the second half of the tenth century. But despite convincing mentions of specific royal edicts in the chronicle texts, and the surviving physical manifestations of rulers' capacities to enforce them, these states produced no codifications of written royal orders dating to this era. The first secular law books from Poland and Russia date from the thirteenth century, and even these look more like codifications of existing custom than monuments to royal power; and prevailing practice, even this late, seems to have left much real legal power in the hands of more local authorities. Again, comparisons with western Europe help put matters into perspective. Church legal texts came to Anglo-Saxon England with the missionaries at the start of the seventh century, but it was not until the tenth that royal law-making started to take a consistently written form, and the later twelfth and the thirteenth that the English monarchy instituted the complex legal bureaucracy and record-keeping required both to make, and to make it possible for, people to bring their cases to centrally organized law courts.[16]

Bureaucratic underdevelopment, however, is not the main reason for regarding these new entities as only a limited form of state organization. Looking at the overall narrative of their collective histories in the period 950 to 1050, what's really striking is their capacity to trade vast tracts of land between themselves, seemingly at the drop of a hat. Take, for instance, Moravia – broadly what is now Slovakia. This fell under Bohemian Premyslid control in the time of Boleslav I (929/35–967/72), then under Polish control under Boleslaw Chrobry in 1003, back to Premyslid in 1013, Piast again in 1017 and Premyslid again two years later. Moravia saw the fastest-moving game of Pass the East European Parcel, but other territories had analogous histories. Silesia and Wroclaw were under Premyslid control in the mid-tenth century, passed to the Piast Miesco I in 989/90, back to the Premyslids in 1038, and were only definitively ceded to the Piasts in return for an annual payment of two hundred and thirty kilos of silver and fourteen of gold in 1054. Cracow in southern Poland suffered from a similar Piast/Premyslid identity crisis. What is now south-eastern Poland, from the Upper Bug to the Carpathians, was similarly swapped, but this time between the Piasts and the Rurikids. Under Rurikid control from the time of Vladimir in 981, it swapped back to the Piasts in 1018, then back again to the Rurikid Yaroslav the Wise in the 1030s.

Similar patterns are observable, if on a slightly different scale, in the outlying regions of Jelling territory. Southern Norway around the Oslo Fjord was always contested with rival lords established further west: first Olaf Tryggvasson in the 990s, then the dynasty of Olaf Haraldsson from whom medieval kings of Norway were destined to descend. The west coast of what is now Sweden, likewise, was eventually wrested from Jelling control by kings of Sweden based further east.[17] What all this makes clear is that it is anachronistic to think of these states as possessing clearly defined territorial boundaries. Over much of central and eastern Europe, the lordship of any particular dynasty was a highly contingent phenomenon.

At the same time, each of our dynasties' landed possessions comprised a much more intensively governed core, over which rulers were able to maintain a consistent authority and which rarely, if ever, passed into the hands of dynastic rivals. The heartland of the Piasts was Great Poland, the territory centred on Gniezno between the Rivers Oder, Warthe and Vistula that Otto III visited in the year 1000. Its extent is clearly marked out by the spread of tenth-century Piast castles (Map 20). Premyslid rule in Bohemia, likewise, had the region around Prague as its core, a zone again defined by the spread of early Premyslid strongholds. Kievan Russia had a double core, as we saw in the last chapter: Novgorod in the north, the Middle Dnieper around

Kiev in the south. Even in the much smaller Denmark, the Jelling dynasty ruled Jutland and the major islands much more directly and with a firmer grip than the larger region that at different moments found itself incorporated into Cnut's Baltic Empire. In the worst Premyslid dynastic crisis of all, in 1003/4, Piast Polish garrisons came as far as Prague, but this was only the briefest of phenomena, as was a parallel Bohemian annexation of Gniezno in 1038. Otherwise, these central areas were securely under the authority of their respective dynasties, and we clearly need to think of these states in terms of 'core' and 'periphery': core territories subject to permanent, more intensive control, and peripheral ones that were liable to fall under the control of others as the power of individual dynasts waxed and waned.

This is a common early medieval pattern, typical of entities that rely less on bureaucratic structures for their cohesion and more on the power and charisma of individual monarchs. The latter was classically expressed by regular patterns of itineration, with the ruler making the circuit of his kingdom, consuming food renders with his attendant military retinues and involving himself personally, as he went, in the needs and desires of his greater subjects. This kind of personal government worked perfectly well in small kingdoms, but characteristically generated patterns of core and periphery when geographical scale increased, to the extent that it's a broad rule of thumb that an early medieval ruler really governed only where he regularly travelled. All our evidence suggests itineration was the key mechanism of government in the new entities of northern and eastern Europe. The main economic right of the ruler referred to in the earliest Bohemian and Polish texts, for instance, consisted of food renders – the basic means by which an itinerant ruler fed himself and his entourage. For logistic reasons, food renders were always consumed close to source rather than transported to one designated royal centre. The larger Piast and Premyslid castles presumably served as the local collection centres for food renders.[18]

Kievan Russia had different origins, a circuit of political itineration not being central to the original Scandinavian merchants' gathering of furs, slaves and other trade goods, even if these did tend to be gathered on winter circuits. By the later tenth century, however, itineration and a more regular pattern of early medieval government were being established. When all of the necessary logistic structure was put in place is unclear. The *RPC* records, however, that, apart from avenging herself upon the Derevlians for killing her husband, Igor's widow Olga (c.890–969, regent 945–c.963) did much to establish towns, trading posts and hunting grounds in their territories, both much further to the north around Novgorod and further south around the River Dnieper and its tributary the Desna. Hunting was the main royal entertainment, and the main occupation of rulers' retinues on most afternoons. The will of Vladimir Monomachus tells us that he used to go hunting a hundred times a year. The establishment of royal hunting preserves, therefore, was – in a bizarre way – an important moment in instituting a regular cycle of government. I suspect that Olga's actions extended over a much wider area the kinds of institutions of rule and support that were already in place closer to the main governmental centre in Kiev.[19]

Danish kings of the Jelling dynasty, likewise, eventually became itinerant, and some of their early constructions, such as the Ravning Edge Bridge, were clearly all about making land travel more efficient, quite possibly with royal itineration in mind. It's hard to see what else the Trelleborg fortresses were for, if not for a monarch's itinerations. When first discovered, they were identified as purpose-built bases for the military forces of Svein and Cnut, who undertook the conquest of England. Their real date is actually too early for this, however, since they were constructed under Harold Bluetooth, Svein's father. Nor could their regular layout have served any straightforward military purpose, as has often been noted. On closer examination, the deceptively identical interior buildings actually served a wide variety of purposes: some were equipped with fireplaces as residences or for entertaining, others served as storage sheds and yet others for craftsmen such as blacksmiths and even goldsmiths.[20] The likeliest answer to the puzzle, in my view, is that they were built to extend Harold Bluetooth's capacity to express practical political power by itineration, an interesting moment in the territorialization of the Jelling dynasty's control.

The new states of northern and eastern Europe present us, then, with something of a paradox. Capable of highly impressive acts of government and of building power structures over huge geographical areas, they were at the same time fragile. Bureaucratically underdeveloped, they could govern only relatively small areas with full intensity, and larger peripheral areas were always liable to be lost to rival powers in moments of dynastic crisis. The rule of the itinerant dynasts provides most of the explanation for their at first sight paradoxical nature, but still leaves unanswered questions. Where had these dynasties come from, and how did they build up their power bases in the first place?

## Dynasty

The year is 995, the place eastern Bohemia at the confluence of the Libice and Elbe Rivers on the morning of St Wenceslas Day. But there's nothing cool, crisp or even about it, since Wenceslas Day falls on 28 September. Nor are we anywhere near the forest fence or St Agnes' fountain. We're with a group of men standing quietly outside the wooden castle of Libice, headquarters of the powerful Slavnik family, currently led by Sobibor, son of Slavnik. Four of his seven brothers are inside the compound, though he himself is on a visit to the Emperor in Germany. The quiet is broken by shouts and violence, orchestrated by Boleslav II, current head of the other power-ful Bohemian dynasty the Premyslids, and nephew of Good King Wenceslas himself. The action is swift and decisive. At its close, the compound and castle are burned out, the Slavnik males and their retainers destroyed. Slavnik power had been eliminated once and for all in what was arguably the most efficient hit of all time: certainly on a par with that February morning in 1929 when six members of Bugs Moran's North Side German/Irish gang were lined up against a garage wall – along with an unfortunate mechanic who happened to be in the wrong place – and gunned down by footsoldiers of the South Side Italian gang. The only thing missing in 995 was any pretence of an alibi. Unlike Al Capone, Boleslav II didn't bother to arrange a holiday; in any case, there were no packages to Florida currently available.[21]

Not only is it a great story, but the St. Wenceslas Day massacre represents the culmination of the political process behind the emer-gence of Premyslid-dominated Bohemia. Thanks to its position close to the Frankish imperial frontier and its own precocious literary tradition, which gives us two clusters of home-grown texts from the tenth century (one surrounding Wenceslas in the 930s, the other Adalbert at the back end of the century), Bohemia also provides the best-documented case study of dynastic emergence. It also gets us in the right frame of mind for thinking more generally about the emergence of all the new dynasties of central and eastern Europe.

There were some important differences of detail in the political processes involved, clearly, but there was also enough in common for Bohemia to provide us with a general model of how the new game of dynasty was being played right across central and eastern Europe.

From the historical sources, one dimension of the story is easy enough to tell, and pretty well known. As it emerged from the Avar Empire following its destruction at the hands of Charlemagne in the years after 800, Bohemia was subdivided into a number of separate political units with their own leaders (called *duces* in Frankish sources, but with the general meaning of 'leader' rather than something as grand and hereditary as the modern English 'duke' implies). The ninth- and tenth-century sources give us a series of snapshots, which between them strongly imply that the Premyslids emerged from a Darwinian process whereby these different ducal lines eliminated each other, until only one remained.

The first snapshot comes from 845, when fourteen *duces* from Bohemia presented themselves for baptism at the Easter court of the Frankish King Louis the German. Fourteen 'leaders' strongly implies that each ruled only a relatively small area, but ducal numbers quickly declined. In 872 only five Bohemian princes turned up at the court of Louis the German, and by 895 there were only two. Part of this picture of ducal decline may be historiographical accident. I am not convinced that the sources are full enough, for instance, for us to be certain that there were only two pre-eminent leaders left in the game as early as 895. This would imply that Premyslids and Slavniks then managed a century of coexistence before their final showdown, and this seems unlikely. But the basic picture is clear enough. State formation in Bohemia was the result of a political process – played out over pretty much two hundred years from Charlemagne's destruction of the Avar Empire – which saw one ducal line eliminating its peers to bring an ever larger core region under its control. As with similar processes affecting Germanic groups earlier in the millennium, each stage need not have been as violent as the St Wenceslas Day massacre. Some of the other, originally peer, families may have been willing to accept demotion rather than demolition. Nonetheless, there is every reason to suppose that violence regularly punctuated the process.[22]

As far as we can tell, similar dynastic games underlay the creation of the two of our other new states that emerged from the wreck of the Avar Empire: Great Moravia and Poland. Great Moravia was the first to appear, in the middle decades of the ninth century. Carolingian sources for c.800–20 mention in passing a whole series of regionally based small-scale political leaders at the head of their own groupings, as Avar dominion in central Europe unwound. One called Vojnomir supported the Franks against the Avars, a certain Manomir appears briefly, while a major revolt against Carolingian rule was led by Ljudevit. The sources are nothing like full enough for us to attempt a political narrative of how these different dynasties combined and eliminated one another to produce the much larger power that was Great Moravia. But that they did is clear enough and, again, we are given the odd snapshot. The first really prominent Moravian ruler, perhaps the real founder of dynastic pre-eminence, was called Mojmir, and Carolingian sources record what was clearly a highly significant moment in the 830s (the incident can be dated no more tightly than 833–6) when he drove a rival prince, Pribina, out of Nitra in Slovakia to bring a broader region under his direct control. Using this greater power base, the dynasty continued to extend its control, as and when it could. Carolingian power kept its westerly ambitions in check through most of the ninth century, but as that Empire waned in the early 890s the Moravians extracted the right to exercise hegemony over Bohemia. From then on, a still more exciting range of ambitions might have been open to this ruling line, had not its career been cut decisively short from 896 by the arrival of the nomadic Magyars as a major force in central Europe.[23]

If we had nothing but the available historical sources, the emergence of Piast Poland would be particularly mysterious. The Piast state suddenly jumps into Ottonian narrative sources in the 960s, already fully formed under the control of the Piast Miesco I. With a heartland west of the Vistula, beyond the immediate border region between the Elbe and the Oder, the new Polish state was simply too far away from imperial dominions for our chronicle sources to observe its growing pains. Not even the *Anonymous Bavarian Geographer* knew the political layout of lands so far to the east. Thanks to the wonders of dendro-chronolgy, however, archaeological evidence – which is usually so much better at observing long-term development than the immediately political – has in this case brilliantly illuminated at least the final stages of the rise of the Piasts. Because the dynasty built its castles of wood – as pretty much everyone else in Europe was still doing in the first half of the tenth century – it has become possible, within just the last decade, to date their construction precisely. The results are revolutionary.

The emergence of the first Polish state used to be construed as a long, slow process of political consolidation, which gradually brought ever larger areas together under the control of a single dynasty. Long-term developments, as we shall examine in a moment, were certainly of critical importance to create the necessary conditions, but the archaeology has shown with striking clarity that the last stage of the Piast rise to power was sudden and violent. Piast castle construction clusters in the second quarter of the tenth century, demonstrating that the dynasty expanded its control over broader areas of Great Poland very quickly, from an originally narrow base (Map 20). More than that, in many of these localities Piast castles replaced a much larger kind of fortified centre, often dating back to the eighth century, many of which seem to have been destroyed exactly at the moment of Piast construction. The conclusion seems inescapable. The creation of Piast Poland, the entity that suddenly bursts into our histories in the mid-tenth century, involved the destruction of long-standing local societies and the imposition of Piast military garrisons upon them. How many of these local societies were 'tribes', for want of a better word – the kind of unit listed in the *Bavarian Geographer* for more westerly regions of the Slavic world – is unclear, as is how they were distributed across the landscape.[24] Just like Great Moravia and Bohemia, then, the new Polish state emerged by violent dynastic self-assertion, as the Piasts eliminated their rivals at the heads of those other, older political units.

Much is also obscure about the rise of the Riurikids. As we saw in the last chapter, the *Russian Primary Chronicle* (*RPC*) is both too Kiev-focused and too much composed from the hindsight of achieved Riurikid domination to provide a straightforward route into the complexities of early Rus history. Nor – at this stage at least – is the archaeological picture so arrestingly precise as that for Piast Poland. Nonetheless, the basic outlines of Scandinavian intrusion into Russia are clear enough, and hence too the key political developments that made possible the Rurikid state.

Amongst its other problems, as we saw, the *RPC* provides a thoroughly unconvincing account of both the date and circumstances by which political power came to be transferred to Kiev from Gorod-ishche in the north. The *Chronicle* both places the transfer a generation too early and seems to be hiding dynastic discontinuity or at least disruption in its odd and seemingly sanitized account of the relationship between Oleg, the first major political figure associated with Kiev, and Igor, Riurik's son and heir. The story also presents Oleg as gathering an army in the north and taking control of the Middle Dnieper by force. Yet it closes by saying that, at the conclusion of these operations, an annual tribute of three hundred *grivny* was imposed by Oleg on Novgorod in return for peace. This, the *Chronicle* notes, was paid until the death of Prince Yaroslav in 1054, which is late enough to fall virtually within living memory of the compiler of the *Chronicle* in the early twelfth century. So the payment is presumably historical. But why would a ruler who came from the north to conquer in the south, as the story has it, end up imposing a tribute on the north?

There are two other big problems besides. First, the trade treaties with Byzantium confirm that, well into the tenth century, non-Riurikid Scandinavians ruled their own Russian settlements with a great deal of independent power, since they had to be represented individually in the negotiations. Second, before the end of the tenth century the *Chronicle* preserves only a very simplified version of Riurikid dynastic history. From that point on, the transmission of power from one generation to the next always involved many contenders and civil war, but before that date, even though we know that the early princes were multiply polygamous (as indeed were their successors), the *Chronicle* mentions only one son at each moment of succession and nothing but a smooth transition of power.

None of this is credible. The 944 trade treaty with Byzantium tells us that Igor had two nephews important enough to rate a separate mention. There is no record of them or their subsequent fate in the rest of the *Chronicle*, and it's hard to resist the conclusion that history has been edited to give an impression of secure and smooth Rurikid dominance. Likewise, the Oleg story: was he a collateral relative of Riurik who first conquered Kiev and then imposed his rule on the north? Or was he a complete outsider who perhaps married into the dynasty so as in some way to legitimize his rule after the fact? And how, then, did power pass from him to Riurik's son Igor? It is also hard to believe that Oleg didn't have heirs of his own, so what happened to them? The politics of early tenth-century Russia were clearly much messier than the *Chronicle* would have us believe, with independent Viking leaders and a self-assertive dynasty all jockeying violently for position.

The full details of these internal political struggles will for ever escape us, but the kind of world we should be envisaging is clear. At this stage, as one commentator has evocatively called it, it was not so much a state as a 'glorified Hudson Bay company', composed of essentially independent trading operations located at various centres along the main river routes, loosely linked together by having to pay protection money to the most powerful among them. They acted in concert only in certain circumstances, such as when using their collective muscle to extract advantageous trade terms from the Byzantines, and no doubt also to engage in a little price-fixing. The Rus state began life, therefore, as a hierarchically organized umbrella organization for these merchants, no doubt established originally by force. Even so, the original merchant adventurers, or their descendants, were left with considerable powers and independence, and as late as 944 still ran their own localities.[25]

By the eleventh century, however, this stratum of independent non-Riurikid rulers in their own settlements had disappeared. By this date, the preferred solution to the dynastic mayhem which characteristically accompanied transfers of power between different Rurikid generations took the form of giving their own centre of power to each eligible contender. This was already happening by the year 1000, the *Chronicle* providing us with an exhaustive list of the twelve cities that were granted by Vladimir to his twelve sons, the products of five of his more official liaisons. How many other children he had generated from the 300 concubines he kept at Vyshgorod, the three hundred at Belgorod and the two hundred at Berestovoe is not recorded. At some point in the tenth century, then, the independent power of the descendants of the founding merchant princes had been curtailed, turning their formerly self-governing settlements into dynastic appanages. In fact, this was probably a steady process, which played itself out over a lengthy period. Oleg's suppression of Askold and Dir, to the extent that this story might be taken as historical example, provides us with an early instance of this kind of action. The *RPC* also records some later instances of exactly the same thing. In the civil war between Sviatoslav's two sons Yaropolk and Vladimir, new merchant settlements continued to be founded. Two Scandinavian leaders by the names of Rogvolod (Ragnvaldr) and Tury established their own trading centres at Polotsk and Turov. Their subsequent fate is not recorded, but both centres were among the twelve distributed in the next generation to the various sons of Vladimir, by which time their founders had clearly lost out. As part of the same civil war, another such locally dominant line, apparently a family established for a much longer period, that of Sveinald, also met its demise.[26] The full story of the suppression of the independent merchant lines is hidden from us, but it clearly happened, and it represented the final stage in the evolution of mercantile settlements into a fully fledged political union. Although the unique origins of the Rus state meant that the Rurikids began as one set of merchant princes among several – rather than as the leaders of one regional tribal group among several, as was the case with the Piasts and Premyslids – nonetheless violent dynastic self-assertion was central to the process of state formation.

The same was true of the last of these new states, Denmark, although here, too, the process differed substantially from that unfolding in the Avar successor states. In the small settlement of Jelling in central Jutland stands a not very substantial church and two huge mounds: the northern one 65 metres in diameter and 8 metres high, the southerly 77 by 11. Within the northern mound there is a wood-lined chamber dated by dendrochronology to 958, which was nearly the last resting place of King Gorm. Gorm's son and heir Harold Bluetooth originally buried him there, but transferred the body to the church when he himself converted to Christianity, probably around 965. Like the Mormons, Harold was taking no chances that his ancestors might be deprived of the joys of his new religion. Apart from shifting the corpse, he also erected a fabulous runestone whose inscription is still there to be read: 'Harold had these monuments erected in memory of Gorm his father and Thyre his mother, that Harold who won for himself all Denmark and Norway, and Christianized the Danes.'

The case of Denmark differs substantially from the other states, by providing a timely warning against the assumption that political developments always move in a straight line. As we have seen, a powerful centralizing political structure had existed in southern Jutland before the Viking Age, from at least the mid-eighth century when the Danevirke was first constructed. But this monarchy was destroyed by flows of new Viking wealth into Scandinavia. Wealth translated pretty much directly into warriors, and warriors into power, so that new wealth in sufficient quantities could not but generate political revolution. The old monarchy fell because so many 'kings' could now buy in so much military muscle that political stability evaporated.[27]

By the mid-tenth century, there are further signs of substantial change. For one thing, there seem to have been fewer kings. Viking-period sources demonstrate that a multiplicity of royals had existed in ninth-century Scandinavia. Apart from the one extended, or possibly two, separate dynastic lines found competing for power in southern Jutland (Godfrid, Haraldr and their descendants), there were more independent kings in the Vestfold west of the Oslo Fjord in Norway in the ninth century, and on the island of Bornholm. Birka and Sweden, further east, likewise, also had kings. A large number of other kings also appeared in western waters in the Great Army period, from the 860s onwards, and these must all have had their origins in some particular corner of Scandinavia. By my reckoning about a dozen of them are named, at different points: not enough to suggest that 'king' was a status that just anyone might claim, especially as we also meet men of slightly lesser status – jarls – who held back from claiming to be royalty. From the time of Harold Bluetooth, by contrast, the historical narrative throws up other 'kings' consistently in Sweden only, and occasionally in Norway. It would appear, therefore, that the word had undergone a change of meaning (as it did in other cultural contexts, too) from something like 'person from an extremely import-ant family' to 'ruler of a substantial territory', the normal meaning of the word today.[28]

That said, the Jelling dynasty did seemingly build up its power by bringing under its control disparate territories that had had their own leaderships in the chaos of the later ninth century. It may have been the dynasty's success, of course, that brought about the substantive change of meaning in the word 'king'. Gorm's wife Thyre is called in another inscription 'the pride of Denmark'. It has been convincingly argued, on the basis of contemporary usage, that in c.900 the 'mark' element in 'Denmark' meant 'regions bordering the Danish kingdom'; in other words, somewhere other than the main centres of the Danish monarchy – perhaps northern Jutland or the southern Baltic islands. Like our other dynasties, therefore, despite the substantial differences in historical context, the political activities of the Jelling dynasty were fundamentally accumulative – putting together regions that had previously been independent. This process was begun by Gorm and carried on by subsequent members of the dynasty. Harold Bluetooth added control of southern Norway to the dynasty's portfolio of assets after the battle of Limfjord, but ruled it indirectly through the Jarls of Lade. Svein and Cnut maintained this hegemony through most of their reigns, and at times dominated the west coast of what is now Sweden as well. Even so, the heritage of old independence did not disappear overnight. From the narratives of Danish history in the eleventh century, it emerges very clearly that Jutland and the islands of Fyn and Sjaelland were still functioning on occasion as separatist power centres.[29]

The political processes behind all these new states, therefore, were similar. In each case, one dynastic line was able to demote or eliminate a peer group of geographically proximate rivals to bring a larger region under its control. The vagaries of this process further explain the propensity of the states it created to swap intervening areas amongst themselves. Given that all these areas were originally independent, it is easy to see why some of them might maintain a capacity for autonomous political activity long after they first accepted a new dynasty's domination, especially in a context where itineration and personal charisma rather than developed bureaucratic structures were being used to govern them. But while full of arresting stories and individuals of striking charisma, political narratives of achieved dynastic ambition do not remotely begin to tell the full story of state formation in the north and east at the end of the first millennium. History is littered with ambitious individuals trying to build their power and thereby eclipse every rival. In most cases, however, such ambition does not lead to new and impressively powerful state structures. Apart from looking at narratives of personal ambition, then, we also need to think about the broader structural transformations that made it possible for entirely ordinary ambitions to achieve such unusual outcomes.

## State-building

Many of these changes were similar to those that had generated the larger political structures on the fringes of the Roman Empire in the first half of the millennium. Taking the long view, social and economic transformations of the most profound kind were structurally critical to the process of state formation in northern and eastern Europe. This is most obviously true of the Slavic-speaking world, but to a considerable extent applies to Scandinavia as well.

Up to the mid-first millennium, Slav or Slavic-dominated societies were characterized by little in the way of obvious social inequality. Whatever their exact geographical origins, the Slavic-speaking groups who burst on to the fringes of the Mediterranean in the sixth century had clearly emerged from the undeveloped, heavily wooded regions of eastern Europe, where settlements were small – no more than hamlets – and whose Iron Age farmers were operating at little above subsistence level and with few material markers of differing social status. This state of affairs had already begun to change radically in the sixth century, as a direct result of the migratory processes that brought some Slavic-speakers into a direct relationship with the more developed Mediterranean. From this, an unprecedented flow of wealth – the profits, more or less equally, of raiding, military service and diplomatic subsidy – quickly generated inequalities around which new social structures began to form. These showed themselves initially after c.575 in the rise of a new class of military leader, controlling quite substantial areas and groups several thousand strong – even if there is also some reason to think that other elements within Slavic society, represented by Korchak remains, retained older, more egalitarian social forms and were even using alternative kinds of migration, and in different directions away from the east Roman frontier, as a means to preserve them.[30]

The new Slavic states of the ninth and tenth centuries were constructed on a marked accentuation of these initial inequalities. This shows up most obviously in the existence of military retinues: that classic vehicle of social and political power, which had played such an important role in the transformation of the Germanic world. Presumably the new Slavic leaders of the sixth century had their henchmen, but large permanent retinues do not figure in any of the historical sources as a major force, military or social. The contrast with the ninth and tenth centuries is striking. The Arab geographers report that Miesco of Poland maintained a personal force of three thousand warriors – and this is just one account among many, stressing the importance of retinues at this time. In Bohemia, the fourteen dukes presenting themselves for baptism in 845 did so 'with their men', and the early Bohemian texts associated with Wenceslas refer both to his retinue and to that of his brother, Boleslav I. Frankish texts, similarly, mention the 'men' of both Mojmir and his nephew Zwentibald among the Moravians, and retinues were just as important in Russia. Again, Arab geographers pick out the four hundred men of the dominant Rus prince in the north in c.900, and retinues appear as important political pressure groups for several of the early kings in the narratives of the *RPC*. It was the need to satisfy the demands of his 'men', for instance, that led Igor to increase the tribute he customarily imposed upon the Derevlians. He may have regretted giving in, since, as we have seen, it led to his death at the hands of the aggrieved taxpayers. And as we saw among the Germani around the Roman Empire, the rise of permanent military retinues greatly increased the capacity of rulers both to bring rival dynasts into line and to enforce a range of obligations (such as army and labour services) upon the broader population. As such, it obviously played a critical role in the process of state formation, not least – again as among the Germani – in creating a much stronger dynastic component to power at the top. There is no sign among even the late sixth-century Slavs that power was in any sense hereditary, even if particular individuals could build up striking power bases.[31] But by the ninth and tenth centuries, dynasties dominated politics, and hereditary power was the order of the day.

But retinues were only one aspect of a broader process of social change. Part of the problem in understanding this bigger picture as fully as one would like to stems from uncertainties about its starting point. The idea of a highly egalitarian Slavic world in c.500 AD is strongly entrenched in both the scholarly literature and more popular mythology. It underlies the 'happy hippy' vision of Slavicization, and finds real support particularly from east Roman sources which note that sixth-century Slavic society was marked by a lack of structured social differentiation, as well as being unusually willing to take on prisoners as free and equal members. But such visions of Slavic equality need to be tempered with some caution. To echo a point made earlier in the case of the Germani, there are entirely non-material ways in which higher status can be all too real – if those enjoying it had to work less hard, enjoyed more food, and if their word counted for more when it came to settling disputes within the group.[32]

But even if we factor in a less egalitarian starting point for the evolution of Slavic society from c.500 (and as we have seen, any pre-existing egalitarianism was being undermined rapidly at this point by the twin processes of migration and development), much had clearly changed by the tenth century. Not only was political leadership now hereditary and its clout more wide-reaching thanks to its permanent military retinues, but Slavic society as a whole was marked by the evolution of clearly differentiated, and therefore presumably also hereditary, hierarchically arranged social categories.

At the bottom of the social scale, unfree population groups now played a prominent role in all our late first-millennium Slavic and Scandinavian societies. The slave trade was a major phenomenon of central and eastern Europe from the eighth century onwards. Likewise, as the new state structures evolved, a major component of their economic makeup (as we shall explore in more detail in a moment) became the unfree 'service village'. Given the available sources, it is not entirely clear whether the populations of these villages enjoyed a higher status than the slaves who were often exported – perhaps a status akin to those of the permanent 'freed' (better, 'semi-free') populations we encountered in the Germanic world. Either way, a large part of Slavic humanity had clearly been permanently relegated to hereditary lesser status (or statuses, if slaves and service villagers need to be distinguished) by the tenth century. However you model Slavic society in c.500 AD, the extent of change here can hardly be overemphasized.

Equally permanent at the other end of the social scale was a class of high-status individuals, often styled *optimates* in our sources. These men are recorded, for instance, attending assemblies in Bohemia to give their approval to their choice of Adalbert the Slavnik as Bishop of Prague in 982, and feature as the rulers of their own settlements under overall Rurikid rule in Russia (some of them independent enough to send their own ambassadors to Constantinople when the trade treaties were negotiated). Certain individuals with the same kind of high status also appear in the train of the King of Poland in the early eleventh century, and were presumably the kind of men Polish and other kings customarily offered hospitality to as they feasted their way round their kingdoms. Their existence a century earlier in Moravia is possibly also reflected archaeologically in the five so-called princely dwellings found in the hundred-hectare outer area at Mikulčiče, although these could have belonged to junior members of the ruling dynasty. The evidence suggests that this group coalesced out of originally three component elements. First, there were the close supporters of the new dynasty from within their home group. These were reinforced, second, by the elites of originally independent units (whether of Slavo-Scandinavian trading enterprises in Russia or 'tribal' units in Bohemia, Moravia and Poland), who accepted the new dynasty's domination; and, third, junior members of the ruling line. Before and even after they accepted Christianity, polygamy was usual – which made such junior royals a correspondingly numerous group, especially with a ruler like Vladimir who, as we know, numbered his concubines in the hundreds. Over time, the three became indistinguishable, between them eventually providing the nobility of the fully fledged kingdoms.

As in the earlier Germanic world, there was also an extensive free class operating in between the nobility and the unfree. They appear in some of the written legal sources from all the major kingdoms, except Moravia, which didn't last long enough to have any. Based on parallels with the rest of late first-millennium Europe, this group probably provided the bulk of military forces deployed by these kingdoms, beyond the specialist military retinues of the rulers. Elsewhere, it was customary for unfree populations to perform lower-status functions, such as providing the labour with which many of the striking monuments of these kingdoms were presumably constructed. Military service, by contrast, was higher-status, despite its obvious dangers.[33]

Even if you don't believe in an entirely egalitarian sixth century, Slavic society underwent a total restructuring between the years 500 and 1000. The sixth-century Slavic world evolved leaders who rose and fell in their own lifetimes, with no markedly hereditary element to their power. There is also no sign of a hereditary nobility, or of permanently unfree population groups. This might still have been true of at least some Slavic groups in the seventh century. The fact that a Frankish merchant, a complete outsider, like Samo, could still at this date be elected overall leader among a multiplicity of other Slavic *duces* would seem to indicate that such men were not sitting on top of a strongly hierarchical or hereditary social pyramid. But this had changed by the tenth century, and, equally important, the new states of the later period could never have appeared without these intervening transformations. Heritable dynastic power, the social and military clout of retainers and nobles, and a differentiated population who could be forced and/or persuaded to undertake necessary functions such as providing food and labour or military service: all of these were key elements of the new state structures, and none had existed in the sixth century.

The question of when the different elements of the restructuring had happened is very difficult to answer. The likeliest answer, as is so often the case, would appear to be mixed. Some of the change looks on balance to have had long roots. When it emerged from Avar control after Charlemagne's campaigns of the 790s, central European Slavic society already had the capacity to throw up powerful princes. Within a couple of decades, the chronicle sources give us a cluster of leaders – Voinomir, Manomir and Liudevit – capable of mobilizing significant military power for a variety of ends. This degree of control seems unlikely to have sprung up overnight and had probably been generated during the Avar period. This is also suggested by the fact that in both Moravia and Bohemia we find leaders – *duces* – with well-entrenched hereditary power over particular localities as early as the mid-ninth century. On the other hand, this observation needs to be balanced by the fact that most of the hillforts built in the Slavic world up to the ninth century appear to have been communally generated places of refuge. On excavation they characteristically lack any sign of an elite dwelling (often any permanent dwellings at all) or any other sign that the guiding hand of some great man was behind the project.[34] If a class of hereditary leader had emerged by c.800, then, it is important not to overestimate the extent of its social power.

Equally important, state-building had powerfully transformative social effects. Most obviously, the increasing wealth of particular dynasties led to the generation of retinues of increasing size and power. At the same time, much of the nascent nobility of the new states was a by-product of dynastic self-assertion, whether from the promotion of supporters and junior relatives, or the demotion of previously independent regional leaders. Castle-building in Bohemia, Moravia and Poland also involved the destruction of the old communal refuge-type hillforts and their replacement with new dynastic castles. And while the slave trade had certainly begun in the eighth century, it gathered pace dramatically in the ninth and tenth. Both of these latter developments probably played a major role in increasing the number of the unfree in the population (if not, perhaps, in initially generating them). My own best guess, therefore, would be that a longer, slower process of evolution had generated a body of hereditary group leaders by c.800 AD, but that the process of state formation after the collapse of the Avar Empire further revolutionized the situation.

How much of this broad model of social transformation is applicable to Denmark is a different question. State formation in Denmark differed substantially that in other cases, because there it was a question of state re-formation. A state-like structure comparable to the Slavic and Scando-Slavic ones already existed in southern Jutland and the islands from the eighth century, before being destroyed by the new wealth introduced into Scandinavia in the Viking period. As this would suggest and the sources confirm, Scandinavian society entered the last two centuries of the millennium with more entrenched social inequalities than was true of the Slavic world. Viking-period sources show us kings, jarls, freemen and unfree (thralls) already fully in existence. This makes good sense, not only because state-like structures already existed there but also because Scandinavia, or Denmark at the very least, had been part of the Germanic world (if belonging to its outer rather than inner periphery), interacting with the Roman Empire in the first half of the millennium, and had participated – as flows of Roman goods and bog deposits of weapons indicate – in some of the earlier processes of sociopolitical transformation. State formation in Denmark in the later ninth and the tenth century was probably much more a story of the promotion and demotion of existing power blocks and the dynasties at their heads, than of the fundamental social change that was central to the process among neighbouring Slavs.[35]

Social revolution, part cause and part effect, was absolutely necessary, therefore, to state formation at this time, at least in Slavic lands. But social change on this scale is never possible without parallel economic restructuring, and, again, there is plenty of evidence of this from contemporary central and eastern Europe. As with the social transformations, some of this preceded the formation of states and was a necessary precondition for their existence. Further change was then instituted by states themselves.

The hardest to document in a precise way is the development of the agricultural economy: food production. Not least, of course, is the fact that Slavic-speakers had come to dominate such a huge territory, with such a vast range of environments, that farming did not and could not have developed everywhere along a single trajectory. Nonetheless, the evidence indicates strongly, if at this point still rather generally, that farming outputs increased dramatically. At different speeds in different contexts, a revolution was under way that was bringing more land into production and instituting more productive farming practices, both in terms of the technologies employed and the management of land fertility. Most obviously, there was a substantial amount of forest clearance in central and eastern Europe in the second half of the millennium. In those parts of Poland with the right kind of lakes for taking pollen cores, the ratio of grass and tree to cereal pollen declined dramatically in these centuries from 3:1 to much more like 1:1, suggesting a doubling in the amount of cultivated land. This result can't be simply applied to the whole of Slavic Europe. I would expect the degree of change to have been less, for instance, as you moved north and east. Nonetheless, even within Mother Russia, the spread of Slavic-type cultures in northerly and easterly directions was closely associated with the spread of full-scale agriculture in the wooded steppe and reasonably temperate forest zones of the East European Plain. The phenomenon of general agricultural expansion is clear enough, then, even if it is impossible to put figures and dates on its impact in particular localities.[36]

The spread of more efficient farming techniques, too, is easy enough to document in outline. Initial contacts between Slavic-speakers and the Mediterranean world led some Slavs to adopt more efficient ploughs, types that turned the soil over so that rotting weeds and crop residues released their nutrients back into it. This increased both the yields that could be expected and the length of time particular fields might be cultivated. Further improvements had not yet worked themselves out fully by the time these states came into existence in the ninth and tenth centuries. The height of medieval sophistication in arable production, for instance, was the manor. Its advantages lay in the fact that it was a self-contained, integrated production unit with a large labour force, where farming strategies could be centrally directed towards greatest efficiency, particularly when it came to crop rotation for maintaining fertility, and costs (particularly of ploughing equipment) could be pooled and minimized. It was also an instrument for brutal social control, but that's another story. For present purposes, the point is that arable production in central and eastern Europe became fully manorialized only from the eleventh century onwards – after the new states had come into being. This finding came as a nasty shock for doctrinaire Marxists, since these were all supposed to be 'feudal' states, whose development was only made possible by manorializing agriculture, but the chronology is secure enough. Even if manorialization was still only nascent in the ninth and tenth centuries, however, we do have evidence that some key preparatory changes were under way. In particular, the amount of rye found in pollen cores in the second half of our period increases steadily. The use of rye, sown in the autumn rather than the spring, is associated with moves towards three-crop rather than two-crop rotation schemes. Three-crop schemes both increased the amount of land under cultivation at any one time (two-thirds rather than just a half) and preserved better fertility. This development perhaps also underlies the observation of the Arab geographers that Slavic populations gathered not one but two harvests each year.[37] There were important further developments yet to come, but much more food was being produced in central and eastern Europe by the year 1000 than had been the case five hundred years earlier.

This was critical to state formation in a number of ways. Until food surpluses were generated in substantial quantities, it was quite impossible (as was also the case with the Germanic world in the first half of the millennium) for leaders to maintain large specialist military retinues and other functionaries not engaged in primary agricultural production. Without economic surpluses, likewise, it was impossible for social differentiation to become entrenched. More food also meant more people,[38] and state formation could probably never have happened as it did without this increased population. It provided all the extra manpower required for ambitious construction projects. More important, but harder to measure in concrete terms, increasing the population density in central and eastern Europe increased substantially the competition for available resources. The need to belong to a group in order to flourish has always been a powerful reason why individuals are willing to accept the costs that usually accompany group membership. Put simply, one reason why peasants – or some of them – were willing to pay food renders and do labour service for rising dynasts was that they offered sufficient military organization to guarantee safe land retention in return.[39]

But much more changed in barbarian Europe between 500 and 1000 than the appearance of more people producing more food. Other economic developments were just as important to state-building, or nearly so. Military retinues, for instance, needed arms and armour, and, as we have seen, the new rulers of the tenth century controlled substantial reserves of precious metals (witness the gold cross erected by Boleslaw Chrobry over Adalbert's tomb) as well as all the other resources, apart from the mere physical labour, required to erect, decorate and furnish prestige projects such as the cathedrals and palace complexes that are such a marked feature of the period. In part, the rulers' capacity to do so arose from some general processes of economic development affecting the whole of central and eastern Europe at this time, processes beyond their control. In part, it was fostered by particular policies adopted by the dynasts themselves.

The biggest non-agricultural economic phenomenon in these years was the rise of an international trade network in furs and slaves. Some of its western axes began to operate in the seventh century, but it was in the eighth that it stretched into the Baltic, and the early ninth before it exploded more generally across eastern Europe. We've already encountered the role of waterborne Scandinavians in making this network's longer-distance connections work, and its central role in the whole Viking phenomenon. Consequently, the period saw a huge outflow of raw materials – largely people and furs – from northern and eastern Europe, and a flood, in return, of due payment. Large quantities of Byzantine silks were presumably one part of this, but few traces of these materials survive in our written sources, and none archaeologically. Beautifully finished silks were the main item Byzantium had to offer in exchange for imported items. What the archaeological record has produced in vast quantities, however, is silver coinage, above all from the Muslim world but from western Europe as well. These coins survive in quite astonishing quantities: as we saw in Chapter 9, over 220,000 Muslim coins in hoards of five or more according to recent estimates. This is all the more impressive given that silver has never been without value. The coins that survive are probably no more than the tip of a silver iceberg that has been reworked many times in the intervening centuries.

Kings, of course, were hugely interested in such massive flows of wealth. Not least, they could milk it for tolls, offering merchants safe places for making their exchanges and charging fees in return. Right at the beginning of the ninth century, the then King of pre-collapse Denmark, Godfrid, forced merchants who'd previously operated on Slavic territory at the trading centre called Reric to move to his newly built trading station at Hedeby in southern Jutland. The move is recorded in a contemporary source, and has found archaeological confirmation. The dendrochronology dates of early timbers recovered from Hedeby show that, as the text reports, it was built in c. 810 when Godfrid was at the height of his powers. The king's interests here can only have been financial. Prague, likewise, one of the key centres of the Premyslid dynasty of Bohemia, was also, as the Muslim geographers report, a major entrepôt in the slave trade. The tolls must greatly have swelled the coffers of the dynasty, and the trade's importance was such that one of the reasons given for Wenceslas' killing is that he was attempting to outlaw it.

Kiev, too, new home of the Rurikids in the tenth century, was a trading entrepôt of huge importance. Byzantine and Russian sources both confirm that it was the starting point for the Rus trade fleets that came to Constantinople every spring from the early tenth century onwards. And by the early eleventh, Thietmar of Merseburg tells us, the city boasted no fewer than eight markets. Only in the case of Poland do we lack explicit textual evidence of its participation in the new international trade networks, but this can only be an accident of (non-)survival. The territory of the Piasts has thrown up such a density of Muslim silver coin finds that there is no doubt that its population was in some way involved in the new trading networks.[40] So all of our new dynasties effectively tapped in to the new wealth being generated.

Nor was their role confined merely to taking tolls. They also sometimes interfered actively to reshape, as it were, the networks and maximize their own profits. This is easiest to demonstrate in the case of the Rurikids. In the tenth century the dynasty mounted collective military action on two occasions, in 911 and 944, to force the Byzantine authorities in Constantinople to grant Rus traders increasingly favourable trade terms, including the stipulation that they would get free bed and board inside the city for a month while conducting business. Not surprisingly, given the origins of Scandinavian interest in Russia, the treaties show us that members of the Rurikid dynasty (and not just its current head) were themselves active traders, so they had every reason to want to increase activity and market share. But I would not jump to the conclusion that this was an enterprise limited to the Rurikids. Byzantine–Rus trade connections just happen to be comparatively well documented, and it seems to me entirely likely, although undocumented, that other dynasts took an equally active interest in developing international trade links along the particular lines that best suited them.[41]

Even though we don't know as much about this as we would like to, a good case can be made that all these dynasties took a proactive role in organizing the economies of at least their dynastic heartlands.

The picture has emerged from a mix of historical sources and archaeological investigation. Looked at archaeologically, the tenth-century
dynastic heartlands of Poland and Bohemia are striking for the relative
density of their populations. Once again, this observation is based upon
detailed knowledge of pottery chronologies, whose spread gives you a
reasonable guide to the existence of settlements. The evidence suggests
that this population density was not an accident, but the outcome of
deliberate interference. As the archaeology has shown, a key moment
in the rise of both Premyslid and Piast dynasties came when they
destroyed the defended centres associated with the old sociopolitical
structures, or 'tribes', and replaced them with their own chain of
castles, in the later ninth and the earlier tenth century respectively.
This process, it seems, was accompanied by the deliberate transfer of
at least some of the subdued population groups to the dynasty's
heartland. Some transfers are mentioned in our sources. The *RPC*, for
instance, associates Prince Vladimir in the late tenth century with a
mass transfer of various population groups – Slavs, Krivichi, Chud and
Viatichi – to different places along the River Desna. Here, persuasion
rather than force may have provided sufficient incentive for the move.
In other cases – Poland and Bohemia – all we have is the archaeological
reflection of the effects of such a process in the sudden creation of an
unusually dense population cluster, but early texts (all gifts to monasteries) from both these kingdoms (and, indeed, from Russia too) make
clear the purpose of these resettlements. The classic economic form to
emerge from these early texts is the 'service village', already mentioned. These unfree villagers were required to fulfil particular economic functions for the king, such as bee-keeping or horse-breeding,
in addition to providing standard food renders. The fact that they were
unfree strongly suggests their origins lay in forced resettlements.[42]

Kings – or kings and their advisers – were economically alert
enough, therefore, to maximize the exploitation of their dynastic
heartlands. The way this was done suggests that they were operating
in a world where there was little in the way of a functioning market
economy in agricultural goods, since instead of simply being able to
purchase the required items, specialist tasks had to be assigned to
particular settlements. This is not surprising. The same was true of the
ninth-century Carolingians who were still using service villages in
certain areas, and is in line with both the coinage evidence and the fact
that peasants owed the king food renders rather than cash taxes. North

and eastern Europe was still at the time an economy lacking small change. Muslim silver coins were plentiful enough, but these were of much too high value to do your everyday shopping with. Use one of them at the baker's and you'd come home with a few sackfuls of bread, which would have gone stale long before you ate it. Likewise, although kings generally preferred cash taxes because they were infinitely more flexible, they could demand them only when the possibility existed for peasants to sell on any surplus production to merchants.

All of this adds another dimension, of course, to the tendency of these late first-millennium states to operate with a distinct centre–periphery dichotomy. Not only was this an accidental offshoot of the logistic limitations of itineration, but it reflected something more fundamental about the states' construction. Thanks to the policies of the triumphant dynasties, core and periphery were also distinct in population density and economic organization. In the case of the Kievan Rus state, because of the peculiarities of its origins, the process of core creation had an additional importance. Up to the mid-tenth century, the Riurikid dynasty displayed a distinct capacity to shift its centre of operations about. It first came to prominence in the north with an initial seat, it seems, at Gorodishche (old Novgorod) before transferring, as we have seen, south to Kiev on the River Dnieper in the late ninth century, when Oleg came south with his army.

The reasoning behind this transfer requires more than a little puzzling out. At first sight, it seems an odd move, since Gorodishche, as noted earlier, was better placed for controlling trade flows along the Volga to the Muslim world, which was a far richer trade route than its counterpart along the Dnieper to Constantinople. Kiev, however, had other advantages. Situated on the wooded steppe, Kiev was excellently placed to dominate the surrounding regions of what is now Ukraine, which had become home in the seventh and eighth centuries to a large Slavic agricultural population. This was organized into units with their own substantial political structures before the arrival of any Scandinavians. The Polian dominated the area immediately around Kiev, the other groups in the vicinity being the Derevlians, Severians, Radimichi and Dregovichi (Map 19). While less well placed in purely trade terms, Kiev offered Scandinavian dynastic wannabes far more in the way of exploitable human and economic resources. Already in the time of Oleg, the *RPC* tells us, the Grand Prince's army consisted not just

of Scandinavians, but of Slavic- and Finnic-speakers. For the Grand
Prince, who wanted to be much more than a merchant prince, Ukraine
had much more to offer than the north. Even so, the Riurikids were
not quite yet ready to give up the gypsy life. Oleg's son and heir
Sviatoslav engaged in wide-ranging campaigns, as far east as the Volga
and south all the way to the Caucasus. The *RPC* reports that, just
before his death, he was contemplating relocating the capital of the
dynasty a third time – to the Danube. The work of Sviatoslav's son
and eventual heir Vladimir, in generating a much stronger economic
core in and around Kiev along the Desna, had the particular effect of
rooting the Riurikid state once and for all in its Ukrainian heartlands.[43]

There is, of course, much else we'd like to know about how state-
building intersected with the economic development unfolding in the
later first millennium. One huge gap is the lack of detailed information
about iron-mining and steelworking. The kinds of armies deployed by
the new dynasts imposed a huge demand for these items, but there is
no good information on how this was satisfied. Nonetheless, the big
picture is clear enough in outline. State-building would have been
impossible without a number of pre-existing social and economic
transformations of fundamental importance: the generation of a much
more productive agriculture, the substantial population increase that
followed on from this, a huge increase in the amount of movable
wealth, and the more developed social hierarchies that formed around
its unequal distribution.

But if these huge changes provided the necessary backdrop, the
dynasts were themselves responsible for further social and economic
developments of profound importance. On the trading front, they not
only milked the new international networks for all the tolls they could
get, but actively extended them, as and when they could. At home,
likewise, agricultural production in the core areas of their kingdoms
was maximized. None of these processes was complete by the year
1000. Not only was agricultural production reorganized on a manorial
basis from the eleventh century, but the grandsons and great-grandsons
of the dynasts would also famously employ recruiting agents to bolster
output still further by making hundreds of thousands of German
peasants offers they could not refuse to move eastwards.[44] Even if all
this was still work in progress by 1000, we have arrived at a partial
answer to our question. Normal dynastic ambition produced entirely
abnormal results during this period because deeply rooted social and

economic transformation meant that the dynasts were pushing at a door that was already opening.

But this, at best, is still only half an answer. Dynastic ambition provided the activating mechanism for state formation; being both cause and effect of the political revolution we have been observing, massive social and economic transformation was its necessary backdrop. But what underlay those initial social and economic transformations that gave such free range to dynastic wannabes to remake the map of central and eastern Europe?

## THE RISE OF THE STATE

In Soviet days, everything was so simple. From the fifth century onwards, often living alongside an existing population, egalitarian Slavs took possession of the landscape of what would become Slavic Europe. Then followed a long, slow process of internal social and economic evolution over the next four to five hundred years, until classes formed around manorial estate-based agriculture and the first states appeared, based on the unequal distribution of control of the agricultural means of production. This always looked more like a Marxist fairytale than anything to do with historical reality, and all the more recent work has only emphasized what a dramatic story state formation actually was. In many places, even initial Slavicization occurred maybe a hundred and fifty years later than used to be thought, manorialized agriculture followed state formation rather than preceding it, and archaeology has brought to light a sudden and violent final stage, where rising dynasts used military muscle rather than long-term socioeconomic evolution to destroy one sociopolitical order and replace it with their own. What we have to explain, all this emphasizes, is why in the ninth and tenth centuries dynasties were suddenly able to grasp the reins of power with so much vigour. Just as with the appearance of larger political structures in the Germanic world in the first half of the millennium, a key role was played by an increasingly dense network of contacts that grew up between Slavic Europe and its more developed imperial neighbours.

## Empire Games

In central Europe, the Slavic world was in direct contact with two successive imperial states: the Carolingians in the eighth and ninth centuries, and the Ottonians in the tenth. Neither was as robust as their Roman predecessor, but each was more than powerful enough in their heyday for their military and diplomatic priorities to have major consequences for neighbouring Slavic and Scandinavian societies. Just as in the Roman period, the most immediate type of contact between Carolingians and Ottonians and their neighbours was imperial aggression. Both these late first-millennium empires built their internal political coherence around the distribution of gifts to local elites, who not only ran their localities but also provided emperors with military muscle.

But Carolingian and Ottonian emperors lacked not only the huge financial reservoir that control of the developed Mediterranean world had brought their Roman counterpart, but also any thoroughgoing powers of taxation even over such lands as they did control. As a result, their gifts to local elites often took the form of non-renewable assets such as land from the royal fisc, which generated a tendency for these empires to fragment from within, as power built up in local hands. The only thing that could square this circle was expansion, providing rulers with an alternative form of renewable wealth to large-scale taxation, and allowing them to reward local elites and maintain their own power at the same time. If anything, therefore, the maintenance of central power was actually predicated more upon expansion in both of these later empires than was the case even with Rome, and both preyed upon their neighbours as and when they could. In the ninety years separating the accession to power of Charles Martel in 715 and the later years of his grandson the Emperor Charlemagne, Carolingian armies were predatorily active in the field for all but five of them. In the first half of the tenth century, likewise, a steady *Drang nach Osten* on the part of what was originally the ruling ducal dynasty of Saxony was a key reason why Henry I and his son Otto I were able to beat off all comers and turn themselves into the Carolingians' imperial heirs.[45]

Predatory expansion always produced pillage, but its real benefit was more structured, long-term exploitation. Even territories not fully subdued were part of the story. From the time of Henry I, Bohemia had to pay an annual tribute, and after 950 owed military support to the dynasty. For about a decade from the mid-960s, likewise, Miesco I of Poland was cast in the role of tributary. For territories more thoroughly under the imperial thumb, the weight of exploitation was correspondingly heavy. Successful campaigns against the so-called Elbe Slavs (small-scale groups who lived broadly between the Rivers Elbe and Oder (Map 14) in the first half of the tenth century) allowed the Ottonians to establish nine major collection centres (called 'towns', *urbes* – or burgwards in our sources) east of the Elbe. These received what the charters euphemistically call 'annual gifts' from the Slavs, some of the proceeds of which were divided between the Ottonians' two favourite ecclesiastics, the Archbishops of Magdeburg and Meissen. It is the charters granted these sees by Otto that document the arrangement. Nor was it just ecclesiastical institutions that benefited from the flow of the new wealth. Frontier commands in what can only be called this colonial situation – called 'marches' – were in huge demand among Otto's magnates because of the opportunities for enrichment they offered. Their distribution was even the source of ferocious feuds within magnate families, when one branch received a nice juicy plum but another did not. Most famously, this was the origin of the bad blood between two brothers, Herrman and Wichman Billung. Herrman got the key appointment and was for ever loyal to Otto; jealousy led Wichmann throughout his long and bitter life into the camp of any opposition to Otto, whatever the issue.[46]

It is not the effects of expansionary policies upon the empires that we're primarily interested in, however, but how the exploited populations responded to this asset-stripping. They reacted exactly as you might expect, attempting to resist imperial expansion outright, and/or to minimize its effects when total resistance was impossible. In particular – and this is why imperial exploitation is so relevant to political consolidation, the subject matter of this chapter – uniting several originally independent, small-scale political units into a smaller number of large ones was one of the most effective strategies available to those seeking to fend off unwanted imperial attention.

The best example is provided by what proved in the long term to be a failed state formation: the Elbe Slavs again. As we've just seen, they felt the full weight of Ottonian imperialism. In 983, however, taking advantage of the dynasty's difficulties elsewhere, they rose in massive and – in the short term – successful rebellion. Their resentment against Ottonian rule, and especially against the Church institutions that had been profiting so substantially from their exploitation, manifested itself in a series of atrocities against churches and churchmen that are lovingly chronicled in our Christian sources. What's particularly striking about this revolt, though, is the element of political restructuring that was central to its success. When the Elbe Slavs fell under Ottonian domination, they comprised a group of small-scale political societies. The success of the revolt, however, was predicated on the generation of a new alliance among them, manifest in the new label 'Liutizi' which our sources start to give them in its immediate aftermath. The Liutizi were not a new people, but old ones reorganized. As their counterparts among the Germani on the fringes of the Roman Empire had come to appreciate so long ago, so had the Elbe Slavs learned from bitter experience that hanging around in larger numbers made it possible more effectively to resist imperial aggression.[47]

Nor, when any initial phase of expansion and conquest was over, was it necessarily any easier to have such imperial neighbours. The reign of Otto III was marked by a spell of excellent relations between himself and both the Bohemians and the Poles, culminating in the Emperor's progress to the tomb of Adalbert. After Otto's death, however, imperial policy changed dramatically. He left no son, and from the accession of his cousin Henry I in 1003 there followed some twenty years of pretty continuous warfare between the Empire and the Piast state, in which the new Emperor was happy to use the pagan Elbe Slavs as allies against his erstwhile Christian brothers. Henry, of course, had his reasons, but this kind of inconsistency in policy reflected the fact that populations beyond the Elbe were viewed as substantially second-class citizens, which meant that the desire to exploit them was always likely to be perceived as legitimate and hence to reassert itself. This underlying attitude was not informed by such a thoroughgoing, denigrating ideology as that of the Romans, whose entirely coherent, and equally unpleasant, vision of 'barbarians' allowed them to be treated like beasts, if that was convenient. The Poles and Bohemians were partly protected by being Christian. It was no accident that it was the pagans of the Elbe and Baltic regions, in later centuries, who would eventually feel the full brutal weight of an ideologically self-righteous form of imperialism: the so-called Northern Crusades

which saw Christian Teutonic knights, amongst others, burn and kill
their way north and east. Nonetheless, even Christian Slavic states
suffered from second-class status, and could never be sure that the
instinctive imperial desire to profit from the exploitation of outsiders
might not reassert itself at their expense.[48] And, in fact, the diplomacy
of the ninth and tenth centuries throws up many examples of the same
kind of change in imperial policy that the Poles suffered from in the
early eleventh.

In the later eighth century, for instance, when Charlemagne was
engaged in his long and tortuous conquest of Saxony, one particular
group of Elbe Slavs, the Abodrites, were key allies. Established on the
Saxons' eastern border, where the Carolingians were attacking from
the south and west, the Abodrites provided an extremely useful second
front, and Charlemagne was duly grateful for their support. In return
he gave them extra territory, direct military and diplomatic support
and trading privileges. Once Saxony had been absorbed into the
Empire, and particularly when it became the seat of Empire, the
Abodrites found themselves surplus to strategic requirements. Instead
of useful allies, they started to look like potential subjects, and imperial
policy swung 180 degrees. Even when they were not being conquered
outright, aggressive diplomacy became the order of the day, reaching
its culmination in a murderous banquet organized by one frontier
commander, the Margrave Gero, at which thirty of their leading men
were assassinated. This dwarfs the dinner-party assassinations even of
the Roman era, which were regular events but usually took out only
one leader at a time. The uncertainty of life on the edge of the Empire
was central to the experiences of successive rulers of the Moravians in
the next century, too. Take the early years of King Zwentibald. He
first came to power with the help of the east Carolingians in 870; then,
in just three years, as imperial policies shifted, found himself impris-
oned for several months before we finally see him raiding Bavaria in
retaliation for his treatment.[49] It was living close to a powerful Empire
but holding – in the view of a large section of its citizenry – second-
class status that laid you particularly open to these kinds of dangerous
changes of policy. It was always possible for some faction within the
Empire's ruling circle to make political capital for itself by championing
a harder – and more profitable – line towards you.

Examples could be multiplied, but there's no point. What's interesting here is the overall effect of imperial predation on the societies

at the sharp end. The Elbe Slavs' revolt provides a particularly arresting example of well-founded resentment in action, but the effects were similar elsewhere. The natural suspicion of the Moravian dynasty, for instance, shows up in the religious sphere. Along with many of our new dynasties, the new ruling line quickly decided to opt for Christian conversion. Rather than simply accepting it from the Carolingians, however, they explored every other possible avenue, famously importing the Byzantine missionaries Cyril and Methodius, with papal blessing, in 863. This was done in the teeth of sustained Carolingian resentment, however, and shows very clearly the suspicion in which the Empire and all its doings were held. Eventually, after Methodius' death, the Moravians were forced into religious line and his remaining disciples expelled in favour of Frankish clergy in 885, but the expectation of imperial exploitation remained, manifest not least in the incident of 882 with which this study began, when Zwentibald the Duke of the Moravians and his men captured the Frankish Counts Werinhar and Wezzilo and cut off their tongues, right hands, and genitals.

They were out for revenge because of the way Engelschalk had treated them when he had been in charge of the same frontier region, and were trying to prevent Engelschalk's sons from seizing their father's old job. The Moravians had an entirely coherent agenda here, and their revenge was very symbolic. I am obviously not privy to the mindset of your average ninth-century Moravian, but this was clearly a case, in the best Mafia tradition, of mutilation with a message. My best guess would be that cutting off the right hand and tongue emphasized that neither deed nor word could be trusted, while removing the genitals expressed the hope that this line would have no further progeny. Taken to these lengths, natural resentment against imperial military and diplomatic aggression could become a building block, both practical and ideological, by which new dynasties could extract consent for their rule. Becoming part of a larger entity always involved taking on obligations of service, but these might be acceptable if, as a result, the worst effects of predation were fended off. And although the Elbe Slavs and the Moravians provide the most explicit instances, there is every reason to suppose that imperial predation had the same effect in all of the border states: Poland, Bohemia and Denmark as well.

If this, what you might call 'negative benefit', was the main effect of military and diplomatic contact with Empire on the capacity of our dynasties to build their state structures, there were also more positive ones. On occasion, when imperial policy was in your favour, there were great photo opportunities. Otto III's great progress to the tomb of Adalbert was a stupendous international occasion, and Boleslaw Chrobry, like many a modern leader at a summit meeting, must have been extremely happy to have his subjects see how highly he was regarded by the reigning Emperor. On the other hand, of course, it may just have been the sight of that massive cross of solid gold hanging over the tomb that set calculators whirring in the brains of some of the Emperor's entourage as they worked out exactly how much wealth might be won from a successful war against the Piasts (leading eventually to twenty years of warfare, but that's another story).

Not, of course, that the violence ran only in one direction. Just like their imperial contemporaries, these new dynasts had to win political support from their magnates to rule effectively, with gift-giving just as much the order of the day east of the Elbe as west of it. Their marriage policies, if anything, made the problem worse. Under the influence of Christianity, they did begin the move from outright polygamy to serial monogamy, but multiple wives and plentiful offspring were the rule – if not quite on the scale of the seventh-century Samo, who ended up with twelve wives and thirty-seven children. This marital profligacy meant that succession disputes and dynastic infighting were extremely common. Yaroslav the Wise, son of Vladimir, for instance, secured his power in 1018 only after a lengthy civil war against his half-brother Sviatopolk that saw many ups and downs and the deaths of at least three other brothers and half-brothers. And Vladimir himself had had to fight a similar war in the 970s against his half-brother Yaropolk, with similar numbers of dynastic casualties. These kinds of wars could be won only by mobilizing a wide range of support among magnates and retinues, which required wealth distribution on a considerable scale. And, just as was the case in the Roman period, leading successful raids on to the richer and more developed soil of an imperial neighbour was an extremely effective mechanism when it came to securing that perfect gift without bankrupting yourself. Accounts of the counter-raids of the Elbe Slavs, not surprisingly, focus on their propensity for smash-and-grab, but the same was true, in only a slightly more structured way, of all our other frontier dynasties. Each outbreak of trouble with the Moravians in the ninth century, or the Bohemians and Poles in the tenth, was accompanied by its due measure of wealth liberation.[50]

Aside from wealth and prestige, close contact with an imperial neighbour also helped secure the power of new dynasties in some more precise ways. Two leap out of the source material. First, the tenth-century Slavic states were entirely up to date in their modes of warfare, possessing armoured knights aplenty. This had not been the case before 800 AD. In the ninth century, even Saxon contingents within east Frankish, Carolingian armies at first took the form only of infantry and light cavalry. The heavily armed, mailed Saxon cavalry of the Ottonian period emerged only in the late ninth and the early tenth century, as the Saxons finally caught up with the times. Against this backdrop, it is very striking that tenth-century Bohemian and Polish armies also boasted at least some heavy armoured cavalry. We know little, if anything about Slavic warfare before 800, but it's a pretty fair bet that if even the Saxons didn't have the latest military hardware at that point, then neither did the Slavs. So where did knowledge of it, and access to it, come from over the next hundred years? The likeliest answer is that it actually came from the Empire, slipping eastwards over the Elbe. Already in 805, in a capitulary issued at Thionville, the Emperor Charlemagne attempted to limit trade with the Slavic world to a number of designated points along the Elbe frontier, including Bardowick, Magdeburg, Erfurt, Hallstadt, Forchheim, Regensburg and Lorch, not least because he professed himself worried about arms shipments. This immediately makes you think that arms were flowing pretty freely across the frontier, since even imperial states of the first millennium lacked the bureaucratic machinery to maintain effective border controls. Obviously, the idea of state-of-the-art Carolingian hardware was highly attractive for Slavic groups who might have to fight off Frankish armies, but such imports also had important internal political effects. Not for nothing did early modern European populations associate standing armies with royal autocracy. Acquiring the kind of military equipment that made his forces militarily dominant also put a nascent dynast in the perfect position to face down internal rivals and suppress dissent. Importing imperial military technology, therefore, directly advanced the process of state formation in the periphery.[51]

With this in mind, the economic organization of the core areas of these new states is also interesting. As we have seen, all quickly evolved a loose pattern of great estates, where particular service villages fulfilled specialist functions in addition to providing basic food supplies. This mode of organization was also prevalent in the ninth-century Carolingian Empire, particularly in its less economically developed reaches east of the Rhine. This was, perhaps, just a sensible way to ensure vital products in pre-market-economic conditions, and arrived at entirely independently east of the Elbe. There must be at least some chance, however, that we are looking here at further, slightly more unexpected fruits of close contact between Empire and periphery.

Compared with the Roman period, what's missing from this cocktail of contacts is the kind of diplomatic manipulation in which Roman emperors excelled, systematically promoting particular dynasts by rearranging prevailing political geographies in their favour because they seemed to promise the best hope of medium-term frontier security. Carolingian and Ottonian emperors did at times promote their particular favourites, such as the Abodrites, but there is no sign in the sources that they attempted consistently to interfere with the political structures of their neighbours. There is a good chance, however, that the diplomatic agendas of a different Empire may have played an important role in the earlier stages of these processes of transformation. Moravia, Bohemia and, to an extent, Poland, can all be seen as successor states to the Avar Empire destroyed by Charlemagne just before the year 800. We don't know a huge amount about the internal running of the Avar Empire, but what there is would suggest that it functioned very much along the lines of that of the Huns. Certainly, like the Huns, the Avars operated an unequal confederation where the military power of their originally nomadic core was mobilized to hold a range of initially unwilling subjects to an Avar political allegiance. There was a range of more and less favoured statuses that subjects might occupy within this overall pattern. The most interesting snapshot of its operations that we have describes how one group, descendants many of them of Roman prisoners, achieved free (as opposed to slave) status, and were granted thereby their own group leader. This does sound like the Hun Empire too, and would suggest that, lacking any complex government machinery, the Avars tended to rule their subjects through trusted allied princes. If so, it is very likely that Avar rule will have cemented further the power of the kind of leaders who were appearing anyway in some Slavic groups by c.600, as they began to control the flows of new wealth coming across the east Roman frontier in particular. This combination – of sixth-century development reinforced by subsequent Avar diplomatic manip-ulation – is the likeliest explanation, in my view, of why the collapse of Avar rule was marked by the swift appearance of a series of Slavic leaders of seemingly substantial and established authority.[52]

Overall, military and diplomatic contact between these new states and the adjacent Empire thus took many forms. Imperial attentions were in general predatory, resulting in a huge groundswell of aggression flowing across from the imperial side of the frontier. This was matched, when conditions were right, by a countervailing tend-ency on the part of the new states, or factions within them, to raid the rich assets available west of the Elbe. So much is only what you might expect, but both phenomena had a strong tendency to advance state formation, giving nascent dynasts ideological cement or just plain cash to employ in advancing the process. Alongside these major themes of contact went some subthemes that also pushed the process forward: exports of military and other technologies, and occasional moments when benevolent imperial attention advanced the capital of particular dynasts.

Looking at the broader patterns of development from the ninth century onwards, two other points are worth making. First, as regards the two effects of proximity to an empire, the 'negative benefit' – using its aggression as ideological cement for your own state formation – and the 'positive benefit' – being able to raid it as a source of ready funds – a comparison of the fate of the Elbe Slavs with the Piast and Premyslid states suggests that the former was the more important. While the Elbe Slavs were in the better position for raiding, being situated right on the imperial frontier, and indulged in it aplenty, this also meant that it was too easy for the Empire to get at them in return. And, of course, the whole point about an imperial power is that, when it put its mind to it, and other factors were not interfering, it was that much more powerful than any surrounding states. There could only be one victor, therefore, in a head-to-head collision between the Empire and the Elbe Slavs. Poland was significantly further away, insulated geographically from immediate imperial aggression, while the upland basin of Bohemia enjoyed the stratigraphic protection of the Bohemian Forest, the Ore and the Krkonoše Mountains. By itself, then, ready access to raiding was not a sufficient basis for state formation. It was a useful additional resource, but only if you could survive imperial counterattack and use to your benefit all the resentment that this would generate.

Second, these different types of contact, both positive and negative, pushed the target societies in the same direction in the longer term – providing, that is, you were in a position to survive attempted imperial conquest. The unifying force of the struggle to survive, the effects of occasional imperial approbation, the flows of raided funds, exports of military hardware and administrative acumen: all strongly facilitated the ability of nascent dynasts to advance towards regional domination. Nor was this pro-dynastic effect limited just to military and diplomatic interaction.

## Globalization

It is clear that for their state-building operations to be successful, the dynasts needed the consent of some of the population groups caught up in the process. In the cases of Moravia, Bohemia and Poland, at least, the new dynasts initially rose to prominence within their own local grouping, or 'tribe', and were then able to win consent for their wider regional ambitions, depending, presumably, on the degree of success they had already achieved. Even when the larger state structures had come into being, rulers still needed that consent, certainly from the *optimates* of the core heartland, and probably also from a wider free class, if we are right in seeing such a social grouping as playing a major role in Slavic society at the turn of the millennium. At the same time, other dimensions of state-building were based on the exercise of brute force. Not least, extending power beyond your original group involved destroying the hillfort refuges of nearby populations and resettling many of them in your own core areas. Large and well-equipped military retinues were a key component in the new state structures, and it is hard to conceive of these shock forces not playing a major role in the destruction of the old political order and accompanying population displacements.

What all this highlights is the overwhelming importance of the dynasts' ability to accumulate wealth in unprecedented concentrations. Military retinues used up huge amounts of it. Obviously, they required feeding, lots of feeding. All the comparative evidence on warrior retinues, and some specifically relating to the new states, suggests that being fed on a heroic scale was a basic expectation. This was not just a matter of greed. They tended to spend mornings hitting large bits of wood with double-weight swords (to build skill and muscle strength) and engaging in mind-expanding activities, all of which used up a lot of calories. Feeding the brutes, however, was not the half of it. As we have seen, a striking feature of the retinues of these new kingdoms is their state-of-the-art arms and armour, especially the defensive armour, which was massively expensive, whether bought – as one suspects it was in the first instance, given the Thionville capitulary – from Frankish gun-runners or produced at home, as it eventually must have been. It was the military potential of the retinues that allowed the rapid, violent expansion that is so characteristic of Premyslid, Piast and even Moravian state formation. But creating them required huge amounts of cash. The obvious questions, therefore, are where did it all come from, and how did the dynasts manage to get their hands on it?

Looking at central and eastern Europe between 800 and 1000, far and away the most likely answer is that they were drawing funds from the new international trade networks in furs and slaves. Again, there are some similarities between this phenomenon and the processes that earlier transformed the largely Germanic societies on the fringes of the Roman Empire. There, the Roman standing armies were a constant source of demand for agricultural products and for labour of all kinds, whether in the form of extra soldiers or just as slaves. As we have noted, the steady flow of payments back across the frontier then helped create the new social structures that underpinned the larger Germanic confederations in the later Roman period. There are, however, some key differences between the two contexts. First and foremost, there is the size of the operation. The fur and slave trades of the later period operated on a much greater geographical and monetary scale than any Roman counterpart. Slaves, of course, were always expensive items, but the fur trade, unmentioned in sources from the first half of the millennium, was much more valuable than any Roman trade. Also, there is no sign that slaves were coming from as far north and east during Roman times. I am not inclined to think it accidental, therefore, that the operations of the later trade networks should have left more trace in our sources, both historical and archaeological, than any of the earlier commerce.

Second, and one of the reasons why the scale was so much larger, the late first-millennium network operated with multiple sources of imperial demand for its high-value goods. Demand seems to have originated in western Europe, with goods even from northern Russia being shipped there from the mid-eighth century. The trading station at Staraia Ladoga came into being a couple of generations before any Muslim connection had been established. This makes perfect sense, since increasing demand in western Europe at this point coincides with the rise of the Carolingian dynasty. But an Islamic dimension soon came into play. Not long after 800, Muslim silver coins started to flow north in vast numbers, part of the trade having now been diverted to a second set of customers, the elites of the Abbasid Empire. This was the greatest state of its age, and so demand from there soon dwarfed the west's, to judge at least by the amount of Muslim silver that ended up in the Baltic region. The Muslim connection was not broken even when the Abbasid Caliphate collapsed in the early tenth century, since a great successor state quickly arose under the control of the Samanid dynasty of eastern Iran whose silver mines made them fabulously wealthy. Sometime in the mid- to late ninth century, finally, Constantinople came into the picture. Much less wealthy than the Muslim world, it was nonetheless a distinct third centre of elite demand.[53]

The relative proliferation of sources also allows us to explore the operations of this trading network in more detail than was possible for its Roman-era counterparts. We have already come across some of the major waterborne routes that Scandinavian adventurers opened up in the ninth century: particularly, down the Volga and its tributaries to the Muslim world, and down the Dnieper and across the Black Sea to Constantinople. There were also land routes running through central Europe into the west, on which Prague was a major staging post. We can also, importantly, say something about where the slaves were generally being captured. The Arab geographers report that the Rus raided westwards for their victims, while the 'western Slavs' raided eastwards. Confirmation of this picture is provided by the distribution of the Muslim silver coins that came back north in return for all the slaves and furs. Striking concentrations emerge. Two are where you might expect: along the Volga and its tributaries, and in Scandinavia. A third, however, lay between the Oder and the Vistula, right in the heartland of the Piast state. Even more arresting is the complete absence of coins in the immense tracts of territory east of the Vistula and north and west of the Dnieper. Pretty straightforwardly, then, the coin distributions confirm the reports of the Arab geographers. The areas without coins are precisely those from which the slaves were being extracted, caught between the rock of the Rus and hard place of the west Slavs.[54]

This suggests some further thoughts about how, precisely, the new dynasts were making money out of these international networks. All were busy extracting tolls, but the Rurikids, as we have seen, were doing much more than that. Active participants in the networks, they were also to be found developing markets, not just taxing them. And given that much of what was being traded was actually slaves, there might well have been an intimate link between the evolution of the new networks and those eminently important military retinues. Violence and terror are the order of the day with slave trading, not just because individuals resist capture, but also because the cowed and terrified are that much easier to transport. I remember as an undergraduate picking up the standard textbook on medieval slavery and glancing through it in an idle way because it was written in French and the subject was not absolutely central to that week's work. But my attention was attracted by a map that appeared to have a series of battle sites marked by the usual crossed-swords symbol. This seemed odd. On closer inspection, the symbols were not crossed swords, but scissors, and the legend read 'points de castration'. This does not need translation. Nor did women fare much better. The Arab geographers certainly enjoyed the barbarous nature of the northern societies they were describing and deliberately underlined the total ghastliness of the Rus slave traders. Ibn Fadlan describes them as the filthiest of God's creatures, emphasizing the unpleasantness of their personal hygiene habits. He also refers only to females and children among the slaves being sold down the Volga, taking a voyeur's delight, too, in how much sex went on between the slavers and their victims.

It's hard to know quite what to make of this. The literary accounts could make you think that the trade with the Islamic world was entirely in women, but I don't know whether to believe this or not. Perhaps the huge distances involved meant that shipping males was just too dangerous, since, although moving on water, the potential refuge of riverbanks was never that far away, unlike in the later Atlantic slave trade. I don't have any doubt, however, that sexual exploitation was a major feature of the action. It always is, in the case of women and slavery, and you have to wonder where Vladimir obtained the three hundred concubines he kept at Vyshgorod, the three hundred at Belgorod and the two hundred at Berestovoe.[55]

The real point, though, is that highly trained, well-equipped military retinues were an excellent tool not only for state-building, but for capturing slaves as well. Some of the raiding was done by intermediaries, but the Rus did a fair amount of their own dirty work, and there is every reason to suppose that this was also true of the west Slavs, probably the retainers of both Piasts and Premyslids. As we have seen, many Muslim coins have turned up on Piast territory, and their lands were conveniently near to the areas from which both texts and the absence of coins tell us that slaves were being taken. To my mind, it is not too much of a stretch to suppose that, like their Rurikid peers, the Piasts built up the military capacity of their retinues not only from toll revenues but also by actively participating in the international slave trade.

The point about the new trading connections is not just that they generated new wealth. At least as revolutionary as the wealth itself was the multiplier effect stemming from the fact that new power structures evolved to maximize and control the direction of the flow. Just as in modern globalization, new connections generated big-time winners but also decided losers. The biggest winners were the new dynasties and their chief supporters: the leading men behind them and their military retinues. The chief losers were of course the slave-producing populations, but also the ascendant dynasts' near-neighbours, who lost their independence and became the occupants of the unfree service villages. And, again like today's globalization, the new interconnections between the more and the less developed were not just economic. Ideas, too, crossed the frontier, and here also the transformative effect of the new contacts was extremely powerful.

The most important set of ideas to bridge the gap in these centuries was undoubtedly, as has long been recognized, the Christian religion. Christianity had been formally adopted by rulers across most of Scandinavia and central and eastern Europe by the year 1000. The Piast dynasty converted in the 970s, the Danes under Harold Blue-tooth at more or less the same time, the Premyslids a generation or so earlier, and the Rurikids half a generation later under Vladimir. The Moravians, of course, had picked up Christianity in the mid-ninth century. For all its triumphant progress among them, however, the new dynasts of non-imperial Europe found one dimension of their new religion potentially problematic. From the person of Charlemagne onwards, although it was not then a new idea, the imperial title carried the connotation that its possessor wielded the highest authority, having been personally chosen by God to rule in His stead on earth. To accept Christianity, therefore, was implicitly to recognize the legitimacy of imperial overlordship, and this naturally made the dynasts hesitate. There was also the practical consideration, if you didn't have an entirely independent ecclesiastical province, that part of any revenues generated (by tithes, for instance) for religious purposes in your domain would in practice pass outside of your control, since they were owed to the archiepiscopal see. Archbishops also, at least notionally, had a strong say in the appointment of bishops, so an 'imperial' archbishop could interfere with the choice of bishops within your territory.

These potential problems certainly got in the way of the Moravian dynasty's acceptance of Christianity. They tried to resolve them by getting their Christianity via a combination of the papacy and Byzantium, rather than the all too adjacent Franks. It was perhaps for similar reasons that Anglo-Saxon missionaries, not the nearby imperial churchmen, played a key role in the early stages of Christianization in Scandinavia. In the long run, however, nearby imperial patronage usually proved too hard to resist, and the best option was to accept your Christianity from that quarter, but – like Poland – extract the right to your own archbishop, thus insulating yourself from the worst hazards.[56]

But why accept Christianity at all? We have already met one obvious benefit. Accepting the religious orientation of rich, imperial, developed Europe was an important move if you wanted to escape the category of 'barbarian' and win admittance to the club of Christian nations. Even if you then faced possible problems of imperial hegemony – or the claims of it, at least – this was probably still a better option than remaining in the barbarian category, where no holds would be barred whenever it seemed a good idea to some influential faction within the Empire's structures to look to profit at your expense. This, of course, was the problem that led to the longer-term demise of the Elbe Slavs, even if, at the start of the eleventh century, they briefly benefited from Henry I's desire to curb Piast power. It has also long been canonical to identify a series of specific advantages for ambitious dynasts in adopting Christianity when it came to the internal administration of their realms.

These fall into three broad categories. First, conversion to Christianity brought kings and rulers a degree of ideological promotion. It was a commonly accepted Christian idea in the first millennium that no ruler could win power without God's will. Converting to Christianity thus allowed rulers to claim to be God-chosen, putting ideological blue water between themselves and their nearest rivals. This was potentially useful in the political context, most career-minded dynasts having risen only recently above a pack of peers, and mostly by brute force. Second, Christianity was a religion of the Book: all its basic texts, the commentaries on them, and the practical rules that had evolved over the centuries to organize its operations, came in written form. Christian churchmen as a whole, therefore, operated at a higher degree of literacy than the average even elite population of early medieval Europe. Clerics could thus make useful royal servants, and in all the cases we know about came to be employed as such by their converted rulers. In the longer term, it would in fact be the literacy of churchmen that would make it possible to sustain more bureaucratic forms of administration – particularly useful when it came to assessing and raising tax in the form of cash. Third, and this flows on naturally from the second, Christianity was a high-maintenance religion. Buildings, books, full-time clergymen: all this was very expensive. So the institution of Christianity always involved establishing new taxes – by the late first millennium, often in the form of tithes – by which the religion's activities could be funded. Everything suggests that kings kept some of these revenues for their own purposes, sometimes directly by appropriating part of the tithe, sometimes indirectly. The indirect method worked well because kings often kept the right to appoint leading churchmen such as bishops and abbots, could then appoint their personal supporters to these positions, and thus be sure of their financial and other compliance.[57]

I've always been suspicious of this list. Claims, for instance, always have to be tested. Just because converted rulers claimed extra respect by styling themselves as God-chosen, this doesn't mean that anyone actually gave it to them, and in most documented cases conversion made precious little difference to prevailing political cultures. Post-conversion kings were just as likely to be opposed, deposed and murdered as their pre-conversion predecessors. It was particularly rich, for instance, that Boleslav II chose to take out the Slavniks on St Wenceslas day. It was surely deliberate, and you might be tempted to think that doing it on the name day of the Premyslids' royal saint gave the act a kind of legitimacy, notwithstanding its brutality. But Boleslav II was the son and heir of Boleslav I, Wenceslas' brother, murderer and replacement, so maybe the line of Boleslav I just liked to kill its rivals in late September, with the choice of day a reminder to all potential rivals of how they had always dealt with them. The second area of proposed advantage, likewise, was far too long-term to have been in the forefront of any converted dynast's calculations. Given that the time lag between Christian conversion and the appearance of a convincingly developed literate administration in the well-documented Anglo-Saxon case, for instance, was several centuries, it does seem unlikely that initial converts were much seduced by visions of a potential revolution in government.[58]

Of the advantages generally seen in conversion, therefore, only the third seems to carry much weight, and this, like escaping barbarian status, was a real factor in the minds of dynastic converts of the ninth and tenth centuries. By then, the forms of Christian taxation were so well established in imperial Europe that extending them to a new area was an entirely straightforward move, and one that held considerable potential advantages for kings.[59] I strongly suspect, however, that both of these advantages paled into relative insignificance next to another dimension of conversion that is not so often discussed. Its importance emerges, slightly paradoxically, from contexts in which the new religion was actively resisted.

As the literate religion of the developed imperial world, backed by all the ideological cachet that perceived success imparts by association, Christianity usually 'won' in the culture clashes of the early Middle Ages: in much the same way, I suspect, that Levi's and McDonald's have been adopted the world over because of their association with the winning world brand that is America. Just occasionally, though, exposure to Christianity generated a violent and opposite backlash (as sometimes does American success in the modern world). We came across one example earlier, when the leadership of the fourth-century Gothic Tervingi started to persecute Christians because they associated the religion with Roman hegemony. Another couple of examples of the same phenomenon can be observed six hundred years later. An overt anti-Christian ideology was central, for instance, to the revolt of the Elbe Slavs against Ottonian rule after 983, when churches and monasteries were robbed and burned and even dead bishops exhumed, despoiled and insulted. Given that the Church was an instrument of colonial exploitation in these marcher lands, the degree of anger is perhaps not surprising. A slightly different, ruler-directed anti-Christianity had also surfaced in Russia at more or less the same time. Although Igor's widow Olga had converted to Christianity under Byzantine influence and was perhaps baptized on a visit to Constantinople in 957, two of her sons, Sviatoslav and Vladimir, ruling successively after her death, positively championed the claims of non-Christian religion against their mother's choice. Here the issue would appear to have been more cultural than practical, since no colonial Byzantine Church structure had yet reared its ugly head in Kiev.[60]

What's fascinating about these examples of aggressive anti-Christianity, however, is that even to begin to compete with the Christian challenge, the nature of prevailing non-Christian religion had itself to change. To unite his many and varied peoples against Christian influence, Vladimir did not outlaw all their different gods, but he did elevate Perun, an old Baltic and Slavic god of thunder and lightning, into a supreme god, and force his subjects to pay homage. Vladimir was pulling together Scandinavians, Slavic-speakers, Finnic-speakers and goodness knows who else, so any impulse towards an anti-Christian religious unity was bound to involve picking one from the no doubt wide range of cults being followed within his highly disparate following. And even among the culturally much more homogeneous Elbe Slavs, anti-Christianity involved major religious change. Again, it was not that all other cults were outlawed, but the new confederation of the Liutizi was held together now by common adherence to one overarching cult, that of Rethra. Dues were owed by everyone to the god's priests and temples, and Rethra was consulted before any and every act of war and presented with a tithe of any spoils. We don't know a huge amount about Slavic paganism before conversion, but as this need to generate a new overarching cult to fight off Christianity confirms, everything suggests that there was a wide variety of cults, each sociopolitical grouping – 'tribe' – having its own.[61]

Against this backdrop, Christianity offered another powerful attraction to dynasts seeking to unite the unprecedentedly large territories under their control. The huge variety of non-Christian cults with which they were faced was part of a cultural structure belonging to the previous and long-established political order. An attractive feature of Christianity in this context was its licensed intolerance: the refusal to accept the validity of any other religious cult. Adopting Christianity permitted a ruler to stamp out pre-existing cultic practices, whether or not he yet had enough Christian priests around to substitute for them a fully functioning Christian Church. As such, it allowed him to break down one of the main cultural barriers that might otherwise have restricted his attempts to create a new political order. Alongside the other more 'positive' attractions, Christianity brought with it an entitlement to destroy existing religious structures, which made it the perfect ideological accompaniment to a process of political unification.

## PEERS AND PERIPHERIES

The new states that appeared in northern and eastern Europe towards the end of the first millennium were the products of long and complex processes of transformation, some of whose roots went back a very long way. The migratory expansions of the late fifth and sixth centuries kick-started the appearance of substantive social differentiation among Europe's Slavic-speakers. The Avar Empire then seems to have established a new kind of hereditary leadership amongst those Slavic groups subject to its dominion, and the new states of the ninth and tenth centuries were able greatly to increase food production and population levels in parts of what had been barbarian Europe's least developed region. At least some of these transformations may have resulted in larger sociopolitical units, built largely on consent, individuals accepting the burdens inherent in being part of a larger mass of humanity for the economic and political security that such allegiances offered. This much, at least, is indicated by the kinds of hillfort being erected up to the year 800, which look essentially communal in inspiration, refuges born of common need, not fortifications built at the orders of some grandee.

Thus far, the process of state formation is reasonably compatible with the models for social change that are sometimes given the jargon heading 'peer polity interaction'. What this means, translated from the original Martian, is that you're looking at a world where change is brought about through a gradual process of competition between social units that are more or less of the same size and power.[62] This evolutionary process was rapidly overtaken, however, in the last two centuries of our period by a series of dramatic developments for which the catalyst was increasingly complex contacts with the outside world. First, Charlemagne destroyed the Avar Empire, letting loose a power struggle among its dependent subjects. And while this struggle was being fought out, new trade networks, combined with military and diplomatic ties, brought a vast amount of new wealth into eastern and northern Europe, not least in the form of precious metals. Cornering the market in this wealth then allowed the most successful dynasties to arm themselves to a degree far beyond any yet seen in the region, and to spread their domination suddenly and by force.

Within this two-stage process, your key move, as a participating dynast, was to establish yourself in a position – geographic and/or economic – from which to maximize profits from the new wealth flowing up and down the international trade networks. Of the four dynasties that flourished so dramatically in the last two centuries of the millennium (not counting the shorter-lived Moravians), three, certainly, emerged in perfect positions to benefit. Prague, home of the Premyslids, was a major entrepôt in the overland slave routes established across central Europe. The Rurikids were intimately involved in the slave and fur trades, while hints in the Arab sources and a suspiciously high density of Arab coin finds indicate that the Piasts, too, had their fingers firmly in the pie. The same may well have been true of the Moravian ruling line, since the routes intersecting at Prague also ran through their heartlands, but for this there is no explicit evidence. Within mainland largely Slavic Europe, there is a strong correlation between a type-A position in the trade networks and successful state formation.

The biggest mystery in this respect is perhaps the Jelling dynasty of Denmark, for whose involvement in the new commercial set-up we have no specific evidence. State formation in Jutland and its attendant islands had much deeper roots than its counterparts in northern and eastern Europe. Given that there was some kind of state there in the pre-Viking period, state formation in Denmark may have been about reactivating something that had never quite died, and was hence less dependent on cornering new wealth so as to build military capacity. It can be argued, however, that the fate of the Jelling dynasty too was intimately bound up with the international trade networks. About the time that Sviatoslav, Grand Prince of the Rus, launched his aggressive campaigns east towards the Volga in the 960s, silver stopped flowing northwards into Scandinavia, although it continued into Russia. It is hard to escape the conclusion that, as with their assaults on Constantinople, the Riurikids' wars here were linked at least in part to market share, designed, amongst other things, to cut Scandinavian traders out of the Volga route. After the brief hiatus, Scandinavian merchants clearly found a new route to the south, and the silver began flowing again for a decade or so. Then, in the 980s, the flows of Muslim silver into the Baltic came to a definitive halt.

It is precisely at this point that Scandinavian raiders started to trouble western European waters again, particularly the prosperous Anglo-Saxon kingdom of Ethelred the Unready, from whom the Scandinavians consistently demanded silver coins and bullion. We owe our detailed knowledge of Ethelred's coinage to these tenth-century Vikings, in fact, since tens of thousands of them survive in Scandinavian contexts. This pattern suggests that the drying-up of Muslim silver, arguably the result of Rurikid intervention on the Volga, led northern Scandinavians to look for alternative sources, and the Jelling dynasty put itself at the head of this enterprise. In doing so, it avoided the fate of the Godfrid dynasty in the first half of the ninth century, whose established power base was undermined by the first flows of Viking-era wealth back to the Baltic. More pointedly, the fact that the Jelling dynasty led the new western attacks also suggests that its power was dependent in some way on the Muslim silver flows that had just been cut off. This came probably from the income from tolls, but also from direct trading of tribute goods for its own benefit, just like the Rurikids.[63] If so, the Danish dynasty was not so different from our other tenth-century success stories.

Other forms of contact with imperial Europe were also important to dynastic success. Exploiting imperial aggression, unless – like the Elbe Slavs – you were too close to it, was an excellent mechanism for generating internal consent if your dynasty was able to offer effective leadership. New military technologies, economic advances, imperial Christianity, not to mention wealth derived from raiding richer, neighbouring imperial lands – all of these were forms of interaction with imperial Europe that drove the engine of state formation, and provided a crucial catalyst for the transformation of largely Slavic-dominated eastern and northern Europe in the ninth and tenth centuries. And, of course, even the beginnings of social stratification in the sixth century, and the importing of better ploughing techniques, can be traced to an earlier round of such contacts. In analytical jargon, a centre–periphery model – where you're dealing with partners to an exchange who are substantially unequal in power – better fits the data from the late first millennium than 'peer polity interaction', and two particular character-istics of this second model need to be stressed. First, the interactions encompassed a wide range of different contacts. This is not a model, as some earlier varieties tended to be, predicated on economic exchange – trade – alone. Political, ideological, even technological contacts all played a role, and all pushed sociopolitical change in broadly the same direction. Second, as with the Germani earlier in the millennium, non-imperial Europe should be cast as anything but passive receptors of imperial gifts. Quite the opposite: northern and eastern European populations, or elements among them, were active agents in all these exchanges, seeking to maximize their beneficial impacts and minimize drawbacks.[64]

It remains, finally, to think a bit further about the role of migration in this unfolding drama. Compared with the generation, say, of the western successor states to the Roman Empire in the fifth century, migration played only a small part in the final stages of state formation in northern and eastern Europe. Of the five state structures explored, only one – that of the Rurikids – took on its distinctive shape because of the intervention of immigrants, and even there, as we have seen, Scandinavian immigrants arrived only in relatively small numbers. It is hard to see Novgorod and Kiev becoming interlinked, even loosely, without the decisive intervention of Scandinavian traders and their determination to take cuts from each other's operations. But there were not enough of them to dominate even the military forces of the new state, which drew on Slavs, Finns and everyone else besides. This was migration operating on a much smaller scale, even, than in those Roman successor states created by partial elite replacement. And the Danish, Polish, Bohemian and Moravian states were all created from entirely indigenous population groups. Indeed, the migration element would seem to be smaller even than that involved in the appearance of larger Germanic powers on the fringes of the Roman Empire in the second and third centuries AD.

In that first revolution among Europe's barbarians in late antiquity, migration sometimes played a larger role, and sometimes a smaller one, and always sat alongside processes of socioeconomic and political transformation. But there was usually some kind of population transfer, characteristically in the direction of the Roman frontier, where wealth-producing contacts with the developed Mediterranean world could be maximized. The Slavic era began with an analogous pattern of migration in the late fifth and sixth centuries, as Slavic-speakers moved into contact with the east Roman Empire and found ways of prospering from that proximity, which set off a profound transformation of their own societies. But when state formation accelerated so dramatically in the ninth and tenth centuries, this kind of migration pattern is conspicuous only by its absence. The new Slavic and Scandinavian states formed where they stood, with no drift towards the magnetic pole of more developed imperial Europe.

This leaves us with one final problem to explore as this study of barbarian Europe comes to its conclusion. Why was it that long-established patterns of migration, so common in the first two-thirds of the millennium, ceased to operate in its last centuries?

# 11

# THE END OF MIGRATION AND
# THE BIRTH OF EUROPE

IN THE MID-890S, the latest nomad menace burst into the heart of Europe. Following in the footsteps of Huns and Avars, the Magyars shifted their centre of operations from the northern shores of the Black Sea to the Great Hungarian Plain. For the most part, the results were everything that past experience of nomad powers would lead you to expect:

> [The Magyars] laid waste the whole of Italy, so that after they had killed many bishops the Italians tried to fight against them and twenty thousand men fell in one battle on one day. They came back by the same way by which they had come, and returned home after destroying a great part of Pannonia. They sent ambassadors treacherously to the Bavarians offering peace so that they could spy out the land. Which, alas!, first brought evil and loss not seen in all previous times to the Bavarian kingdom. For the Magyars came unexpectedly in force with a great army across the River Enns and invaded the kingdom of Bavaria with war, so that in a single day they laid waste by killing and destroying everything with fire and sword an area fifty miles long and fifty miles broad.[1]

The populations of the Great Hungarian Plain and surrounding regions, not least Great Moravia centred in Slovakia, were quickly subdued, and an orgy of equine-powered aggression saw Magyar raiding parties sweep through northern Italy and southern France with a ferocity not seen since the time of Attila, while full-scale Magyar armies defeated their East Frankish counterparts three times within the first decade of the tenth century.

But one element in the usual mix of nomad pastimes is missing from the Magyars' European tour. Five hundred years before, the two pulses of Hunnic movement westwards – first on to the northern shores of the Black Sea in the 370s, and then on to the Great Hungarian Plain a generation later – had thrown semi-subdued, largely Germanic-speaking clients of the Roman Empire across its frontiers in extremely large numbers. Two hundred years later, the arrival of the Avars west of the Carpathians would prompt the departure of the Lombards for Italy and a widespread dispersal of Slavic-speakers in every direction: south into the Balkans, west as far as the Elbe, north towards the Baltic, and even eastwards, it seems, into the Russian heartland. Destructive as it was in so many ways, the arrival of the Magyars generated no documented population movements whatsoever (apart, of course, from those of the Magyars themselves). Why not? The answer lies in the dynamic interaction between migration and development which had played itself out across the European landscape over the previous thousand years.

# MIGRATION

The absence of any secondary migration associated with the Magyars is all the more surprising because it is one of the central findings of this study that, contrary to some recent trends in scholarship on the period, migration must be taken seriously as a major theme of the first millennium. This trend has not eliminated migration entirely from accounts of first-millennium history, but certainly incorporates a powerful tendency to downplay its importance. In some quarters even the word itself is avoided wherever possible, because 'migration' is associated with the simplistic *deus ex machina* of the 'invasion hypothe-sis' model of explanation, which was so prevalent up until the early 1960s. In this view, migration meant the arrival of a large mixed group of humanity – a 'complete' population: men and women, old and young – who expelled the sitting tenants of a landscape and took it over, changing its material cultural profile more or less overnight. This model was massively overused, and trapped the developing discipline of archaeology into migrato-centric models that crippled creativity. Besides, as many archaeologists have since pointed out, the model didn't really explain anything anyway, because it never properly addressed the issue of *why* large groups of human beings might have behaved in such a fashion. This being so, it has been both reasonable and natural for subsequent archaeologists to concentrate upon other possible reasons for material cultural change. And these are legion. Everything from religious conversion to agricultural innovation and social development can have profound effects upon material cultural profiles. A highly suspicious attitude towards migration has also crossed the boundaries between disciplines. Some early medieval historians are now also so convinced that nothing like the old invasion hypothesis could ever have happened, that they are happy to suppose that historical sources must be misleading whenever they seem to be reporting possibly analogous phenomena.

A central aim of this study, however, has been to re-examine the evidence for first-millennium migration with a more open mind, and above all to reconsider it in the light of everything that can be learned about how migration works in the modern world. And from this point of view, one of its key conclusions is that the evidence for migration in the first millennium is both much more substantial and much more comprehensible than has sometimes been recognized in recent years. A deep-seated desire to avoid mentioning migration (a more successful version of Basil Fawlty and the war) has thus been wrenching discussion of some pivotal moments of first-millennium history away from the most likely reconstruction of events, and, in so doing, hampering analysis of the broader patterns of development that were under way.

It is an inescapable conclusion from all the comparative literature that a basic behavioural trait of *Homo sapiens sapiens* is consistently to use movement – migration (mentioned it again, but I think I got away with it . . .) – as a strategy for maximizing quality of life, not least for gaining access to richer food supplies and all other forms of wealth. The size of migration unit, balance of motivation, type of destination, and other detailed mechanisms will all vary according to circumstance, but the basic phenomenon is itself highly prevalent. In practice, two particular migration models have been retained in even the most minimizing of recent discussions: 'elite replacement' for larger-group movement, and 'wave of advance' for smaller migration units. Part of the attraction of both has been that they are safely different from the old invasion hypothesis. Elite replacement suggests both that not very many people in total were involved in the action, and that their migratory activity didn't really have that much effect. If you just replace one elite with another, what's the big deal? The wave-of-advance model employs mixed migratory units – essentially families – but their colonization of landscapes is piecemeal, slow, by and large peaceful, and decidedly not deliberate – intention being one of the elements of the old invasion model which revisionists find most problematic. How much of first-millennium European migration can be successfully described by employing these models?

## Migration Modelling

Some of it, certainly. Cheating only slightly in chronological terms, the classic, superbly documented example of elite replacement is the Norman Conquest of England in 1066. In the following twenty years or so, as *Doomsday Book* shows, an immigrant, basically Norman elite took over the agricultural assets of the English countryside, evicting or demoting the existing landholders. But the overwhelming majority of the indigenous population remained exactly where they had been before the Normans arrived. Likewise, at least some elements of Wielbark expansion in the first and second centuries AD and of its later Slavic counterpart, particularly the spread of Korchak-type farmers through the largely unoccupied central European uplands, probably had a wave-of-advance quality about them. Looking at the millennium as a whole, however, these models are both too simple and too narrow to describe the totality of recorded migratory action.

First, the models themselves need a substantial overhaul. They either collapse different situations into undifferentiated confusion, or are of such limited applicability as to be more or less useless – at least for first-millennium Europe. As currently construed, elite replacement fails to distinguish the particularity of a case such as the Norman Conquest, where the invading elite could fit easily into existing socio-economic structures, leaving them intact, and any broader effects on the total population remain correspondingly small, if not so minimal as those wanting to undermine the importance of migration might think.[2] But this kind of elite replacement applies only when the incoming elite was of broadly the same size as its indigenous counterpart, and I strongly suspect, even if I could never prove it, that, over the broad aeons of human history, this will have been true only in a minority of instances.

Certainly the first millennium AD throws up more examples of a different kind of case, where the intruding elite, if still a minority – and even quite a small one – compared to the totality of the indigenous population, was still too numerous to be accommodated by redistributing the available landed assets as currently organized. In these cases, existing estate structures had to be at least partially broken up and the labour force redistributed. As a result of this process, the entire balance between elite and non-elite elements of the population was restructured, and the overall cultural and other effects of the migration process were likely to be correspondingly large. This kind of elite migration could not but have huge socioeconomic consequences, and potentially also much greater cultural ones as the indigenous population came into intense contact with an intrusive elite, which was more numerous than its old indigenous counterpart. It was this intense contact, seen in Anglo-Saxon England and Frankish Gaul north of Paris from the fifth century, and perhaps to a lesser extent the Danelaw after 870, that generated substantial cultural, including linguistic, change, as the indigenous population was forced into modes of behaviour dictated by a new and relatively numerous foreign elite living cheek by jowl among them.[3]

Different again were cases of only partial elite replacement, particularly common in more Mediterranean regions of the old Roman west in the fifth and sixth centuries. Here there was some economic restructuring to accommodate the intruders – Goths, Vandals, Burgundians and others – but considerable elements of the old Roman landowning elites survived. In the longer term, it was the immigrants in these cases who struggled to hold on to their existing culture, and long-term linguistic change moved in the other direction. That is not to say, however, that this – the most limited form of migration on display in the first millennium – had only negligible consequences for the areas affected. In the first instance, high politics were dominated by the intrusive elites at the expense of their indigenous counterparts, at least when it came to matters like royal succession, and the overall political effect was sufficient to initiate major structural change. The disappearance in the medium to longer term of large-scale, centrally organized taxation of agricultural production, and the consequent weakening of state structures in the post-Roman west, are best explained in terms of the militarization of elite life that followed the creation of those structures at the hands of intrusive new elites.

The wave-of-advance model requires an equally substantial theoretical overhaul. The basic problem with it, even with ostensibly relevant cases such as Slavic Korchak expansion in the fifth and sixth centuries, or Wielbark expansion in the first and second, is that the Europe of the first millennium AD retained few if any uncontested landscapes of the kind that may have existed when the first farmers had been operating four thousand years before. By the year 1000, there were still plenty of forests, and we take our leave of European history at a moment when a further wave of agricultural expansion was in the process of hacking great swathes through them. But farmers had been clearing the landscape for millennia by this date and many of the best spots had long since been claimed. In this kind of context, random, uncontested expansion, even by small groups, was rarely an option. Korchak-type family or extended family groups probably did spread in largely uncontested fashion, but they did so by moving in a thoroughly non-random fashion through less sought-after, more marginal habitats of upland central Europe. And even here, the total subsequent subjugation of landscapes to the Slavic cultural model, combined with the documented aggression of Slavic groups in other contexts, strongly suggests that a degree of coercion might still have been involved. The same was probably also true of earlier Wielbark groups. Early Wielbark expansion seems to have been carried forward by small social units, but adjacent northern Przeworsk communities certainly came into Wielbark cultural line as a result of their activities. This could have been voluntary, but I suspect that examples of small-scale migration from the Viking period give us a more likely model for what was going on.

Small-scale Scandinavian migration units began carving out territories for themselves in northern Scotland and the northern and western isles of Britain from pretty close to the start of the ninth century. In this case, the logistic problem of getting access to shipping imposed constraints that did not apply in the Korchak or Wielbark cases. Hence, as is documented in subsequent Scandinavian expansion into Iceland and Greenland, the migration units, even if small, did have to be organized by jarls or lesser landowners (holds) who had sufficient wealth to gain access to shipping. But whereas Iceland and Greenland were more or less unpopulated landscapes, northern Scotland and the isles were not, and, even if the migrating units were individually small, Scandinavian expansion into these territories was certainly aggressive. Older suggestions that the result was ethnic cleansing are outdated, but the indigenous population was forcibly demoted to lesser status, and, over time, absorbed into the invaders' cultural patterns. Small-scale migration need not, therefore, necessarily mean peaceful migration. As long as they confronted an indigenous population who did not have larger-scale, regionally based political structures, small migration units could still insert themselves successfully by aggressive means. Alongside a wave-of-advance model for small-scale migration that was random in direction and peaceful in nature, therefore, we need to add small-scale migration flows that were non-random or aggressive, or both. This kind of model is potentially highly applicable to the generally already-occupied landscape of first-millennium Europe, relevant not only to Wielbark, Korchak, and some Viking expansions, but also perhaps to the early stages of eastern Germanic expansion towards the Black Sea in the third century, of Elbe Germani into the *Agri Decumates*; or of Slavic groups north and east into Russia in the seventh to the ninth centuries.

What also emerges from the evidence is that too clear a line cannot be drawn between wave-of-advance and larger-scale migration. Just because an expansion began with small-scale migration units, does not mean that it stayed that way. The best-documented case here is provided by the Vikings. Initial Scandinavian raiding and settling, in the late eighth and early ninth centuries, were all carried forward by small groups. The earliest recorded violence involved the crews of three ships – perhaps a hundred men – and there is no reason to think that the settlements around Scotland and the isles need have been carried forward by groups much larger than this. But, as resistance and profits both built up, and the desire eventually formed to settle more fertile areas of the British Isles, where larger political structures in the form of Anglo-Saxon kingdoms barred the way, more important Scandinavian leaders became involved in the action, and larger coalitions formed among the migrants. This reached its climax during the Great Army period from 865, when coalitions formed with the idea of carving out settlement areas first in Anglo-Saxon England and then in northern Francia. If the early raids were undertaken by groups of no more than a hundred strong, the series of Great Armies each comprised much more like five to ten thousand men. The water-borne nature of the action in the Viking era always needs to be kept in mind because it imposed logistic problems that did not apply in other cases, but the evolution from raiding parties to great armies nonetheless provides a well-documented model of how – on the back of evident and growing military and financial success – originally small-scale expansion might eventually suck in much larger numbers of participants. The evidence is not so good for some of the earlier expansions, and these were not affected by the problems of water transport. Nonetheless, the expanding momentum of Viking-era migration provides a helpful model for understanding a series of other first-millennium migratory phenomena, not least the second- and third-century Gothic, and fourth- and fifth-century Lombard expansions, which again, it seems, started small, but grew in scale until forces large enough to fight major battles against Roman armies and regional competitors (such as the Carpi), came to be involved. Anglo-Saxon expansion into former Roman Britain can also be partly understood with such a model in mind, and it is potentially applicable to the third-century Alamanni.

Even without venturing into really contentious areas, therefore, the full range of first-millennium evidence suggests some major revisions to now-standard migration models. But in addition to small-scale migration, elite replacements, and migration flows of increasing momentum, first-millennium sources do periodically report large, mixed groups of human beings on the move: 10,000 warriors and more, accompanied by dependent women and children. Not only do such reports arouse suspicion because they seem uncomfortably close to the old invasion hypothesis, but this particular type of migration unit does not figure in modern migratory patterns, where large, mixed groups of migrants are seen only when the motivation is political and negative – when populations are fleeing oppression, pogrom and massacre, as in Rwanda in the early 1990s. This is not what is reported in first-millennium sources, which describe both a more positive motivation and a greater degree of organization among groups intruding themselves in predatory fashion into other people's territory. Can we believe what the sources seem to be telling us? Should we retain large, mixed and organized groups of humanity as part of the overall picture of first-millennium migration?

## Invasion

Even when employing the most up-to-date methods – DNA or steady-state isotope analysis – the kind of evidence that archaeological investigation brings to this debate is at best only a blunt tool. It remains hotly disputed whether much usable DNA will ever be recovered from human remains of first-millennium vintage laid down in the damp and cold of northern Europe. And too much has happened in demographic terms since the first millennium for the percentage distributions of modern DNA patterns to give much clear insight into the relative proportions of their progenitors 1,500 years ago, except perhaps in the highly exceptional case of Iceland, where there was no human population before the Viking era.[4] Steady-state isotopes, likewise, only reveal where someone came to dental maturity. The children of two immigrants will have fully indigenous teeth, and this kind of analysis will always carry an in-built tendency to underestimate the importance of migration. Arguments based on more traditional types of archaeological investigation – the transfer to new regions of items or customs originally characteristic of another – are also unlikely to be any more conclusive.

The reasons are straightforward. By the birth of Christ, most of Europe had been settled and farmed, after a fashion, for millennia. And since even the most aggressive and dominant of immigrants usually still had a use for indigenous populations as agricultural labour, migration did not tend to empty entire landscapes. Furthermore, as all comparative study has emphasized (and modern experience shows), when migrants move into an occupied landscape, the result – in material and non-material cultural terms – is always an interaction. There are only a relatively few items in any particular group's material cultural profile that are so loaded with meaning that they will be held on to, for good or ill, in the longer term. Everything else is open to change under the stimulus of new circumstances, so you can hardly expect migration to involve the complete transfer of an entire material culture from point A to point B in normal first-millennium European conditions. There will always be some elements of continuity in the material cultural profile of any region subject to migration, and this makes it entirely possible, if you are so inclined, to explain any observable change in terms of internal evolution. Goods and ideas can move without being attached to people, and if what you observe archaeologically is no more than a limited transfer of either, it will always be possible to explain it in terms of something other than population displacement. But the fact that it will always be *possible* to do this does not mean that it will necessarily be *correct* to do so, and the inherent ambiguity of archaeological evidence is sometimes misinterpreted. Ambiguity means exactly that. If the archaeological evidence for any possible case of migration is ambiguous – which it usually will be – then it certainly does not prove that migration played a major role in any observable material cultural change – but neither does it disprove it. What all this actually amounts to is that archaeological evidence alone cannot decide the issue. It is important to insist on this point because there has been a tendency in some recent work to argue that ambiguous archaeological evidence essentially disproves migration, when it absolutely does not. Overall, of course, this forces us back on to the historical evidence. How good a case can be made from historical sources for the importance of large, organized and diverse groups of invaders on the move in the first millennium?

The answer has to be complex. There are some clear instances where a migration topos, a misleading invasion narrative, has been imposed on more complex events. Jordanes' account of Gothic expansion into the northern Black Sea region in the late second and third centuries is a classic case in point, as is the picture of the fourth- and fifth-century Lombard past to be found in Carolingian-era sources and beyond. But in other cases, the historical evidence in favour of distinct pulses of large-scale migration involving 10,000-plus warriors and a substantial number of dependants is infinitely stronger: the Tervingi and Greuthungi who asked for asylum inside the Roman Empire in 376, for instance, or the movement of Theoderic the Amal's Ostrogoths to Italy in 488/9. In both these cases, attempts have been made to undermine the credibility of our main informants, respectively Ammianus and Procopius, but they lack conviction. Ammianus described many different barbarian groups on the move on Roman soil in the course of his historical narrative and only on this one occasion does he refer to very large mixed groups of men, women and children. The idea that he was infected by some kind of migration topos in this instance, but not elsewhere, takes a lot of believing. Likewise Procopius: he is not in fact the only source to describe Theoderic's Ostrogoths on the march to Italy as a 'people' in a quasi-invasion-hypothesis sense of the term (a large, mixed grouping of men, women and children). One contemporary commentator even described them as such in person to Theoderic and other actual participants gathered at his court. You wouldn't want to hang anyone in a court of law on this kind of evidence, but its credibility is pretty much as good as anything else we get from the first millennium. To reject it on the basis of a supposed migration topos is arbitrary.[5]

Not quite in the same category of solidity, but still well within the usual limits of first-millennium plausibility, likewise, is a range of evidence indicating that moves of a similar nature were made by large, organized Vandal and Alanic groups on to Roman soil from 406, and by Radagaisus' Goths in 405.[6] And while more argument is certainly again required, by far the likeliest reconstruction of Alaric the Visigoth's career indicates that it was founded on mobilizing the Tervingi and Greuthungi of 376, settled in the Balkans by treaty in 382, into a series of further moves from 395 onwards. These are all instances of large, mixed-group movement that pass muster on all the normal rules of first-millennium evidence. There are also enough of them to require us not to dismiss too quickly a series of other cases, where the evidence is a notch or two weaker: in particular the population movements associated with the rise and fall of the Hunnic Empire, which saw the gathering-in of armed, largely Germanic groups, and their subsequent departures from the Great Hungarian Plain as competition built up among them in the era of Hunnic collapse. Here the evidence for large group migration is either partial (the cases of the Rugi or Heruli), or implicit rather than explicit (those of the Sciri, Sueves, and Alans). Although we can find some convincing cases where the action has been mistakenly cast in the form of an invasion-hypothesis-type population movement, therefore, there are many others where there is no good reason to think that this has happened. And, in fact, even the Goths and Lombards are worth a closer look.

In both instances, we are dealing with highly retrospective miscastings of the action. Jordanes was writing about events that happened three hundred years before his own lifetime, and the Lombard authors in the ninth century and beyond about migratory activity that was then four to five hundred years in the past. On one level, it is easy to see why mistakes might have crept in, but there is more to say here than just that. For in neither case was it complete fantasy to be thinking in terms of migration of some kind. The totality of the evidence for both the second- and third-century Goths and the fourth- and fifth-century Lombards does indicate that substantial population displacement played a major role in these eras of their respective pasts.

The evidence is better for the Goths. Here we have contemporary accounts locating Goths in northern Poland in the first and second centuries, but north of the Black Sea from the mid-third. There was also a major material cultural revolution north of the Black Sea in the third century, in the course of which a whole series of customs and items became prominent in the region, which had not previously been part of its characteristic profiles. Some of the more distinctive among the new features, moreover, had been well-established aspects of life and death in first- and second-century Poland. These archaeological indications cannot prove that Gothic migration took place from the Baltic to the Black Sea regions, but, taken in conjunction with the contemporary historical evidence, they amount to a very serious argument to that effect. And while that historical evidence clearly indicates, as we have seen, that, even if there were many separate groups involved in the action rather than one 'people', and that some of them were perhaps originally numerically challenged, this did not remain the case throughout the migratory process. The third-century Goths provide, in fact, an excellent case of a migration flow of increasing momentum, which didn't really stop until the Gothic Tervingi had displaced the Carpi as the dominant grouping between the Danube and the Carpathians in the decades either side of the year 300. Though much less detailed, the Lombard evidence is similar.

Lombards are well attested in the Lower Elbe region, just south of modern Denmark, in the first and second centuries AD. In this case, there are no contemporary historical indications at all of any major population displacements from this region in the Roman period, and what archaeological evidence there is might suggest only a series of relatively small ones, like the first Gothic flows towards the Black Sea. Yet again, however, Lombards were present on the Upper Elbe in sufficient numbers by the 490s to move in and destroy the hegemony of the Heruli in the western half of the Great Hungarian Plain through main force. Whatever its earlier forms, therefore, Lombard expansion towards the Danube, like that of the Goths towards the Black Sea, eventually took the form of much larger pulses of population. Neither Jordanes nor our Lombard sources invented the concept of large-scale migration from nothing, therefore, even if they miscast its form. And, just to push their rehabilitation one stage further, subsequent Gothic and Lombard migrations, occurring between these initial flows and our sources' composition, had taken the form of large, composite group moves, both in the direction of Italy: the Ostrogoths in 488/9 and the Lombards some eighty years later.[7]

When examined more closely, therefore, neither Jordanes nor the Lombard sources give us reason to deny the reality of the large-group migrations recorded in other sources. That said, it is very important to recognize that even our *echt* examples of large-group first-millennium migration do not conform exactly to the old invasion-hypothesis model. Not even the largest groups were whole 'peoples' moving from one locality to another untouched by the process. They could both shed population and gain it. This was presumably even more true of drawn-out migration flows, such as the second- and third-century Goths and fourth- and fifth-century Lombards, but the pattern is only explicitly documented for some of the large-group moves. Decisions to move on such a scale were never lightly, and often caused splits. The Tervingi who crossed into the Empire in 376 left behind them north of the Danube a significant minority of the old group's membership who adhered to the old leadership. Theoderic the Amal's father caused another split when he moved the then Pannonian Goths into the Roman Balkans in 473, and Theoderic himself left behind at least some elite Goths who were absorbed into the military-political hierarchies of the east Roman state. When it comes to gathering recruits, the Lombards were joined by a mixed group of 20,000 Saxons for their move to Italy, together with descendants of much of the flotsam and jetsam left over by the post-Attilan struggles for power in the Middle Danube. Theoderic the Amal, likewise, added a body of Rugi to the Gothic following built up over two generations by his uncle and himself. Similarly, the relationship between the two Vandal groups and the Alans who crossed the Rhine together became much tighter in the face of Roman counterattack in Spain, so that, by the time they invaded North Africa in 429, the survivors, united behind the Hasding monarchy, were much more of a cohesive political unit than the loose alliance they had been twenty-three years before. As much recent work has emphasized, there was as much of the snowball to these migratory movements as the billiard ball.

Another significant departure from the old invasion model is the fact that, when looked at closely, these large groups were mixed not only in age and gender, but also in status. Visions of the Germanic *Völkerwanderung* produced in the great era of nationalism in the nineteenth and early twentieth centuries had in mind large invasion groups of free and equal warriors with their families in tow. But within the larger groups, two separate status-categories of warrior are documented, and there is reason to suppose that non-militarized slaves also participated in at least some of the moves. It is only the higher warrior class that fell into the 'free' category, and the fact that they were by definition an elite class suggests that this group was some kind of minority. The key decisions about migration in the period were being taken, therefore, only by a minority of the participants, with lesser warriors and slaves having little if any influence. Recognizing the reality and significance of these status distinctions also imposes clear limits on the extent to which currently fashionable ideas about the freedom with which group identities could be chosen and discarded can really have applied in practice. What kind of idiot would have chosen to be of lesser-warrior or slave status if group identity was entirely a matter of individual choice? By extension, this also indicates that we need to be careful as to how far we suppose snowball-type phenomena to have operated. Since much of the population of barbarian Europe was not in control of its own destiny, the right to join or not join in large-group migration must have been exercised only by certain, more elite elements among participating populations.[8]

The final modification that must be made to the old invasion-hypothesis model of large-group migration concerns its supposition that large-scale intrusions drove out existing populations. There are several good examples of large-scale invasion in the first millennium, but none where the evidence suggests mass ethnic cleansing. Indigenous populations were often faced with a choice between accepting subjugation or moving on, a choice which would have felt particularly brutal to indigenous elites who had most to lose from the arrival of a new set of masters. But there is no convincingly documented case where the response to this choice led to the complete evacuation of an extensive landscape. At the very least, indigenous populations supplied good agricultural labour, and many of our immigrant groups anyway had lower social-status categories into which newly subjugated indigenous populations could easily be slotted.

These alterations are important, but they remain modifications rather than denials of the basic proposition that the evidence for large, mixed, and organized migrant groups from the first millennium is, ostensibly, periodically convincing. Nationalist visions of whole ancestral 'peoples' clearing out new landscapes for themselves to enjoy can be consigned to the recycle bin of history. The groups documented in our sources were political entities, which could grow or fragment,

which contained individuals occupying lesser- and higher-status categories, and which inserted themselves in correspondingly complex
ways into new but already thoroughly inhabited environments.
Though fair enough on the basis of the available historical evidence
(and not denied by the archaeological), can this proposition still be
maintained in the face of the non-appearance of such phenomena in
modern migratory patterns? The answer to this question is bound up,
in my view, with that to a far larger one: Why did European migration
take the forms it did in the first millennium? Answering this question
requires us to set the observable patterns of demographic displacement between the birth of Christ and the year 1000 against all that
comparative study can teach us about migration as a general human
phenomenon.

## Migration Mechanics

There are a myriad detailed ways in which the mechanics of first-
millennium migration correspond to what has been observed in better-
documented case studies of early modern and more recent migration.
Not least of these, the crucial importance of active fields of information
in dictating precise destinations is just as prominent in the first
millennium as in later eras. Germanic expansion towards the Black Sea
in the third century was clearly exploiting information about the region
which had built up through the operations of the Amber Route. Slavic
groups first came to know the Roman Balkans as raiders before
exploiting that knowledge to turn themselves into settlers as and when
political conditions permitted. Scandinavian expansion to the west in
the Viking era likewise operated on the back of intelligence acquired
by participation in the emporia trading networks of the eighth century,
while those working to the east took a generation or so to find their
way down the river routes of western Russia to the great centres of
Islamic demand for northern goods, having originally opened up the
eastern hinterland of the Baltic to feed western markets. To these
entirely uncontroversial examples, I would also add some others. A
major contributory factor to the apparently odd stop/start migratory
patterns of some of the groups entering Roman territory either side of
the year 400 was the need to acquire information about further possible
destinations before hitting the road again. The Goths, especially the

Tervingi who entered the Empire in 376, already knew about the Balkans, for instance, but not about Italy and Gaul, to where they moved on in the next generation. It took twenty years (and their participation in two Roman civil wars that took some of them lengthy distances in that direction) before they were ready to take the next step. Likewise the Vandals and Alans: Spain marked the end of their original migratory ambitions, and it again took twenty years and some exploratory sea raids before they were prepared to venture across the Straits of Gibraltar to North Africa. More generally, the whole broader phenomenon of migration flows of increasing momentum is clearly a product of growing knowledge. It was precisely the fact that exploratory expansionary ventures into a new region produced profitable outcomes for the pioneers that encouraged others to participate. In some modern cases, such as the spread of the Boers northwards from the Cape, the pioneers were deliberately recruited scouts, sent to check the viability of larger-scale expansion. The same effect could also be achieved, however, by a less formal grapevine.

The study of modern migration also devotes much effort to the key issue of why some people from any particular community choose to move, whereas others in more or less identical circumstances stay put. Tackling this complex issue fully requires the kind of detailed information which is simply unavailable for the first millennium, but it is worth pointing up the relevance of the issue. In the cases of large-group migration reported in any detail in our sources, there is no instance where the decision to move did not generate some kind of split among the affected population group. The same is true, only more so, of the more extended migration flows. For all the Germani of Polish origin who ended up by the Black Sea in the third century, there were many others who stayed behind, shown by the fact that the Wielbark and Przeworsk cultural systems continued to operate. Likewise, many Angles and Saxons did not relocate to England in the fifth and sixth centuries, and Scandinavia was not emptied in the Viking period. Such divergences of response were only natural, of course, given the magnitude of the decisions involved, and first-millennium populations clearly felt the same stress of migration as modern ones, even if we can't explore their reactions in detail.

Stress also manifests itself in the modern world in the phenomenon of return migration. Looked at closely, all modern migration flows see substantial numbers of immigrants returning to their original homelands. Again, the level of information is not sufficient to allow us to discuss this topic properly for the first millennium, but aspects of the Viking period emphasize that it, too, needs to be recognized as a real phenomenon. The initial phases of Scandinavian expansion were all about gathering wealth, whether by raiding or trading, or both. Having gathered their wealth, different individuals then made different choices about how to invest it. Some chose, even early on, to stay put at their points of destination in the east and west (as shown by the early settlements in northern Scotland and the isles), whereas others chose to take their new wealth back home to Scandinavia, eventually prompting a massive shake-up in Baltic politics. With this example in mind, I (as others) would be happy to believe reports that some incoming Anglo-Saxons also eventually chose to return to the continent.[9]

Closely related, too, to the stress of migration, but this time something we can explore in greater detail, is the highly significant influence on patterns of movement of an ingrained migration habit. In modern migration flows, an existing tradition of mobility often plays a vital role in dictating which individuals within a particular group of people will decide to move. Individuals who have moved once are more prone to move again within their own lifetimes, but, less intuitively obvious, the habit is also passed on between generations. The children and grandchildren of migrants are much more likely than the average to move again themselves. A tradition of personal or familial mobility clearly generates a greater propensity to attempt to solve life's problems, or look for greater opportunity, by moving to new localities. Anyone might move if the stimulus to do so is large enough, but the required stimulus is smaller for those with established migration habits.

The effects of this factor can be seen at work on at least two different levels in the first millennium. First, at least two of the broader population flows, those of the Wielbark and Przeworsk Germani in the second and third centuries, and of the early Slavs three hundred years later, involved populations whose farming techniques were then insufficient to maintain the fertility of any individual piece of arable land for more than a generation or two. A general, periodic local mobility was simply a fact of life for these populations, and there is every reason to suppose that this facilitated the eventual transformation of a more random wave-of-advance-type expansion into a channelled migration flow when information began to filter back about the opportunities available at an entirely new set of longer-distance destinations. Second, a more specific tradition of distinct, longer-distance relocation clearly built up among some particular first-millennium populations. The fourth-century Gothic Tervingi are probably most famous for the fact that a majority of them decided to seek asylum inside the Roman Empire in 376. That decision was greatly facilitated, however, by active memories of recent migrations. This same Gothic group had taken possession of their existing lands in Wallachia and Moldavia between the Lower Danube and the River Dniester only in the decades either side of the year 300, and a generation or so later, in the 330s, had attempted to move bodily to new locations on the fringes of the Middle Danube region. It was the children of those who had moved into Moldavia and Wallachia who were on the move again in the 330s, and their children and older grandchildren who decided to seek a new life inside the Roman Empire in 376. Similar observations apply to many of the other groups caught up in the rise and fall of the Hunnic Empire, both those who fled inside Roman borders in the crises of 376–80 and 405–8, and those who moved first to the Middle Danube under Hunnic influence and/or duress, and then out of it after Attila's death. The willingness of some Norse to move on to Iceland and Greenland in the later ninth century was likewise facilitated by the fact that they were the immediate descendants of Viking immigrants to Scotland and the isles. In fact, examples like the Goths or Slavs demonstrate how moves that were initially generated by general traditions of local mobility could then spawn the more specific traditions of larger-scale mobility that underlay the move of many Tervingi on to Roman soil in 376, in the same way that internal migrants within the European landscape provided many of the recruits for the trek to North America in the nineteenth century.

Aside from the emotional costs of migration, financial ones were also a major factor in any migrant's calculations. Most first-millennium migration that we know anything about was a question, more or less, of walking and wagons. It involved no major transportation costs, apart from wear and tear to animals, peoples and wheels, and participation was consequently open to many. It nonetheless involved many indirect costs, above all the potential food shortages that were bound to result when movement disrupted normal agricultural activity. As a result, food stocks had to be maximized before moving, unless circumstances were completely overwhelming, and this meant that autumn was the classic moment to make a move – just after the current year's harvest had been gathered and while there was still a chance of some grass growing to feed the oxen pulling the wagons and other animals. Alaric's Goths moved into Italy in both 401 and 408 in the autumn, Radagaisus' Goths in autumn 405. The Vandals, Alans, and Sueves who crossed the Rhine at the very end of 406 likewise presumably began their trek from the Middle Danube in the autumn of that year.[10]

As usual, there is little information about the impact of migration costs beyond this very basic point, but logistic problems do show themselves from time to time in the available data. Above all, extended periods of movement left groups particularly vulnerable in economic terms. Flavius Constantius was able to bring Alaric's Goths – now led by Athaulf and Vallia – to heel by starving them out in 414/15. By that date, they had been living off the land without planting crops for six or seven years. Later in the fifth century, similarly, after the collapse of the Hunnic Empire, the surviving sources give us just a little insight into the logistic strategies adopted by Theoderic the Amal. His grouping journeyed around the Balkans with wagonloads of seedcorn in the 470s, and one dimension of its diplomatic negotiations with the Roman state involved providing it with agricultural land. Even on the march, noticeably, this group always sought to establish more regular economic relationships with Balkan communities, rather than merely robbing them. This meant that the communities could keep on farming and producing surpluses, from which the Goths could siphon off a regular percentage, whereas destroying them by pillage would only have fed Theoderic's followers once.

Logistic factors had a still bigger impact upon population flows requiring more than land transport. Mass access to sea transport did not even become a possibility until the advent of steerage class in the enormous transatlantic liners of the later nineteenth century. Before that point, travel costs necessarily limited participation in any kind of maritime-based expansion. Again, the Viking period provides the best-documented first-millennium example. Ships were highly expensive, and even specialist cargo ships could carry only limited numbers of people and their goods. Thus Viking raiding required the less well-off to come to some kind of joint arrangement for funding the purchase or hire of a ship (though how many shipowners, I wonder, would be willing to hire out shipping for raiding ventures?), or to attach themselves to a leader of higher status.[11] Logistic limitations figured even more strongly when it came to the settlement phases, when so many more types of people and a wider range of bulky farming equipment were required. The relevant shipping costs alone make Stenton's suggested phase of large-scale Norse peasant settlement in the Danelaw pretty much inconceivable. Who would have bothered to pay for this when there was a subdued, low-status Anglo-Saxon labour force already in situ? We also see the effects of logistics on the Icelandic settlements, where each immigrant unit was headed by a higher-status individual who could presumably cover the large initial investment costs of transportation. Logistics may also have limited the number of Scandinavian women who participated in the Norse migration flow compared to the other land-based movements of our period. Modern DNA patterns suggest that only one-third of immigrant women to Iceland came all the way – directly or indirectly – from Scandinavia, with the rest moving a shorter distance from the British Isles. This may reflect the fact that it was too expensive for more than a minority of warriors to bring their Scandinavian sweethearts with them. On the other hand, given that the men involved were relatively wealthy, and that they were pagan and polygamous, it may be that women outnumbered men early on, with each Scandinavian male bringing with him not only his Scandinavian sweetheart but a couple of British or Irish babes besides.

As frustratingly limited as all the Viking-period evidence is, our other major first-millennium examples of maritime movement – Anglo-Saxon moves across the North Sea and the expedition of Vandals and Alans across the Straits of Gibraltar – are not even illuminated in this much detail. The impact of logistic demands must, though, have been similar. Possibly the Vandals and Alans were in a position to use intimidation to requisition some transport, but I doubt that they were able to avoid having to meet most of their costs themselves. And there is reason to think that the fact that they could only move a relatively few people at a time dictated their initial choice of landfall: Morocco, far away from the better-defended heartland of Roman North Africa, which was their ultimate destination. The logistic impossibility of moving many people at once was probably also a major factor in the drawn-out nature of Anglo-Saxon migration into southern Britain.

So far, so good: there are a whole series of ways in which the comparative literature sheds light on first-millennium migration, even given the limited data set available. But this still leaves some big questions to answer. Above all, can we in fact accept what the sources appear to be telling us: that the first millennium occasionally saw large, mixed, and organized population groups take to the road? And, if so, how are we to explain this phenomenon both in its own context, and the fact that it has not been observed in more modern and better-documented eras? Again, modern migration studies, in my view, can help answer these questions, but a fully satisfactory explanation also requires us to explore first-millennium migration patterns against the backdrop of a much wider set of transformations that were unfolding simultaneously in barbarian Europe.


## MIGRATION AND DEVELOPMENT


Comparative studies provide two basic points of orientation when thinking about the likely causes of any observable migration flow. First, it is overwhelmingly likely that a substantial difference in levels of economic development between adjacent areas will generate a flow between the two, from the less-developed towards its richer neighbour. What 'adjacent' means will vary enormously in different eras according to what transport is available, and a situation that would otherwise generate a 'natural' flow of people may be interfered with by political structures at either end, or by the availability of information. All things being equal, however, a flow of population will be one result of different levels of development, the result of *Homo sapiens sapiens'* inherent tendency to use movement as a strategy for maximization. The second point is equally basic. In the vast majority of cases, the precise motivation of any individual migrant will be a complex mixture of free-will and constraint, of economic and political motives. There are exceptions, not least when political refugees are driven forward by fear of imminent death, but most migrants are motivated by some combination of all four factors. Taken together, what both of these observations stress above all is that migration will almost always need to be understood against prevailing patterns of economic and political development. Taking this approach, in my view, provides satisfactory explanations for both the general geographical 'shape' of first-millennium migration, and the seemingly odd nature of its characteristic migration units.

## Migration in Roman Europe

At the start of the first millennium, the most highly developed region of Europe – in both economic and political terms – was the circle of the Mediterranean united under Roman domination, to which the largely La Tène landscapes of the south and west had recently been added. La Tène Europe featured developed agricultural regimes whose surpluses could support relatively dense populations, together with considerable production and exchange in other sectors of the economy. The Romans did not only conquer La Tène populations as they moved north, but it is a fact – and not an accidental one – that their conquests ran out of steam more or less at the outer fringes of La Tène Europe. The reason was simple: beyond that zone, the profits of conquest ceased to be worth the costs. Beyond La Tène Europe lay the territories of the largely Germanic-speaking post-Jastorf world. There was a large degree of variation in economic patterns across this zone, not least because some of its populations had been in substantial engagement with their La Tène neighbours for a considerable period. In general terms, however, political units were smaller in scale here than those of La Tène Europe, even before the latter was incorporated into the Roman Empire, and agricultural productivity was lower. General population density was therefore less, and there are fewer signs either of non-agricultural production and exchange, or of marked differences of wealth (at least as expressed in material cultural terms). Beyond Jastorf Europe, the northern and eastern reaches of the European landscape were still host to Iron Age farming populations (as far as ecological conditions permitted), but they operated still less productive agricultural regimes, their settlements were smaller and even more short-lived, and they possessed little in the way of material cultural goods.

Faced with this distinctly three-speed Europe (Map 1), comparative migration studies would lead you to expect flows of population from its less developed regions to the more developed (i.e. in broadly southerly and westerly directions). And in the Roman period – the first three centuries AD – this is essentially what occurred. The economic and sociopolitical structures of more developed Roman Europe sucked in population from its less developed neighbours in a variety of forms, particularly from adjacent, largely Germanic-dominated post-Jastorf Europe. Many individuals entered the Empire as voluntary recruits for Roman armies on the one hand, or involuntary slaves for a variety of economic purposes on the other. These population flows are well known and require no further comment here. But the larger and more contentious Germanic population flows of the second and third centuries also fall into line with this pattern, in the general sense that they too moved broadly south and west towards more developed Europe. A full understanding of their particular history, however, also requires an understanding of how a broader set of interactions with the Roman Empire had in the meantime been transforming the three-speed pattern which prevailed at the birth of Christ.

For one thing, the military and political structures of the Roman Empire fundamentally explain the geographically asymmetrical outcome of Germanic expansion in these years. The forces behind the expansion seem to have been operating very generally in Germanic-dominated central Europe, but the resulting population flows had much more dramatic effects in the south-east, and particularly north of the Black Sea, than in the south-west. Where Germanic immigrants took over no more than the *Agri Decumates* in the south-west, further east Dacia was abandoned and political structures north of the Black Sea were entirely remade. There may have been some difference in the scale of the migratory flows in operation in each direction, but this, too, was reflective of the more fundamental cause of the different scale of outcome. Flows south and east were operating against the clients of Rome's inner frontier zone, rather than directly against the military power of the Empire itself. As a result, the likelihood of success was that much greater than in the south-west, where the Empire's military power had to be tackled directly.

Why the successful leaders of these expansion flows were generally willing to settle for outcomes that left them largely on the fringes of Empire, instead of pressing on permanently across the frontier, also comes down in part to the longer-term effects of interaction with the Roman world in the first two centuries AD. The operations of trading mechanisms – both in longer-distance luxury goods and shorter-distance largely agricultural products – opportunities for raiding richer

Roman territories, and the Empire's own propensity for bolstering the power of its clients with diplomatic subsidies all meant that in the first two centuries of the Empire's existence new wealth built up at the courts of Germanic kings in the immediate vicinity of the frontier. Three-speed Europe thus developed a fourth gear in the form of an inner zone of clients whose wealth outstripped those of their former peers in what now became the outer periphery of post-Jastorf Europe. Not only was it militarily much less dangerous for the leaders of Germanic expansion to restrict their operations to areas beyond the imperial frontier, but two centuries of interaction with the Empire, and the subsequent accumulations of wealth, had made the frontier zone an attractive target for predatory expansion in its own right. Before these processes had unfolded, there would have been little point for ambitious Germanic warlords in moving, say, from northern central Europe to southern central Europe, or from north of the Carpathians to the south-east, since the potential material gains for such efforts would have been minimal.

Understanding the action of the later second and third centuries in this way also explains the apparently odd form taken by at least some of the units participating in these migration flows. The first recorded attempt from the outer periphery to tap into the new wealth building up closer to the imperial frontier took the form of a raid. As the power of King Vannius of the Bohemian-based Marcomanni weakened in his dotage, an ousted political rival was able to organize a warband from central Poland (and possibly northern Poland too) to ransack the movable wealth around his court, much of it the proceeds of diplomatic subsidies and his cut from the activities of Roman merchants. Although I cannot prove it, I would be willing to bet that this was but one example of a far from uncommon phenomenon. Hit-and-run raids were not, however, the most effective way to tap into all the new wealth accumulating in the immediate hinterland of the Empire. For entirely structural reasons to do with trade, Roman diplomatic methods and even ease of raiding Roman territory, the best opportunities to benefit from the new wealth-generating interactions with the Roman Empire were all limited geographically to the immediate frontier zone, and any greater ambitions towards wealth acquisition among groups and leaders in the outer periphery required their permanent relocation towards the frontier. It is therefore hardly surprising that raiding gave way to migration in the second and third centuries as more ambitious leaders and followings from the outer periphery looked to win control of the new Rome-centred wealth flows operating in barbarian Europe.

But by the end of the first century AD, there was no potentially lucrative spot along the frontier that was not already occupied by a warlord of some kind, and no sitting tenants were likely to surrender their highly advantageous position without a fight. Any permanent relocation towards Rome's frontier therefore necessarily required the destruction of existing political structures, and this explains why the second- and third-century migration flows eventually encompassed substantial military forces numbered in the thousands, rather than warbands of just one or two hundred men. Warbands might raid effectively enough, but their power was insufficient to remake an entire political structure, so that ambitious wannabes from the outer periphery had no choice but to recruit larger expeditionary forces to achieve their aims.

It is worth pausing to consider this pattern of migratory expansion in the light of more recent and better-documented examples. This kind of intentional, predatory intrusion on the part of thousands of armed individuals is not generally seen in the modern world, and this is sometimes put forward as an objection to supposing that it ever occurred in the past. Half of the answer to this objection is that, though not common, this kind of activity has indeed been seen in the relatively modern world: it is exactly the same basic kind of migratory pattern observable among the Boers of the Great Trek. In that case, the intrusive units could be smaller because the Boers enjoyed a massive advantage in firepower over their Zulu and Matabele opponents. In the second and third centuries, any technological advantage was probably more likely to have lain with the groups of the inner periphery being targeted, since they may well have been buying Roman weaponry, so that the intrusive forces from the outer periphery had to be more or less as large as those deployed by the sitting kings of the frontier region.

The other half of the answer comes from thinking about precisely why modern migratory flows, even if cumulatively large, tend to operate on the basis of small individual migration units of just a few people at a time. They do so because the migration-unit size is dictated by the way in which modern migrants seek to access wealth from the more-developed economies to which they have been attracted. In the

modern context, wealth is accessed by individual immigrants finding
employment in the industrial or service sectors of an economy, which
is well-paid at least from the relative perspective of the immigrant him-
or herself. The underlying principle here is not that migration-unit
sizes are always likely to be small, but, rather, that they will be
appropriate to the means by which the wealth of the more developed
economy is going to be accessed. All the economies of first-millennium
Europe were essentially agricultural, and extremely low-tech. As a
result, even in the developing periphery of the Roman Empire, they
did not offer many even relatively well-paid jobs for individual
migrants, except for a few who could attach themselves to the military
followings of frontier kings. For those with ambitions to unlock the
wealth of this world on a much larger scale, coming as an individual
immigrant, or merely within a small group, was a pointless exercise.
In such a context, you had to arrive with enough force to defeat the
sitting tenant, and prompt the Empire to identify you now as its
preferred trading and diplomatic partner on your particular sector of
the frontier. Although this kind of migrant group is not commonly
seen in the modern world, therefore, it actually accords with the
fundamental principles behind all observed migration flows. Large-
scale predatory intrusion was as appropriate to wealth acquisition via
migration in the first millennium, as individual movement is now.

Levels of development also explain the other fundamental oddity
of these second- and third-century population flows: that many of the
warriors were accompanied by women and children. Germanic-
dominated Europe of the early centuries AD was a world of low-tech,
small-scale farms producing only limited food surpluses. As a result,
the economy could not support large warrior retinues; the kind of
food renders available even to fourth-century kings could support only
one or two hundred men. Again like the Boers, therefore, the kind of
larger military expeditions that were required to take over a revenue-
producing corner of the Roman frontier could never have been
mounted using just the small numbers of military specialists that
existed in the Germanic world. Recruits were required from a broader
cross-section of society, many of whom already had dependants. These
participants would obviously not have wanted to leave their dependants behind in the long term – aside, perhaps, from a few of the
younger teenage ones – but even to have left them in the short term,
while the expedition reached a hopefully successful conclusion, would

have been to expose them to substantial risks. In context again, therefore, it was only natural for Germanic expeditionary forces of more than one or two hundred men to be accompanied by numerous familial dependants.[12] There were a few women even on the Boer scouting expeditions, but the larger trekking parties were always mixed, and the women, in fact, were far from bystanders when it came to fighting; they loaded the flintlock rifles and even shot them when necessary. Germanic women of the second century had no rifles to load, but they no doubt had their own key roles to play, even on substantially military expeditions. Although the recorded nature of these Germanic migration flows looks odd, both in size and composition, in the light of some of the comparative literature, it does accord with the fundamental principles behind observed migratory behaviour, once due allowance is made for differences between the first and third millennia.

## Völkerwanderung and Beyond

The evolving patterns of development and migration unfolding in the Roman era came to a head in the so-called Völkerwanderung. In the later fourth and fifth centuries, documented European history is marked by the appearance of a whole series of migrant groups comprising 10,000 or more warriors and a large number of dependants, which were powerful enough to survive direct confrontation with the military and political structures of the Roman imperial state. Seen in the broadest of terms, these extraordinary pulses of large-group migration were produced by the intersection, at a critical moment, of a number of related lines of development. First, by the mid- to late fourth century, processes of economic and political development among the Germani had reached a point where political structures had sufficient strength to hold together such enormous groups of warriors and their dependants within a reasonably solid edifice. But, second, these structures had been generated by the expansionary processes of the second and third centuries, and were close enough in time to those events to retain a tradition of migration that could be mobilized when circumstances were appropriate or demanded it. And, third, perhaps the other side of the same coin, their economic structures were not yet so rooted in the arable cultivation of any particular landscape that it was impossible for them to conceive of shifting their centre of operations to another locality.

Viewed against the backdrop of long-term development in the Germanic world, and particularly against the more immediate events of the third-century crisis, the existence and activities of these very large migrant groups are certainly explicable, but that should not take away from the extraordinary nature of the action. For, though larger and more cohesive than their counterparts of the first century, none of the groups that initially emerged from the imperial periphery was in itself large enough to confront the Roman Empire with success, and yet the aggregate outcome of their collective activities, as we have seen, was the destruction of the west Roman state. This highly unpredictable outcome was itself the result of further intersections between contingent historical events and longer-term patterns of development.

First, it took the unintentional stimulus provided by the Huns to get sufficient numbers of these largely Germanic groups from beyond Rome's Rhine and Danube frontiers moving on to Roman soil at broadly the same time to make it impossible for the Roman state merely to destroy them. Had these groups – even given that they were larger and more cohesive – arrived separately on Roman territory, the result would eventually have been their destruction, and there were still far too many of them to organize any unified plan for the Empire's destruction. The key element missing from the Germanic world of the imperial periphery, as opposed to its Arab counterpart, was the lack of a Muhammad to provide an alternative and unifying ideology to that of the Roman state. But, second, once established on Roman soil, the processes of political amalgamation that had been unfolding over the long term beyond the frontier reached a relatively swift climax. This key point was missed in much of the traditional nationalist historiography. By insisting on treating the groups who eventually founded successor states to the western Roman Empire as ancient and unchanging 'peoples',[13] this historiography missed the fact that most of them were explicitly documented as new coalitions which formed on Roman territory out of several groups – usually three or four – and who had been independent of one another beyond the frontier. Visigoths and Ostrogoths, Merovingian Franks, the Vandal–Alan coalition – all represented a further step-change in the organization of barbarian political structures, and it was this further evolution which really produced groups that were large enough (deploying now 20,000 warriors and more) to destroy the western Empire.[14]

Contingent as much of this was – there is no sign that there would have been such an influx on to Roman soil without the intrusion of the Huns – one dimension of the action was far from accidental. The new and much larger political formations that became the basis of the successor states could not have come into being on the far side of the frontier. The level of economic development prevalent in the periphery of the Empire in the fourth century did not produce sufficient surplus to allow political leaderships enough patronage to integrate so many followers in that context. Only when the economy of the Empire could be tapped directly for extra wealth, and when the Roman state was providing extra political stimulation towards unification in the form of a real outside threat, was there a sufficient economic and political basis for these larger entities to come into existence. Political structures were the product of, and limited by, prevailing levels of development, and the new state-forming groups could not have emerged in a purely barbarian context.[15]

But if there is a real sense in which the *Völkerwanderung* can be seen as the culmination of Roman-era patterns of development in barbaricum, its outcomes nonetheless revolutionized broader patterns of development across Europe as a whole. To start with, the new states that emerged on former Roman territory made imperial Europe considerably less imperial. The epicentre of supraregional power in western Europe shifted decisively north around the year 500, the second half of the millennium being marked not by Mediterranean-based imperial power, but a series of broadly Frankish dynasties whose prominence was based on economic and demographic assets located north of the Alps between the Atlantic and the Elbe. Again, this can be seen as a culmination of trends of development set in place in the Roman period. The fact that the new imperial power of western Europe should be based on a combination of a chunk of former Roman territory with a substantial part of its ex-periphery is a clear sign of how profoundly that periphery had been transformed by its interaction with Roman power in the preceding centuries. At the birth of Christ, this landscape on either side of the Rhine could never have supported an imperial power, not being remotely wealthy or populous enough, but Roman-era development on both banks of the river radically transformed this situation. At the same time, the political structures of post-Roman Frankish-dominated western Europe, particularly the militarization of its landed elites, meant that this new imperial state was different in kind to its Roman predecessor. Lacking the power to tax agricultural production systematically, it was a less dominant and less self-sufficient kind of entity, which required the profits of expansion to provide its rulers with enough patronage to integrate its constituent landowners. And when broader circumstances did not allow for expansion, fragmentation followed, with power quickly seeping away from the centre to the peripheral localities. Periods of great central authority and external aggression – the hallmarks of empire – thus alternated with others of disunity in the second half of the millennium, where Roman imperialism had previously presented a more consistently cohesive face. There is a real sense in which the pre-existing inequalities of the first half of the millennium were in part eroded from the top, as it were, by the fact that imperial Europe became less consistently imperial.

More fundamentally, and also more interesting given that it has been so much less discussed, is the effect of the *Völkerwanderung* upon barbarian Europe. By the sixth century, Germanic-dominated Europe as it had stood in the Roman era had almost completely collapsed. Where, up to the fourth century, similar socioeconomic and political structures had prevailed over a huge territory from the Rhine to the Vistula in the north and to the River Don at their fullest extent in the south, by c.550 AD, their direct descendants were essentially restricted to lands west of the Elbe, with an outlying pocket on the Great Hungarian Plain, which was about to be terminated by the arrival of the Avars (Map 15). The *Völkerwanderung* had played a central role in this revolution, though not by actually emptying these landscapes of all their inhabitants. Settlement did completely disappear in some restricted localities, but, even making maximum assumptions, the exodus from Germanic Europe from the fourth to the sixth century was not on a large enough scale to denude central and eastern Europe of its entire population. What the *Völkerwanderung* clearly did do, however, was empty much of the old inner and outer peripheries of the Empire of the armed and organized, socially elite groupings which had previously run them. From the perspective of barbarian Europe, the period saw not just the collapse of the Roman Empire, but also the collapse of the larger state-like structures and organizations of its periphery, the vast majority of which relocated themselves, in the course of the migrations, on to parts of just the old inner periphery – between the Rhine and the Elbe, and the Great Hungarian Plain – and actual, largely western Roman territory.

This first extraordinary revolution in barbarian Europe marked a caesura in over half a millennium of broadly continuous development over large parts of central and eastern Europe. It also allowed a second and equally dramatic transformation. In the aftermath of Germanic collapse, population groups from the third zone of Europe as it stood at the start of the Roman era started to develop, for the first time as far as we can see, substantial political, economic and cultural interactions with the rest of Europe. The Romans had some kind of knowledge of the Venedi who inhabited that part of Europe's low-speed zone closest to them. Tacitus in the first century knew that they were out there, beyond the Vistula and the Carpathians; Ptolemy a couple of generations later could add the names of a few of their broader social groupings. But, remarkably, there is no evidence at all that these populations were sucked into the political events of the first half of the millennium in any shape or form. Venedi mounted no known raids into Roman territory, find no mention in narratives of the Marcomannic War or the third-century crisis, and do not even seem to have participated in the structures of Attila's Empire, which incorporated so many of the other population groups of central and eastern Europe. Nor do the distribution maps of Roman imports suggest that these European population groups from east of the Vistula and north of the Carpathians played a major role in any of the trade networks stretching out into barbaricum in the Roman era, though some of the routes surely passed through their territories.

More or less immediately after the collapse of Germanic Europe, however, Slavic-speakers started to emerge from the low-speed zone to take an increasingly important role in recorded narratives of broader European history. By about 500 AD, they had moved south and east of the Carpathians into direct contact with the east Roman frontier, and were beginning to raid across it. Their capacity to do so may have been the result of preceding interactions with Goths and others of the more organized groups of the Germanic periphery to the Roman Empire, which pass more or less unmentioned in our historical sources.[16] Be that as it may, the new contacts with the east Roman Empire massively accelerated any nascent processes of development already operating among those Slavic groups involved, as raiding and diplomatic subsidies brought in unprecedented quantities of movable wealth, and stimulated among them both militarization and the formation of larger political structures, both of which allowed profits from the new relationship with Constantinopolitan territories to be maximized. All this ran parallel to some of the kinds of transformation seen in the Germanic world in the early Roman period, and, following the collapse of Germanic Europe, Slavic-speakers had already emerged by 550 as the main barbarian 'other' confronting east Rome's civilization in south-eastern Europe.

At this point, a second nomadic 'accident' bent existing processes of development substantially out of shape, and acted as a crucial catalyst in the further transformation of barbarian Europe. Like the Huns, the Avars swiftly built a powerful military coalition in central Europe, one of whose main effects was to siphon off still larger amounts of Mediterranean-generated wealth into now largely Slavic-dominated central Europe. This, of course, further stimulated the competition for control of that wealth, which had already been producing a new kind of military kingship in the Slavic world even before the Avars appeared. Equally important, and just like the Huns, the Avars lacked the governmental capacity to rule their large number of subject groups directly, operating instead through a series of intermediate leaders drawn in part from those subject groups. We lack much in the way of detailed information, but there is every reason to suppose that this would have had the political effect of cementing the social power of chosen subordinates, further pushing at least their Slavic subjects in the direction of political consolidation.[17] The third major effect of the Avars was both to prompt and to enable a wider Slavic diaspora, as some Slavic groups moved further afield to escape the burden of Avar domination. Large-scale Slavic settlement in the former east Roman Balkans – as opposed to mere raiding – only became possible when the Avar Empire (in combination with the Persian and then Arab conquests) destroyed Constantinople's military superiority in the region. But at least some of these Slavs were as much negatively motivated by a desire to escape Avar domination as they were by a positive desire to move on to Roman territory. Elsewhere we lack historical narratives, but the same desire to escape Avar domination surely played a substantial role in the widespread further dispersals of Slavic groups from c.550 onwards: westwards towards the Elbe, northwards to the Baltic, and even eastwards into the heart of Russia and Ukraine. It remains unclear to what extent this eastern expansion represented the first intrusion of Slavic-speakers into western Russia, or whether we are really looking at the expansion of particular groups of Slavic-speakers who had been made more politically organized and militarily potent through their interactions with the East Romans and Avars, and were thus able to assert their dominance over fellow Slavic-speakers who had not participated in the same process.

Either way, the process of Slavicization – the establishment of the dominance of Slavic-speaking groups across vast areas of central and eastern Europe – again combined processes of migration and development in intimate embrace. Interaction with the Roman Empire's more developed economy generated new wealth flows which prompted political consolidation and militarization among at least some Slavs. But the groups who benefited from this new wealth were only able to do so because they had already physically moved into a tighter Roman orbit after the collapse of the Hunnic Empire, presumably in order to make precisely these kinds of gain. The sociopolitical revolution they experienced as a consequence then pre-prepared them, especially under the extra stimulus provided by the Avars, to spread their domination by further migration across broad swathes of central and eastern Europe. Some of this certainly involved the absorption of the clearly numerous indigenous populations that had survived the processes of Germanic collapse. Some of that absorption will have been peaceful, as some east Roman sources suggest, but at the same time many Slavic groups were becoming increasingly militarized, and the results of Slavicization were strikingly monolithic. If some Slavic groups, particularly of the Korchak type, remained peaceful small-scale farmers up to the year 600 and beyond, many others were undergoing rapid transformation as new wealth brought social differentiation and militarization. Much of the subsequent Slavicization of Europe was clearly brought about by the armed and dangerous Slavs, not the Korchak farmers – not least in those parts of Russia where Slavic domination was advanced by communities of a few hundred pushing one fortified settlement after another into clearly hostile territory.

# The Birth of Europe

East Roman wealth and Avar interference marked only the beginning of a much broader development process, which unfolded right across the vast area of Slavic-dominated Europe in the second half of the millennium. By the tenth century, this had produced the first state-like dynastic structures that much of northern and eastern Europe had ever seen. These new entities still operated with major limitations by the year 1000, distinct patterns of centre and periphery being discernible across the vast territories notionally under their control. A governmental mechanism based on itineration was not capable of governing such large territories with even intensity, and this shows up in their regular propensity to swap control of very large intermediate territorial zones between them. Nonetheless, these states were capable of centrally organized activities that are straightforwardly impressive. Much bigger in geographical scale than the Germanic client states that emerged on the fringes of the Roman Empire in the fourth century, they were also capable of greater acts of power. They built more and bigger buildings, supported larger, better-equipped, and more professional armies, and quickly adopted some of the cultural norms of more developed, imperial Europe: above all the Christian religion.

Everything suggests that the transformative mechanisms that produced these new entities were similar in nature to those that had generated the larger Germanic client states of the fourth-century Roman periphery. In both cases, a whole range of new contacts – via trading, raiding, and diplomacy – led to unprecedented flows of wealth into the non-imperial societies. The internal struggle to control these flows of wealth then led to both militarization and the emergence of pre-eminent dynasts, who eventually used their domination of this wealth to generate permanent military machines that could institutionalize their authority by destroying and/or intimidating pre-existing, more local authority structures. As a result, potential rivals were steadily eliminated and power was increasingly centralized.

But if the basic processes were the same, the second half of the millennium saw the Slavic world develop further and faster than its largely Germanic counterpart had done in the first. The explanation for this disparity in part lies in the broader range of stimuli operating in barbarian Europe after 500 AD. Western parts of the Slavic world established a full range of economic, military and diplomatic contacts with a sequence of Frankish imperial powers in western Europe. At the same time, two hundred years of Avar imperial domination at the heart of central Europe had important effects on a broader Slavic clientele, as did interaction with a further, if lesser, European imperial power: the Byzantine Empire. Equally, if not more important, more distant parts of the largely Slavic-dominated barbaricum were interacting with a fourth and still greater imperial power in the form of the Islamic Caliphate. There is no sign of any large-scale trade networks in either slaves or furs operating out of central and eastern Europe to feed Near Eastern as well as Mediterranean sources of demand in the first half of the millennium, so these later networks represented flows of wealth with no precedent in the Roman era. And to judge both by the staggering numbers of Islamic silver coins that survive and their correlation with the core areas of the new Slavic states, there is every reason to suppose this extra-European imperial stimulus played a major role in the transformation of Slavic Europe.

The other obvious explanation for the faster development of Slavic Europe is the impact of the new military technologies of the last two centuries of the millennium – notably armoured knights and castles – which made it much easier for those dynasts who could establish control over the new wealth flows to intimidate potential opponents. For even if the new states all encompassed less intensively governed peripheries, the power that they could exercise in dynastic core territories is (horribly) impressive. The brutal power inherent in the destruction of old tribal strongholds and their replacement with new dynastic ones – in both Bohemia and Poland – emerges strikingly from the dramatic archaeological evidence that has become available in recent years. Dynastic power is equally apparent in the movement of subdued populations into core zones of the new states, and their general economic organization, illustrated this time by a combination of archaeological evidence and the earliest strata of documentary evidence preserved from the new states.

The nature and overall significance of these processes of development could hardly be clearer, and their consequences were myriad. In broadest terms, the most important of these might well be the first emergence of Europe as a functioning entity. By the tenth century, networks of economic, political and cultural contact were stretching right across the territory between the Atlantic and the Volga, and from the Baltic to the Mediterranean. This turned what had previously been a highly fragmented landscape, marked by massive disparities of development and widespread non-connection at the birth of Christ, into a zone united by significant levels of interaction. Europe is a unit not of physical but of human geography, and by the year 1000 interaction between human populations all the way from the Atlantic to the Volga was for the first time sufficiently intense to give the term some real meaning. Trade networks, religious culture, modes of government, even patterns of arable exploitation: all were generating noticeable commonalities right across the European landscape by the end of the millennium.

For the purposes of this study, however, the processes of development are more immediately important for the role they played in bringing to an end the kind of conditions that had generated the large-scale often predatory forms of migration – whether in the concentrated pulse form of the *Völkerwanderungen* or the more usual flows of increasing momentum – which had been a periodic feature of first-millennium Europe. Inequalities of development across the European landmass had not completely disappeared, but they had been greatly reduced. Essentially, the new trade networks, combined with more general agricultural expansion (the latter still very much a work in progress), meant that politically organized power structures in central and eastern Europe were now able to access wealth in large quantities in their existing locations. Agricultural and broader economic development also meant that they were busy entrenching themselves in some entirely new ways in some specific geographical zones of operation, at least in their core territories.

As a result, the kinds of positive stimulation that had periodically prompted large-group migration had been structurally removed, or at least massively eroded. Migration was never an easy or universally prevalent option in first-millennium Europe, but rather a strategy that was sometimes adopted when the gains were worth the stress of mounting expeditions into only partly known territory with no absolute guarantees of success. Once social elites could access wealth without the extra insecurity of relocation, they became much less likely to resort to that strategy. And, of course, the less they did so in practice, the less they were ever likely to, as previously ingrained migration habits unwound both among themselves, and among the broader population under their control as more intense patterns of arable farming were generating more permanent patterns of cultivation. Overall, both elites and broader populations within barbarian Europe were becoming much more firmly rooted in particular localities, and, as a result, were much less likely to respond by migration even when faced with powerful stimuli that might in other circumstances have led them to shift location.

This, to my mind is the underlying explanation of the particular problem with which this chapter began. Where many Goths and other Germani (though certainly not all) responded to the Hunnic menace, and the Slavs to its Avar counterpart, by seeking new homes elsewhere, the arrival of the nomadic Magyars on the Great Hungarian Plain engendered no known secondary migration. The actions, nature and eventual fate of the Moravian state encapsulate the difference. Rather than run away, the Moravians stood and fought the Magyars, just like the armies of Frankish imperial Europe. They lost (as, initially, did many of their Frankish counterparts), but the fact that the Moravians stayed put reflects the deeper roots they had sunk in their own particular locality, and the fundamentally different nature of political power in barbarian Europe as it had developed by the end of the first millennium. Earlier, the prevailing limitations of agricultural technique in barbarian Europe generated a broad local mobility, and large disparities in levels of wealth and development had encouraged the more adventurous periodically to attempt to take over some more attractive corner of the landscape, closer, usually, to imperial sources of wealth. The Moravians, by contrast, built castles and churches in stone, on the back of wealth generated by more intense agricultural regimes and wider exchange networks. With so much invested where they stood, it was not going to be easy to shift their centre of operations. The same was true of the other new dynasties of the late first millennium too. All were much more firmly fixed in particular localities than their earlier counterparts, both because of developing agricultural technique and because trade networks made other types of wealth available well beyond the imperial borderlands. In overall terms, processes of development had both eliminated the massive inequalities that had previously made long-distance, large-group migration a reasonably common option for Europe's barbarians, and rooted central and east European populations more deeply in particular landscapes.

Not, of course, that any of this really spelled the end of migration.

Some human beings are always on the move in search of greater prosperity or better conditions of life, and European history from the tenth century onwards is still marked by migration on a periodically massive scale. From late in the first millennium onwards, however, medieval migration generally took one of two characteristic forms. On the one hand, we see knight-based elite transfers. The Norman Conquest is a particularly large-scale and successful example of this phenomenon. Much more usual were bands of one or two hundred well-armed men looking to establish small principalities for themselves by ousting sitting elites and/or establishing their rights to draw economic support from a dependent labour force. The productive rootedness of peasantry and the empowering effect of new military technologies were key factors in dictating the characteristics of this particular migratory form. Castles and armour allowed them to establish a form of local domination based on quite small numbers of men that was extremely hard to shift. The other common form of migration was the deliberate recruitment of peasantry to work the land, with lords offering attractive tenurial terms to provide the incentive, and employing agents to run recruiting campaigns. Again, new patterns of development were of crucial importance here, since the extra agricultural productivity of the new arable farming technologies being put into practice in the late first millennium made it highly desirable for the masters of the landscape to secure sufficient labour to maximize agricultural outputs. Though they had come a long way, the new Slavic states still lagged behind western and southern Europe in levels of economic development. They therefore figured among the chief customers for the new peasant labour being mobilized from more developed parts of Europe where higher population levels reduced opportunities for ambitious peasants to get more land on better terms. As a result, hundreds of thousands of peasants from west-central Europe would be attracted eastwards by the offer of land on much better terms than could be secured at home, and the Slavicization of much of old Germanic Europe that had occurred in the early Middle Ages was partly reversed by an influx of Germanic-speaking peasants.[18]

## NEWTON'S THIRD LAW OF EMPIRES?

Both of these later medieval forms of migration are very well evidenced, operating, as they did, in an era when literacy was intensifying across most of Europe, so their importance within developing European history cannot be contested in the way that that of their earlier counterparts of the first millennium has come to be. The prevalence of these different forms in a later era, however, is no objection to the broader argument of this book, that larger-scale, socially more broadly based predatory forms of migration than knight-based expansion had played a hugely important role in the making of Europe in the first millennium. The later migratory forms were entirely appropriate to the economic and political conditions prevailing across the Europe of the central Middle Ages. The kinds of large-scale predatory migration flow studied in this book – essentially combining peasants and elites within the same migrating groups, where the later Middle Ages saw them move separately – were equally appropriate to their own area. In the first millennium, highly disparate patterns of development then combined with a lack of agricultural rootedness and relatively low agricultural outputs. This meant that the economy of barbarian Europe could support only very few military specialists, so that it was necessary and possible for ambitious leaders to put together large and hence necessarily broad-based expeditions to secure wealth-generating positions on the fringes of more developed, imperial Europe. This in turn generated forms of migration that were different from those operating in the central Middle Ages, and different again from those we are used to in the modern world. Migration in the first millennium looks thus not because our sources were infected with a distorting cultural reflex, but because prevailing circumstances contrasted in some key ways from those operating subsequently. They entirely conform to the basic principles of modern migration, however, in that direction of movement and form of the migration unit were both largely dictated by prevailing patterns of development.

In short, there is every reason to respond to the limitations of the old invasion-hypothesis model not by rejecting migration as an important explanatory factor in first-millennium history, but by bringing a series of more complex migration models back into the picture. Deployed in more analytic fashion, migration ceases to be a catch-all, simplistic alternative to 'more complex' lines of explanation focusing on social, economic and political change. Understood properly, and this is the central message screaming out from the comparative literature, migration is not a separate and competing form of explanation to social and economic transformation, but the complementary other side of the same coin. Patterns of migration are dictated by prevailing economic and political conditions, and another dimension in fact of their evolution; they both reflects existing inequalities, and sometimes even help to equalize them, and it is only when viewed from this perspective that the real significance of migratory phenomena can begin to emerge. A further line of thought that follows from this is that prehistorians should perhaps not be too quick to reject predatory migration either as a periodic contributor to the shaping of Europe's deeper past. If the argument is correct that the predatory forms of migration observable periodically in the first millennium were generated by a reasonable degree of geographical proximity between zones of highly disparate levels of development, combined with the existence of societies where those who farmed also fought and were not deeply rooted in one particular patch of soil, then these are conditions which are likely to have existed in many other ancient contexts too, and periodic predatory migration could reasonably be expected as one natural consequence.

That is no more than a side issue for this study, however, and thinking about the transformation of barbarian Europe in the first millennium in overall terms, there is no doubt that development played a profoundly more important role in the process than migration. Old narratives had this the other way round, emphasizing the arrival of named peoples at their assigned places across the map of Europe at different points within the millennium, until all the modern nations were in place. In this view, movement and arrival were the events of key historical importance, and what happened subsequently was so much detail. This was deeply mistaken. Much more important than these occasional moments of arrival, many of which led precisely nowhere, were the dynamic interactions between the imperial powers of more developed Europe and the barbarians on their doorstep: Germanic, largely, in the first half of the millennium, then Slavic, largely, in the second. It was these interactions, not acts of migration, that were ultimately responsible for generating the new social, economic and political structures which brought former barbarian Europe much more to resemble its imperial counterpart by the end of the millennium. This is not to say that these transformations were inherently a good thing, or that there was something inherently better about imperial Europe, but the evidence leads directly to the conclusion that it was new connections with imperial Europe, and the responses to those new connections on the part of elements within barbarian societies, that ultimately demolished the staggering disparities in development that had existed at the birth of Christ. This in a nutshell is the second major argument I have been attempting to make. Not everywhere in Europe was Christian and full of states built around castles, knights and a productive peasantry by the year 1000, but this was true to an extent that would have astonished Tacitus in the first century AD. He thought that eastern Europe was home to creatures with 'human faces and features, but the bodies and limbs of beasts'; in his terms, barbarian Europe was barbarian no longer.[19]

Migration had played a role – sometimes a very major one – in this unfolding story. Especially if you take the definition of mass or significant migration offered in the comparative literature – and I have found this extremely helpful – migration can be understood as central to the action at various key points in the millennium. Perhaps above all, the Hunnic 'accident' threw enough more organized Germanic groupings on to Roman soil in a short enough space of time both to undermine the central Roman state and to generate a massive collapse in the old power structures of barbarian central Europe. This in turn allowed for an extraordinary Slavic diaspora whose cultural effects – the widespread Slavicization of central and eastern Europe – remain a central feature of the European landmass to this day. These are hardly minor phenomena. Even so, migration should generally be given only a secondary position behind social, economic and political transformation when explaining how it was that barbarian Europe evolved into non-existence in the course of the millennium. For one thing, aside from particular and unusual moments like the Hunnic or Avar accidents, patterns of migration were entirely dictated by and secondary to patterns of development. It was only when nomadic intruders added a much stronger shade of politically motivated migration into the picture that the relationship was reversed, and migration started to dictate patterns of development, undermining both the west Roman state and Germanic Europe in one fell swoop.

Even without the Huns, moreover, these processes of development would eventually have undermined the Roman Empire. Looked at in the round, what emerges from the first-millennium evidence is that living next to a militarily more powerful and economically more developed intrusive imperial neighbour promotes a series of changes in the societies of the periphery, whose cumulative effect is precisely to generate new structures better able to fend off the more unpleasant aspects of imperial aggression. In the first millennium, this happened on two separate occasions. We see it first in the emergence of Germanic client states of the Roman Empire in the fourth century, and again – this time to more impressive effect – in the rise of the new Slavic states of the ninth and tenth. This repeated pattern, I would argue, is not accidental, and provides one fundamental reason why empires, unlike diamonds, do not last forever. The way that empires tend to behave, the mixture of economic opportunity and intrusive power that is inherent in their nature, prompts responses from those affected which in the long run undermine their capacity to maintain the initial power advantage that originally made them imperial. Not all empires suffer the equivalent of Rome's Hunnic accident and fall so swiftly to destruction. In the course of human history, many more have surely been picked apart slowly from the edges as peripheral dynasts turned predator once their own power increased. One answer to the transitory nature of imperial rule, in short, is that there is a Newtonian third law of empires. The exercise of imperial power generates an opposite and equal reaction among those affected by it, until they so reorganize themselves as to blunt the imperial edge. Whether you find that comforting or frightening, I guess, will depend on whether you live in an imperial or peripheral society, and what stage of the dance has currently been reached. The existence of such a law, however, is one more general message that exploring the interactions of emperors and barbarians in the first millennium AD can offer us today.

# MAPS

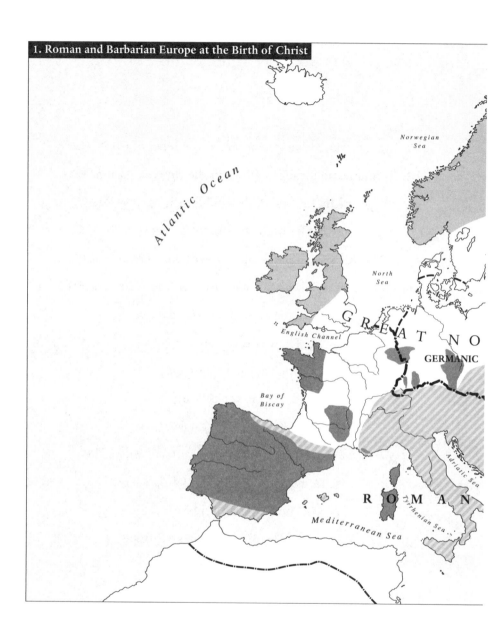

**1. Roman and Barbarian Europe at the Birth of Christ**

RUGII   Germanic political groupings

▬▬▬▬▬   Amber routes

  Concentrations of Roman goods

▬▬▬▬   Roman empire

**2. Germanic political groupings in the time of Tacitus**

3. Germanic Europe in the mid-fourth century

600 kilometres

400 miles

Finds of Germanic glass

4. The Marcomannic War

5. The Agri Decumates and Elbgermanic Triangle

Roman frontier abandoned c. 270
Roman frontier line 4th C

160 kilometres
100 miles

ELBGERMANIC TRIANGLE

THURINGIA

RAETIA

NORICUM

CENTRAL EMPIRE

AGRI DECUMATES

GALLIC EMPIRE

Baltic Sea

Warta
Oder
Spree
Havel
Elbe
Elbe
Weser
Rhine
Mouse
Meuse
Cologne
Trier
Mainz
Main
Lech
Danube
Limes
Limes

6. Third Century Germanic expansion to the Black Sea

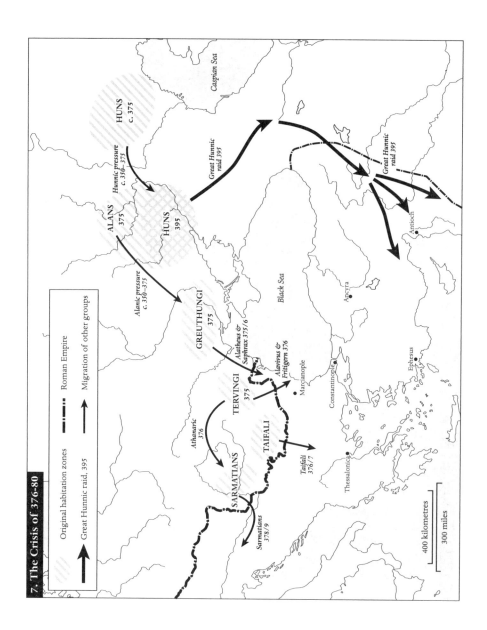

**7. The Crisis of 376-80**

8. The Crisis of 405-8

9. Repeat Migrations

10. Attila's subjects

**11. Early Anglo-Saxon England**

BERNICIA    Known Anglo-Saxon kingdoms
            c.600 AD

*SPALDA*     Possible early kingdoms
             <u>Cemeteries</u>
   ■         Large / inhumation
   □         Small / inhumation
   ▲         Inhumation with few cremations
   ●         Large / cremation
   ○         Small / cremation
   △         Cremation with few inhumations
   ◆         Large / mixed
   ◇         Small / mixed

150 kilometres

100 miles

BERNICIA

*Irish
Sea*

DEIRA
York

*North
Sea*

*PECSÆTE*          LINDSEY

                MIDDLE
MERCIA          ANGLIA
*WREOCENSÆTE*                *NORTH GYRWE*
        *TOMSÆTE*      *SOUTH GYRWE*        EAST
*PENCERSÆTE*                              ANGLIA
            *SWEORORA*
                   △ *SPALDA*
*MAGONSÆTE*              *WEST    EAST*
              *GIFLA   WILLA*
HWICCE            *HICCA*
⦿Gloucester  *CILTERNSÆTE*
                        ESSEX
                  London
WESSEX                        KENT
    ⦿Winchester
            SUSSEX

*English Channel*

**12. Discontinuity in Northern Gaul**

Amsterdam

Cologne Rhine Trier Strasbourg Rhine

Antwerp Meuse

Brussels

London English Channel Seine Paris Orléans

Nantes Loire

150 kilometres

100 miles

○ Cemeteries falling out of use c. 400 / 450 AD

▲ New cemeteries of the Merovingian period

■ New cemeteries containing late 5th–century materials

⌇⌇ Area of Episcopal discontinuity

—·—· New western boundary of Germanic language line

Areas with Germanic place names in Northern Gaul

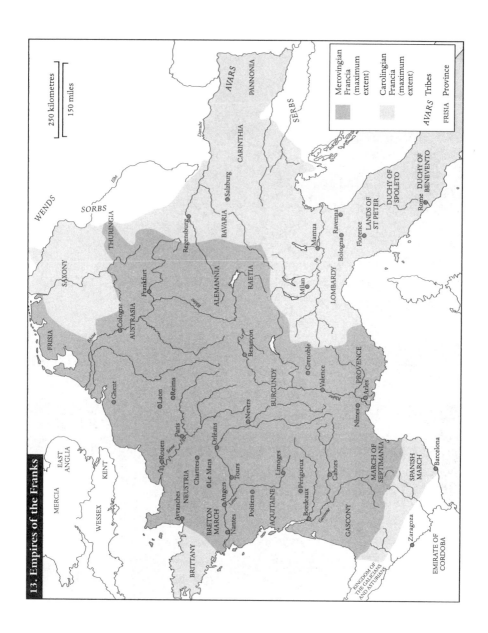

13. Empires of the Franks

14. The Ottonian Empire

250 kilometres

150 miles

BILLUNG MARCH

Hamburg

Bremen

NORTH MARCH

SAXONY

Elbe

FRISIA

Hildesheim

Magdeburg

POLAND

LOWER LOTHARINGIA

Cologne

Rhine

THURINGIA

LAUSITZ MARCH

Oder

FRANCONIA

MEISSEN MARCH

Mainz

Bamberg

Trier

Würzburg

BOHEMIA

UPPER LOTHARINGIA

Regensburg

ALSACE

Danube

BAVARIA

Danube

SUABIA

Salzburg

Constance

CARINTHIA

HUNGARY

Rhône

VERONA

Po

Slavic marches

Ottonian Empire

Duchies

15. The strange death of Germanic Europe

16. Slavic Europe in 900 AD

Legend:
- Slavic dominated areas
- East Francia
- Baltic-speakers
- Areas of Baltic hydronyms

500 kilometres
300 miles

VOLGA
Don
KHAZARS
Don
Dnieper
PECHENEGS
Dniester
Black Sea
Danube
MAGYARS
Vistula
Oder
Baltic Sea
Elbe
Danube
EAST FRANCIA
Adriatic Sea

17. Proposed Slavic Homelands

A  Borkovsky – Bohemia
B  Rybakov – Cernjachov
C  Rusanova – Polesia
D  Tretiakov – Kievan
E  Kostrzewski – Przeworsk
F  Korosec – Pannonia
G  Baran/Godlowski – Carpathian
H  Curta – Danubian

Proposed Slavic homelands

Maximum area of Slavic domination

Area of Baltic hydronyms

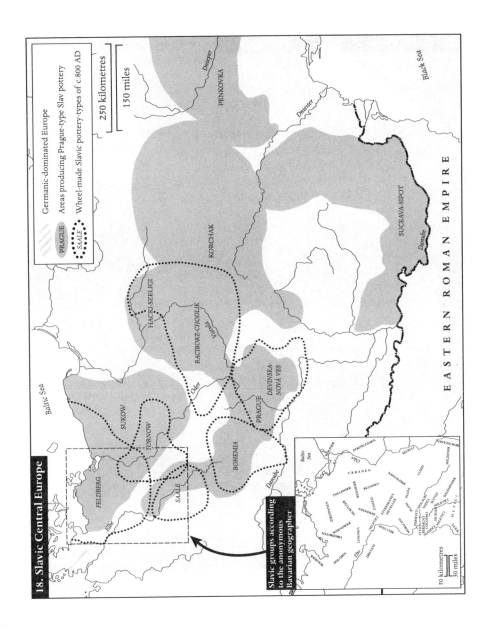

**18. Slavic Central Europe**

Germanic-dominated Europe
Areas producing Prague-type Slav pottery
Wheel-made Slav pottery-types of c.800 AD

PRAGUE
SAALE

250 kilometres
150 miles

Baltic Sea

Dnieper

PENKOVKA

Dniester

Black Sea

HACKI-SZELIGI

RACIBORZ-CHODLIK

KORCHAK

SUCEAVA-SIPOT

Vistula

Oder

DEVINSKA-NOVA VES

PRAGUE

SUKOW

TORNOW

BOHEMIA

Danube

FELDBERG

SAALE

Elbe

Danube

E A S T E R N   R O M A N   E M P I R E

Slavic groups according
to the anonymous
Bavarian geographer

Baltic Sea

Oder

PYRZYCZANEN

SELPOLI

NINVIZUNBIR

UKRANEN

NINVIZBIR

LUSIZI

TOLLENSER

REZANEN

PLONI

WILZENEN

MORIZANI

ZIRZIPANEN

ZANIZZI

STODORANEN HVELLI

PLONI

OPOLINI

HEFELDI

LINONEN

MILZANE

FRAGA

BEHEIMARE

DADOSESANI

GOLENSIZI

LENDIZI

SLENZANE

WOSTROCONZI

PHESNUZI

SITTICI

DALMENSA

BETHENICI

WERIZANE

FRAGA

OROCIOLINI

NELETICI

SEBBIROZI

UNLIZI

POLABEN

DRVVANI

MILZANE

Elbe

BESUNZANE

WCRIATI

50 kilometres
30 miles

19. Slavic western Russia in the tenth Century

Area of Baltic hydronyms

Zones of Slavic pottery

**KRIVICHI**   Slavic tribal names

Baltic
Sea

*Dvina*

SLOVIANE

VIATICHI

KRIVICHI

*Niemen*

RADIMICHI

DREGOVICHI

DEREVLIANE

POLIANE

SEVERIANE

VOLYNIANE

*Dnieper*

TYVERCY

*Dniester*

Sea of
Azov

250 kilometres

150 miles

*Black Sea*

20. State Formation in Eastern Europe

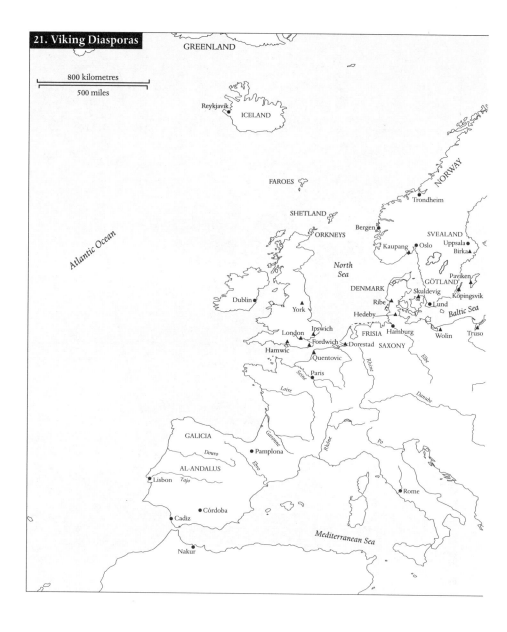

**21. Viking Diasporas**

GREENLAND

800 kilometres

500 miles

Reykjavik

ICELAND

FAROES

SHETLAND

ORKNEYS

Atlantic Ocean

North Sea

NORWAY

Trondheim

Bergen

Kaupang

Oslo

SVEALAND

Uppsala

Birka

Paviken

GÖTLAND

Köpingsvik

DENMARK

Skuldevig

Ribe

Lund

Dublin

York

Hedeby

Baltic Sea

Ipswich

London

Fordwich

Hamwic

Quentovic

FRISIA

Dorestad

Hamburg

Wolin

Truso

SAXONY

Elbe

Paris

Seine

Loire

Rhine

Danube

GALICIA

Douro

Garonne

Rhône

Po

Pamplona

Ebro

AL-ANDALUS

Lisbon

Tajo

Rome

Córdoba

Cadiz

Mediterranean Sea

Nakur

# NOTES

1 *Annal of Fulda* 882 for the incident with Poulik (1986) on the archaeology.

## 1. MIGRANTS AND BARBARIANS

1 Bohning (1978), 11.
2 For useful summaries of the modern evidence, see Salt and Clout (1976); King (1993); Collinson (1994), 1–7, 27–40; Holmes (1996); Cohen (1995), (1996), (1997), (2008); Vertovec and Cohen (1999). Canny (1994) provides an introduction to early modern migration evidence. 200,000 Germanic-speaking peasants: Kuhn (1963), (1973); Bartlett (1993), 144–5; and see, more generally, Phillips (1988), (1994).
3 For an introduction to the pre-Roman world of the Celts, see e.g. Cunliffe and Rowley (1976); Cunliffe (1997); James (1999). In fact, there is no one-to-one equation between Celts and the Oppida culture, and Roman conquest did advance just beyond its bounds: see Heather (2005), 49–58.
4 For useful introductions to the early Germanic world, see Hachmann (1971); Todd (1975), (1992); Krüger (1976), vol. 1; Pohl (2000). Note, though, that there is a strong tendency in some of this literature to avoid discussing Germanic groups around the Vistula and further east – a squeamishness resulting from the Nazi era, when the fact that ancient Germanic speakers had once dominated these lands was used as an excuse for territorial aggression.
5 For an excellent, recent overall introduction, see Batty (2007); on the broader cultural role played by Scythia in the formation of the Greek world view, see Braund (2005).
6 Khazanov (1984) provides an excellent introduction to the world of the steppe.
7 'The Veneti have taken': Tacitus, *Germania* 46.2 (cf. 46.4 on what lay beyond); see also Pliny, *Natural History* 4.97; Ptolemy, *Geography* 3.5.1 and 7. On the geography and ancient archaeological patterning of the society and economy of these regions, see Dolukhanov (1996). Within the Russian forest zone, many of the river names are actually Balt rather than Slavic in origin, even in areas where Slavs would be dominant by the year 1000 AD. It is thus unclear whether Tacitus' Veneti are likely to have been Slavic-speakers, Balt-speakers, or speakers of a tongue ancestral to them both (see Chapter 8).
8 Nomads too played their part: the Huns in the fall of the Roman Empire, the

Avars in the slavicization of central and eastern Europe, and the Magyars and Bulgars in laying the foundations of two substantial political entities whose lengthy histories underlie the existence of modern Hungary and Bulgaria.

9   The literature on the cultural significance of the rise of nationalism is now vast, but for introductions, see Gellner (1983); Anderson (1991); Geary (2002).

10  Early modern and modern accounts of Germanic migration consistently pictured migrants as family groups, while more contemporary Roman sources, when they said anything, also sometimes recorded the presence of women and children alongside the warriors. (I have simplified here, and the actual evidence will be surveyed in subsequent chapters.) Students of the collapse of the Roman Empire are broadly divided between viewing the Germanic invasions as its cause, and as its result. For useful overviews of the range of opinion, see Demandt (1984) and Ward Perkins (2005). With regard to the Slavs, one body of opinion has wanted to identify a very large, if submerged, population of Slavic-speakers throughout central and eastern Europe since the Bronze Age, but the evidence remains unconvincing (see Chapter 8). For a useful survey of traditional approaches to the Vikings, see Sawyer (1962), chapter 1. Nationalist conflicts also led to the downplaying of the so-called 'Normanist' view, that Vikings were responsible for the first Russian state: see Melnikova (1996), chapter 1 (and see also my Chapter 9).

11  Childe (1926), (1927).

12  See note 9 above. The general point is accepted even by those, such as Smith (1986), willing to conceive of relatively solid and sizeable group identities in at least some corners of the pre-nationalist past.

13  Leach (1954); 'evanescent situational construct': Barth (1969), 9. For more recent overviews, see e.g. Bentley (1987); Kivisto (1989); Bacall (1991).

14  That hypothesis was already marked in the work of Kossinna himself: see especially Kossinna (1928). It showed itself even more strongly in the equally influential work of Gordon Childe (see note 11 above), who generalized many of Kossinna's ideas, while dropping some of his assumptions about Nordic racial superiority. On Kossinna's legacy, see e.g. Chapman and Dolukhanov (1993), 1–5; Renfrew and Bahn (1991).

15  For an overview of these intellectual developments, see Shennan (1989); Renfrew and Bahn (1991); Chapman and Dolukhanov (1993), 6–25 (which includes an instructive difference in emphasis on the part of the two authors); Ucko (1995). The work of Ian Hodder – especially (1982) and (1991) – has been particularly important in rehabilitating the view that patterns of similarity and difference in material cultural items might sometimes reflect important aspects of human organization.

16  Clark (1966) represents a key turning point away from the invasion hypothesis. For accounts of the range of explanatory hypotheses that have been tried since, see e.g. Renfrew and Bahn (1991); Preucel and Hodder (1996); Hodder and Hutson (2003).

17  Halsall (1995b), 61; and see his further comment: '[The invasion hypothesis] is rarely given much credence in archaeological circles today. It is too simplistic, rather on a par with asserting that the change from neo-classical to neo-Gothic architecture or from classical to romantic art in the nineteenth century was the

result of an invasion' (p. 57). This 'before' and 'after' approach to migration is quite common. See, for a further example, the comments of Nicholas Higham in Hines (1997), 179, where a reinterpretation of a set of remains that had excluded migration from its discussion is lauded as 'more complex'. The discussion in question is in Hines (1984).

18 Wenskus (1961); cf., amongst others, Wolfram (1988) on the Goths, and Pohl (1988) on the Avars.

19 Geary (1985) and (1988) provide introductory essays composed from this perspective, Halsall (2007) a full-scale study of the fourth to sixth centuries. The migration topos features in Amory (1997) and Kulikowski (2002).

20 On the 'wave of advance' model, see, most famously, Renfrew (1987), chapters 1–2, 4 (summarizing previous approaches), and 6 (the model itself).

21 For a detailed case study of 'elite transfer', see my Chapter 6.

22 See note 13 above. Smith (1986) explores some historical applications of this more solid vision of group identity; Bentley (1987), 25–55 uses Bourdieu's concept of the *habitus* as the basis of a theorized approach towards how identity might be programmed into the individual by the society in which they grow up. When talking about the kinds of differences that prevent the individual from changing group identity so easily (religion, language, social values and so on) the 'primordialists' can sound as though they are still stuck in the intellectual world of pre-1945, making out checklists and ticking boxes. But in the primordialist view, it is not these 'things' themselves that decide identity, but the individual's reaction to them. In most of Europe, being a Catholic or Protestant is not a major determinant of group affiliation, but in Northern Ireland, for particular historical reasons, the same religious difference functions as a strong symbol of communal allegiance. It is not the item ticked in a box that decides group affiliation, but how individuals react to that item.

23 On the Greeks and Romans, see Sherwin-White (1973). Halsall (1999) objects to my earlier use of this analogy, but he doesn't seem to realize that Gastarbeiter and migrants without green cards don't enjoy remotely full citizenship rights in the societies in which they live, and ignores substantial evidence that even in the first millennium group identity was sometimes made the basis of differentiated rights in culturally complex contexts: see Chapter 5. He also takes the to my mind bizarre view that just anyone could turn up to claim a share when barbarian conquerors of different parts of the Roman west were handing out economic assets: see Heather (2008b).

24 Cf. Antony (1990), 895–9; Antony (1992) notes that these revised understandings render obsolete many older theoretical discussions that assumed much starker archaeological correlates of migration.

25 Härke (1998), 25–42, offers a fascinating insight into which contemporary archaeological traditions are more accepting of migration as a possible engine of change, and which more dismissive. British 'immobilism' – rejection of migration – finds parallels in the old Soviet Union and Denmark; the German tradition still incorporates migration as one of its basic paradigms.

26 Jerome (1926).

27 A recent five-hundred page book devoted to migratory activity around the fall of the Roman west, for instance, contents itself with drawing on a few

summaries of the literature drawn up for archaeologists rather than engaging with it at first hand: Halsall (2007), 417–22. By contrast, the same book devotes an entire chapter to the group-identity question, based on intense (and insightful) engagement with the specialist literature.

28 On Irish and Dutch migrants, see Bailyn (1994), 1–2. On overall patterns in modern instances, see Fielding (1993a); King (1993), 23–4; Rystad (1996), 560–1. On the historical parallels, see Canny (1994), especially 278–80 (with full references).

29 On the calculation of costs, see Rystad (1996), 560–1; Collinson (1994), 1–7 (both with useful further references.). On return migration, see e.g. Gould (1980); Kuhrt (1984).

30 For reviews of changing policies towards migrants in Western Europe, and their overall effects, see Cohen (1997); King (1993), 36–7; Fielding (1993b); Collinson (1994), chapter 4; Rystad (1996), 557–62; Cohen (2008). Obviously in recent years, EU enlargement has led to a huge influx of Eastern European migrants.

31 'Gives a shock': King and Oberg (1993), 2. For general discussions of a qualitative definition of mass migration, see e.g. King and Oberg (1993), 1–4; Fielding (1993a).

32 For discussion, though, of the high Middle Ages, see Phillips (1988), (1994); Bartlett (1993), 144–5.

33 In the 1990s there were discussions of how an end to Fordist mass-production techniques in industry were likely to affect future migration flows: Fielding (1993a). We now partly know the answer, with skilled labour being sucked into Western Europe, for instance, while the demand for mass labour in the Middle East continues to grow apace: Cohen (2008).

34 On Spanish migration to the new world, and British migration to Australia and New Zealand, see Sanchez-Albornoz (1994); Borrie (1994), 45ff. The convict ships to Australia were another kind of involuntary state-assisted scheme.

35 Bartlett (1993), 134–8.

36 Helpful general discussions of motivation include Fielding (1993a); Collinson (1994), especially 1–7; Voets et al. (1995), especially 1–10; Rystad (1996); Vertovec and Cohen (1999); Cohen (2008). Some case studies are provided by the essays of Atalik and Beeley, Cavaco, Montanari and Cortese, Oberg and Boubnova, in King (1993).

37 See e.g. Cohen (1996), (2008).

38 See e.g. Rystad (1996), 560–1; Bailyn (1994), 4–5.


## 2. GLOBALIZATION AND THE GERMANI

1 Ammianus 16.12.23–6. For attempts at localizing these early units, see Krüger (1976–83), vol. 1, 44–55, 202–19. For the view that little changed between the first and fourth century, see e.g. James (1989), 42, after Thompson (1965), 40.

2 The literature on Arminius and Maroboduus is enormous, but for introductions, see Krüger (1976–83), vol. 1, 374–412; Pohl (2000), 21–4. On early kingship, and its general lack, see Green (1998), chapter 7. On Maroboduus' lack of heirs, see Tacitus, Germania 42.

3 Chnodomarius, Serapio and Mederichus: Ammianus 16.12.23–6; Vadomarius and Vithicabius: Ammianus 27.10.3–4; Gundomadus: Ammianus 16.12.17. *Optimates*: Ammianus 16.12.23–6. This view of hereditary canton kingship would be accepted by the vast majority of scholars working in the field: see e.g. Pohl (2000), 29–30, 102ff.; Drinkwater (2007), 117ff. (with full references). Some of the old sub-group names within the Alamanni (Brisigavi, Bucinobantes, Lentienses) survive as modern place names (Breisgau, Buchengau, Linzgau).

4 On the first- and second-century leagues and alliances, see e.g. Tacitus, *Germania* 38–40 (on the Sueves). For more general commentary, see e.g. Hachmann (1971), 81ff.; Krüger (1976–83), vol. 1, 374–412; Pohl (2000), 65f. The revolt of Julius Civilis, for instance, combined elements from the Batavi, Frisians, Caninefates, Bructeri and Tencteri (Tacitus, *Histories* 4.18; 21) but no unity survived his fall.

5 'There fell in this battle': Ammianus 16.12.60; Julian's diplomacy is recounted at Ammianus 17.1, 17.6, 17.10 and 18.2. Vadomarius: Ammianus 21.3–4; Macrianus: Ammianus 28.5, 29.4, 30.3.

6 Early Medieval Ireland and England provide, respectively, more and less articulated examples: see e.g. Binchy (1970a) and the papers in Bassett (1989) for an introduction. I take here a very different view to the minimalist line in germanophone scholarship, a full introduction to which is provided by Humver (1998), and to Drinkwater (2007), 121ff., who argues that there was no urge to unification among fourth-century Alamanni, although he does admit that once Roman manipulation was removed in the fifth century, unification happened.

7 See Wolfram (1988), 62ff., with further arguments in Heather (1991), 97ff. against e.g. Thompson (1966), 43–55; cf. Thompson (1965), 29–41. The three generations are: Ariaricus (in power in 332), Ariaricus' anonymous son, and the son's son Athanaric. For this particular reconstruction of Gotho-Roman relations, which is again argued against Thompson (1966), see Heather (1991), 107–21. Others would reconstruct Gotho-Roman relations differently, but none doubts that the Tervingi survived heavy defeat at the hands of Constantine, or that the position of 'judge' survived.

8 Batavi: Tacitus, *Histories* 4.12; *Germania* 29. Chatti, Bructeri and Ampsivarii: Tacitus, *Annals* 58; *Germania* 33. Hermenduri: Tacitus, *Annals* 13.57.

9 On Ejsbøl Mose, see Ørsnes (1963). Sacrifices of the weapons of a defeated enemy are reported at Caesar, *Gallic War* 6.17; Tacitus, *Annals* 13.57.

10 Chnodomarius: Ammianus 16.12.60. Drinkwater (2007), 120–1 supposes that the king and his three friends had fifty followers each, rather than Chnodomarius having all two hundred, but if that were the case, it is hard to see why he was king. Tervingi: *Passion of St Saba*. On retinues more generally, see e.g. Hedeager (1987); Todd (1992), 29ff. (with references). The contrast with the public bodies of the early Roman period is very striking: see Thompson (1965), 29ff.

11 See Green (1998), chapter 7; cf. Wolfram (1997), chapter 1; Pohl (2000), 66ff. 'They chose kings': Tacitus, *Germania* 7 ('reges ex nobilitate duces ex virtute sumunt').

12 See Chapter 6 below on the rise of Clovis. Clovis operated on Roman soil, however, which meant that he could support a much larger retinue, whereas a Germanic economic context (see below) would have imposed tighter economic constraints and perhaps made this impossible.

13 On Chnodomarius' armour, see Ammianus 16.12.25; we will return to these swords on p. 78.

14 On Odry, see Kmiecinski (1968). In these eastern areas of Germania, the cemeteries were much more permanent than any settlements in the first two centuries AD, and are marked by large stone circles which contained few if any burials. It has been plausibly suggested that this reflects the fact that cemeteries rather than settlements provided the locus for social gatherings.

15 The fullest discussion is Haarnagel (1979).

16 On Wijster, see Van Es (1967). See more generally the relevant studies in Krüger (1976–83): compare vol. 1, chapter 11 with vol. 2, chapter 5; Myhre (1978); Steuer (1982), 258ff.; Hedeager (1988), (1992), 193ff.; Todd (1992), chapter 4. There is a useful discussion of the Roman side of the frontier in Carroll (2001), chapter 4.

17 Goffart (2006), 26–32 objects to old-style assumptions, based on the famous Jordanes, Getica 4.25, that Scandinavia in particular and Germania in general was a womb of nations, endlessly producing future invaders of the Roman Empire until it was overwhelmed. As a comment on old-fashioned historiography, this is fair enough, though his work does not engage with the detailed archaeological evidence.

18 See Urbanczyk (1997b).

19 On the Pietroasa treasure, see Harhoiu (1977). On *fibula* production at the Runder Berg (see note 24 below), see Christlein (1978), 43–7, 171. On pottery, see Heather and Matthews (1991), chapter 3 (Cernjachov); Drinkwater (2007), 89–93; cf., more generally, Krüger (1976–83), vol. 2, 123ff.

20 On glass, see Rau (1972). On combs, see Palade (1966).

21 The groundwork was laid by Steuer (1982).

22 For an introduction to the historiography, see Thompson (1965). I strongly suspect that measuring social status via artefacts will tend to place the basic erosion of human equality (to the extent that it ever existed) at far too late a date in the history of *Homo sapiens sapiens*.

23 For useful surveys, see Thompson (1965), chapters 1–2; Todd (1992), chapter 2; for more detailed discussions, see Gebuhr (1974); Hedeager (1987), (1988), (1992), chapters 2–3; Hedeager and Kristiansen (1981); Steuer (1982), 212ff.; Pearson (1989). For Odry, see note 14 above.

24 On Runder Berg, see Christlein (1978); Siegmund (1998); and cf. Brachmann (1993), 29–42; Drinkwater (2007), 93–106, which point out that there must have been other lowland Alamannic elite sites, none of which has yet been identified. On Feddersen Wierde, see Haarnagel (1979). On Gothic areas, see Heather (1996), 70ff. (with references). For more general discussion, see Krüger (1976–83), vol. 2, 81–90; Hedeager (1988), (1992), chapter 4; Todd (1992), chapter 6; Pohl (2000).

25 The two classic and highly influential general accounts are the solidly Marxist interpretation of Fried (1967), and the more optimistic line adopted by Service (1975). These studies set the agenda for more detailed subsequent studies of intermediate societies (between the very small and the more modern). The four areas I identify represent a distillation from the helpful collections of papers in Claessen and Skalnik (1978), (1981); Claessen and van de Velde (1987); Skalnik (1989); Earle (1991); Claessen and Oosten (1996).

26 This is true whether (see previous note) one adopts Service's view of the process (by which a wider range of functions is more efficiently fulfilled) or Fried's less optimistic Marxist view (whereby the growth of the bureaucracy entails the further rigidification of power structures).

27 The key term here is 'reciprocity', meaning that ruler and ruled exchange something that is of mutual value. This probably won't be (and certainly doesn't have to be) an equal exchange, but even the act of exchanging makes the interaction honourable. If it is one-sided, then it is demeaning.

28 Alamanni: Ammianus 16.12. Tervingi: Heather (1991), 109 (on pre-376 AD, based on Ammianus 20.8.1, 23.2.7, and 26.10.3), 146. Drinkwater (2007), 142–4 proposes that there were 15,000 Alamanni and allies at Strasbourg. He consistently downplays Alamannic numbers on the basis of his prior assumption that they posed no real threat to Roman frontier security, which is in my view a circular and unconvincing approach: see Heather (2008a). The evidence strongly suggests that these societies possessed slaves and that slaves were not normally liable for military service. We do not know the proportion of slaves, but they are likely enough to have been a significant portion of the population, so that merely to number fighting men will be to underestimate the total of young adult males in these societies.

29 For waterborne summits, see Ammianus 27.5.9 (cf. Themistius, *Orations* 10), 30.3.4–6. For Burgundian/Alamannic boundaries, see Ammianus 28.5.11.

30 For an introduction to the evidence, see Heather & Matthews (1991), chapter 5.

31 On the Gothic contingents, see note 28 above, with Heather (1991), 107ff. for the crucial link that military service was something imposed on the Goths by the Romans when they held the diplomatic upper hand. On the Alamannic contingents, see Heather (2001). On the loan word, see Green (1998), chapter 11.

32 Vannius: Tacitus, *Annals* 12.25. On Roman imports on elite Gothic sites, see Heather (1996), 70–2. On trade and diplomacy, see Heather (1991), 109. Of course, Chnodomarius may possibly just have been offering a share of war booty rather than cash up front.

33 On the 'wall' of Athanaric, see Ammianus 31.3.8, with Heather (1996), 100 for the identification. On Runder Berg and other sites, see note 24 above.

34 Based on a trawl through the literature cited in note 25 above. Not even the famously inert Irish kings of the Middle Ages – so wonderfully caricatured by the late Patrick Wormald as a 'priestly vegetable' – failed to exercise powers over dispute settlement. In the famous tract on Irish kingship, *Crith Gablach*, one day was reserved for this function: see Binchy (1970b); cf. Wormald (1986).

35 For an introduction to early Anglo-Saxon tax systems, see Campbell (2000); Blair (1994). These kinds of arrangement have also been found in areas of Britain that never fell under Roman rule: see Barrow (1973).

36 The mobility of Alamannic kings is suggested by the difficulty the Romans faced in trying to kidnap one of their number: see Ammianus 29.4.2ff. For an excellent introduction to the immense bibliography on itineration, see Charles-Edwards (1989).

37 See Thompson (1966); cf. Heather (1991), 177ff. (with full references). For Gundomadus, see note 3 above. Even if one accepts the hypothesis of Drinkwater (2007), 142–4 that there were 24 Alamannic canton kings, they would

have produced no more than 4,800 retinue warriors between them. On the range of material in burials, see e.g. Steuer (1982); Weski (1982); Harke (1992). On burials entirely empty of goods, see e.g. Heather and Matthews (1991), 62, for some examples from Gothic-dominated territories.

38 A quick read of the relevant law collections from the Visigothic, Frankish, Lombard, Burgundian, and Anglo-Saxon kingdoms brings out the importance of this group, who also feature in materials from the 'smaller' political entities, such from Thuringia, Bavaria, and Alamannia.

39 On the proportion of freemen to slaves, see Heather (1996), 324–5, after Procopius, *Wars* 3.8.12 (1 elite to 4 subordinates in one Gothic force); 8.26.12 (close to 1:1 in a Lombard force). On this warfare, see Heather (1996), especially Appendix I (collecting the evidence for two classes of warrior being mentioned in Roman narrative sources). For charter evidence, see Wickham (1992); (2005), part 3. Post-Roman society did not immediately fall under the sway of the much smaller landowning elite, who can be seen to be dominant from the Carolingian period of c.800 and beyond: see for example Chapter 6 above on the growth of landed estates, which was the basis of aristocratic/gentry domination in Anglo-Saxon England and northern Francia; and, for more general comment, Wickham (2005), part 2.

40 The village community at least attempted to protect the Christians in their midst: see *Passion of St Saba* 4.4; Heather and Matthews (1991), chapter 4.

41 See Ammianus 31.3.8.

42 The law codes again show that social value varied substantially with age, with women's value famously being highest during child-bearing years. But age was clearly important to men too: older men were buried with spurs but not weapons, for instance, suggesting that there was an age limit to military obligation: see Hedeager (1988). Children were likewise sometimes not buried in cemeteries: see e.g. Siegmund (1998), 179ff.

43 On the general importance of feasting as part of 'reciprocity' (see note 27 above), see Earle (1984), (1991). The first-century evidence is discussed in Thompson (1965). On Anglo-Saxon ideologies and realities, see Charles-Edwards (1989); Campbell (2000), chapter 8.

44 For the early Roman period, see Thompson (1965), 37ff. On Roman control of assemblies, see Dio 72.19.2; 73.2.1–4. On fourth-century village assemblies, see *Passion of St Saba*; cf. Heather and Matthews (1991), chapter 4. On the decision to cross into the Empire, see Ammianus 31.3.8: 'diuque deliberans' (see Chapter 4 below). Thompson (1965), (1966) emphasizes the absence of reference in fourth-century sources (which basically means Ammianus) to regular councils among the Goths and other Germani. While a correct observation, it does not mean they weren't happening.

45 The literature on sacral kingship is huge, but see e.g. Wenskus (1961) and Wolfram (1994). The terminology and concept of *heilag* is nevertheless clear: see Green (1998), chapter 7 for the linguistic evidence; and cf. Pohl (2000) and Moisl (1981) for a practical application. On the actual (as opposed to invented) history of the Amal dynasty, see Heather (1991), chapters 1–2, and part 3; Heather (1996), chapters 6, 8 and 9.

46 See Gregory of Tours, *Histories* 2.9; the Chatti are also mentioned at Ammianus

20.10. Salii: Ammianus 17.8; cf., amongst a huge range of possible secondary literature, James (1988), chapter 1, and the relevant papers in Wieczorek et al. (1997). The political processes behind the generation of the Alamanni may not have been totally dissimilar. No old names survived into the fourth century, but the confederation does seem to have built up gradually over time. In the third century, for instance, the Iuthingi (itself a new name) seem to have been a separate grouping, but by the fourth were operating as an integral part of the broader confederation: see Drinkwater (2007), 63ff.

47 For Gargilius' cow, see Boeles (1951), 130, plate 16, cited in Geary (1988), 3; the calculation of legionaries' demands is from Elton (1996).

48 Julian's treaties are discussed in more detail in Heather (2001). On the frontier and its operations, see generally Whittaker (1994); Elton (1996); Wells (1999), chapter 6; Carroll (2001), of which the two latter focus greater attention on the Roman side of the Rhine.

49 On loan words and trade, see Green (1998), 186f. and chapter 12. On iron production, see Urbanczyk (1997b); cf. more generally Krüger (1976–83), vol. 2, 157ff.

50 On the forced drafts of recruits, see Heather (2001).

51 See Green (1998), chapter 12.

52 Caesar, *Gallic War* 4.2; Tacitus, *Germania* 5 (who notes, however, that interior Germanic groups still did not value Roman silver coins); cf. Green (1998), chapter 12. On fourth-century coin concentrations, see Drinkwater (2007), 128–35; Heather and Matthews (1991), 91–3.

53 On the Tervingi and trade, see Themistius, *Orations* 10, with the commentary of Heather (1991), 107ff. For general orientation on Roman imports and their patterns, see Eggers (1951); Hedeager (1988); von Schnurbein (1995); Wells (1999), chapter 10; Drinkwater (2007), 34ff.

54 For Roman goods and social status, see Steuer (1982). For the amber causeways, see Urbanczyk (1997b). For tolls, see Green (1998).

55 See Caesar, *Gallic War* 6.17; Tacitus, *Annals* 13.57. For the bog deposits, see Orsnes (1963), (1968); Ilkjaer and Lonstrup (1983); Ilkjaer (1995); for more general comment, see e.g. Hedeager (1987); Steuer (1998); Muller-Wille (1999), 41–63.

56 For a thoughtful critique of the importance of trade, see Fulford (1985). On ninth- and tenth-century beneficiaries, see Chapter 10 above. For an introduction to 'agency', and its more particular problems, see Wilson (2008).

57 For a detailed report of the find, see Kunzl (1993); for an English summary, see Painter (1994).

58 For a more detailed account, with full references, see Heather (2001).

59 Ammianus 17.12–13, with Heather (2001). On the removal of potentially dangerous leaders, see Ammianus 21.4.1–5; 27.10.3; 29. 4.2 ff.; 29.6.5; 30.1.18–21.

60 On the rationale of hostage-taking, see Braund (1984). On subsidies, Klose (1934) collects the evidence from the early period, Heather (2001) for that of the later Empire.

61 'So eagerly did our forces': Ammianus 19.11. For further comment on the balance between resettlement and exclusion, see Chapter 3 above; and cf. e.g. Heather (1991), chapter 4, on standard Roman immigration policies; and Carroll

(2001), 29ff., on the amount of organized restructuring of adjacent populations that went on as Rome created its German frontier.

62 Valentinian's reduction of gifts: Ammianus 26.5; 27.1. For commentary, see Heather (2001); and Drinkwater (2007), chapter 8 (who seeks, in my view damagingly, to demonstrate that the Alamanni could never have represented any kind of threat).

63 On the Rhine–Weser, see Drinkwater (2007), 38–9. On fifth-century economic expansion in Alamannia, see ibid., 355–44.

64 See Wells (1999), chapters 10–11, following von Schnurbein (1995), who stresses the increase in imports of Roman weaponry into Germanic contexts after the mid-second century.

65 Athanaric: Ammianus 27.5; Macrianus: Ammianus 30.3. In both cases, though, the relevant emperor was being pressed by problems elsewhere – Valentinian in the Middle Danube, and Valens in Persia: see Heather and Matthews (1991), chapter 2.

## 3. ALL ROADS LEAD TO ROME?

1 'They were expecting . . .': Dio 32. 8–10.

2 For a good introduction, see Birley (1966), chapters 6–8, with Appendix III; see also Böhme (1975).

3 See Dio 72.20.1–2 (on the stationing of troops); 72.11–12, 72.20.2, 72.21 (on the movements of the Asdingi, Quadi, and Naristi respectively); 72.15, 72.16.1–2, 72.19.2, 73.3.1–2 (on trading privileges and neutral zones); 72.19.2, 73.2.1–4 (on assemblies).

4 'Not only were . . .': *Historia Augusta*: Marcus Aurelius 14.1; for an introduction to the trickeries of this text, see Syme (1968), (1971a), (1971b). For Roman aggression, see Drinkwater (2007), 28–32, who adds further thoughts on the possible impact of the plague, and Marcus' sense of duty, to the argument.

5 On Rhine frontier damage, see Carroll (2001), 138; and cf., on the legions and Marcus' self-monumentalization, Birley (as note 2 above). See also Chapter 2, note 28 above.

6 For the first-century homeland of the Langobardi, see Tacitus, *Germania* 40. That group of 6,000 clearly did not represent more than a subgroup, and they would be followed south by more Langobardi in the fifth century (see Chapter 5 below). These later Langobardi invaded the Middle Danube proper from intermediate settlements in Bohemia, but it is unknown whether this was true also of the second-century group. For references to permanent displacements, see note 3 above.

7 See Dio 72.3.1a.

8 See e.g. Barford (2001), introduction and chapter 1.

9 Of fundamental importance here is the work of the late Kazimierz Godlowski, especially his general treatment of north-central Europe in the Roman period: Godlowski (1970). Shchukin (1990) supplies a good general survey, building on Godlowski's pioneering work. The argument continues over details, and many more 'cultures', and phases within 'cultures', have acquired much more precise

and absolute dates. In pioneering days, only Roman coins provided any indication of absolute chronology. Since 1945, the chronological development of Roman wheel-turned pottery became better understood, both for fine wares (dinner services) and amphorae (storage jars for olive oil and wine). Two later techniques supply still more precise dates: carbon-14 (which produces a date-range) and dendrochronology, based on tree rings (which tells you precisely when a given tree was cut down). Combined with Godlowski's general method, these technical advances have generated a wealth of knowledge that would have astonished previous generations of scholarship.

10  In technical dating terms, the expansion occurred in Roman Iron Age periods B2, B2/C1a. These paragraphs distil information in two important collections of papers: *Peregrinatio Gothica* 1 and 2; and cf. Shchukin (2005).

11  For a fuller discussion, see Heather (1996), 35–8. There is a range of fragmentary references in classical sources indicating that Gothic groups were moving south and east: see Batty (2007), 384–7.

12  The relevant literature is huge. For a brief introduction, with full references, see Heather (2005), chapter 2.

13  For a recent comprehensive treatment, with full refererences, see Drinkwater (2007), chapter 2. (Note his important argument on pp. 43–5 that a group called the Alamanni clearly existed already in the 210s, a point to which we shall return.) On the brutal violence, see ibid., 78f. (with further examples); Carroll (2001), chapter 9.

14  On Alamannic origins, see Drinkwater (2007), 48f., 108–16 (with full references).

15  Argaith and Guntheric: Jordanes, *Getica* 16.91 (cf. *Historia Augusta*: Gordian 31.1 on 'Argunt', which probably represents a conflation of the two). Cniva: Zosimus 1.23; Jordanes, *Getica* 18.101–3; Zonaras, *Chronicle* 12.20.

16  The principal source is Zosimus 1.31–5. For additional sources and commentary, see Paschoud (1971–89), vol. 1, pp. 152ff., n. 59ff.

17  Zosimus 1.42–3, 46, with Paschoud (1971–1989), vol. 1, pp. 159ff. n. 70ff.

18  *Historia Augusta*: Aurelian 22.2. There is no evidence that he was related to the Cniva who had been operating in the same region a generation before: see note 15 above. On all these third-century attacks, see Batty (2007), 387–95.

19  Eutropius, *Breviarium* 8.2.

20  For first- and second-century references to the Goths, see Tacitus, *Germania* 43–4; Strabo, *Geography* 7.1.3 ('Butones'); Ptolemy *Geography* 3.5.8. Kulikowski (2007), chapters 3–4; cf. Jordanes, *Getica* 4.25–8 (on Filimer: see p. 122).

21  For more detail on the Tervingi, see Chapter 2 above. Jordanes' anachronisms were first demonstrated in Heather (1991), chapters 1–2 (where I show my own scepticism of Jordanes, *pace* Kulikowski).

22  On the first and second century, see Shchukin (1990); and cf. Batty (2007), 353ff. on Bastarnae, Sarmatians, and Dacians of various kinds (with full references, and noting the distorting political agendas that have sometimes been applied to these materials). For an introduction to Ulfila and his Bible, see Heather and Matthews (1991), chapters 5–7.

23  For the first- and second-century placement of Goths, see note 20 above. Rugi: Tacitus, *Germania* 44. Vandals: Courtois (1955), chapter 1. (Kulikowski does not discuss the broader range of evidence.)

24  Carpi: see note 38 below. On the 330s, see *Anonymous Valesianus* I.6.30.376, chapter 4. On the migration habit, see above, p. 30.

25  In technical terms, these transformations occurred in period B2–C1a/b. For fuller discussion, see Heather (1996), 43–50, drawing on the materials mentioned in note 9, and now supplemented by Shchukin (2005). Kulikowski (2007), 60ff. dismisses the importance of the archaeological evidence in very general terms without discussing the phenomenon of Wielbark expansion.

26  For introductions to this material, see Kazanski (1991); Shchukin (2005), with a fuller literature listed at Heather (1996), 47–50.

27  See Kazanski (1991); Heather (1996), 47–50; Shchukin (2005).

28  Jordanes, *Getica* 4.25–8.

29  Jordanes, *Getica* 16–17.90–100 records the third-century triumphs of the Amal King Ostrogotha. The king is entirely mythical, however, invented to explain why the Ostrogoths were so called, and his name has been added to known historical events: see Heather (1991), 22–3, 368.

30  For more detail, see Heather (1991), chapter 1 and 84–9.

31  Batavi: Tacitus, *Histories* 4.12, *Germania* 29. Chatti, Bructeri and Ampsivarii: Tacitus, *Annals* 58, *Germania* 33.

32  The element of fragmentation under Filimer is quoted on p. 122. Berig: *Getica* 4.25–6, with 17.94–5. Goffart (1988), 84ff. is reasonably concerned to undermine old assumptions that Gothic oral history suffuses the *Getica*, but is arguably a little too dismissive: see Heather (1991), 5–6, 57–8, 61–2.

33  See e.g. Borodzej et al. (1989); Kokowski (1995); Shchukin (2005).

34  See Drinkwater (2007), chapter 2 and 85–9 (with references).

35  See Ionita (1976).

36  On Heruli casualties, see George Syncellus, *Chronicle*, ed. Bonn, I.717. For other figures from the Aegean expedition (2,000 boats and 320,000 men), see *Historia Augusta*: Claudius 8.1. Cannabaudes' defeat is said to have cost 5,000 Gothic dead: *Historia Augusta*: Aurelius 22.2. Much of this material derives from the contemporary account of Dexippus. If the parallel with Viking activity is to be taken to the ultimate, one would suspect that relatively small groups made the initial moves, only for their very success to encourage larger entities to participate in the action. The state of the third-century evidence, however, does not make such a chronological progression certain. For further commentary on scale, see Batty (2007), 390ff.

37  Langobardi: Dio 72.1.9. Quadi: Dio 72.20.2 (explicitly *pandemei*, 'all the people').

38  For the protest of the Carpi, see Peter the Patrician fr. 8. For the exodus on to Roman soil, see Aurelius Victor, *Caesars* 39.43; *Consularia Constantinopolitana*, s.a. 295. See, more generally, Bichir (1976), chapter 14. A total of six campaigns were fought against the Carpi during the reign of the Emperor Galerius (293–311).

39  Naristi: see p. 98. Limigantes: see p. 85. On the Greek cities, the classic works of Minns (1913) and Rostovzeff (1922) remain essential. For an introduction to the archaeological evidence that has since become available, see Batty (2007), 284–9 (with references).

40  Drinkwater (2007), 43–5 rightly rejects the recent tendency to claim that Alamanni did not exist before the 290s, but then attempts to make all the action

of the third century, including the whole settlement of the Agri Decumates, into the result of warband activity. This argument fails to convince.

41 See above Chapter 9.

42 For female burial costume, see note 26 above. For an introduction to the Gothic Bible, see Heather and Matthews (1991), chapters 5–7. The contrast with the originally Norse Rurikid dynasty, who quickly took Slavic names (see above Chapter 10), is extremely striking. See also Chapter 6 below for discussion of the linguistic evidence from the Anglo-Saxon conquest of lowland Britain.

43 Quadi: Dio 72.20.2. Hasding Vandals: Dio 72. 12.1.

44 'Commonsense': Drinkwater (2007), 48. For Burgundian linguistic evidence, see Haubrichs (2003), (forthcoming).

45 For a qualitative definition of 'mass' migration, see pp. 31–2 above. If 'mass' sounds too redolent of the invasion hypothesis, then alternative terms might be found (perhaps 'significant'?), but there is surely virtue in bringing first-millennium usage into line with the norms prevailing in specialist migration studies.

46 Panegyrici Latini 3 [11].16–18.

47 See above Chapter 2.

48 On military inscriptions, see Speidel (1977), 716–18; cf. Batty (2007), 384–7. On shipping, see Zosimus 1.32.2–3.

49 I would therefore strongly argue that the 'interaction' theme that has been so marked a feature of frontier studies in recent years – e.g. Whittaker (1994); Elton (1996) – must be balanced with a proper appreciation of the frontier's equally real military function.

50 See pp. 43ff. Oddly, Drinkwater (2007), 48–50, while accepting the evidence for increased competition within the Germanic world, refuses to recognize that this would naturally lead to increased pressure on the Roman frontier, amongst other areas, as groups sought to escape the heightened dangers of their existence. Wells (1999), chapter 9 is similarly – and equally oddly – 'internalist' in interpretation, seeking to locate the causes of third-century disturbances within the frontier zone, and particular the Roman side of it.

51 Ammianus 26.5, 27.1; cf. Drinkwater (2007), chapter 8.

52 Tacitus, Annals 12.25.

53 See e.g. Anokhin (1980); Frolova (1983); Raev (1986).

54 Peter the Patrician fr. 8.

55 The rhythms of Roman frontier management perhaps aided the process. Thinning out the frontier zone periodically, as the Romans did, to reduce overcrowding and the potential for violence (see p. 85), can only have made it easier for more peripheral groups eventually to build up a sufficient manpower advantage to overthrow established Roman clients.

56 Cf. Chapter 2 above, p. 101. I would in any case strongly argue that freeman and retinue society were unlikely to be completely separate.

57 Jordanes, Getica 55.282 ('ascitis certis ex satellitibus patris et ex populo amatores sibi clientesque consocians').

58 For references, see note 10 above, with Kmiecinski (1968) on Odry. Descriptive terms like 'semi-nomad' are sometimes used, but to my mind misleadingly. What we're talking about here are mixed farming populations, who kept many animals, perhaps measured their wealth in cattle, but also engaged in extensive

arable agriculture, despite lacking the techniques to maintain the fertility of individual fields over the long term.

## 4. MIGRATION AND FRONTIER COLLAPSE

1 Before these tumultuous events of the late fourth century, the western border of Alanic territory lay on the River Don. This just about made them outer clients on Rome's Lower Danube frontier, especially since the Empire retained strong contacts with the southern Crimea. But they can only be classed as complete outsiders when it comes to the convulsion of 405–8, which affected the Middle Danubian frontier region.

2 The same basic vision of the crisis can be found, amongst other sources, in Ammianus 31; Eunapius frr. (and Zosimus 4.20.3 ff., which is largely but not completely dependent on Eunapius); Socrates, *Historia Ecclesiastica* 4.34; Sozomen, *Historia Ecclesiastica* 6.37. The total figure of 200,000 is provided by Eunapius fr. 42, whose account is generally vague and rhetorical, and therefore unconvincing by itself: see Paschoud (1971–89), vol. 2, 376 n. 143. The figure has, however, been accepted by some: see e.g. Lenski (2002), 354–5 (with references). On the 10,000 warriors, see Ammianus 31.12.3; these may have represented only the Tervingi: see Heather (1991), 139. On the wagon trains, see Ammianus 31.7, 31.11.4–5, 31.12.1ff. On social dependants, see e.g. Ammianus 31.4.1.ff.; Zosimus 4.20.6.

3 Matthews (1989) stresses Ammianus' literary artistry, where Barnes (1998) stresses his lack of candour. These two most recent studies disagree on many things but both stress that Ammianus is not a straightforward read. For further comment, see Drijvers & Hunt (1999); G. Kelly (2008).

4 For the 'more secret' archive, see Ammianus 14.9.1. For career documents, see Ammianus 28.1.30. For military dispatches, see Sabbah (1978).

5 On the migration topos, see Kulikowski (2002). On causation, see Halsall (2007), chapter 6.

6 For examples of the migration topos in action, see pp. 122 and 251 above. Ammianus on warbands: e.g. 14.4; 17.2; 27.2; 28.5. Ammianus on Strasbourg: 16.12.7; 31.8.3.

7 The recruitment of this extra mercenary support has sometimes been confused with the arrival of the Greuthungi alongside the Tervingi. This is a serious mistake: see Heather (1991), 144–5, and Appendix B.

8 On the split of the Tervingi, see Ammianus 31.3.8ff.; 31.4.13. The Greuthungi seem also to have fragmented, in that a leader called Farnobius and his followers, found alongside the main body as it crossed the Danube, then suffered an entirely different fate from the rest: see Ammianus 31.4.12; 31.9.3–4.

9 Only Kulikowski (2002) really dares to suggest that Ammianus might be completely misleading, and even he seems to backtrack substantially in Kulikowski (2007), 123ff., which, while wanting to minimize any unity among the Goths, still accepts that they formed a mixed group of humanity 'numbered at least in the tens of thousands, and perhaps considerably more' (p. 130). Among the other anti-migrationists, Halsall (2007) is willing to think in terms of over

10,000 warriors and a total mixed group of 40,000 people; while Goffart (1981), (2006) has never treated the events of 376 in any detail.

10 See Halsall (2007), 170ff., drawing particularly on the analysis of Socrates, *Historia Ecclesiastica* 4.33 in Lenski (1995).

11 I therefore remain entirely happy with the analysis of the 'Ammianus versus Socrates' issue I offered, with references, in Heather (1986). Halsall's desire to avoid a sequence of events that would put predatory migration at the heart of causation seems to provide the principal reason for rejecting the contemporary and more detailed Ammianus in favour of the later and less detailed Socrates, but he offers no good reasons based on the historical evidence, and in my view this line of argument allows preconception to justify unsound methodology.

12 Ammianus 31.3.8.

13 Zosimus 4.20.4–5.

14 Ammianus 31.3.2–8.

15 On the Caucasus raid, see Maenchen-Helfen (1973), 51–9 (who does think they came from the Danube). For other Goths north of the Danube in 383, see (Arimer) Achelis (1900); and (Odotheus) Zosimus 4.35.1, 4.37–9.

16 Some Hunnic groups did operate further west before 405–8, but the numbers were very small up to about 400: just the mercenaries who joined the Goths south of the Danube in autumn 377 (see note 7 above) and another Hunnic/ Alanic warband found near Raetia in the 380s (Ambrose, *Epistolae* 25). Uldin's force from c.400 was clearly a bit larger, but even his command paled compared to the Hunnic forces that arrived in the Middle Danube after 405–8: see above Chapter 5. In general terms, all of this suggests to me that the action of 376 should be viewed rather along the lines of Caesar's description of the move of the Tenctheri and Usipetes west of the Rhine in the mid-first century BC. In that case, an extended series of smaller-scale raids and attacks, rather than one outright invasion, convinced them that they could no longer live securely east of the Rhine: Caesar, *Gallic War* 4.1.

17 On discussion, see Ammianus 31.3.8. On persuasion, see Heather (1991), 176–7,179–80.

18 On the archaeology and group identity, see above Chapter 1. The particular items within the Cernjachov culture that strike me as a priori promising for distinguishing the immigrant groups are its bone combs, particular *fibulae* and north European, Germanic longhouse types. Unfortunately, no detailed mapping of these items has yet been made.

19 For an introduction to Ulfila, see Heather and Matthews (1991), chapter 3. I suspect that the alternative view, of a swift social amalgamation, involves a degree of wishful thinking, largely inspired in reaction to the horrors of the Nazi era, that shrinks from accepting such unequal relationships between relatively bounded groups of human beings. The eastern expansions of the Goths and other Germanic groups in the late Roman period were enthusiastically seized upon by Hitler's propagandists to justify the poisonous activities of the Third Reich: see Wolfram (1988), chapter 1. But a laudable determination to condemn Nazi atrocities becomes muddled thinking if we try to make the past conform to our wish rather than to the reasonable probability of its evidence.

20 Different grades of warrior are not specifically mentioned in the Hadrianople campaign, but they do feature in the evidence for Radagaisus' Gothic force of 405 (Olympiodorus fr 9.) and Theoderic the Amal's Ostrogoths (see Chapter 5), as well as in later Visigothic laws. Moreover, the *Historia Augusta*'s vivid account of third-century mass Gothic migratory bands, complete with families and slaves, may well be based on fourth-century events (*Historia Augusta*, Claudius 6. 6, 8.2; cf. Chapter 3 above), and I strongly suspect it was those of lower status that the hard-pressed Tervingi were selling into Roman slavery in return for food on the banks of the Danube: Ammianus 31.4.11.

21 On Carpo-Dacai, see Zosimus 4.34.6. On Cernjachov continuity, see Kazanski (1991).

22 For the Carpi, see Chapter 3 above. On the Sarmatian move, see *Anonymous Valesianus* 6.31.

23 For Goths in the fourth century, see Chapter 2. The point about information is also applicable to the minority under Athanaric who moved into Sarmatian territory: this is what the Tervingi as a whole had tried in 332, only to be frustrated by Roman counteraction (see previous note).

24 Noel Lenski (2002), 182ff., 325f. seeks to locate the reason for Valens' aggression towards Persia in the Goths' arrival, and thoughts of the extra recruits he could muster from them. I find the argument unconvincing, and remain confident that the Gothic crisis left Valens with very little room for manoeuvre: see Heather (1991), 128ff.

25 Kulikowski (2007), 123ff. implies that the Tervingi and Greuthungi came to the Danube and requested asylum on separate occasions, so that Valens had sequential decisions to make, but this is not what Ammianus' account suggests (31.4.12–13; 31.5.2–3).

26 Ammianus 31.10; cf. more general frontier studies such as Whittaker (1994).

27 Ammianus 31.5.3–4. This might possibly be Roman paranoia; I don't think it is.

28 For example, the Goths of Sueridas and Colias (Ammianus 31.6.1); perhaps also the Alamannic unit under Hortarius (Ammianus 29.4.7).

29 I suspect, but am unable to prove, that this would have been particularly true of indigenous groups who merely paid some tribute to the Goths and were otherwise left substantially alone. For a similar range of relationships between the Huns and their different subjects, see Chapter 5.

30 For full references, see *PLRE* 2, 934.

31 For Vandals in Raetia, see Claudian, *Gothic War* 278–81, 363–5, 400–4, 414–29. On the identity of the Sueves, see most recently Goffart (2006), 82–3, who adopts the most plausible Marcomanni/Quadi approach. The Rhine crossing is generally dated 31 December 406 on the basis of Prosper, *Chronicle* AP 379; for the argument that the chronicler might have meant 31 December 405, see Kulikowski (2000a), 328–9. Following the counterargument of Birley (2005), 455–60, however, Kulikowski (2007), 217 n. 37 appears less sure.

32 For Uldin, see Sozomen, *Historia Ecclesiastica* 9.25.1–7; *Codex Theodosianus* 5.6.3. On Burgundians, see Demougeot (1979), 432; 491–3.

33 On Olympiodorus, see, above all, Matthews (1970), with the further thoughts of Blockley (1981), (1983).

34 For Vandal losses, see Gregory of Tours 2.29. The 1:5 ratio was customarily

employed, e.g. by Schmidt (1933), 286, 293. For Vandal/Alanic numbers, see Procopius, *Wars* 3.5.18–19; Victor of Vita, *History of the Persecution* 1.2. For Burgundian numbers, see Orosius 7.32.11. On Radagaisus' following, see note 30 above.

35  Jerome, *Chronicle* 2389 (= 371 AD).

36  On the '*distributio*' and its significance, see Jones (1964), Appendix III. Jones's argument is unaffected by Kulikowski (2000b) since it works from the comparison of two well-dated sections of the *Notitia*: the eastern field army of c.395, and its western counterpart of c.420. For the thirty '*numeri*', see Zosimus 5.26.4. For the 12,000 followers of Radagaisus, see Olympiodorus fr. 9.

37  Victor of Vita, *History of the Persecution* 1.2. I therefore take a more optimistic view of Victor than does Goffart (1980), Appendix A.

38  Halsall (2007), 206, for example, has Radagaisus leading 'a large force', characterizing the Rhine crossers as a 'huge force' (p. 211). It is really only Drinkwater (2007), especially 323–4, who thinks that warbands will adequately explain the action.

39  Zosimus 5.26.3 has Radagaisus engaged in widespread recruitment prior to attacking Italy (although I remain slightly worried that he is here confusing Radagaisus and the Rhine crossing). *Codex Theodosianus* 5.6.3 makes clear that Uldin's following was a mixture of Huns and Sciri, and therefore a new, post-376 alliance.

40  On Radagaisus' followers: Zosimus 5.35.5–6. On Alans in Gaul: Paulinus of Pella, *Eucharisticon* 377–9. On Vandals and Alans in North Africa: Victor of Vita, *History of the Persecution* 1.2. For Burgundians, see notes 34 and 35 above, together, of course, with the fact that this group were able to preserve their east German dialect throughout these moves: see Chapter 3 above. No one doubts Ammianus' report that the Goths of 376 also came with women and children in tow (31.3–4), so the basic principle that Germanic and Alanic armed forces might have moved with their dependants seems well enough established. Against this, the assertions of Drinkwater (1998), especially 273, that it is commonsense that only warriors took part in the action are underwhelming. Cf. Drinkwater (2007), 323–4.

41  Both points – i.e. the Middle Danubian origins of the crisis, and the subsequent appearance there of the Huns – were first argued by Heather (1995a), and are now been generally accepted: see for example Goffart (2006), chapter 5; Halsall (2007), 206ff. The crucial passage of Claudian which has been misunderstood to refer to Huns on the Danube is *Against Rufinus* ii.26ff. (especially 36ff.)

42  Heather (1995a).

43  Goffart (2006), chapter 5, especially 75–8 (Huns appear in Middle Danube shortly after the crisis); 78–80 (Radagaisus); 94–5 (summarizing the knock-on effect among the expectations of other groups of the fact that the Goths had survived their arrival on Roman soil with their coherence more or less intact).

44  Halsall (2007), 195–212; cf. Halsall (2005), particularly on the disruptive effects of ending subsidies.

45  On Tribigild, see Heather (1988); Synesius, *De Regno* 19–21.

46  The first practical help from the east consisted of 4,000 soldiers who arrived in Ravenna in 409/10: Zosimus 6.8.

47  For slaves, see Orosius 7.37.13ff.

48  Either Constantine III or Flavius Constantius has usually been considered responsible for the transfer: see Chastagnol (1973); cf. Kulikowski (2000a). Halsall (2007), 209 raises doubts, but offers no specific evidence in their support.

49  On Constantine III, see Zosimus 6.1, which specifically identifies British, Gallic and Spanish military forces as sufficiently united behind him to drive the Vandals, Alans and Suevi into Spain, and to take the usurper to the brink of Empire: see Matthews (1975), 312ff. On the general role of subsidies in Roman diplomacy, see Heather (2001).

50  The relevant sources are, above all, Ammianus 17.12–13; *Anonymous Valesianus* 6.31–2. For a recent discussion of the Vandals in the fourth century, see Goffart (2006), 82–7, who convincingly concludes that the evidence places them in Silesia and on the Upper Tisza.

51  For Vandals in Raetia, see note 31 above. For their fourth-century placement, see previous note.

52  For fourth-century Goths, see for example Heather (1991), chapter 3. For Alans, see Goffart (2006), 89–90, with Ammianus 31.3.1, who records that the western-most group of Alans in c.375 were called 'The Don People' (Tanaites).

53  For the Alans in 377, see Ammianus 31.8.4ff., with Heather (1991), 144–5 and Appendix B; and in 378, see Ammianus 31.11.16. For their drafting into the Roman army, see Zosimus 4.35.2.

54  The identity of Uldin's followers emerges from Sozomen, *Historia Ecclesiastica* 9.25.1–7 and *Codex Theodosianus* 5.6.3.

55  Ammianus 17.12–13 (Constantius' arrangements in 358); 19.11.1–3 (the return of the Limigantes in 359).

56  On the differences between the cyclical movements inherent in a nomad economy and 'real' migration, see pp. 208–12).

57  Ammianus 31.4.13; I take it these are the Sarmatians defeated by Theodosius prior to his elevation: Theodoret, *Historia Ecclesiastica* 5.5; *Panegyrici Latini* 12(2).12.9–10.

58  The nomadic character of the Alans' economy makes one expect a priori that they had a different social structure from agricultural Germani such as the Vandals or Goths, and this is strongly implied, if in a rather general way, by Ammianus 31.2.25.

59  On the Sciri, see *Codex Theodosianus* 5.6.3. The contrasting fates of the 'better' among Radagaisus' following who were drafted into the Roman army, versus the many others sold into slavery, might suggest that the latter had had little choice over whether to participate in the action.

60  On Uldin's force, see Sozomen, *Historia Ecclesiastica* 9.25.1–7; and *Codex Theodosianus* 5.6.3. Radagaisus: Olympiodorus fr. 9 for the 'best', as against Orosius 7.37.13ff., who records the miserable fate of the mass of the rank and file sold into slavery. 'Best' translates Olympiodorus' *optimates*, which has sometimes been translated as 'nobles', but to reckon so many nobles is absurd, so the word can only make sense as a reference to the higher-grade caste of warriors: see Chapter 2 above. The elites of both the Rhine crossers and the Burgundians, neither of whom of course were faced with as powerful and immediate a

Roman counterattack as Radagaisus or Uldin, showed no obviously similar propensity to abandon the migrant mass.

61 The only group for whom any case can be made for an invitation is the Tervingi, by Valens, in 376, but in my view even here Valens had no real choice: see p. 169 above.

62 Cf. Heather (1991), chapter 5, and Appendix B. I don't believe that the Emperor Gratian made a separate peace agreement with the Greuthungi in the summer of 380. That this adjustment in traditional Roman policy affected only these particular Goths is well understood: see Stallknecht (1969). Kulikowski (2002) and Halsall (2007), 180ff. have recently tried to argue that nothing out of the ordinary was granted in 382, but the case does not stand up to scrutiny: see Heather (forthcoming).

63 It may well be, then, that local Roman landowners cut a deal with the invaders to prevent less organized and hence inherently more damaging assaults upon their property. Cf. Hydatius, *Chronicle* 41[49]: the settlement saw particular groups of invaders settle in particular provinces, so it is possible that the Spanish provincial councils were responsible for the Roman provincial side of the negotiations.

64 See for example Kulikowski (2002); Halsall (2007), chapters 7–8.

65 Claudian, *De Bell. Get.* 166ff., 610ff. (dating to 402); Synesius, *De Regno* 19–21 (dating to 399), with Heather (1988). Neither Kulikowski (2002) nor Halsall (2007), 189–94 offers any explanation of the fundamental distortion they suppose these authors to be incorporating.

66 Zosimus 5.5.4. Privileging the short, non-contemporary and confused Zosimus over the more contemporary sources is the basic approach adopted (even if leading to slightly different interpretations of Alaric's career) in Liebeschuetz (1992); Kulikowski (2002); Halsall (2007), 191–4. Amongst other problems, Zosimus conflates Stilicho's two campaigns against Alaric (in 395 and 397) and wipes out ten years of the history of Alaric's Goths in making the join between his two main sources here: Eunapius and Olympiodorus (at Zosimus 5.26.1: see Heather (1991), 210). To say that Zosimus had no real grasp of Alaric's career, therefore, is an understatement.

67 The activities of Gainas are well covered, if certainly with hostility, in Synesius, *De Providentia*; cf. Cameron and Long (1993).

68 To my mind, this is why Liebeschuetz (1992) cannot be correct in viewing Alaric as leading no more than a regiment or two of Gothic auxiliaries in 395. Halsall (2007), 192–3 tries to wriggle round this problem by continuing to deny the overlap with the Goths of 382 while accepting that Alaric's armed following must have been large, mostly Gothic and from the Balkans. Having accepted these points, he is in fact most of the way to the conclusion that Alaric led the 382 Goths in revolt. He resists this conclusion because he doesn't believe there was a peace deal in 382 which licensed Gothic autonomy, but see the next note.

69 Themistius, *Orations* 16.211. Continuing Gothic autonomy up to and beyond c.390 is signalled, beyond Themistius, in sources both sympathetic to Theodosius and his treaty such as Pacatus, *Panegyrici Latini* 12.(2).22.3–5 (where the Goths are one of a series of foreign peoples serving Theodosius), and hostile to them:

Synesius, *De Regno* 19–21, with the commentary of Heather (1988). Halsall (2007), 180–4 oddly argues that there is no evidence that any continued Gothic autonomy was licensed in 382; he appears not to have read the closing words of Themistius' speech closely enough. Cf. Kulikowski (2002).

70 For Roman policies towards leaders, see Heather (2001). Neither the original leaderships (Athanaric, the dynasty of Ermenaric) nor their immediate successors (Fritigern, Alatheus and Saphrax) survived the struggles of 376–82: for more detail, see Heather (1991), 188–92.

71 Fritigern: Ammianus 31.12.8–9, with Heather (1991), 175–6, 179–80. The best example of the post-382 jockeying is provided by the quarrel between Fravitta and Eriulph. Both led factions and both held different views over the proper ordering of Gotho-Roman relations: see Eunapius fr. 59, dated by the summary of it at Zosimus 4.56. For further discussion, see Heather (1991), 190–1. That Theodosius should have held such a banquet undermines the contention of Halsall (2007), 188–9 that Alaric couldn't have been the leader of the Goths of 382 in revolt, because there is no evidence that their sociopolitical hierarchies had continued in place after that date (Halsall does not discuss the incident). For Sarus and Sergeric in more detail, see Heather (1991), 197–8. Neither Kulikowski (2002) nor Halsall (2007) bothers to discuss its potential significance. In my view, extracting Roman recognition of his leadership was also precisely the significance of the generalship that Alaric periodically demanded of compliant Roman regimes – probably along with the financial package for his followers that came with it. But note that the generalship was an optional extra that he was willing to drop to make a deal: see Heather (1991), chapter 6.

72 Kulikowski (2002) – largely followed by Halsall (2007), 187–9 – denies large-scale Gothic military service in the years between the 382 treaty and Alaric's revolt in 395, but this involves too much special pleading to be convincing. *Panegryrici Latini* 12.(2)32.3–5 strongly implies that the main Gothic contingent was recruited only for the campaign against Maximus (especially Pacatus' explicit comment that it would have been dangerous to leave the Goths behind), while Eunapius fr. 55 and Zosimus 4.45.3 note Maximus' attempts to undermine the recruited Goths' loyalties, which again implies that this was something unusual. A range of sources note the participation of large numbers of Goths in the campaign against Eugenius (Zosimus 4.58; John of Antioch fr. 187; Orosius 7.37.19), and Theodosius' banquet for the Gothic leaders (see note 71 above) was held precisely when Theodosius was mulling over his answer to Eugenius' envoys (Zosimus 4.56). In my view, the banquet was probably a first move towards securing Gothic participation.

73 For Maximus' revolt, see Eunapius fr. 55; Zosimus 4.45.3, 48–9. Alaric of course led the revolt after the Eugenius campaign. The arguments of Kulikowski (2002) and Halsall (2007), 187–93 comment neither on the Maximus revolt nor on the significance suggested by the exact chronology of the banquet quarrel.

74 Orosius 7.35.19 (casualties confirmed at Zosimus 4.58). Neither Kulikowski (2002) nor Halsall (2007), 187–93 discusses this backdrop to the Gothic revolt.

75 In recent times, we have seen one successful example of this kind of diplomatic strategy in the Good Friday Agreement in Northern Ireland, and one so far unsuccessful example in the Oslo Accords on the Middle East.

76  Zosimus 5.5.5ff.

77  Themistius, *Orations* 16.211.c–d.

78  Whether this made any practical difference to Alaric's position in Illyricum in the short term is unclear; having been commanding general there, he was perhaps in a position to retain control of the levers of power.

79  For this argument in more detail, see Heather (forthcoming).

80  See in more detail Heather (1991), chapter 6.

81  Fravittas, Sarus and Modares: *PLRE* 1, 605; 372–3. On the 402 battle, see Claudian, *VI cons. Hon.* 229ff.; cf. Cameron (1970), 186–7.

82  It disappeared to the extent that of the sources that discuss the events of 376, only Ammianus knew there were originally two separate groups of Goths. In my view, both Greuthungi and Tervingi were settled under the treaty of 382 and Alaric's revolt in 395 involved and definitively united both. An alternative view sees the unification happening when Alaric summoned his brother-in-law Athaulf from Pannonia in 408: Zosimus 5.37.1ff.

83  Zosimus 5.35.5–6. *Pace* Kulikowski (2002), it is hard to see who this large body of barbarian soldiery in Roman service was, if not mainly the 12,000 followers of Radagaisus drafted by Stilicho: Olympiodorus fr. 9.

84  Heather (1991), 151ff. looks to unravel Zosimus' confusions.

85  Gothic subgroups were destroyed by Frigeidus (Ammianus 31.9), Sebastianus (Ammianus 31.11) and Modares (Zosimus 4.25), and there is no reason to think this a comprehensive list. On this process in general, see Heather (1991), 213–14, 223–4, 314ff.

86  Zosimus 5.45.3; cf. Liebeschuetz (1990), 75ff.; Kulikowski (2002).

87  Exactly how much larger this Gothic force was involves a huge amount of guesswork, but if it is right to calculate the military manpower of fourth-century Gothic units at around 10,000, then the Visigoths who formed around Alaric could certainly field at least twice this number of soldiers, and possibly between three and four times as many.

88  Victor of Vita, *History of the Persecutions* 1.2.

89  Hydatius, *Chronicle* 77 [86].

90  On the mid-410s: Hydatius, *Chronicle* 59–60 [67–8]; on the 420s: ibid. 69 [77]; on the 440s and 460s: Heather (2005), 289ff. and 390ff.

91  Suevi: Hydatius, *Chronicle* 63 [71]. Alans: see the convenient listings of Bachrach (1973).

## 5. HUNS ON THE RUN

1  Jordanes, *Getica* 50.261–2.

2  Uldin's Huns and Sciri: Sozomen, *Historia Ecclesiastica* 9.5; *Codex Theodosianus* 5.6.3. Huns' Gothic subjects in 427: Theophanes AM 5931; cf. Procopius, *Wars* 3.2.39–40, with Croke (1977). The date could be either 421 or 427. The best general survey of Attila's subject peoples is Pohl (1980).

3  See Maenchen-Helfen (1973), chapters 8–9, who also notes that leaders like Attila could easily have had 'proper' Hunnic names as well as Germanic nicknames; Attila means 'little father' in Germanic.

4   Ammianus 31.2.1–2; Zosimus 4.20.3–5 (cf. Eunapius fr. 42); Jordanes, *Getica* 24.121–2.

5   Ammianus 31.2.3ff.

6   The Alanic digression: Ammianus 31.2; the Saracen digression: Ammianus 14.4. In treating this material, the approach of Maenchen-Helfen (1945) was much more critical than that of Thompson (1995), even though it was Maenchen-Helfen who noticed the meat being placed under saddles. For further comment, and recent bibliography, see G. Kelly (2008), chapter 2.

7   For some orientation on nomadism, particularly of the Eurasian-steppe variety, see Cribb (1991); Khazanov (1984); Krader (1963); Sinor (1977), (1990).

8   Bury (1928).

9   Avars: Pohl (1988). Magyars: Bakony (1999).

10   For general accounts, see Thompson (1995); Maenchen-Helfen (1973); cf. Heather (1995a) on relations with Aetius.

11   Attila's more or less complete indifference to additional territorial gains emerges with striking clarity from the surviving fragments of Priscus' history.

12   Huns up to 376: Ammianus 31.3. Huns and Alans in 377: Ammianus 31.8.4ff. Huns and Carpo-Dacians: Zosimus 4.35.6.

13   'Improvised leaders': Ammianus 31.2.7. Jordanes does place a Hunnic king called Balamber in this era, but these are really events of c.450 and Balamber is in fact the Gothic king Valamer: see Heather (1989), and p. 234 above.

14   Uldin: Sozomen, *Historia Ecclesiastica* 9.5, with further comment and full references in Heather (1995a). Analogous phenomena occurred in the Viking era, when leaders thrown up in the first generation of small-scale expansion were quickly subdued as larger numbers under more important leaders joined in the flow: see Chapter 9.

15   Olympiodorus fr. 19; cf. Priscus fr. 11.2, p. 259 (on the Akatziri).

16   On the Huns' bow, see Heather (2005), 154–8, with further references.

17   For some calculations based on grazing room on the Great Hungarian Plain, see Lindner (1981). On the great raid of 395, see Maenchen-Helfen (1973), 51–9.

18   On nomad devolution in general, see the literature cited in note 7 above.

19   See Heather (2005), 325ff., with full references.

20   Procopius, *Wars* 8.5 seems to preserve by an indirect route the story originally told by the contemporary Eunapius, which was cast after Herodotus 5.9 (on the Sigynnae).

21   On the third-century Heruli, see Chapter 3. Sciri: Zosimus 4.35.6. Rugi: Tacitus, *Germania* 43. On likely placements within the Middle Danubian region, see Pohl (1980).

22   We will return to the Amal-led contingent in more detail. Bigelis: Jordanes, *Romana* 336. For the third group under Dengizich's control, see Priscus fr. 49.

23   Dengizich: *PLRE* 2, 354–5. Hernac: Jordanes, *Getica* 50.266, with *PLRE* 2, 400–1. Hormidac: *PLRE* 2, 571. Bigelis: see previous note.

24   Jordanes, *Getica* 50.264. Pohl (1980) suggests – in a compromise – that the Amal-led Goths may have moved at this point only from Transylvania. Much ink has been spilled on the relationship between the surviving Gothic history of Jordanes and the Gothic history of one Cassiodorus, which we know to have been written down at Theoderic's court in Italy. In my view, the textual evidence indeed

suggests that Jordanes worked using Cassiodorus' text (as he claims) and I find the various conspiracy theories that have been offered against this unconvincing: see Heather (1991), chapter 2; Heather (1993). The archaeological evidence for such a late Gothic move to the Middle Danube is indecisive. Kazanski (1991) has placed the end of the Cernjachov culture as late as c.450, but this is not the usual view, and the argument is essentially circular since it is based on Jordanes' report that there were still Goths east of the Carpathians at this date.

25  Odovacar: *PLRE* 2, 791–3. On the Balkan adventures of the Amal-led Goths, see Heather (1991), part 3.

26  For full references, see *PLRE* 2, 457 and 484–5.

27  The Lombards should strictly be called Langobards. The narrative source is Paul the Deacon, *History of the Lombards* 1.19. For modern commentary, see e.g. Christie (1995); Jarnut (2003); Pohl and Erhart (2005).

28  Procopius, *Wars* 6.14–15. Cf. Pohl (1980): the archaeological evidence suggests that the Gepids were slowly expanding south into Transylvania at this point.

29  An earlier exception would be the Goths rescued from Hunnic domination in 427: see note 2 above. These may also be the same as the Thracian Goths, as we shall shortly see. The Gepids too engaged in expansion within the region: see previous note.

30  'He was a Greek trader . . .': Priscus fr. 11.2.422–35. Edeco: *PLRE* 2, 385–6.

31  You can tell how people were dressed by where they wore their safety pins, which is all that tends to survive of clothing in most graves. Possible reasons for archaeological invisibility can range from the dramatic (where bodies are left exposed to the elements and wild animals) to the prosaic (cremation followed by scattering of ashes), or the generation of customs where bodies are buried without any chronologically identificatory gravegoods (something which often makes medieval cemeteries undatable in northern Europe once populations convert to Christianity). The horizons of the Hunnic Middle Danube are differentiated from one another by slight changes in the manner in which broadly similar sets of gravegoods were decorated. In chronological order (and there are overlaps between them), the sequence starts with the Villafontana horizon, succeeded in turn by those of Untersiebenbrunn and Domolospuszta/Bacsordas. For introductions to this material, see Bierbrauer (1980), (1989); Kazanski (1991); Tejral (1999). There are excellent illustrations in Wolfram (1985).

32  Many of the Germanic groups of central Europe had practised cremation in the first to the third century, but inhumation was already spreading more widely before the arrival of the Huns.

33  Historical sources do occasionally supply enough information, however, which can be used in conjunction with the archaeological evidence approximately to identify some particular groups.

34  See most recently Halsall (2007), 474–5; for a similar view of the Avar Empire, see Pohl (1988), with Pohl (2003).

35  Priscus fr. 14.

36  Priscus fr. 11.2, p. 259. See Chapter 4 for the Tervingi and Greuthungi; cf. the junior status and grimmer treatment handed out to the Sciri after Uldin's defeat: see above, note 2.

37  For references, see note 2 above; and see p. 248.

38  Priscus fr. 2, p. 225.

39  Priscus fr. 2, p. 227.

40  Priscus fr. 2, p. 227.

41  Priscus fr. 49.

42  The Romans provided Attila with a succession of secretaries, and a prisoner called Rusticius wrote the odd letter (Priscus fr. 14, p. 289). This governmental machine could keep lists of renegade princes who had fled to the Romans, and could keep track of the supplies required from subject groups, but little more. Akatziri: Priscus fr. 11.2, p. 259. Goths: Priscus fr. 49.

43  Jordanes, *Getica* 48.246–51, with Heather (1989), (1996), 113–17, 125–6.

44  Gepids: Jordanes, *Getica* 50.260–1.

45  Franks: Priscus: fr. 20.3. Akatziri: see note 42 above. Of the subject groups in between, the most dominated were apparently the Goths who appear in Priscus fr. 49, part of which is quoted above; the least dominated were the Gepids, who led the revolt against Attila's sons (see previous note). In between were the Pannonian Goths of Valamer: see note 43 above.

46  *Miracles of St Demetrius* II.5.

47  See e.g. Agadshanow (1994).

48  For further discussion, see Heather (2005), 324ff., with references.

49  As we have seen, modern anthropological evidence indicates that the most you will sometimes find in such circumstances is that a very few particular items have significance for signalling group identity, but that does not mean that the group identity is in any sense unreal: above, p. 26, after, in particular, Hodder (1982).

50  While Attila could extract annual subsidies measured in thousands of kilos of gold, the most that even a successful Hunnic successor group like the Amal-led Goths could manage was three hundred: Priscus fr. 37.

51  Jordanes, *Getica* 50.265–6. Jordanes himself came from this Balkan military milieu, and there is every reason to suppose this catalogue correct. When exactly in the 450s or 460s these settlements occurred is not clear: that of Hernac is firmly dated to the later 460s, however, and it may be that they all belong to the post-465 meltdown of Hunnic power that also saw moves into Roman territory by Bigelis and Hormidac. Hernac's willingness to have his power base broken up might explain why he was treated more favourably than Dengizich (see note 23 above).

52  Jordanes, *Getica* 53.272; cf. Agathias 2.13.1ff.

53  Paul the Deacon, *History of the Lombards* 2.26ff.; cf. Jarnut (2003). It is a consistent theme both within Paul's narrative and some of the other early Lombard texts that victory led to the inclusion of warriors in the group, but not always on terms of equality: see e.g. *Origo Gentis Langobardorum* 2 (as *aldii*: 'half-free'); *History of the Lombards* 1.20, 1.27, 5.29.

54  Goths: Heather (1996), Appendix 1. Lombards: ibid., and see previous note. See also Chapter 2 above.

55  Lombards: see e.g. Jarnut (2003), who argues that kingship among the Lombards may have been a temporary phenomenon restricted to the leading of expeditions. Goths: Heather (1989), (1996), chapters 8–9.

56  For the Rugi joining Theoderic in 487: John of Antioch fr. 214.7; on their still

being identifiable in 541: Procopius, *Wars* 7.2.1ff. (they had swapped sides twice during the Gothic conquest of Italy). Heruli: Procopius, *Wars* 6.14–15.

57 The account of the Heruli is doubted by Goffart (1988), 84ff.; that of the Rugi by Halsall (1999). See Chapter 1 above for general comments on modern understandings of group identity.

58 The Gundilas papyrus (translated by him as Appendix 1) is central to Amory (1997). But see also Heather (1996), chapter 9, and Appendix 1, (2003).

59 Malchus fr. 20, p. 446.215ff. (the 6,000 men), p. 440.83ff. (non-combatants and baggage). Cf. Jordanes, *Getica* 55.281–2 (Theoderic had earlier also used 6,000 men in the expedition that proved his manhood following his return from being a hostage in Constantinople). For further commentary, see Heather (1991), chapter 7.

60 See Amory (1997); but see also, in addition to Procopius, *Wars* 5.1.6ff., Ennodius, *Panegyric on Theoderic* 26–7 and *Life of Epiphanius* 118–19 (cf. 111–12).

61 The east Romans captured 2,000 wagons in a surprise attack (Malchus fr. 20), but there is nothing to suggest that this was the total baggage train. The Goths were offered 'unoccupied' land, which strongly implies that they were to do their own farming, as do all the negotiations between Theoderic and Constantinopolitan representatives: Malchus fr. 18.3, p. 430.5ff.; fr. 20, p. 438.55ff., p. 446.199ff.; cf. Heather (1991), 244ff.

62 For fuller discussion and complete references, see Heather (1991), 259–63; for Bigelis, see note 22 above.

63 For pay and rations for 13,000, and 910 kilos of gold per annum, see Malchus fr. 18.4, p. 434.12ff. and fr. 2, p. 408.22ff. For full discussion and references, see Heather (1991), 253–6.

64 For Strabo's death, and Recitach's assassination, see John of Antioch fr. 211.4 and fr. 214.3. For Theoderic's forces in Italy, see Hannestad (1960). For full discussion, see Heather (1991), 300–3.

65 For references, see notes 22 and 23 above.

66 On Herule numbers in 549: Procopius, *Wars* 7.34.42–3. It is generally tempting to think that the Heruli were smaller than the Amal-led Goths because the latter are portrayed as so victorious in the post-Attilan competition on the Middle Danubian plain. Our only source for this, however, is Jordanes, and it may be that Theoderic's following only acquired superpower status when he added the Thracian Goths to his following.

67 The migration topos entirely suffuses Paul the Deacon's *History of the Lombards*: the brothers Ibor and Agio lead the first move from Scandinavia, Agilmund the second into Bohemia, Godo takes them into Rugiland, Tato fights the Heruli, and Wacho leads the annexation of part of Pannonia. For modern secondary comment, see the works cited in note 27 above.

68 See especially Jarnut (2003), with references, and for the thought – as note 55 above – that early Lombard kings may fundamentally have been expedition leaders; cf. Christie (1995), 14–20.

69 See Curta (2001), 190–204, with his figure 18.

70 On various occasions, groups of Ostrogoths, Heruli, Huns, Rugi, and Lombards all fall into this category of mass migration. Lombard migration may well have taken the form of an initial flow that had to reorganize itself in mass form when

it was necessary to fight the Heruli head-on. In this, it resembles the third-century Goths: see Chapter 3.

71  Vidimer: Jordanes, *Getica* 56.283–4. Procopius, *Wars* 1.8.3 explicitly names Bessas and Godigisclus among the Thracian Goths who didn't follow Theoderic; see Heather (1991), 302 for some other contenders.

72  The Amal-led Goths were receiving 136 kilos of gold per annum in the 460s (Priscus fr. 37), while the Thracian *foederati* pulled in 910 (see note 63 above). On Theoderic and the wealth of Italy, see Heather (1995b).

73  For Hun-generated wealth, see note 31 above. It is possible, however, given their seemingly non-centralized political structures, that the further spread of Lombard groups south of the Danube into old Roman Pannonia may have again taken the form of a variegated flow rather than a single directed movement.

74  *Life of Severinus* 6.6.

75  For references, see note 56 above. Alternatively, it may be , given Theoderic's subsequent success, that they had no real choice in the matter.

76  For markets, see Priscus fr. 46. For other references, see note 23 above.

77  On Theoderic's spell as a hostage, and its ending, see Heather (1991), 264–5. On his mention of Italy in 479, see Malchus fr. 20.

78  Rodulf of the Rani: Jordanes, *Getica* 3.24.

79  For the route of the 473 trek: Jordanes, *Getica* 56.285–6.


## 6. FRANKS AND ANGLO-SAXONS: ELITE TRANSFER OR *VÖLKERWANDERUNG?*

1  Campbell (1982), chapter 2.

2  The old maximalist tradition runs from scholars such as Freeman (1888) to Stenton (1971). It never went unchallenged, but scholars such as Higham (1992) and Halsall (2007), especially 357–68, are representative of the more substantial minimizing tradition of recent years. Recent scholars thinking in terms of large-scale migration include Campbell (1982), Härke (1992), Welch (1992). Hills (2003) is representative of an ultra-minimalist position adopted by some younger archaeologists. A good introduction to the variety of opinion is Ward Perkins (2000).

3  See Woolf (2003).

4  H. R. Loyn, quoted in P. Sawyer (1978). The best introduction to late Roman Britain remains Esmonde-Cleary (1989).

5  For an overview of Anglo-Saxon settlement and the development of place names, see Hooke (1998).

6  See Heather (1994).

7  Esmonde-Cleary (1989) is very balanced on the end of Roman Britain, as is Halsall (2007), 79–81, 357ff. For an introduction to the literature on systems collapse, see amongst others Faulkner (2000); Jones (1996); Higham (1992). Dark (2002) stands against this position.

8 One recent example is Halsall (2007), 519ff., with references to some of the alternatives.

9 For an introduction to such materials, see Dumville (1977).

10 Campbell (1982), chapter 2 provides a clear introduction to the *Chronicle*.

11 For useful introductions to this material, see Campbell (1982), chapter 2; Arnold (1997); Welch (1992).

12 This much is accepted even by such a general anti-migrationist as Halsall (1995b), (2007), 357ff.

13 See e.g. Arnold (1997), 21ff.

14 *Ine's Law* 24.2 (cf. 23.3); cf. Arnold (1997), 26ff., with discussion of Warperton.

15 Compare, for example, Weale et al. (2002) with Thomas et al. (2006). The sample was of men whose pre-Industrial Revolution ancestors can be shown to have been living in the same area as the modern descendant.

16 One other line of thought has therefore taken a more indirect route, attempting to identify and analyse so-called 'epi-genetic' features of the skeletal remains unearthed from the inhumation cemeteries of the fifth to seventh centuries. Such factors reflect the impact of inherited genes rather than diet or environmental factors. The work was able to establish that the element of the population buried with weapons was noticeably taller than those buried without. The argument continues as to whether the height differences should be explained genetically – i.e. as a sign that the weapons-bearers were an intrusive population – or by something else, such as differences in diet, and no firm conclusions have yet emerged: see Härke (1989), (1990).

17 For 446 AD, see Bede, *Ecclesiastical History* 2.14; 5.23, 24 (after Gildas, *Ruin of Britain* 20). For 450 AD, see *The Greater Chronicle*, year of the world 4410; cf. *Anglo-Saxon Chronicle* (449 AD) for the arrival of the Kentish dynastic founders, Hengist and Horsa.

18 Everything is reasonably clear up to about 409, when Zosimus 6.5 records a British revolt. Controversy really begins with Zosimus 6.10, which is traditionally interpreted as Honorius telling the British provincials to look after their own defence, although the text is corrupt. For an introduction to these events and the historiography, see Salway (2001).

19 Gildas, *Ruin of Britain* 23–6.

20 On the Saxon attacks in c.410, see *Gallic Chronicle* of 452 (though this chronicle does not always date events to individual years). For the first datable remains, see Welch (1992), chapter 8. The appendix to Halsall (2007) attempts to extend the generally accepted sequence still further, arguing that Gildas' unnamed tyrant, who issued the invitation, usually thought of as a post-Roman figure, was in fact the usurping Emperor Maximus (383–7), and that it was Maximus who brought the first Saxon mercenaries to Britain. This is not an impossible reading, but neither is it the most obvious, so the jury is still out. The further arguments which Halsall erects on the back of this first hypothesis are unconvincing: see notes 44 and 46 below.

21 Gildas' report that Roman Britain's final appeal to the central imperial authorities came when Aetius was (or had been) consul for the third time (446 or after) might provide some further confirmation that the 440s were a period of

particular disaster. The British leader on the Loire was Riotamus: see *PLRE* 2, 945.

22 See e.g. Campbell (1982), chapter 2; Higham (1994); Halsall (2007), Appendix.

23 See Dumville (1977).

24 Gregory of Tours, *Histories* 4.42; cf. Paul the Deacon, *History of the Lombards* 2.6ff.

25 Bede, *Ecclesiastical History* 1.15 (Angles, Saxons and Jutes); 5.9 (the others).

26 Higham (1992), 180–1.

27 Gregory of Tours, *Histories* 5.26, 10.9; Procopius, *Wars* 8.20.8–10; cf. especially Woolf (2003).

28 Famously, the supposed Gothic migration from Scandinavia is also said to have taken place in three ships: Jordanes, *Getica* 1.25, 17.95.

29 See Chapter 4 above.

30 For Norse DNA evidence, see Chapter 9. For language change, see p. 296 above.

31 Gildas, *Ruin of Britain* 23–6.

32 On the Saxon attack on Gaul: Ammianus 28.5. For introductions to the 'Saxon Shore', see Johnston (1977); Rudkin (1986).

33 On coastal inundation, see the excellent discussion of Halsall (2007), 383ff. On Frankish pressure: Gregory of Tours, *Histories* 4.10, 14.

34 Carausius: *PLRE* 1, 180. On parallel phenomena in the Viking period, see Chapter 9.

35 Gildas, *Ruin of Britain* 20. The archaeological evidence for Pictish and especially Scottish (= Irish) intrusion into western Britain is irrefutable, even if there is little in the way of historical evidence. A good recent account is Charles-Edwards (2003), Introduction and chapter 1.

36 See Woolf (2003), 345f.

37 On the nautical evidence, see Jones (1996), though his discussion includes neither a consideration of Roman ships nor the extended nature of the Anglo-Saxon migration flow. For Goths and the Black Sea, and Vandals and North Africa, see above Chapter 4.

38 For further exploration of these issues, see e.g. Dark (2002); Woolf (2003).

39 See e.g. Higham (1992); Halsall (1995a), (2007), 357ff.

40 An excellent general survey is Hooke (1998).

41 Relevant general surveys include Hooke (1998); Williams (1991). An excellent case study is Baxter (2007), chapter 7. On the demotion of the peasantry, see Faith (1997), chapter 8.

42 For introductions to this issue, see Hooke (1997); Powlesland (1997).

43 See Esmonde-Cleary (1989), 144–54; cf. Loseby (2000) and Halsall (2007), 358f., both with references, on attempts to generate a substantial post-Roman urbanism.

44 On the peasants' revolt, see e.g. Jones (1996); cf. Halsall (2007), 360ff.

45 Constantius, *Life of St Germanus* 13–18, 25–7. For the Romance-speaking elite, see note 3 above. The famous Llandaff charters may provide further confirmation of essential sub-Roman continuity, although this has been disputed: see Davies (1978).

46 'Is simply to dispose . . .': Halsall (1995), 61. This 'before' and 'after' approach to migration is quite common. For another example, see the comments of Higham in Hines (1997), 179, where a reinterpretation of a set of remains – by Hines

(1984) – is praised as 'more complex' because it ejected migration from its usual role in their discussion. See pp. 160 and 192 for two instances where the determination to minimize the importance of migration has led scholars, including Halsall again, to make methodologically problematic choices in their handling of the evidence.

47  There are many parallel examples, but for a recent overview of the decline of Roman structures in the Balkans, see Heather (2007).

48  See the review of the literature in Woolf (2007), 123ff., which draws on, amongst others, Denison (1993) and Hall (1983), which have effectively countered the attempts of Preussler (1956) and Proussa (1990) to detect deeper Celtic influences on Old English. On later medieval cases of language change, see Bartlett (1993), 111ff.

49  See further Chapter 2 above.

50  This emerges with huge clarity from all the literary sources – everything from critiques of individual kings in historical narratives to the value systems underlying heroic poetry. Introductions to the mix of land and cash expected over the course of an individual's lifetime are provided by Charles-Edwards (1989); Campbell (2000), chapter 10.

51  For a general introduction to the pre-Viking great powers, see Campbell (1982), chapters 3–4.

52  See Hooke (1998), chapter 3; Powlesland (1997); Esmonde-Cleary (1989).

53  For weapons burials, see Härke (1989), (1990). For continental parallels, see Chapter 2 above.

54  Ward Perkins (2000).

55  See e.g. Kapelle (1979).

56  Woolf (2007), 127ff.

57  Even the land-grabbing that followed the Norman Conquest was not under William's control, despite his relatively great authority, and the need for clarity as to who now held what was one of the reasons for the great survey that underlay the *Doomsday Book*: *Anglo-Saxon Chronicle* 1085 AD. I would imagine that the land-grabbing process of the fifth and sixth centuries was infinitely more chaotic, given that central authority among the incoming Anglo-Saxons was so much weaker than among the eleventh-century Normans, and that the land-grabbing followed piecemeal in the wake of many small victories rather than a single decisive one like the battle of Hastings.

58  This is also the conclusion of Woolf (2007), as, of course, of all of those writing in the tradition that does not seek to minimize the importance of Anglo-Saxon migration.

59  Julian and the Franks: Ammianus 17.8.3–5. This is an isolated incident, however, and it is therefore impossible to say whether the Franks had the same kind of functioning confederative structure as the Alamanni, although it is certainly possible. For introductions to early Frankish history and archaeology, see Zollner (1970); Perin (1987); James (1988); Ament (1996); Reichmann (1996); R. Kaiser (1997).

60  For materials and commentary on Childeric's grave, see Perin and Kazanski (1996); Halsall (2001).

61  On Childeric's career, see PLRE 2, 285–6, with referencess. The 'Roman' Clovis

has been argued for by Halsall (2001), (2007), 269–71, 303–6. On Gundobad, see *PLRE* 2, 524–5.

62  James (1988) started the controversy, and it has drawn counter-arguments from Perin (1996); MacGeorge (2002).

63  Gregory of Tours, *Histories* 2.40–2.

64  On the dating controversies surrounding Clovis' conversion, see Shanzer and Wood (2002), with more general commentary on his career in Wood (1985); Halsall (2001).

65  On the parallel rise of Theoderic and the Amal family, see Chapter 5.

66  See Halsall (2007), 346f. On the rise of Marseilles, see Loseby (1992), (1998).

67  For a general introduction, see Halsall (2007), 347ff. Halsall (1995a) looks at the re-emergence of the landed basis of real aristocracy in northern Gaul in the seventh century.

68  On the inscriptions at Trier, see Handley (2001), (2003). On Remigius, see Castellanos (2000). On the broader cultural changes, specifically on language, see Haubrichs (1996). On the disruption to ecclesiastical structures, especially bishoprics, across northern France, see Theuws and Hiddinck (1996), 66f.

69  The most recent general surveys are Perin and Feffer (1987), vol. 2; Wieczorek et al. (1997).

70  For introductions to rural settlement, see Van Ossel (1992); Van Ossel and Ouzoulias (2000); Lewitt (1991).

71  Werner (1950); Böhme (1974). The grander of these Frankish officers met with in historical sources are Fraomarius, Erocus, Silvanus, Mallobaudes, Bauto and Arbogast.

72  Halsall (2007), 152–61, with references; the argument was first made in Halsall (1992). Reichmann (1996), 61–4 discusses the funerary habits of Frankish groups before the rise of the Merovingians.

73  On 'tutulus' brooches, see Halsall (2007), 157–9; cf. Böhme (1974). Furthermore, as Halsall observes, even if it were established that the brooches signified Germanic origin, the appearance of weapons would still remain to be explained, since this would then become a 'new' habit adopted on Roman soil.

74  See Chapter 5, and p. 271 above.

75  On the Armorican revolt: Zosimus 6.5. On the 410s: Exsuperantius, *PLRE* 2, 448. On the subsequent history, see MacGeorge (2002).

76  Slightly different views of the phenomenon of Bagaudae have been adopted by Van Dam (1985), 16–20, 25f.; Drinkwater (1989), (1992); Minor (1996), all of whom nevertheless step back from the old Marxist, class-warfare analysis to think instead in terms of local self-help in the face of Roman central control's fragmentation.

77  For policies towards Alamannic overkings, see Chapter 2.

78  For general surveys, see note 69 above.

79  The historiography of the study is discussed by James (1988).

80  Pirling (1966) and Pirling and Siepen (2003) summarize the ongoing investigations.

81  James (1988), 25–8 surveys the tradition, which runs through Werner (1935); Bohner (1958); Perin (1980). Frénouville was the work of Buchet: see James (1988), 110f. For a useful overview, see Perin (1987), 138ff.

82 See p. 311 above.

83 For the 'social-stress' interpretation, see Halsall (2007), 350ff.

84 For the traditional argument, see e.g. Perin (1996) or Wieczorek (1996); for its critique, see Halsall (2007), 269f.

85 For references, see note 69 above.

86 For the ending of cremation in England, see e.g. Welch (1992).

87 For an excellent recent survey, see Haubrichs (1996). For the earlier emergence of structured estates, see Halsall (1995a).

88 I will return to this broader issue in the following chapter.

89 Ammianus 17.8.3–5.

90 See Holt (1987).

## 7. A NEW EUROPE

1 The radical wing on identity and the supposed migration topos is led by Amory (1996), and Kulikowski (2002), (2007), but the germanophone tradition had long been thinking in terms of very fluid group identities: see Wenskus (1961); Wolfram (1988). The idea that the fall of the western Empire was a surprisingly peaceful process is particularly associated with Goffart (1980), (1981), (2006). In a different combination of these trends, Halsall (2007) sees the Empire coming apart from the edges because of its own internal divisions, particularly that between east and west, with barbarian invasion as consequence rather than cause. In various combinations, these ideas have been exercising a huge influence over the scholarship of the last twenty years or so, on which see the excellent Ward Perkins (2005).

2 We have already encountered these examples in Chapters 4, 5 and 6. The idea that the western Empire was actually going to end really only dawned on much of the Roman west after the defeated attempt to conquer North Africa in 468: see Heather (2005), chapter 9.

3 Heather (2005), 375–84.

4 See Chapter 4 above.

5 See Halsall (2007), chapter 7, with Chapter 4 above.

6 By my reckoning, the eleven campaigns comprise: Ad Salices (377); Hadrianople (378); the Macedonian defeat of Theodosius (381); Frigidus (393); the Macedonian campaign (395); Epirus (397); Verona and Pollentia (402); the defeat of Radagaisus (406); the sack of Rome (409/10); the assault of Flavius Constantius (413/15); and the savaging of the Vandals (416–18).

7 See Chapter 5.

8 The same was broadly true, with different date ranges, of the smaller migrant' groups the Suevi and Burgundians. A third stage, where the migrantsí new states engaged in competition with one another, was also carried forward largely by violence, and occasionally generated further migration, such as that of the Visigoths to Spain – see Heather (1996), chapter 9 – but that is beyond the limits of the story being explored here.

9 For further discussion of this model, see Heather (1995). I should note that this account of how the Empire unravelled does not significantly differ from that,

for example, of Goffart (1981), from the point at which barbarian groups were already on Roman soil.

10 See Jones (1964), vol. 3, Appendix III.

11 For more detailed discussion, see Heather (2005), chapter 6.

12 For lowland Britain, see Chapter 6.

13 In the 430s, the Burgundians first suffered a heavy military defeat at the hands of the Huns, and were then resettled on Roman soil: for an introduction, see Favrod (1997).

14 On the creation of these new and larger groups, see pp. 189ff.

15 See Chapter 5 above.

16 On the developing understanding of group identity, see Chapter 1 above.

17 It is well documented that the Goths' motivation for moving in 376 was political and negative. In my view, the same can be deduced with a high degree of probability for the migrants of 405–8, although the lack of explicit evidence means that other views of causation are possible (see above Chapter 5). These other views have no effect on my account of the amount of migration under way in the middle of the first decade of the fifth century.

18 There is no evidence for the Sueves, but the fact that so many other groups moved with women and children must make it a reasonable probability.

19 See Chapter 6.

20 See Chapter 4 note 20 above for the suggestion that the *Historia Augusta*'s description of migrant Goths with large numbers of slaves, which ostensibly relates to the third-century migrations, actually relates to events after 376.

21 The distinction – but simultaneous intersection – between local Roman life and the structures of the state is often missed, but is a deeply important historical phenomenon. Just to give one example, the effects of wrenching the Church out of its Roman context show up vividly in the highly fragmented western Christendom examined in Brown (1996) and Markus (1997).

22 Goffart (1980) made the initial case, responding to the some of the critiques in Goffart (2006), chapter 6, which are well summarized, with much extra value besides, by Halsall (2007), 422–47.

23 Among Theoderic's Ostrogoths in Italy, who are better documented than most other intrusive groups, there is good evidence for the existence of intermediate leaders who stood in between the king and their own personal followings among the rank and file. These leaders would presumably have been responsible for distributions of booty and property which affected their own men. See Heather (1995a).

24 Victor of Vita, *History of the Persecution* 1.13, with Moderan (2002).

25 For an outline of this view, together with the settlement evidence, see Heather (1996), chapter 8. It should be noted in passing that Goffart (2006), chapter 6 has commented that there is no evidence of public rather than private land ever being recycled to barbarians. However, this ignores *Novels of Valentinian* 34, which records that the Roman state precisely compensated displaced landowners from Proconsularis with incomes from publicly owned land.

26 On the Burgundian settlement, see Wood (1990); cf. Halsall (2007), 438ff. on the Visigothic material.

27 For the conflict in Spain, see p. 204 above. For the conquest of North Africa, see Heather (2005), chapter 6.

28 For Ostrogoths, see Chapter 5 above. Wood (1990) gives some thought to the trauma suffered by the Burgundians.

29 To this extent, we are seeing here an extension of third-century patterns, but with the added negative stimulus imparted by the Huns (see Chapter 3).

30 Or, at least, the capacity to create large enough forces, combined with the ability to exploit further movement: see p. 189ff.

31 For the Ostrogoths and the Franks, see pp. 248 and 309 respectively.

32 As we have seen, Priscus' evidence makes it entirely clear that Attila's chief aim in attacking the Roman Empire was to siphon off some of its wealth.

33 'You [Anastasius] are the fairest . . .': Cassiodorus, *Variae* 1.1., trans. Hodgkin (1886); cf. more generally Heather (1996), chapter 8, with full references.

34 See Chapter 2, but note that the third-century migrations had partly collapsed the outer periphery into the inner zone.

35 On Theudebert in particular, see Collins (1983); cf., more generally on the growth of Merovingian power, Wood (1994), chapters 3–4.

36 Justinian's decision to attack in the west was a highly contingent one: see Brown (1971). On the collapse of Theoderic's quasi-imperial edifice, see Heather (1996), 248ff., with Wood (1994), chapters 3–4 on Frankish expansion.

37 As Rome's capacity to conquer most of the known world on the back of its Mediterranean assets makes clear.

38 See Wood (1994), chapters 4 and 10.

39 In my view, this process can broadly be characterized as its transformation from an outright conquest state to something more like a community of provincial communities, built on consent: see Heather (2005), chapters 1 and 3.

40 For a useful outline narrative, see Wood (1994), chapters 13 and 15.

41 For more detailed discussion, especially on the nature of Charles Martel's rule and the strategies used to cement his control, see Wood (1994), chapter 16; Fouracre (2000).

42 Famously, seizing the crown involved an appeal to the Pope, Zacharias, who replied that kingship should reside in the hands of a man wielding real power, not in a figurehead. Less famously, but probably more important at the time, the change of dynasty was also sanctioned by a major Frankish assembly. For a good account, see McKitterick (1983).

43 On all this, see most recently Collins (1998).

44 For an excellent introduction, see Dunbabin (2000).

45 For useful introductions to the Ottonian Empire, see Leyser (1989) and Reuter (1991).

46 See Reuter (1985), (1990).

47 The phenomenon of culture collapse, with its more precise chronology, was identified by Kazimierz Godlowski: see e.g. Godlowski (1970), (1980), (1983). One anomaly within the overall pattern is the so-called 'Olsztyn group'. Established in Mazovia on the south-east shores of the Baltic east of the Vistula, and beyond the long-standing limits of Germanic domination, the material culture of this group is characterized by the presence of some of the traditional

Germanic items and also a fair quantity of Mediterranean imports, both of which date this group firmly to the sixth century. What remains unclear, of course, is whether the remains were deposited by a group of newly arrived Germanic immigrants to the area, or else represent some locals (perhaps Baltic-speakers) who adopted a new kind of material culture. Either way, the group was relatively short-lived, since no Olsztyn remains can be dated to the seventh century: see Barford (2001), 33, with references.

48 See e.g. Koch and Koch (1996); Wieczorek (1996); Hummer (1998).

49 Those Saxons who were never completely conquered by the Merovingians, although brought under Frankish hegemony, insulated the Scandinavian world from any explicit Frankish interference.

50 For primary references, see note 47 above, taken further by Parczewski (1993), 120ff., (1997).

51 Historical sources also provide a possible analogy to explain the Olsztyn group. As we have seen (above, Chapter 5), one fragment of the Heruli, defeated by the Lombards in 508, moved north from the Middle Danube region, eventually establishing themselves in Scandinavia. It is perfectly conceivable, therefore, that other Germanic-speakers, taking a similar option, might have ended up further east.

52 See e.g. Urbanczyk (1997b), (2005).

53 The case of Frankish migrants into northern France also deserves comment, though it is unclear whether these came from the areas that suffered from culture collapse, so I have omitted them from this thought experiment.

54 See above Chapter 4

55 See Batty (2007), 39–42. For Greater Poland, which fell within the areas of the Przeworsk and Wielbark culture collapse, an extensive field-walking and survey-ing project prompts the parallel conclusion that its population density after culture collapse was still around 1 person per square kilometre: see Barford (2001), 89–91 (with references). This again suggests that the departure of half a million people might well be significant, but, representing a maximum one-third of the population, would not have generally emptied the landscape, while many of the more southern areas affected are likely to have had larger populations.

56 See pp. 64ff above.

57 See Chapter 8 above.

58 For a good recent account, see Kennedy (2007).

59 Why the long-established habit of limited warfare between the two empires should have given way to such a mutually destructive conflict thus becomes a central question.

60 This emerges very clearly from Sartre (1982).

61 For useful introductions, see Whittow (1996); Haldon (1990).

62 The great expansion of the tenth century came when the Abbasid Caliphate had fragmented as a political entity, and itself fell apart when the Seljuks restored a measure of Islamic unity in the eleventh.

63 For an introduction, see Kennedy (2004).

64 Not at least since the second century, when formal relations between Vandals and Empire are recorded during the Marcomannic war: see Chapter 2 above.

## 8. THE CREATION OF SLAVIC EUROPE

1 These remains were originally labelled 'Prague' by Borkovsky, who first identified them in what is now the Czech Republic in a study of 1940. On the change of name, see note 9.

2 Especially since much of the third zone of Europe, beyond Rome's outer periphery, had been inhabited by people living this kind of life. Hence it is unsafe to assume the kind of exclusive, one-to-one association between 'the' Slavs and Korchak remains that would have been posited in the old world of culture history (see Chapter 1).

3 The map is after Barford (2001), 326. The collapse of the Iron Curtain has made it possible to discuss these matters with much greater candour. For good introductions in English to the politicized history of Slavic studies, see e.g. Barford (2001), especially the introduction and chapter 13; Curta (2001), chapter 1.

4 Kostrzewski (1969) provides a good summary of his position, drawn up at the end of his highly eventful life. Having studied with Kossinna from 1910, he spent the Second World War in hiding from the Gestapo since his visions of an early, utterly Slavic Poland were considered unacceptable.

5 Shchukin (1975), (1977). In Poland, the work of Godlowski on the Przeworsk system and early Slavic cultures was crucial; its results are most easily accessible to English-speakers through Godlowski (1970). Thanks to the work of him and his pupils, the Wielbark and Przeworsk systems have come to be understood as thoroughly dominated by Germanic-speakers, with earlier archaeological 'proofs' that the latter comprised just a very few migrants from southern Scandinavia being overturned. Godlowski was also responsible for demonstrating how huge an archaeological upheaval separated the Germanic-dominated Poland of the Roman period from the Slavic-dominated Poland of the early Middle Ages.

6 Procopius, *Wars* 8.40.5 mentions that attacks began in the time of Justin. Slavic raids of different kinds feature regularly in Procopius' narrative of Justinian's reign: Curta (2001), chapter 3 offers a good recent analysis.

7 See Barford (2001), 41f.; Curta (2001), 228–46.

8 Jordanes, *Getica* 5.34–5; cf. Tacitus, *Germania* 46.2 (on the Venedi) and 46.4 (on what lay beyond). For further references to the Venedi, see Pliny, *Natural History* 4.97; Ptolemy, *Geography* 3.5.1 and 7.

9 The 'tree argument' was first made by the Polish botanist Rostafinski in 1908: Curta (2001), 7–8. Rusanova published entirely in Russian; for discussion of her work with full references, see Curta (2001), 230ff.

10 See Curta (1999), (2001), especially 39–43 (Jordanes); 230ff. (Rusanova); chapters 3 and 6 (the Slavs' dynamic transformation via contact with eastern Rome).

11 Godlowski (1983); Parczewski (1993), (1997: an English summary); Kazanski (1999), chapter 2; cf. Barford (2001), 41ff. (who remains open-minded).

12 Jordanes, *Getica* 48.247 (Boz and the Antae), with Heather (1989) establishing the chronology (see p. 234 above); 50.265–6 (Hunnic and other settlements on the Danube: see p. 223 above).

13 Dolukhnaov (1996) is good on the background of the long-term development of the simple farming cultures of eastern Europe.

14 For useful introductions to the linguistic evidence, see Birnbaum (1993); Nichols (1998).

15 Procopius, *Wars* 7.29.1–3 (547 AD); 7.38 (548 AD); 7.40 (550 AD). Procopius elsewhere reports that the raids were annual: *Secret History* 18.20; cf. Curta (2001), 75–89.

16 Turris: Procopius, *Wars* 7.14.32–5. On forts more generally, see Curta (2001), 150ff.

17 On the Avars, see e.g. Pohl (1988), (2003); Whitby (1988); with Daim (2003) for an introduction in English to the archaeological materials of the Avar Empire.

18 See Whitby (1988), especially 156ff.

19 On the Persian war, see Chapter 7 above. On the disasters of the 610s: John of Nikiu, *Chronicle* 109; *Miracles of St Demetrius* I.12, 13–15; II.1, 2. The siege of Constantinople is recounted in *Chronicon Paschale* AD a. 626.

20 *Miracles of St Demetrius* II.4, 5. Miracle II.4 names the Runchine, Strymon and Sagoudatae Slavs as attacking Thessalonica at this point; Miracle II.1 adds the names of the Baiounitae and Buzetae. For the transplanting, see Theophanes, *Chronicle* AM 6180 (687/8 AD). Justinian later tried to use them to fight the Arabs, but they changed sides at the crucial moment in the battle of Sebastopol in 692: Theophanes, *Chronicle* AM 6184 (691/2 AD), where the figure of 30,000 appears. For archaeological materials from the north and west Balkans, see Kazanski (1999), 85–6, 137; Barford (2001), 58–62, 67ff.

21 The seven Slavic tribes: Theophanes, *Chronicle* AM 6171 (678/9 AD). For the developing archaeological picture, see Kazanski (1999), 138; Barford (2001), 62ff., with references. For an introduction to the Bulgars, see Gyuzelev (1979).

22 *Miracles of St Demetrius* II.4, with *De Administrando Imperio* 49–50 on Patras. For the archaeology, see Kazanski (1999), 85f., 137; Barford (2001), 67f.; and in particular the correctly critical account of Curta (2001), 233–4, responding in part to overly enthusiastic past attempts to use these materials to 'prove' the *Chronicle of Monemvasia*'s account of an early and massive Slavicization of the Peloponnese: see e.g. Charanis (1950).

23 *De Administrando Imperio* 30 and 31 (respectively Croat and Byzantine versions of the arrival of the Croats); 32 (the Serbs). Samo: Fredegar, *Chronicle* 4.48; cf. 4.72 (on the Bulgars). For further comment, see Pohl (2003). Scholarly opinion divides on how much credence to give the *De Administrando*'s account.

24 For further comment, see Barford (2001), 73–5; Curta (2001), 64–6, with references. An Iranian origin to some of the names recorded of Antae leaders has also been argued for, but the etymologies continue to be contested.

25 For references, see note 21 above.

26 The Geographer's information underlies all accounts of ninth-century Slavic central Europe, and discussion of the preceding centuries is always framed with this outcome in mind. Ninth-century Carolingian diplomatic manoeuvring concentrated on groups within this area: the Elbe Slavs, the Bohemians, and the Moravians.

27 For the tenth century, see Chapter 10. For the Roman era, see Map 1.

28  512 AD: Procopius, *Wars* 6.15.1–2. Hildegesius: Procopius, *Wars* 7.35.16–22; cf. Curta (2001), 82, with full references to other secondary literature, on Slovakia as his likely recruiting ground. Samo: Fredegar, *Chronicle* 4.48, 68.

29  The literature is enormous, but for recent general accounts see Brachmann (1997); Parczewski (1997); Kazanski (1999), 83–96; Barford (2001), 39–44; Brather (2001). These draw on and update such earlier accounts as Donat and Fischer (1994); Szydlowski (1980); Brachmann (1978); Herrmann (1968)

30  On the new wheel-turned potteries, see Barford (2001), 63ff., 76–9, 104–12; Brather (2001); cf. Brather (1996). For the older view of a second migration, see Brachmann (1978), with references.

31  For a general discussion, see Godlowski (1980), (1983), with pp. 371ff above. The departure of the Lombards for Italy in 568 greatly changed the complexion of archaeological patterns in the Middle Danube region.

32  Barford (2001), 53–4, 65–6, with references.

33  For the basic information, see Kobylinski (1997); Barford (2001), 65–7, 76–7. For an introduction to older views, see Herrmann (1983). Sukow-Dziedzice burial customs are not known; they must have have consisted of some archaeologically invisible rite such as surface disposal or cremation of the body without any additional, identifying objects.

34  See Kobylinski (1997).

35  For references, see note 33 above.

36  For useful introductions, see Franklin & Shepard (1996), 71ff.; Goehrke (1992), 34–43.

37  For the linguistic evidence, see note 14 above.

38  For the evidence, see Goehrke (1992), 14–19; Parczewski (1993); Kazanski (1999), 96–120; Barford (2001), 55–6, 82–5, 96–8. The term 'Slavic-dominated' is a carefully chosen formulation to remind the reader that the old assumptions of culture-historical interpretation may be as misleading in the Slavic era as in its Germanic predecessor: see Chapter 1 above.

39  For an outline and further information, see Goehrke (1992), 20–33; Barford (2001), 85–9, 96–9.

40  The different possible answers are nicely defined by two recent books on early Slavic history. Kazanski (1999), especially 120–42, argues that overall similarities in lifestyle between the Prague-Korchak, Penkovka, and Kolochin cultures suggests that if the first two were Slavic, then so was the third. In his view, much of the East European Plain, the territory covered by the Kolochin culture, was already Slavic-speaking in c.500 AD (cf. Map 16). Korchak/Penkovka expansion from the seventh century onwards represented a political but not a linguistic revolution. Barford (2001) would identify the generation of Prague–Korchak itself as a moment of primary Slavicization, when Balts and Slavs really came to distinguish themselves from one another. For him, therefore, the spread north and east of Prague-Korchak in the seventh century, followed by the generation of the Luka Raikovetskaia, Volyntsevo, and Romny-Borshevo traditions, represents not just a political revolution, but the moment when Slavs first came to dominate the landscape, albeit while absorbing much of the indigenous population into their new social structures.

41  The mixed group of 1,600 Huns, Antae and Sclavenes: Procopius, *Wars* 5.27.1; the 3,000 Slavs: Procopius, *Wars* 7.38. Hildegesius: Procopius, *Wars* 7.35.16–22. The 5,000 Slavs at Thessalonica: *Miracles of St Demetrius* I.12.

42  Possibly also consistent with some kind of 'wave of advance' model is the fact that the same names seem to have been used by different Slavic groups who found themselves in very different places at the end of the migration process. The usual explanation adopted for this phenomenon is that originally unified groups split into fragments, which moved in different directions as Slavic migration progressed. Such a process might also explain why Prague-Korchak, Penkovka, and even some Kolochin materials have been found intermixed with one another in the Balkans (see note 40 above). The problem remains, however, that the best-documented examples of multiply appearing names refer to Serbs and Croats, who appear to have been military specialists (see pp. 424–5 above), rather than the small conservative type of social grouping that carried Korchak culture in its complete form across the European landscape.

43  *Strategicon of Maurice* 11.4. Given the relatively small size of the groups in which they operated, this preference presumably reflected a desire for additional protection, rather than an inherent love of difficult terrain. On the Indo-European wave of advance, see Renfrew (1987).

44  For references, see notes 20 and 22 above. The political context also provides good reasons why the Balkan settlements would have been undertaken by larger units. In the case of the Peloponnese, likewise, the named Slavic groups were distinct from a local Greek-speaking population, so, once again, the named units would appear to have been properly Slavic, as opposed to the result of any reorganization among native and immigrant populations.

45  Musocius: Theophylact 6.8.13–6.9.15. Ardagastes: Theophylact 1.7.5, 6.7.1–5, 6.9.1–6. Perigastes: Theophylact 7.4.8 ff. Dabritas: Menander fr.21. The quarrel over the prisoners: Theophylact 6.11.4–21. On the sociopolitical transformation of the Slavs nearest the east Roman frontier, see Curta (2001), especially chapter 7. To keep matters in proportion, a total group population of c.10,000 individuals could not have fielded more than one or two thousand fighting men, and was much smaller – by as much as a factor of ten – than some of the migrant groups attested among the Germani of the Hunnic era (see Chapter 4).

46  For references, see notes 23 and 24 above; for the 5,000 'elite' Slavs at Thessalonica, see note 41 above.

47  For general references, see note 39 above. For Novotroistkoe, see Liapushkin (1958).

48  Maurice, *Strategicon* 11.4.

49  For Bohemia, see Godja (1988); cf., more generally, Kolendo (1997). For pollen studies, see Brachmann (1978), 31–2; Herrmann (1983), 87–9. Discontinuity is also the theme of Henning (1991). On Germanic culture collapse, see also pp. 371ff.

50  Fredegar, *Chronicle* 4.48. On agriculture and its expansion, see Barford (2001), chapter 8, (2005), with full references. Really good information on population expansion is limited to only a few areas, but the field-walking and surveying project in Greater Poland has established that population densities increased from less than 1 person per square kilometre in c.500 AD to 3 per square kilometre by 900 AD, to 7 per square kilometre by 1200 AD: see Barford (2001),

89–91, with references. Indications from agricultural technology tell the same story in qualitative terms. For example, ploughs only came into use at all in the more northerly reaches of the Russian forest zone with the spread of Slavic dominance there in the second half of the first millennium: see Levaskova (1994).

51 For references, see note 33 above.

52 See Halsall (2007), 383ff.

53 On the *Chronicle of Monemvasia*, see Charanis (1950). For Patras and Ragusa, see *De Administrando Imperio* 49–50; cf. (on the Salona evacuation) Whitby (1988), 189–90, with references.

54 See Chapter 4 above.

55 Urbanczyk (1997b), (2005). There is no explicit historical evidence to support this view of an exploited Germanic peasantry, but, as a kind of parallel, highly exploited Roman peasantry certainly sometimes sought refuge in (perhaps relative) tax havens beyond the frontier. One aspect of the Emperor Constantius' activities north of the Danube in 358, as we have seen, was to 'liberate' peasantry who had cleared off north of the frontier: see Chapter 3.

56 Fredegar, *Chronicle* 4.48; cf. Urbanczyk (2002).

57 This might also explain how Slavs came to take over some Germanic river and place names, the island of Rügen and Silesia, for example, seemingly named after the Rugi and the Siling Vandals respectively.

58 See Henning (1991), correcting and exposing the political bias of the DDR era in Herrman (1984), (1985), 33ff.

59 Topirus: Procopius, *Wars* 7.39. The events of 594: Theophylact, 7.2.1–10.

60 This provides an alternative explanation – and a much more convincing one – to the ideologically generated nationalist models of 'submerged' Slavs living under the rule of just a small Germanic-speaking elite.

61 See Chapter 10.

62 For an excellent overview, see Barford (2001), chapters 3–8.

63 'When [Vinitharius] attacked . . .': Jordanes, *Getica* 48.247, with note 12 above.

64 *Chronicon Paschale* (626 AD); cf. the more general accounts of Avar–Slav relations in Whitby (1988), 80ff.; Curta (2001), 90ff.

65 Fredegar, *Chronicle* 4.48.

66 The Mogilany group predates the arrival of the Avars, but they may have given added momentum to the generation of the Sukow-Dziedzice system, although, as we have seen, the internal chronology is as yet too unclear to allow too much emphasis to be given to this point: for references, see note 33 above.

67 For useful introductions to the history and archaeology of the Avar Empire, see Pohl (2003); Daim (2003).

68 See p. 203 above.

69 On Dulcinea, see Curta (2006), 56–7.

70 The Slavs' dugouts: *Chronicon Paschale* (626 AD); *Miracles of St Demetrius* II.1.

71 Buko (2005), chapter 3.

## 9. VIKING DIASPORAS

1 'From Hernar in Norway one should keep sailing west to reach Hvarf in Greenland and then you are sailing north of Shetland, so that it can only be seen if visibility is very good; but south of the Faroes, so that the sea appears halfway up their mountain slopes; but so far south of Iceland that one only becomes aware of birds and whales from it': from the fourteenth-century *Hauksbok*, quoted in Bill (1997), 198.

2 There is a strong tendency from a British perspective to distinguish two ages of major Viking invasion: one in the ninth century, and another right at the end of the tenth and the beginning of the eleventh. The latter, however, was substantially different in character, being organized by a centralized Danish monarchy and involving little in the way of actual migration; it will therefore be considered in Chapter 10.

3 On the logistics of sailing these northern waters, see Crawford (1987), chapter 1.

4 There is an almost infinite bibliography on the Viking raids in the west, but, between them, Nelson (1997), Keynes (1997) and O Corrain (1997) provide an excellent introduction, usefully supplemented by the appropriate chapters in Forte et al. (2005) and Loyn (1995).

5 See Crawford (1987), chapter 4 (place names); 136ff. (types of settlement); cf. Ritchie (1993). Hints of what must have been happening in the north emerge from the action unfolding in Ireland (see following note).

6 See for example the *Chronicle of Ireland* for the years 807, 811, 812 and 813; the record of attacks becomes pretty much annual from 821, suggesting that the assault on Ireland intensified just a little before that on England and the continent. The *Chronicle of Ireland* (848 AD) calls the Viking leader Tomrair a *tanaise rig*, in Irish terms an heir apparent or second in command to a king (Charles-Edwards (2006), vol. 2, 11). He may well have been an 'earl' (Old Norse, *Jarl*), therefore, rather than a 'king': see further below. The action in England and on the continent is well covered in Nelson (1997); Keynes (1997).

7 For further detail, see Nelson (1997); Keynes (1997); Coupland (1995), 190–7.

8 See O Corrain (1997), with the very helpful commentary of Charles-Edwards (2006) in the notes to his translation of the *Chronicle of Ireland*. On the two kings, see the ground-breaking work of Smyth (1977). Something more of the actual death of Reginharius is reported in the *Translatio* of St Germanus: see Nelson (1997).

9 For useful summaries, see Coupland (1995), 197–201; Keynes (1997). The narrative of the *Anglo-Saxon Chronicle* is itself excellent (in early medieval terms!) for these years.

10 On the nature of the Great Armies, see especially Brooks (1979); cf. Smyth (1977). The switching of manpower back and forth between England and the continent can be followed in more detail in Nelson (1997) and Keynes (1997).

11 Studies of Alfred's reforms abound, but Brooks (1979) is an extremely helpful introduction. It can be supplemented in greater detail by e.g. Smyth (1995); Abels (1998). Many of the relevant texts are conveniently collected and translated in Keynes and Lapidge (1983).

12  For further detail, see Nelson (1997); O Corrain (1997).

13  For Brittany, see J. Smith (1992), 196–200; Searle (1988), 29–33. For (somewhat) contrasting introductions to the history of Normandy, see Bates (1982); Searle (1988), especially chapters 5 and 8.

14  For Orkney, see Crawford (1987), 51ff., with Rafnsson (1997) on Iceland and the Atlantic diaspora.

15  For a broad summary, see O Corrain (1997); for a much more detailed, indeed slightly controversial treatment, see Smyth (1979).

16  Various materials have come down to us in excerpts made in the Middle Ages from Ibn Rusteh – see Wiet (1957) – Ibn Jaqub – see Miquel (1966) – and Ibn Fadlan – see Canard (1973); cf. Melnikova (1996), 52–4.

17  For the 'rapids', see *De Administrando Imperio*, chapter 9. For trade treaties, see *Russian Primary Chronicle* (911 and 944 AD). For an introduction to the debate, with full sources, see Franklin and Shepard (1996), 27–50; Melnikova (1996), 47–9; Duczko (2004), 3ff.

18  Ibn Fadlan also makes the Rus sound like Nordic stereotypes: tall and fair, with reddish complexions.

19  *Russian Primary Chronicle* (860–2 AD). For the textual tradition, see the introduction to the translation of Cross and Sherbowitz-Wetzor (1953), with the further thoughts of Franklin and Shepard (1996), 27ff.; Melnikova (1996), chapters 7–8.

20  Noonan (1997) provides an excellent introduction; the comprehensive treatment is now Duczko (2004).

21  Ibn Jaqub, *Relation* (see note 16).

22  *Life of St Anskar* 30. On Ottar, see Lund (1984); cf. Melnikova (1996), 49–52.

23  As we shall see in Chapter 10, there is good reason to suppose that many of the slaves were also being acquired from indigenous intermediaries.

24  Ibn Jaqub, *Relation* (see note 16). For the winter circuit of the Rus in the first half of the tenth century, see *De Administrando Imperio* 9.

25  *Russian Primary Chronicle* (911 and 944 AD); for detailed comment, see Franklin and Shepard (1996), 106ff. and 118ff.: comparison shows, amongst other things, an increase in the numbers of Rus trading with Constantinople.

26  *De Administrando Imperio* 9.

27  For an excellent introduction, see Noonan (1997).

28  On the archaeological evidence for this earliest phase of Scandinavian activity in northern Russia, see Duczko (2004), chapter 2. For the comparison between Constantinople and the Caliphates as potential markets, see Chapter 7.

29  Swedish Vikings: *Annals of St Bertin* AD a 839. (It must be questioned whether this was the first time that the Dnieper route was actually tried.) The death of Sviatoslav: *Russian Primary Chronicle* (972 AD).

30  The relevant boats will presumably have been Slavic 'monoxyla', hollowed from single tree trunks, however, rather than the longships so prominently deployed in the west.

31  On the Abaskos attack and its aftermath, see Franklin and Shepard (1996), 50ff.; Duczko (2004), chapter 1.

32  On the anarchy at Samarra, see Kennedy (2004).

33  On these coin flows, see Noonan (1997).

34 On the archaeological evidence for Scandinavian settlers from this era, see Franklin and Shepard (1996), 91ff.; Duczko (2004), chapters. 3–5.

35 See Franklin and Shepard (1996), chapter 3; Melnikova (1996), 54–60; Duczko (2004), chapter 6.

36 See Likhachev (1970); Melnikova (1996), 105–9.

37 Quoted in O Corrain (1997), 94.

38 See Sawyer (1962).

39 *Chronicle of Ireland* ad a. 848.

40 Healfdan: *Anglo-Saxon Chronicle* (878 AD). The argument for the scale of the Great Armies was made in full by Brooks (1979); cf. Smyth (1977) on their structure, with the identifications of Olaf and Ingvar. (The data has since been accepted by Sawyer.) On the continent, likewise, when the Franks won their great victory at the Dyle, they killed two Viking kings and captured sixteen royal standards.

41 Settlement entries: *Anglo-Saxon Chronicle* (876, 877 and 880 AD). Estimates based on *Doomsday Book* suggest that the total population of England in 1086 was perhaps a million and a half, and the settlements did not affect the whole country.

42 *Anglo-Saxon Chronicle* (896 AD).

43 See Vince (2001); Leahy and Paterson (2001); cf. the more general studies of Hart (1992); and for a good survey of the place-name evidence, with full references, see Fellows-Jenson (2001).

44 See O Corrain (1997), (1998); Smyth (1979).

45 For a useful introduction, see Ritchie (1993), 25–7.

46 *Chronicle of Ireland* (856, 857, 858 AD); cf. O Corrain (1998), 326–7; Charles-Edwards (2006), vol. 2, 4–5.

47 For the DNA evidence, see Helgason et al. (2000), (2001), (2003); Goodacre et al. (2005).

48 For a useful introduction, see Rafnsson (1997).

49 The Great Army: *Anglo-Saxon Chronicle* (892 AD). For the DNA evidence, see note 47. As we have seen in the case of the Anglo-Saxon evidence (Chapter 6), there is a substantial margin for error in reading modern proportions as a direct reflection of those in the past.

50 See note 28 above.

51 And to suggest that the Norse had in fact arrived here before any Slavic immigrants: see note 34 above.

52 For references, see note 35 above.

53 Such commemorative runestones were put up in far larger numbers in the late Viking period: see B. Sawyer (1991).

54 See Wormald (1982).

55 For introductions to post-Viking history in England and Scotland respectively, see Campbell (1982); Broun et al. (1998). Davies (1990), chapter 4 tackles the same issue for Wales.

56 For references, see notes 13 and 14 above.

57 See e.g. P. Sawyer (1982), (1997a); Sawyer and Sawyer (1993), chapter 2, with references.

58 On the dirhems, see Noonan (1997), 145 (and cf. the comments of Arab

travellers on the astonishing silver wealth of Rus merchants: see note 16 above).
On Francia, see Nelson (1997), 37.

59  For the background of the Roman period, see Chapter 2.

60  For useful introductions, see Crawford (1987), chapter 1; Bill (1997); Rafnsson (1997).

61  See Melnikova (1996), 3–18 (for the mixture of practical information, amidst the learned and biblical material, in medieval Scandinavian geography), and 31–44 (for a brilliantly evocative account of the main Russian river routes and their interconnections).

62  The Anglo-Saxon expansion into England nevertheless bears some comparison: see Chapter 6.

63  Asser Saxe: Aarhus runestone no. 6; cf. Roesdahl (1991), 58. *Sodalitates*: *Annals of St Bertin* (862 AD); cf. Nelson (1997), 36.

64  For Asser Saxe, see previous note. On ship types, see Bill (1997). For *monoxyla*, see note 26 above; cf. Melnikova (1996), 33. Because of the rapids, shallows and sandbanks of the River Volkhov, ships had to be changed for rivercraft precisely at Ladoga.

65  For a useful introduction, see Bill (1997).

66  For an excellent recent survey, see Wickham (2005), 680–90, 809–11, with full references to the excavations, most of which have happened within the last scholarly generation.

67  'Emporia' were centres of movable wealth, so it is at least possible that initial accident turned into eventual design here; that would certainly be my best guess.

68  See Wormald (1982). For an introduction to this 'first' Danish state, see Roesdahl (1982), especially chapters 5 and 8; Hedeager (1992); Lund (1995), 202–12.

69  Anoundas: *Life of St Anskar* 19. Reginharius: see note 8 above.

70  This phenomenon has generated the concept of 'New Medievalism' in international-relations theory, a conceptualization of the fact that Third World states in particular find that they have in practice no monopoly of power or authority within their notional territorial space. For an introduction to these debates, see Friedrichs (2004), chapter 7.


## 10. THE FIRST EUROPEAN UNION

1  Thietmar, *Chronicle* 4.45–6.

2  The classic treatment in English of all three of these kingdoms remains Dvornik (1949); cf. Dvornik (1956). The available literature is now immense, and the references below are largely restricted to those written in western European languages, in which most of the main players in the Slavic world have anyway always tended (and now increasingly tend) to write, at least at regular intervals. Important supplements to Dvornik are provided, firstly, by useful general works such as Barford (2001); Curta (2006); and, secondly, by collections of papers dealing with a range of Slavic states: Manteuffel and Gieysztor (1968); Settimane (1983); Brachmann (1995); Urbancyzk (1997a), (2001); Curta (2005); Garipzanov et al. (2008). Then, thirdly, there are the studies devoted to individual kingdoms,

as follows. Poland: Manteuffel (1982); Urbancyzk (2004). Bohemia: Wegener (1959); Graus and Ludat (1967); Turek (1974); Sasse (1982); Prinz (1984); Godja (1988), (1991). Moravia: Dittrich (1962); Bosl (1966); Graus and Dostál (1966); Poulik et al. (1986); Bowlus (1995); M. Eggers (1995). These works provide the basis of my understanding of state formation in eastern Europe in the late first millennium; I will only footnote very specific points in the rest of this chapter, but this literature will always be implicit.

3 Dvornik was well aware of this point, although he did not treat Denmark in the same detail as his Slavic kingdoms. Papers relevant to Scandinavian state formation appear in some of the secondary sources listed in the previous note. In addition, the following studies, from an immense literature, of the early Danish state's emergence from the Viking period, are particularly useful: Randsborg (1980); Roesdahl (1982); Hedeager (1992); Sawyer and Sawyer (1993); Rumble (1994); Lund (1997).

4 Dvornik treated the history of the first Rus state in some detail (see note 2 above, with the supplementary works detailed there). For further information, see e.g. Kaiser and Marker (1994); Franklin and Shepard (1996); Melnikova (1996); Duczko (2004); cf., on legal structures, D. Kaiser (1980), (1992).

5 The first homegrown historian of the Danish state, Saxo Grammaticus, worked about seventy-five years later than his Slavic counterparts.

6 For an introduction to the new cultural patterns of the Carolingian era and beyond, see McKitterick (1989), (1994).

7 For a useful commentary on Thietmar's *Chronicle*, see Schröder (1977). Dvornik was immensely interested in the conversion of these states to Christianity: with the works cited in note 2 above, see especially Dvornik (1969). Many of the studies cited in notes 2–4 deal with Slavic conversion, but useful additional information and analysis can be found in e.g. Wolfram (1979), (1995); Kantor (1990); Urbancyzk (1997b); Wood (2001).

8 In addition to the studies cited in note 3 above, there are several useful papers in Scragg (1991) and Cooper (1993), especially those of Sawyer (1993) and Lund (1993). See, too, in Rumble (1994), the papers of Sawyer (1994) and Lund (1994). The rehabilitation of the reputation of Aethelred – see e.g. Keynes (1987) – only emphasizes the military capacity of the Danish monarchy.

9 On the fortifications of Dux Rastiz of Moravia: *Annals of Fulda* 869 (cf. ibid 855). For Slavic and Danish fortifications, see notes 2–4 above, but particularly helpful are Kurnatowska (1997a); Dulinicz (1997); Petrov (2005). For the Alamanni, see Chapter 2. Admittedly, the political unity of the Tervingi collapsed when their leader induced them to build fortifications, but only when they were simultaneously faced with Hunnic assault: Ammianus 31.3.8, and see Chapter 4 above.

10 See Ibn Fadlan, *Relation*, with Thietmar, *Chronicle* 4.46 (quoted on p. 515). Polish forces in 1003: Thietmar, *Chronicle* 5.36–7. For other sources of revenue, see pp. 563ff above.

11 One Byzantine source reports that the Rus force assisting Basil II numbered 6,000 men: Franklin and Shepard (1996), 161–3. Territorial contingents: *Russian Primary Chronicle* (1015 AD, 1068 AD). Retinues appear regularly in the Bohemian sources translated by Kantor (1990).

12 *Encomium of Queen Emma* II.4. Lund (1986), (1993) argues firmly for a solely

mercenary army, but the descriptions in the *Encomium* sound more like a mixed force, and it is worth noting that the much less powerful earls of Orkney had imposed carefully defined military obligations on their populations from an early date: Crawford (1987), 86–91. I think it is in the nature of the Danish state, as with its Slavic peers, that there are likely to have been substantial differences between separate parts of the kingdom: see pp. 526ff above.

13 On the Tithe Church, see Franklin and Shephard (1996), 164–5. For other references, see notes 2–4 above, with Kurnatowska (1997a); Shepard (2005); Font (2005).

14 For Danish transport infrastructure, see Randsborg (1980), 75ff.; Roesdahl (1982), chapter 3.

15 For an introduction, see Dvornik (1949), 105–10, with Appendix 5, though the details of the territories it defines are much disputed.

16 On Moravia and Bohemia, see Jirecek (1867) and Friedrich (1907) for some of the texts, with Kantor (1983). (1990) for commentary. On Russia, see D. Kaiser (1980), (1992).

17 The pattern does not apply to Moravia, however, whose capacity to operate as state centre was destroyed by the rise of Magyar power in the 890s, after which it became one of the territories to be swapped.

18 For a more detailed narrative in English, see Dvornik (1949). Randsborg (1980), 75ff. is excellent on the principles on itineration. For Bohemian documents, see note 16 above. For excellent commentaries on the Polish information, see Lowmianski (1960); Gorecki (1992).

19 *Russian Primary Chronicle* (945–55 AD).

20 See e.g. Roesdahl (1982), 147–55. One-quarter of the buildings in Fyrkat were residential, for instance, and one-third for storage.

21 Sobibor would later die in Prague in 1004 fighting the expelled Premyslid Jaromir, having returned to Prague with a Polish army: Thietmar, *Chronicle* 6.12. For a general account, see Urbanczyk (1997c).

22 *Annals of Fulda* (845, 872, 895 AD), with secondary references as note 2 above.

23 For commentaries, see Wolfram (1995); cf. the different geographical reconstructions of Bowlus (1995); M. Eggers (1995). Wherever it is placed, however, the basic political process stays the same.

24 The traditional picture was of 30 small 'tribes' in the seventh century, eventually evolving into 8 greater ones, according to Marxist principles, in the ninth. This was mostly guesswork based on extrapolation from the *Anonymous Bavarian Geographer*, which didn't cover lands beyond the Oder (see Chapter 8), and by analogy with Bohemia: cf. Barford (2001), chapter 12. The pattern may not be so far from the historical reality, except that we must reckon with a much more violent finale: see especially Kurnatowska (1997a); Dulinicz (1994), (1997).

25 On the emergence of the Rus state, see Franklin and Shepard (1996), chapter 3.

26 *Russian Primary Chronicle* (974 AD: Sveinald); 978 AD: Rogvolod/Ragnvaldr and Tury; 993 AD: the concubines).

27 For fuller discussion of the Jelling dynasty, see references in note 3 above. On the fate of the ninth-century state, see p. 511 above.

28 On the kings associated with the ninth-century Great Armies, see Chapter 9. For more detail on tenth-century patterns, see the literature cited in note 3 above.

29  For general references, see previous note. For the 'mark' in Denmark, see Lund (1984), 21–2; cf. Lund (1997).

30  See Chapter 8 above, with Curta (2001), chapter 7.

31  Miesco: Ibn Jaqub. Bohemia: *Annals of Fulda* (845 AD), with the texts translated in Kantor (1990). Moravia: *Annals of Fulda* (894 AD). Russia: Ibn Fadlan, *Relation*; *Russian Primary Chronicle* (945–6 AD). The fourth-century Germani: see Chapter 2 above. The sixth-century Slavs: Curta (2001), chapter 7.

32  For further discussion, see Chapter 8, and Chapter 1 (on the early Germanic world).

33  For fuller discussions, see the literature cited in notes 2–4 above. On the Germanic world, see pp. 64ff above.

34  For post-Avar leaders, see the literature cited in note 23 above. Wiztrach and his son ruled their own *civitas* in Bohemia: see *Annals of Fulda* (857 AD). On Moravia, see the studies cited in note 2 above. For excellent introductions to the changing patterns of hillforts, see Godja (1991), chapter 3; Kurnatowska (1997a), with full references. Nothing similar has been found in the early Slavic world to the Runder Berg and other *Herrenhöfe* of the leaders of the fourth-century Alamanni: see Chapter 2.

35  See, in particular, Roesdahl (1982); Hedeager (1992); Sawyer and Sawyer (1993).

36  For pollen, see Donat (1983); cf. Barford (2001), 153–9, both with full references.

37  In addition to the literature cited in note 2 above, see most recently, on agricultural expansion, Henning (2005); Barford (2005). These studies show that full manorialization followed rather than preceded state formation (as Marxist orthodoxy required). Agricultural expansion did, however, take other forms between the sixth and tenth centuries.

38  For the reasons we have previously encountered, the availability of food is one of the most basic limiting factors on possible population sizes.

39  For similar processes among the Germani, see Chapter 2.

40  Hedeby: *Royal Frankish Annals* (808 AD), with Roesdahl (1982), 70–6. Prague: Ibn Rusteh. Kiev: *De Administrando Imperio*, chapter 9; cf. Thietmar, *Chronicle* 8.2. Poland's participation in these networks is clear from the silver dirham distribution map: see Map 16.

41  *Russian Primary Chronicle* (911 and 945 AD). As far back as 808, Godfrid had moved the merchants to Hedeby because he wanted the toll revenue: see previous note.

42  For literature on the destruction of tribal castles, see note 24 above. On Vladimir's transfers, see *Russian Primary Chronicle* (1000 AD). On service villages and the organization of the heartlands of Bohemia and Poland, see respectively Godja (1991), chapters 3–4; Kurnatowska (1997a).

43  Oleg's army: *Russian Primary Chronicle* (880–2 AD). Sviatoslav: *Russian Primary Chronicle* (971–2 AD). For Vladimir, see previous note, with general commentary in Franklin and Shepard (1996), chapter 4.

44  For an introduction, see Bartlett (1993), chapter 5. A top estimate is that some 200,000 German peasants were eventually attracted east of the Elbe by the excellent terms on offer.

45  On Carolingian expansion and its structural importance, see Reuter (1985), (1990).

46  On the feuds, see Leyser (1989). On the burgwards, see Reuter (1991).

47  For an introduction to the Elbe Slavs, and a convenient collection of the relevant materials, see Lübke (1984–88), with Lübke (1994), (1997) for further analysis.

48  Dvornik (1949) provides a useful narrative. For the Northern Crusades, see e.g. Christiansen (1980).

49  Gero: Widukind of Corvey 2.20, with Heather (1997) more generally on the Abodrites. Zwentibald: *Annals of Fulda* (870–2 AD).

50  On the Christianization of Moravia, see the references in note 2. Werinhar's mutilation: *Annals of Fulda* (882 AD). Violence and plunder are regular features in all the warfare of this period, as recorded in Thietmar's *Chronicle*, the *Russian Primary Chronicle*, Adam of Bremen's *History of the Bishops of Hamburg* and Helmold's *Chronicle of the Slavs*, the two latter both having much to report on the plunderings and wars between the Empire and the Elbe Slavs.

51  On Saxon military evolution, see Leyser (1982), essays 1 and 2. For the Capitulary of Thionville, see Boretius (1883), 44.7.

52  *Miracles of St Demetrius* II.5; cf. the swift appearance of powerful leaders such as Liudewit: for references, see note 23 above.

53  For further discussion, and references, see Chapter 9.

54  On the slave raids of the Rus and Western Slavs: Ibn Jaqub; cf. McCormick (2001), on the general importance of these new connections.

55  Ibn Fadlan, *Relation*; cf. *Russian Primary Chronicle* (993 AD), on Vladimir. If the trade was essentially in women, the Rus presumably had to carry their own boats round the Dnieper rapids, but this may just be the literature of shock. Certainly the western slave trades – overland and by sea – involved males as well as females; cf. Verlinden (1955), the source of the map in question.

56  For introductory references, see note 7 above. The same tendency of trying to avoid taking your Christianity from a near imperial neighbour is also visible in the case of the Bulgarians, who did the same, trying to avoid a Byzantine connection: see e.g. Browning (1975), for an introduction. The Bulgarians equally failed to avoid the imperial connection, but, like the Poles, were eventually granted their own archbishop.

57  The availability of Bede's extraordinary narrative and a host of other sources from the early conversion period in England means that the Anglo-Saxon case study has often been a vehicle for exploring these ideas. For an excellent introduction, see Mayr Harting (1972); cf. Mayr-Harting (1994) for a comparison with Bulgaria.

58  There is little sign that conversion to Christianity changed the nature of immediate political competition in the Slavic context, any more than it did in the Anglo-Saxon, on which see the wonderful paper of Wormald (1978). On the administrative front, the last of the Anglo-Saxon kingdoms was brought to Christianity in 681, when Wessex conquered the Isle of Wight, but the beginnings of an administrative system that was working convincingly via literacy are, to my mind, visible only two or three generations later, and it is really only in the ninth and tenth centuries that the evidence multiplies.

59  Carolingian imperial rule had established tithing as a norm from the later eighth century: see McKitterick (1977). This made the later Slavic conversions different examples, like that of the Anglo-Saxons, where religious taxation was not yet so firmly established.

60  For the Tervingi, see Chapter 2. For the 983 revolt, see Reuter (1991); Lübke (1994), commenting particularly on the narrative of Thietmar, *Chronicle* 3.17ff. The *Russian Primary Chronicle* is the basic source of information on the Russian case, upon which Shepard (2005), with full references to the earlier literature, provides an excellent recent treatment.

61  Vladimir: *Russian Primary Chronicle* (978–80 AD); with Shepard (2005) for commentary. For the Elbe Slavs, see the references in note 47 above.

62  For an introduction to the concept of 'peer polity interaction', and some case studies, see Renfrew and Cherry (1986).

63  For a detailed discussion of coin flows, see Noonan (1997), (1998).

64  For comparative case studies, both ancient and modern, see Gottmann (1980); Rowlands et al. (1987); Bilde et al. (1993); Champion (1995). It is extremely important, however, to factor in a generalized concept of agency: cf. Wilson (2008).


## 11. THE END OF MIGRATION AND THE BIRTH OF EUROPE

1  *Annals of Fulda* (900 AD).

2  See Faith (1997) on the extent to which the Normans rewrote the rules by which peasant life was governed.

3  See in particular Chapters 6 and 9.

4  As we saw in Chapter 6, the 50–75 per cent spread of possibly 'Anglo-Saxon' Y chromosomes recorded in samples of the modern English population can be accounted for by an invading group that was anywhere between 50–75 per cent of the fifth-/sixth-century population, or only 10 per cent if you give them even a marginal breeding advantage.

5  These key cases reported by Ammianus and Procopius are explored in detail in Chapters 4 and 5.

6  In these cases, the evidence is currently not good that the groups actually crossed the frontier, but reliable contemporaries describe at least their subsequent moves, to Spain and North Africa respectively, and to join Alaric, in precisely such terms.

7  The Gothic and Lombard migration flows are discussed in Chapters 3 and 5.

8  The ideas set out here, and through earlier chapters, are discussed in more detail in Heather (2008a).

9  For Anglo-Saxon return migration, see Chapter 6 above.

10  Autumn 376, although this has been challenged, is also the likeliest time for the move of the Gothic Tervingi: see Heather (2005), 153.

11  This presumably limited the amount of fundamental social (as opposed to political) change that was generated by the flows of new wealth into Scandinavia, since the wealth was bound initially to fall largely into the hands of those who where already reasonably wealthy.

12 And possibly also by non-militarized slaves: see Chapter 4 above.

13 Of course, Jordanes' migration topos gave more than an excuse to do so: see Chapter 3.

14 The one successor state not founded by a new coalition created on the march was that of the Burgundians, but there is a crucial lack of narrative evidence to help us understand fifth-century Burgundian history, which was certainly traumatic.

15 Hunnic imperial history confirms the point, since the huge supraregional power created by Attila and his predecessors was entirely dependent upon large-scale flows of Mediterranean wealth for its continued existence: see Chapter 5.

16 Just one surviving vignette illustrates Gotho-Slav interaction: Jordanes, *Getica* 48.247, with p. 234 above.

17 The sources suggest, however, that some Slavic groups had already developed a considerable degree of political and military organization on the back of the new wealth flows of the sixth century: see Chapter 8.

18 Bartlett (1993), especially chapters 2 and 5, provides an excellent introduction to these new patterns.

19 Tacitus, *Germania* 46.4.

# PRIMARY SOURCES

Following normal conventions, specific editions and translations of standard classical works are not listed in the bibliography, though all those works cited in this book appear below, and most are translated in either or both of the Loeb and Penguin Classics series. All Christian authors are available, if sometimes in outdated form, in *Patrologia Latina* or *Patrologia Graeca* editions. More recent (sometimes competing) editions of most of the texts cited in the introductions and notes can be found in *GCS* (*Die Griechischen Christlichen Schriftsteller der ersten Jahrhunderte*), CSEL (*Corpus Scriptorum Ecclesiasticorum Latinorum*), CC (*Corpus Christianorum*), and SC (*Sources Chrétiennes*). Many are translated in the *Nicene and Post-Nicene Fathers*, and *Library of the Fathers* collections. Otherwise, the following editions and translations of late Roman and early medieval sources have been used.

Adam of Bremen, *History of the Bishops of Hamburg*, ed. Schmeidler (1917); trans. Tschan (1959)

Agathias, *History*, ed. Keydell (1967); trans. Frendo (1975)

Ammianus Marcellinus, ed. and trans. Rolfe (1935–39)

*Anglo-Saxon Chronicle*, ed. and trans. Whitelock et al. (1961)

*Annals of Fulda*, ed. Pertz and Kurze (1891); trans. Reuter (1992)

*Annals of St Bertin*, ed. Waitz (1883); trans. Nelson (1991)

*Anonymous Bavarian Geographer*, ed. Bielowski (1946)

*Anonymous Valesianus*, ed. and trans. in Rolfe (1935–39), vol. 3

Aurelius Victor, *Caesars*, ed. Pichlmayr (1911); trans. Bird (1994)

Bede, *Ecclesiastical History*, ed. and trans. Colgrave and Mynors (1969)

Caesar, *Gallic War*

Cassiodorus, *Variae*, ed. Mommsen (1894b); trans. Hodgkin (1886); Barnish (1992)

*Chronicle of Ireland*, trans. Charles-Edwards (2006)

*Chronicle of Monemvasia*, ed. and trans. Charanis (1950)

*Chronicon Paschale*, ed. Dindorf (1832); trans. Whitby and Whitby (1989)

Claudian, *Works*, ed. and trans. Platnauer (1922)

*Codex Theodosianus*, ed. Mommsen and Kreuger (1905); trans. Pharr (1952)

Constantius, *Life of St Germanus*, ed. Noble and Head (1995), 75–106

*Consularia Constantinopolitana*, ed. Mommsen (1892)

Cosmas of Prague, *Chronicle of Bohemia*, ed. Bretholz and Weinberger (1923)

*Crith Gablach*: ed. Binchy (1970).

*De Administrando Imperio*, ed. and trans. Moravcsik and Jenkins (1967)

Dio Cassius, *Roman History*, ed. and trans. Cary (1914–27)

*Encomium of Queen Emma*, ed. and trans. Campbell (1949)

Ennodius, *Works*, ed. Vogel (1885)

Eugippius, *Life of Severinus*, ed. Noll and Vetter (1963); trans. Bieler (1965)

Eunapius, *Histories*, ed. and trans. Blockley (1982)

Eutropius, *Breviarium*, ed. Santini (1979); trans. Bird (1993)

Fredegar, *Chronicle*, ed. and trans. Wallace-Hadrill (1960)

*Gallic Chronicle of 452*, ed. Mommsen (1892)

Gallus Anonymous, *Chronicle*, ed. Maleczynski (1952); trans. Knoll and Schaer (2003)

Gildas, *Ruin of Britain*, ed. and trans. Winterbottom (1978)

Gregory of Tours, *Histories*, ed. Krusch and Levison (1951); trans. Thorpe (1974)

Helmold, *Chronicle of the Slavs*, ed. Lappenberg and Schmeidler (1909); trans. Tschan (1966)

Herodotus, *Histories*

*Historia Augusta*, ed. and trans. Magie (1932)

Hydatius, *Chronicle*, ed. Mommsen (1894); trans. Burgess (1993)

Ibn Fadlan, ed. and trans. Canard (1973)

Ibn Jaqub, ed. and trans. Miquel (1966)

Ibn Rusteh, ed. and trans. Wiet (1957)

Jerome, *Chronicle*: an online edition and English translation may be found at http://www.tertullian.org./fathers/jerome_chronicle_oo_eintro.htm

John of Antioch, ed. Mueller (1851–70); trans. Gordon (1966)

John of Nikiu, *Chronicle*, trans. Charles (1916) (from the Ethiopian)

Jordanes, *Romana* and *Getica*, ed. Mommsen (1882); *Getica*, trans. Mierow (1915)

*Laws of Ine*, ed. Liebermann (1903–16); trans. Whitelock (1955)

*Life of Anskar*, ed. Trillmich et al. (1978); trans. Robinson (1921)

Malchus, ed. and trans. Blockley (1982)

Menander Protector, ed. and trans. Blockley (1985)

*Miracles of St Demetrius*, ed. Lemerle (1979–81)

*Notitia Dignitatum*, ed. Seeck (1962)

*Novels of Valentinian III*, ed. Mommsen and Kreuger (1905); trans. Pharr (1952)

*Origo Gentis Langobardorum*: see Paul the Deacon.

*Olympiodorus of Thebes*, ed. and trans. Blockley (1982)

Orosius, *Against the Pagans*, ed. Arnaud-Lindet (1990–91); trans. Defarri (1964)

*Panegyrici Latini*, ed. and trans. Nixon and Rogers (1994)

*Passion of St Saba*, ed. Delehaye (1912); trans. Heather and Matthews (1991)

Paul the Deacon, *History of the Lombards*, ed. Bethmann and Waitz (1878); trans. Foulke (1974)

Paulinus of Pella, *Eucharisticon*, ed. and trans. Evelyn White (1961), vol. 2

Peter the Patrician, ed. Mueller (1851–70)

Pliny, *Natural History*

Priscus, ed. and trans. Blockley (1982)

Procopius, *Works*, ed. and trans. Dewing (1914–40)

Prosper Tiro, *Chronicle*, ed. Mommsen (1892)

Ptolemy, *Geography*

*Royal Frankish Annals*, ed. Kurze (1895); trans. Scholz (1972)

*Russian Primary Chronicle*, trans. Cross and Sherbowitz-Wetzor (1953)

Saxo Grammaticus, *History of the Danes*, ed. Knabe et al. (1931–57); trans. Fisher (1996) (Books I–IX); Christiansen (1980–81) (Books X–XVI)

Socrates, *Historia Ecclesiastica*, ed. Hansen (1995); trans. in *Nicene and Post-Nicene Fathers*, vol. 2

Sozomen, *Historia Ecclesiastica*, ed. Bidez and Hansen (1995); trans. in *Nicene and Post-Nicene Fathers*, vol. 2

Strabo, *Geography*

*Strategicon of Maurice*, ed. Dennis (1981); trans. Dennis (1984)

Synesius of Cyrene, ed. Garzya (1989)

Tacitus, *Annals*; *Histories*; *Germania*

Themistius, *Orations*, ed. Schenkl et al. (1965–74); trans. Heather and Matthews (1991) (*Orations* 8 and 10); Heather & Moncur (2001) (*Orations* 14–16 and 34)

Theodoret, *Historia Ecclesiastica*, ed. Parmentier and Hansen (1998); trans. in *Nicene and Post-Nicene Fathers*, vol. 3

Theophanes, *Chronographia*, ed. Niebuhr (1839–41); trans. Mango and Scott (1997)

Theophylact Simocatta, *History*, ed. De Boor and Wirth (1972); trans. Whitby and Whitby (1986)

Thietmar of Merseburg, *Chronicle*, ed. Holtzmann (1935); trans. Warner (2001)

Victor of Vita, *History of the Persecution in Africa*, ed. Petschenig (1881); trans. Moorhead (1992)

Widukind of Corvey, ed. Lohmann and Hirsch (1935)

Zonaras, *Chronicle*, ed. Weber (1897)

Zosimus, *History*, ed. Paschoud (1971–89); trans. Ridley (1982)

# BIBLIOGRAPHY

Abels, R. (1998). *Alfred the Great: War, Kingship and Culture in Anglo-Saxon England* (London)

Achelis, H. (1900). 'Der älteste deutsche Kalender', *Zeitschrift für die neutestamentliche Wissenschaft* 1, 308–35

Adamson, S. et al., eds. (1990) *Papers from the 5th International Conference on English Historical Linguistics* (Amsterdam)

Agadshanow, S. G. (1994). *Der Staat der Seldschukiden und Mittelasien im 11.–12. Jahrhundert* (Berlin)

Ament, H. (1996). 'Frühe Funde und archäologische Erforschung der Franken in Rheinland', in *Die Franken: Wegbereiter Europas: vor 1500 Jahren, König Chlodwig und seine Erben* (Mainz), 22–34

Amory, P. (1997). *People and Identity in Ostrogothic Italy, 489–554* (Cambridge)

Anderson, B. (1991). *Imagined Communities: Reflections on the Origin and Spread of Nationalism* (London)

Anokhin, V. A. (1980). *The Coinage of Chersonesus* (Oxford)

Antony, D. W. (1990). 'Migration in Archaeology: the Baby and the Bathwater', *American Anthropologist* 92, 895–914

————— (1992). 'The Bath Refilled: Migration in Archaeology Again', *American Anthropologist* 94, 174–6

Arnaud-Lindet, M-P., ed. and trans. (1990–91). *Orose: Histoires contre les païens* (Paris)

Arnold, C. J. (1997). *An Archaeology of the Early Anglo-Saxon Kingdoms*, 2nd ed. (London)

Arnold, E. (1973). *The Kingdom of the Scots: Government, Church and Society from the Eleventh to the Fourteenth Century* (London)

Bacall, A. (1991). *Ethnicity in the Social Sciences: A View and a Review of the Literature on Ethnicity* (Coventry)

Bachrach, B. S. (1973). *The Alans in the West* (Minneapolis)

Bailyn, B. (1994). 'Europeans on the Move, 1500–1800', in Canny (1994), 1–5

Bakony, K. (1999). 'Hungary', in Reuter (1999), 536–52

Barford, P. (2001). *The Early Slavs* (London)

————— (2005). 'Silent Centuries: The Society and Economy of the Northwestern Slavs', in Curta (2005), 60–102

Barnes, T. D. (1998). *Ammianus Marcellinus and the Representation of Historical Reality* (Ithaca; London)

Barnish, S. J. B. (1992). *The Variae of Magnus Aurelius Cassiodorus Senator* (Liverpool)

Barrett, J. C. et al., eds. (1989). *Barbarians and Romans in North-west Europe from the Later Republic to Late Antiquity* (Oxford)

Barrow, G. W. S. (1973). *The Kingdom of the Scots: Government, Church and Society from the Eleventh to the Fourteenth Century* (London)

Barth, F., ed. (1969). *Ethnic Groups and Boundaries: The Social Organization of Ethnic Difference* (Boston)

Bartlett, R. (1993). *The Making of Europe: Conquest, Colonization and Cultural Change 950–1350* (London)

Bassett, S., ed. (1989). *The Origins of Anglo-Saxon Kingdoms* (London)

Bates, D. (1982). *Normandy before 1066* (London)

Batty, R. (2007). *Rome and the Nomads: The Pontic-Danubian Realm in Antiquity* (Oxford)

Baxter, S. (2007). *The Earls of Mercia: Lordship and Power in late Anglo-Saxon England* (Oxford)

Bentley, G. C. (1987). 'Ethnicity and Practice', *Comparative Studies in Society and History* 29, 25–55.

Bethmann, L. and Waitz, G., eds. (1878). *Pauli Historia Langobardorum*, Monumenta Germaniae Historica: Scriptores rerum Germanicarum (Hanover)

Bichir, G. (1976). *The Archaeology and History of the Carpi* (Oxford)

Bidez, J. and Hansen, G. C., eds. (1995). *Sozomenus Kirchengeschichte* (Berlin)

Bieler, L. (1965). *Eugippius: The Life of Saint Severinus* (Washington)

Bielowski, A., ed. (1946). *Descriptio civitatum et regionum ad septentrionalem plagam Danubii*, Monumenta Poloniae Historica 1, 10–11

Bierbrauer, V. (1980). 'Zur chronologischen, soziologischen und regionalen Gliederung des ostgermanischen Fundstoffs des 5. Jahrhunderts in Sudosteuropa', in Wolfram and Daim (1980), 131–42

——— (1989). 'Ostgermanische Oberschichtsgräber der römischen Kaiserzeit und des frühen Mittelalters', in *Peregrinatio Gothica 2, Archaeologia Baltica* 8 (Lodz), 40–106

Bilde, P. et al. (1993). *Centre and Periphery in the Hellenistic World* (Aarhus)

Bill, J. (1997). 'The Ships', in P. Sawyer (1997a), 182–201

Binchy, D. A. (1970a). *Celtic and Anglo-Saxon Kingship: the O'Donnell Lectures for 1967–8 delivered in the University of Oxford on 23 and 24 May 1968* (Oxford)

———, ed. (1970b). *Crith gablach* (Dublin)

Bird, H. W. (1993). *Eutropius Breviarium* (Liverpool)

——— (1994). *Liber de Caesaribus of Sextus Aurelius Victor* (Liverpool)

Birley, A. R. (1966). *Marcus Aurelius* (London)

——— (2005). *The Roman Government of Britain* (Oxford)

Birnbaum, H. (1993). 'On the Ethnogenesis and Protohome of the Slavs: the Linguistic evidence', *Journal of Slavic Linguistics* 1.2, 352–74

Blair, J. (1994). *Anglo-Saxon Oxfordshire* (Oxford)

Blench, R. and Spriggs, M., eds. (1998). *Archaeology and Language II: Correlating Archaeological and Linguistic Hypotheses* (New York)

Blockley, R. C. (1981). *The Fragmentary Classicizing Historians of the Later Roman Empire: Eunapius, Olympiodorus, Priscus and Malchus*, vol. 1 (Liverpool)

——— (1983). *The Fragmentary Classicizing Historians of the Later Roman Empire: Eunapius, Olympiodorus, Priscus and Malchus*, vol. 2 (Liverpool)

——— (1985). *The History of Menander the Guardsman* (Liverpool)

Boeles, P. C. J. A. (1951). *Friesland tot de elfde eeuw* (Gravenhage)

Böhme, H.-W. (1974). *Germanische Grabfünde des 4 bis 5 Jahrhunderts zwischen untere Elbe und Loire. Studien zur Chronologie und Bevölkerungsgeschichte* (Munich)
———— (1975). 'Archäologische Zeugnisse zur Geschichte der Markomannenkriege (166–80 n. Chr.)', *Jahrbuch des römischgermanischen Zentralmuseums Mainz* 22, 155–217

Bohner, K. (1958). *Die frankischen Altertumer des Trierer Landes*, 2 vols. (Berlin)

Bohning, W. R. (1978). 'International Migration and the Western World: Past, Present and Future', *International Migration* 16, 1–15.

Boretius, A., ed. (1883). *Capitularia regum Francorum* (Hanover)

Borodzej, T. et al. (1989). *Période romaine tardive et début de la période des migrations des peuples (groupe de Masłomecz)* (Warsaw)

Borrie, W. D. (1994). *The European Peopling of Australasia: A Demographic History, 1788–1988* (Canberra)

Bosl, K. (1966). *Das Grossmährische Reich in der politischen Welt des 9. Jahrhunderts* (Munich)

Bowlus, C. (1995). *Franks, Moravians, and Magyars: the Struggle for the Middle Danube, 788–907* (Philadelphia)

Brachmann, H. (1978). *Slawische Stämme an Elbe und Saale: zu ihrer Geschichte und Kultur im 6.–10.* (Berlin)
———— (1993). *Der frühmittelalterliche Befestigungsbau in Mitteleuropa: Untersuchungen zu einer Entwicklung und Function im germanisch-deutschen Gebiet* (Berlin)
————, ed. (1995). *Burg – Burgstadt – Stadt: zur Genese mittelalterlicher nichtagrarischer Zentren in Ostmitteleuropa* (Berlin)
———— (1997). 'Tribal Organizations in Central Europe in the 6th–10th Centuries AD: Reflections on the Ethnic and Political Development in the Second Half of the First Millennium', in Urbanczyk (1997a), 23–38

Brather, S. (1996). *Feldberger Keramik und frühe Slawen: Studien zur nordwestslawischen Keramik der Karolingerzeit* (Bonn)
———— (2001). *Archäologie der westlichen Slawen: Siedlung, Wirtschaft und Gesellschaft im früh- und hochmittelalterlichen Ostmitteleuropa* (Berlin)

Braund, D. C. (1984). *Rome and the Friendly King: The Character of Client Kingship* (London)
———— (2005). *Scythians and Greeks: Cultural Interactions in Scythia, Athens and the early Roman Empire (Sixth Century BC–First Century AD)* (Exeter)

Bretholz, B. and Weinberger, W., eds. (1923). *Die Chronik der Böhmen des Cosmas von Prag*, Monumenta Germaniae Historica: Scriptores rerum Germanicarum, n.s. 2 (Berlin)

Brooks, N. (1979). 'England in the Ninth Century: The Crucible of Defeat', *Transactions of the Royal Historical Society*, 5th series, 29, 1–20

Broun, D. et al., eds. (1998). *Image and Identity: The Making and Re-making of Scotland through the Ages* (Edinburgh)

Brown, P. (1971). *The World of Late Antiquity: from Marcus Aurelius to Muhammad* (London)
———— (1996). *The Rise of Western Christendom: Triumph and Diversity, AD 200–1000* (Oxford)

Browning, R. (1975). *Byzantium and Bulgaria: A Comparative Study across the Early Medieval Frontier* (London)

Buko, A. (2005). *Archeologia Polski* (Warsaw)

Burgess, R. (1993). *The Chronicle of Hydatius and the Consularia Constantinopolitana* (Oxford)

Bury, J. B. (1928). *The Invasion of Europe by the Barbarians* (London)

Cameron, A. D. E. (1970). *Claudian: Poetry and Politics at the Court of Honorius* (Oxford)

Cameron, A. D. E. and Long, J., with a contribution by Sherry, L. (1993). *Barbarians and Politics at the Court of Arcadius* (Berkeley)

Campbell, A. (1949). *Encomium Emmae Reginae* (London)

Campbell, J., ed. (1982). *The Anglo-Saxons* (Oxford)

———— (2000). *The Anglo-Saxon State* (London)

Canard, M. (1973). *Miscellanea Orientalia* (London)

Canny, M., ed. (1994). *Europeans on the Move: Studies on European Migration 1500–1800* (Oxford)

Carroll, M. (2001). *Romans, Celts and Germans: The German Provinces of Rome* (Stroud)

Cary, E. (1914–27). *Dio's Roman History* (London)

Castellanos, S. (2000). 'Propiedad de la tierra y relaciones de dependencia en la Galia del siglo VI. El Testamentum Remigii', *Antiquité Tardif* 8, 223–7

Chadwick-Hawkes, S., ed. (1989). *Weapons and Warfare in Anglo-Saxon England* (Oxford)

Champion, T. C. (1995). *Centre and Periphery: Comparative Studies in Archaeology* (London)

Champion, T. C. and Megaw, J. V. S., eds. (1985). *Settlements and Society: Aspects of West European Prehistory in the First Millennium* BC (Leicester)

Chapman, R. and Dolukhanov, P., eds. (1993). *Cultural Transformations and Interactions in Eastern Europe* (Aldershot)

Charanis, P. (1950). 'The Chronicle of Monemvasia and the Question of the Slavic Settlements of Greece', *Dumbarton Oaks Papers* 5, 141–66

Charles, R. H. (1916). *The Chronicle of John, Bishop of Nikiu* (London)

Charles-Edwards, T. C. E. (1989). 'Early Medieval Kingships in the British Isles', in Bassett (1989), 28–39.

————, ed. (2003). *After Rome* (Oxford)

———— (2006). *The Chronicle of Ireland* (Liverpool)

Chastagnol, A. (1973). 'Le repli sur Arles des services administratifs gaulois en l'an 407 de notre ère', *Revue Historique* 97, 23–40

Childe, V. G. (1926). *The Aryans: A Study of Indo-European Origins* (London)

———— (1927). *The Dawn of European Civilization* (London)

Christiansen, E. (1980). *The Northern Crusades: The Baltic and the Catholic Frontier, 1100–1525* (London)

———— (1980–81). *Saxo Grammaticus: Danorum Regum heroumque historia: Books X–XVI* (text and translation), 3 vols. (Oxford)

———— (2002). *The Norsemen in the Viking Age* (Oxford)

Christie, N. (1995). *The Lombards: The Ancient Longobards* (Oxford)

Christlein, R. (1978). *Die Alamannen* (Stuttgart)

Claessen, H. J. M. and Skalnik, P. (1978). *The Early State* (The Hague)

———— (1981). *The Study of the State* (The Hague)

Claessen, H. J. M. and van de Velde, P. (1987). *Early State Dynamics* (Leiden)

Claessen, H. J. M. and Oosten, J. G. (1996). *Ideology and the Formation of Early States* (Leiden)

Clark, G. (1966). 'The Invasion Hypothesis in British Archaeology', *Antiquity* 40, 172–89

Cohen, R., ed. (1995). *The Cambridge Survey of World Migration* (Cambridge)

————, ed. (1996). *Theories of Migration* (Cheltenham)

————, ed. (1997). *The Politics of Migration* (Cheltenham)

———— (2008). *Global Diasporas: An Introduction*, 2nd ed. (Abingdon)

Colgrave, B. and Mynors, R. A. B., eds. (1949). *Bede's Ecclesiastical History of the English People* (Oxford)

Collins, R. (1983). 'Theodebert I, "Rex Magnus Francorum"', in P. Wormald (ed.), *Ideal and Reality in Frankish and Anglo-Saxon Society* (Oxford), 7–33

———— (1998). *Charlemagne* (Basingstoke)

Collinson, S. (1994). *Europe and International Migration*, 2nd ed. (London)

Constantinescu, M. et al., eds. (1975) *Relations Between the Autochthonous Population and the Migratory Populations on the Territory of Romania* (Bucharest)

Cooper, J., ed. (1993). *The Battle of Maldon: Fiction and Fact* (London)

Coupland, S. (1995). 'The Vikings in Francia and Anglo-Saxon England', in McKitterick (1995), 190–201

Courtois, C. (1955). *Les Vandales et l'Afrique* (Paris)

Crawford. B. (1987). *Scandinavian Scotland* (Leicester)

Cribb, R. J. (1991). *Nomads in Archaeology* (London)

Croke, B. (1977). 'Evidence for the Hun Invasion of Thrace in AD 422', *Greek, Roman and Byzantine Studies* 18, 347–67

Cross, S. H. and Sherbowitz-Wetzor, O. P., eds. (1953). *The Russian Primary Chronicle: Laurentian Text* (Cambridge, MA)

Cunliffe, B. (1997). *The Ancient Celts* (Oxford)

Cunliffe, B. and Rowley, T., eds. (1976). *Oppida: The Beginnings of Urbanization in Barbarian Europe: Papers Presented to a Conference at Oxford, October 1975* (Oxford)

Curta, F. (1999). 'Hiding behind a Piece of Tapestry: Jordanes and the Slavic Venethi', *Jahrbücher für Geschichte Osteuropas* 47, 1–18

———— (2001). *The Making of the Slavs: History and Archaeology of the Lower Danube Region, c.500–700* (Cambridge)

————, ed. (2005). *East Central and Eastern Europe in the Early Middle Ages* (Ann Arbor)

———— (2006). *Southeastern Europe in the Middle Ages 500–1250* (Cambridge)

Daim, F. (2003). 'Avars and Avar Archaeology: An Introduction', in Goetz et al. (2003), 463–570

Dark, K. R. (2002). *Britain and the End of the Roman Empire* (Stroud)

Davies, W. (1978). *An Early Welsh Microcosm: Studies in the Llandaff Charters* (London)

———— (1990). *Patterns of Power in Early Wales* (Oxford)

De Boor, C. and Wirth, P., eds. (1972). *The History of Theophylact Simocatta* (Stuttgart)

Defarri, R. J. (1964). *Orosius: Seven Books of History Against the Pagans* (Washington).

Delehaye, H. (1912). 'Saints de Thrace et de Mesie', *Analecta Bollandia* 31, 161–300

Demandt, A. (1984). *Der Fall Roms: die Auflösung des römischen Reiches im Urteil der Nachwelt* (Munich)

Demougeot, E. (1979). *La Formation de l'Europe et les invasions barbares: II. Dès l'avènement de Dioclétien (284) à l'occupation germanique de l'Empire romain d'Occident (début du VIe siècle)* (Paris)

Denison, D. (1993). *English Historical Syntax* (Harlow)

Dennis, G. T., ed. (1981). *Das Strategikon des Maurikios* (Vienna)

———— (1984). *Maurice's Strategikon: Handbook of Byzantine Military Strategy* (Pennsylvania)

Dindorf, L., ed. (1832). *Chronicon Paschale* (Bonn)

Dittrich, Z. R. (1962). *Christianity in Great Moravia* (Groningen)

Dolukhanov, P. M. (1996). *The Early Slavs: Eastern Europe from the Initial Settlement to the Kievan Rus* (London)

Donat, P. (1983). 'Die Entwicklung der Wirtschaftlichen und Gesellschaftlichen Verhältnisse bei den slawischen Stämme zwischen Oder und Elbe nach archäologischen Quellen', in *Settimane* (1983), 127–45

Donat, P. and Fischer, R. E. (1994). 'Die Anfänge slawische Siedlung westlich der Oder', *Slavia Antiqua* 45, 7–30

Drijvers, J. W. and Hunt, D., eds. (1999). *The Late Roman World and its Historian: Interpreting Ammianus Marcellinus* (London)

Drinkwater, J. F. (1989). 'Patronage in Roman Gaul and the Problem of the Bagaudae', in *Patronage in Ancient Society*, ed. A. Wallace-Hadrill (London), 189–203

———— (1992). 'The Bacaudae of Fifth-Century Gaul', in Drinkwater and Elton (1992), 208–17.

———— (1998). 'The usurpers Constantine III (407–411) and Jovinus (411–413)', *Britannia* 29, 269–98

———— (2007). *The Alamanni and Rome 213–496* (Oxford)

Drinkwater, J. F. and Elton, H., eds. (1992) *Fifth-Century Gaul: A Crisis of Identity?* (Cambridge)

Duczko, W. (2004). *Viking Rus: Studies on the Presence of Scandinavians in Eastern Europe* (Leiden)

Dulinicz, M. (1994). 'The Problem of Dating of the Strongholds of the Tornow Type and Tornow-Klenica Group', *Archeologia Polski* 39, 31–49 (English summary)

———— (1997). 'The First Dendrochronological Dating of the Strongholds in Northern Mazovia', in Urbanczyk (1997a), 137–42

Dumville, D. N. (1977). 'Kingship, Genealogies and Regnal Lists', in Sawyer and Wood (1977), 72–104

Dunbabin, J. (2000). *France in the Making, 843–1180*, 2nd ed. (Oxford)

Dvornik, F. (1949). *The Making of Central and Eastern Europe* (London)

———— (1956). *The Slavs: Their Early History and Civilization* (Boston)

———— (1969). *Les légendes de Constantin et de Méthode vues de Byzance*, 2nd ed. (Hattiesburg, MS)

Earle, T. K., ed. (1984). *On the Evolution of Complex Societies: Essays in Honor of Harry Hoijer, 1982* (Malibu)

————, ed. (1991). *Chiefdoms: Power, Economy and Ideology* (Cambridge)

Eggers, H. J. (1951). *Der römische Import im freien Germanien*, Atlas der Urgeschichte 1 (Berlin)

Eggers, M. (1995). *Das 'Grossmährische Reich': Realität oder Fiktion?: eine Neuinterpretation der Quellen zur Geschichte des mittleren Donauraumes im 9. Jahrhundert* (Stuttgart)

Elton, H. (1996). *Frontiers of the Roman Empire* (London)

Esmonde-Cleary, S. (1989). *The Ending of Roman Britain* (London)

Evelyn White, H. (1961). *The Works of Ausonius* (London)


Faith, R. (1997). *The English Peasantry and the Growth of Lordship* (Leicester)

Farrell, R. T., ed. (1978). *Bede and Anglo-Saxon England* (Oxford)

————, ed. (1982). *The Vikings* (London)

Faulkner, N. (2000). *The Decline of Roman Britain* (Stroud)

Favrod, J. (1997). *Histoire politique du royaume burgonde (443–534)* (Lausanne)

Fellows-Jenson, G. (2001). 'In the Steps of the Vikings', in Graham-Campbell et al. (2001), 279–88

Fielding, A. (1993a). 'Mass Migration and Economic Restructuring', in King (1993), 7–18

———— (1993b). 'Migrations, Institutions and Politics: The Evolution of Emigration Policies', in King (1993), 40–62

Fisher, P., trans., ed. Davidson, H. E. (1996). *Saxo Grammaticus: The History of the Danes: Books I–IX* (Woodbridge)

Font, M. (2005). 'Missions, Conversions, and Power Legitimization in East Central Europe', in Curta (2005), 283–296

Forte, A. et al. (2005). *Viking Empires* (Cambridge)

Foulke, W. D. (1974). *History of the Lombards* (Philadelphia)

Fouracre, P. (2000). *The Age of Charles Martel* (Harlow)

————, ed. (2005). *The New Cambridge Medieval History: vol. 1, c.500–c.700* (Cambridge)

Franklin, S. and Shepard, J. (1996). *The Emergence of Rus 750–1200* (Harlow)

Freeman, E. A. (1888). *Four Oxford Lectures 1887* (London)

Frendo, J. D. (1975). *Agathias History* (Berlin)

Fried, M. H. (1967). *The Evolution of Political Society: An Essay in Political Anthropology* (New York)

Friedrich, G. (1907). *Codex Diplomaticus et Epistolaris Regni Bohemiae*, vol. 1 (Prague)

Friedrichs, J. (2004). *European Approaches to International Relations Theory: A House With Many Mansions* (London)

Frolova, N. A. (1983). *The Coinage of the Kingdom of Bosporos AD 242–341/2* (Oxford)

Fulford, M. (1985). 'Roman Material in Barbarian Society c.200 BC–AD 400', in Champion and Megaw (1985), 91–108


Garipzanov, I. et al., eds. (2008). *Franks, Northmen, and Slavs: Identities and State Formation in Early Medieval Europe* (Turnhout)

Garzya, A. (1989). *Opere di Sinesio di Cirene: epistole, operette, inni* (Turin)

Geary, P. (1983). *Ethnic Identity as a Situational Construct in the Early Middle Ages* (Vienna)

——— (1988). *Before France and Germany: The Creation and Transformation of the Merovingian World* (New York)

——— (2002). *The Myth of Nations: The Medieval Origins of Europe* (Princeton)

Gebuhr, M. (1974). 'Zur Definition alterkaiserzeitlicher Fürstengräber vom Lubsow-Typ', *Prähistorische Zeitschrift* 49, 82–128

Gellner, E. (1983). *Nations and Nationalism* (Ithaca)

Geuenich, D., ed. (1998). *Die Franken und die Alemannen bis zur 'Schlacht bei Zulpich'*

Gillet, A., ed. (2002). *On Barbarian Identity: Critical Approaches to Ethnicity in the Early Middle Ages* (Turnhout)

Godja, M. (1988). *The Development of the Settlement Pattern in the Basin of the Lower Vltava (Central Bohemia) 200–1200* (Oxford)

——— (1991). *The Ancient Slavs: Settlement and Society* (Edinburgh)

Godlowski, K. (1970). *The Chronology of the Late Roman and Early Migration Periods in Central Europe* (Cracow)

——— (1980). 'Das Aufhören der Germanischen Kulturen an der Mittleren Donau und das Problem des Vordringens der Slawen', in Wolfram & Daim (1980), 225–32

——— (1983). 'Zur Frage der Slawensitze vor der grossen Slawenwanderung im 6. Jahrhundert', in Settimane (1983), 257–302

Godman, P. and Collins, R., eds. (1990). *Charlemagne's Heir* (Oxford)

Goehrke, C. (1992). *Frühzeit des Ostslaventums* (Darmstadt)

Goetz, H.-W. et al., eds. (2003). *Regna and Gentes: The Relationship between Late Antique and Early Medieval Peoples and Kingdoms in the Transformation of the Roman World* (Leiden)

Goffart, W. (1980). *Barbarians and Romans AD 418–584: The Techniques of Accommodation* (Princeton)

——— (1981). 'Rome, Constantinople, and the Barbarians in Late Antiquity', *American Historical Review* 76, 275–306

——— (1988). *The Narrators of Barbarian History (AD 550–800): Jordanes, Gregory of Tours, Bede, and Paul the Deacon* (Princeton)

——— (2006). *Barbarian Tides: The Migration Age and the Later Roman Empire* (Philadelphia)

Goodacre S. et al. (2005). 'Genetic Evidence for a Family-Based Scandinavian Settlement of Shetland and Orkney during the Viking Periods', *Heredity* 95, 129–35

Gordon, D. C. (1966). *The Age of Attila* (Ann Arbor)

Gorecki, P. (1992). *Economy, Society and Lordship in Medieval Poland 1100–1250* (New York)

Gottmann, J., ed. (1980). *Centre and Periphery: Spatial Variation in Politics* (London)

Gould, J. D. (1980). 'European Inter-Continental Emigration, The Road Home: Return Migration from the USA', *Journal of European Economic History* 9.1, 41–112

Graham-Campbell, J. et al., eds. (2001). *Vikings and the Danelaw* (Oxford)

Graus, F. J. and Dostál, A. (1966). *Das Grossmährische Reich: Tagung der wissenschaftlichen Konferenz des Archäologischen Instituts der Tschechoslowakischen Akademie der Wissenschaften, Brno-Nitra, 1.–4.x.1963* (Prague)

Graus, F. and Ludat, H., eds. (1967). *Siedlung und Verfassung Böhmens in der Frühzeit* (Wiesbaden)

Green, D. H. (1998). *Language and History in the Early Germanic World* (Cambridge)

Gyuzelev, V. (1979). *The Proto-Bulgarians* (Sofia)

Haarnagel, W. (1979). *Die Grabung Feddersen Wierde : Methode, Hausbau-, Siedlungs- und Wirtschaftsformen sowie Sozialstruktur* (Wiesbaden)

Hachmann, R. (1971). *The Germanic Peoples* (London)

Haldon, J. F. (1990). *Byzantium in the Seventh Century: The Transformation of a Culture* (Cambridge)

Hall, C. (1983). *Periphrastic Do: History and Hypothesis* (Ann Arbor)

Halsall, G. (1992). 'The Origins of the Reihengräberzivilisation: Forty Years On', in Drinkwater and Elton (1992), 196–207

———— (1995a). *Settlement and Social Organization: The Merovingian Region of Metz* (Cambridge).

———— (1995b). *Early Medieval Cemeteries: An Introduction to Burial Archaeology in the Post-Roman West* (Skelmorlie)

———— (1999). 'Movers and Shakers: The Barbarians and the Fall of Rome', *Early Medieval Europe* 8, 131–45

———— (2001). 'Childeric's grave, Clovis' Succession and the Origins of the Merovingian Kingdom', in Mathisen and Shanzer (2001), 116–33

———— (2005). 'The Barbarian Invasions', in Fouracre (2005), 35–55

———— (2007). *Barbarian Migrations and the Roman West 376–568* (Cambridge)

Handley, M. (2001). 'Beyond Hagiography: Epigraphic Commemoration and the Cult of the Saints in Late Antique Trier', in Mathisen and Shanzer (2001), 187–200

———— (2003). *Death, Society and Culture: Inscriptions and Epitaphs in Gaul and Spain, AD 300–750* (Oxford)

Hannestad, K. (1960). 'Les forces militaires d'après la guerre gothique de Procope', *Classica et Mediaevalia* 21, 136–83

Hansen, G. C., ed. (1995). *Sokrates: Kirchengeschichte* (Berlin)

Harhoiu, R. (1977). *The Treasure from Pietroasa, Romania* (Oxford)

Härke, H. (1989). 'Early Saxon Weapon Burials: Frequencies, Distributions and Weapon Combinations', in Chadwick-Hawkes (1989), 49–61.

———— (1990). ' "Warrior Graves?" The Background of the Anglo-Saxon Weapon Burial Rite', *Past and Present* 126, 22–43

———— (1992). *Angelsächsische Waffengräber des 5. bis 7. Jahrhunderts* (Cologne)

———— (1998). 'Archaeologists and Migrations: A Problem of Attitude?', *Current Anthropology* 39.1, 19–45

Hart, C. (1992). *The Danelaw* (London)

Haubrichs, W. (1996). 'Sprache und Sprachzeugnisse der merowingischen Franken', in *Die Franken: Wegbereiter Europas: vor 1500 Jahren, König Chlodwig und seine Erben* (Mainz), 559–73.

———— (2003). 'Remico aus Goddelau: Ostgermanen, Westgermanen und Romanen im Wormser Raum des 5./6. Jahrhunderts', in *Runica – Germanica – Mediaevalia*, ed. W. Heizmann and A. van Nahl (Berlin), 226–42

———— (forthcoming). 'Ein namhaftes Volk: Burgundische Namen und Sprache des 5. und 6. Jahrhunderts', in *Die Burgunder: Ethnogenese und Assimilation eines Volkes*, ed. V. Gallée (Worms), 135–84

Heather, P. J. (1986). 'The Crossing of the Danube and the Gothic Conversion', *Greek Roman and Byzantine Studies* 27, 289–318

———— (1988). 'The Anti-Scythian Tirade of Synesius' De Regno', *Phoenix* 42, 152–72

———— (1989). 'Cassiodorus and the Rise of the Amals: Genealogy and the Goths under Hun Domination', *Journal of Roman Studies* 79, 103–28

———— (1991). *Goths and Romans 332–489* (Oxford)

———— (1993). 'The Historical Culture of Ostrogothic Italy', in *Teoderico il grande e i Goti d'Italia, Atti del XIII Congresso internazionale di studi sull'Alto Medioevo* (Spoleto), 317–53

———— (1995a). 'The Huns and the End of the Roman Empire in Western Europe', *English Historical Review* 110, 4–41

———— (1995b). 'Theodoric King of the Goths', *Early Medieval Europe* 4.2, 145–73

———— (1996). *The Goths* (Oxford)

———— (2001). 'The Late Roman Art of Client Management and the Grand Strategy Debate', in Pohl and Wood (2001), 15–68

———— (2003). 'Gens and regnum among the Ostrogoths', in Goetz et al. (2003), 85–133

———— (2005). *The Fall of Rome: A New History* (London)

———— (2007). 'Goths in the Roman Balkans c.350–500', in Poulter (2007), 163–90

———— (2008a). Review of John Drinkwater (2007), *Nottingham Medieval Studies* 52, 243–5

———— (2008b). 'Ethnicity, Group Identity, and Social Status in the Migration Period', in Garipzanov et al. (2008), 17–50

———— (forthcoming). 'Why Did the Barbarian Cross the Rhine?', *Late Antiquity*

Heather, P. J. and Matthews, J. F. (1991). *The Goths in the Fourth Century: Translated Texts for Historians* (Liverpool)

Heather, P. J. and Moncur, D. (2001). *Politics, Philosophy, and Empire in the Fourth Century: Select Orations of Themistius, Translated Texts for Historians* (Liverpool)

Hedeager, L. (1987). 'Empire, Frontier and the Barbarian Hinterland: Rome and Northern Europe from AD 1–400', in Rowlands et al. (1987), 125–40

———— (1988). 'The Evolution of Germanic Society 1–400 AD', in Jones R. F. J. et al. (1988), 129–44

———— (1992), trans. John Hines. *Iron-Age Societies: From Tribe to State in Northern Europe, 500 BC to AD 700* (Oxford)

Hedeager, L. and Kristiansen, K. (1981). 'Bendstrup – A Princely Grave from the Early Roman Iron Age: Its Social and Historical Context', *Kuml* (1981), 150–62

Helgason, A. et al. (2000). 'Estimating Scandinavian and Gaelic ancestry in the male settlers of Iceland', *American Journal of Human Genetics* 67, 697–717

———— (2001). 'mtDNA and the Islands of the North Atlantic: Estimating the Proportions of Norse and Gaelic Ancestry', *American Journal of Human Genetics* 68, 723–37

———— (2003). 'A Reassessment of Genetic Diversity in Icelanders: Strong Evidence from Multiple Loci for Relative Homogeneity caused by Genetic Drift', *Annals of Human Genetics* 67, 281–97

Henning, J. (1991). 'Germanen-Slawen-Deutsche: Neue Untersuchungen zum frühgeschichtlichen Siedlungswesen ostlich der Elbe', *Praehistorische Zeitschrift* 66, 119–33

——— (2005). 'Ways of Life in Eastern and Western Europe during the Early Middle Ages: Which Way was Normal?', in Curta (2005), 41–59

Herrmann, J. (1968), *Siedlung, Wirtschaft und gesellschaftliche Verhältnisse der slawischen Stamme zwischen Oder/Neisse und Elbe* (Berlin)

——— (1983), 'Wanderungen und Landnähme im Westslawischen Gebiet', in Settimane (1983), 75–101

——— (1984), *Germanen und Slawen in Mitteleuropa* (Berlin)

Hermann, J. et al., eds. (1985). *Die Slawen in Deutschland: Geschichte und Kultur der slawischen Stämme westlich von Oder und Neisse vom 6. bis 12. Jahrhundert*, 2nd ed. (Berlin)

Higham, N. (1992). *Rome, Britain and the Anglo-Saxons* (London)

——— (1994). *The English Conquest: Gildas and Britain in the Fifth Century* (Manchester)

———, ed. (2007). *The Britons in Anglo-Saxon England* (London)

Hills, C. (2003). *The Origins of the English* (London)

Hines, J. (1984). *The Scandinavian Character of Anglian England in the pre-Viking Period* (Oxford)

———, ed. (1997). *The Anglo-Saxons from the Migration Period to the Eighth Century: An Ethnographic Perspective* (Woodbridge)

Hodder, I. (1982). *Symbols in Action: Ethnoarchaeological Studies of Material Culture* (Cambridge)

——— (1991). *Reading the Past: Current Approaches to Interpretation in Archaeology* (Cambridge)

Hodder, I. and Hutson, S., eds. (2003). *Reading the Past: Current Approaches to Interpretation in Archaeology* (Cambridge)

Hodges, R. and Bowden, W., eds. (1998). *The Sixth Century: Production, Distribution, and Demand* (Leiden)

Hodgkin, T. (1886). *The Letters of Cassiodorus: A Condensed Translation* (London)

Holmes, C., ed. (1996). *Migration in European History* (Cheltenham)

Holt, J. C. (1987). '1086' in Holt, ed., *Doomsday Studies* (Woodbridge), 41–64

Holtzmann, R., ed. (1935). *Thietmari Merseburgensis episcopi chronicon*, Monumenta Germaniae Historica: Scriptores rerum Germanicarum, vol. 9 (Berlin)

Hooke, D. (1997). 'The Anglo-Saxons in England in the Seventh and Eighth Centuries: Aspects of Location in Space', in Hines (1997), 65–99

——— (1998). *The Landscape of Anglo-Saxon England* (London)

Hummer, H. J. (1998). 'The Fluidity of Barbarian Identity: The Ethnogenesis of Alemanni and Suebi AD 200–500', *Early Medieval Europe* 7, 2–26

Ilkjaer, J. (1995). 'Illerup Adal (Danemark). Un lieu de sacrifices du IIIe siècle de n.è. en Scandinavie meridionale', in Vallet and Kazanski (1995), 101–12

Ilkjaer, J. and Lonstrup, J. (1983). 'Der Moorfund im Tal der Illerup-A bei Skanderborg im Ostjutland', *Germania* 61, 95–126

Ionita, I. (1975). 'The Social-Economic Structure of Society During the Goths' Migration in the Carpatho-Danubean Area', in Constantinescu (1975), 77–89

James, E. F. (1988). *The Franks* (Oxford)
——— (1989). 'The Origins of Barbarian Kingdoms: The Continental Evidence', in Bassett (1989), 40–52
James, S. (1999). *The Atlantic Celts: Ancient People or Modern Invention?* (London)
Jarnut, J. (2003). 'Gens, Rex, and Regna of the Lombards', in Goetz et al. (2003), 409–28
Jerome, H. (1926). *Migration and Business Cycles* (New York)
Jirecek, H. (1867). *Codex Juris Bohemici*, vol. 1 (Prague)
Johnston, D. E., ed. (1977). *The Saxon Shore* (London)
Jones, A. H. M. (1964). *The Later Roman Empire: A Social Economic and Administrative Survey*, 3 vols. (Oxford)
Jones, M. E. (1996). *The End of Roman Britain* (Ithica).
Jones R. F. J. et al., eds. (1988). *First Millennium Papers: Western Europe in the First Millennium* (Oxford)

Kaiser, D. H. (1980). *The Growth of the Law in Medieval Russia* (Princeton)
———, ed. (1992). *The Laws of Rus': tenth to fifteenth centuries* (Salt Lake City)
Kaiser, D. H. and Marker, G., eds. (1994). *Reinterpreting Russian History: Readings 860s–1860s* (Oxford)
Kaiser, R. (1997). *Die Franken: Roms Erben und Wegbereiter Europas?* (Idstein)
Kantor, M. (1983). *Medieval Slavic Lives of Saints and Princes* (Ann Arbor)
——— (1990). *The Origins of Christianity in Bohemia* (Evanston)
Kapelle, W. E. (1979). *The Norman Conquest of the North: The Region and Its Transformation 1000–1135* (Chapel Hill, NC)
Kazanski, M. (1991). *Les Goths (Ier–VIIe siècle après J.-C.)* (Paris)
——— (1999). *Les Slaves: les origines, Ier–VIIe siècle après J.-C.* (Paris)
Kelly, C. (2008). *Attila the Hun: Barbarian Terror and the Fall of Rome* (London)
Kelly, G. (2008). *Ammianus Marcellinus: The Allusive Historian* (Cambridge)
Kennedy, H. (2004). *The Court of the Caliphs: The Rise and Fall of Islam's Greatest Dynasty* (London)
——— (2007). *The Great Arab Conquests: How the Spread of Islam Changed the World We Live In* (London)
Keydell, R., ed. (1967). *Agathias Historiae, Corpus Fontium Historiae Byzantinae* (Berlin)
Keynes, S. (1986). 'A Tale of Two Kings: Alfred the Great and Aethelred the Unready', *Transactions of the Royal Historical Society* 36, 195–217
——— (1997). 'The Vikings in England, c.790–1016', in Sawyer (1997a), 48–81
Keynes, S. and Lapidge, M., eds. (1983). *Alfred the Great: Asser's Life of King Alfred, and Other Contemporary Sources* (London)
Khazanov, A. M. (trans. Julia Crookenden, with a foreword by Ernest Gellner) (1984). *Nomads and the Outside World* (Cambridge)
King, R., ed. (1993). *Mass Migration in Europe: The Legacy and the Future* (London)
King, R. and Oberg, S. (1993). 'Europe and the Future of Mass Migration', in King (1993), 1–4

Kivisto, P. (1989). *The Ethnic Enigma: The Salience of Ethnicity for European-Origin Groups* (Philadelphia)

Klose, J. (1934). *Roms Klientel-Randstaaten am Rhein und an der Donau: Beiträge zu ihrer Geschichte und rechtlichen Stellung im 1. und 2. Jhdt. n. Chr.* (Breslau)

Kmiecinski, J. (1968). *Odry: cmentarzysko kurhanowe z okresu rzymskiego w powiecie chojnickim* (Lódz)

Knabe, C. and Herrmann, P., eds. (1931–57). *Saxonis Gesta danorum* (Copenhagen)

Knoll, P. W. and Schaer, F. (2003). *Gesta principum Polonorum* ['The deeds of the princes of the Poles'] (Budapest)

Kobylinksi, Z. (1997). 'Settlement Structures in Central Europe at the Beginning of the Middle Ages', in Urbanczyk (1997a), 97–114

Koch, R. and Koch, U. (1996). 'Die frankische Expansion ins Main und Neckargebiet', in *Die Franken: Wegbereiter Europas: vor 1500 Jahren, König Chlodwig und seine Erben* (Mainz), 270–84

Kokowski, A. (1995). *Schätze der Ostgoten* (Stuttgart)

Kolendo, J. (1997). 'Central Europe and the Mediterranean World in the 1st–5th Centuries AD', in Urbanczyk (1997a), 5–22

Kossinna, G. (1928). *Ursprung und Verbreitung der Germanen in vor- und frühgeschichtlicher Zeit* (Leipzig)

Kostrzewski, J. (1969). 'Über den gegenwärtigen Stand der Erforschung der Ethnogenese der Slaven in archäologischer Sicht', in Zagiba (1969), 11–25

Krader, L. (1963). *Social Organization of the Mongol-Turkic Pastoral Nomads* (The Hague)

Kristiansen, K. and Paludan-Muller, C., eds. (1978). *New Directions in Scandinavian Archaeology* (Copenhagen)

Krüger, B. et al., eds. (1976–83). *Die Germanen: Geschichte und Kultur der germanischen Stämme in Mitteleuropa*, 2 vols. (Berlin)

Krusch, B. and Levison, W., eds. (1951). *Gregory of Tours: Historiae*, Monumenta Germaniae Historica: Scriptores rerum Merovingicarum 1.1 (Berlin)

Kuhn, W. (1963). 'Die Siedlerzählen der deutschen Ostsiedlung', in *Studium Sociale. Karl Valentin Muller dargebracht* (Cologne), 131–54

——— (1973). *Vergleichende Untersuchungen zur mittelalterlichen Ostsiedlung* (Cologne)

Kuhrt, D., ed. (1984). *The Politics of Return: International Return Migration in Europe* (New York)

Kulikowski, M. (2000a). 'Barbarians in Gaul, Usurpers in Britain', *Britannia* 31, 325–45

——— (2000b). 'The Notitia Dignitatum as a Historical Source', *Historia* 49, 358–77

——— (2002). 'Nation versus Army: A Necessary Contrast?', in Gillet (2002), 69–84

——— (2007). *Rome's Gothic Wars* (Cambridge)

Kunzl, E., ed. (1993). *Die Alamannenbeute aus dem Rhein bei Neupotz*, 4 vols. (Mainz)

Kurnatowska, Z. (1995). 'Frühstadische Entwicklung an den Zentrum der Piasten in Grosspolen', in Brachmann (1995), 133–48

——— (1997a). 'Territorial Structures in West Poland Prior to the Founding of the State Organization of Miesco I', in Urbanczyk (1997a), 125–36

——— (1997b). 'Die Christianisierung Polens im Lichte der Materiallen Quellen', in Urbancyzk (1997a), 101–121

Kurze, F., ed. (1895). *Annales Regni Francorum 741–829*, Monumenta Germaniae
  Historica: Scriptores rerum Germanicarum, vol. 6 (Hanover)

Lappenberg, J. M. and Schmeidler, B., eds. (1909). *Helmoldi presbyteri Bozoviensis
  Cronica Slavorum*, 2nd ed. (Hanover)

Leahy, K. and Paterson, C. (2001). 'New Light on the Viking presence in
  Lincolnshire: the Artefactual Evidence', in Graham-Campbell et al. (2001),
  181–202

Leach, E. R. (1954). *Political Systems of Highland Burma: A Study of Kachin Social
  Structure* (London)

Lemerle, P. (1979–81). *Les plus anciens recueils des miracles de Saint Démétrius* (Paris)

Lenski, N. (1995). 'The Gothic Civil War and the Date of the Gothic Conversion',
  *Greek Roman and Byzantine Studies* 36, 51–87

——— (2002). *Failure of Empire: Valens and the Roman State in the Fourth Century* AD
  (Berkeley)

Levaskova, V. P. (1994). 'Agriculture in Rus', in Kaiser and Marker (1994), 39–44

Lewitt, T. (1991). *Agricultural Production in the Roman Economy* AD 200–400 (Oxford)

Leyser, K. (1982). *Medieval Germany and its Neighbours, 900–1250* (London)

——— (1989). *Rule and Conflict in an Early Medieval Society: Ottonian Saxony*
  (Oxford)

Liapushkin, I. I. (1958). *Gorodishche Novotroitskoe* (Moscow).

Liebermann, F., ed. (1903–16). *Die Gesetze der Angelsachsen* (Halle)

Liebeschuetz. J. H. W. G. (1990). *Barbarians and Bishops: Army, Church, and State in
  the Age of Arcadius and Chrysostom* (Oxford)

——— (1992). 'Alaric's Goths: Nation or Army?', in Drinkwater and Elton (1992),
  75–83

Likhachev, D. S. (1970). 'The Legend of the Calling-in of the Varangians', in K.
  Hannestad et al. (eds.), *Varangian Problems*, 178–85

Lindner, R. (1981). 'Nomadism, Huns, and Horses', *Past & Present* 92, 1–19

Lohmann, H.-E. and Hirsch, P., eds. (1935). *Widukindi monachi Corbeiensis Rerum
  Gestarum Saxonicarum*, Monumenta Germaniae Historica: Scriptores rerum
  Germanicarum, 5th ed. (Hanover)

Loseby, S. T. (1992). 'Marseille: a Late Antique Success Story?', *Journal of Roman
  Studies* 82, 165–85

——— (1998). 'Marseille and the Pirenne Thesis I: Gregory of Tours, the
  Merovingian kings and 'un grand port', in Hodges and Bowden (1998), 203–29

——— (2000). 'Urban Failures in late Antique Gaul', in Slater (2000), 72–95

Lowmianski, H. (1960). 'Economic Problems of the Early Feudal Polish State', *Acta
  Poloniae Historica* 3, 7–32

Loyn, H. (1995). *The Vikings in Britain* (Oxford)

Lubke, C. (1984–88). *Regesten zur Geschichte der Slaven an Elbe und Oder (vom Jahr 900
  an)* (Berlin)

——— (1994). 'Zwischen Triglav und Christus: Die Anfänge der Christianisierung
  des Havellandes', *Wichmann-Jahrbuch des Diozesangeschichtsverein Berlin*, n.f. 3,
  Jahrgang 34–5, 15–35

——— (1997). 'Forms of Political Organization of the Polabian Slavs (until 10th c.)',
  in Urbanczyk (1997a), 115–124

Lund, N. (1984). *Two Voyagers at the Court of King Alfred: Othere and Wulfstan* (York)
———— (1986). 'The Armies of Swein Forkbeard and Cnut: leding or lith?', *Anglo-Saxon England* 15, 105–18
———— (1993). 'Danish Military Organization', in Cooper (1993), 109–26
———— (1994). 'Cnut's Danish Kingdom', in Rumble (1994), 27–42
———— (1995). 'Scandinavia', in McKitterick (1995), 202–27.
———— (1997). 'The Danish Empire and the End of the Viking Age', in Sawyer (1997a), 156–81
Lund Hansen, U. (1987). *Römischer Import im Norden: Warenaustausch zwischen dem Römischen Reich und dem freien Germanien während der Kaiserzeit unter besonderer Berücksichtigung Nordeuropas* (Copenhagen)

McCormick, M. (2001). *Origins of the European Economy: Communications and Commerce,* AD *300–900* (Cambridge)
MacGeorge, P. (2002). *Late Roman Warlords* (Oxford)
McKitterick, R. (1977). *The Frankish Church and the Carolingian Reforms, 789–895* (London)
———— (1983). *The Frankish Kingdoms under the Carolingians, 751–987* (London)
———— (1989). *The Carolingians and the Written Word* (Cambridge)
————, ed. (1994). *Carolingian Culture: Emulation and Innovation* (Cambridge)
————, ed. (1995). *The New Cambridge Medieval History. Vol. II, c.700–c.900* (Cambridge)
Maenchen-Helfen, O. J. (1945). 'Huns and Hsiung-nu', *Byzantion* 17, 222–43
———— (1973). *The World of the Huns* (Berkeley)
Magie, D. (1932). *The Scriptores Historiae Augustae* (London)
Maleczynski, K., ed. (1952). *Anonima tzw. Galla Kronika* (Cracow)
Mango, C. and Scott, R. (1997). *Chronographia: The Chronicle of Theophanes Confessor* (Oxford)
Manteuffel, T., translated with an introduction by A. Gorski (1982). *The Formation of the Polish State: The Period of Ducal Rule, 963–1194* (Detroit)
Manteuffel, T. and Gieysztor, A., eds. (1968). *L'Europe aux IX.–XI. siècles aux origines des états nationaux: Actes du Colloque international sur les origines des états européens aux IX.–XI. siècles, tenu à Varsovie et Poznan du 7 au 13 septembre 1965* (Warsaw)
Markus, R. A. (1997). *Gregory the Great and his World* (Cambridge)
Mathisen, R. W. and Shanzer, D., eds. (2001). *Society and Culture in Late Roman Gaul: Revisiting the Sources* (Aldershot)
Matthews, J. F. (1970). 'Olympiodorus of Thebes and the History of the West (AD 407–425)', *Journal of Roman Studies* 60, 79–97
———— (1975). *Western Aristocracies and the Imperial Court* AD *364–425* (Oxford)
———— (1989). *The Roman Empire of Ammianus* (London)
Mayr Harting, H. (1972). *The Coming of Christianity to Anglo-Saxon England* (London)
———— (1994). *Two Conversions to Christianity: The Bulgarians and the Anglo-Saxons* (Reading)
Melnikova, E. A. (1996). *The Eastern World of the Vikings* (Gothenburg)
Mierow, C. C. (1915). *Jordanes: Getica* (New York)

Minns, E. H. (1913). *Scythians and Greeks: A Survey of Ancient History and Archaeology of the North Coast of the Euxine From the Danube to the Caucasus* (Cambridge)

Minor, C. (1996). 'Bacaudae – A Reconsideration', *Traditio* 51, 297–307

Miquel, A. (1966). 'Ibn Jacub', *Annales* 23, 1048–63

Moderan, Y. (2002). 'L'établissement des Vandals en Afrique', *Antiquité Tardif* 10, 87–122

Moisl, H. (1981). 'Anglo-Saxon Royal Genealogies and Germanic Oral Tradition', *Journal of Medieval History* 7, 215–48

Mommsen, T., ed. (1882). *Jordanes Romana et Getica*, Monumenta Germaniae Historica: Auctores Antiquissimi 5.1 (Berlin)

———, ed. (1892). *Chronica Minora 1*, Monumenta Germaniae Historica: Auctores Antiquissimi 9 (Berlin)

———, ed. (1894a). *Chronica Minora 2*, Monumenta Germaniae Historica: Auctores Antiquissimi 11 (Berlin)

———, ed. (1894b). *Cassiodori Senatoris Variae*, Monumenta Germaniae Historica: Auctores Antiquissimi 12 (Berlin)

Mommsen, T. and Kreuger, P., eds. (1905). *Codex Theodosianus* (Berlin)

Moorhead, J. (1992). *Victor of Vita History of the Persecution in Africa* (Liverpool)

Moravcsik, G. and Jenkins, R. J. H., eds. (1967). *Constantine Porphyrogenitus: De administrando imperio* (Washington)

Mueller, K., ed. (1851–70). *Fragmenta Historicorum Graecorum*, vols. 4–5 (Paris)

Muller-Wille, M. (1999). *Opferkulte der Germanen und Slawen* (Darmstadt)

Myhre, B. (1978). 'Agrarian Development, Settlement History and Social Organization in Southwest Norway in the Iron Age', in Kristiansen and Paludan-Muller (1978), 224–35, 253–65

Nelson, J. L. (1991). *The Annals of St-Bertin* (Manchester)

——— (1997). 'The Frankish Empire', in Sawyer (1997a), 19–47

Nichols, J. (1998). 'The Eurasian Spread Zone and the Indo-European Dispersal', in Blench and Spriggs (1998), 220–66

Niebuhr, B. G., ed. (1839–41). *Theophanes Chronographia* (Bonn)

Nixon, C. E. V. and Rodgers, B. S. (1994). *In Praise of Later Roman Emperors: The Panegyrici Latini* (Berkeley)

Noble, T. F. X. and Head, T., eds. (1995). *Soldiers of Christ: Saints and Saints' Lives from Late Antiquity and the Early Middle Ages* (Pennsylvania)

Noll, R. and Vetter, E., eds. (1963). *Eugippius Vita Sancti Severini, Schriften und Quellen der Alten Welt* 11 (Berlin)

Noonan, T. S. (1997). 'Scandinavians in European Russia', in Sawyer (1997a), 134–55

——— (1998). *The Islamic World, Russia and the Vikings, 750–900: The Numismatic Evidence* (Aldershot)

O Corrain, D. (1997). 'Ireland, Wales, Man, and the Hebrides', in Sawyer (1997a), 83–109.

——— (1998). 'The Vikings in Scotland and Ireland in the Ninth Century', *Peritia* 12, 296–339

Ørsnes, M. (1963). 'The Weapon Find in Ejsbøl Mose at Haderlev: Preliminary Report', *Acta Archaeologica* 34, 232–48

——— (1968). *Der Moorfund von Ejsbøl bei Hadersleben. Deutungsprobleme der grossen nordgermanischen Waffenopferfunde: Abhandlung der Akademie der Wissenschaft in Göttingen* (Göttingen)

Painter, K. (1994). 'Booty from a Roman Villa found in the Rhine', *Minerva* 5, 22–7

Palade, V. (1966). 'Atelierele pentru lucrat pieptini din os din secolul at IV-leas e.n. de la Birlad-Valea Seaca', *Arheologia Moldovei* 4, 261–77

Parczewski, M. (1993). *Die Anfänge der frühslawischen Kultur in Polen* (Vienna)

——— (1997). 'Beginnings of the Slavs' Culture', in Urbanczyk (1997a), 79–90

Parmentier, L. and Hansen, G. C., eds. (1998). *Theodoret: Kirchengeschichte*, 3rd ed. (Berlin)

Paschoud, F. (1971–89). *Zosimus: Historia Nova*, 6 vols. (Paris)

Pearson, M. P. (1989). 'Beyond the Pale: Barbarian Social Dynamics in Western Europe', in Barrett (1989), 198–226

*Peregrinatio Gothica 1.* (1986). *Archaeologia Baltica* VII (Lodz)

*Peregrinatio Gothica 2.* (1989). *Archaeologia Baltica* VIII (Lodz)

Perin, P. (1980). *La datation des tombes mérovingiennes* (Geneva)

——— (1987). *Les Francs à la Conquête de la Gaule* (Paris)

——— (1996). 'Die Archäologische Zeugnisse der frankischen Expansion in Gallien', in *Die Franken: Wegbereiter Europas: vor 1500 Jahren, König Chlodwig und seine Erben* (Mainz), 227–32.

Perin, P. and Feffer, L. C. (1987). *Les Francs à l'Origine de la France*, 2 vols. (Paris)

Perin, P. and Kazanski, M. (1996). 'Das Grab Childerichs I', in *Die Franken: Wegbereiter Europas: vor 1500 Jahren, König Chlodwig und seine Erben* (Mainz), 173–82

Pertz, G. H. and Kurze, F., eds. (1891). *Annales Fuldenses, sive, Annales regni Francorum orientalis ab Einhardo, Ruodolfo, Meginhardo Fuldensibus, Seligenstadi, Fuldae, Mogontiaoi conscripti cum continuationibus Ratisbonensi et Altahensibus* (Hanover)

Petrov, N. I. (2005). 'Ladoga, Ryurik's Stronghold, and Novgorod: Fortifications and Power in Early Medieval Russia', in Curta (2005), 121–37

Petschenig, M., ed. (1881). *Victoris Episcopi Vitensis Historia persecutionis Africanae provinciae* (Vienna)

Pharr, C. (1952). *The Theodosian Code and Novels, and the Sirmondian Constitutions* (New York)

Phillips, J. R. S. (1988). *The Medieval Expansion of Europe* (Oxford)

——— (1994). 'The Medieval Background', in Canny (1994), 9–25

Pichlmayr, F., ed. (1911). *Sexti Aurelii Victoris liber de Caesaribus* (Leipzig)

Pinder, M., ed. (1897). *Ioannis Zonarae Epitomae historiarum libri XVIII* (Bonn)

Pirling, R. (1966). *Das römisch-fränkische Gräberfeld von Krefeld-Gellep* (Berlin)

Pirling, R. and Siepen, M. (2003). *Das römisch-fränkische Gräberfeld von Krefeld-Gellep 1989–2000* (Stuttgart)

Platnauer, M. (1922). *The Works of Claudian* (London)

*PLRE: The Prosopography of the later Roman Empire*, ed. A. H. M. Jones et al., 3 vols. (Cambridge, 1971–92)

Pohl, W. (1980). 'Die Gepiden und die Gentes an der mittleren Donau nach dem Zerfall des Attilareiches', in Wolfram and Daim (1980), 239–305

———— (1988). *Die Awaren: ein Steppenvolk im Mitteleuropa, 567–822 n. Chr.* (Munich)

———— (2000). *Die Germanen* (Munich)

———— (2003). 'A Non-Roman Empire in Central Europe: The Avars', in Goetz et al. (2003), 571–595.

Pohl, W. and Erhart, P. (2005). *Die Langobarden : Herrschaft und Identität* (Vienna)

Pohl, W. and Wood, I. N., eds. (2001) *The Transformation of Frontiers from Late Antiquity to the Carolingians, Proceedings of the Second Plenary Conference, European Science Foundation Transformation of the Roman World Project* (Leiden)

Poulik, J. et al., eds. (1986). *Grossmähren und die Anfänge der tschechoslowakischen Staatlichkeit* (Prague)

Poulter, A., ed. (2007). *The Transition to Late Antiquity on the Danube and Beyond* (Oxford)

Powlesland, D. (1997). 'Early Anglo-Saxon Settlements: Structures, Forms, and Layout', in Hines (1997), 101–24

Preucel, R. and Hodder, I., eds. (1996). *Contemporary Archaeology in Theory* (Oxford)

Preussler, W. (1956). 'Keltischer Einfluss im Englischen', *Revue des Langues Vivantes* 22, 322–50

Prinz, F. (1984). *Böhmen im mittelalterlichen Europa* (Munich).

Proussa, P. (1990). 'A Contact-universals Origin for Periphrastic Do, with Special Consideration of OE-Celtic Contact', in Adamson (1990), 407–34


Raev, B. A. (1986). *Roman Imports in the Lower Don Basin* (Oxford)

Rafnsson, S. (1997). 'The Atlantic Islands', in Sawyer (1997a), 110–33

Randsborg, K. (1980). *The Viking Age in Denmark: The Formation of a State* (London)

Rau, G. (1972). 'Körpergräber mit Glasbeigaben des 4. nachchristlichen Jahrhunderts im Oder-Wechsel-Raum', *Acta praehistorica et archaeologica* 3, 109–214

Reichmann, C. (1996). 'Frühe Franken in Germanien', in *Die Franken: Wegbereiter Europas: vor 1500 Jahren, König Chlodwig und seine Erben* (Mainz), 55–65

Renfrew, C. (1987). *Archaeology and Language: The Puzzle of Indo-European Origins* (London)

Renfrew, C. and Bahn, P. (1991). *Archaeology: Theories, Methods and Practice* (London)

Renfrew, C. and Cherry, J. F., eds. (1986). *Peer Polity Interaction and Socio-Political Change* (Cambridge)

Reuter, T. (1985). 'Plunder and Tribute in the Carolingian Empire', *Transactions of the Royal Historical Society*, 75–94

———— (1990). 'The End of Carolingian Military Expansion', in Godman and Collins (1990), 391–407

———— (1991). *Germany in the Early Middle Ages c.800–1056* (London)

———— (1992). *The Annals of Fulda* (Manchester)

————, ed. (1999). *The New Cambridge Medieval History: vol. 3, 900–1024* (Cambridge)

Ridley R. T. (1982). *Zosimus: New History* (Canberra)

Ritchie, A. (1993). *Viking Scotland* (Bath)

Robinson, C. H. (1921). *Anskar: The Apostle of the North, 801–865* (London)

Roesdahl, E., trans. S. Margeson and K. Williams (1982). *Viking Age Denmark* (London)

————, trans. S. Margeson and K. Williams (1991). *The Vikings* (London)

Rolfe, J. C., ed. (1935–39). *Ammianus Marcellinus* (London)

Rostovzeff, M. I. (1922). *Iranians and Greeks in South Russia* (Oxford)

Rowlands, M. et al., eds. (1987). *Centre and Periphery in the Ancient World* (Cambridge)

Rudkin, D. (1986). *The Saxon Shore* (London)

Rumble, A. R., ed. (1994). *The Reign of Cnut: King of England, Denmark and Norway* (London)

Rystad, G. (1996). 'Immigration Policy and the Future of International Migration', *International Migration Review* 26.4, 555–86

Sabbah, G. (1978). *La méthode d'Ammien Marcellin: recherches sur la construction du discours historique dans les Res Gestae* (Paris)

Salt, J. and Clout, H., eds. (1976). *Migration in Post-War Europe: Geographical Essays* (Oxford)

Salway, P. (2001). *A History of Roman Britain* (Oxford)

Sanchez-Albornoz, N. (1994). 'The First Transatlantic Transfer: Spanish Migration to the New World', in Canny (1994), 26–36

Santini, C., ed. (1979). *Eutropius Breviarium ab urbe condita* (Stuttgart)

Sartre, M. (1982). *Trois études sur l'Arabie romaine et byzantine: Revue d'Études Latines* (Brussels)

Sasse, B. (1982). *Die Sozialgeschichte Böhmens in der Frühzeit: Historisch-archäologische Untersuchungen zum 9.–12. Jahrhundert* (Berlin)

Sawyer, B. (1991). 'Viking-Age Rune-Stones as a Crisis Symptom', *Norwegian Archaeological Review* 24, 97–112

Sawyer, B. and Sawyer, P. H. (1993). *Medieval Scandinavia: From Conversion to Reformation c.800–1500* (Minneapolis)

Sawyer, P. H. (1962). *The Age of the Vikings* (London)

———— (1978). *From Roman Britain to Norman England* (London)

———— (1982), 'The Causes of the Viking Age', in Farrell (1982), 1–7

———— (1993). 'The Scandinavian Background', in Cooper (1993), 33–42

———— (1994). 'Cnut's Scandinavian Empire', in Rumble (1994), 10–22

————, ed. (1997a). *The Oxford Illustrated History of the Vikings* (Oxford)

———— (1997b). 'The Age of the Vikings, and Before', in P. Sawyer (1997a), 1–18

Sawyer, P. H. and Wood, I. N., eds. (1977). *Early Medieval Kingship* (Leeds)

Schenkl, H. et al., eds. (1965–74). *Themistii Orationes* (Leipzig)

Schmeidler, B., ed. (1917). *Adam von Bremen: Gesta Hammaburgensis ecclesiae pontificum*, Monumenta Germaniae Historica: Scriptores rerum Germanicarum (Hanover)

Schmidt, L. (1933). *Geschichte der deutschen Stämme bis zum Ausgang der Völkerwanderung: Die Ostgermanen*, 2nd ed. (Munich)

Scholz, B. W. (1972). *Carolingian Chronicles* (Ann Arbor)

Schröder, F. J. (1977). *Völker und Herrscher des östlichen Europa im Weltbild Widukinds von Korvei und Thietmars von Merseburg* (Munster)

Scragg, D. (1991). *The Battle of Maldon, AD 991* (Oxford)

Searle, E. (1988). *Predatory Kinship and the Creation of Norman Power 840–1066* (Berkeley).

Seeck, O., ed. (1962). *Notitia dignitatum* (Frankfurt am Main)

Service, E. R. (1975). *Origins of the State and Civilization: The Process of Cultural Evolution* (New York)

Settimane [Centro italiano di studi sull'alto Medioevo: Settimane di studio] (1983). *Gli Slavi occidentali e meridionali nell'alto medioevo, Atti del xxx Congresso internazionale di studi sull'alto Medioevo* (Spoleto)

Shanzer, D. and Wood, I. N., eds. and trans. (2002). *Avitus of Vienne: Letters and Selected Prose* (Liverpool)

Shchukin, M. (1975). 'Das Problem der Cernjachow-Kultur in der sowjetischen archäologischen Literatur', *Zeitschrift für Archäologie* 9, 25–41

—— (1977). 'Current aspects of the Gothic Problem and the Cherniakhovo Culture', *Arkheologichesky sbornik* 18, 79–92 (English summary)

—— (1990). *Rome and the Barbarians in Central and Eastern Europe: 1st Century BC–1st Century AD* (Oxford)

—— (2005). *The Gothic Way: Goths, Rome, and the Culture of the Chernjakhov/ Sintana de Mures* (St Petersburg)

Shennan, S. (1989). *Archaeological Approaches to Cultural Identity* (London)

Shepard, J. (2005). 'Conversions and Regimes Compared: The Rus' and the Poles, ca. 1000', in Curta (2005), 252–82

Sherwin-White, A. N. (1973). *The Roman Citizenship*, 2nd ed. (Oxford)

Siegmund, F. (1998). 'Social Structure and Relations', in Wood (1998), 177–98

Sinor, D. (1977). *Inner Asia and its Contacts with Medieval Europe* (London)

—— (1990). *The Cambridge History of Early Inner Asia* (Cambridge)

Skalnik, P., ed. (1989). *Outwitting the State* (New Jersey)

Slater, T., ed. (2000). *Towns in Decline AD 100–1600* (Aldershot).

Smith, A. D. (1986). *The Ethnic Origin of Nations* (Oxford)

Smith, J. M. (1992). *Province and Empire: Brittany and the Carolingians* (Cambridge)

Smyth, A. P. (1977). *Scandinavian Kings in the British Isles, 850–880* (Oxford)

—— (1979). *Scandinavian York and Dublin: The History and Archaeology of Two Related Viking Kingdoms* (New Jersey)

—— (1995). *King Alfred the Great* (Oxford)

Speidel, M. P. (1977). 'The Roman Army in Arabia', *Aufstieg und Niedergang der Antiken Welt* II. 8

Stallknecht, B. (1969). *Untersuchungen zur römischen Aussenpolitik in der Spätantike* (Bonn)

Stenton. F. (1971). *Anglo-Saxon England* (Oxford)

Steuer, H. (1982). *Frühgeschichtliche Sozialstrukturen Mitteleuropa* (Göttingen)

—— (1998). 'Theorien zur Herkunft und Entstehung der Alemannen: Archaeologische Forschungsansatze', in Geuenich (1998), 270–334

Stockwell, S., ed. (2008). *The British Empire: Themes and Perspectives* (Oxford)

Syme, R. (1968). *Ammianus and the Historia Augusta* (Oxford)

—— (1971a). *Emperors and Biography: Studies in the Historia Augusta* (Oxford)

—— (1971b). *The Historia Augusta: A Call for Clarity* (Bonn)

Szydlowski, J. (1980). 'Zur Anwesenheit der Westslawen an der mittleren Donau im ausgehenden 5. und 6. Jahrhundert', in Wolfram and Daim (1980), 233–7

Tejral, J. et al., eds. (1999). *L'Occident romain et l'Europe centrale au début de l'époque des Grandes Migrations* (Brno)

Theuws, F. and Hiddinck, H. (1996). 'Der Kontakt zu Rom', in *Die Franken:*

*Wegbereiter Europas: vor 1500 Jahren, König Chlodwig und seine Erben* (Mainz), 64–80

Thomas, M. G. et al. (2006). 'Evidence for an Apartheid-like Social Structure in Early Anglo-Saxon England', *Proceedings of the Royal Society* 273, 2651–7

Thompson, E. A. (1965). *The Early Germans* (Oxford)

——— (1966). *The Visigoths in the Time of Ulfila* (Oxford)

——— (1995). *The Huns* (Oxford)

Thorpe, L. (1974). *Gregory of Tours: The History of the Franks* (London)

Todd, M. (1975). *The Northern Barbarians 100 BC–AD 300* (London)

——— (1992). *The Early Germans* (Oxford)

Trillmich, W. et al., eds. (1978). *Quellen des 9. und 11. Jahrhunderts zur Geschichte der hambürgischen Kirche und des Reiches*, 5th ed. (Darmstadt)

Tschan, F. J. (1959). *Adam of Bremen: History of the Archbishops of Hamburg-Bremen* (New York)

——— (1966). *Helmold, Priest of Bosau: The Chronicle of the Slavs* (New York)

Turek, R. (1974). *Böhmen im Morgengrauen der Geschichte von den Anfängen der slawischen Besiedlung bis zum Eintritt in die europäische Kulturgemeinschaft (6. bis Ende des 10 Jahrhunderts)* (Wiesbaden)

Ucko, P. 1995). *Theory in Archaeology: A World Perspective* (London)

Urbanczyk, P., ed. (1997a). *Origins of Central Europe* (Warsaw)

——— (1997b). 'Changes of Power Structure During the 1st Millennium AD in the Northern Part of Central Poland', in Urbanczyk (1997a), 39–44

———, ed. (1997c). *Early Christianity in Central and East Europe* (Warsaw)

———, ed. (2001). *Europe around the Year 1000* (Warsaw)

———, ed. (2004). *Polish Lands at the Turn of the First and the Second Millennia* (Warsaw)

——— (2005). 'Early State Formation in East Central Europe', in Curta (2005), 139–51

Vallet, F and Kazanski, M., eds. (1995). *La noblesse romaine et les chefs barbares du IIIe au VIIe siècle* (Paris)

Van Dam, R. (1985). *Leadership and Community in Late Antique Gaul* (Berkeley)

Van Es, W. A. (1967). *Wijster: A Native Village Beyond the Imperial Frontier 150–425 AD* (Groningen)

Van Ossel, P. (1992). *Etablissements ruraux de l'antiquité tardive dans le nord de la Gaule* (Paris)

Van Ossel, P. and Ouzoulias, P. (2000). 'Rural Settlement Economy in Northern Gaul in the Late Empire: An Overview and Assessment', *Journal of Roman Archaeology* 13, 133–60

Verlinden, C. (1955). *L'Esclavage dans l'Europe Médiévale* (Bruges)

Vertovec, S. and Cohen, R. (1999). *Migration, Diasporas, and Transnationalism* (Cheltenham)

Vince, A. (2001). 'Lincoln in the Viking Age', in Graham-Campbell et al. (2001), 157–80

Voets, S. et al., eds. (1995). *The Demographic Consequences of Migration* (The Hague)

Vogel, F., ed. (1885). *Ennodius Opera*, Monumenta Germaniae Historica: Auctores Antiquissimi 7 (Berlin)

von Schnurbein, S. (1995). *Vom Einfluss Roms auf die Germanen* (Opladen)

Waitz, G., ed. (1883). *Annales Bertiniani* (Hanover)

Wallace-Hadrill, J. M. (1960). *The Fourth Book of the Chronicle of Fredegar* (London)

Ward Perkins, B. (2000). 'Why did the Anglo-Saxons not become more British?', *English Historical Review* 115, 513–33

——— (2005). *The Fall of Rome and the End of Civilization* (Oxford)

Warner, D. A. (2001). *Ottonian Germany: The Chronicon of Thietmar of Merseburg* (Manchester)

Weale, M. E. et al. (2002). 'Y Chromosome Evidence for Anglo-Saxon Mass Migration' *Molecular Biology & Evolution* 19.7, 1008–21

Wegener, W. (1959). *Böhmen/Mähren und das Reich im Hochmittelälter* (Cologne)

Welch, M. (1992). *English Heritage Book of Anglo-Saxon England* (London)

Wells, P. S. (1999). *The Barbarians Speak: How the Conquered Peoples Shaped Roman Europe* (Princeton)

Wenskus, R. (1961). *Stammesbildung und Verfassung: Das Werden der frühmittelalterlichen gentes* (Cologne)

Werner, J. (1935). *Münzdatierte austrasische Grabfunde* (Berlin)

——— (1950). 'Zur Entstehung der Reihengräberzivilisation', *Archaeologica Geographica* I, 23–32

Weski, T. (1982). *Waffen in germanischen Gräbern der älteren römischen Kaiserzeit südlich der Ostsee* (Oxford)

Whitby, L. M. (1988). *The Emperor Maurice and his Historian: Theophylact Simocatta on Persian and Balkan Warfare* (Oxford)

Whitby, L. M. and Whitby, J. M. (1986). *The History of Theophylact Simocatta* (Oxford)

——— (1989). *The Chronicon Paschale* (Liverpool)

Whitelock, D., ed. (1955). *English Historical Documents, vol. 1, c.500–1042* (London)

Whitelock, D. et al. (1961). *The Anglo-Saxon Chronicle: A Revised Translation* (London)

Whittaker, C. R. (1994). *Frontiers of the Roman Empire: A Social and Economic Study* (Baltimore).

Whittow, M. (1996). *The Making of Orthodox Byzantium, 600–1025* (London)

Wickham, C. (1992). 'Problems of Comparing Rural Societies in Early Medieval Western Europe', *Transactions of the Royal Historical Society*, 6th series 2, 221–46

——— (2005). *Framing the Early Middle Ages: Europe and the Mediterranean, 400–800* (Oxford)

Wieczorek, A. (1996). 'Die Ausbreitung der frankischen Herrschaft in den Rheinland vor und seit Chlodwig I', in *Die Franken: Wegbereiter Europas: vor 1500 Jahren, König Chlodwig und seine Erben* (Mainz), 241–61

Wiet, G. (1957). *Les Atours Précieux* (Cairo)

Williams, A. (1991). *The English and the Norman Conquest* (Woodbridge)

Wilson, J. (2008). 'Agency, Narrative, and Resistance', in Stockwell (2008), 245–68

Winterbottom, M., ed. and trans. (1978). *Gildas: The Ruin of Britain, and other works* (London)

Wolfram, H. (1979). *Conversio Bagoariorum et Carantanorum: das Weissbuch der*

*Salzburger Kirche über die erfolgreiche Mission in Karantanien und Pannonien* (Vienna)

———— (1985). *Treasures on the Danube: Barbarian Invaders and their Roman Inheritance* (Vienna)

————, trans. T. J. Dunlap (1988). *History of the Goths* (Berkeley)

———— (1994). 'Origo et Religio: Ethnic Traditions and Literature in Early Medieval Texts', *Early Medieval Europe* 3, 19–38

———— (1995). *Salzburg, Bayern, Österreich: die Conversio Bagoariorum et Carantanorum und die Quellen ihrer Zeit* (Vienna)

————, trans. T. J. Dunlap (1997). *The Roman Empire and its Germanic Peoples* (Berkeley)

Wolfram, H. and Daim, F., eds. (1980). *Die Völker an der mittleren und unteren Donau im fünften und sechsten Jahrhundert, Denkschriften der Osterreichischen Akademie der Wissenschaften*, phil.-hist. Kl. 145 (Vienna)

Wolfram, H. and Pohl, W., eds. (1990). *Typen der Ethnogenese unter besonderer Berücksichtigung der Bayern, Denkschriften der Osterreichischen Akademie der Wissenschaften*, phil.-hist. Kl. 193 (Vienna)

Wood, I. N. (1985). 'Gregory of Tours and Clovis', *Revue Belge de Philologie et d'Histoire* 63, 249–72

———— (1990). 'Ethnicity and the Ethnogenesis of the Burgundians' in Wolfram and Pohl (1990), 53–69

———— (1994). *The Merovingian Kingdoms* (London)

————, ed. (1998). *Franks and Alamanni in the Merovingian Period: An Ethnographic Perspective* (Woodbridge)

———— (2001). *The Missionary Life: Saints and the Evangelization of Europe, 400–1050* (Harlow)

Woolf, A. (2003). 'The Britons: from Romans to Barbarians', in Goetz et al. (2003), 345–80

———— (2007). 'Apartheid and Economics in Anglo-Saxon England', in Higham (2007), 115–29

Wormald, C. P. (1978). 'Bede, Beowulf and the Conversion of the Anglo-Saxon Aristocracy', in Farrell (1978), 32–95

———— (1982). 'Viking Studies: Whence and Whither', in Farrell (1982), 128–53

———— (1986). 'Celtic and Anglo-Saxon Kingship', *Studies in Medieval Culture* 20, 151–83

Zagiba, F., ed. (1969). *Das heidnische und christliche Slaventum* (Wiesbaden)

Zollner, E. (1970). *Geschichte der Franken bis zur Mitte des sechsten Jahrhunderts* (Munich)

# INDEX